THE KURDS

THE KURDS:
A CONCISE HANDBOOK

Mehrdad R. Izady

Department of Near Eastern Languages and Civilizations
Harvard University

CRANE RUSSAK

Taylor & Francis International Publishers
Washington • Philadelphia • London

USA	Publishing Office:	Taylor & Francis, Inc.
		1101 Vermont Ave., Suite 200
		Washington, DC 20005-3521
	Sales Office:	Taylor & Francis, Inc.
		1900 Frost Road, Suite 101
		Bristol, PA 19007-1598
UK		Taylor & Francis Ltd.
		4 John Street
		London WC1N 2ET

THE KURDS: A Concise Handbook

1 2 3 4 5 6 7 8 9 E B E B 9 8 7 6 5 4 3 2

Interior design by Designers Workshop. Cover design by Michelle Fleitz.

Printing and binding by Edwards Brothers, Inc.

A CIP catalog record for this book is available from the British Library.

⊗ The paper in this publication meets the requirements of the ANSI Standard Z39.48-1984(Permanence of Paper).

Library of Congress Cataloging-in-Publication Data

Izady, Mehrdad
   The Kurds : a concise handbook / Mehrdad Izady
   Includes bibliographical references.

   1. Kurds—Handbooks, manuals, etc. 2. Middle East—Ethnic relations. I. Title.
DS59.K86I93 1992
956'.0049159—dc20   92-8174
ISBN 0-8448-1729-5 (case)   CIP
ISBN 0-8448-1727-9 (paper)

CONTENTS

Chapter 1: **GEOGRAPHY**

Chapter 2: **LAND & ENVIRONMENT**

Chapter 3: **HISTORY**

Chapter 7: **SOCIETY**

Chapter 8: **POLITICAL AND CONTEMPORARY ISSUES**

Chapter 9: **ECONOMY**

Chapter 10: **CULTURE AND ARTS**

List of Maps

List of Tables

List of Figures

PREFACE

Since before the dawn of recorded history the mountainous lands of the northern Middle East have been home to a distinct people whose cultural tradition is one of the most authentic and original in the world. Some vestiges of Kurdish life and culture can actually be traced back to burial rituals practiced over 50,000 years ago by people inhabiting the Shanidar Caves near Arbil in central Kurdistan.

Despite their antiquity and cultural vitality there are very few reference works on the Kurds today. A major reason for such a gap is that the Kurds have lacked the organized apparatus of a sovereign state, which allowed Turkey, Syria, Iraq, and Iran to produce symbolic scholarly justifications of their "distinct" collective national identities in the eyes of outsiders. These works in turn engendered the binding glue of pride to help create "nations" from the disparate elements found within their boundaries when they were created.

In the same stroke, these very same nation-states have attempted to stop the growth of the Kurdish people as a distinct and separate national entity. Often they have tried to do away with them altogether.

They have glossed over the Kurdish past, denying the originality of this ancient culture, and preventing original research on any topic of national importance to ethnic Kurds. They have created and foisted false identities onto the Kurds—such as the labels "Mountain Turk" in Turkey, and "Umayyad Arab" in Syria and Iraq for the Yezidi Kurds. They have simply denied the Kurds separate ethnic existence in Iran, Soviet Azerbaijan, and Turkmenistan. In doing this these modern nation-states have done plenty to confuse even the Kurds themselves.

It is an astonishing fact, if not an outright embarrassment, that not a single archaeological object has ever been identified as "Kurdish" in any museum anywhere in the world—not even a broken arrowhead, a pottery shard, or a piece of mosaic. This omission is made more glaring by the fact that every other ethnographic grouping of people, including the stone-age cultures of pre-Columbian North America, Australia, the Pacific islands, and Africa, has had historical artifacts identified for it in museums.

Except for rugs, and (very recently) paintings, the same omissive treatment continues for modern specimens of Kurdish artistic creation as well. Despite the Kurdish origin of over three-quarters of the hand-made rugs and kilims produced in contemporary Turkey, no specimen is actually identified as Kurdish within the boundaries of that state.

In this work I have tried to identify and delineate the heritage of the Kurds, now thoroughly submerged in the accepted and standard models for subdividing Middle Eastern civilization, none of which is designed to accommodate the stateless Kurds.

As to who *is* a Kurd and who is not, this work respects the claim of anyone who calls himself a Kurd, regardless of the dialect he speaks, religion he practices, or state where he lives. As to who *was* a Kurd, I treat as Kurdish every community that has ever inhabited the territory of Kurdistan and has not acquired a separate identity to this day, or been unequivocally connected with another identifiable nation the bulk of which is or was living outside the territories of Kurdistan. This is consistent with what is accepted by consensus for the identification of ancient Egyptians or Greeks and the relationship they have to modern Egyptians and Greeks.

By the same certainty that we accept the inhabitants of pharaonic Egypt as the unquestionable forbearers of the modern Egyptians, despite the fact that they spoke a different language, practiced a different religion, and had different racial characteristics, the ancient inhabitants of Kurdistan ought to be equally treated as the forbearers of the modern ones. This topic is elucidated in the section on **National Identity**.

This book is meant to serve as a reference manual to provide a reasonably brief but documented insight into matters Kurdish, beginning always with their historical background and, if relevant, geographical setting. Only the main points and the major causes and effects are discussed here. As one might expect, no people can be described fairly in the space of a single volume. But even the most basic knowledge of the Kurds is scanty. Not even now, at the end of the second millennium and in the age of space travel, is anyone sure how many Kurds there are. It is hoped this book will be a useful contribution and basis for further research.

This work is targeted at the widest possible audience: the public, the press, teachers, students, scholars, and even travelers. It is a source to check one's data quickly or simply provide oneself for the first time with an understanding of the people and land of Kurdistan.

A more complete reference/textbook, *A Basic Study of the Land and People of Kurdistan*, is under preparation by this author. It is hoped that it will provide readers with a far more detailed view of the Kurds, their land, history, and culture. A companion *Atlas of the Kurds* is also under preparation.

While the final editorial revisions of this work were underway, the Soviet Union, the last of the great European empires, joined history. Since it will be long before a stable alternative state takes hold in the former Soviet territories, the name "Soviet Union" and the adjective "Soviet" are used in this work for what they represented before the recent changes.

Cambridge
December 1991

Notes on Sources, Spelling and
Other Observations

The bibliographies and suggested further readings given after each entry in this work include those sources used in its preparation as well as other sources of value. It is crucial to note, however, that these are by no means only those works that agree with the ideas or support the views entertained in this handbook. On the contrary, in view of the relative infancy of the field of Kurdish studies, many of these sources hold positions, even on fundamental issues, at variance with those presented here, and as often with each other. Some authors cited have also reversed their own earlier stands in later works. On the important issue of the origins of the modern Kurdish language, the linguist David N. MacKenzie, for example, wrote in 1961 of connections he saw with the Median language, only to reverse himself in a mere footnote in 1989 (in Peter A. Andrews, ed., *Ethnic Groups in the Republic of Turkey* (Wiesbaden: Ludwig Reichert, 1989, p. 531, n. 1). All those sources that are of value, therefore, are listed here, regardless of their stance, to help readers in examining all existing positions and hypotheses on any given topic. The citation of a source in the body of the text also falls within this same approach.

Some general works are cited at the end of each major topical division with some relevant observations on their merit. Utmost effort has been made to provide sources only in English. On occasion, this has not been possible, and therefore some important sources from French, German, and Russian have also been supplied. Bibliographies do not contain sources in Middle Eastern languages, since this would be an exercise in futility for most readers. Works of the classical Greco-Roman and the medieval Islamic authors, on the other hand, are too well-known to need a separate entry in the bibliographies of this work.

The exceptions to the omission of sources in Middle Eastern languages in the suggested readings are locally produced maps, census data, and atlases.

The publisher's names for books are provided only if they have been published in the past 30 years, or by multiple publishers at different times. Sources published by university and museum publishers always have the name of the publisher, as these institutions usually have the books available for sale far longer than commercial publishers. City or country of publication is always cited for the lesser-known journals and periodicals.

Maps, figures, and tables in the present study are original. The primary data sources for their creation are duly credited at the bottom of each map or table, unless the data have been compiled from many diverse sources and interpreted by me to create the map, table, or figure. For these the souces are those found in the bibliographies at the end of the relevant entry. The boundaries of Kurdistan are based on reliable and primary sources, as indicated in the section on **Geography**.

Cross-references are provided rather lavishly, and I urge readers to benefit from them. Not only do they aid further investigation, but on some occasions they are also quite critical for elucidating the full dimensions of a topic.

Since it is impossible for a reader unfamiliar with the languages of the Kurds, Persians, Arabs, and Turks to ascertain the correct pronunciation of proper names by any system of transliteration that could be devised here, and since such an attempt would at any rate be out of place in this nonphilological, nonlinguistic work, I refrain from burdening the reader with any undue explication of orthographic peculiarities.

In rendering names I have followed as closely as possible the standard American English spellings for familiar sounds—consonants, vowels, and diphthongs.

Only one simple diacritical marking has been retained. This is the letter *â* which stands for the sound of *a* in the English words *car*, *bar*, or *far*. An *a* without the mark is pronounced like the *a* in the English words *add*, *bad*, and *sad*.

The place names are all spelled as they are pronounced by the Kurds, except for non-Kurdish localities or those that are Kurdish but have standard and accepted spellings already, such as Arbil and Mahâbâd, two major Kurdish cities that are called, respectively, Hawlar and Sablâkh by the Kurds themselves. In order to assist readers, all the more common spelling variations of town and city names are given under the entry **Urbanization & Urban Centers**.

Tribal names are rendered as closely as possible to the classical Kurdish set forth by the 16th-century Kurdish historian Sharaf Khân Bitlisi, or earlier in the works of medieval Islamic authors. The reason for this choice is the multifarious pronunciations and thus spellings of the same tribal name by various branches of the tribe, particularly if the branches are separated from each other by long distances. An example is the Rashwand tribe, now found from the Mediterranean coast to the Caucasus and Soviet Central Asia. They are currently referred to by various names, such as Rashven, Rashvend, Reshwan, Reshvand, Reshkân, and Rashkân. By retaining these variations, one would inadvertently hide the inherent unity of the tribe, and its eventful history, which has dispersed its members over an area 2000 miles wide.

The spellings based on the standards set forth in the *Encyclopaedia of Islam*, and now common for classical Islamic historians, geographers, and other luminaries, have been retained for the sake of uniformity. These are few, and the spelling is clear enough for those unfamiliar with the intricacies of the *Encyclopaedia*'s transliteration system.

Acknowledgments

The valuable resources at the Kurdish Library and Museum in Brooklyn, New York were generously made available to me, and much gratitude and appreciation I owe this institution.

Both Dr. Vera Beaudin Saeedpour, my long-time colleague, and Miss Anahid Akasheh, my charming wife, were most encouraging and helpful with their comments and observations, for which I duly thank them.

I must also acknowledge my gratitude to Professor Wheeler Thackston for his insightful comments regarding the organization of this work, and my faithful friend, Dr. Lawrence Potter, for always posting me with the latest developments regarding Kurdish affairs.

I am also indebted to Mr. Todd Baldwin, my astute editor, for his outstanding attention to detail, precision, and insightful comments.

Chapter 1

GEOGRAPHY

BOUNDARIES & POLITICAL GEOGRAPHY

The vast Kurdish homeland consists of about 200,000 square miles of territory. Its area is roughly equal to that of France, or of the states of California and New York combined (see Map 1).

Kurdistan straddles the mountainous northern boundaries of the Middle East, separating the region from the former Soviet Union. It resembles an inverted letter V, with the joint pointing in the direction of the Caucasus and the arms toward the Mediterranean Sea and the Persian Gulf (Map 2).

In the absence of an independent state, Kurdistan is defined as the areas in which Kurds constitute an ethnic majority today. Kurdish ethnic domains border strategically on the territories of the three other major ethnic groups of the Middle East: the Arabs to the south, the Persians to the east, and the Turks to the west. In addition to these primary ethnic neighbors, there are many smaller ethnic groups whose territories border those of the Kurds, such as the Georgians (including the Lâz) and the Armenians to the north, the Azeris to the northeast, the Lurs to the southeast, and the Turkmens to the southwest (Map 3).

The range of lands in which Kurdish populations have predominated has, historically, fluctuated. Kurdish ethnic territorial domains have contracted as much as they have expanded, depending on the demographic, historical, and economic circumstances of given regions of Kurdistan (Map 4). A detailed analysis of migrations, deportations, and integration and assimilation is provided under **Human Geography**.

In the north of Kurdistan, Kurds now occupy almost half of what was traditionally the Armenian homeland, that is, the areas immediately around the shores and north of Lake Vân in modern Turkey. On the other hand, from the 9th to the 16th centuries, the western Kurdish lands of Pontus, Cappadocia, Commagene, and eastern Cilicia were gradually forfeited to the Byzantine Greeks, Syrian Aramaeans, and later the Turkmens and Turks. This last trend, however, has begun to reverse itself in the present century.

Vast areas of Kurdistan in the southern Zagros, stretching from the Kirmânshâh region to Shirâz (in Fârs/Pârs/Persis country) and beyond, have been gradually and permanently lost to the combination of the heavy northwestward emigration of Kurds and the ethnic metamorphosis of many Kurds into Lurs and others since the beginning of the 9th century AD. The assimilation process continues today and can, for example, be observed among the Laks, who, although they still speak a Kurdish dialect (see **Laki**) and practice a native Kurdish religion (see **Yârsânism**), have been more strongly associated with the neighboring Lurs than with other Kurds (Map 4). The distinction between the Kurds and their ethnic neighbors remains most blurred in southern Kurdistan in the area where they neighbor the Lurs, that is, on the Hamadân-Kırmânshâh-Ilâm axis.

Since the 16th century, contiguous Kurdistan has been augmented by two large, detached enclaves of (mainly deported) Kurds. The central Anatolian enclave includes

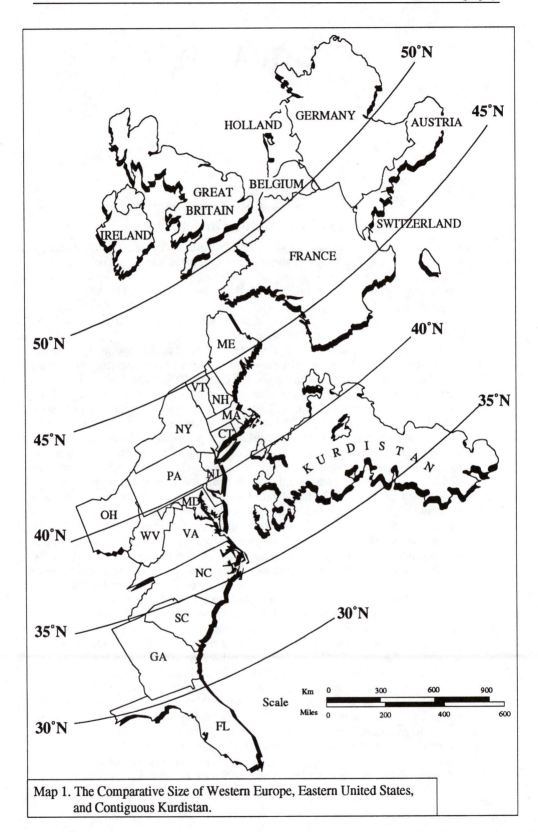

Map 1. The Comparative Size of Western Europe, Eastern United States, and Contiguous Kurdistan.

the area around the towns of Yunak, Haymâna, and Cihanbeyli/Jihânbeyli, south of the Turkish capital of Ankara (the site of ancient Cappadocia). It extends into the mountainous districts of north-central Anatolia (the site of ancient Pontus), where it is bounded by the towns of Tokat, Yozgat, Çorum, and Âmâsyâ in the Yisilirmâq river basin. The fast-expanding north-central Anatolian segment of the enclave now has more Kurds than the older segment in central Anatolia. It is doubtful that, except for some very small Dimili-speaking pockets, this colony harbors any of the ancient Pontian Kurds who lived here until the Byzantine deportations of the 9th century.

The north Khurâsân enclave in eastern Iran is centered on the towns of Quchân and Bujnurd and came into existence primarily as a result of deportations and resettlements conducted from the 16th to the 18th centuries in Persia.

Since World War I, Kurdistan has been divided among five sovereign states (see **Modern History**), with the largest portions of Kurdish territory in Turkey (43%), followed by Iran (31%), Iraq (18%), Syria (6%), and the former Soviet Union (2%). These states have at various stages subdivided Kurdistan into a myriad of administrative units and provinces. Only in western Iran has the Kurdish historical name, even though corrupted, been preserved, in the province of "Kordestan," with its capital at Sanandaj (Map 5).

A rather peculiar and confusing by-product of the division of Kurdistan among contending states and geopolitical power blocs (see **Geopolitics**) is its four time zones (five if Khurâsân in Turkmenistan is also counted). The continental United States, 15 times larger than Kurdistan, also has four time zones. Geographically, Kurdistan fits perfectly into one time zone, 3 hours ahead of Greenwich, England. The standard - 3-hour time zone is defined as the area between 35 and 50 degrees east of Greenwich. With its western and eastern borders at, respectively, 36 and 49 degrees east, Kurdistan should naturally fall into a single time zone.

Plotting the Geographical Distribution of Kurds. Like many other aspects of their national existence and identity, the extent of the areas in which Kurds constitute the majority is the subject of dispute. While neighboring ethnic groups, in particular those in a ruling position, have consistently underestimated the extent of areas with a Kurdish majority, the Kurds have often tended to exaggerate them. This problem has naturally affected the works of non-local scholars as well.

Surprisingly, it is not difficult to plot the extent of Kurdish lands. There are plenty of old and new primary and reliable data available for such an attempt.

In the last century and the first half of the present, many trustworthy scholars and institutions have provided detailed lists of Kurdish tribes, their locations, distributions, and populations in various corners of Kurdistan (see **Tribes**). There were also attempts to plot these statistics and lists on maps: one of the best results was a large, multicolored British Royal Geographical Society ethnic map of this area, entitled *Map of Eastern Turkey in Asia, Syria, and Western Persia (Ethnographical)* (1906), which serendipitously is centered on Kurdistan. Few changes need be made today to this extremely valuable map, except of course to account for the obliteration of the Armenian ethnic element from around Lake Vân and other corners of eastern Anatolia as a result of World War I.

In the course of the 1960s, the Turkish government embarked on a project entitled *Köy Envanter Etüdleri*, or "village inventory studies," which was later aborted and suppressed after 1967. Still, the "inventory" provided a great deal of information on the ethnic composition of Turkey down to the village level. In a data-packed work, Nestmann (in *Ethnic Groups in the Republic of Turkey*, P. Andrews, ed., 1989) provides a convincing ethnic map of Kurdistan in Turkey (excluding the central Anatolian enclave), utilizing the very same village inventory. The data in the inventory closely support the depictions of Anatolia in the 1906 British Royal Geographical Society map mentioned above. The only difference, and a surprising one, is that the inventory depicts the Kurdish ethnic

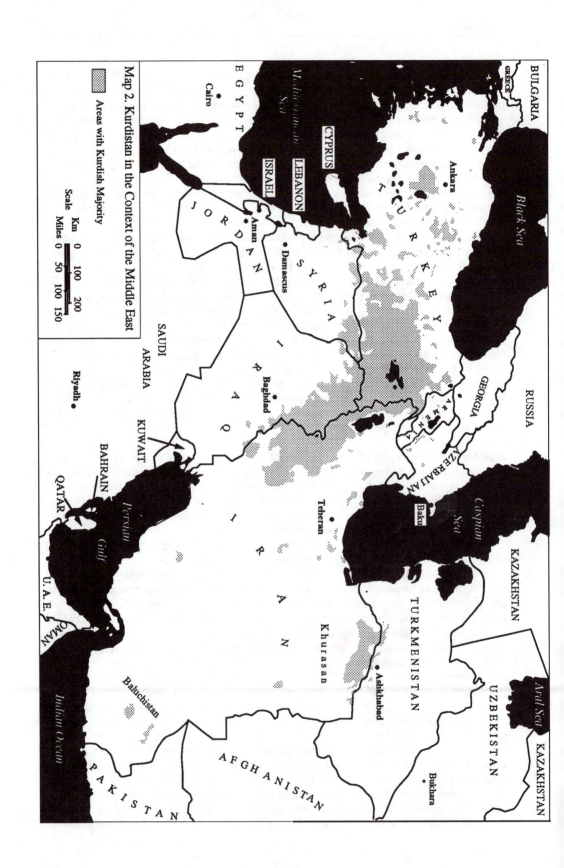

Map 2. Kurdistan in the Context of the Middle East

Areas with Kurdish Majority

Scale
Km   0   100   200
Miles 0 50 100 150

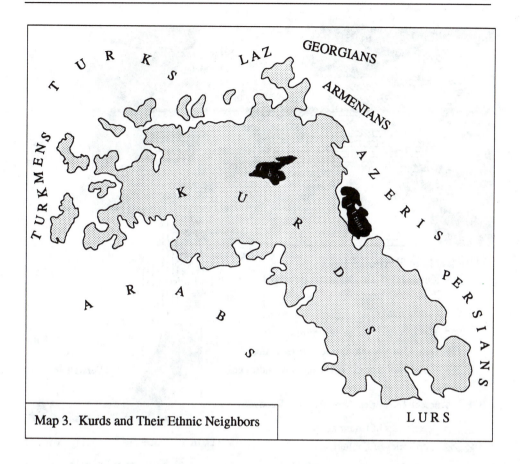

Map 3. Kurds and Their Ethnic Neighbors

domain as being even larger than on the British map. This may be an inadvertent reflection of the large-scale deportations and resettlements of Kurds within Turkey in 1929-38, and the relatively recent Kurdish demographic revolution (see **Deportations & Forced Resettlements** and **Demography**).

The Iranian Armed Forces Geographical Bureau carried out a similar project in the 1940s, and the results appeared in the ten-volume *Geographical Dictionary of Iran* (A. Razmara, ed., 1949–1951). This was later supplemented by the *Village Gazetteer of Iran* (Iranian Statistical Center, 1968–present). The British colonial government of the Mandate of Iraq and the French in Syria (which included the Antioch district before its transfer to Turkey in 1938) provided sufficient data on the ethnic breakdown of those areas to refine the boundaries and extent of Kurdistan.

Russian maps created in the 1960s, utilizing just such primary data, also demarcate Kurdish regions, and have served ever since as models for others, including the U.S. Central Intelligence Agency's published ethnic maps of the region. The best such Soviet material is found in the works of Bruk, *Narody Peredney Azii* (1960), with an accompanying sheet map at 1:5,000,000 scale, and Bruk and Apenchenko, *Atlas Narodov Mira* (1964). Both of these works also provide population figures for various segments of Kurdistan.

Maps provided for the present study have been based on these reliable sources.

Further Readings and Bibliography: *Map of Eastern Turkey in Asia, Syria, and Western Persia (Ethnographical)* (London: Royal Geographic Society, 1906, updated in 1914), with full-color sheet map at 1:2,000,000 scale; *Ethnographische Karte der Türkei: Vilayet Darstellung der amtlichen Türkischen*

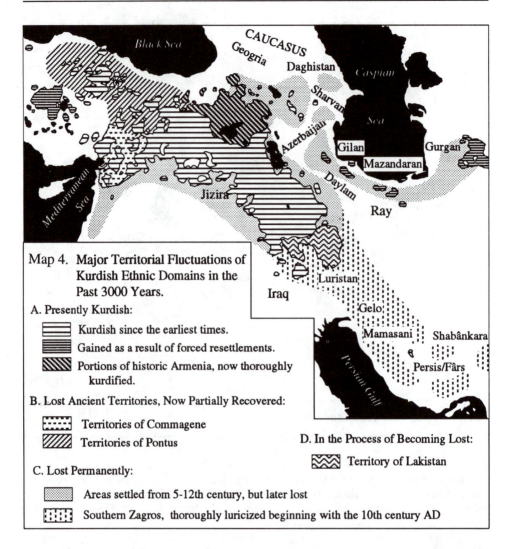

Map 4.   Major Territorial Fluctuations of
         Kurdish Ethnic Domains in the
         Past 3000 Years.

A. Presently Kurdish:

Kurdish since the earliest times.

Gained as a result of forced resettlements.

Portions of historic Armenia, now thoroughly
kurdified.

B. Lost Ancient Territories, Now Partially Recovered:

Territories of Commagene

Territories of Pontus

C. Lost Permanently:

Areas settled from 5-12th century, but later lost

Southern Zagros, thoroughly luricized beginning with the 10th century AD

D. In the Process of Becoming Lost:

Territory of Lakistan

Statistik 1935 (Berlin: Presse E. Zagner, n.d.), with sheet map at 1:2,500,000 scale; S. I. Bruk and V. S. Apenchenko, *Atlas Narodov Mira* (Moscow: Academy of Science, 1964); S.I. Bruk, *Narody Peredney Azii* (Moscow: Ethnographical Institute, 1960), with sheet map at 1:5,000,000 scale; J. F. Bestor, "The Kurds of Iranian Baluchistan: A Regional Elite," unpublished masters thesis, based on the author's field work (Montreal: McGill University, 1979); W. Barthold, *An Historical Geography of Iran* (Princeton: Princeton University Press, 1984); G. Le Strange, *The Lands of the Eastern Caliphate* (London: Cass, 1966, reprint of the 1905 original); H.W. Hazard, *Atlas of Islamic History* (Princeton: Princeton University Press, 1951); L. Nestmann, "Die ethnische Differenzierung der Bevölkerung der Osttürkei in ihren sozialen Bezügen," in Peter Andrews et al., *Ethnic Groups in the Republic of Turkey* (Wiesbaden: Reichert, 1989); *Annual Abstract of Statistics, 1970* (Baghdad: Government of Iraq, 1971); *Statistical Abstract 1973* (Damascus: Government of Syria, 1973); *Population Census 1970* (Damascus: Government of Syria, 1972); Captain Bertram Dickinson. "Journeys in Kurdistan," *Geographical Journal* 35 (1910), with map of Kurdistan at 1:2,000,000 scale; Captain F.R. Maunsell "Kurdistan," *Geographical Journal* 3-2 (1894), with map at 1:3,000,000 scale; Captain F.R. Maunsell "Central Kurdistan," *Geographical Journal* 18-2 (1894), with map at 1:1,000,000 scale; Lieut. Col. J. Shiel, "Notes on a Journey from Tabriz, through Kurdistan via Vân, Bitlis, Se'ert and Erbil, to Suleïmaniyeh, in July and August 1836," *Journal of the Royal Geographical Society* 8 (1838), with map at 1:4,060,000 scale; T.F. Aristova and G.P. Vasil'yeva, "Kurds of the Turkmen SSR," *Central Asian Review* 13-4 (1965).

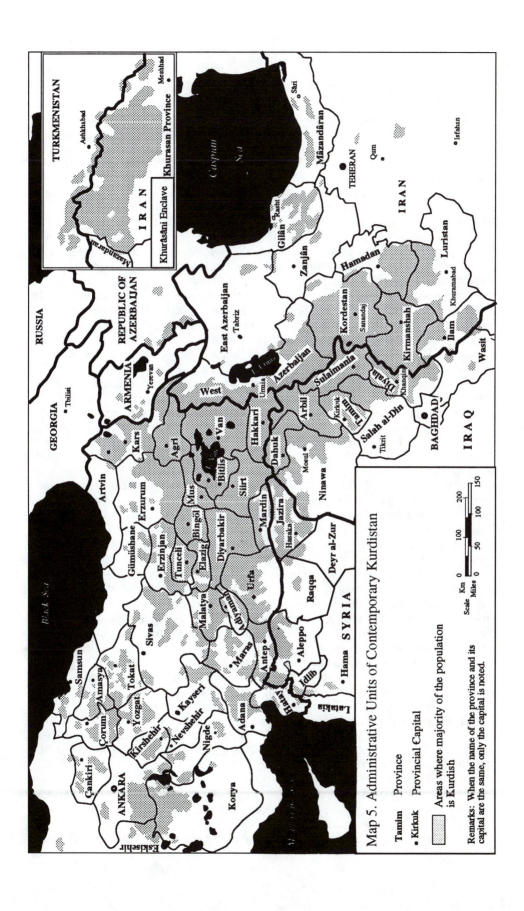

Map 5. Administrative Units of Contemporary Kurdistan

Tamim   Province

• Kirkuk   Provincial Capital

Areas where majority of the population
is Kurdish

Remarks: When the name of the province and its
capital are the same, only the capital is noted.

INTERNAL SUBDIVISIONS

Kurdistan can be divided historically, and on a socioeconomic, cultural, and political basis, into five major subdivisions: southern Kurdistan centered historically on the city of Kirmânshâh, central Kurdistan centered on Arbil, eastern Kurdistan centered on Mahâbâd, northern Kurdistan centered on Bâyazid, and western Kurdistan centered on Diyârbakir. The two large, detached Kurdish enclaves in Khurâsân and central Anatolia merit separate treatment (Map 6).

There exist "fossilized" records of two major historical subdivisions of Kurdistan, each following an epoch of ethnic homogenization. They have left their marks in the dialects spoken by the Kurds, their material culture, the elements of their religious beliefs, and their world outlook. Detailed analyses of the elements causing and/or fortifying the contemporary internal subdivisions, as well as the earlier ones, are found in the sections on **Language, Religion, Urbanization & Urban Centers, Historical Migrations,** and **Deportations & Forced Resettlements**.

A long episode of southeast-to-northwest migration of the Kurds culturally homogenized Kurdish society by the end of 3rd century AD. This homogeneity was subsequently diluted by a four-centuries-long separation of northern and western Kurdistan in Anatolia, which had come under the jurisdiction and/or influence of the Byzantines, from the rest of Kurdistan in the Muslim domains (see **Medieval History**). This ultimately resulted in the modern north-south split between the Kurmânji dialect groups, with the Greater Zâb river in Iraq marking the current linguistic and old cultural boundaries.

The boundaries drawn between Persian and Ottoman territories in the course of the 16th century proved to be as lasting—and divisive to the Kurds—as the older ones between the Byzantines and Muslims. The result is now a very perceptible east-west divide, which runs from Lake Urmiâ, intersecting the older north-south division, south along the present Iran-Iraq border.

Southern Kurdistan. Southern Kurdistan is now the last domain of the Gurâni-Laki language, and the center of the Yârsân religion. Here, South Kurmânji is the language of a rather small minority, and it may in fact be less common than Persian, a non-native language. The area is urbanized and its people cosmopolitan. Its inhabitants have a strong sense of history, informed primarily by its close contact with Persian culture over the past five centuries.

Eastern Kurdistan. Large portions of eastern Kurdistan, particularly south from the Bijâr-Marivân axis, were culturally part of southern Kurdistan until recently. South Kurmânji is now almost the only language there, and Sunni Islam the religion of a vast majority. The country folk, with their nomadic background, are markedly alien to the city people, creating a double-personality. While cities like Sanandaj, Bijâr, and Marivân have the feel and open culture of southern Kurdistan, the countryside is conservative and stark. The failure of many Kurdish political parties formed in this area is attributable to their difficulty in gaining allegiance from both sectors of their local society. The point of cultural inspiration for the area is surely Iran, but the links are not as strong as in southern Kurdistan, particularly with respect to the country people.

Central Kurdistan. Central Kurdistan has always tilted towards Mesopotamia, and its history is connected to that region. Like southern Kurdistan, it has an urban-oriented past, but the climate and terrain are not very much like southern Kurdistan. Central Kurdistan is the least mountainous, and on average, the warmest part of Kurdistan. In fact, the area is often referred to as *garmasir*, or "warm country." Culturally, however, central and southern Kurdistan are in many respects extensions of one another, despite five centuries of Persian political rule over southern Kurdistan. (Prior to the Persian-Ottoman division, and since the beginning of recorded history, southern Kurdistan also showed a cultural tilt towards Mesopotamia.)

While Sunni Islam is the religion of the majority in central Kurdistan, Shi'ite Islam,

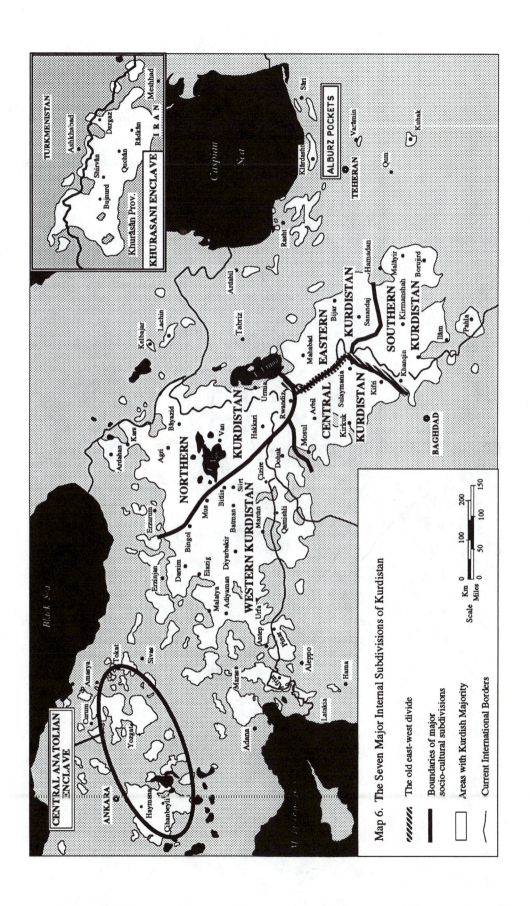

Map 6. The Seven Major Internal Subdivisions of Kurdistan

////// The old east-west divide

▬▬▬ Boundaries of major
    socio-cultural subdivisions

☐ Areas with Kurdish Majority

⌒ Current International Borders

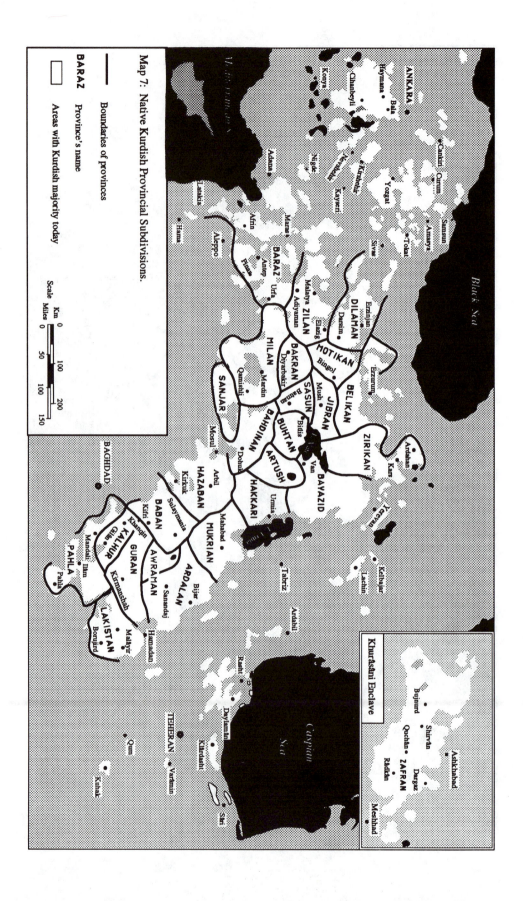

Map 7: Native Kurdish Provincial Subdivisions.

—————— Boundaries of provinces

BARAZ Province's name

☐ Areas with Kurdish majority today

Yârsânism, Alevism, Yezidism, Christianity, and Judaism are all present. In addition, every major dialect of Kurdish is spoken there, rendering it the one area linking together, culturally as well as geographically, all the subdivisions of Kurdistan.

Western Kurdistan. Western Kurdistan is Mediterranean in outlook, although geographically it ranges from the Mediterranean coast near Alexandretta to mountain elevations of over 11,000 feet just north of Darsim. Throughout, the climate is benign, agriculture bountiful, and woodlands plentiful. Historically, it has been urban-centered, and its many large cities have always been populous and worldly, looking toward the West and the Mediterranean for inspiration, whether from Antioch, Rome, Byzantium, or Istanbul.

There are about as many followers of Alevism in this subdivision as there are Sunni Muslims. Linguistically, the area is divided between Dimili and North Kurmânji speakers, but since there is presently only a weak correlation between language and religion, the internal differences have not manifested themselves as clear-cut social or cultural divisions.

Western Kurdistan is physically isolated from the rest of Kurdistan, despite its long borders with northern Kurdistan. This is due to the desolate character of northern Kurdistan and the mountains that separate the two regions.

Northern Kurdistan. Northern Kurdistan has the harshest, most inhospitable land and climate of contiguous Kurdistan. Large portions of this subdivision, particularly the shores of Lake Vân and the area north of it, are historical Armenia. They have gotten their almost exclusively Kurdish character only since the end of World War I. The area once had a strong agricultural sector and an urban-based, trade-oriented economy, which was devastated by the past five centuries of wars, deportations, and massacres, as well as through environmental abuse (see **Early Modern History** and **Land & Environment**). The inhabitants are inward-looking, strongly tribal, and the least developed economically and technologically in Kurdistan.

Although the town of Vân is the largest in the area, it is a bit misleading to point to a city as the center or hub of northern Kurdistan. There are no cities of note in the region, but there are numerous city ruins. Northern Kurdistan is the land of many great past cultural centers. Even a smaller town like Bâyazid (modern Dogu Bâyazit) was once a major city and cultural center, to which was born Ahmad Khâni, perhaps the greatest Kurdish poet and the versifier of the national epic *Mem o Zin* (see **Literature**).

Khurâsân. Of the two large detached enclaves of Kurds, the one in northeastern Iran in the province of Khurâsân owes its existence to the deportations from mainly northern and western Kurdistan of the 16th to 18th centuries by the Safavid monarchs. This enclave spills over the Iranian borders into the Republic of Turkmenistan, onto the heights overlooking the Turkmen capital of Ashkhâbâd. This enclave is as large in area as eastern Kurdistan, with half its population. The area is milder, and environmentally less abused, than northern Kurdistan, has a respectable number of cities for its size (including Quchân, Shirvân, and Bujnurd), and rich agriculture. It has also had a far less tumultuous history in the past few centuries than the northern Kurdistan most of its inhabitants left behind. The Khurâsâni Kurdish community preserves a tradition now lost to its original home, as their deportations coincided with the beginning of a sustained cataclysmic military ravaging of northern Kurdistan by the Persian and Ottoman empires. The milder customs and intricate costumes of these Kurds preserve for posterity a glance at what northern Kurdistan might have been, had it been spared this devastation.

Almost all the Kurdish population in Khurâsân therefore speaks North Kurmânji, but centuries of exposure to the Shi'ite Persian community of Khurâsân and the proximity to the Shi'ite holy city of Mashhad have rendered the community a mixture of Sunni and Shi'ite Muslims, with a peppering of Alevi adherents.

The Khurâsâni enclave also is home to some smaller communities of Laki-speaking Yârsân Kurds. These were deported here from southern Kurdistan during the reign of the

Afshârid monarchs of Persia in the middle of the 18th century. Indeed, Karim Khân, the founder of the Zand dynasty of Persia that succeeded the Afshârids, was himself born to a family of these Lak deportees (of the Zand tribe). After ascending the Peacock Throne, Karim brought most of his people back to their original home. Those who chose to stay behind are the ancestors of the modern Laks of the Khurâsâni enclave and Birjand in Qohistân.

Central Anatolia. The enclave in central and north-central Anatolia in Turkey is a two-lobed entity with two personalities. The southern lobe is on the arid and inhospitable lands to the west of Lake Tuz Gölü (south of Ankara), with the impoverished towns of Cihanbeyli, Yunak, and Haymâna being its major urban settlements. The northern lobe is by contrast on the agriculturally rich and populous highlands in a quadrangle between the towns of Tokat, Yozgat, Çorum, and Âmâsyâ. The cities of Yozgat and Tokat, although not yet having a Kurdish majority, are the focal points of the northern lobe.

The southern lobe owes its existence to the same 16th-18th-century deportations that created the Kurdish community in Khurâsân, while the northern lobe is more the result of a natural and steady migration of Kurds into the region from contiguous Kurdistan. The northern lobe is bustling and dynamic, with the highest overall living standards among Kurds. It is fast expanding today.

The overwhelming majority of the Kurds in the central Anatolian enclave speak North Kurmânji, but Dimili is also spoken by perhaps 10% of the community. Sunni Islam may be the religion of the majority of these Kurds, with Alevism retaining a sizable minority.

Each of the major internal subdivisions delineated above is further subdivided and informally administered by an array of large and small tribal organizations with deep historical roots. In the absence of a sovereign Kurdish government, the traditional internal subdivisions and large tribal domains may be properly perceived to serve as the national Kurdish substitute for administrative units, similar to the ordinary provincial entities devised for modern state administration. After all, these units have come into existence on the basis of historical and cultural realities, some thousands of years old (see **Tribes**) (Map 7).

General Bibliography

H.V. Handel-Mazzetti. "Zur Georgraphie von Kurdistan," *Petermann's Geographische Mitteilungen* 58 (1912); Walter Harris, "A Journey in Persian Kurdistan," *Geographical Journal* 6-5 (1895); Major Kenneth Mason, "Central Kurdistan," *Geographical Journal* 154-6 (1919); E. Smith, "Contribution to the Geography of Central Koordistan," *Journal of the American Oriental Society* II (1851); J.G. Taylor, "Travels in Kurdistan, with Notices of the Sources of the Eastern and Western Tigris, and Ancient Ruins in their Neighbourhood," *Journal of the Royal Geographical Society* 35 (1865); Jacques de Morgan, *Relation sommaire d'un voyage en perse et dans le kurdistan* (Paris, 1895).

Chapter 2

LAND & ENVIRONMENT

TERRAIN

The most prominent geophysical feature of Kurdistan is clearly its mountainousness. Kurdistan at present is composed primarily of the area of the central and northern Zagros, the eastern two-thirds of the Taurus and Pontus, and the northern half of the Amanus mountains. The two large, detached Kurdish enclaves are in the Rivand heights of the eastern section of the Alburz mountains of northeastern Iran, in the province of Khurâsân, and in the central Pontian mountains in central and north-central Anatolia, neighboring the Turkish capital of Ankara (see Map 8). In addition to these, there have been for centuries many smaller Kurdish enclaves in areas ranging from the volcanic highlands of western Baluchistan, to the central Alburz range in northern Iran, to the Ulu Mountains on the Aegean coast of western Turkey.

In contiguous Kurdistan, as well as in the many far-flung Kurdish settlements, mountains are the single most important natural phenomenon, and they have shaped the Kurdish history, people, tradition, and culture. Kurdish domains end abruptly where the plains begin.

Northern Kurdistan has the highest average elevation. In the words of William Eagleton, this is the home of "roaring torrents, shadowed canyons and suspension bridges." Central Kurdistan, on the other hand, has the lowest average elevation, with the warmest, often balmy, climate in all of Kurdistan. The other sections of the land range between these two extremes. The Kurdish mountains form a rampart to the Iranian and Anatolian Plateaus to the east and west, respectively, separating them from the flat plains of Arabia to the south and southwest, and the Black Sea basin to the north. The central massif runs the entire length of Kurdistan from one end to the other like a mighty spinal column.

The highest points in Kurdistan are, respectively, Mt. Alvand in the south (in Iran) at 11,745 feet, Mt. Halgurd (or Algurd) in north-central Kurdistan (in Iraq) at 12,249 feet, Mt. Munzur in the west (in Turkey) at 11,644 feet, and Mt. Ararat in the north (in Turkey) at 16,946 feet (Map 9).

Further Readings and Bibliography: Y. Abul Haggag, "North-east Iraq: A Physiographical Study," *Bulletin de la Societe de Geographie d'Egypte* 33 (1960); H. Bobek, "Forshungen im Zentralkurdischen Hochgebirge zwischen Van- und Urmia-See (Sudest-Anatolien und West-Azerbaidjan)," *Petermann's Geographische Mitteilungen* 84 (1938); R. Clayton, "The Mountains of Kurdistan," *Alpine Journal* (1887); Francis Halley, "The Gorge of the Qal'a Cholan and its Confluence with the Lesser Zab. Notes of a Tour in South Kurdistan in 1921," *Geographical Journal* 86-2 (1935); Jacques de Morgan, *Relation sommaire d'un voyage en perse et dans le kurdistan* (Paris, 1895).

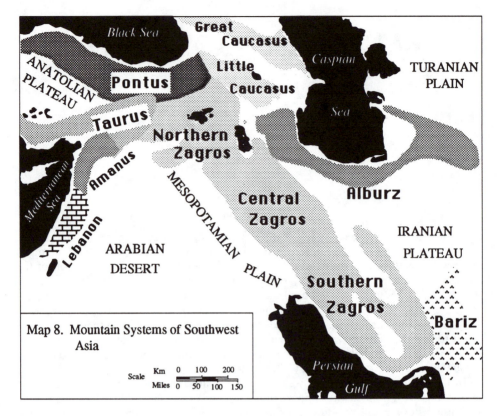

Map 8. Mountain Systems of Southwest Asia

GEOLOGY

Kurdistan is geologically quite active. The land straddles the subduction zone between the colliding Eurasian and African tectonic plates. Locally, the breakaway Arabian microplate is being subducted under the Iranian and Anatolian microplates at the rate of a few inches a year, and as a result the Zagros mountains and Kurdistan—the point of this collision—are being compressed and pushed upward several inches a year. This continental collision, which began about 15 million years ago, pushed up the area of Kurdistan from the bottom of the Tethys Sea, which covered southwest Asia, and is still adding elevation to the young mountains of Kurdistan.

   The geologic province of the Kurdish foothills which faces the Arabian platform, is basically a continuation of the same land formation that lies farther south under the Persian Gulf—a remnant of the ancient Tethys Sea with its wealth of hydrocarbons. These formations run almost unchanged from the east coast of the Mediterranean Sea at Antioch to the Straits of Hormuz. In fact, the waters of the Persian Gulf washed the Kurdish foothills until very recently in geologic terms, when they joined the Indian Ocean to the Mediterranean Sea and the Atlantic, separating Eurasia from Africa and Arabia. The petroleum-bearing geologic strata of the Persian Gulf thus ought to be credited for the wealth of petroleum and natural gas deposits in Kurdistan.

   Massive volcanic outpourings have resurfaced large portions of Kurdistan in the north and northeast. The greater and lesser Ararat peaks, as well as Mt. Nimrod (or Nimrut Dâgh) on the shores of Lake Vân, are three prominent results of this active geology. Also, Lake Vân and Lake Urmiâ are both the results of the natural damming of river channels by lava flows in the geologically recent past The rest of the land is thoroughly folded, with numerous fault lines crossing Kurdistan, mainly in a northwest-southeast direction, but more or less east-west in western Kurdistan. Igneous outpourings have enriched the land with many commercially valuable mineral resources (see **Natural Resources**). They have also painted the landscape with such richness in rock colors that it continues unfailingly to astonish outsiders on their first visit.

Its active geology has also rendered Kurdistan an earthquake-prone land. One result of this is that very few archaeological monuments stand above ground. At Kangâwar in southern Kurdistan, the vast temples of the goddess Anahita bear dramatic witness to the force and persistence of these tremors. The far-thrown columns, shattered grand staircases, and crumbled masonry platforms and walls are vivid illustrations of 2,200 years of ceaseless quakes. The mangled colossal statues at Mt. Nimrut Dâgh (not to be confused with Mt. Nimrod, above) north of Adiyâman in far western Kurdistan are other examples. The persistent folk tales and legends of cities and villages that were "swallowed up by the earth" all point to this geologic activity throughout the ages.

Further Readings and Bibliography: Celâl Sengör, *The Cimmeride Orogenic System and the Tectonics of Eurasia* (Boulder: Geological Society of America, 1984); *The International Petroleum Encyclopedia*; Christopher Ryan, *A Guide to the Known Minerals of Turkey* (Ankara: Mineral Research and Exploration Institute of Turkey, 1960); I. Altin et al., "Ölçekli Türkiye Jeoloji Haritasi" ("Explanatory Text of the Geological Map of Turkey"), sheets published loose at 1:500,000 scale for each Turkish province, accompanied by explanatory texts (Ankara: Mineral Research and Exploration Institute of Turkey, 1960-70); *Seismotectonic Atlas of Iran* (Teheran: Geological Survey of Iran, 1976); Herbert Wright, "Geologic Aspects of the Archaeology of Iraq," *Sumer* XI (1955).

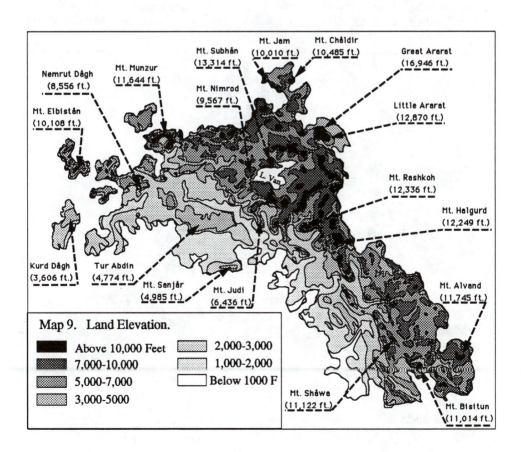

Map 9. Land Elevation.

CLIMATE & RAINFALL

Mean annual temperatures in Kurdistan vary sharply with elevation, decreasing as one ascends the central massif. The summers in the lower elevations can be oppressively hot and semi-humid, while it stays pleasantly cool in regions deep inside the mountains. The winters, except in small marginal regions facing the plains, are bitterly cold and snowy (Map 10).

This contrast in climates has been progressively heightened by the destruction of the forests and overgrazing in the lower elevations. Many areas known until very recently for their agreeable climates are now semi-barren, denuded landscapes that alternate between summer heat and winter freezes.

The coldest regions, with mean annual temperatures below the freezing point, are almost all in northern Kurdistan in Anatolia, and this allows for permanent glacier fields on the highest elevations. The coldest regions constitute about 5% of the land.

The regions with a mean annual temperature between the freezing point and 5° Celsius (40° Fahrenheit) constitute about 15% of Kurdistan. These are spread primarily across northern Kurdistan in Turkey and into Iran, but include long spurs stretching into northwestern Kurdistan at Darsim, and south into Iraq. These regions can have snow 7 months of the year. The cities of Kârs and Ardahân are inside this zone.

In northern Kurdistan, the winter months are colder on average than in Anchorage and Juneau, Alaska. The vivid reports of the Greek historian Xenophon, as he and 10,000 Greek soldiers struggled desperately with the cold on their retreat (BC 401) through Kurdistan (*Anabasis*, IV.1-3), are supplemented by Plutarch's report of the Roman Lucullus' expedition there about two centuries later. On that occasion, winter fell as early as late September, Plutarch relates, "with storms and frequent snows, and even in the most clear days, hoarfrost and ice, which made the waters scarcely drinkable for the horses by their exceeding coldness, and scarcely passable through the ice breaking and

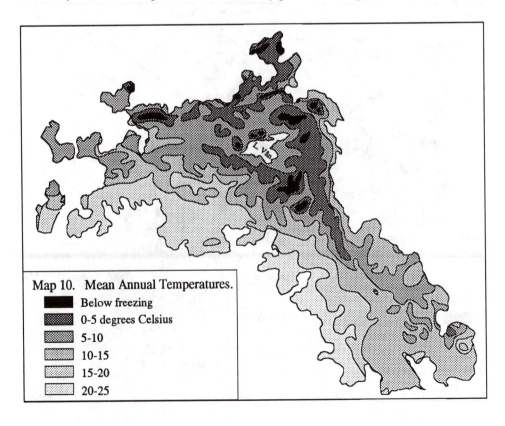

Map 10.   Mean Annual Temperatures.
- Below freezing
- 0-5 degrees Celsius
- 5-10
- 10-15
- 15-20
- 20-25

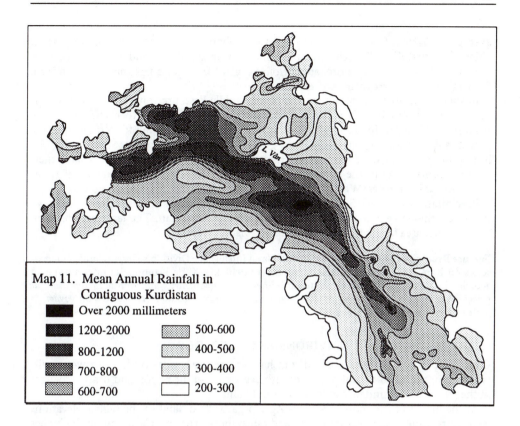

Map 11. Mean Annual Rainfall in
Contiguous Kurdistan

■ Over 2000 millimeters

■ 1200-2000   ▥ 500-600

■ 800-1200   ▥ 400-500

■ 700-800   □ 300-400

▥ 600-700   □ 200-300

cutting the horses' sinews" (*Lives*, "Lucullus"). The Roman army mutinied, resulting in a retreat. Late in the Middle Ages, the Venetian traveller Marco Polo described cold "past all bounds" (*Travels*, I.vi)

The rest of northern Kurdistan has mean annual temperatures of 5-10°C (40-48°F), as do large portions of western and eastern Kurdistan, stretching south in pockets to Hamadân. This climatic zone comprises about 20% of the overall area of contiguous Kurdistan. The cities of Darsim, Bitlis, Mus, Bingöl, Âgri, Vân, Hakkâri, and Qala Diza, as well as Bijâr, Sardasht, Marivân, Bâna, and Hamadân are within this zone. There is an average of 5 months of snow in these areas most years.

Perhaps the most pleasant part of Kurdistan is the zone with mean annual temperatures of 10-15°C (48-57°F). This is the largest single zone, comprising 40% of Kurdistan, including almost two-thirds of southern Kurdistan and half of western Kurdistan. The central Anatolian and Khurâsâni enclaves are also primarily inside this zone. This zone includes the cities of Malâtya, Adiyâman, Antep, Elâzig, Zakho, Dohuk, Amâdiya, Halabja, Mahâbâd, Saqqez, Sanandaj, Kirmânshâh, Shâhâbâd, and Kangâwar, as well as Quchân, Bujnurd, and Shirvân (in the Khurâsâni enclave), and Cihânbeyli, Haymâna, Polâtli, Yozgat, and Tokat (in the Anatolian enclave) (see **Urbanization & Urban Centers**). These regions can have up to 4 months of snow.

The warmest major zone in Kurdistan has mean annual temperatures of 15-20°C (57-65°F). All of Syrian Kurdistan, half of central Kurdistan in Iraq, and about 15% of western Kurdistan is located in this warm zone. It contains the cities of Diyârbakir, Siirt, Mârdin, Urfâ, Qamishli, Afrin, Sanjâr, Sulaymânia, Arbil, Qasri Shirin, Ilâm, Gelân, and Pahla. Here one can expect up to 2 months of snow.

A rather small zone, comprising less than 10% of Kurdish lands and consisting of the border region between Kurdistan and the neighboring lowlands, has temperatures averaging 20-25°C (65–74°F). It is almost entirely in Iraqi Kurdistan. The important cities of Kirkuk, Kifri, Tuz Khurmâtu, Khânaqin, Mandali, Badra, and Mehrân, however, fall within this zone, where orchards of olives, citrus fruits, and figs can be maintained. Snowfalls there are irregular and very brief.

In sharp contrast to most other parts of the Middle East, precipitation in Kurdistan is regular and bountiful. It follows a Mediterranean regime, with a winter-spring maximum. Most precipitation is in the form of snow, which can fall for 6 months of the year in some areas, forming permanent glaciers on the highest peaks. Summer has the least rain, but because of melt water from the higher elevations, the rivers have their maximum discharge in the summer, supplying reliable and bountiful irrigation water (see **Natural Resources: Water**).

Precipitation averages 50–80 inches per year in the central massif, down to 20–40 inches on the descent to the lowland boundaries of Kurdistan. The least precipitation occurs in the area facing the Mesopotamian lowland (Map 11).

Further Readings and Bibliography: British Naval Intelligence Division's *Geographical Handbook* series on Iran, Iraq, Turkey (2 vols.), and Syria (1940-43); X. de Planhol, "Limites antique et actuelle des cultures arbustives mèditerranèennes en Asie Mineure," *Bulletin de l'Association de Gèographes français* 239-40 (Paris, 1954). Jacques de Morgan, *Relation sommaire d'un voyage en perse et dans le kurdistan* (Paris, 1895).

ENVIRONMENT & ECOLOGY

Over the past 100,000 years, Kurdistan has seen several cycles of dry and wet spells, resulting in the advance and retreat of lush vegetation in the region and drastic changes in the nature and abundance of local flora and fauna.

At the height of the most recent Ice Age, large tracts of land in the higher elevations were barren due to the persistent cold and much more extensive glaciation on the higher points. The lower regions received less precipitation, because of a shift in the climatic zones and a southward shift in the jet stream.

At the time of the the the domestication of crops and animals in Kurdistan, around 12,000 years ago, a good deal of glacial ice was still present, and there existed a precipitation regime not dissimilar to that of today, although its seasonal pattern was quite different. The most prominent feature of the ecosystem at this time was its pervasive and rich grassland, with a wealth of seed grasses and plantago weed, as well as bulbed and other kinds of flowers (Wright 1968, 334-339). Large herds of wild sheep, goats, boars, carnivorous mammals, and migratory birds were present to tap this wealth of food. The area was ideal for the invention of two new and revolutionary technologies: agriculture and livestock domestication. The territory of Kurdistan, along with the adjacent lowlands of Mesopotamia and Syria-Palestine, took the historical title of "Fertile Crescent" for this reason (see **Early Technological Development**).

The last episode in climatic and ecological change began around 8000 years ago, with the final retreat of the glaciers and the return in full force of warm, rain-bearing clouds stimulated by a northward shift of the jet stream. This Asian monsoon regime advanced well onto the Iranian plateau to the east of Kurdistan around 6000 years ago, creating vast inland lakes. This greatly accelerated the retreat of the ice and the proliferation of vegetation up the slopes of Kurdistan by adding adequate summer rainfall to the already generous winter and spring precipitation on these mountains.

The cold tundra and sparse grasslands gave way to thick forests of cedar, pine, juniper, oriental cyprus, ash, poplar, sycamore, and most importantly, chestnut and oak. Large stands of fruit and nut trees also appeared in the more protected valleys. New animals, such as brown and black bear, proliferated with the new forests. The higher elevations now became the grasslands.

The Asian monsoons began a slow retreat back south about 4000 years ago, dramatically cutting the summer rains. While the vegetation in the higher elevations in Kurdistan could tolerate this reduction of rainfall because of lower annual temperatures (and thus evaporation rates), the lower grounds and valleys were left in a fragile state. The neighboring Iranian plateau was devastated. The long and slow trend toward desiccation continues to the present day.

The extant literature from the cuneiform archives of Mesopotamian civilizations, beginning with the 4000-year-old epic of Gilgamesh, all celebrate the Zagros as the land of the "Cedar Forest," which stretched "for ten thousand leagues in every direction" (see **Popular Culture** and **National Character**). "Together they went down into the forest and they came to the green mountain. There they stood still, they were struck dumb; they stood still and gazed at the forest, at the mountain of cedars, the dwelling place of the gods. The hugeness of the cedar rose in front of the mountain, its shade was beautiful, full of comfort; mountain and glade were green with brushwood" (Sandars, trans. and ed., *The Epic of Gilgamesh*, "The Forest Journey," 1972).

To the ancients these thick, dark mountain woods must have seemed an inexhaustible source of timber for construction and charcoal for brick furnaces and domestic use. But exhausted they became. In fact, by the beginning of the first millennium BC, the cedar forests of the Zagros (*konâr* in Kurdish) were so exhausted (or the victims of climatic change) that later versions of the Epic, despite clear geographical discrepancy, ascribe the "Cedar Forest" to Lebanon, where the prized timbers could still be logged in abundance at the time. In fact, some modern scholars, noting the geographical discrepancy but perplexed by the long absence of any large cedar stands in the Zagros, have come to interpret the ancient words of the epic as "Pine Forest" rather than as "Cedar Forest."

By the time of the advent of the Achaemenians (550 BC) (see **Ancient History**), who adhered to the time-honored tradition of using cedar beams for roofing, Kurdistan no longer provided the wood. For his palaces at Susa and Persepolis, the Achaemenian king Darius I had to import cedar from far-off Lebanon. It did not, at any rate, take long for the Lebanese cedars to meet the fate of the Kurdish cedars.

Many Kurdish forests are relics of a more humid past and are unable to renew themselves once they have been clear-cut in large tracts. Once the forests are clear-cut, the micro-climate and the ecosystem they maintain literally evaporate. As such, most of these woods are not a renewable resource in the strict sense of the word, and great care must be given to the exploitation and management of these old forests. First, there went the cedars, followed by the pine. An approximate date for the destruction of the pine forests can be set at about the 3rd or 4th century BC, by noting that pines are depicted as the tree of choice, and pine cones as a favorite motif, in the palace bas reliefs during the Assyrian, Median, and Achaemenian periods, ending in 330 BC—but not later.

This deterioration in plant cover has naturally had a strong and adverse effect on the general climate and the ability of the ecosystem to mend the damage (see **Climate & Rainfall**). The damage done in the 19th- and 20th century has dwarfed the total effects of all previous abuses since antiquity. A quick comparison of the current environment with the accounts of European travelers in the past century horrifies the reader with the degree of negative change in the plant and animal wealth of the region. The fertile topsoil, devoid of its protective plant cover, washes away catastrophically under the heavy down-pours of spring, and winter snow avalanches alternate with spring mud avalanches to block roads and damage settlements below. The valuable topsoil dumped into the network of rivers carries away not only the future natural productivity of the land but also clogs at alarming rates the dams built to tap the region's vast hydraulic potentials (see **Natural Resources: Water**).

Kurdistan is not, of course, alone on this destructive path, as the ecosystems of the neighboring regions, in fact the world over, similarly bear the brunt of human abuse.

Very little has been spent on the preservation or revival of plant cover. The perennial existence of a state of siege or outright war in the region has not helped either. The movement of heavy military equipment, bombardments, and intentional fires in the course of military operations have all contributed to the deterioration of the fragile environment.

Further Readings and Bibliography: Herbert Wright, "Pleistocene Glaciation in Kurdistan," *Eiszeitalter und Gegenwart* XII (Wiesbaden, 1961); K. Wasylikowa, "Late Quaternary Plant Macro-Fossils from Lake Zeribar, Western Iran," *Review of Palaeobotany and Palynology* 2 (1967); Herbert Wright, "Late Quaternary Climates and Early Man in the Mountains of Kurdistan," *Report of the VI International Congress on Quaternary Epoch, Warsaw, 1961* (Lödz, 1964); H. Wright, "Modern Pollen Rain in Western Iran and its Relation to Plant Geography and Quaternary Vegetational History," *Journal of Ecology* 55 (1969); Charles Reed and R. Braidwood, "Toward the Reconstruction of the Environmental Sequence of Northeastern Iraq," in Braidwood and Howe, eds., *Prehistoric Investigations in Iraqi Kurdistan* (Chicago: University of Chicago Press, 1960); C. Brooks, *Climate Through the Ages* (London: Ernest Benn, 1949); Arlette Leroi-Gourhan and Ralph Solecki, "Palaeoclimatology and Archaeology in the Near East," *Annals of the New York Academy of Sciences* XCV (1961); Clark Howell, "Pleistocene Glacial Ecology and the Evolution of Classic Neanderthal Man," *Southwestern Journal of Anthropology* VIII-4 (1952); Werner Nützel, "The Climatic Changes of Mesopotamia and Bordering Areas: 14,000 to 2,000 BC," *Sumer* xxx:1-2 (Baghdad, 1976); X. de Planhol, "Limites antique et actuelle des cultures arbustives mèditerranèennes en Asie Mineure," *Bulletin de l'Association de Gèographes français* 239-40 (1954); *Climatic Atlas of Iran* (Teheran: Teheran University Press, 1970); Ali Tanoglu, Sirri Erinç, and Erol Tümertekin, *Türkiye Atlasi* (Istanbul: Milli Egilim Basimevi, 1961); *The Epic of Gilgamesh*, translated and edited by N.K. Sandars (Baltimore: Penguin, 1972); H. Wright, "Natural Environment of Early Food Production North of Mesopotamia," *Science* 161:334-339 (1968); W. van Zeist, "Late Quaternary Vegetation History of Western Iran," *Review of Palaeobotany and Palynology* 2 (1967); H. Bobek, "Die gegenwärtige und eiszeitliche Vergletscherung im Zentralkurdischen Hochgebirge (Osttaurus, Ostanatolien)," *Zeitschrift für Gletscherkunde* 27 (1940); Jacques de Morgan, *Relation sommaire d'un voyage en perse et dans le kurdistan* (Paris, 1895).

FLORA & FAUNA

Enough stands of oak, dwarf oak, chestnut, juniper, pine, cedar, and wild fruit trees have survived in Kurdistan today to convey a glimpse of the ancient forests (see **Environment & Ecology**). Oak and dwarf oak are now the most common trees in the remaining Zagros forests. The oak forests are the ideal ecosystems for several highly prized fungi, such as truffles (*chema*), which are available in abundance and are, along with wild chestnuts, a food of the poor. A large array of wild fruits, berries, and nuts, such as grapes, cherries, pears, quince, mulberries, blackberries, hazel nuts, walnuts, and almonds, are also collected in the forests.

The land has been known since ancient times for its wealth of luxurious flowers (see **Popular Culture**). Kurdistan was probably the site of the domestication of many bulb flowers, such as tulips, hyacinths, gladioli, and daffodils, and medicinal herbs such as valerian and cowslip. Its abundance of aromatic flowers and herbs may be the source of the renowned pleasant scent of Kurdistan's dairy products (see **Agriculture**).

The fauna still retains its richness, with an abundance of black and brown bears, wolves, hyenas, boars, foxes, beavers, jackals, cheetahs, leopards; migratory and resident birds such as eagles, bustards, larks, bluebirds, quail, and partridges; and reptiles such as small and giant turtles, lizards, and snakes. In addition, a variety of fresh-water lake and river fish like carp, trout, and over forty different spring and subterranean-cave fish, including blind fish, are found in local bodies of water.

Ancient Kurdish pottery and Assyrian bas reliefs depict a number of animals no longer present in Kurdistan. From the archaeological evidence, elephants (of genus *Loxodonta)* and ostriches seem to have been hunted out of the Kurdish foothills in the beginning of the third millennium BC, while lions (genus *Felis leo Persica*) seem to have survived until perhaps the beginning of the last century. The great mammals were the primary targets for hunts, some of which took the proportions of massacres. Assyrian monarch Tiglath-pileser I (r. 1114-1076 BC), for example, asserts in one of his surviving inscriptions that he killed four wild bulls, ten elephants, and 920 lions, in one hunting season.

Tigers (genus *Felis tigris Tigris*) of the Tigris river basin (whence the animal's name in European languages) seem to have survived only until late classical times. The tigers presented at the staged hunting games held in Roman cities must have come from this source. It is possible, however, that these Kurdish tigers were not in the strict sense tigers at all, but rather the large leopards that are still found in Kurdistan, albeit in dwindling numbers. The name *tiger* first coined for them was later retained by the Romans for the real tigers from the Caspian-Hyrcanian forests after the Kurdish source of other, similar game animals dried up.

The wing bones of some large birds, probably used in religious ceremonies (see **Yezidism**), have been unearthed in the upper strata of the Shanidar-Zâwi Chami caves in central Kurdistan, and have been dated to about 10,800 years ago. These include bearded vultures, griffon vultures, white-tailed sea eagles, small eagles, and great bustards. Most of these birds are now extinct in Kurdistan, but the two largest of these great birds, the *halo'i homâ* or cliff eagle, which served as the model for the coat of arms of king Saladin and the Ayyubid Kurdish dynasty (see **Medieval History**), and the *shawât* or great bustard (*Otis tarda*), have survived in small numbers in the more inaccessible regions of the land. The wing spans of these two impressive birds are over 8 feet, which makes it understandable that they were used in ancient religious practices in Kurdistan.

Further Readings and Bibliography: M.B. Rowton, "The Woodlands of Ancient Western Asia," *Journal of Near Eastern Studies* 26 (1967); P.F. Turnbull and C.A. Reed, "The Fauna for the Terminal Pleistocene of Palegawa Cave," *Fieldiana Anthropology* 63 (1974); T.C. Young, "Survey in Western Iran, 1961," *Journal of Near Eastern Studies* 25 (1966); Dexter Perkins, "Prehistoric Fauna from Shanidar, Iraq," *Science* CXLIV-3626 (1964); H. Wright, H. McAndrews, and W. van Zeist, "Modern Pollen Rain in Western Iran, and Its Relation to Plant Geography and Quaternary Vegetational History," *Journal of Ecology* LV (1967); H. Walter, "Vegetationgliederung Anatoliens" ("Plant Distribution in Anatolia"), *Flora* 143 (1956); Jacques de Morgan, *Relation sommaire d'un voyage en perse et dans le kurdistan* (Paris, 1895).

General Bibliography

Some very good sources on the land and nature of Kurdistan in general are the British Naval Intelligence Division's *Geographical Handbook* series on Iran, Iraq, Turkey (2 vols.), and Syria (1940-43). The sheet maps and the accompanying text books of the *Tübinger Atlas des Voerderen Orients* (TAVO) (Wiesbaden, Ludwig Reichert Verlag, ongoing) are valuable resources for this and many other topics discussed in this work. Also see Ali Tanoglu, Sirri Erinç and Erol Tümertekin, *Türkiye Atlasi* (Istanbul: Milli Egilim Basimevi, 1961); Sirri Erinç, *Dogu Anadolu Cografyasi* ("Geography of Eastern Anatolia") (Istanbul: Istanbul University Press, 1953).

Chapter 3

HISTORY

Reconstruction of the Kurdish history is a difficult task. It frequently involves interpolation and extrapolation among a variety of sources written neither for nor about Kurds. Middle Eastern history has all too often (although not always) been written by its hegemons, and most recently the modern nation-states. The Kurds have not been hegemons for over 800 years. The result is that Kurdish contributions to history have been ignored, or worse, appropriated by other peoples (as to who or what is considered Kurdish in the present work, consult the **Preface** and **National Identity**). Any pioneering effort to reconstruct Kurdish history from fragments long buried and neglected is bound to raise questions and generate controversy, no matter how meticulous the research. This is to be expected because it challenges the status quo. If this work serves to encourage further scholarly investigation, it will have served its purpose.

PREHISTORY & EARLY TECHNOLOGICAL DEVELOPMENT: 10,000-3000 BC

This is by far the most noteworthy period in the history of Kurdistan. The technological advancements and discoveries made in the Kurdish highlands in the 7000 years preceding the rise of Mesopotamia (3000 BC) forever changed the course of human history, and altered the very face of the planet. Much that was achieved later by the civilization of lowland Mesopotamia starting 5000 years ago began 7000 years before that, in the bordering mountains and valleys of Kurdistan. The archaeological and zoological-botanical evidence of Kurdistan's crucial importance to the development of civilization is bountiful and well documented.

Paleolithic and Mesolithic cave habitats (i.e., those dated prior to 10,000 BC) dot southern and central Kurdistan in large numbers. The cave habitations at Behistun (Mt. Bisitun) in the south are dated to about 100,000 years ago, while those at Shanidar are as old as 55,000 years. The technological development and artistic expression of these Paleolithic and Mesolithic cultures are more or less parallel to those of other settlements in the Middle East and southern Europe.

The Neolithic period in Kurdistan was by contrast of a fundamentally different nature. The Neolithic revolution appears now to have had Kurdistan as a primary, if not *the* primary, locus. The inhabitants of this land went through an unexplained stage of accelerated technological evolution, prompted by yet uncertain forces. They rather quickly pulled ahead of their surrounding communities, the majority of which were also among the most advanced technological societies in the world, to embark on the transformation from a low-density, hunter-gatherer economy to a high-density, food-producing economy.

Kurdistan, the mountainous northern perimeter of the historic Fertile Crescent, was the site of the development and application of many early domestic and industrial technologies as well as modes of food production. A significant body of archaeological evidence points to the Kurdish mountains as the site of the invention of agriculture approximately 12,000 years ago (Braidwood 1960). From the Kurdish mountains, this revolutionary technology later spread into the neighboring lowlands of Mesopotamia, the hills of western Anatolia, and the plateau of Iran. By about 8000 years ago it had further spread into North Africa, Europe, and the Indian subcontinent. As such, Kurdistan is the point of origin for many common crops and domesticated animals (Ucko and Dimbleby 1969; Berg and Protsch 1973; Wright 1969).

The transition from food-gathering to food-production began within the natural geographical ranges of the wild ancestors of the early domesticates, which is in the general area of the Zagros mountains (Braidwood and Howe 1960, 1962; Braidwood 1972). Additionally, the present evidence strongly points to the foothills and intermontane valleys along the Kurdish mountain chains (with a spur stretching down into Samaria) as the main geographic context of this transition (Whallon 1979).

Agriculture of course necessitated domestication of the requisite flora and fauna. The ancestors of modern-day wheat, barley, rye, oats, peas, lentils, alfalfa, and grapes were first domesticated by the ancestors of the modern Kurds shortly before the 9th millennium BC. Wild species of most common cereals and legumes still grow as weeds in the Zagros and eastern Taurus, and to a lesser degree in the Amanus mountains (see **Land & Environment**).

The remains of some of the first domesticated goats, sheep, dogs, and pigs have been found at three major archaeological sites in Kurdistan: Çayönü (near modern Diyârbakir in western Kurdistan), Ganj Dara (northwest of Kirmânshâh in southern Kurdistan, dating to 10,000 years ago), and Jarmo (north of modern Sulaymânia in central Kurdistan, dating to 8000 years ago).

By the early 8th millennium BC many agricultural communities in Kurdistan had domesticated animals. The wealth of remains of agricultural and grain processing equipment, millstones, mortars and pestles, add to pollen records as firm evidence for the establishment of agriculture in Kurdistan by this time.

The extraordinary boom in population and production engendered by these advances led to the exploration and invention of many more technologies. The civilization of Kurdistan continued on its revolutionary technological course to invent or greatly contribute to the invention of metallurgy, common weaving, and fired pottery, as well as advances in architecture, urbanization, and writing.

The community at Çayönü became one of the two earliest in the world in which the existence of metallurgy has been proven (Braidwood 1969, Caldwell 1967). Copper instruments discovered there date to the first half of the 5th millennium BC. Bronze, an alloy of copper and tin, is harder and more useful than copper, and melts at a lower temperature, making it easier to work. Bronze instruments appear in Çayönü early in the 4th millennium BC—a full 2000 years ahead of their appearance in Europe.

The advances in metallurgy were facilitated by the proximity of the necessary ores. While the alluvial plains of Mesopotamia are utterly devoid of metal deposits, the Zagros, Taurus, and Amanus mountains, as well as the Judean volcanic formations, are teeming with just such deposits. In fact, the area centered on Çayönü can very properly be called the oldest living industrial site in the world, since the copper smelting and copper alloy goods manufacturing which started there over 7000 years ago continues to this day (see **Natural Resources: Minerals**).

In Çayönü as well as Ganj Dara (on the opposite side of Kurdistan near Kirmânshâh), meanwhile, fired pottery (along with small fired clay figurines) makes its first appearance, in the early 8th millennium BC (Majidzadeh 1975). While in the Neolithic period vessels were normally of stone or wood, plaster, or basketry, the introduction of durable, versatile pottery revolutionized domestic life, and the technology proved to be dearly sought by other communities. It spread at a very rapid rate into the neighboring regions and became widespread throughout the Middle East in the space of less than 1000 years, by about 7000 BC (Roaf 1990, 42).

Near Ganj Dara, at the ancient mound of Seh Gâbi, the very first example of glazed pottery in the world also appears, in about 3500 BC, predating by 2000 years the glazing technology in Mesopotamia and China (Vandiver 1990; Levine 1974). Kurdistan's involvement in the development of weaving technology is detailed under **Rugs & Fabrics**.

By the late 8th millennium BC society in Kurdistan had become sufficiently complex to need records for commercial transactions. These records first appear in Kurdistan as variously shaped clay tokens, each shape signifying an item of trade and a number. The tokens began carrying extra markings on them by 7500 years ago. As the messages they carried became more complex for each transaction, the tokens were encased in clay casings, and sometimes strung through a central hole so that the sequence of tokens could form a sentence (Schmandt-Besserat 1986, Nissen, 1986). By 3000 BC, the clay casing itself had become the record, replacing the tokens. The earliest cuneiform clay tablets still preserve the bulging appearance of the old token casings, without having any tokens inside. Writing in the modern sense had thus begun.

The earliest cuneiform, pictographic markings are actually impressions of the tokens, but they soon evolved into more symbolic forms and increased in complexity (Green 1981). As in other fields, Mesopotamia by the beginning of the 3rd millennium BC was surpassing Kurdistan in the development of writing. In Kurdistan and the Zagros mountains, the more primitive and indigenous token system continued to be used as the primary means of record keeping for a longer time. Writing underwent rapid development in Mesopotamia, and in Kurdistan was used only in conjunction with the tokens. Clay tablets bearing records written in a pictographic script known, for the lack of a better term, as "proto-Elamite" made their first known appearance in southern Kurdistan at Godin, near modern Kangâwar, about 4500 years ago. This dating, if we regard the token system per se as non-writing, renders Kurdistan the site of one of the earliest literate communities in the world, second only to neighboring Mesopotamia, and with a yet unknown level of influence on similar developments in the neighboring Iranian Plateau.

Vast food resources and high living standards allowed the population in Kurdistan to boom. In a relatively short time, it increased at least tenfold, from approximately 15,000 in 10,000 BC to about 150,000 in 9000 BC. The first states, or rather city-states, came into being by about 8th millennium BC (Wright 1977).

The sites of Cayönü, Oylum Höyük, Titrish (in western Kurdistan), Jarmo, Tapa Gawra (in central Kurdistan), Ganj Dara, and Giyân (in southern Kurdistan), along with Jericho in Judea, became the first urban communities on the planet, even though these "cities" were very modest in size (1000-1500 residents). Most of the rest of the world was of course limited to cave dwelling at this time. These urban sites had modest temples and very clearly followed a plan for the spatial relationship of the buildings to one another and to their general surroundings. They were also strategically located on the landscape to optimize their advantage for trade, agriculture, and defense.

The natural bounty of the land and ease of defending the mountainous landscape made unnecessary the expansion of the emergent bureaucracies and armies, keeping the local governments small and their jurisdictions limited. By contrast, in the neighboring alluvial plains of Mesopotamia, the need for constant management of scarce resources (via irrigation works and flood control) and the defense of the exposed landscape necessitated a great deal of bureaucratic organization and a standing military force. As the governments grew, so did the cities. The earliest Mesopotamian cities, of the Sumerians and the Akkadians, like Eridu, Nippor, Ur, and Uruk were on average 10 times more populous than the cities in Kurdistan, having around 10,000-15,000 inhabitants and formidable defense systems.

The civilization of Kurdistan came to full bloom during what is termed the Halaf cultural period, ca. 6000-5000 BC. The period is named after the ancient mound of Halaf in western Kurdistan, west of Mardin (Map 12). Halaf culture is marked by the spread of

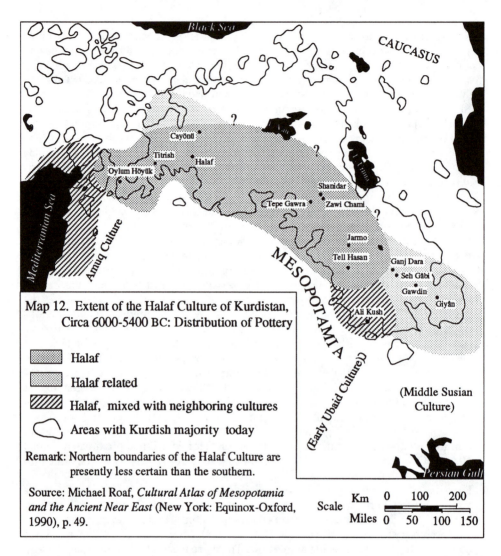

Map 12. Extent of the Halaf Culture of Kurdistan,
          Circa 6000-5400 BC: Distribution of Pottery

▓▓ Halaf

▓▓ Halaf related

▨▨ Halaf, mixed with neighboring cultures

⌒ Areas with Kurdish majority today

Remark: Northern boundaries of the Halaf Culture are
         presently less certain than the southern.

Source: Michael Roaf, *Cultural Atlas of Mesopotamia
and the Ancient Near East* (New York: Equinox-Oxford,
1990), p. 49.

Scale   Km   0   100   200
        Miles 0   50   100   150

uniform, well-constructed circular residential units and the production of masterfully
manufactured and exquisitely painted potteries. The first firm evidence of cultural
homogenization of the inhabitants of Kurdistan dates from the Halaf period, consisting
in the uniformity of artistic expression and material culture found from one end of
Kurdistan to the other (Roaf 1990, 51). This unity in architecture and the decorative arts
is so strong as to have prompted many archaeologists to suggest also an ethnic unity of
the people who practiced them (von Oppenheim 1931). Surprisingly, many of the
decorative elements of the Halaf culture survive in contemporary Kurdish art (Mellaart
1975) (see **Decorative Designs & Motifs**).

By the conclusion of the Halaf period, the level of civilization and technological sophistication of lowland Mesopotamia had come to match that of highland Kurdistan. It
clearly had surpassed Kurdistan by the beginning of what is termed the Historical Era,
ca. 4000 BC, and the opening of the Hurrian cultural period in Kurdistan. This new era
coincided with the widespread introduction of writing, expansion of government,
institutionalization of religion, urban explosion, and what is commonly termed "literate
civilization," moving from "Prehistory" into the "Historical Era."

Agricultural Technology and the Spread of the Indo-European Language. Several new theories, championed by Colin Renfrew (1988) now propose that the original spread of the Indo-European languages was powered by a new technology: agriculture. These theories maintain that the speakers of the original proto-Indo-European language, the illusive "*Ursprache*," expanded their realm by spreading into the thinly populated, non-agriculturalist Europe and subsequently the Eurasian steppes from the densely populated agriculturalist Anatolia. As such, they place the original homeland of the Indo-European family of languages in an area centered on Çatal Hüyük in south-central Anatolia. Farming at Çatal Hüyük, as is admitted by Renfrew and originally proposed by its excavator, James Mellaart (1975), is dated to only the 7th millennium BC—over 2000 years after many proven archaeological sites in nearby Kurdistan (such as Çayönü near Diyârbakir), show the existence of sophisticated agricultural communities with subsidiary advanced technologies. Agricultural technology spread from Kurdistan towards western Anatolia nearly 3000 years after its invention there. Two Soviet authors, T. Gamkrelidze and V. Ivanov (1990) have now joined the group which attaches the origin and spread of the Indo-European languages to the invention of agriculture. These two, however, place the original homeland on the eastern flank of Kurdistan and the southern Caucasus. Perplexingly, both ignore the well-documented fact that agriculture was present in force in the interior of Kurdistan much earlier than in the peripheral regions in the Caucasus and Çatal Hüyük.

These theories, although strongly contested, inadvertently elevate eastern Anatolia, i.e., Kurdistan, the home of the earliest agriculture, to the rank of the motherland of this all-important family of languages. I fully concur with Mallory (1989) in rejecting this otherwise attractive model, as it leaves behind far more questions than it addresses. Additionally, faulty methodologies, coupled with a number of important geographical and historical discrepancies, render these theories suspect at best.

Further Readings & Bibliography: Richard Lee and Irven DeVore, eds., *Man the Hunter* (Chicago: Aldine, 1968); Robert Braidwood, "The Iranian Prehistoric Project," *Iranica Antiqua* I (1961); Robert Braidwood and Bruce Howe, *Prehistoric Investigations in Iraqi Kurdistan* (Chicago: The University of Chicago Press, 1960); Henry Field, *Ancient and Modern Man in Southwest Asia* (Coral Gables, Florida, 1956); Dorothy Garrod, "The Palaeolithic of Southern Kurdistan: Excavations in the Caves of Zarzi and Hazer Merd," *Bulletin of American Schools of Prehistoric Research* 6 (1930); Patty Jo Watson, *Archaeological Ethnography in Western Iran* (Tucson: University of Arizona Press, 1979); Clark Howell, "Pleistocene Glacial Ecology and the Evolution of Classic Neanderthal Man," *Southwestern Journal of Anthropology* VIII-4 (1952); Carleton Coon, ed., *Cave Explorations in Iran in 1949* (Philadelphia: University of Pennsylvania Museum, 1951); Carleton Coon, *The Seven Caves* (New York: Knopf, 1957); T.C. Young and P. Smith, "Research in the Prehistory in Central Western Iran," *Science* CLIII (1966); T. Cuyler Young, *Excavations at Godin Tepe, Progress Report* I-II, Art and Archaeology Occasional Papers 17 and 26 (Toronto: Royal Ontario Museum, 1969, 1974); L.D. Levine, "The Excavations at Seh Gabi," in *Proceedings of the III Annual Symposium on Archaeological Research in Iran* (Chicago: University of Chicago Press, 1974); T. Cuyler Young, Jr., "An Archaeological Survey of the Kangavar Valley," in *Proceedings of the III Annual Symposium on Archaeological Research in Iran* (Chicago: University of Chicago Press, 1974); L.D. Levine and M. McDonald, "The Neolithic and Chalcolithic Periods in the Mahidasht," *Iran* XII (1974); Colin Renfrew, *Archaeology and Language: The Puzzle of Indo-European Origins* (New York: Cambridge University Press, 1988); J.P. Mallory, *In Search of the Indo-Europeans: Language, Archaeology and Myth* (London: Thames and Hudson, 1989); Thomas Gamkrelidze and V. Ivanov, *The Indo European Language and the Indo-Europeans* (London: Mouton, 1990); Thomas Gamkrelidze and V. Ivanov, "The Migrations of Tribes Speaking Indo-European Dialects from Their Original Homeland in the Middle East to Their Historical Habitations in Eurasia," *Journal of Indo-European Studies* 13 (1985); I.M. Diakonov, "On the Original Home of the Speakers of Indo-Europeans," *Journal of Indo-European Studies* 13 (1985); Jared Diamond, "The Earliest Horsemen," *Nature* 350 (London, 28 March 1991); Michael Roaf, *Cultural Atlas of Mesopotamia and the Ancient*

Near East (New York: Equinox-Oxford, 1990); P. Ucko and G. Dimbleby, eds., *The Domestication and Exploitation of Plants and Animals* (London: Duckworth, 1969); R. Berger and R. Protsch, "The Domestication of Plants and Animals in Europe and the Near East," *Orientalia* 42 (1973); J. Harlan and D. Zohary, "Distribution of Wild Wheats and Barley," *Science* 153 (1966); D. Perkins, "The Beginnings of Animal Domestication in the Near East," *American Journal of Archaeology* 77 (1973); W.A. Wigram and T.A. Edgar, *The Cradle of Mankind: Life in Eastern Kurdistan* (London, 1914); Y. Majidzadeh, "The Development of Pottery Kiln in Iran from Prehistoric to Historic Period," *Paleorient* 3 (1975-1977); R. J. Braidwood et al., *Prehistoric Archeology Along the Zagros Flanks* (Chicago: Oriental Institute, 1980); R. J. Braidwood, "Seeking the World's First Farmers in Persian Kurdistan: A Full-Scale Investigation of Pre-Historic Sites near Kirmanshah," *Illustrated London News* (October 22, 1960); R.J. Braidwood, "The Early Village in Southwestern Asia," *Journal of Near Eastern Studies* 32 (1973); Braidwood, "The Joint Istanbul and Chicago Prehistoric Project," *The Oriental Institute Report for 1968-69* (Chicago: University of Chicago Press, 1969); G.A. Wright, "Origins of Food Production in Southwestern Asia: A Survey of Ideas," *Current Anthropology* 12 (1971); P. Mortensen, "Excavations at Tepe Gurân, Luristan: Early Village Farming Occupation," *Acta Archaeologica* 34 (1964); Robert Whallon, *An Archaeological Survey of the Keban Reservoir Area of East-Central Turkey*, Memoirs of the Museum of Anthropology, No. 11 (Ann Arbor: University of Michigan Press, 1979); Robert Braidwood and Gorden Willey, ed., *Courses Toward Urban Life* (Chicago: Aldine, 1962); Willem van Zeist, "Palaeobotanical Results of the 1970 Season at Çayönü, Turkey," *Hellenium* 12:3-19 (1972); Fuad Safar, "Pottery from Caves of Baradost," *Sumer* VI-2 (1950); Herbert Wright, "Recent Research on the Origin of the State," *Annual Review of Anthropology* 6 (1977); Charles Reed, "Animal Domestication in the Prehistoric Near East," *Science* CXXX-3389 (1959); H. Wright, "Natural Environment of Early Food Production North of Mesopotamia," *Science* 161: 334-339 (1968); Max von Oppenheim, *Der Tell Halaf* (Leipzig, 1931); James Mellaart, *The Neolithic of the Near East* (New York: Scribner, 1975); Pamela Vandiver, "Ancient Glazes," *Scientific American* 262:4 (April 1990); J. Oates, "The Background and the Development of Early Farming Communities in Mesopotamia and the Zagros," *Proceedings of the Prehistoric Society* XXXIX (1973); Denise Schmandt-Besserat, "Numbers and Measures in the Earliest Written Records," *Scientific American* (February 1984); Denise Schmandt-Besserat, "An Ancient Token System: The Precursor to Numerals and Writing," *Archaeology* (November/December 1986); M.W. Green, "The Construction and Implementation of the Cuneiform Writing System," *Visible Language* xv.4 (1981); Hans Nissen, "The Development of Writing and of Glyptic Art," in U. Finkbeiner and W. Rölling, eds., *Gamdat Nasr: Period or Regional Style?* (Wiesbaden: Reichert, 1986); Hans Nissen, "The Archaic Texts from Uruk," *World Archaeology* 17 (1985-86).

ANCIENT HISTORY: 3000-400 BC

This period marks the progressive technological and commercial overshadowing of Kurdistan by neighboring Mesopotamian cultures. It also heralds a power struggle between the military forces of the mountains (Kurdistan) and the plains of the Fertile Crescent (Mesopotamia and Syria) for political and economic control of this most civilized and richest of the planet's corners. Successive advances and retreats by both sides in the struggle for supremacy continue to this day. The ancient period also marks the coming of the Aryans and the beginning of the transformation of Kurdistan into an Indo-European-speaking society, which culminated in the classical period.

The content of those written tablets excavated so far in Kurdistan and tentatively labeled "proto-Elamite" has not been deciphered and translated. These primary sources for early Kurdish history therefore remain inaccessible at this time. Consequently, the history of this period must be reconstructed using the records of the neighboring civilizations inasfar as they make reference to the inhabitants of the Kurdish mountains. Many such references can now be linked only to the names of certain modern Kurdish tribes, localities, and the like. The name *Qutil*, however, may present us with the earliest version of the ethnic term *Kurd* (see **National Identity**).

Among the many independent kingdoms and city-states in Kurdistan before the arrival on the scene of the unifying Medes (ca. 1100 BC) were the kingdoms of Kummuhu,

Melidi, Gurgum, Ungi (Unqi), Kamanu, Kasku, Nairi, Shupria, Urkish, Mushku, Urartu, Namar, Saubaru, Qurtie, Mardu, Lullubi, Kardu, Zamua, Ellipi, and most importantly the Manna and the Qutil. These are presently known primarily through their Mesopotamian names, with their native names waiting to be discovered. Some have, on the other hand, left their imprints in the name of modern Kurdish localities and/or tribes. The name Mushku survives today in the city and region of Mush (Mus) in northwest Kurdistan. Before their conquest by the Assyrian Tiglath-pileser I (r. 1114-1076 BC), this kingdom was able to field 20,000 soldiers and is now believed to have brought about the final downfall of the Hittites in Anatolia (Roaf 1990). Mardu's name is preserved in Kurdish mythology as the anthropomorphic character Mard, one of the progenitors of the nation. It also survives in the name of the city of Mardin in western Kurdistan. Melidis have given their name to the city of Malâtya, also in western Kurdistan, while the Lullubis' name is preserved in the ethnic name of the Lurs (Map 13).

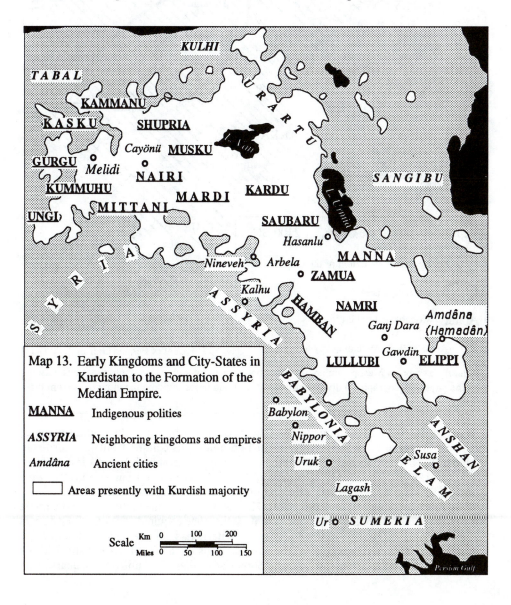

Map 13. Early Kingdoms and City-States in Kurdistan to the Formation of the Median Empire.

MANNA   Indigenous polities

ASSYRIA   Neighboring kingdoms and empires

Amdâna   Ancient cities

☐ Areas presently with Kurdish majority

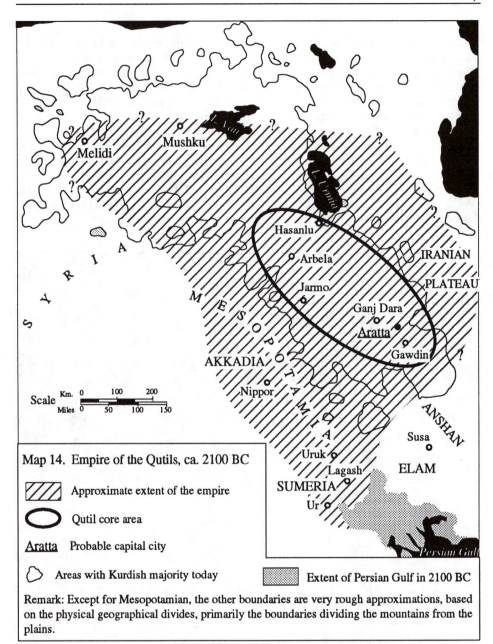

Map 14. Empire of the Qutils, ca. 2100 BC

⬛ (hatched) Approximate extent of the empire

⬭ Qutil core area

Aratta Probable capital city

Areas with Kurdish majority today

Extent of Persian Gulf in 2100 BC

Remark: Except for Mesopotamian, the other boundaries are very rough approximations, based on the physical geographical divides, primarily the boundaries dividing the mountains from the plains.

Late in the 3rd millennium BC, the Qutils succeeded in politically uniting many of their city-states and subsequently launched an ambitious conquest outside Kurdistan (Map 14). They established a new ruling dynasty in Sumeria and Akkadia lasting from 2250 to 2120 BC. The Qutils' conquests of lowland Akkadia and Sumeria are the only ones for which historical records exist, but may not be the only ones achieved.

The Akkadian king Naram Sin (r. 2291–2255 BC) writes of the Qutils: "… in the midst of the mountains they grew up, they became virile, they acquired stature…." Five years after the death of Naram Sin, these very mountaineers had conquered his kingdom. The Sumerians mention at least one of the warring clans of the Qutils that is still with us today. These are the Zibâris, whom the Sumerians called the Subiru or Saubaru. The

Zibâris still live in the same general location indicated by four-thousand-year-old Sumerian inscriptions—north of the Iraqi city of Arbil in central Kurdistan. The name of a king of the Qutils, Tirigan, also is preserved by the Sumerian tablets. This is also the name of an important Kurdish tribe of the late classical period, the Tirikân, who still live to the north of the Zibâris. This tribe may have also given its name to another ruler of Kurdish origin, Tigrân, the king of the Armenians (2nd century BC) (see **Tribes** and **Classical History**).

The energetic exploits of the Qutils came at the zenith of a homogenization period of Kurdish society as the result of the Hurrian migrations. The Hurrians were speakers of a language, or a group of languages, of northeast Caucasian origin, related to modern Georgian, Checheni, and Avari (Diakonov and Starostin 1986). The Hurrians spread to cover all Kurdistan and bring about a cultural, and perhaps also linguistic, change to all peoples of the ancient Zagros, unifying them under a new identity (see **Historical Migrations**) (Wilhelm 1989). The only surviving native terminology belonging to these early times is one of statecraft. It is the Qutil word *ianzi* or *yânzi*, meaning a "ruling person" of these city-states in the Zagros. A far more important vestige of the seemingly liberal political culture of these early states in Kurdistan has survived. From the Assyrian tablets we indirectly learn that, contrary to the contemporary despotic political tradition of the Mesopotamian lowlanders, at least the ruler of the Mannaean state of eastern Kurdistan (with its capital perhaps at the archaeological site of Hasanlu) occupied a much more democratic office. The citizens took an active part in public life. "The Mannaean king seems to have ruled not as an autocrat, but with power limited by a council of elders," writes I.M. Diakonov, the authority on the Median and other Zagros states' history. In a diplomatic request to the Assyrian king, the Mannaean king addresses himself not personally but together with his "Patricians, elders, and councillors of his country" (Diakonov 1985, 73). This Mannaean tradition of pluralism and comparatively liberal political culture is encountered time and again among the important ruling houses with their roots in Kurdistan, from the Mannaeans to the Adiabenes, to the Ayyubids, to the Zands, and so on.

By 653 BC, the Babylonians, judging by their surviving tablets, had extended the term *Qutil* to designate all Kurdish mountains and their inhabitants, including the Medes, who by this time had firmly spread their influence to the shores of Lake Vân in northern Kurdistan. But they also maintained a parallel, and more recent, designator for the Kurds, which was *Qardu* or *Qarduk*, likely evolved from the same ancient term *Qutil*. The element *Qard* in the name may have some connection with the Semitic Akkadian word *qard* and the Indo-European Persian word *gurd*, both of which mean a hero, or a warrior.

Qardu or *Kardu* also appears with variations in the Talmud. In fact, good early sources on the Kurds are the Old Testament and the Talmud. The Talmud, for example, has, "On his return to Assyria, Sennacherib found a plank, which he worshipped as an idol, because it was part of the ark which had saved Noah from the deluge. He vowed that he would sacrifice his sons to this idol if he prospered in his next ventures. But his sons heard his vows, and they killed their father, and fled to *Kardu*." Also, "Haman's son Parshandatha, who was governor of *Kardunya*, where the Ark rested." Or, "Our father Abraham was imprisoned for ten years, three in Kutha and seven in *Kardu*." And finally, "Proselytes may be accepted from among the *Karduyyim*." (The very large, until recently, community of Kurdish Jews may properly find their roots in these accounts.)

The material attraction of the Zagros kingdoms made them frequent targets of expeditions and plundering by the various Mesopotamian states. Late Akkadian tablets dated around 1400 BC (cf. the Amarna archives of Egypt) report a mountain kingdom of *Qortie* or *Kortie* to the north of Mesopotamia all the way to the shores of Lake Vân, as being one of the regions conquered by their Kassite rulers. Three centuries later, during the reign of king Tiglath-pileser I (r. 1114-1076 BC), the Assyrian sources also report these *Kortei* as inhabiting the neighboring northern mountains which were conquered by him. The last

Babylonian tablets before the fall of the fabled city (early 6th century BC) list the *Kardaka* among their royal guards.

The hostilities between the Kurdish highland states and lowland Mesopotamia throughout this period involved lasting military invasions, looting, destruction, and slave gatherings, with Mesopotamia often getting the upper hand and causing large-scale damage to the economy and civilization of Kurdistan. With many of its cities destroyed, large numbers of captives and slaves taken from the land, and the economy disrupted in this manner, Kurdistan had ripened for easy picking by the invading Aryans, particularly the Medes and the Scythians. Kurdistan was inundated, for over 2000 years ending only about the 3rd century AD, by progressive waves of Indo-European-speaking people like the Medes in such numbers that the archaic local languages were replaced by an ancient, Indo-European form of Kurdish. The process of linguistic switch did not ebb until shortly before the beginning of the Christian era. The appearance by about the 3rd century BC of Indo-European, Iranic toponymic terms in the far corners of Kurdistan, such as the river name *Arâsân* of the early Armenian records for the Murât River in northwestern Kurdistan, Ptolemy's report of *Harâz* for the modern Araxes in the far north, *Arâz* for the Khâbur River in west-central, and *Orontes* (Haravant) for the Asi River in far southwestern Kurdistan, may well mark the completion of this process.

The full force of the Aryan nomadic immigration in the Zagros and neighboring regions was felt between 1200 and 900 BC, when the physical destruction and material, social, and commercial disruption drove Kurdistan, and subsequently the rest of southwest Asia, into a social and economic depression (Roaf 1990). Many centers of culture and bustling commercial loci were deserted. The numerical and martial strength of these Aryan settlers overwhelmed the old cultural and ethnic components of Kurdistan, as well as the rest of the Iranian and Anatolian plateaus (see **Historical Migrations**). At the close of this period, by 900 BC, the Kurds had become aryanized.

The Aryan settlers and the aryanized Kurds expanded their power and dominion in the 7th century BC to cover most of the Middle East, under the Medians. The full-fledged expansion of the Median state (founded ca. 727 BC) was preceded by the establishment of other smaller Indo-European-speaking royal houses in and around Kurdistan. The Mitannis (in western Kurdistan) and the Hittites (in northwestern Kurdistan and central Anatolia) are just the better-known examples.

The first known elected Median ruler (the Medes elected their head of state, as attested by Herodotus I. 97.8) was Deioces or Diyâoku (r. 727-675 BC). He embarked on a program of unification of all the inhabitants of Kurdistan against the ceaseless onslaught of the invincible Neo-Assyrian Imperial forces (745-606 BC). This quickly brought the alarmed Assyrians to challenge and eventually destroy him. His successor, Phraortes or Khshathrita (r. 674-653 BC), followed Deioces' course and met the same end at the hands of the Assyrians. Next came Cyaxares the Great (or Huvvakhshathrita, r. 624-585 BC), who finally succeeded in driving out and finally annihilating the Assyrians by occupying their capital Nineveh in 612 BC. The Old Testament celebrates this by the dire predictions of the Jewish prophet Nahum of the imminent destruction of "wicked Nineveh."

The 1500-year dominance of Mesopotamia over the Kurdish highlands (since the fall of the Qutils) was reversed, and would remain so until the Islamic invasion reversed it yet again in the 7th century AD. A crucial element in the success of this epoch-making event was the Medians' brilliant use of people's militias or guerrillas. These are called the *kâra* in the Behistun inscription in southern Kurdistan (Diakonoff 1985,115). This is the earliest record of this form of warfare, which since has become the preferred form of defense of Kurdistan up to the present day, in the form of the Kurdish *peshmerga,* or "guerrilla warriors."

Cyaxares expanded the limit of his empire to include all the areas of Kurdistan to the banks of the Halys (modern Kizilirmaq) River near Ankara, and much beyond Kurdistan to the east (Map 15).

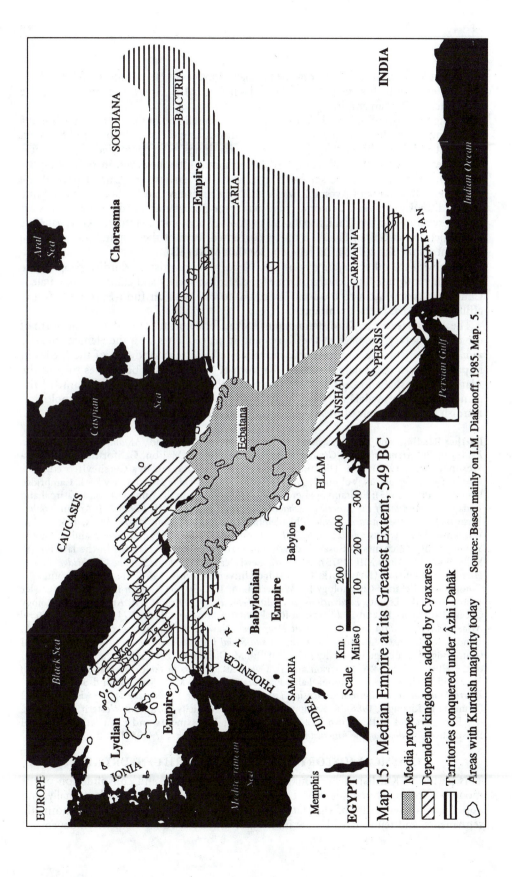

Map 15. Median Empire at its Greatest Extent, 549 BC

Media proper

Dependent kingdoms, added by Cyaxares

Territories conquered under Âzhi Dahâk

Areas with Kurdish majority today

Source: Based mainly on I.M. Diakonoff, 1985. Map. 5.

Scale Km. 0   100 200   300 400

Miles 0   200   300

EUROPE

Black Sea

Mediterranean Sea

Memphis

EGYPT

IONIA

Lydian

Empire

PHOENICIA

SAMARIA

JUDEA

SYRIA

Babylonian

Empire

Babylon

CAUCASUS

Caspian Sea

Ecbatana

ELAM

ANSHAN

PERSIS

CARMANIA

MAKRAN

Aral Sea

Chorasmia

SOGDIANA

BACTRIA

ARIA

Empire

Persian Gulf

Indian Ocean

INDIA

The last Median ruler, Rshti-vegâ Âzhi Dahâk (Astyages of Herodotus, r. 584–549 BC), lost his empire to his half-Persian grandson Cyrus the Great, the founder of the Achaemenian Persian empire.

During the reign of Âzhi Dahâk, the native Kurdish religion of the Cult of Angels had a strong impact on the nascent Zoroastrianism, introducing the priestly office of the Magi into that religion. The Zoroastrian Achaemenian kings, who succeeded the Medians, attempted to reverse this influence, but they achieved little, however, in reinstating the original Zoroastrianism, as set forth in *Gathas*, the earliest and purest part of the Zoroastrian holy book of Avesta. It was at this time probably that the honorific royal title of *Âzhi Dahâk* was given a demonic character by the Zoroastrians, and embedded as such in that religion and the Iranian national mythology and epic literature. Âzhi Dahâk is still venerated as Sultân Sahâk, a much corrupted form of the original name, by the adherents of the Kurdish Yârsân religion (see **Cult of Angels**).

Along with the other Aryan groups, the Medes and pre-existing Kurdish people were thoroughly integrated, which transformed the Kurdish society and culture from a Paleo-Caucasian group, akin to modern Georgian, to one with an Indo-European, Iranic affiliation that has lasted to this day.

The Median legacy in Kurdistan remains indeed fundamental, as evident in the form of the contemporary language of the Kurds and in place names with the element *mâh* or *mâi*, i.e., Median. The Scytho-Alanic heritage is a close second to that of the Medes in impact. Modern place-names such as the town of Saqqez and tribal names such as the Alans of Pirânshahr in central Kurdistan recall this heritage, as does the name of the princely house of Ardalân ("great Alans"), and even in the name of the mythological Kurdish hero of the epic of *Mem o Zin* (i.e., *Memi Alan*, "Mam the Alan").

Further Readings and Bibliography: L.D. Levine and T.C. Young, ed., *Mountains and Lowlands: Essays in the Archaeology of Greater Mesopotamia*, Vol. 7 (Malibu, California: Bibliotheca Mesopotamica, 1977); I.M. Diakonov (Diakonoff), "Media," in Ilya Gershevitch ed., *The Cambridge History of Iran*, Volume 2, *The Median and Achaemenian Periods* (New York: Cambridge University Press, 1985); Ephraim Speiser, "Southern Kurdistan in the Annals of Ashurnasirpal and Today" *The Annual of the American Schools of Oriental Research* VIII (1926-27); Arthur Tobler, *Excavations at Tepe Gawara*, 2 vols (Philadelphia: University of Pennsylvania Press, 1950); W.A. Wigram, *The Assyrians and Their Neighbors* (London: G. Bell, 1929); H. Weiss and T. Cuyler Young, "The Merchants of Susa: Godin V and Plateau-Lowland Relations in the late Fourth Millennium BC," *Iran* XIII (1975); W. Hinz, "Persia, ca. 2400-1800 B.C.," *The Cambridge Ancient History*, 3rd edition (New York: Cambridge University Press, 1984); T. Cuyler Young, "A Comparative Ceramic Chronology for Western Iran, 1500-500 B.C.," *Iran* III (1967); T. Cuyler Young and L.D. Levine, *Excavations at Godin Tepe*, *Progress Report* I-II, Art and Archaeology Occasional Papers 17 and 26 (Toronto: Royal Ontario Museum, 1969, 1974); M. Roaf, *Cultural Atlas of Mesopotamia and the Ancient Near East* (New York: Equinox-Oxford, 1990); M.A. Dandamaev and V.G. Lukonin, *The Cultural and Social Institutions of Ancient Iran*, trans. P. Kohl (Cambridge: Cambridge University Press, 1989); I.M. Diakonov, "Evidence of the Ethnic Division of the Hurrians," in M.A. Morrison and D. Owen eds., *Studies in the Civilisation and Culture of Nuzi and the Hurrians...* (Winona Lake: Eisenbrauns, 1981); M.I. Diakonov and S.A. Starostin, *Hurro-Urartian as an Eastern Caucasian Language. Münchner Studien zur Sprachwissenschaft* 12 (Munich: R. Kitzinger, 1986); K. Kamp and N. Yoffee, "Ethnicity in Ancient Western Asia During the Early Second Millennium BC: Archaeological Assessments and Ethnoarchaeological Prospectives," *Bulletin of the American Schools of Oriental Research* 237 (1980).

CLASSICAL HISTORY: 5TH CENTURY BC-6TH CENTURY AD

This period in Kurdish history marks the homogenization and consolidation of the modern Kurdish national identity. The ethnic designator *Kurd* is established finally, and applied to all segments of the nation. After over a millennium of Aryan nomadic settlements, and rejuvenated by the infusion of the Aryan ethnic element, independent and vital Kurdish kingdoms resurfaced after three centuries of eclipse under Achaemenian and Seleucid rule. This revival reached its apex in the 1st century BC, when Kurdish political hegemony stretched from Greece and Ukraine to the Straits of Hormuz. Toward the end of this period, Kurdish influence over southwest Asia shifted from politics to religion and demography, which stretched well into the medieval period.

At the onset of the classical era, the Greek general and historian Xenophon personally encountered the Kurds when, heading a 10,000-strong Greek army, he chose to cut across Kurdistan in 401 BC. The local inhabitants he calls the Karduchoi, adding that even though living in the geographical heartland of the Persian Achaemenian Empire, "they are fully independent and pay no homage to the Persian kings"(*Anabasis*, "Passage Through Kurdistan"). Another Greek historian, Diodorus, adds shortly afterwards that the Kurds "in their highland fastnesses were more trouble than they were worth to the foreign armies and empires" and that it was "sufficient to keep them by force or agreement from troubling the plain."

Soon after Xenophon's observation, the geographer and historian Strabo writes in the 3rd century BC: "The Kurtioi of Persis [southwestern Iran], and the Mards [of north-central Kurdistan in modern Turkey] of Armenia who call themselves by the same name, are of the same character" (see **Historical Migrations**). By other accounts of Strabo, we learn that Kurds, called by their late classical name *Kurt,* are already present in the territories of Anatolia, Armenia, northern Syria, Iraq, and in large stretches of western and southwestern Iran. The historian Polybius in 220 BC also cites the Kurds, whom he calls *Kurti,* as the inhabitants of Media and eastern Anatolia (where they are still today). By consensus, the term *Kurt* (written *Cyrtii* in Latin texts) is the direct ancestor of the modern term *Kurd.* Kurds are also called *Kurt* by the Middle Persian sources of pre-Islamic times. In fact, in modern Turkish the term for the Kurds is the same as in the Middle Persian sources, albeit with a rounded U sound, i.e., *Kürt.*

Despite the establishment of *Kurt* as a common designator for the Kurds, variations persisted up to the modern era. The Roman historian Pliny, for example, writes of this transitional process at the beginning of the 1st century BC: "Joined to the Adiabene [central Kurdistan in northern Iraq] are the people formerly called the Carduchi and now the Cordueni, past whom flows the river Tigris" (Natural History, VI.xviii.44).

The 4th century BC and the fall of the Achaemenians at the hands of Alexander the Great roughly mark the end of ancient Kurdish history and the beginning of the classical period. The decaying Seleucid empire, established by one of the generals of Alexander the Great after his death in 332 BC, over his conquered Asiatic lands, was by the end of the 3rd century BC steadily losing its eastern domains to the rising star of Parthia. An Iranic people like the Kurds, the Parthians were in many ways similar to the Kurds, and different from the other Iranic peoples, like the Persians, particularly in the laxness of their political rule. Most Kurds either struck an alliance with the expanding Parthian Federation or were seized by it during its expansion beginning in the 3rd century BC. The eastern two-thirds of Kurdistan ended up within the territories of the Federation. In the four centuries of the Parthian era (247 BC to AD 226), the Kurdish kingdoms and principalities of Gordyene/Cordueni (modern Bitlis and Siirt), Adiabene (modern Arbil), Mâda (Media), Elymais (modern Luristân), Kerm (modern Kirmânshâh), Mukriyân (modern Mahâbâd), Shahrazur (modern Sulaymânia), Bârchân (modern Bârzân), and Sanak (modern Sahna and Kangâwar) were active semi- or fully independent members of the Parthian Federation for about three centuries (Map 16).

The Kurdish kingdom of Adiabene, with its capital at Arbela (modern Arbil), merits the most attention here, particularly for its fascinating religious history. Following the conversion of its aristocracy to Judaism in the 1st century BC, large portions of the general Kurdish population of the kingdom followed suit. During the Roman conquest of Judea and Samaria (68-67 BC), it was only Adiabene that sent provisions and troops to their res-

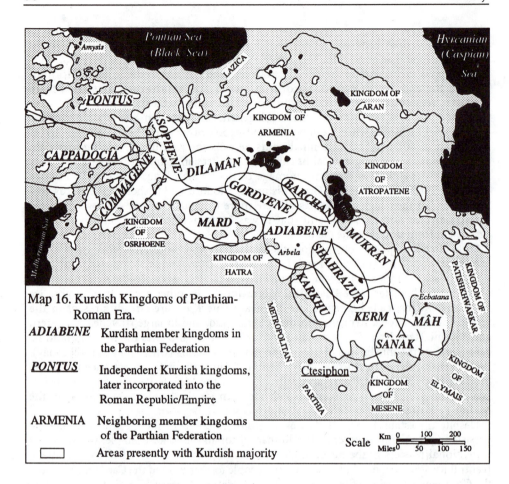

Map 16. Kurdish Kingdoms of Parthian-
        Roman Era.

ADIABENE   Kurdish member kingdoms in
             the Parthian Federation

PONTUS   Independent Kurdish kingdoms,
             later incorporated into the
             Roman Republic/Empire

ARMENIA   Neighboring member kingdoms
             of the Parthian Federation
             Areas presently with Kurdish majority

cue. Adiabene also participated in the hopeless defense of Galilee (Grayzel 1968, 163).

By the 4th century, however, Adiabene had become largely Christian, and the church records of this period are among the most valuable historical records, clarifying this period of Kurdish history (see **Judaism** and **Christianity**). The latinized term *Adiabene* is a corruption of the Kurdish tribal name *Hadhabân* or *Hazawân/Hazâwand*. This populous Kurdish tribe had arrived in central Kurdistan in the 3rd century BC from the southern Zagros. Some remnants of the Hadhabânis were still found in the southern Zagros in the late medieval era (see **Tribes**). The Hadhabânis quickly established their political and military supremacy in the region, and took ancient Arbela as their capital, imparting for a time their own ethnic name to the city. Arbela came to be known as Hazâ until the Sasanian conqueror of the kingdom, Ardashir I, renamed it after himself, *Notar Artakhsher.* (In Islamic times the old Assyrian name, *Arbela,* was eventually restored, as *Arbil.*)

Despite their eventual eclipse by the Sasanian Persians in the 3rd century AD, the Hadhabânis rose again in the 11th century, giving rise to the Ayyubid dynasty of King Saladin (see **Medieval History**).

At about the same time that the eastern two-thirds of Kurdistan was gradually merging with Parthia, three western Kurdish kingdoms (Cappadocia, Commagene, and particularly Pontus) were expanding their fully independent domains toward the Aegean Sea and beyond. However, they collided with and were eventually subdued by the expanding Roman Republic. It took three successive Roman generals and councils, Marius, Lucullus, and Pompey, to receive final submission from these western Kurdish states. At its zenith under Mithridates the Great (Mithridates VI, Eupator, r. 121-63 BC), the Pontian kingdom stretched as far as Greece, the Caucasus, and southern Ukraine (Map 17).

It must be noted that the ancient Greco-Roman sources refer to Mithridates (and several other kings of Kurdish origin in this period) as "Persian." They did so for two simple reasons. First, they used the term *Persian* loosely to mean any one of Iranic cultural and genetic background. Kurds were and are Iranic. The Kurdish language was then even closer to Persian than it is now. In fact, Strabo at about this time echoes the old words of Herodotus when he asserts that "Medes and Persians can understand each other's language" with little difficulty, while simultaneously calling the Kurds/Cyrtii, the inhabitants of Media and Persis (Persia proper). The second reason is that the great Kurdish migrations from the southeastern Zagros were bringing Kurds from as far south as Persis into Pontus and other regions of eastern and central Anatolia.

The expanding boundaries of the Roman Republic and the Parthian Federation soon met on the Euphrates in 57 BC. A century of bloody wars followed, ravaging western Kurdistan and eventually establishing the Euphrates as the border between the two powers. Thus, the western one-third of Kurdistan fell under Roman jurisdiction. The affected Kurds included the Pontians, Cappadocians, and Commagenes, but also the less known, and often neglected, Kurds of the Amanus mountains on the Mediterranean coast.

It appears that since ancient times, the Amanus highland areas around Antioch and along the Mediterranean coast have been a homeland for the western Kurds. The ... modern *Asi*) for the major Syrian ... ce there at the time of Alexander ... ack as the Halaf Period, ca. 8000 ... with other segments of Kurdistan ... lexander the Great's conquest, the ... control of the Amanus mountains.

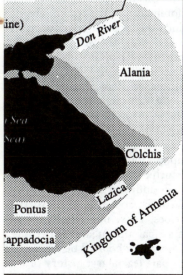

17: Pontian Kurdish Empire under
   King Mithridates VI, ca. 86 BC.
   Under direct Pontian rule
   Pontian vassal territories
gia Provinces

Hellenistic Seleucid monarchs, particularly Antiochus II, also tried to settle these Kurds in their newly established city of Antioch and the port of Alexandretta (ca. 300 BC). Many influential Kurdish families, particularly those of the princely houses of Veras (modern Barâz confederacy) and Belcanae (modern Belikân confederacy) eventually took up residence in these bustling commercial centers, and developed strong bonds with the new Roman administrators of the region. This Kurdish-Roman relationship was to last until the beginning of the 8th century AD, and the final demise of Roman/Byzantine rule in the area. In both Persian sieges, of AD 260 under Shapor I and AD 538 under Chosroes I, the Kurds of the surrounding Amanus mountains participated in defense of Appamea and Antioch, the latter being by then the third largest city of the Roman/Byzantine Empire.

The inclusion of western and northern Kurdistan in the Roman lands provided a golden opportunity for the native Kurdish Cult of Angels (see **Religion**) to absorb the old Greco-Roman pantheon in the guise of Mithraism. For centuries the Cult had been in contact with these religions on its western frontiers. Expanding from western Kurdistan, Mithraism carried the tenets of the Cult as far as Britain. It more or less succeeded in absorbing the old religion of the Romans. Prior to the declaration in the 4th century of Christianity as the state religion of the Empire, Mithraism had become the most important religion in the Empire.

To the events of this historical period must be added a special note on the massive Kurdish population movement from the southeastern toward the northwestern Zagros and into the Taurus and Pontus ranges. Northern and western Kurdistan in Anatolia were the terminal points of this Kurdish internal migration, which brought multitudes of Kurds from as far south as the mountains of Persis (modern Fârs). This massive migration succeeded in homogenizing the Kurdish people and culture from one end of the land to the other. It established Pahlawâni as the dominant tongue in Kurdistan (see **Language**), spread the Cult of Angels to all corners of the lands (see **Religion**), and to a large degree unified the national literature, art, and ethos. By the end of the 8th century AD, this homogenization manifested itself in the form of a renewed Kurdish political dominance of the region, absent since the downfall of the Medians. The details of this and other population movements of the Kurds are given under **Historical Migrations**.

By about the 3rd century BC, Commagene, Cappadocia, and Pontus to the far northwest had already absorbed large numbers of immigrating Kurdish tribes. The Kurdish Pontian king Mithridates, in a single alliance against the Romans, received the allegiance of 14 of these tribes. The tribal forces became the vanguards of his regular army, carrying out raids on the Roman forward territories before the Pontian regular forces made their advance. Along with several sea-borne divisions from Cilicia, these tribal irregulars carried out raids on the Ionian coastal towns, before crossing over into Europe. Plutarch, calling them thieves and pirates, writes "they offered strange sacrifices upon Mount Olympus, and performed certain secret rites or religious mysteries, among which those of Mithras" (see **Cult of Angels**).

In addition to the territories in the northwest of Kurdistan, Armenia, southern Georgia, and Aran also experienced steady settlement by a large number of Kurdish tribes. These immigrants played a crucial role in the history of those nations in the classical and medieval periods. The early medieval Armenian historian, Moses of Chorene (who lived between 490 and 760 AD), offers an interesting account of the early, in part legendary, history of the Armenians, in which he makes a strong connection between the house of the Median king Âzhi Dahâk and the early Armenian kings and aristocratic houses. Moses writes that the ancestors of the Armenian king Tigrân were related to Âzhi Dahâk, but eventually escaped from his realm because of his oppression (*History,* 114-139).

In the epic of *Shâhnâma*, the Persian poet Firdawsi places the home of Âzhi Dahâk in the general area of southern and south-central Kurdistan, near Hamadân, where in fact

Âzhi Dahâk reigned. Moses' account thus can be interpreted to place the home of Tigrân's ancestors in the same general area in southern Kurdistan.

In the reorganization of the Armenian kingdom under King Valarshak, the second rank in the state is explicitly reported by Moses to have gone to "the seed of Azhdahâk" in the form of the Muratsean aristocratic family. Another Armenian king mentioned is Eruand, who fights the Parthian king Artashes (ca. 2nd century AD). Eruand seeks and receives the support of the Muratsean, Median-Armenian aristocracy, but defeated, he is reported by Moses to have fallen back to his native land of "Eruandavan." *Eruand* is a corruption of *Haravand* or *Halvand/Alvand*, the name of the tallest and most sacred mountain in Media, overlooking the ancient capital of Hamadân. The term *Eruandavan* (more correctly, *Arvandâvand*), is a typical Kurdish tribal name of south Kurdish origin.

The attempt has been made to assign the ethnic origins of Tigran to the Persians. As was briefly shown above and also under **Tribes** and **Historical Migrations**, the Kurdish connection is quite clear. Further, it must be noted that during the four-centuries-long Parthian period, ending in 224 AD, ethnic Persians were a minor nationality in the far southern reaches of the Parthian Federation, more than a thousand miles from Armenia, with the interceding space teeming with ethnic Kurds. As has already been noted on the question of the ethnic origin of the Pontian Mithridates VI, what is implied by the term *Persian* for Tigrân's ethnicity, is *Iranic*—a larger ethnic designator which includes the Kurds.

The Armenian histories are, at any rate, exceedingly valuable resources for reconstructing the history of the Kurds and their population movements in the classical and medieval periods.

The aristocratic Kurds immigrating from the south also played a role perhaps similar to that of the German aristocratic houses in Europe up until the turn of the present century. They provided many kings, dukes, and princes to intermarry with the royal houses of such ethnic groups as the Georgians, or directly ruled newly formed states in need of a king with a noble lineage. They possessed the necessary bloodlines for rule, while lacking the troubling allegiances to contending empires and kingdoms of the time. This practice continued until the end of the medieval period.

The Bagrâtids, like the Adiabenes mentioned earlier, are of special note. They originally ruled the populous and eponymous Kurdish tribe Bagrâwand. They rather quickly established local leadership, and established a ruling house, which developed into that of the Bagrâtids. The Bagrâwands imparted their tribal name to the region on the upper course of the Tigris, mentioned as *Bagrauandene Regio* by Ptolemy. Like the Hadhabânis, they renamed their capital, ancient Amida, after themselves. Diyârbakir (from *Diyâri Bakr*, "the Land of the Bakrân") is still the largest city in Anatolian Kurdistan. The Bagratids ruled, with major gaps in their tenure, over the Georgians until AD 1801 and the Russian takeover of Georgia.

These early Kurdish immigrant luminaries were often assimilated quickly into their new ethnic surroundings. The history of the medieval Ayyubid dynasty (which is much better documented than that of the Bagratids) is a good example of how fast a Kurdish dynasty in a foreign setting can lose almost every vestige of its Kurdish ethnic personality. Tigrân the Great, the greatest king of the Armenians, although of Kurdish origin, sympathized in all likelihood with the Armenians. The only controverting evidence is his decision to build his new capital, Tigranocerta, deep in the Kurdish territories (in *Gordena-Gordyei Regio* of Ptolemy, *Cordueni* of Pliny) and outside Armenia proper. This can be interpreted as a sign that he felt his Kurdish past more than has been thought. Assimilated Kurds, at any rate, continued to reach important positions under their new identities during the medieval period, and in fact do so today (see **Integration & Assimilation**).

The founder of the Persian Sasanian Empire, Ardashir I, who succeeded in replacing the aged Parthian Federation in AD 224, immediately challenged what he called the

"King of the Median Kurds." This swiftly unified under the leadership of the kingdom of Kerm (modern Kirmânshâh) an impressive array of Kurdish principalities and kingdoms from Bârchân (modern Bârzân) and Hakâr (Hakkâri) to Mukrân (Mukriyân), Sanak (Sahna), and Shahrazur (Sulaymânia). Ardashir had to carry out a two-year war (AD 224-226) against the Kurds before he finally received suzerainty from the various Kurdish kingdoms. He did so only by agreeing, against his strict policy of direct central rule through appointed governors, to reinstate a local Kurdish prince, Kayus, as an autonomous tributary king to rule the Median Kurds. The House of Kayus continued as a semi-independent principality in central and southern Kurdistan until AD 380, when Ardashir II (r. AD 379-383) removed the last member of this Kurdish dynasty. The dynasty's last member (with the title of "Wisamakân of Dumbâwand from the family Kavosakân") was cited by the early Armenian sources as a contemporary of the Armenian king Arshak II (r. ca. 353-367 AD). His was the last semi-independent Kurdish ruling house for the next five centuries.

This momentous event in Kurdish history is commemorated by a skillful carving on the living rock at Tâq Bustân, the site of the historic capital of Kerm and the Kayosid dynasty (see cover photograph). This event (despite an as yet unexplained discrepancy of seven years) marks the beginning of the Kurdish national calendar, according to which we are now (1992) in the year 1604 (see **Festivals & Celebrations**).

There still can be found in the vicinity of the ancient city of Dinawar, northeast of Kirmânshâh, a series of elaborate tombs cut into the living rock of the mountains that the local tradition ascribes to the House of Kâvos or Kayus.

A point of interest is the term by which the Kurdish fighters are referred to in the original text of King Ardashir's battle chronicle, the *Kârnâmak*. The term is *jânspâr*, a Persian equivalent of the modern Kurdish term for their fighters, i.e., *peshmerga*, both meaning "self-sacrificer" to the cause.

Curiously, the last of the Parthians accused Ardashir himself of being "a Kurd, born to the Kurds, raised in the tent of the Kurds" (cf. *Kârnâmak* and al-Tabari, *History*). As already observed, Kurds at this time actually did live in Ardashir's home country of Persis, and the *Kârnâmak* holds that his father spent a good deal of his youth with the Kurds (*Kurtân*). However, there is no direct evidence that he was actually connected to them ethnically.

After the removal of the the house of Kayus in AD 380 and until the fall of the Sasanians in AD 651, no Kurdish entity is known to have governed independently or autonomously in Kurdistan, or any where else. Under Byzantine rule in Anatolia even the Christian Armenians were denied home rule, let alone the primarily non-Christian Kurds. The Kurds had to wait until the Arab forces of Islam destroyed the Sasanians and chased off the Byzantines before they could reassert their home rule.

By the late 4th century, a massive influx of nomads from the north and east of the Byzantine and Sasanian empires had begun to press their borders. Meanwhile, a century of internal political and economic strife, and the diversion of the military forces to remote border areas to counter the pressure from the steppe nomads of the north, allowed the Kurds to exploit their numerical and economic advantages within these empires. Kurds soon began raiding neighboring territories. They also began to advance on cultural and religious grounds.

The great ecological and economic catastrophes of this period naturally entailed many social upheavals as well, particularly in the Sasanian domains. From the Zagros mountains came a social revolutionary, Mazdak, who founded a new movement on the basis of the native Kurdish Cult of Angels. This soon evolved into the second major attempt to overtake Zoroastrianism (after its earlier, and more effective, movement late in the Median period). For a time, it appeared that the Cult might succeed in overwhelming Zoroastrianism, particularly when the Sasanian king Kavât (r. AD 488-531) became one of its converts (see **Cult of Angels**). Kavât's son and successor, Chosroes I Anoshervân, a champion of orthodox Zoroastrianism, pursued a policy of massive pogroms against the Mazdakites, which had already started toward the end of Kavât's own reign, circa 528. Anoshervân coupled these anti-Mazdakite pogroms with major socioeconomic reforms to undercut the socialistic appeal of the movement to the poverty-stricken citizenry. Some modern scholars, like Christensen (1925) and Klima (1957), have actually called the Mazdakite movement the first Communism.

These pogroms and repressions only succeeded in pushing the movement underground. It quickly resurfaced upon the destruction of the Sasanians at the hands of the Muslim forces, and then challenged in full force the Islamic Caliphate.

Further Readings and Bibliography: E. Sachau, "Die Chronik von Arbela," *Abhandlungen der Preussische. Akademie der Wissenschaften* 6 (Berlin, 1915); A.H.M. Jones, *The Cities of the Eastern Roman Provinces* (Oxford, 1937); A. Christensen, *Le règne du roi Kawadh I et le communisme mazdakite* (Copenhagen, 1925); O. Klima, *Mazdak* (Prague, 1957); F. Altheim, *Ein asiatischer Staat* (Wiesbaden, 1954); N.C. Debevoise, *A Political History of Parthia* (Chicago, 1938); L.D. Levine and T.C. Young, eds., *Mountains and Lowlands: Essays in the Archaeology of Greater Mesopotamia*, Vol. 7 (Malibu, California: Bibliotheca Mesopotamica, 1977); H. Luschey, "Iran und der Western von Kyros bis Khosrow," *Archäologische Mitteilungen aus Iran, Neue Folge* 1 (1968); Arshak Safarastian, *Kurds and Kurdistan* (London, 1948); Moses Khorenats'i, *History of the Armenians*, edited and translated by Robert Thomson (Cambridge: Harvard University Press, 1979); Solomon Grayzel, *A History of the Jews* (New York: Mentor, 1968); Movses Dasxuranci, *The History of the Caucasian Albanians*, edited and translated by C.J. Dowsett (London: Oxford University Press, 1961); N. Pigulevskaya, *Goroda Irana v Pannem Crednevekovie* (Leningrad, 1955), French translation by Claude Cahen (Paris: Édition scientifique, 1962).

MEDIEVAL HISTORY: 6TH TO 16TH CENTURY

This vibrant period of Kurdish history is marked by the reemergence of Kurdish political power from the 7th to 9th century, after three centuries of decline under the centralized governments of the Sasanians of Persia and the Byzantine Empire. It culminated in three centuries, the 10th through the 12th, that can rightfully be called Islam's Kurdish centuries. Through steady emigrations and military conquests, their political rule extended from central Asia to Libya and Yemen.

Kurds established powerful dynasties that defended the Middle Eastern heartland against outside invaders such as the Crusaders, and produced a golden age of Kurdish culture, during which Kurds excelled in the fields of history, philosophy, music and musicology, architecture and civil engineering, mathematics, and astronomy, among others. Among the noteworthy Kurds of this period are the historians Abul-Fida, Ibn Athir, Ibn Shaddâd, and Abu Hanifa al-Dinawari; the philosophers al-Suhrawardi and Badi' al-Zamân al-Hamadâni; explorer Ibn Fadhlân; musicologists Safi al-Din Urmawi and Muhammad al-Khâtib Arbili; musicians Ibrâhim and Is'hâq Mawsili, and Zeriyâb; architect and civil engineer Munis; mathematician and astronomer Muhi al-Din Akhlâti; biographer Ibn Khalkân; encyclopedist Ibn Nadim; and the social (and religious) revolutionaries Bâbak and Nârseh. In his work *'Uyun al-Akhbâr*, for example, Ibn Qutayba, a Kurd from Dinawar, writes in the 9th century on the subjects of natural and mechanical sciences, including details on blast furnaces, techniques of refining steel and casting iron and bronze—fields with long roots in Kurdistan (see **Prehistory & Early Technological Development**).

This period also saw the culmination of the religious movements that had begun in the late Sasanian period under Mazdak. Two new champions, Bâbak and Nârseh, led the movement under the aegis "*Khurramiyyah*." Beginning with Bâbak's announcement in Azerbaijan in AD 817 that he was an avatar of the divinity, he initiated an uprising against the 'Abbâsid caliphs that lasted over a century. In fact, *Bâbak* was only the title conferred upon this revolutionary man; his given name was Hasan. *Bâbak* may well be a diminutive form of *bâbâ*, an "avatar" of the divinity. *Bâbak*, therefore, most likely means "minor avatar," precisely what Hasan could have considered himself to be (see **Cult of Angels**).

While Bâbak's religious affiliation as a follower of the Cult of Angels is clear, his ethnic origin is not. The claim that Bâbak was a Kurd is made on the following basis. First, Azerbaijân had at that time been a terminus of heavy Kurdish migrations for nearly three centuries. The Savalân mountains of Azerbaijân were settled by the Belikân and Badh Kurdish tribes (still extant as the Belikân, Bâz, and Bazayni tribes; see Table 3), which had imparted their tribal name to the towns of Baylaqân and Badh, the latter serving as Bâbak's capital. Second, those of Bâbak's commanders whose ethnic origins are mentioned in the medieval Muslim sources are identified as Kurds. The governor of Marand in Azerbaijân and Bâbak's chief military commander, for example, is mentioned as "Ismah the Kurd" by Ya'qubi.

Bâbak was joined by Nârseh (recorded as "Nasir the Kurd" by the Muslim historian Mas'udi), who rose up in rebellion in southern Kurdistan, the heartland of the native Kurdish Cult of Angels. The 'Abbâsid caliphal armies succeeded in 833 in putting down Nârseh, but not before 60,000 of his followers had been killed, as Muslim historian Tabari records. Nârseh fled with a large number of his remaining followers to the Byzantine territories, where they formed the Kurdish contingent of the Emperor Theophilus' army, which invaded the domains of the Muslim 'Abbasid caliphate in 838 to help the crumbling movement of Bâbak (Rekaya 1974, Rosser 1974). The intercession of Theophilus was to no avail, however, as Bâbak was defeated decisively by the 'Abbâsid.

The Byzantines settled Nârseh and his followers in Pontus in north-central Anatolia. Byzantine sources indicate that this location was chosen so that the refugees could be settled among "their own people" (Bury 1912). The ancient Kurdish community of Pontus must therefore have preserved its Kurdish identity until the mid-9th century, despite its conversion to Christianity, for the Byzantines to have reckoned them the same people as Nârseh's group from southern Kurdistan. Nonetheless, too much of the evidence is circumstantial to warrant a definitive conclusion on the question of the Pontian ethnic identity of the time. Nârseh himself, at any rate, is reported to have converted to Christianity, taking up the name *Theophobus*.

Bâbak's movement and the massive Kurdish presence in Azerbaijân were the result of a much earlier episode of Kurdish population movements. By about the beginning of the 4th century AD, as a result of many centuries of immigration of southern Kurds (see **Classical History**), and favorable socioeconomic conditions, northern and western Kurdistan in Anatolia entered a period of great population surplus (see **Demography**). The flow of Kurdish tribes into the northwest had pushed the population levels to a critical mass, at which the slightest weakness in the organized military power of the Sasanian and Byzantine empires, which held the population at bay on the east and west, respectively, would have resulted in a great human march.

The breaking point in Persia came about with the political, religious and economic upheavals of the late 5th and early 6th centuries. Many decades of environmental deterioration, droughts, and famines, as well as nomadic invasions from Central Asia and the Caucasus, had steadily weakened the Sasanians. While not experiencing adverse climatic and environmental changes, the Byzantines had come under heavy attack from those who were. The cousins of the Kurds, the Sarmatians, Âlâns, and Sorbs, along with various Germanic tribes, came pouring into the Byzantine lands from the European plains farther north, economically and militarily weakening the empire. The floodgates to massive Kurdish emigrations, however, were thrown open with the collapse of the Sasanian Empire in 651 AD at the hands of Arab Islamic forces.

After the advent of Islam in the 7th century, the energetic emigrants from Kurdistan acceded to power in kingdoms and principalities outside Kurdistan proper. In fact this exodus shaped the course of Muslim history in the area from Khurâsân to the Mediterranean coast for three centuries, beginning with the 10th. While the eastern Iranic lands in Central Asia and Afghanistan/Sistân were ruled by the Persian-speaking Soghdian (e.g., Sâmânid) and Sacae (e.g., Tâhirid, Saffârid) dynasties, the western Iranic land, and later also the Fertile Crescent, had become the almost exclusive domain of several independent Kurdish dynasties. The period from the 10th to the 12th century in the political history and life of the Islamic heartland should rightfully be called Islam's Kurdish centuries, as the Kurds ruled and defended the Islamic heartlands against the Byzantines, the Rus, and finally the Crusaders.

The most important of the Kurdish dynasties were the early medieval Daylamites (or Dilami), who established a number of kingdoms, the most famous of which was the house of the Buwâyhids, more commonly (and less accurately) known as the Buyids (AD 932–1062). The Buwâyhids succeeded in subduing the Islamic 'Abbâsid caliphate of Baghdad. Under King Panâ Khusraw (Adud al-Dawlah, r. 949-983), the Buwâyhid Kurdish empire stretched from Anatolia and Mesopotamia to the shores of the Indian Ocean. (Map 18).

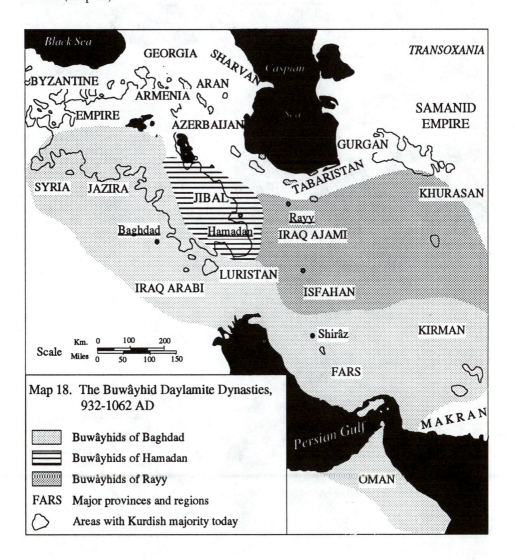

Map 18. The Buwâyhid Daylamite Dynasties, 932-1062 AD

Buwâyhids of Baghdad

Buwâyhids of Hamadan

Buwâyhids of Rayy

FARS   Major provinces and regions

Areas with Kurdish majority today

Confusion surrounds the origins of the Daylamites. Their military and political expeditions during Islamic times were launched from the Alburz Mountains in Gilân, overlooking the Caspian Sea; however, if traced to pre-Islamic periods, they clearly originated in the upper Tigris River area in Anatolia, the home of their modern descendants, the Dimila (Zâzâ) Kurds. The Zoroastrian holy book, *Bundahishn,* places *Dilamân* (i.e., the later Daylamân) at the headwaters of the Tigris, and not in the Caspian Sea coastal mountain regions. The church archives of the late classical Christian Arbela (modern Arbil) also refers to this same area north of Sanjâr (headwaters of the Tigris) as *Beth Dailômâye,* i.e., "the land of the Daylamites." Further, the tiny corner of the western Alburz mountains (a land about the size of Long Island, New York) traditionally thought to be the home of the Daylamites, is physically and ecologically incapable of sustaining a population large enough to cover an area from the Nile to Central Asia with many colonies, as the Daylamites did in a short period of time. Many Buwâyhids, such as Sharaf al-Dawla Sherzil or Sherzili (r. AD 983-990), clearly have Kurdish names, with *zil,* the

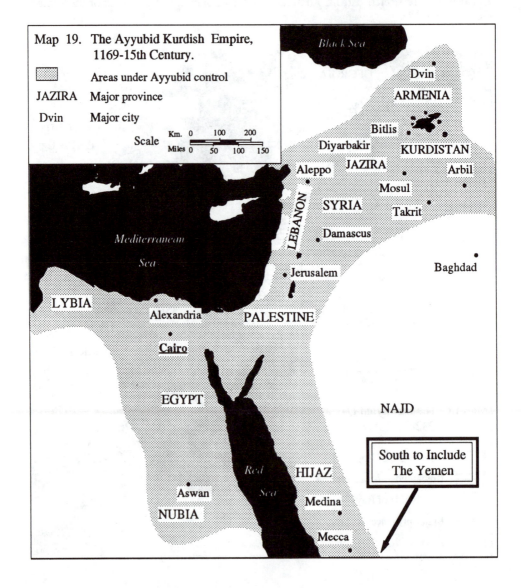

Map 19. The Ayyubid Kurdish Empire, 1169-15th Century.

second segment of his given name, being exclusively Dimili and meaning heart (Awrâmani *zili*, Gurâni, *Dhill*, Kurmânji *zird*; see **Language**), rendering the name as meaning "lionhearted." The early medieval historian Abu'l Fidâ, discussing the various hypotheses on their origins and racial connection, places the Kurds and the Daylamites together as one (*Al-Tawârikh al-Qadima*). Abu'l Fidâ was himself an ethnic Kurd, and well qualified to pass an opinion on the topic of Kurdish ethnicity.

Most, if not all, Daylamites appear to have been adherents of the native Kurdish Cult of Angels, with some minor Shi'ite doctrinal influence (see **Religion**). This may well account for the puzzlement of modern scholars as to why when they subjugated of the Sunni 'Abbâsid caliphate of Baghdad, the Daylamite Buwâyhid kings did not replace it with a Shi'ite house. It may also explain why they received so much praise from staunch Sunni writers like the medieval politicians Sâhib ibn 'Abbâd and Nizâm al-Mulk, who never spared Shi'ites in their influential writings. Being themselves non-Muslim, the Daylamites could not afford to affront further the Sunni majority by bringing on a caliph of another minority religion, i.e., Shi'ism. It is well known that about this same time some Daylamite rulers, such as the Ziyârid king Mardâwij and the Kâkuyid king Mâkân, intended to wipe out Islam altogether (and lost their lives trying to do it).

The religion of the Daylamites remained different from that of their lowland neighbors, the Gilânis and the Tâlishis, who were Sunni Muslims from early dates (Minorsky 1953:112). In fact, while the Gilânis later converted to the Zaydi (Fiver) branch of Shi'ite Islam, the Tâlishis remain Shafi'ite Sunnis to this day. As late as the 15th century, Muslim geographer, historian, and administrator Hamdullâh Mustawfi, whose home town Qazvin was only a few tens of miles from the borders of Alburz Daylamân, reckons the Daylamites as non-Muslims and polytheists. Taking their non-Muslim religion as the pretext, the Gilâni Zaydi ruler, prince Kiyâ, embarked on a ruthless massacre of the remaining Alburz Daylamites in the 14th century.

Today, the population of this part of the Alburz mountains is still Kurdish, and a majority of these Kurds follow the non-Muslim religions of Yârsânism and Alevism, albeit with some Twelver Shi'ite and Ismâ'ili influence. These Kurds are, however, late arrivals, dating only to the 16th century. They nevertheless fortify the notion that this area has long been the terminus for Kurdish migrations from the central and northern Zagros. It is fascinating that among these new Kurds inhabiting the Alburz mountains, one also finds speakers of Dimili, the closest language to the old Daylami.

Daylamân in the Alburz mountains also served as the location of the most important Ismâ'ili fortress, the Castle of Alamut, the legendary abode of the "Old Man of the Mountain" (*Alamut* means "eagle's nest" in Dimili).

Among other Daylamite Kurdish dynasties of importance were the Bâvandids of the southern Caspian Sea region (AD 665–1349), the Ziyârids of Tabaristân and Gurgân (927-1090), the Kangarids (also known as the Musâfirids or Sallârids) of Azerbaijan and northwest Iran (916–1090), the Jastânids of Gilân, Ruyân, and Tâlishân (ca. 6th-12th century), the Shabânkâras of Fârs and Kirmân, and the Kâkuyids of central and southern Iran (1008–1119).

After the Buwâyhids, the Ayyubids are the most illustrious of the medieval Kurdish dynasties. The Ayyubids derived from the Hadhabâni Kurdish tribe and royal house that ruled the eponymous kingdom of Adiabene (central Kurdistan) seven centuries earlier, during its centuries of membership in the Parthian Federation (227 BC–AD 224) (see **Classical History**). Bursting out of Kurdistan to recapture the Holy Lands from the Crusaders, the founder of the empire, King Saladin (r. 1169-1193), defeated Richard the Lionhearted of England and went on to expand his domain to occupy, in addition to Kurdistan, Egypt, Iraq, Syria, the Holy Lands, Arabia, and the Yemen. The Ayyubids ruled these lands from AD 1169 through the end of the 15th century (Map 19).

These medieval Kurdish dynasties displayed an unusual degree of religious liberalism, as demonstrated by their exemplary treatment of Christians and Jews in their domain.

The Shaddâdids' equal treatment of the Christian Georgians and Armenians in their domains is attested by the contemporary Christian sources.

The Ayyubid treatment of the Crusaders won for King Saladin the title of the "Prince of Chivalry" from the Christians. In recognition of this, 711 years after the capture of Jerusalem by him, when Kaiser Wilhelm II of Germany visited Damascus in 1898, he ordered the crumbling tomb of Saladin rebuilt. A silver lamp suspended on the sarcophagus bore the Kaiser's own insignia and that of the Ottoman sultan, for "Saladin was the closest example of the Noble Enemy as could be found" (Newby 1983, 13).

Parallel to the great Daylamites and the Ayyubids, other Kurds also succeeded in establishing important dynasties in and around Kurdistan. The most important of these were the Shaddâdids of Armenia, Sharvân, and Arân (in the Caucasus) (951–1174), the Mamlânids (also known as the Rawwâdids) of Azerbaijan and the southern Caucasus (ca. 920–1071), and the Hasanwâyhids (less accurately known as the Hasanuyids and Badirkhânids) of central and southern Kurdistan (959-1015) (Map 20).

There were also many minor Kurdish princely houses, numerous enough to warrant a study of their own. The smallness of their domains, however, does not, by any means imply unimportance or an ephemeral rule. A Kurd named Bâdh or Badh from the historic Bâdh tribe (which had probably earlier also given birth to Bâbak), established in 983 a dynasty to rule the area in and around the city of Akhlât (Khelât) on the northern shore of Lake Vân. It later expanded and came to be known as the Marwânid dynasty, ruling the territories between the Euphrates and Lake Urmiâ (983-1085). The Marwânids then evolved into the Rozhakis with their capital at Bitlis, followed by the Badirkhânids. The Rozhaki/Badirkhânid dynasty fell only in 1846 (see **Early Modern History**). The original House of Bâdh, however, remained as the emirs of the city-state of Akhlât on Lake Vân. Their reign was not broken until 1847, when the Ottomans imposed direct rule on the area and removed the last Kurdish prince of the House of Bâdh—864 years after its foundation. This small principality easily outranks in longevity any of the resilient local dynasties of the 'Abbâsids and the Ottomans. The tribe from which Bâdh sprung today survives as the Bâz and Bazayni tribes in northern and western Kurdistan (see Table 3).

Toward the middle of the 12th century, the term *Kurdistan* emerged for the first time, to refer to only southern Kurdistan, centered upon Kirmânshâh, Dinawar, and Hamadân. Although much has been made of it by authors writing on the Kurds, in reality this fact has absolutely no historical significance for the Kurds. The Iranic *stân* or *istân* meaning "land" or "country," was used indiscriminately at about that time, and when added to the name of an ethnic group, signified, rather clumsily, an administrative unit and its inhabitants. Hence the term Kurdistan came to parallel other ethnic designations for large segments of southwest Asia (i.e., Armenistân, Turkistân, Arabistân, Sakistân (Sistan), Baluchistân, etc.), and was used strictly for administrative purposes by the late Seljuks.

By the beginning of the 13th century, the Kurdish period of Islamic history has closed, and there began four Turkic centuries. Kurdistan—in fact all Asiatic parts of the Middle East—entered into four centuries during which it was inundated by Turkic nomads, who wiped out many cultures and ethnic groups. Kurdistan became a corridor through which a vast number of Turkic nomads passed to enter and eventually destroy the Byzantine Empire and turkify its domains.

While the major Kurdish dynasties vanished, smaller Kurdish principalities continued their political lives. They paid loose homage to the great Turkic and Mongolian royal houses of the Seljuks, Khwârazmshâhids, Ilkhânids, and Timurids. Annual tributes and occasional conscripts were all that were given by the Kurds in return for domestic autonomy. Most Kurdish principalities were quick to use any weakness in Turkic dominance to establish full independence. Among these were the Ahmadyals of eastern Kurdistan and Azerbaijan (a branch of the Rawwâdids, until ca. 1201), the Zangana or

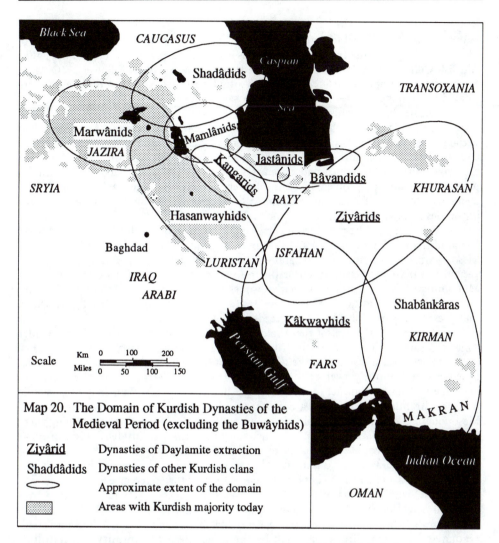

Map 20. The Domain of Kurdish Dynasties of the
Medieval Period (excluding the Buwâyhids)

Ziyârid — Dynasties of Daylamite extraction

Shaddâdids — Dynasties of other Kurdish clans

— Approximate extent of the domain

— Areas with Kurdish majority today

Zangids of Mosul (1127-1250), the Kukborids of Arbil and Kirkuk (1144-1232), the Bakrids of Diyârbakir and Urfâ (1101-1312), and the long-lasting Ardalâns (1168-1867).

Even the Mongol invasion of the eastern lands of the Middle East did not diminish self-rule in Kurdistan. The Mongol forays into Kurdistan were brief and superficial in impact. Kurdistan was in fact far enough from the targets of Mongol activities that the last Khwârazmshâhid king, Jalâl al-Din Mangüberti, sought refuge there. The Kurds, who found his ruthless pillaging of the Kurdish countryside as menacing as the specter of Mongol invasion, prepared under the leadership of Prince Muzafar al-Din Kukborid of Arbil to ward him off. But the prince was defeated and captured. To attract Kurdish cooperation, Jalâl al-Din returned the Kukborids to Arbil and made recompense for his rough treatment of the Kurdish countryside.

However, Jalâl al-Din had greater designs on Kurdistan. He soon sieged and destroyed Akhlât, the old capital of the historic Bâdh principality, which had by then become tributary to the Ayyubids. He failed to take Bitlis from the Rozhaki princes, but promised to return and wipe out the city. This last major Middle Eastern monarch battling the Mongols met his death a year later in 1231, at the hands of the Kurds who found this ruthless king more than they could tolerate.

While Kurdish political fortunes in the late Middle Ages sank under the suzerainty of the Turkic dynasties, the religion of the Kurds expanded impressively. In fact, the native Kurdish Cult of Angels very nearly absorbed Shi'ite Islam and its followers. (Only an extraordinary campaign of ideological and ritual purification of the middle and late Safavid court in the course of the 17th century saved Shi'ism.)

The Cult has had an inherent capacity for transforming and absorbing alien religions through its fundamental belief in reincarnation of the soul (see **Cult of Angels**). It had declared the Prophet Muhammad, his only surviving child, Fatima, and his son-in-law and the first Shi'ite imam, Ali (along with many others, including the Judeo-Christian supreme figures), to be reincarnated avatars of the religion's "Universal Spirit." It did not pose any fundamental problems for the followers of the Cult, particularly the Alevis and, to lesser extent, the Yârsâns, to attempt to first "reform" the Shi'ites of their Koranic impurities and then absorb them and their religion.

The campaign had begun during the gradual collapse of authority of the Mongol Ilkhânid dynasty of Persia (1256-1353) over its domain, which included Kurdistan, Mesopotamia, Persia ,and other neighboring regions. A group of "pseudo-Shi'ite" Alevis vengefully instituted a daily curse on the venerated companions of the Prophet Muhammad from the pulpit of their mosques. Their purpose was to scandalize and forcefully convert traditional Muslim Shi'ites (and even Sunnis) to their religion, which they presented as true Islam. They succeeded for a time.

The Alevis found the zeal of the Anatolian Turkmen converts a crucial boon. Under King Jahânshâh (r, 1438-67) of the Turkmen Qara Qoyunlu dynasty (1380-1468), they spread their political domain to the gates of Herat (in modern Afghanistan), the capital of the greatest Sunni power of the time, the Timurids. Terrorized by these "Shi'ite pretenders'" bloody conduct and scandalized by the religion's manifestly non-Islamic nature, the Sunnis mounted a counterattack. Sunni theologians of Anatolia, Mesopotamia, Persia, and central Asia began to attack the "Shi'ite" Alevis, calling them not Shi'ites, but *Râfidis*, "apostates." Their call to punish the "infidels," soon brought down the Qara Qoyonlu at the hands of another Turkmen dynasty, the Aq Qoyunlu, in 1468. This reversal was not to last, and Alevi propaganda soon succeeded in cutting into Sunni Turkmen and Kurdish support of the Aq Qoyunlu through conversions.

The Aq Qoyunlu capital of Diyârbakir in western Kurdistan was taken in 1508 by a powerful new Alevi king, Ismâ'il I, who founded the Safavid empire in Persia (r. 1501-1524). Ismâ'il, who claimed to be a new avatar of the divinity and a living "Time Lord" (still recognized and worshipped as such by the large Alevi community of Anatolia), commanded a formidable army of fanatically devoted soldiers, known as the Qizilbâsh. (*Qizilbâsh*, "red heads" in Turkish, were so called for the red headgear they wore, and which is still worn by the traditionalist Kurdish Alevis of Anatolia; see **Costumes & Jewelry**).

Kurdish and Turkmen proselytes streamed out of Anatolia and Kurdistan to join Ismâ'il in his messianic undertaking. Kurdistan could well afford this, as the Kurdish population was increasing at unprecedented rates, of nearly 20% between 1425 and the time of Ismâ'il, to an all-time high of 3.1 million (see **Demography**). In a few years, the numerous and dreaded Qizilbâsh enlarged Ismâ'il's domain from central Anatolia and the Black Sea coast, to central Asia and the coasts of the Indian Ocean. Nothing seemed able to stop Ismâ'il's sword and the spread of Alevism at the expense of conventional Islam, when from the western horizons appeared the canons of the orthodox Sunni Ottomans.

Further Readings and Bibliography: For the dynastic lists of medieval Kurdish royal houses and a very succinct account of their histories, C.E. Bosworth, *The Islamic Dynasties* (Edinburgh: Edinburgh University Press, 1967) is the best source. More detail of the same nature can be found in Stanley Lane Poole's *The Mohammadan Dynasties: Chronological and Genealogical Tables with*

Historical Introductions (London 1893), Eduard von Zambaur, *Manuel de généalogie et de chronologie pour l'histoire de l'Islam* (Hanover, 1927), and Eduard Sachau, "Ein Verzeichnis Muhammedanische Dynastien," *Abhandlungen der Preussischen Akademie der Wissenschaften* I (Berlin, 1923). V. Minorsky, *A History of Sharvân and Darband in the 10th and 11th Centuries* (Cambridge, UK: Heffer, 1958); V. Minorsky, *Studies in Caucasian History: New Light on the Shaddâdids of Ganja, The Shaddâdids of Ani, Prehistory of Saladin* (London: Taylor & Francis, 1953); V. Minorsky, *Persia in A.D. 1478-1490: An Abridged Translation of Fadlullâh b. Ruzbihân Khunji's Târikh-i Âlam-Ârây-yi Amini* (London: Luzac, 1957); C.E. Bosworth, *The Medieval History of Iran, Afghanistan and Central Asia* (London: Variorum, 1977), including material on the Daylamites and the Baluchis; Aram Ter-Ghewondian, *The Arab Emirates in Bagratid Armenia*, translated by N. Garsoïan (Lisbon: Livraria Bertrand, 1976); P.H. Newby, *Saladin and His Time* (Boston: Faber and Faber, 1983); W. Madelung, "The Minor Dynasties of Northern Iran," in *The Cambridge History of Iran*, Vol. 4, ed. R. Frye, (New York: Cambridge University Press, 1975); C.E. Bosworth, "Dailamis in Central Iran: The Kâkuyids of Jibâl and Yazd," *Iran* VIII (1970); C.E. Bosworth, "Military Organisation under the Buyids of Persia and Iraq," *Oriens* XVIII-XIX (1965-6); C.E. Bosworth, "The Kufichis or Qufs in Persian History," *Iran* XIV (London, 1976); M. Rekaya, "Mise au point sur Thèophobe et l'alliance de Bâbek avec Thèophile (839/840)," *Byzantion* 44 (1974); J.B. Bury, *A History of the Eastern Roman Empire from the Fall of Irene to the Accession of Basil I: AD 802-867* (Brussels, 1935); H. Grègoire, "Manuel et Thèophobe et l'ambassade de Jean le Grammairien chez les Arabes," in A. Vasiliev, *Byzance et les Arabes*, vol. 1 (Brussels, 1935); J. Rosser, "Theophilus' Khurramite Policy and Its Finale: The Revolt of Theophobus' Persian Troops in 838," *Byzantia* 6 (1974); W.A. Wright, "Bâbak of Badhdh and al-Afshin during the Years 816-41 AD: Symbols of Iranian Persistence against Islamic Penetration in North Iran," *Muslim World* 38 (1948).

EARLY MODERN HISTORY: 1497-1918

This period in the history of the Kurds is one of steady decline in every aspect of their national life, with the possible exception of literature. An important proportion of the nation also found itself deported to far-away regions in the course of the 250 years from ca. 1500 to 1750 (see **Deportations & Forced Resettlements**).

An energetic, industrious, and reasonably worldly Kurdish society at the beginning of the period had turned into one of the most backward and devastated societies in the Middle East by the end of the period. There were two primary causes of this decline: 1) the division of the Middle East into two, warring empires, Persians and the Ottoman, with their line of fire being the heartland of Kurdistan, and more importantly, 2) the utter economic isolation of Kurdistan resulting from the epoch-making shift in international trade routes.

The crossing of the Cape of Good Hope by Vasco da Gama in 1497 is a calamitous date in the national life of the Kurds, as it is in those of other local ethnic groups. This date marks the beginning of the rapid shift of international commerce toward sea transportation, and away from the long-established land routes like the Silk Road between East and West.

The heavy traffic in goods and technology between Europe and the Orient, and all the lands in between, suddenly ceased to cross Kurdish lands, bypassing its markets altogether. Kurdistan quickly became a mountainous irrelevancy. The commercial wealth that once leaked out throughout the land trade routes, benefitting everybody on the way, now was directly funnelled to the trading destination country in Europe or Asia, leaving everybody else high and dry. While Europe began to sink in gold, Kurdistan and every other country on the old land routes went bankrupt and became impoverished—and not just financially.

It was not the transit revenues alone that were lost. The entire infrastructure that supported and supplemented the heavy commerce—the roads, the educated bureaucrats who administered the wealth, and the need for stable local and national states to maintain a free flow of commerce—also withered away. The shift stopped the inflow of new technologies, information, and ideas through the arteries of the country, as well as news of new developments from distant corners of the known world and samples of the latest products for local use and replication.

The shift also resulted in the reduction in quantity and quality of most prized local products because of the loss of their markets. Many old and reputable commodities, technologies, and capital-generating activities became irrelevant when faced with only the local Kurdish demand. Even the nature of the Kurdish traditional weaving was changed (see **Rugs & Fabrics**). Many classes of artisans simply ceased to practice their trade and vanished. This development greatly diminished the Kurdish middle class. It is only now that Kurdistan is pulling out from the effects of the many centuries of progressive isolation wrought by the change. (The resumption of the international trade in Kurdish mineral deposits and other natural resources isplaying not a small role in this process; see **Natural Resources**).

However, the shift in trade routes was not alone responsible for the decline of Kurdistan. The Persian Empire was revived under the Safavids in 1501 after four centuries, more or less, of Turkic nomadic upheaval.

A few words must be said here on the question of the Safavid dynasty's ancestry and ethnic affiliation vis-a-vis the Kurds. The only pre-Safavid, and thus reliable, source extant on the ancestry of the dynasty's patriarch, the Sufi holy man Shaykh Safi al-Din (d. 1334), is the *Safwat al-Safâ* of Ibn Bazzâz Ardabili. Ibn Bazzâz had as a child visited the Shaykh in 1325. He completed the *Safwat al-Safa* shortly after 1357, and well before the Safavid conquest. Although the Safavids altered the work in later copying, the original clearly establishes Safi al-Din's ancestry as Kurdish (Kasravi, 1927). Later works contain "historical corrections" necessitated by the Safavid dynasty's sensitive station. These works consist of court-fabricated, politically corrected genealogies that artfully connected the Shaykh on one hand to the seventh Shi'ite imam and on the other to the Turkmen tribes that were increasingly constituting the bulwark of the dynasty's support (at the expense of the Kurds). (These doings of the Safavids might explain how the Bagratids and Tigrân passed as Georgian and Armenian in the classical period; see **Classical History**.)

According to Ibn Bazzâz, Shaykh Safi al-Din's Kurdish ancestor, Piroz Shâh Zarrin-Kulâh, had emigrated, along with a large Kurdish clan, from the Sanjâr region in modern Syria in the 10th century. The clan, most likely Dimila, settled the mountain regions to the southwest corner of the Caspian Sea near Ardabil. This could well have been among the last migrations of the great medieval Kurdish tribes and ruling houses to this general area. Safi al-Din lived the life of a Muslim holy man in Ardabil, following the rites of Shafi'ite Sunni Islam, as the majority of Kurds do today, but probably did not then. The few extant lines of poetry by him are in a language much closer to Dimili than the Kurmânji dialect that now predominates in the Sanjâr region (see **Language**). There is still today a small Dumbuli (Dimili) clan living in the Sanjâr mountains in Syria. The Alevism of the Safavid house even before its rise to royal station is more akin to a Dimila, Alevi background than to Sunni Kurmânj. The founder of the Safavid dynasty, Ismâ'il I, claimed to be a deity reincarnate, and is still venerated by the modern Alevis as being so.

The Kurdish presence has not disappeared from the Ardabil area, despite the thorough turkification of the plains of Azerbaijan to the west since the time of Safi al-Din. Even today there are two Kurdish tribes, Shatrânlu and Kurdbeglu, living in the mountains south of Ardabil.

Shortly after the accession in Azerbaijan and Sharvân of Ismâ'il I, he extended his political dominance westward to destroy the Sunni Aq Qoyunlu dynasty in 1508 and recover Kurdistan (see **Medieval History**).

The progressive influence of traditional Shi'ism on the Safavid princes through their up-bringing by the court's Persian regents, teachers, and ministers culminated in Abbâs the Great (1588-1629) disbanding the Alevi Qizilbâsh and hiring the services of traditional Shi'ite Muslim theologians from all over the Middle East. These religious thinkers progressively expunged the Alevi elements from the state religion. Although these developments saved Shi'a Islam from complete absorption into Alevism, the Alevi influence lasts until this day.

The westward expansion of the nascent Safavid Empire was challenged in 1514 by the eastward-expanding Ottoman Empire on the battlefields of Châldirân in northeastern Kurdistan. The classical-era East-West conflict between the Persians and the Romans/Byzantines was thus revisited, with the Kurds again caught in between. The difference was that at Châldirân the Ottomans, the successors of the Byzantines, scored a decisive victory over Ismâ'il I and the Safavid Persians, pushing them farther east beyond the Tigris. After an ensuing century of wars, the border between the two empires was fixed at more or less the western borders of modern Iran by the Treaty of Zohâb in 1639. This left three-quarters of Kurdistan under Ottoman suzerainty, which lasted until that empire's breakup at the end of World War I.

In the formative early wars between the Persian and Ottoman Empires, the Alevi Kurds gave their allegiance to the Safavids, and the Sunni Muslim Kurds often sided with the Ottomans, whose rule was more lax than that of the fanatical Alevi and Shi'ite dynasties of Persia. Additionally, most Kurds, Alevi and Sunni alike, suffered gravely at the hands of the Safavids, primarily because of their strategic location and the geopolitical realities of the time.

With an army made up largely of highly mobile light cavalry, the Safavid forces tended to be much smaller than the Ottoman forces, which were made up basically of slow-moving, cannon-laden infantry. Because of this, the larger and slower Ottoman forces had to collect provisions en route to battle. Otherwise, the very size of the provision trains (and their cost) would limit how many men an Ottoman army could field on any Persian battlefield. To counter Ottoman firepower, the Safavids pursued a "scorched earth" policy, to prevent the Ottomans from collecting these provisions. The scorched earth policy effectively balanced the power between the two empires, and in fact on occasion tipped it toward the smaller, less populous Persia. Its speedy, light cavalry could with little difficulty cross the scorched, no-man's land, to carry out raids on the cumbersome Ottomans. It just happened that Kurdistan was the earth that needed to be scorched for them to succeed.

Vast numbers of Kurds were deported by the Safavids to far-away corners of their domain. The frightening degree of destruction in northern and western Kurdistan persuaded the remaining Kurds there to support the Ottomans. The vanguard in mobilizing the Kurds to side with the Ottomans was led by Prince Idris, the Rozhaki emir of Bitlis and grandfather of Sharaf Khân, the author of the first-known pan-Kurdish history *Sharafnâma* (see **Literature**).

One episode of Safavid maltreatment of the Kurds has now attained the stature of a national epic: the *Ballad of Dem Dem*. The fortress of Dem Dem, 110 miles south of Urmiâ, was attacked by the Safavid Abbâs I in 1608. During the year-long siege, the Kurdish defenders of Dem Dem fought to the last living person under the leadership of the Emir Khân of Barâdost, the legendary "Khân with the Golden Arm." The epic combines the heroic elements of the *Iliad* and the fruitless, single-minded persistence of the defenders of Massada.

Because of their strong cultural and even religious affinities with Persia, the population of central and southern Kurdistan usually sided with that state. But even these were at times turned against the fanatical early Safavid rule. Soon after the death of Shâh Ismâ'il I in 1524, the Kurdish prince Zulfaqâr Khân of the Kalhur tribe rebelled against the Safavids. He was able to conquer Baghdad, and placed himself and his domain under Ottoman suzerainty. This brought Ottoman sultan Süleyman the Magnificent in 1533 to snatch Iraq, which remained under Ottoman control for the most part until 1917.

In fact, the Ottoman sultan Selim the Grim (r. 1512-1520) allowed a great measure of autonomy to the Kurds, who thus sided with him. However, the Ottoman promise of fair conduct soon was broken too, in fact by Selim himself. Toward the end of his reign, large numbers of Kurds were forcibly removed to central and northern Anatolia, where they became the nucleus of the large Kurdish enclaves now there. Some were deported as far as Bulgaria.

From among these Ottoman deportees rose in 1519 at Tokat in northern Anatolia a certain Jalâl, who claimed to be an avatar of the Spirit. It is fascinating to note that Jalâl arose from the exact same area of ancient Pontus that had served in the 9th century as the headquarters of the Khurramite Nârseh (Theophobus) and his deported Kurdish followers, and that they preached basically the same religious and social ideology based on the Cult of Angels (see **Medieval History** and **Cult of Angels**). Jalâl took up the name Shâh Ismâ'il, after the defeated Safavid king. He claimed to have received the royal glory that had departed the king earlier, causing his disastrous defeat at Châldirân in 1514. Jalal attempted to avenge that defeat. As a Dimila Alevi, Jalâl's main support came from the agriculturalists and urbanites. Despite his initially considerable success, he was defeated and killed with thousands of his followers. His revolt, called the Jalâli (Celâli) movement after his given name, resurfaced periodically over the next two centuries in the Ottoman lands. Many Jalâli revolts were lead by individuals who claimed to be avatars (Bâbâ) of the Spirit such as Bâbâ Zonnun at Bozok and Qalandar Chalabi (Kalender Çelebi) in 1526-27 in Elbistan in Cilicia. The Jalâli followers, however, came increasingly from Turkmen and Turkish ethnic groups, losing their direct relevance to Kurdish history.

The ongoing destructive events of this era on Kurdish soil precipitated also a new idea among Kurdish thinkers: a pan-Kurdish government. The idea of a nation to be ruled by a national government dedicated to the welfare, safety, and cultural survival of that ethnic body was in fact a very uncharacteristic and anachronistic thought, especially in the Muslim Middle East, where *umma*, the nation of believers, was to be the only point of greater loyalty.

Shortly after the Islamic conquests of the 7th century, a movement among the Iranic people also developed to champion the national cause of the greater "Erân," as home to a culture and people distinct from those of the Arabian domains and cultural sphere. This was best embodied in Firdawsi's epic of *Shâhnâma*. This, however, can be distinguished from the national awakening of the Kurds, as *Shâhnâma* did not pertain to a single ethnic group, but rather to a collection of ethnic groups who shared the greater Iranic civilization. *Shâhnâma*, at any rate, never promoted the idea of a single government or political entity to unify and protect these peoples and civilization. Facing a much more destructive tide, the Kurdish writers of the 17th century doubtless did.

The first pan-Kurdish history, *Sharafnâma*, was written in 1596-97 by Prince Sharaf al-Din (Sharaf Khân) of Bitlis—a city located at the eye of the devastating, century-long hurricane of destruction, deportations, and violence. Sharaf Khân laments the lot of the Kurds and their strategic homeland. Intermittently, Bitlisi speaks of the idea of a pan-Kurdish king. He laments its absence, and then, believing that Islam and the distracting idea of *umma* may be the problem, metonymically blames it on a curse set on the Kurds by none other than the Prophet Muhammad. "The Prophet Muhammad, disconcerted by the warlike and awesome looks of a Kurdish visitor," Bitlisi writes, "asked the Almighty to place a curse of disunity on the Kurds, since in unity, the Prophet feared, they will overcome the world."

A century later, in 1694, the Kurdish lyricist Ahmad Khâni observes in the epic of *Mem o Zin*: "Behold! From Arabia to Georgia is the Kurdish home. But when the Persian ocean and the Turkish seas get rough, only the Kurdish country is spattered with blood." Khâni openly blames the sorry lot of his Kurdish compatriots, caught in between the vengeful armies of the Safavids and the Ottomans, on the absence of a Kurdish state (*hukumet*). Born to disunity among the Kurdish princely houses of the time, he proposed unity under a single Kurdish king who could then protect the people and their national and cultural heritage. Ahmad Khâni's use of almost exclusively patriotic themes at this time of utter national distress is the first concrete expression, along with Bitlisi's *Sharafnâma*, of a pan-Kurdish national awareness, if not of nationalism in the modern sense (see **Literature**).

With the abatement of Perso-Ottoman hostilities after the mid-17th century, this prototype of modern nationalism among the Kurdish intellectuals fell upon the deaf ears. Declining levels of culture and literacy, and the extinction of the once-vibrant urban middle class spawned an ever-widening intellectual gap between these luminaries and their impoverished, largely nomadized compatriots of the following generations.

Among the Kurdish autonomous princely houses of this period, the Ardalâns of Shahrazur in central and southern Kurdistan were famous for their patronage of the fine arts. The Shamdinâns of Hakkâri of eastern and north-central Kurdistan supported many Kurdish poets and writers. Sharaf al-Din Bitlisi, as has been observed, was himself a prince of the Rozhaki dynasty of Bitlis in western Kurdistan (Map 21).

Of the degree of autonomy of these Kurdish ruling houses, the French traveller Tavernier observed in 1676 that the prince of Bitlis "recognized neither Shah [i.e., Persia] nor Padishah [i.e., the Ottomans], and could put into the field a force of 20-25000 cavalry." According to Fleurian, writing in 1694, the Jesuits who visited the city of Bitlis in 1683 reported that the nominal vassalage of the ruler to the Ottomans was preserved only in that he sent them tribute on his accession.

After the Treaty of Zohâb, a relative calm descended upon Kurdistan and its autonomous principalities, to be broken relatively briefly, but very harshly from 1722 and

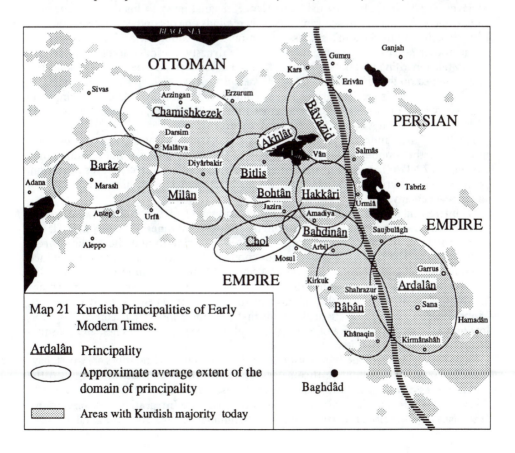

Map 21 Kurdish Principalities of Early Modern Times.

<u>Ardalân</u> Principality

⬭ Approximate average extent of the domain of principality

▦ Areas with Kurdish majority today

the fall of the Safavids, to 1750 and the rise of the Zands in Persia. The power vacuum caused by the fall of the Safavids brought the Ottomans to annex the Safavid western provinces, placing for a few years all of Kurdistan under Ottoman rule.

The energetic founder of the Afshârids of Persia, Nâdir Shâh (r. 1736-1747), soon challenged the Ottomans in Kurdistan and Iraq. The destruction of the post-Châldirân years was all but revisited on the Kurds, this time ravaging southern, eastern, and central Kurdistan. Cities and villages were destroyed and entire tribes deported. The few bastions of the old Kurdish culture and civil life that had miraculously escaped the havoc of the 16th and 17th centuries (because they happened to remain outside the main battlegrounds) were annihilated. Total darkness had now descended on Kurdistan, and would last into the 20th century.

So much of the national heritage was lost and forgotten in this period, and what was left was so fragmented, that only the medieval terminologies for the native religion (*Yazdâni*, "Cult of Angels") and the old language of the Kurds (*Pahlawâni*) remained. No equivalent terms were employed thereafter; only the titles of the denominations of the religion (e.g., Yârsânism, Alevism, and Yezidism) survived, as have the names of the dialects (e.g., Dimili, Gurâni, and Laki) of the old language (see **Religion** and **Language**).

From one of the tribes deported by the Safavids to Khurâsân, the Zands of the Deh Pari region of southeastern Kurdistan, unexpectedly rose the last Kurdish dynasty comparable in size and nature to the medieval Ayyubids and Buwâyhids. Muhammad Karim Khân (r. 1750-1779) founded in Persia the Zand dynasty, which ruled an area comparable to modern Iran and far southern Iraq until 1794 from their capital Shirâz (Map 22). The Laki-speaking Zand tribes are still found in various localities of southern Kurdistan from Kifri to Malâyer (see **Tribes**). In personal benevolence, magnanimity to his defeated enemies, valor—and political naivete— Karim uncannily reminds one of another Kurdish monarch, King Saladin. While Saladin's successors demonstrated enough Machiavellian political sophistication to ensure the continuation of their dynasty, Karim's successors lacked his valor while inheriting his political naivete. Karim in fact never adopted the title of king, but instead settled on the unprecedented title of *Vakil al-Ru'âyâ*, i.e., "deputy of the people," or *Vakil* for short. This recalls Karim's ancient ancestor, the Kurdish Mannaean king who addressed himself not personally but together with his "patricians, elders, and councillors of the country" to the Assyrian despots (see **Ancient History**).

The last of the Zands, the young and highly gifted Lutf Ali, was defeated and tortured to death by the founder of the Qâjâr dynasty of Persia, the dreaded Âghâ Muhammed Khân (r. 1779-1797). Âghâ Muhammed had spent his youth, and received his education, at the court of Karim Khân, who had cast his benevolence upon him as the son of a vanquished enemy.

An interesting trait of the Zands was their inclusion of women in military campaigns. A very ancient and venerated Kurdish custom (see **Status of Women & Family Life**), it was even practiced by Karim Khân himself, whose first bride fought the Afghan forces alongside him. The Zands are also noted for another, characteristically Kurdish, conduct: tolerance of religions beside their own. A Shi'ite Muslim (or quite possibly Yârsân) dynasty, the Zands were noted in 1766 by the Danish archaeologist and traveler Niebuhr as giving "no attention to the religion of their men under arms, be it Christian, Mohammedan, or Jewish." He further adds that after the Zands had occupied Basra following a long siege, "no place of worship, including synagogues, churches, and mosques of various Muslim denominations were desecrated, or given to loot."

Since the beginning of the 18th century, the Laks, of which the Zand tribes are a part, have been progressively distancing themselves from the Kurds and assimilating into the communities of the neighboring Lurs, who themselves had lost their Kurdish identity through an ethnic metamorphosis at an even earlier date (see **Integration & Assimilation**). Historians have therefore had a difficult time determining the ethnicity of the Zand dynasty.

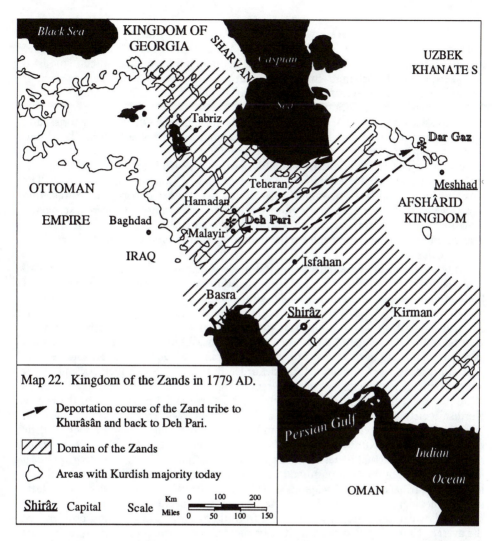

Map 22. Kingdom of the Zands in 1779 AD.

Deportation course of the Zand tribe to Khurâsân and back to Deh Pari.

Domain of the Zands

Areas with Kurdish majority today

Shirâz Capital   Scale   Km 0   100   200
                            Miles 0 50 100 150

From the beginning of Zand rule, Kurdistan sank into a dubious kind of peace, more like the peace of a wilderness. This was mainly the result of the three centuries of calamitous military operations and economic devastations. The people were so decimated and the land so impoverished that Kurdistan had turned into remote and poor frontier marches of little value to either empire, Ottoman or Persian. These empires were themselves fast losing their gloss to the rising star of the European colonial empires and their technological prowess. The decline in Kurdistan was more or less on a par with the general decline of the East, if more rapid as a result of the wars and depopulations.

The 19th Century. A reawakening of the Kurds took place toward the turn of the 19th century. The Russian Empire was pushing its frontiers deep into the northern Middle East in the Caucasus and central Asia. In 1813, after a nine-year war between the Russians and the Persians, the Treaty of Gulistân transferred Georgia, North Azerbaijan (old Sharvân), and Daghistân from Persia to the Russian Empire. Kurds thus first passed into the Russian Empire. These were the ancient Kurdish colonies in the areas of Ganja and Sharvân (now the Republic of Azerbaijan), where a thousand years earlier they had given rise to the royal Kurdish house of the Shaddâdis (see **Medieval History**).

The second Russo-Persian war (1826-1828) culminated in the Treaty of Turcomanchây. The treaty transferred Persian Armenia (now the Republic of Armenia) into the Russian Empire, and with it a much larger Kurdish population, contiguous to the heartland of Kurdistan. Interestingly, at the time, even in this part of ancient Armenia, according to Bournoutian, Kurds outnumbered Armenians (25,000 Kurds to 20,000 Armenians) (Bournoutian 1982, 76).

The Russians soon extended their hold into the neighboring Ottoman territories, and by annexing the districts of Kârs and Ardahân, moved unmistakably inside Kurdistan proper, acquiring a relatively large Kurdish community.

This movement of the boundaries of a European state, even if the most backward one, into the Kurdish territories ended the two centuries of isolation of the Kurds. The Russians brought with them, among other things, new Western ideas. The reawakening effects were quickly felt deep inside Kurdistan, where new technologies were fast making it possible for the central Persian and Ottoman governments to exert an ever more overbearing and obtrusive central rule on the traditionally autonomous Kurds and their local principalities.

Ethnic nationalism of the European kind made its debut at this time in the works of Hâji Qâdir Koy'i (1817-1897). He championed this nationalism by promoting unity of the common people, and rejecting the traditional ruling classes and religious leaders as obstructive and misguided irrelevancies. He also called for a fully independent, pan-Kurdish state, which was to implement secular education in the Kurdish language at the expense of the established Middle Eastern lingua francas. Kurdish was also to be adopted as the state language in this pan-Kurdish state (Hassanpour 1989, 55). These sounded like outlandish ideas, even to many educated Kurds. But Koy'i was just the first, and scores like him emerged by the turn of the 20th century.

Despite their growing numbers, people like Koy'i remained isolated from the rest of Kurdish society. Most of them travelled and lived in the Western European capitals, and often were better versed in the history and culture of these alien societies than in their own. The common Kurds, who were then living at the tail end of several centuries of national and intellectual regression, were completely unfamiliar with their novel political ideas. At the end of the 19th century, those who were at the helms of the Kurdish political leadership—tribal chiefs and religious shaykhs—were far closer to their plebeian subjects in their ideological awareness than to these modern intellectuals. The intellectuals were perceived as detached dreamers, alienated from the realities and common problems of the average Kurds. They were thought to be more aware of what was happening in Paris or Vienna than in their own home towns in Kurdistan.

As visionaries like Koy'i experimented with modern nationalism, the last of the Kurdish princely houses were being reduced to little more than refugees in their capital cities. The Ardalâns (founded AD 1168) were forced out of their capital of Senna (modern Sanandaj) in 1867 in favor of direct Persian rule from Teheran. Shortly before that, in 1847-48, the last major Kurdish princely houses in the Ottoman domain, i.e., the houses of Bâbân of Sulaymânia, the historic Rozhaki (Badirkhânids) of Bitlis (founded ca. AD 1034), and the Bâdh of Akhlât (founded AD 983), had been forced out of their capitals and their territories placed under direct rule from Istanbul.

This fundamental change in the nature of Kurdish leadership, the extinction of the native tradition of orderly government, merits a great deal of attention because of its decisive role in retarding the process of Kurdish social and political evolution. These native institutions went back thousands of years, and were the most important source of development, promotion, and dissemination of culture, new technology, and new ideas in Kurdistan. The defunct princely houses tamed unruly tribal chiefs, checked the ambitions of fanatical religious leaders, and maintained economic contact with the outside world. The members of these houses were usually highly educated and cultured individuals and can be credited with most cultural achievements of the Kurdish past. Sharaf Khân Bitlisi was an older example already given. The Badirkhânid princes must be cited for their invention of the modern, Latin-based, Kurdish writing system. They were also the founders of most early Kurdish newspapers, and the organizers of the first Kurdish political party in the modern sense, the Khoyboun (see **Education, Press & Electronic Mass Media**, and **Political Parties**). The princely houses also fostered a well-informed and cosmopolitan political culture that could quickly fill any power gap that emerged in the region, be it among Kurds or non-Kurds.

The tradition of religious tolerance among the Kurdish princes continued only until the middle of the 19th century, when the old order of local government was abolished. Bitlis, for example, was transformed from the seat of the cultured Badirkhânids/Rozhakis to a center for fanatical religious activities under the direction of the Sufi masters of the Naqshbandi mystic order (see **Sufism**). The home of Sharaf Khân, Bitlis had served as home to Italian Priest Maurizio Garzoni, who lived and worked among the Kurds for 18 years. He received the same fair treatment as the Jesuits, who established a mission in Bitlis in 1683. In 1858 an American Protestant mission was established there. Many of the earliest linguistic works, dictionaries, and translations of the Bible into Kurdish were the creations of these missionaries (McCarus 1960). Yet by 1880, Bitlis had become a base for the fanatical uprising staged by Shaykh Ubaydullâh. Sulaymânia, the capital of the defunct Bâbâns, and Sanandaj, of the exiled Ardalâns, underwent similar metamorphoses.

The religious figures who rose to primacy in 19th century Kurdistan had no need for tolerance. Religious bigotry was an important tool in the demagogic hands of the Kurdish religious leaders, whose powers were now unchecked by the old princely rulers. In Ottoman Kurdistan, their wrath turned first against the Yezidi Kurds. Massacres perpetrated against them, with the tacit support of Ottoman authorities and religious leaders, forced into Russia most of those they did not kill (see **Deportations & Forced Resettlements**). The ruthless massacre of 5000 Assyrians in 1842 at the hands of the chieftain Nurullâh heralded a campaign against the Christians. Then came the Shi'ites, Alevis, and finally the Jews and the Bâbis.

In 1880, Shaykh Ubaydullâh, who had risen to power by opposing the progressive intrusion of the centralizing Ottoman government, found supporters even among the politically decapitated Kurds of Persia, albeit those adjacent to Anatolia, the home base of Ubaydullâh. The local Kurdish religious leaders in these corners of Persia had even more reason to fan religious extremism. They were living as a small Sunni minority in a country with a Shi'ite majority, magnified by the proverbial religious militancy of their ethnic neighbors, the Azeris.

In Anatolia per se, Ubaydullâh carried out oppressive measures against non-Sunni Muslim Kurds as well as others. The Kurdish Alevi community witnessed so many killings, forced conversions, and seizures of property in the course of the 1880's that it sided with Atatürk's secular republic in 1925 in order to protect itself from yet another Kurdish religious leader, Shaykh Sa'id. Their fears were so great that they took part in the actual combat against Sa'id alongside the Turkish republican forces.

With the encouragement of the mullâhs and shaykhs, the Shakâk tribal chief Ismâ'il Âghâ Simko, before his execution by the Iranian monarch Reza Shah in 1930, carried out enough atrocities in his 15-year political life to place him alongside such historical villains as Attila the Hun. In one instance, Simko persuaded the Assyrian minority of northern Kurdistan to send him a delegation to reach a mutual entente. He then treacherously killed every single member of the peace party, including the Assyrians' most revered patriarch, Mar Benyamin Sham'un, then over ninety years of age. He then proceeded to drink the patriarch's blood as a demonstration of his rage. Simko bears a disproportionate degree of the blame for tainting the tradition of liberal tolerance in Kurdish society.

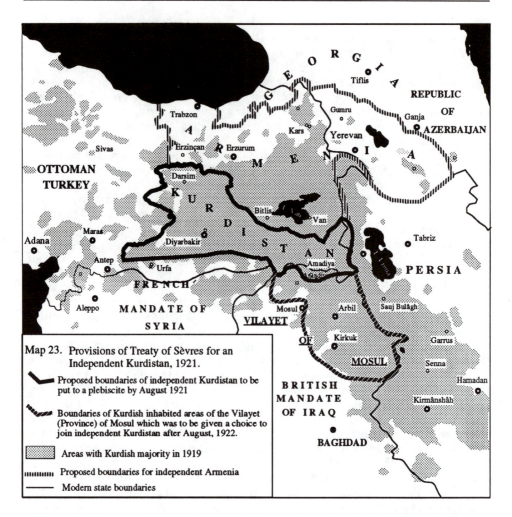

Map 23. Provisions of Treaty of Sèvres for an Independent Kurdistan, 1921.

Proposed boundaries of independent Kurdistan to be put to a plebiscite by August 1921

Boundaries of Kurdish inhabited areas of the Vilayet (Province) of Mosul which was to be given a choice to join independent Kurdistan after August, 1922.

Areas with Kurdish majority in 1919

Proposed boundaries for independent Armenia

Modern state boundaries

These developments left behind in Kurdistan only major tribal chiefs and religious leaders, *shaykhs, mullahs,* and *qadis,* to fend for the Kurds and their aspirations. None of these leaders was even remotely capable of fathoming the requirements of the fast arriving new world. Instead of individuals like Sharaf al-Din Bitlisi, the spokesmen for an independent Kurdistan at the end of World War I were unpolished, truculent tribal chiefs like Simko, nicknamed "the cannibal," and mullahs like Shaykh Sa'id, whose fanaticism had already alienated the Alevi Kurds. At this historic moment when independent states were being created thanks to the professionalism, wit, and political prowess of other local ethnic leaders, Kurdish politicians could hardly have been any less professional and convincing to the European powers. Had the traditional Kurdish princely houses survived until 1918, this golden opportunity for statehood might not have been squandered.

While the hapless Kurds missed the golden opportunity presented at the end of the World War I and the breakup of the old empires, they were fully involved in its most horrendous devastations. The front line of fire between the Russian and the Ottoman forces moved back and forth across northern and western Kurdistan, from Kârs to Diyârbakir. By 1917 and 1918, British and French forces were also warring on Kurdish soil. The damage to the people and the land left nearly 400,000 dead among the Kurds of Anatolia alone (see **Demography**). The Armenian population of the area was totally annihilated through massacres and forced migrations. Central, eastern, and southern

Kurdistan, although suffering less, nevertheless witnessed looting and destruction of crops by the Russian, Ottoman, and British armies, which caused severe famines in the area.

By 1918, Kurdistan was a land with its infrastructure wrecked, its society in utter disarray, its intelligentsia dispersed, and the tribal chieftains and shaykhs in full control of what was left.

Further Readings and Bibliography: Fleurian, *Estat présent de l'Arménie* (Paris, 1694); Tavernier, *Les six voyages* (Paris, 1676); V. Cuinet, *La Turquie d'Asie* (Paris, 1892); Martin van Bruinessen, "Kurdish Tribes and the State of Iran: the Case of Simko's Revolt," in Richard Tapper, ed., *The Conflict of Tribe and State in Iran and Afghanistan* (New York: St. Martin's Press, 1983); Martin van Bruinessen, *Agha Shaikh and State: On the Social and Political Organization of Kurdistan* (Rijswijk: Europrint, 1978); Ernest McCarus, "Kurdish Language Studies," *The Middle East Journal* (Washington, Summer, 1960); Ibn Bazzâz Ardabili, *Safwat al-Safâ*, ed., Ahmad Kasravi (Teheran, 1927); Sharaf al-Din Bitlisi, *Chèref-nameh [Sharafnâma] ou Fastes de la nation kourde*, translated by Charmoy, 2 vols. (St. Petersburg, 1868-75); Amir Hassanpour, "The Language Factor in National Development: The Standardization of the Kurdish Language, 1918-1985," unpublished doctoral dissertation (Urbana, Illinois, 1989); Carsten Niebuhr, *Reisebeschreibung nach Arabien und anderen umliegenden länder*, vol. 2, "Kurdes" (Copenhagen, 1766); John Perry, *Karim Khan Zand* (Chicago: Chicago University Press, 1979).

MODERN HISTORY: 1919-1959

The idea of a nation-state in the modern sense and on the European model was more or less unknown in the Middle East until the late 19th century. This European political convention had caught on as much with Kurds as with any other nationality in the area at the time of the dismemberment of the Ottoman Empire.

Modern ethno-nationalism of the European kind, which had its earliest champion in Kurdistan in Qâdir Koy'i, had grown to attract a large number of Kurdish intellectuals and modernists. A Kurdish nationalist newspaper, *Kurdistan*, had already started publication in Istanbul in 1898. Kurdish political and literary clubs and societies in the Ottoman domain actively promoted the national aspirations of the Kurds and worked to preserve their culture and identity. After its forced closure in 1920, *Kurdistan* resumed publication immediately in Cairo at one of the earliest Kurdish printing houses, *Al-Matbi'ah al-Kurdi*, "the Kurdish Printing House," run by a Bâhâ'i Kurd, Muhammed Zaki al-Kurdi (see **Bâbism and Bâhâ'ism**). *Kurdistan* was soon joined by two other Kurdish papers printed in Sulaymânia, promoting the same goals (see **Press & Electronic Mass Media**).

Two factors prevented a Kurdish nation-state in the settlement following World War I. One was internal, resulting from the absence of credible, worldly statesmen following the demise of the princely houses three generations earlier. The other was external.

U.S. President Woodrow Wilson had vigorously promoted the idea of "self-determination" for all nationalities living within the boundaries of the defunct empires of the Germans, Austrians, Ottomans, and Russians. As such, he categorically and repeatedly demanded independent states for the "Arabs, Armenians, and the Kurds." The Treaty of Sèvres (August 10, 1920), which dismantled the defeated Ottoman Empire, clearly recognized this. Section III, Articles 62-64, provided for the creation of a Kurdish state on the Kurdish territories (Map 23). Article 64 reads as follows:

> If within one year from the coming into force of the present Treaty the Kurdish peoples within the areas defined in Article 62 [comprising western Kurdistan] shall address themselves to the Council of the League of Nations in such a manner as to show that a majority of the population of these areas desires independence from Turkey, and if the Council then considers that these peoples are capable of such independence and recommends that it should be granted to them, Turkey hereby agrees to execute such a recommendation, and to renounce all rights and title over

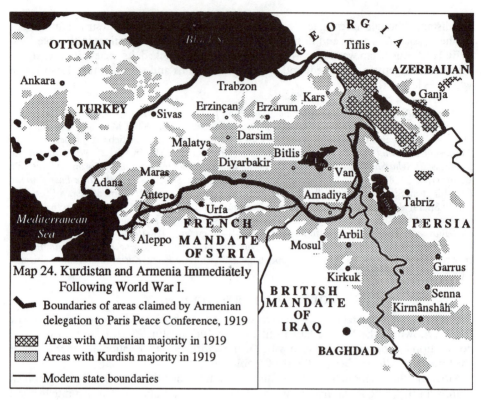

Map 24. Kurdistan and Armenia Immediately
Following World War I.

Boundaries of areas claimed by Armenian
delegation to Paris Peace Conference, 1919

Areas with Armenian majority in 1919

Areas with Kurdish majority in 1919

Modern state boundaries

these areas. The detailed provisions for such renunciation will form the subject of a separate agreement between the principal Allied Powers and Turkey. If and when such renunciation takes place, no objection will be raised by the principal Allied Powers to the voluntary adhesion to such an independent Kurdish State of the Kurds inhabiting that part of Kurdistan which has hitherto been included in the Mosul Vilayet [comprising central Kurdistan].

This treaty was signed by the moribund Ottoman Sultanate in Istanbul, but the successor to the Ottomans, the newly founded Turkish Republic under Mustafa Kemal Pasha (later named Atatürk, i.e., "Father of the Turks") did not consider itself bound to observe it. The terms of the Treaty of Sevres were never enacted.

Having absorbed the richest and most accessible non-Turkish parts of the Ottoman lands, the British and the French tried to bring the United States to the feast, with an offer of a mandate over Armenia and Kurdistan, which the United States failed to take up.

By 1921, however, there were few if any Armenians left in Anatolian Armenia, following their massacre and massive exodus. Except for Soviet Armenia, historic Armenia had become almost exclusively populated by the surviving Kurds, and such an "Armenian" state would inevitably have had a vast Kurdish ethnic majority (Map 24).

The U.S. Congress rejected the mandate because 1) it would unnecessarily involve the still-isolationist United States in the quagmire of world colonial infightings, 2) both Armenia and Kurdistan were remote and hardly accessible by sea, and 3) it would have been unprofitable, since Britain had decided to annex and keep central Kurdistan and its petroleum wealth (Stivers 1982). The failure of the United States to sponsor an independent Kurdistan prompted Britain, the only credible power left on the scene, to proceed with annexing as much of Kurdistan as it found attractive. It took only the ex-Ottoman vilayet (province) of Mosul (central Kurdistan), and with it the petroleum-bearing Kurdish district of Kirkuk. The region was attached to the Arab-dominated British mandate of Iraq, with the League of Nations provision that the national and ethnic aspirations of the Kurdish people be respected by Baghdad.

On June 24, 1923, a new treaty was signed in Lausanne, Switzerland, that ceded all of Anatolia, including northern and western Kurdistan, to Turkey. An independent Kurdistan in Anatolia would almost certainly have destabilized the British hold on central Kurdistan and its vital oil deposits (Nash 1976). Britain therefore willingly allowed the rest of ex-Ottoman Kurdistan to be occupied by the young Turkish Republic. As a face-saving measure, for the European powers to show that they had not completely abandoned Wilson's idealist principle of self-determination for ethnic nationalities, certain guarantees of minority rights were included in Articles 37-44 of the Treaty. None of the ethnic minorities who were summarily handed over to Turkey were mentioned by name in the document.

While Article 38 guaranteed freedom of religion and religious practices for all, and additionally freedom of movement and emigration for non-Muslims, Article 39 guaranteed language rights for all ethnic groups. It reads

> No restrictions shall be imposed on the free use by any Turkish national of any language in private intercourse, in commerce, religion, in the press, or in publications of any kind or at public meetings. Notwithstanding the existence of the official language, adequate facilities shall be given to Turkish nationals of non-Turkish speech for the oral use of their own language before the Courts.

To prevent any future state laws in Turkey from infringing upon these guarantees, Article 37 states that

> Turkey undertakes that the stipulations contained in Articles 38 to 44 shall be recognized as fundamental laws, and that no law, no regulations, nor official action shall conflict or interfere with these stipulations, nor shall any law, regulation, nor official action prevail over them.

As an international mechanism of checks and balances on the enforcement of these and other provisions of the Treaty, Article 44 added that

> Turkey agrees that any Member of the Council of the League of Nations shall have the right to bring to the attention of the Council any infraction or danger of infraction of any of these obligations, and that the Council may thereupon take such action and give such directions as it may deem proper and effective in the circumstances.

However, realizing early the inclination of the Allied powers not to press for observation of Articles 38 and 39, a Turkish official decree on March 3, 1924, less than a year after the signing of the Treaty, banned all Kurdish schools, organizations, and publications, along with their religious fraternities and seminaries. A year later, in February 1925, the Anatolian Kurds staged the first of a series of bloody and calamitous general uprisings against the infant Turkish Republic.

This first general rebellion was led by Shaykh Sa'id, a chief of the Sunni Naqshbandi Sufi order, himself a Dimila Kurd (see **Sufi Orders**). Although the rebels had occupied most of Diyârbakir, Darsim, Bingöl, and Elâzig provinces by March 1925, tribal rivalry limited the effectiveness of the uprising. The Turkish Republican army quickly defeated the revolt, and Shaykh Sa'id and many of his top supporters were hanged in June of the same year.

This revolt was as much, if not more, a religious reaction to the secularizing programs of Atatürk as it was a Kurdish patriotic uprising. In it, the Alevi Kurds sided largely with Atatürk's secular Republic, fearing another Sunni-led episode of pogroms and oppression, as under Ubaydullâh in the 1880's, this time under Shaykh Sa'id. (This by no means meant the Alevi Kurds were any less patriotic than the others. In fact, it was the Alevis who staged the first nationalistic uprisings of the post-World War I era, albeit within much more limited area, when in 1920 the populous Kuchkiri Alevi tribes rose up in rebellion. It was also the Alevis who later became the victims of the most horrific anti-Kurdish campaigns of the young Turkish Republic in the 1937-38 Darsim massacre, discussed below). Shaykh Sa'id's general uprising of 1925, at any rate, proved to be just a prelude.

In 1919 a group of Kurdish aristocratic intellectuals and modernists (they included tribal leaders, and some descendants of the old Kurdish princely houses) living in Paris, in exile or otherwise, established a political party named *Khoyboun* (also spelled *Hoybun* or *Hoyboon*, i.e., "independence"). Following the fall of Shaykh Sa'id, they declared from their headquarters in Lebanon the formation of a Kurdish government in exile in 1927 and moved to gain popular support for an armed insurgency against Turkey the following year.

Khoyboun's uprising was distinguished from that of Shaykh Sa'id by its modernist approach to the Kurdish national dilemma, seeking an end to tribal rivalry among the Kurds and the creation of a single, independent Kurdish state, with secular inclinations. The credit for this approach undoubtedly goes to two representatives of the old Rozhaki-Badirkhânid princely houses of Bitlis, Sorayyâ, and Kamurân, who also helped to establish many important Kurdish journals and papers to educate their fellow Kurds in the realities and requirements of the modern times (see **Press & Electronic Media**).

Khoyboun's military forces, led by General Ihsân Nuri Pâshâ, a former Kurdish member of the "Young Turk" movement, swiftly secured Bitlis, Vân, and most mountainous regions of the land from around Lake Vân all the way to Mount Ararat. Their success proved to be short-lived.

Kurds from outside Anatolia, like Shaykh Ahmad Bârzâni of (now) Iraqi Kurdistan, provided some military assistance to Khoyboun, but soon were restrained by French and British administrations under Turkish pressure. Then the Iranian government of Reza Shah withdrew its support as well. Iran swapped its support for political and territorial concessions by Turkey, including the ceding to Iran of the fertile district of Dustân and the strategic Qotour Heights northwest of Urmiâ. (Turkey received the useless Little Ararat peak as nominal "compensation.") With no outside help, the revolt was crushed in the summer of 1932 by the Turkish Army, which had been allowed to cross Iranian borders to encircle the last stronghold of the rebels at Mount Ararat. General Nuri Pâshâ went into permanent exile in Teheran (Nouri Pasha 1986).

Following the rebel defeat, a program of pacification was quickly put into action in the Kurdish provinces of Turkey. The severity of the Turkish military actions created a tense atmosphere, which culminated in the massacres and destruction of the inaccessible mountainous district of Darsim, the heartland of the Dimila Kurds and the original home of the medieval Daylamite warriors and dynasties (see **Medieval History**).

The army had begun a "preventive" action in this area in the spring of 1937 with every weapon in its arsenal, including poison gas, heavy artillery, and even primitive bomber aircraft. By October 1938, the area, which had only been suspected of inclination to revolt, had been "pacified." Accounts abound of refugees immolated in woods, collective suicides of Kurdish villagers throwing themselves off cliffs, and women and girls drowning themselves in rivers from fear of rape. Darsim was so thoroughly and ruthlessly devastated that the Turkish press noted, "*Delenda est Darsim*," or "Darsim is no more," echoing the words of the Roman general Scipio two thousand years earlier on his utter destruction of Carthage (Safarastian 1948, 87). Armed struggle would not resume in Turkish Kurdistan until 1981 (Map 25).

The relative decline of the Kurdish population in Turkey, attributable first to physical

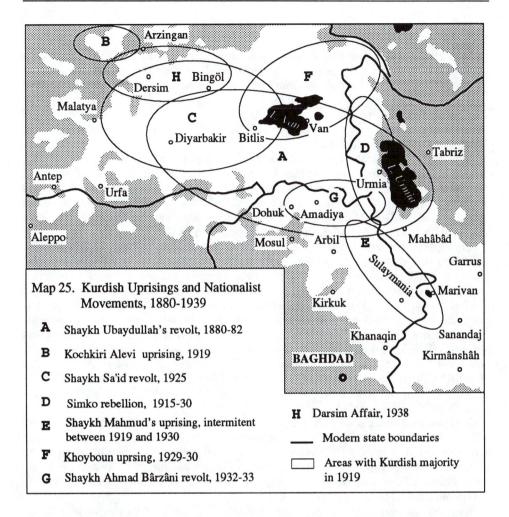

Map 25. Kurdish Uprisings and Nationalist Movements, 1880-1939

A Shaykh Ubaydullah's revolt, 1880-82

B Kochkiri Alevi uprising, 1919

C Shaykh Sa'id revolt, 1925

D Simko rebellion, 1915-30

E Shaykh Mahmud's uprising, intermitent between 1919 and 1930

F Khoyboun uprsing, 1929-30

G Shaykh Ahmad Bârzâni revolt, 1932-33

H Darsim Affair, 1938

_____ Modern state boundaries

☐ Areas with Kurdish majority in 1919

violence and after 1940 to much lower rates of natural increase, appeared by the 1950's to be sending the Kurdish community into assimilation and oblivion. Noting this, Premiers Menderes and Bayar relaxed many strict government policies. Some publications even appeared in Kurdish. However, the demographic decline was a temporary phenomenon, and the Kurds began to increase again in absolute, but much more importantly, in relative numbers (see **Demography**). The only tangible evidence that the Government worried about the reversal of the Kurdish demographic **increase** per se came after 1965, when the state census ceased reporting the ethno-linguistic breakdowns altogether.

The military regime of Cemal Gürsel, brought into power in a 1960 coup, reinstated the forceful older policies, given renewed Kurdish population growth. Many Kurdish tribal elites were deported, and 26 intellectuals were executed between 1961 and 1963. A series of unstable civilian governments holding office in Turkey during the remainder of the 1960s, then alternately instituted programs of oppression in Kurdistan or relaxed the tension heightened earlier by Gürsel.

In Iraq, almost from the moment of its formation as a British mandate, the British had to deal with Kurdish unrest in the north. However, the Kurds there were never a match for the technologically and numerically superior British imperial troops. In fact, a decade before the Turkish use of airpower against Darsim, the Iraqi Kurds were history's first civilian targets of bomber aircraft, when the British Royal Air Force in Iraq bombed

Kurdish villagers in central Kurdistan (Olson 1989, 163).

In northern Iraq a Kurdish kingdom was announced in 1922 by Shaykh Mahmud. Although he had no connection with the old Kurdish princely houses, Mahmud sprang from an illustrious Qâdiri Sufi religious house, that of Barzanja. Mahmud thus enjoyed supreme religious status when he sought political station as well. His power base was in the South Kurmânji-speaking, less tribal and more urbane, southern portion of Iraqi Kurdistan (where he was a precursor of Jalâl Tâlabâni and the Patriotic Union of Kurdistan; see **Political Parties**).

Mahmud was originally chosen by the British authorities to subdue and supervise the Kurds for them in their newly acquired Mandate of Iraq. He did subdue and supervise the local Kurds, but not for the British authorities. He was quickly arrested and sent to exile in India, only to be brought back a year later by the British, who hoped to co-opt him. Instead, in 1922 Mahmud, under the banner of the "Free Kurdistan Movement," declared the independence of Kurdistan, with himself as its king.

Throughout his twelve-year struggle, Mahmud had to fight as much against Kurdish tribal chiefs as the British forces, and could claim real authority only in his home district of Sulaymânia. He was a representative of the old society, and aroused considerable animosity among the modernist Kurdish intellectuals, who blamed the Kurdish predicament on just the values that Mahmud and traditionalists like him stood for and promoted. The local tribal chieftains did not see much difference between giving up their semi-independence to Mahmud or to London, Baghdad, and Ankara. Mahmud's strong and specific religious background could not have helped his cause among those Kurds who were not Sunni Muslim of the Qâdiri Sufi order. Yet despite all these handicaps, "in Southern Kurdistan," reported Sir Arnold Wilson, the British Political Officer in Baghdad, "four out of five people support Sheikh Mahmoud's plans for independent Kurdistan" (Wilson 1931, 137).

Meanwhile, Atatürk's forces had entered Mosul Province (Iraqi Kurdistan) to enforce the Turkish claim over the territory, against the British plans. The Turkish nationalism and secularism promoted by Atatürk combined with the savagery demonstrated by his forces in that region prompted many Kurds to switch their allegiance toward the laissez faire British. They thus abandoned Shaykh Mahmud, who still opposed the British. Mahmud's capital Sulaymânia fell in 1924.

In 1926, the League of Nations Commission, citing the cruel treatment of both the Assyrian Christians and the Kurds in the contested territories at the hands of the Turks, awarded Mosul Province to Iraq and its British government. The League required Iraq to allow cultural and social autonomy in the Kurdish regions.

Naively having hoped to receive central Kurdistan as his independent kingdom from the League of Nations, Mahmud moved his headquarters across the border into Iran to begin anew. There he staged a revolt in the town of Marivân in eastern Kurdistan. Beaten back by the Persian forces, he moved once again to Sulaymânia, where he was put down one more time by the British in the spring of 1930.

As early as 1927, the North Kurmânji-speaking northern section of Iraqi Kurdistan was the scene of another, rather peculiar, uprising led by the charismatic religious leader of the Bârzâni tribe, Shaykh Ahmad, the elder brother of the well-known Kurdish political leader, General Mustafa Bârzâni, and a leader of the influential Naqshbandi Sufi order. Ahmad took on the British, Turks, Arabs, as well as fellow Kurds (the rival Baradost tribe). As if that were not enough, Ahmad also challenged traditional Islam by instituting a new religion, which was to bring together Christianity, Judaism, and Islam in one. Possibly hoping to unite the religiously fragmented Kurds, he also included elements of the old Cult of Angels by declaring himself the new avatar of the Universal Spirit (see **Cult of Angels**). (He was not alone in this claim. In 1939 the Alevi Nusayri leader Sulaymân Murshid of Syria, then under the French Mandate, also claimed to be a Divine avatar; Hourani 1947, 88.)

Ahmad's forces were put down by British and Iraqi troops after several years of fighting. The British and Iraqis were supported by the Royal Air Force bombers, whose appearance alone stunned the Kurdish villagers more than the destruction their bombs brought to their lives and property.

Defeated, Shaykh Ahmad escaped to Turkey, but later was arrested and sent into exile in southern Iraq. His legacy within the Bârzâni tribe was passed on to his brother Mustafâ, who raised the specter of Kurdish home rule as early as 1940, but mainly in the course of 1960s, which stretches to this day (see **Recent History**).

A harsh result of Mahmud's and Ahmad's fierce and long struggle against the British in central Kurdistan, however inadvert, was that it weakened British resolve to grant local Kurdish autonomy, as expressed in the League of Nations' articles of incorporation of central Kurdistan into the State of Iraq. The new Anglo-Iraqi Treaty of 1930, which provided for the independence of Iraq from the British by 1932, did not include any specific rights of autonomy, or in fact of any kind, for the Kurds.

Protesting the terms of the treaty of Iraqi independence, the seemingly unsinkable Mahmud rose one last time in 1931. Having finally scaled down his expectations following a dozen years of fruitless struggle, Mahmud this time asked for only an autonomous Kurdistan. The British refused, and it took them a full year to gain the final downfall of the war-seasoned Mahmud and his forces. By December 1931, Mahmud had been broken for good—16 months after the defeat of the Khoyboun uprising in Turkey.

It shall never be known why at the very end, and after the final demise of Mahmud in late 1931, British politicians included an eleventh-hour amendment to the Iraqi independence treaty of 1932, to provide for the teaching of Kurdish in the schools and for election of local Kurdish officials in Iraqi Kurdistan. It may be that Mahmud's tenacity in the face of all odds finally gained admiration and sympathy from his European adversary (see **National Character**).

After 1932 a relative calm descended upon ravaged countryside of central Kurdistan, for the first time since 1914.

The Mahâbâd Republic. By the fall of 1940, as a result of the Allied invasion of Iran, the Iranian Kurds initiated an independence movement. Having suffered from a lack of security, the interference of Soviet forces in the local economy, and the resulting famines, the Iranian Kurds established in 1945 an independent Kurdish republic in Mahâbâd. Republican forces quickly expanded their domain south towards Sanandaj and Kirmânshâh. Beaten back at the battle of Divândara, they retreated to a rather tiny enclave behind the Soviet defense lines in their occupied zone in Iran (Map 26). The Republic lasted for one year (December 1945-December 1946), during which time Kurdish state apparatuses and ministries were formed and functioned, until their destruction at the hands of the Iranian forces. Or so has the myth enshrouding this political entity in the Kurdish national consciousness.

In reality, however, the Mahâbâd Republic, as it is commonly called, was a creation of the Soviet forces occupying Iran (the Soviets also created a neighboring Azerbaijan Democratic Republic centered on Tabriz). These unquestionably were to have been incorporated into the Soviet Union when the dust from World War II had settled. It is rather naive to believe there would have been any chance of survival for this Kurdish polity once its loss by Iran had been acknowledged, or as happened, the Soviet Union withdrew its supportive military umbrella. Iranian troops took Mahâbâd with ease, hanging President Qâzi Muhammad and many of his aides in the city's main public square. The Mahâbâd Republic was disbanded.

The period following the fall of the Republic and before the rise of the Mustafâ Bârzâni-led Kurdish insurgency in Iraq in the 1960s is the least eventful period of modern Kurdish history. Except for some minor skirmishes, limited local armed and unarmed

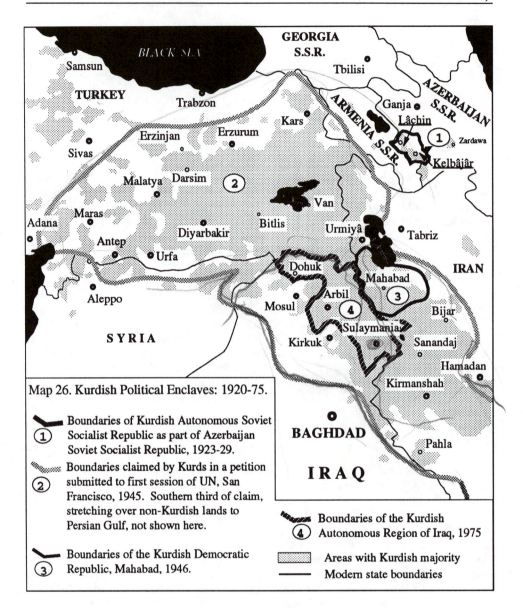

Map 26. Kurdish Political Enclaves: 1920-75.

(1) Boundaries of Kurdish Autonomous Soviet Socialist Republic as part of Azerbaijan Soviet Socialist Republic, 1923-29.

(2) Boundaries claimed by Kurds in a petition submitted to first session of UN, San Francisco, 1945. Southern third of claim, stretching over non-Kurdish lands to Persian Gulf, not shown here.

(3) Boundaries of the Kurdish Democratic Republic, Mahabad, 1946.

(4) Boundaries of the Kurdish Autonomous Region of Iraq, 1975

Areas with Kurdish majority
Modern state boundaries

protests against various government policies, Kurdistan as a whole experienced a much-needed period of repose. This readied the Kurds for a new and dramatic period of their national life beginning with the decade of 1960's.

Further Readings and Bibliography: William Eagleton, *The Kurdish Republic of 1946* (London: Oxford University Press, 1963); Arshak Safarastian, *Kurds and Kurdistan* (London, 1948); Robert Olson, *The Emergence of Kurdish Nationalism and the Sheikh Said Rebellion, 1880-1925* (Austin: University of Texas Press, 1989); Gerard Challiand, *People Without a Country* (London: Zed Press, 1980); David Adamson, *The Kurdish War* (London: George Allen and Unwin, 1964); Lord Kinross, *Ataturk: The Rebirth of A Nation* (London: Weidenfeld and Nicolson, 1964); Martin van Bruinessen, *Agha Shaikh and State: On the Social and Political Organization of Kurdistan* (Rijswijk: Europrint, 1978); Albert Hourani, *Minorities in the Arab World* (New York: Oxford University Press, 1947); Theodore Nash, "The Effect of International Oil Interests upon the Fate of Autonomous Kurdish Territory: A Perspective on the Conference at Sèvres, August 10, 1920,"

International Problems 15, 1-2 (1976); William Stivers, *Supremacy and Oil: Iraq, Turkey, and the Anglo-American World Order, 1918-1930* (Ithaca: Cornell University Press, 1982); Elmer Bermon Sovill, "The Royal Air Force, the Middle East and Disarmament, 1919-1934," unpublished doctoral dissertation (Kalamazoo: Michigan State University, 1972); Stephen Longrigg, *Iraq, 1900-1950: A Political, Social, and Economic History* (London: Oxford University Press, 1953); Stephen Longrigg, Oil in the Middle East: Its Discovery and Development (London: Oxford University Press, 1968); Ernest Main, *Iraq: From Mandate to Independence* (London, 1935); Sir Arnold Wilson, *Mesopotamia, 1917-1920: A Clash of Loyalties* (London, 1931); William Westermann, "Kurdish Independence and Russian Expansion," *Foreign Affairs* 70-3 (Summer 1991); Ihsân Nouri Pâshâ, *La Revolt d'Agri Dagh* (Geneva: Editions Kurdes, Genev PV, 1986).

RECENT HISTORY: 1960-PRESENT

This period marks a rejuvenation of the Kurdish national life. The trade routes returned to Kurdistan in the 1960's, picking up volume at a dizzying speed in the course of the 1970's. This was due in part to the booming economies of Iran and Iraq since the late 1950's and their need to use the short land routes to European markets via Turkey. This commercial traffic crossed Kurdistan in various points in these states. The trade is driving Kurdistan from centuries of sleepiness into the late 20th century at an astonishing pace (see **Trade**).

The role of international commercial traffic in the revitalization of the Kurdish economy and the subsidiary infrastructure, as well as its social and cultural effects, can hardly be overestimated. The devastating effects of its stoppage have already been demonstrated under **Early Modern History**. The vast economic improvements born from this quiet, but fundamental change have been translated into construction of new roads and communication systems, introduction of many agricultural projects, and urban improvement programs. Meanwhile, urbanization and literacy have been rising steadily. A sizable Kurdish middle class is being born, after having been nearly absent for the past 400 years.

Even though the Kurds of Turkey have benefited the most from this process, the Iraqi Kurds have been the most restive—and visible. Due to its perennial state of turmoil, Iraqi Kurdistan has attracted the most attention from the outside world, despite representing only about 17% of the total number of Kurds. It has thus given the erroneous impression of having played the central role in this period of Kurdish history. The Kurds in Turkey, who are undergoing much more fundamental change, and will play an indisputable role in the future of the Kurdish nation, have been largely ignored by the outside world.

The Iraqi Kurds start this period with rather much hope. In fact, under the military leadership of Abdul Karim Qâsim, the coup leader who toppled the monarchy in Iraq (1958), the Iraqi state flag began carrying as its center piece the Kurdish sun disk (a yellow disk surrounded by seven red rays) between 1959 and 1963. Qâsim is believed to have been an assimilated, arabized Kurd himself (see **Integration & Assimilation**), even though his uncordial policies toward the Kurdish leadership did not endear him or his government to them, resulting in a few, rather minor, insurgencies.

After toppling Abdul Karim Qâsim's military junta in Baghdad, the Ba'ath party leaders decided to reach a comprehensive settlement with the Kurds. The Kurdish sun disk was, however, dropped from the Iraqi state flag upon the removal of Qâsim in 1963.

On March 11, 1970, party representative Saddam Hussein (emerging as the most powerful man in the regime, although not yet the Republic's President) entered and negotiated a deal with Iraqi Kurdish Democratic Party leader General Mullah Mustafâ Bârzâni.

The agreement explicitly declared that "The people of Iraq are made up of two principal nationalities, the Arab and the Kurdish." Kurdish was to be given the status of the second national language alongside Arabic, and an autonomous Kurdish Region was to be established within four years of the signing of the treaty. Only Kurdish-speaking government officials would be appointed to serve within the autonomous region. A Kurd was actually appointed the Vice President of Iraqi Republic.

The agreement was not destined to stand, as each side seemed to think it could have gotten a better deal, and that it had been tricked by the other party. Before the ink of the document had dried, General Bârzâni claimed that the whole of the agreement was "a ruse. I even knew it before signing it." The suspicion was surely mutual, to say the least. Both sides, the following events showed, were just buying time.

General Bârzâni escaped an assassination attempt on September 29, 1971, less than a year after signing the agreement. This event did not diminish his misgivings as to the intentions of Baghdad, and of Saddam Hussein, whom he suspected as the mastermind of the attempt. Interestingly, fingers were pointed first toward Jalâl Tâlabâni, the other Iraqi Kurdish political party leader (Ghareeb 1981, 109).

Bârzâni repudiated his signature in 1973. He quickly established ever more cordial relations, overt and covert, with three archenemies of Iraq—Iran, Israel, and the United States.

At the end of the four-year interim period, Baghdad published in 1974 the details of the law that would govern the Kurdish autonomous area. While the law provided for Kurdish executive and legislative local councils, real power over the internal affairs of the autonomous region was held in Baghdad (Ghareeb 1981, 156-170). The restrictive law conformed with neither the word nor the spirit of the 1970 agreement.

Both sides were itching to show their military muscle, and this provided them with ample excuse. Kurdish forces, under Iraqi KDP direction, reacted within a few weeks by commencing massive guerrilla attacks on government forces and installations. Their alliance with Iran became more and more conspicuous, as cash and arms from the Shah were augmented by U.S. and Israeli intelligence and funding. Seeking regional supremacy and the upper hand in his territorial dispute with Iraq, the Shah found the Iraqi Kurds a suitable thorn to press in the side of Baghdad. He did not, however, want an outright Kurdish victory, as he would then need to deal with the intensified aspirations of his own, more populous, Kurdish minority. He shrewdly milked the Iraqi Kurdish uprising for his country's gain over Iraq, increasing aid to the Kurds when they were in too much trouble, and decreasing it when they were gaining too much ground. The United States and even Israel concurred with this policy and participated in the Iranian tactic. Bârzâni, mean-while, did not see any of this.

With these mighty "friends" Bârzâni appeared to have the Iraqi government at a disad-vantage. He then committed a strategic mistake by ordering a switch from guerrilla to conventional warfare against the central forces. The Kurdish *peshmerga,* adept at elusive guerrilla warfare in the mountains since at least the time of the Medes and the conquest of Assyria (see **Ancient History**), were no match in a conventional war against the clearly superior Iraqi forces, and were soon cut to pieces. By 1975, the Kurdish forces had been chased to within a few miles of the Iranian borders and over.

Realizing the fast-approaching defeat of Bârzâni's forces, and that the war would give him the opportunity to press Baghdad into a treaty on terms favorable to Iran, the Shah correctly concluded that the day in the sun for the Iraqi Kurds had passed. He agreed in Algiers (March 6, 1975) on the terms of a treaty of friendship with Iraq, and for turning his back on the Kurds, received all the land and sea concessions he had wanted. Saddam Hussein, then Vice President, signed for Iraq.

The hapless Kurd might have done better had Bârzâni read his history books. Exactly 45 years earlier, General Ihsân Nuri Pâshâ had entrusted the Khoyboun movement to an-other Iranian monarch, Reza Shah, only to be swapped for territorial and political gains (see **Modern History**). Thus, like Nuri Pâshâ, Mustafa Bârzâni ended up in exile in Teheran on a meager Iranian government stipend. He died of cancer while receiving treatment in Virginia in 1978.

Triumphant, Baghdad embarked on a systematic program of reducing the influence of Kurdish political parties in its domain, while pouring financial and human resources into the region to rebuild and revamp the devastated Kurdish countryside. The hope was to coopt the common Kurdish citizens by giving them a fairly reasonable "piece of the pie." A small "Kurdish Autonomous Region" was created in Iraqi Kurdistan under Baghdad's strict supervision and control. It included about half of the Kurdish-populated lands in Iraq (Map 26). Meanwhile, a government-sponsored program of Arabization of certain Kurdish regions gained momentum. This last program, however, appears in retrospect to have been in vain, despite many population transfers, deportations, and the enticement of Arab immigrants from as far afield as Sudan and Mauritania to settle the Kurdish highlands.

In Iran, from the fall of the monarchy in February 1979 until the Islamic government could tighten its grip on the country by the end of 1982, various degrees of social and military chaos transformed the grievances of several ethnic groups into armed uprisings. In Kurdistan, long-suppressed Kurdish political organizations such as the Kurdish Democratic Party of Iran (KDP-I) and the Komala quickly moved to secure a form of local autonomy for the Kurds while Teheran was still weak and willing to compromise. Negotiations over autonomy were prolonged. As Teheran regained the necessary strength, it used the demand of these parties for a separate currency (which was really nothing more than a bargaining chip) as proof of the Kurdish goal of dismembering the state. It declared all-out war on the Kurds.

Supplied by competing Kurdish groups with information and volunteers, Iranian forces stormed and eventually crushed these Kurds. The area and number of Kurds controlled by the leaders of Komala and the KDP-I (as well as by a new Kurdish religious movement and its leader, Shaykh Izzidin Husayni, who supported the uprising) was rather limited and at no time included more than one-quarter of Iranian Kurdistan or the allegiance of similar proportions of the inhabitants (see **Political Culture & Leadership**). As a result, the overall number of Kurdish casualties was small, perhaps in the range of 1000-2000.

By 1983, the uprising had diminished to just a minor headache for Teheran, which, except for some remote mountain hideouts, had the Kurdish territories firmly under its control .

The start of the war between Iraq and Iran, and the open siding of the Iraqi KDP with Iran, did not help the Kurdish case in the eyes of common Iraqi citizens or Baghdad. This was to have been expected, however, since the KDP had its headquarters in Iran and had derived a good deal of its budget from that source since Bârzâni's 1975 flight from Iraq. While the war was going well for Iraq, Baghdad cared little what the Iraqi KDP was doing in Iran. After the reversal of its fortunes and the invasion of Iraqi territories by Iranian forces, they began to care much more. Iraq attempted to coopt the KDP with a number of peace offerings. Failing to do so, however, Baghdad moved in 1984 to strike a deal with the other Kurdish political party, the Patriotic Union of Kurdistan (PUK), led by Jalâl Tâlabâni.

As the war with Iran went ever more awry, Baghdad was forced to sue for a settlement with the Kurds, almost at any price. Tâlabâni succeeded in extracting from the desperate Saddam Hussein concessions that were much more generous than in the original 1970 agreement with Mustafâ Bârzâni. The Autonomous Region was to expand to include all of the disputed areas—and Kirkuk. The degree of local autonomy was also to be strengthened, to include free elections for the local councils. To the region was also to be allocated 25-30% of overall Iraqi state budget. Nonetheless, since it was made by Saddam under duress, it is doubtful that this generous agreement, had it been signed and ratified, would have been adhered to by Baghdad without major alterations after the cease fire of 1988.

"The break [in Tâlabâni-Baghdad negotiations] came," the *Economist* observed, "when Turkey's foreign minister arrived in Baghdad to assert that the Kurdish autonomous area with the proposed expanded powers was too autonomous for Turkey's liking, and that the agreement, at that point awaiting signature, should not be implemented. Dependent on the pipelines through Turkey for its oil exports, Iraq complied with its big neighbor's wish and dropped the Kurdish deal. It also, the same year, granted Turkey the right of hot pursuit of dissident Turkish Kurds across the frontier" (*Economist,* April 27, 1991, 46).

Fighting between Kurdish and Iraqi troops resumed, lasting for another four years. Between March and August 1988, Baghdad finally put down the insurrection by the use of chemical weapons on civilians and guerrilla fighters alike.

The Iraqi military had used chemical weapons with caution on the Kurdish fighters and then on civilians since 1985. Having been encouraged by silence from the international community and the United Nations while using them regularly on Iranian forces, in March 1988 the Kurdish town of Halabja became the sight of the first extensive use of chemical weapons on civilians since they were outlawed after the horrors of World War I. Up to 5000 people were reported to have perished by them in Halabja.

In a few months time, a cease-fire was declared between Iran and Iraq, ending their eight years of war. Free to act on Kurdish rebels, Baghdad resorted to much more extensive use of the chemicals.

In August 1988, a region to the north of Mosul was victimized. The affected region is a triangle located on the Iraqi borders with Syria and Turkey and on the opposite side of Iraq from the Iranian borders. The Kurdish towns of Zakho, Dohuk, and Amâdiya mark the corners of this triangle. Through this region pass the Iraqi-Turkish oil pipelines to the Mediterranean and the highway connecting Iraq to Europe via Turkey. The only railroad connecting Iraq to Europe, through Syria and Turkey (even though nonoperational now), passes less than 10 miles away. By any account this area is of extreme economic importance to Baghdad. Gas canisters dropped from planes and helicopters on every village, hamlet, and farm in the region were apparently meant to flush out or kill every inhabitant. The attack caused several thousand civilian casualties and an exodus of about 60,000 Kurds across the borders into Turkey.

To enforce better control of the Kurdish populace and deny civilian logistical support to the Kurdish guerrillas, Baghdad since 1988 has embarked on a scorched earth policy in Kurdistan, reminiscent of the Persian policy of the 16th and 17th centuries (see **Early Modern History**). An astonishing amount of work has been dedicated to the destruction of hundreds of villages and the infrastructure supporting life in the countryside of central Kurdistan. Buildings are first blown up and then bulldozed. Cement is then poured neatly into wells and irrigation works to choke them. Power lines are pulled out and burned, if of wood, or dynamited if of concrete. Witnessing such an admirably efficient, and costly, job in even the far corners of Iraqi Kurdistan, one cannot help but laugh bitterly at the tragicomic air of the Kurdish countryside. The area was long in want of just such attention, and such meticulous feats of engineering, as the Iraqis were lavishing on it; but it was needed for construction, not, as it was now receiving it, for destruction.

In August 1990, Iraq invaded its small, but rich neighbor, Kuwait. An international armed response expelled it from Kuwait, and in the process destroyed much of the Iraqi economy and military. In March 1991, less than a week after the February 28 announcement of the Allied powers' cease-fire, the Kurds staged a general uprising in Iraqi Kurdistan. While the elite Iraqi Republican Guards were regrouping and putting down a Shi'ite uprising in the south, the Kurdish forces, which had gathered under a coalition of all major Kurdish political parties in Iraq, took over all Kurdish inhabited areas of Iraq, and more. This was an empty victory. After putting down the Shi'ites in the south, the battle-hardened, dreaded Republican Guards advanced into Kurdistan. A massive flight of Kurds ensued. Nearly half of all Kurds of Iraq ran for the borders of Turkey and Iran, as a horrific picture of mass starvation, freezing, epidemics, and harassment by Iraqi and Turkish troops unfolded. Nearly 1.2 million Kurds passed into Iran. Another 500,000 massed on the Turkish border, with only about 200,000 being allowed in by the Turks, who closed their borders after two days.

Allied forces (mainly British and American) were sent into northern Iraq to protect the Kurds. They also declared the area north of the 36th parallel off limits to the Iraqi air force.

This was a little strange. The ethnic line separating the Kurds from the Arabs in Iraq runs almost north-south. The area thus included a large Arab population, and the multiethnic Mosul, the second largest city in Iraq. Although designated area also included Arbil and a score of smaller towns, it left out over two-thirds of Iraqi Kurdistan, including Sulaymânia, Kirkuk, Kifri, and Khânaqin. Allied forces also occupied a "Security Zone," a sliver of land north of Mosul that included the Kurdish towns of Zakho, Amâdiya, and, more or less, Dohuk—exactly the same area that had been extensively gassed by Baghdad in August 1988. The creation of the Security Zone was to entice Kurdish refugees to return to Iraq. The area was later handed over to Kurdish forces.

Iraqi government functionaries were eventually chased out of the area by the Kurds, prompting a quarantine of all Kurdish-occupied areas by Baghdad. As of the end of 1991, this area had grown to include almost 40% of Iraqi Kurdistan, and to stretch from the Syrian borders, along the Turkish and Iranian borders, to the Diyâla River.

Since the rise to power of Turgut Özal in Turkey, Ankara has embarked on reversing its 70 years of rough handling of the Kurdish question in that country. The shift in its policy of dealing harshly with the Alevi community in 1989, followed by the grant of language rights to the Kurds in November 1990, were the first promising signs.

For centuries, the staunchly Sunni Muslim Ottoman sultans in Istanbul could seldom find a time that was not suitable to torment the much-maligned Alevi community, which had besides its Kurdish adherents, a strong following among the Turkmens in Anatolia (see **Alevism**). The bloody events at Darsim in 1937-38 were just a continuation of the oppressive trends of the past, albeit with a greater degree of bloodshed. Late in 1989, a sudden change of heart took place with respect to the Alevis. Having declared secularism at its inception in 1921, 68 years later the Turkish Republic put it into practice for the first time. It gave official recognition to the Alevi religion (albeit after declaring it to be just an Islamic sect).

While this was great news for the Alevis, Kurds as well as non-Kurds, it also greatly helps Ankara to stave off the rising militarism among yet another unhappy ethno-religious group in Turkey. Many Alevi festivals, like the all-Kurdish *New Ruz* (the new year festival), had taken the form of strong anti-government political expression. By recognizing Alevism, such festivals now receive official recognition too, and on occasion, sponsorship (see **Festivals, Ceremonies, & Calendar**). Indeed, cynics point out that the government is coopting the Alevi Kurdish community and pulling its youths away from radical Kurdish politics, in which they have played a strong role in the past (see **Political Parties**). The Alevis can also be used as a counterweight against their old enemies, the orthodox Sunni Muslims, among whom revolutionary Islamic ideas have risen to alarming proportions in the past decade. Courting the Alevis could also reduce the Alevi Kurds' association with the Muslim Kurds, at whose hands the Alevis have suffered in the recent past.

It is surprising that such policies had not been implemented earlier in Turkey. Iran had carried out a policy of controlled accommodation vis-a-vis its vast Azeri community, with excellent results in gaining state loyalty through economic and political integration (Izady 1988). Ankara now appears to have noted the mutual benefits of this policy, and the Alevi experiment is being further expanded to all Kurds, at a relatively rapid pace.

Following the 1991 ratification of the "Language Law," which allowed for the use of Kurdish in public, Kurdish language publications, after having been banned for decades in Turkey, have been permitted. The past two years indeed have brought signs that finally the Turkish and Kurdish citizens of Turkey are beginning to try to live together in peace. Through mutual understanding and fair conduct by the government in Ankara, there may be left no grounds for criticism or hostile actions using the Kurdish question as a pretext.

In Iran, even the 1988 assassination of Abdul Rahman Ghassemlou, the illustrious leader of the Kurds' most important political party, the KDP-I (see **Political Parties**), while he awaited Iranian peace negotiators, did not move the Kurdish population there. The Iranian state newspapers are now reporting that Ghassemlou's successor, Sa'id Sharafkandi, is suing for a new round of peace negotiations, presumably more certain that he will not be assassinated in the process.

Further Readings and Bibliography: Abdul Rahman Ghassemlou, *Kurdistan and the Kurds* (Prague: Academy of Science, 1965); Edmund Ghareeb, *The Kurdish Question in Iraq* (Syracuse: Syracuse University Press, 1981); David Andrews, *The Lost Peoples of the Middle East: Documents of the Struggle for Survival and Independence of the Kurds, Assyrians and other Minority Races in the Middle East* (Salisbury, NC: Documentary Publications, 1982).

General Bibliography

A valuable source to consult on many Kurdish historical issues is the *Encyclopaedia of Islam* under various headings, particularly "Kurds," "Kurdistan," and "Kurdish"; for historical background on religious movements, "Ahl-i Haqq," "Alevi," "Yezidi," "Gholât," and "Sufism"; and for dynastic information under the names of the dynasties as provided in this study. Also, G.R. Driver, "Studies in Kurdish History," *Bulletin of the School of Oriental Studies*, II (1921-23); Hasan Arfa, *The Kurds, An Historic and Political Study* (London: Oxford University Press, 1966); V. Minorsky, "Les origines des Kurdes," *Actes du XXe Congrès International des Orientalistes* 1938 (1940); H. Arfa, *The Kurds* (Oxford: Oxford University Press, 1966); Drek Ninnane, *The Kurds and Kurdistan* (London: Oxford University Press, 1964); G.R. Driver, "The Name Kurd and its Philological Connexions," *Journal of the Royal Asiatic Society of Great Britain and Ireland* (1923); Basil Nikitine, *Les Kurdes. Etude Sociologique et Historique.* (Paris, 1956); Arshak Safrastian, *Arabs and Kurds and Kurdistan* (London, 1946); *Kurdish Times*, semi-annual journal of the Kurdish Library, Brooklyn, New York 1985-present.

Chapter 4

HUMAN GEOGRAPHY

PHYSICAL ANTHROPOLOGY

By their physical characteristics alone Kurds cannot be distinguished from their neighbors, as all traits and variations among the Kurds can also be found among any one of their major ethnic neighbors. Neither is there any uniformity among Kurds themselves. Even though the Kurds are now predominantly of Mediterranean racial stock, resembling southern Europeans and Levantines in general coloring and physiology, there is yet a persistent recurrence of two racial substrata: 1) a darker, brachy- to mesocephaloid, aboriginal Paleo-Caucasian element, and 2) a more localized occurrence of blondism of the mesocephaloid Alpine type, and occasionally dolichocephaloid Nordic type. This latter physical type is most often encountered in the Zakho-Urmiâ-Shnu and Kirmânshâh-Hamadân regions, as well as extreme northwest Kurdistan in the Pontus mountains. It is least frequently encountered in eastern and western Kurdistan, while central and western Kurdistan are in the middle of the two extremes.

Blondism and submerged blondism (as evidenced by blue or other light-colored eyes with dark hair), for example, appeared in about one-third of the 598 Kurds who were the subject of a study in physical anthropology in Iraq by Henry Field. The frequency of its occurrence diminished from its peak at Zakho toward Kirkuk and Sulaymânia (Field 1952).

Generally speaking, the city and sedentary village people are shorter (average height 5' 3" to 5' 7") than the mountain-dwelling (former) nomads (average height 5' 7" to 6'). A good deal of this difference in stature may be attributable to the nutritional regimes of the two groups, but genetic differences should certainly be taken into consideration as well. Most western travellers of the 19th and early 20th centuries observed in their reports that the Kurdish farmers and city dwellers were a darker, slight-built race, who gave tribute to the migratory nomadic tribes and were occasionally enslaved by them. They were called "Gurâns" by the light-complexioned, much taller tribal people, who called themselves "Kurmânj." This physiological distinction can still be seen in the heartland of the last remaining Gurâni-speaking, agricultural pocket, from Pâwa to Shâhâbâd, where numerous dark-complexioned, small-statured agriculturalists and urbanites live side-by-side with the (now poverty-stricken) light-complexioned ex-nomads. The only difference is that their historical roles have been reversed: the well-to-do Gurâns now hire their domestic help and laborers from among their former nomadic tormentors and overlords, whom they call pejoratively *dâri hull*, i.e., "the pale trees."

The "aryanization" of the aboriginal Paleo-Caucasian Kurds, linguistically, culturally, and racially, seems to have begun by the beginning of the 2nd millennium BC, with the continuous immigration and settlement of many Indo-European-speaking groups such as the Mitânnis, Hittites, Medes, Sagarthians, Scythians, Persians, and Alans. The numbers of these fair-complexioned immigrants must have been so large as to assure a fundamental cultural (although not genetic) metamorphosis.

Despite many episodes of cultural destabilization and homogenization, before and after the coming of the Aryans, genetic homogenization of the Kurds has never taken place. This is self-evident from a cursory look at the contemporary Kurds in various sections of their homeland.

What is noteworthy about the Kurdish ethnic stock is the multiplicity of its origins. This is directly attributable to waves of immigration and invasions of Kurdistan over many millennia. For example, even a peppering of Mongoloid traits is present in many sections of Kurdistan, where many Turkic peoples settled and have been assimilated since the 12th century. The Kurdish ethnic pool is an amalgam into which these peoples have been absorbed.

The most common blood type in Kurdistan is B, followed by A (and the mixed type AB) and O. Type B blood, common among Kurds, appears to provide natural resistance against cholera, a disease which still takes a periodic toll on the Kurds. Type A is resistant to bubonic plague, which explains its prevalence in Europe, hardest hit by the plague, and indicates that the disease had less impact on the Kurdish population in the past. The relative dearth in Kurdistan of type O, which is resistant to smallpox, common throughout the Middle East, indicates that the disease did not often intrude on the Kurdish mountains. This epidemiological evidence must be taken into account in any historical study of Kurdish demography, particularly when adjusting population figures for historical occurrences of high-mortality epidemics (see **Demography**).

Further Readings and Bibliography: C.U. Ariëns Kappers, "Contributions to the Anthropology of the Near East, V: Kurds, Circassians and Persians," *Proceedings of the Section of Sciences* XXXIV (Amsterdam: Koninklijke Akademie van Wetenschappen te Amsterdam, 1931); Henry Field, *The Anthropology of Iran* (Chicago: Field Museum Press, 1939); Henry Field, *The Anthropology of Iraq* (Cambridge: Harvard Peabody Museum of Anthropology, 1952); R.H. Dyson, "Ninth Century [BC] Man in Western Iran," *Archaeology* 17 (1964).

TRIBES

There are a considerable number of clans, tribes, and tribal confederations in Kurdistan today, each with its own defined territory (see Map 27). Many of these tribes have been in existence—with the same names—for several thousand years. The modern Zibâri tribe, for example, is mentioned as the Saubaru/Sibaru by Sumerian and Akkadian sources. Variations of the tribal names of the Buhtân, Mamakân, Hadhabân, Bakrân, Pirân, and Barâz appear in the Greco-Roman, Aramaic, Middle Persian, and Armenian records (as the Bokhtanoi, Mamigonian, Adiabene, Bagrat, Paren, and Virâz). Medieval Muslim sources provide detailed lists of Kurdish tribes from the Straits of Hormuz to the heartland of Anatolia. Almost all of the tribes mentioned in these early lists are still with us today, albeit in different locations. The detailed lists provided by the Kurdish historian Sharaf al-Din Bitlisi in 1596 AD in the *Sharafnâma* (see **Early Modern History** and **Literature**) and by the Ottoman administrator and traveller Evliyâ Chelebi (1611-1682), in his *Siyâhatnâma,* fill the gap of information on the movements and distribution of Kurdish tribes in particular, and the Kurdish people in general, between the medieval and modern periods.

Some interesting information on the earlier locations of certain tribes may also be derived from the surnames of certain medieval Muslim luminaries who carry Kurdish tribal names, and for whom birth places are known. It has been common for tribal names to be adopted for personal and dynastic names since early medieval times, and perhaps much earlier. The historian Ibn Khalkân (of the Khalkân tribe), for example, came from central Kurdistan, while the first known Middle Eastern traveler to the Arctic and Scandinavia, Ibn Fadhlân (of the Fazlân/Fazlun tribe of the Shadâd [modern Shâdlu] confederacy), came from southern Kurdistan. The Fadhlân tribe is now found only in

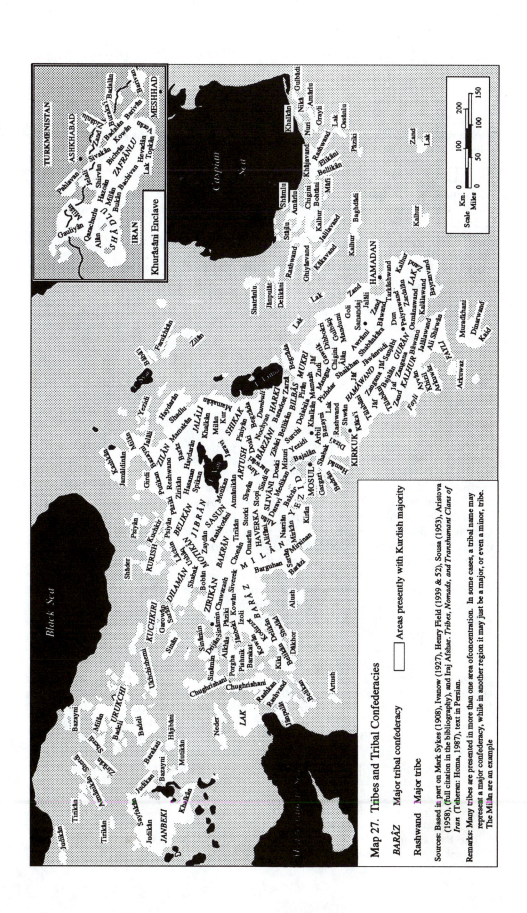

Map 27. Tribes and Tribal Confederacies

BARÂZ   Major tribal confederacy

Rashwand   Major tribe

□   Areas presently with Kurdish majority

Sources: Based in part on Mark Sykes (1908), Ivanow (1927), Henry Field (1939 & 52), Sousa (1953), Aristova (1958), (full citation in the bibliography), and Iraj Afshar. *Tribes, Nomads, and Transhumant Clans of Iran* (Teheran: Homa, 1987), text in Persian.

Remarks: Many tribes are presented in more than one area of concentration. In some cases, a tribal name may represent a major confederacy, while in another region it may just be a major, or even a minor, tribe. The Milân are an example northern Kurdistan and in the Khurâsâni enclave, while the Khalkâns are found in pockets in almost every subdivision of Kurdistan.

An important factor accounting for the modern distribution of the Kurdish tribes, the religions they practice, the dialects they speak, and even the variations in their physical characteristics, has been the episodes of massive migrations within and from without Kurdistan proper. Mass deportations in the past and present have further diversified the tribal makeup of Kurdistan. They have also brought the Kurds into close contact with many other ethnic groups in the region, and fostered links of various kinds among them. A detailed account of these phenomena and their historical background is provided under **Historical Migrations**, **Deportations & Forced Resettlements**, and **Classical** and **Medieval History**.

To trace the movements of the Kurdish tribes is more or less to see living documents and primary sources on the nation's past. The historic Hadhabâni tribe, for example, from which an eponymous royal house ruled central Kurdistan from the 1st century BC to the 3rd century AD, gave its name to the region—Adiabene of the classical Greek and Latin sources. However, a branch of this tribe found itself nine centuries later living near Dvin and Ani in northern Armenia. From this branch came the Ayyubid clan, which migrated back to the territories of ancient Adiabene. The future king Saladin, the founder of the Ayyubid dynasty, was born soon after in Tikrit, a town in the Ayubbid fiefdom. This Hadhabâni tribe is now found, by corrupted forms of the old name, from Khurâsân to Syria.

The Bâvand tribe now living near Kirmânshâh, the Kâkâ'is now living near Kirkuk (as well as Kâkâvand in the Alburz range and in Kirmânshâh), and the Shaddâdân tribe living in Syria and Turkey to the north of Aleppo, are the descendants of those Kurds who established the medieval dynasties of the Bâvandids, Kâkuyids, and the Shaddâdids, which ruled, respectively, the Caspian coastal regions, central Iran, and the Caucasus-Armenia-northern Kurdistan region. The name of the great Bâbân confederacy, which ruled central Kurdistan under Ottoman suzerainty until 1848, may well be a corruption of *Bâvand*. From the Dimila tribes issued the medieval royal house of the Buwâyhids as well as more than half a dozen other dynasties. The main body of the Dimilas are today still in northwestern Kurdistan in Anatolia, and are better known to outsiders as the *Zâzâ*.

On close scrutiny, one encounters several other Kurdish tribal names in the aristocratic and princely houses of Armenia, Georgia, and other neighboring districts. The great Barâz or Verâz tribal chiefs became one of the seven most important feudal families of the long Parthian era (247 BC-AD 224), claiming vast territories from Syria through Armenia to the borders of Adiabene. The modern Kurdish Barâz tribal confederacy still occupies the western half of that earlier domain.

The Mamakân tribe produced an aristocratic feudal family (Armenian *nakharar*), the Mamikonians or Mamigonians, which ruled among the Armenians. This family also produced two Byzantine generals, Vartan and Vahan Mamikonian, in the 6th century, and a saint, St. Vardan Mamikonian, the hero of the Battle of Avarayr (AD 451). The Mamikonians, according to Armenian tradition, ruled the area of "Taik, Taron, Bagravandene, and Acilisene." These are the modern regions of Mush (Mus), Bitlis, Siirt, and Hakkâri, on the borders between northern and western Kurdistan in the environs of Lake Vân. The modern Mamakân tribe is found in this same general area in small pockets to the north, east, and south of Lake Vân. Other older branches of the Mamakân may be the Mamish and the Mamasanis, living in large numbers in the central and southern Zagros. While the Mamikonians spoke Armenian, the Mamasani have adopted the Luri dialect of Persian. The Mamish and the remaining Mamakân are the only Kurdish-speaking branches surviving today.

The Bakrân or Bagrân tribe, which lives in and has given its name to the city of Diyârbakir, also engendered the Bagratid royal house, which ruled intermittently, first over the Armenians, and later over the Georgians, with major interruptions from the 9th through the beginning of the 19th century. The original domain of the early Bagrâtids was in fact the area of Diyârbakir to Bingöl in northwest Kurdistan, according to Ter-Ghewondian. The Bakrâns are the descendants of the Bagrâvand tribe, mentioned as the *Bagrauande* by the geographer Claudius Ptolemy, 22 centuries ago. Their country between Lake Vân and the Tigris River he christened *Bagrauandene Regio*, i.e., the "Region or Country of the Bagrâvands."

"The [modern] Bakrâns' own tradition maintains that they are descendants of the Bagratians [Bagratids]," writes Sykes. "The Armenian clergy generally speak with some certainty of this point." A similar connection between the Tirikân tribe and King Tigrân, the greatest Armenian monarch of ancient times, can be established. "The Tirikâns I visited were kindly disposed to the few Armenians who live among them," wrote Sykes. "The local Armenians state that they are of common origin [with the Tirikans] and that they [the local Armenians] are not of Armenian race; this idea is naturally discouraged by the Armenian clergy and laity of Diyarbakir, but I have it on the authority of a priest and Christian headman of the district" (Sykes 1908, 464). To this interesting hypothesis can be added another name, Tirigan (r. ca. 2255 BC), king of the ancient Qutils (see **Ancient History**). As noted above, it has been common for tribal names to be adopted for dynastic and personal names since at least early medieval times. The Qutil name *Tirigan* may be the first known instance in which a monarch from the Kurdish mountains took up a tribal name, pushing the tradition back by thousands of years. In fact the practice of attaching the tribal name to the first name of every pre-modern Kurd has prompted some, like Ala-Firouz (1977), to suggest that the Kurds were the first ethnic group in the world to use surnames.

Another Kurdish tribe of note that is still present where Ptolemy placed it is the Belikân confederacy. Ptolemy calls their territory *Belcania*, roughly straddling the modern Turkish-Syrian border north and northeast of Aleppo.

In the course of their long history, many important tribes have been fragmented. This has been a result of deportations or voluntary migrations. For example, the Khalkân tribe is found today in pockets near Arbil (in Iraq), near Kirmânshâh (in Iran, under the corrupted name, *Qalkhân*), between Ankara and Konya in Turkey, as well as in Khurasân, Turkmenistan, and Armenia, and on the border between Iran and Turkey near Maku. The earliest available record of the existence of the Khalkâns places them in the general area of Arbil.

In modern times, particularly since the early 1930s, the old tribal organizations and affiliations of the Kurds in Turkey have been to a large degree suppressed. This has not meant, however, that the Kurdish tribes there are no longer in existence. Far from it. Their strong presence has prompted close surveillance by the Turkish government. Extracts from a secret Turkish government survey of Kurdish tribes and their degree of loyalty to the state were recently published illegally in the Turkish journal *Ikibin'e Dogru*, in a report entitled "Top Secret Report. Government Survey: The Traitor and Loyal Tribes" ("*Çok gizli rapor. Devletin gözüyle: Hain ve Yandas Asiretler*," December 1987).

The survey included for each Kurdish tribe its location, number, spoken dialect, religious denomination, leader(s), and past record of loyalty to the state, from the founding of the Turkish Republic to the time of the report. The journal has since been closed and the issue is now the subject of a court action in Turkey. The available portions of the survey are invaluable resources for understanding the current state of Kurdish tribes in Turkey.

In the territories of the former Soviet Union, Kurdish tribal loyalties have survived among the Kurds of Armenia, Georgia, and Turkmenistan, but less among the Kurds of Azerbaijan. The Azerbaijani Kurds were deported in large numbers to various corners of Eurasia, and the Kurdish culture that remains is suppressed by the Azeris. Aristova

TABLE 1: Kurdish Tribes and Tribal Confederacies

Tribes are listed from east to west. With some minor exceptions, only the tribal confederacies and important non-confederated tribes are given. All members of each confederacy are listed below it in alphabetical order. Remarks in parentheses include alternative tribal names, location, language, religion, etc. To these one must also add the Hamkâw Kurds of the Bukhara and Fergana regions (Uzbekistan), for whose tribal affilations I could find nothing. Kurds deported since 1925 are not included here, regardless of whether or not they have maintained their tribal affliation in their new homes.

1. Khurâsâni Enclave

A. NORTHERN KHURÂSÂN
(All tribes are North Kurmânji speaking Sunnis with some admixture of Shi'ites, unless otherwise indicated.)

Zafrânlu (or Za'farânlu, Chemishgezek) Confederacy
(covers the eastern two-thirds of the enclave, in both Iran and Turkmenistan)
  Amârlu (very large)
  Amirân
  Bakrân (or Bichrân)
  Bâchvan (or Bâchyân)
  Bâdelân (or Bâhâdurân)
  Barivan (or Brikân, the old Bahârvand? Laki-speaking Yârsâns)
  Buraka'i (related to the Buraka'is of Eastern Kurdistan. South Kurmânji-speaking, Sunnis)
  Gawliyân (very large)
  Hizolân (or Izoli)
  Hazoan (or Hamzakân; related to the ancient Hazabân/Hadhabân)
  Hevadân (N. Kurmânji-speaking, Yezidi)
  Izân
  Jalâli
  Kaykân
  Kowâ (or Qovânlu, Kâviyânlu, Kowand)
  Kukhban (or Kukhbaniklu, Kuhâniklu)
  Milân (Milli)
  Muzhdakân
  Paluvulân
  Pahlavân (Fayli?)
  Pâlukân
  Qarachurlu (or Qarachul)
  Qarmân (Qahramânlu)
  Qâchkân
  Rashvan (or Rashwand)
  Rutakân
  Sharân
  Shaykhkân
  Shâmlu (Bichrânlu)

  Silseporân
  Sivakân (or Siverek. Dimili-speaking, Alevi)
  Sufiyân
  Topkân (very large)
  Verân
  Zaydân

Shâdlu (Shadâd) Confederacy
(covers the southwestern quarter of the enclave)
  Âlân
  Bughân
  Dirqân
  Garivân
  Gurdân
  Inrân
  Jâbân (or Jâpâ. Possible connection with the great Jâfs)
  Juyân
  Kâghân
  Mitrân
  Qilichân
  Qrabâshlu
  Quprân (Kuprân)

Non-Confederated Tribes
  Lak (Abivard to Chahchaha. Laki-speaking, Yârsâns)
  Qarachurlu (covers the smaller, northwestern sections of the enclave, and some smaller pockets in the west)
  Zand (Abivard to Chahchaha. Laki speaking, Yârsâns)

B. QOHISTAN-BIRJAND REGION
  Bohluli (Qâ'in to Tâybât. Laki-speaking, Yârsâns)
  Manâvand (Manâvand-Khosh Âwa heights, NE of Birjand. Laki-speaking, Yârsâns)
  Rushnavand (Rashawand. Tabas Masinâ district. Laki-speaking, Yârsâns)
  Topkânlu (Kâshmar and Bakrân Kuh south of Birjand. N. Kurmânji-speaking, Sunnis)

2. Alburz Mountains

A. MÂZANDARÂN REGION

Khâjavand Confederacy
(in Nur, Kajur, Klârdasht and Pul. Laki speaking, Yârsâns)
  Dilfân
  Kâkavand (Kâkâvand)
  Lak
  Sultânqulikhâni

Non-Confederated Tribes
(N. Kurmânji-speaking Sunnis, unless otherwise indicated)
  Elikâni (Damâvand and Lâr regions. Dimili-speaking, Alevis)
  Belikân (Gachsar-Kanduwân heights. Dimili-speaking, Alevis)
  Grili (Grayli; on the Nekâ river. S. Kurmânji-speaking, Sunnis)
  Gulbâdi (between Behshahr and Bandar Gaz. S. Kurmânji-speaking Sunnis)
  Larijâni (in heights around Larijân)
  Masha'i (near Bandar Gaz)
  Navâ'i (near Amul)
  Nekâ (on the Nekâ river)
  Nuri (around town of Nur)
  Umrânlu (in Galugâh district)

B. GILÂN REGION

Amârlu Confederacy
(Daylaman, Siyâhkal, to Shâhrud valley. They believe they are an offshoot of the great Bâbân confederacy. N. Kurmânji speaking Sunnis)
  Bahâ Davallu
  Bayshân
  Devalu (Davallu)
  Shâmlu (Shâmkân)
  Shâqulân (Shâhkânlu)
  Stâjlu (Istâjlu)

Non-Confederated Tribes

Bajalân (Gurâni-speaking,
  Yârsâns)
Bohtu'i (Bohtâni. N.
  Kurmânji-speaking,
  Sunnis)
Chigini (north of Shâhrud
  rivers. S. Kurmânji-
  speaking, Sunnis)
Chemishgezek (Dimili-
  speaking, Alevis)
Jalilvand (or Jalâlawand. Laki-
  speaking, Yârsâns)
Kalhur (Gurâni-speaking,
  Yârsâns)
Kâkâvand (Laki-speaking,
  Yârsâns)
Kirmâni (S. Kurmânji-
  speaking, Yârsâns)
Mâfi (related to the Mâfis of
  Kirmânshâh. Laki-
  speaking, Yârsâns and
  Shi'ites)
Qiyâsvand (made of Komâsi
  and Silâkhur branches.
  Laki-speaking, Yârsâns)
Rashwand (Rashvand. N.
  Kurmânji-speaking,
  Sunnis)
Waliyâri (S. Kurmânji-
  speaking, Yârsâns)
Yamini (S. Kurmânji-
  speaking, Sunnis)

C. ZANJAN-KHALKHÂL REGION

Delikân (Khalkhâl region. N.
  Kurmânji-speaking,
  Sunnis)
Jânpulât (or Jumbalât. East of
  Khalkhâl. N. Kurmânji-
  speaking Sunnis)
Kilishâni (N. Kurmânji-
  speaking Sunnis)
Shatrâni (south of Ardabil. N.
  Kurmânji-and Azeri-
  speaking Shi'ites.

3. Central Iranian Plateau

A. KASHAN-QUM REGION

Baghdâdi (or Anjilâvand.
  West of Sâveh. Laki-
  speaking, Yârsâns)
Kalhur (in Qarachây, south of
  Sâveh. Gurâni and S.
  Kurmânji-speaking
  Yârsâns)
Lak (Kohak and Kurdakân
  districts in the Karkas
  Mountains)
Pâzuki (Pâziki or Bâziki.

Around Varâmin, east of
  Teheran. N. Kurmânji-
  speaking, Shi'ites and
  Sunnis)
Ossânlu (Garmsâr and
  Varâmin. Laki-speaking,
  Yârsâns and Shi'ites)
Zand (SW of Qum. Laki-
  speaking,Yârsâns)

B. FÂRS

Kâkâ'i (to the immediate NW
  of Shiraz. Laki-speaking,
  Yârsâns)
Kurdshuli (in Marasurkhi
  heights, Shari Naw, and
  Jahrom. Laki-speaking,
  Yârsâns)

C. BALUCHISTAN

Gurân (Bampour. Gurani &
  Laki-speaking Yârsâns and
  Shi'ites. Serve as the work
  force for the Yelhâni
  chiefs)
Zangana (Bampour. S.
  Kurmânji-speaking,
  Sunnis
Kalhur (Taftân Volcanic
  Heights. Gurâni-speaking
  Yârsâns. Now are being
  Baluchified)
Yelhâni (Bampour. S.
  Kurmânji-speaking
  Sunnis. An elite tribe of
  small size)

4. Eastern Kurdistan
(all S. Kurmânji-speaking,
Sunnis, unless otherwise
indicated)

Bilbâs Confederacy
(SW of Lake Urmia)
Mâmash
Mangur
Ojâq (Ushâk)
Pirân (large)
Ramak
Sinn

Gulbâghi Confederacy
(WNW of Bijâr)
Chukharashi (or
  Chukharashti)
Gâmeli
Jujarash
Kalkeni (Qalqâli)
Kâkâwand (or Kâkâswandi)
Kâmili
Murâd Gurâni
Pitâwasari
Qomri
Sinduli

Jâf Confederacy (Jawânrud to
Sanandaj. A branch of the great
Jâf of central Kurdistan in Iraq)
Bâshugi
Galâli
Hâruni
Inâkhi
Ismâ'il Azizi
Kalâshi (Kalâshin)
Kamâli
Mandumi
Mikâ'ili
Qobâdi (Kowâ)
Rukhzâdi
Shâtiri
Tarkhâni
Valadbagi

Mandumi Confederacy
(SW of Bijâr)
Târimurâdi
Alimurâdi
Lawlarzi

Mukri Confederacy
(south of Lake Urmiâ to
Mahâbâd and Diwândara. This
confederacy has now largely
broken up)
Begzâda
Dehbokri
Jâf (of Mahâbad region)
Qâsimlu

Non-Confederated Tribes
(Most were once members of
the great Ardalân confederacy
until its break-up. All are South
Kurmânji-speaking Sunnis un-
less otherwise indicated)
Ahmadi (near Bâna)
Âlân (near Sardasht)
Ardalân (NW of Sanandaj. A
  relatively new tribe which
  has called itself after the
  old Ardalâns)
Bâbâjâni (Gurâni-speaking,
  Yârsâns)
Bahrâmbegi (in Dizli and
  Chamshâmân, Near Bâna)
Bâlawand (Laki-speaking,
  Yârsâns)
Bâshuki
Bâskula (west of Sardasht)
Biryâhi (Near Sardasht)
Bistârawand
Buraka'i
Dorrâji
Fayzullahbegi (Near Bukân,
  Takâb, and Saqqiz)
Gashki (or Kashki. Near
  Kâmyârân)
Garga'i

Gawurka (or Gewrg. Sardasht
   to Saqqiz and Mahâbâd)
Hamâwaysi
Haydarbegi (near Marivân)
Jalâli (east of Sanandaj)
Kalâli (or Galâli, Jalâli.
   Around Saqqiz)
Kalâsi (near Sardasht)
Kamângar (near Kâmyârân)
Koli (or Guli. NE of
   Sanandaj)
Komâsi (between Marivân
   and Sanandaj)
Lak (Laki-speaking, Yârsâns)
Lotfullâbegi (near Bâna)
Mariwâni (Marivân to
   Panjwin)
Osmanbegi (south of
   Mahâbâd)
Qobâdi
Sursuri
Sarshiv
Zand (around Qurwa. Laki-
   speaking, Yârsâns)
Waladbagi

5. Southern Kurdistan

Arkuvâzi Confederacy
(Mehrân, Badra and Chwâr.
Laki-speaking, Yarsâns)
   Bânsarda (or Bânzarda)
   Bânviza
   Bi
   Karshvand
   Kurdel
   Malikashvand
   Maysami
   Mir
   Muma
   Murt
   Qaytuni
   Qrushvand

Awrâmân Confederacy
(In Awrâmân district. Yârsâns,
speak Awrâmâni dialect of
Gurâni)
   Lahuni (Jafarsultâni)
   Takhti
      Bahrâmbegi
      Hasansultâni
      Mustafâsultâni

Ayvân (Ivân) Confederacy
(Nafti Shâh, Naft Khâna and
Mandali. S. Kurmânji-speaking,
Sunnis)
   Bânsayra
   Chulak

Bajalan (Bajarwan)
Confederacy (Qasri Shirin,

Khânaqin, Quratu, Shaykhân,
Dargazin [near Sulaymânia],
Horin, and Jizani. Gurâni-
speaking, Yârsâns)
   Jomur (or Jomhur)
   Qazânlu

Bayrânvand (Silâkhur)
Confederacy (Medieval
Barâvand. South of Hamadân,
into Silâkhur district of Luristân.
Very large. Laki-speaking
Yârsâns and some Shi'ites)
   Alâyno
   Chaqalvand
   Dasheyno
   Komâsi
   Rashvand (or Rashwand)
   Zand

Gurân Confederacy
(Kirmanshâh to Pâwa. Gurâni-
speaking, Yârsâns)
   Bibiyân
   Biwanij
   Dâniyâli
   Gawâra (Gahwâra)
   Haydari
   Nirzhi
   Qalkhâni Bahrâmi (Khalkân)
   Qalkhâni Speri (Khalkân)
   Shabânkâra (Chupânkâra)
   Tufanghchi
   Yâsami

Holaylân Confederacy
(east of Kirmânshâh, around
Sonqor. Laki-speaking, Yârsâns)
   Bâlawand
   Jalâlawand
   Osmânawand
   Tarhân
   Zardalân

Jomir (or Jomur, Jomhur)
Confederacy (south of
Hamadân. Laki-speaking, Yâr-
sâns)
   Abdâli
   Barâzi
   Guma
   Shâhvaysi

Kalhur Confederacy
(Khânaqin to Kirmânshâh.
Presently perhaps the largest
Kurdish confederation. Yârsâns,
speaking mostly Gurâni with
some S. Kurmânji)
   Abulmuhamadi
   Alirezâwand
   Alwandi
   Barga

Budâghbegi
Chilla'i
Farrukhi
Galladâr
Hârunâbâdi
Jelowgir
Kalapâ
Kallajub
Kamar
Karampanâh
Kâzimkhâni
Kergâ
Khâlidi
Khomân
Krbiyân
Mansuri
Mâydashti (Mâhidashti)
Mirazizi
Mu'mini
Mughira
Mushgir
Pâpirân
Qulâmi
Qumchi
Rajab
Ramazâni
Rizâwand
Rutwand
Saydnâza
Sayyâdân
Sâlka
Shaybâni
Shâhini
Shirzâdi
Shwânkâra (Shwân)
Siyâ Siyâ
Telesh (Tâlish)
Zaynalkhâni

Khizir (Kizil or Kaz'al)
Confederacy (Mandali and
Sumâr. Laki-speaking, Yârsâns)
   Khizirvand
   Murshidvand
   Qolivand
   Shamsivand

Pahla (Fayli) Confederacy
(in pockets from Baquba, north
east of Baghdad to Khuzistân.
Laki-speaking, Yârsâns and
Shi'ites)
   Bâpirvand
   Brâspi
   Châydarvand
   Dustalivand
   Gurân
   Haywari
   Jâbirvand
   Jugi
   Kalkuh
   Khizirvand
   Kowlivand
   Mamasivand

Mami
Mamus
Marâl
Mrâvarzi
Murâdkhâni
Nowruzvand
Osivand
Pâpi
Shakarbegi
Sharaka
Sulaymânkhâni
Zargush

Qalkhâni (Khalkân) Confederacy
(NW of Kirmânshâh, around
Kuzârân. Related to the
Khalkâns. Gurâni-speaking,
Yârsâns)
Âynawand
Bachahâli
Bârawli (Bârwali)
Bizirâbâdi
Dengi
Divaka
Malgi (Maliki)
Najafi
Pashtmâla
Qalazanjiri (Qolozanjiri)
Qari
Qarka
Rustam
Sabza
Sarâwâra
Wistali

Qaralos Confederacy
(Mandali to Tangi Sumâr). S.
Kurmânji-seaking, Sunnis.
Charmawand
Gaw Sawâri
Gesh
Kaytun
Kâkawand
Naftchi

Salâs Confederacy
(west of Kirmânshâh to Kerend.
South Kurmânji-speaking,
Sunnis. Made of three smaller
confederacies)

1. Bâbâjâni
Begzâda
Zamkâni

2. Qobâdi
Bâzâni
Begzâda
Miraki
Takhta
Tangi Izhdahâ
Zilâni

3. Waladbagi (Waladbegi)
Aliâgha'i
Darwish
Delâzhiri
Duru'i
Kâleka
Khalwân (related to the
Khalkân?)
Rashid

Sanjâbi Confederacy
(Pâwa to Mâydasht. Gurâni-
speaking, Yârsâns)
Abbâswand
Aliwand
Allâhyârkhâni (Ilâhikhâni)
Bâghi
Bâwân (Bâvand)
Chalâwi (Châlâbi)
Dataja
Dawlatmand
Dârkhwâr
Haqqnazarkhâni
Jalâlawand (Jalâlwand)
Kalâlawand (Kalâlwand)
Kâkâ
Khusrawi
Kolkol
Nazka/Targa
Siminwand
Sufi
Surkhaki
Surkhawand

Sharafbayâni Confederacy
(Shiwâldir mountains and
Sirwân river, and Shaykhân)
Kuraki
Amirkhân Begi
Aziz Begi
Gakhâri
Nâdiri

Swâramayri Confederacy
(Khânaqin, Shahrabân, and Abu
Jisra). Laki and S. Kurmânji-
speaking, Yârsâns
Kalhur
Tutik
Mamakân (or Mamejân)
Inântir

Tirkashvand Confederacy
(Asadâbâd to Hamadân and
Tusirkân. Laki-speaking,
Yârsâns)
Alijâni
Alimurshid
Rahmati
Sulaymâni
Zand

Zand Confederacy (south and
NW of Hamadân. Laki-speaking
Yârsâns and Shi'ites)
Aliyân
Mamad
Qani
Sâlih Âghâ
Tâhir Khâni

Non-Confederated Tribes
Bâbâni (or Babâni. Small. In
Khânaqin and North of
Kirkuk. S. Kurmânji-
speaking, Sunnis)
Bânzarda (north of Sarpoli
Zohâb. Gurâni and S.
Kurmânji-speaking,
Yârsâns)
Bâwand (Dinawar and
Shâhâbâd. Gurani-
speaking, Yârsâns)
Dinârvand (Dehlurân,
Dâlpari and Dinâr ranges.
Laki-speaking, Yârsâns
and Shi'ites)
Dun (or Dum; around
Dinawar and Kandula.
Gurâni-speaking, Yârsâns)
Gashki (north of
Kirmânshâh. S. Kurmânji-
speaking, Sunnis)
Imâmi (formerly of Jâf
Confed. S. Kurmânji-
speaking Sunnis)
Irâqi (formerly of Jâf Confed.
S. Kurmânji-speaking
Sunnis)
Jawânrudi (formerly of Jâf
Confed. S. Kurmânji-
speaking Sunnis)
Kayd (Musiyân and
Dehlurân. S. Kurmânji-
speaking, Sunnis)
Kâykhurda (suburbs of
Dehlurân. S. Kurmânji-
speaking, Sunnis)
Kerend/Krind (around town
of Kerend. S. Kurmânji-
speaking, Sunnis)
Kolyâ'i (between Sunqor and
Qorwa. S. Kurmanji-
speaking, Sunnis)
Mâfi (east of Kirmânshah.
Laki-speaking, Yârsâns
and Shi'ites)
Ossânlu (Related to Osivand?
Laki-speaking, Yârsâns)
Pâyrawand (north of
Kirmânshâh. S. Kurmânji-
speaking, Sunnis)
Warjâwand (between Sahna
and Kangawar. Laki-
speaking Yârsâns)
Zangana (SW of Kirmânshâh.

Gurâni and S. Kurmânji-
speaking, Yârsâns)
Zardalân (or Bâlawand. Laki-
speaking, Yârsâns)
Zula (SW of Kirmânshâh. S.
Kurmânji-speaking,
Sunnis)

6. Central Kurdistan

(With the exception of the
Hamâwand, most other tribes
here were once members of the
great Bâbân (medieval Bâvand)
confederacy until its break-up
early in this century. All are S.
Kurmânji-speaking, Sunnis
unless indicated otherwise)

Delo Confederacy
(small. Khush mountinas to
Sarkala and Khânaqin)
  Gash
  Jamrezi
  Kârez
  Panjânkushti
  Salim Waysi
  Tarkawand

Diza'i (Dizay) Confederacy
(very populous. Arbil to Tigris
river)
  Gondola (or Gontola)
  Mâman
  Pirân

Hamâwand Confederacy
(large. Chamchamâl to Sirwân
river, and Bazayn region.
Gurâni-speaking, Yârsâns)
  Begzâda
  Chingini
  Kafrushi
  Mâmand
  Piriyâ'i
  Ramawand
  Rashwand
  Safarawand
  Shitabisar
  Sofiawand

Jaf Confederacy
(very large. Sulaymânia to Klâr
and Halabja, stretching into
Southern and Eastern Kurdistan
in large pockets. S. Kurmânji-
speaking, Sunnis)
  Amala
  Badghi
  Bâseri
  Bâshki
  Hâruni
  Isâ'i
  Ismâ'il Uzhayri

Jalâli (or Galâla)
Jâwânrudi (Jawânrudi)
Kamâli
Mikâeli
Murâdi
Nâwroli
Pishtmâle
Rashubâri
Roga'i
Sadani
Safiawand
Shatri
Shaykh Ismâ'ili
Tarkhâni
Tawgozi
Yazdânbakhsh
Yârwaysi
Yusifjâni

Keza (or Kaza) Confederacy
(small. Ski Kifir to Chinchaldân)
  Sandula Begi
  Kokha Bahrâm
  Sarkala

Shwân (Shiwân) Confederacy
(large. North of Kirkuk, between
Khâsa and Zeh rivers)
  Bazayni
  Khâsa

Zand Confederacy
(Kifri to Sirwân river. Laki-
speaking, Yârsâns)
  Alyân (Elyân)
  Gheni (Qini)
  Mamsâlih
  Tayer Khâni

Non-Confederated Tribes
  Ako (large. Around Râniya)
  Bâbân (or Babâni. Small.
    North of Kirkuk and in
    Khânaqin)
  Belikân (or Balik, Balikiyân.
    Large. Between Rawânduz
    and Râyât in Balik
    Heights)
  Barzanji (or Berzinji. Large.
    Khânaqin. Part Yârsân)
  Bayâti (Tuz Khurmâtu to
    Kifri)
  Bazayni (or Shaykh Bazayni.
    Arbil to Kirkuk)
  Boli (small. South of Bilek)
  Chigini (north of
    Sulaymânia)
  Dumbuli (Dunbeli, in
    Shaykhân)
  Daudi (or Dawde. Large. In
    Tawq, Kifri, to Tuz
    Khormâtu)
  Gakhor (Qara Tapa)
  Girdi (north of Arbil and Koy

Sanjaq)
Homermil (Sarkala to Kocha
  Chyân)
Jabbâri (or Jebzâri. ESE of
  Kirkuk to Chamchamâl
  and Laylân)
Kâkâ'i (Kirkuk to Tuz
  Khurmâtu. Yârsâns)
Khalkân (or Khalhâni.
  Northern Balik mountains
  and NE of Arbil)
Khoshnaw (very large.
  Around Shaqlâwa)
Kura (Arbil to Shaqlâwa)
Laylâni (in Laylân)
Palhâni (Zanâbâd to Qara
  Tapa)
Pizhdar (or Peshdar. Around
  Qala Diza)
Salhi (between Kirkuk and
  Qara Hasan. Also in
  Damascus, Syria)
Sherwân (north of
  Rawânduz)
Siyân (north of Kirkuk)
Surchi (very Large. Middle
  course of the Greater Zâb
  river to Rawânduz)
Tâlabâni (large. In pockets SE
  of Kirkuk, NE of Klâr)
Tâlshâni (or Telshâni. Ski
  Kifri to Zardâwa)
Zangana (an extension of the
  Zanganas of Southern
  Kurdistan. Kifri to Klâr.
  Gurâni and S. Kurmânji-
  speaking, Yârsâns)
Zarâri (north of Basturicha)
Zudi (Rawânduz region)

7. Northern Kurdistan

(All North Kurmânji-speaking,
Sunnis unless otherwise
indicated. Most western tribes
living in Turkey have adopted
the Turkish ending -li/lu to
replace Kurdish -kân/ân or -van/
vand/wand. Sometimes the
Turkish ending is added to the
Kurdish ending. The trend has
now reversed and here only the
ending -kân/ân is given.)

Artush Confederacy
(or Hartushi, Hartuch. Very
Large. South of Lake Vân, to
Zakho and Dohuk)
  Âlân
  Azdinân
  Gâvdân
  Grâviyân
  Havishtân
  Hulaylân (or Halilân)

Mamkhorân
Qashurân
Pirân
Sharafân
Shidân
Zawkân
Zhiriki
Zaydân

Bârzâni Confederacy
(on the banks of upper Greater
Zâb river, to western Hakkâri)
Bârushi
Dolamayri
Mizuri (a splinter from the
Mizuri Confederacy of
western Kurdistan)
Nervâ
Raykâni
Sherwâni

Bohtân Confederacy
(on both banks of Bohtân river,
south of Lake Vân. It was once a
major confederacy like those of
Bâbân and Ardalân before the
break-up of all three in the late
19th and early 20th centuries)
Shirnak
Tiyân

Harki Confederacy
(or Herki. Very large. Shnu to
Hakkâri and Rawânduz. Famous
for their elaborate costumes and
ornaments)
Mandân
Sarhaddi (Sihatti)
Saydân (Zaydân)

Jalâli Confederacy
(or Jelâli. Mâku to Bâyazid and
Kârs. Connected with the
Jalâlawands of Southern
Kurdistan and the Gelus of
southern Zagros of pre-Islamic
times)
Alimohâwlu
(Alimuhammadlu)
Belikân
Hasow Khalaf
Jenikânlu
Khalkân (Khalikân. Jalâli
chiefs usually come from
this tribe)
Misrikân
Otâblu
Qadikân
Qizilbâsh
Sâkân (Sakân)

Jibrân (Gibrân, Gawrân)
Confederacy (NE of Bingöl. The
name may be connected with
the Gurâns)
Aliki
Âqâ
Azdinâni
Mamakân (Mamagân)
Mukhil
Shaykhakân
Shâderi
Torini

Milân Confederacy
(NW of Lake Urmia, from Salmâs
to Khoy. This is a distinct
branch of the old Milân or Milli
confederacy of Western
Kurdistan. Alevis)
Dilmaqân (Dimilakân)
Dolân (Dlâyn)
Dudakân
Khalkân
Mamakân (Mamaqân)
Mandulakân
Sârmân
Shaykhakân

Piniyân Confederacy
(or Piniyânishli. Northern
Kakkâri region. Some 5000
members of this confederacy
were reported to have been
Kurdish Christians at the
beginning of the 20th century.
The numbers today are
unknown)
Barkoshân
Bilijân (Belikân)

Shakâk (Rivand) Confederacy
(in district of Dustân and Qotur,
NW of Urmia to Lake Vân. The
old name, *Shâh Kâk* relates them
to the Kâkâ'is of Central
Kurdistan, and the Kâku'is of
the southern Zagros regions.
Abdâwi
Buhtân
Dari
Dolân
Evari
Fanak
Gurik
Honara
Kârkâr
Khalaf
Khedri
Movaqqari
Ne'mati
Nisân
Otamâni
Pachik
Pas Âqa

Shâpirâni (Dilmaqâni)
Shukri

Spikân Confederacy
(or Sipikân. NW of Lake Vân.
Populous, but small in number
of member tribes.
Mamakân
Spikân

Non-Confederated Tribes
Adyâman (north of Bâyazid)
Barâdost (large. Rawânduz to
Hakkâri)
Bâz (Cukurca to Oraman.
The modern appellation
for the historic Bâdh or
Badh tribe)
Bazayni (east of Erzurum and
north of Agri. The modern
appellation for the historic
Bâdh or Badh tribe)
Begzâda (west of Urmia)
Brukân (NE of Vân, and west
of Khoy)
Doski (large. North of Dohuk
and in Hakkâri)
Girdi (north of Agri)
Goyân (north of Uludara)
Halâji (SE of Bitlis)
Hamdikân (between Agri and
Kâqizmân)
Hasanân (very large. In
Malâzgird, Hinis, and
Warto regions)
Hawâtân (SE of Bitlis)
Haydarânlu (north of
Malâzgird)
Hayruni (NW of the town of
Çizre)
Kâkâ (or Kakâ. Hakkâri)
Khaylâni (Near Rowânduz)
Khâniyân (or Khâni. The
tribe of the poet Ahmad
Khâni)
Kourasonni (or Kurishâni.
NW of Khoy)
Mamâkân (or Mamaqân.
West of Khoy)
Manurân (south of Agri)
Mirân (east of Bitlis)
Nushiyân (or Nuchiyân. In
Hakkâri)
Oramar (Hakkâri)
Pâziki (or Bâziki, Pâzuki. SE
of Erzurum)
Rashwand (or Reshven. SE of
Erzurum)
Rowândok (or Rawânduz. In
Hakkâri)
Shamsiki (east of Vân)
Sindi (north or Zakho)
Slopi (or Silopi. East of the
town of Çizre)

Surchi (NE of Arbil and near
Aqra)
Takuli (east of Vân)
Zarzâ (around Shnu. Partly
Dimili-speaking)
Zibâri (large. On middle
course of the Greater Zâb
river)

8. Western Kurdistan

(Most western tribes living in
Turkey have adopted the
Turkish ending *li / lu* to replace
Kurdish *ân* or *van / vand / wand*.
Sometimes the Turkish ending
is added to the Kurdish ending.
The trend has now been
reversed and here only the
ending *ân* is given.)

Barâz Confederacy
(Samsat to Antep, Marash and
Aleppo. N. Kurmanji-speaking
Alevis and some Sunnis)
Alidinli
Didân
Dinân
Kârakichân
Keytkân
Ma'afân
Mir
Okiyân
Pijân
Shadâdân (or Shaddâd)
Shaykhân
Zarwân

Barwâri Confederacy
(Amadiya to Uludara)
Barwâri Bâlâ
Barwâri Jir

Châwarash Confederacy
(north-NW of Adiyâman. Dimili
and N. Kurmânji-speaking
Alevis)
Brimsân
Tashik
Zirâwkân (or Ziroskân)

Darsimli (Dilamân)
Confederacy
(Erzinjân to Darsim and Elazig.
Dimili speaking, Alevis)
Abbâsân
Bakhtiyâri
Bâlâ Ushâghi (or Ushâk or
Ujâq. NE of Darsim)
Farhâd Ushâghi (or Ushak or
Ujâq. East of Darsim)
Gurân (or Gawrân)
Karabâr
Kochman (or Kichir.

Gypsies)
Kuzlichân
Lâchin
Milân
Mirzân
Shabak (or Shawak)
Ushâk (or Ujâgh)

Haverka Confederacy
(or Hawerka. In Tur Âbidin,
Mardin area. N. Kurmânji-
speaking Sunnis)
Aliyân
Dasikân
Girgir
Mahalimi
Mizidagh
Mizizakh
Moman

Kochkiri Confederacy
(very large. West of the
Euphrates toward Sivâs. Dimili-
speaking, Alevis)
Barlân
Garâwan (Garâwand)
Ibân
Sarân

Kuresh Confederacy
(ENE of Erzinjân, towards
Erzurum. N. Kurmânji-
speaking Alevis)
Bâdel
Bâlâbrân
Shâder

Milân (Milli) Confederacy
(from Euphrates to Mardin and
Jabal Sanjâr. N. Kurmânji-
speaking Sunnis)
Alia
Barguhân
Beski (or Sâlârgân)
Bujâgh (or Buchâk)
Chakali
Chamikân
Chiâ Rash
Danân
Dâshi
Derejân
Hâji Bâyrâm
Hoshiyân
Isi Âdat
Izoli
Jânbeki
Kalândilân
Kassiyâni
Kawât
Kelish
Khalkân (or Khalajân)
Kuma Rash
Mandân

Mard
Matmiya
Mânli
Meshkân
Nasriyân
Porgha
Sartân
Sharkân
Shwân (or Shiwân)
Tirkân
Zaydân
Zirâfkân

Motikân (Modki or Moti)
Confederacy (Bingol to near
Diyârbakir. Formed the core of
the old Chemishgezek
confederacy. Primarily Dimili-
speaking, Sunnis. The name may
be connected with the Medes.)
Ariki
Bobân (or Bâbân)
Kayburân
Kusân
Pirmusi
Ruchâba
Zaydân

Silvan Confederacy
(or Slivan. Çizre to Zakho and
Dohuk. N. Kurmânji-speaking
Sunnis)
Dudwâdta
Guli
Saydahr
Sinâ (or Sinân)
Sindi

Yezidi Confederacy
(in pockets from Mosul to
Antioch, with the heaviest con-
centration in the Jabal Sanjâr
region. This is more of a
religious coalition among the N.
Kurmânji-speaking tribes,
whose members practice
Yezidism, than a standard tribal
confederation. These tribes pay
allegiance to the Chol princely
house, who also serve as the
supreme religious leaders)
Âliyân
Anidi (Dannedi)
Balad
Daseni (or Dasna'i)
Dasikân
Dorkân
Khaliti
Mandikân (Mandukiân of the
Medieval Armenian
sources)
Samuga
Sâshili

Non-Confederated Tribes

(all N. Kurmânji-speaking, Sunnis, unless indicated otherwise)

Alikân (southwest of Elazig to Diyârbakir. N. Kurmânji-speaking, Alevis)

Ashita (in Jazira region in Syria)

Atmânikân (very large. In pockets from Diyârbakir to Hakkâri)

Barakat (north of Antep)

Belikân (very Large. North of Bingol, and south and SE of Antep. Dimili-speaking Alevis in Bingol, Kurmânji-speaking in Antep)

Beshni (in Adiyâman and the vicinity)

Dakhori (SW of Diyârbakir to Amuda in Syria)

Delikân (NW and west of Aleppo. Part Alevi)

Derejân (NW of Malâtiya. Dimili and N. Kurmânji-speaking Alevis)

Dudari (NE of Mardin)

Dumbuli (Dunbeli, in Jabal Sanjâr. Dimili-speaking)

Gabbara (around Amuda in Syria)

Goyan (large. In Kilâbân, NE of Silopi. Partly Dimili-speaking)

Guli (or Geli, Gili. Zakho to Peshkhâbur river)

Hawerka (in Jazira region in Syria)

Izoli (Adiyâman to Urfa)

Jalikân (or Jalilkân. South of Adiyâman to Antep)

Jânbegi (Adiyâman to Siverek)

Karagich (or Qaragich. Large. Siverek to Diyârbakir, with pockets in Tur Âbidin. Dimili-speaking, Alevis)

Khidrsor (NW of Adiyâman. N. Kurmânji-speaking Alevis)

Kiki (south of Antep to Aleppo)

Koti (SE of Malâtya)

Kowâ (or Kao or Qovanlu. East of Adiyâman. N. Kurmânji-speaking Alevis)

Lak Kurdi (Ceyhan river basin, east and NE of Adana. Part Laki-speaking, part Kurmânji, Alevis)

Malikân (east of Malâtya)

Mandukân (or Mendikân. In Tall Afar. N. Kurmânji-speaking, primarily Yezidi. Mentioned frequently in the early Armenian histories as having provided to the Armenians the Mandukâniyân aristocracy)

Mardâs (or Mardis. Nârinja to Euphrates. N. Kurmânji-speaking, Sunnis)

Mirân (large. In Cizre)

Mirsinân (south of Diyârbakir)

Mizuri (large. Dohuk region)

Pâziki (or Baziki. Around Samsat. N. Kurmânji-speaking, Alevis)

Pishnik (NW of Adiyâman. N. Kurmânji-speaking, Alevis)

Porqa (south of Malâtya. Dimili and N. Kurmânji-speaking Alevis)

Shabak (or Shavak. North of Elâzig towards Darsim and Bingol. Primarily Dimili-speaking Alevis)

Shuwaysh (around Amuda in Syria)

Sinâmini (or Sinân. Very large. South, NNW of Malâtya and north of Antep. Laki-speaking, Alevis)

Sindi (large. Between Zakho and Peshkhâbur river)

Tirikân (NE of Diyârbakir)

Zaydân (or Zeidân. East of Bingol, north of Mus. A member of the ancient Rozhaki confederation which broke up in the 19th century)

9. Anatolian Enclave

(All are N. Kurmânji-speaking, Sunnis unless otherwise indicated.)

A. SOUTHERN LOBE

Bazayni (east of Lake Tuz Gölü)

Jânbeki (very large, western half of the lobe, from Yunak to Pulâtli)

Judikân (north of Lake Tuz Gölü)

Khalkân (around Cihânbayli)

Motki (SE of Lake Tuz Gölü. Dimili-speaking, Sunnis)

Nâsirli (around town of Bâlâ)

Sinâminli (Sinân) (east of Lake Tuz Gölü. Dimili-speaking, Alevis)

Sayfkâni (around town of Haymâna)

B. NORTHERN LOBE

Atmanikân (NE of Ankara)

Badeli (south and SW of Yozgat)

Barakat (north of Nevshehir across Kizilirmaq)

Bazayni (NW of Corum and west and NW of Kirshahir across Kizilirmaq)

Hâjibâni (or Hadhabâni. North of Kayseri across Kizilirmaq)

Khâtunoghli (south of Yozgat)

Makhâni (around and in Kirshahir)

Milân (or Milli. North of Corum)

Sheveli (west of Corum across Kizilirmaq)

Tirikân (west of Ankara, and south of Cankiri)

Ukhchijemi (NW of Sivas)

Umrânli (or Amarlu, Kirshahir)

Urukchi (very large, Tokat to Amasya and Yozgat)

Zirikân (SE of Cankiri, and west of Samsun)

reported in 1958 of having been able to find only two Soviet Azeri Kurds who could identify the tribes to which their people belonged before the upheavals. But she records an array of tribes and clans for non-Azerbaijani Kurds when she put the question to them.

In Iran, Iraq, and Syria many Kurdish tribal organizations remain intact. A list of all tribal confederacies and major non-confederated tribes is provided in Table 1.

Sykes' 1908 study of Kurdish tribes records their numbers and location and offers brief socio-cultural observations. Although the work does not cover Kurdish regions of Persia, it is precise and especially valuable because it was done well before the divisions and suppressions following the 1920's. Subsequent work, such as the that of Vilechevski, Edmonds, Nikitine, and Mukri, has added more information (albeit sometimes contradictory) to existing knowledge of the tribes. Field, through his anthropological fieldwork in Iran and Iraq, provides some of the best maps, statistics, and surveys on Kurdish tribes in the English language. Many more valuable works are available in local Middle Eastern languages.

Further Readings and Bibliography: Claudius Ptolemy, *Geographia*, trans. E. Stevenson (New York: New York Public Library, 1932); Henry Field and J.B. Glubb, *The Yezidis, Sulubba and other Tribes of Iraq and Adjacent Regions* (Menasha, Wisconsin, 1943); Henry Field, *Contribution to the Anthropology of Iran* (Chicago, 1939); Ahmad Sousa, *Atlas of Iraq* (Baghdad, 1953); Mark Sykes, "The Kurdish Tribes of the Ottoman Empire," *The Journal of the Royal Anthropological Institute of Great Britain and Ireland* XXXVIII (1908); V. Minorsky, "The Tribes of Western Iran," *Journal of the Royal Anthropological Society of Great Britain and Ireland* LXXV (1945); W. Ivanov, "Notes on the Ethnology of Khurasan," *The Geographical Journal* LXVII-2 (London, 1926); *Sovremennii Iran: Spravochnik* ("Contemporary Iran: A Reference Book') (Moscow, 1957); Alexandre Jaba, *Recueil de Notices et Récits kourdes* (St. Petersburg, 1860); Henry Field, *The Anthropology of Iraq* (Cambridge: Harvard Peabody Museum of Anthropology, 1952); J.B. Noel, *Notes on Kurdish Tribes: On and Beyond the Borders of the Mosul Vilayet and Westward to the Euphrates* (Baghdad, 1919); W.D. Hütteroth, "Bergnomaden und Yaylabaurern im mittleren kurdischen Taurus," *Marburger Geographischer Schriften* II (Marburg, 1959); Aram Ter-Ghewondian, *The Arab Emirates in Bagratid Armenia*, trans. N. Garsoïan (Lisbon: Livraria Bertrand, 1976); H.L. Rabino, "A Journey in Mazandaran (from Resht to Sari),"*The Geographical Journal* 42 (1913); J.B. Noel, "A Reconnaissance in the Caspian Provinces of Persia," *Geographical Journal* 57 (1921); Marcel Bazin and Christian Bromberger et al., *Gilân et Âzerbâyjân Oriental: Cartes et Documents Ethnographic* (Paris: Éditions Recherche sur les civilisations, 1982); Mark Sykes, *The Caliph's Last Heritage* (New York: Arno Press, 1973, reprint of the 1915 London edition); Office of the Civil [Iraq's British Administration] Commissioner, *Notes on Kurdish Tribes, on and Beyond the Borders of the Mosul Villages* and *Westward to the Euphrates, and Notes on the Tribes of Southern Kurdistan Between the Greater Zab and the Dialeh* (Baghdad, 1919); Fu'ad Khurshed, *Notes on the Tribes of Southern Kurdistan* (Baghdad, 1919); Sharaf al-Din Bitlisi, *Chèref-nameh [Sharafnâma] ou Fastes de la nation kourde*, French trans. Charmoy, 2 vols. (St. Petersburg, 1868-75); T.F. Aristova and G.P. Vasil'yeva, "Kurds of the Turkmen SSR," *Central Asian Review* 13-4 (1965); Evliyâ Chelebi, *Siyâhatnâma: Narrative of Travels in Europe, Asia, and Africa*, trans. Joseph von Hammer, 3 vols. (London, 1834-50).

HISTORICAL MIGRATIONS

Familiarity with historical Kurdish migration patterns is perhaps the single most important tool in accurately reconstructing Kurdish history. The utter lack of knowledge of and interest in the population movements, and their interconnection with historical and social events in Kurdistan, is surprising, given the availability of information. Ignorance of these historical events has been the source of the puzzlement of most modern writers over questions of Kurdish national identity, the Kurdish role in and contributions to Middle Eastern history, and the complexity of their modern religious, linguistic, and racial composition. The large body of work and attention given to past Turkic migrations, for example, has clarified many otherwise puzzling historical points about those peoples. The same degree of attention to Kurdish migration patterns can also clarify many questions concerning the centuries between the advent of Islam in the 7th century and the opening of the Turkic era of influence in the Middle East in the 12th century. The necessary historical information on the pre-modern and modern composition of Kurdish tribes and tribal confederacies, with their place in the historical records, is provided in the sections on **Classical, Medieval**, and **Early Modern History; Deportations & Forced Resettlements**; and **Tribes**.

Two kinds of migration patterns, external and internal, can readily be recognized in the history of Kurdistan. Among the more important external migrations are the settlement of Kurdistan by the Aryan tribes in late ancient times, and the heavy Kurdish emigration and settlement of neighboring territories in late classical and early medieval times. The Cimmerians (or "the People of the Sea") of early ancient times and the Turkic nomads of late medieval times just passed through Kurdistan, leaving relatively few settlers and almost no cultural legacy.

The internal migrations involved a steady and massive movement of a portion of the Kurdish population within Kurdistan, resulting in extensive homogenization of Kurdish culture, language, economy, and society. These periodic internal migrations have prevented local variations from permanently fragmenting the nation. The internal migrations do not seem ever to have resulted in total cultural homogenization of the Kurds, as the rough nature of the terrain is conducive to rapid cantonization of the society of the inhabitants. There also remain, even today, many substrata of earlier languages, cultures, racial characteristics, and so on, as evidence of the basic plurality of Kurdish society and culture since the earliest times, despite periodic episodes of homogenization.

The two episodes of internal migration during the classical and early modern periods are well understood, while strong evidence indicates another, much earlier, episode. Of the earliest migrations, so far we have only sketchy and indirect evidence. New technological innovations, like the invention of agriculture, that are conducive to sharp demographic growth (which had Kurdistan as their primary locus), could have translated into episodes of emigration from Kurdistan from 10,000 to 8000 BC (see **Prehistory & Early Technological Development**). The change from rectangular to circular house plans throughout Kurdistan at the onset of the period of the Halaf culture (6000-5000 BC) (see **Architecture & Urban Planning**) could imply an episode of massive immigration into Kurdistan, such as that of the Aryans 3500 years later, or a sustained internal migration, like the late classical-early medieval episode (see below).

Evidence is mounting of another episode of massive migration, dating back to about 3000 BC. This is the period of the Hurrian migrations. The Hurrians, whose name is preserved today in the name of Mt. Ararat (*Hurar>Urartu>Ararat*), were speakers of a northeast Caucasian language related to modern Georgian (Diakonov and Starostin 1989). The Hurrians gradually spread throughout Kurdistan, from Anatolia to the Iranian Plateau. They also made some inroads outside the Zagros region. The Hurrian spread was very likely the result of a sustained episode of massive north-to-south internal migration, and not, as is more often suggested, immigration from the Caucasus mountains (Dyson 1989). The exceedingly small area of the thinly populated eastern Caucasus simply could not have produced such massive numbers of emigrants to overwhelm one of the most densely settled areas of the world, Kurdistan of 3000 BC.

Paleo-linguistic and archaeological evidence indicates that the Hurrian migrations resulted in the cultural and linguistic homogenization of Kurdistan (Kamp and Yoffee 1980, Dyson 1989). This soon translated into the emergence of powerful kingdoms in the territories of Kurdistan, culminating in the political unification of Zagros communities under the Qutils, a tribe of "hurrianized" Kurds. The powerful Qutils burst out of Kurdistan to conquer neighboring territories and kingdoms, including those of Mesopotamia. The periodic cultural homogenizations of Kurdistan brought about by massive internal migrations almost always culminated in expansion of Kurdish political and military power. The Hurrian episode is the earliest example of this phenomenon.

From the middle of the 2nd millenium BC, the Indo-European-speaking immigrants from the Eurasian steppes began their heavy settlement of Kurdistan and the neighboring lands. Their scouts were in Kurdistan over a thousand years earlier, but the floodgates did not open wide until this time. These Indo-European settlers are believed to have arrived in Kurdistan from the north, northeast, and northwest. The Zoroastrian holy book *Avesta* holds that they were forced out of their yet mysterious homeland by excessive cold and drought. Archaeological evidence indicates that climatic deterioration of this sort, caused by a southward shift of the Jet Stream, reached its nadir by about 2000 BC in the Eurasian steppes (see **Environment & Ecology**) (Map 28). There is, however, still a lively debate as to the original homeland of the Indo-European language, some of the theories on which are discussed under **Prehistory & Early Technological Development**.

In any case, as a result of these migrations, almost all peoples of the northern Middle East and central Asia, including the Kurds, had become primarily Indo-European-speaking by about 500 BC. Most of these immigrants into Kurdistan, Persia, central Asia, and India called themselves by the ethnic name *Er* or *Aryâ* ("Aryan"), which is preserved in the geographic, linguistic, and ethnic designator *Iran*, or *Iranic*, which includes the modern Kurds (see **Language** and **National Identity**).

The aryanization of the Kurds, which occurred in the 1st millenium BC, is the first major episode of homogenization of Kurdistan of which we have generally accepted evidence. It would have required a large number of immigrants, and we know that the Medians did embark on repopulating central Kurdistan after three centuries of slaughter, slave gathering, and deportation of the local population by the Assyrians (ending in 612 BC). The Median rulers were elected to local office by the leaders and elders of the confederate tribes and principalities within their sphere of influence. As the Kurds constituted the backbone of the Median Empire and their fighting force, it is likely that the route by which the Median Empire expanded is a rough indicator of the extent of the Kurdish ethnic domains of the time. This was almost exclusively along the mountain systems of the Zagros, Pontus, and Alburz. For a more detailed reconstruction of Kurdish population movements, however, one has to wait until the late classical period, when extensive material is available from the Greco-Roman, Middle Persian, and Aramaic sources.

After his final destruction of Assyria in 612 BC, the Median king Cyaxares settled a large number of Sagarthians, a people related to the Medes, in regions of central Kurdistan, particularly in and around Arbil and Kirkuk. The Sagarthians, from whose name *Zagros* is derived, lived primarily in the area of modern Bakhtiyâri and Luristân, and all the way to Kirmânshâh, in the central and southern Zagros.

It is not clear how much of the settlement of central Kurdistan during the Median and Achaemenian periods can be termed "forced." This was, after all, the ebb of the flow of Indo-European-speaking tribes into the general area. The settlements of the Sagarthians and the repopulation of the Kirkuk region by other Aryan tribes were directed by the Median Cyaxares and the Achaemenian Darius I, for whom no other evidence of mass deportations or forced settlements of people is known. These movements then should logically be interpreted as simply one of several instances of migrating Aryan tribes settling new territories, albeit under the direction of these two monarchs. It is clear from the historical record that these Aryan immigrants enslaved or placed under serfdom the old inhabitants of Kurdistan.

The downfall of the Achaemenian empire, brought about by Alexander the Great in the Battle of Arbela (modern Arbil), opened the land to Greek settlement. Kurdistan, particularly western and southern Kurdistan, became one of the regions to receive relatively large numbers of Greek settlers. The Greeks were soon joined by even larger

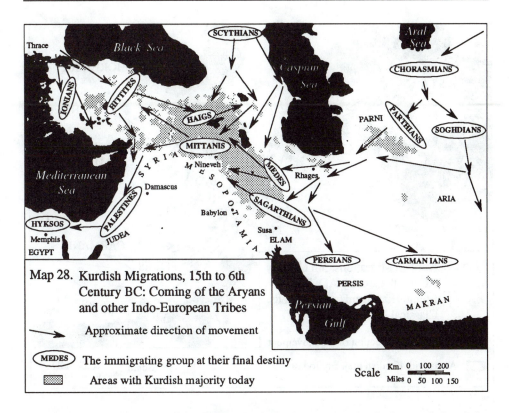

Map 28. Kurdish Migrations, 15th to 6th
Century BC: Coming of the Aryans
and other Indo-European Tribes

→   Approximate direction of movement

(MEDES) The immigrating group at their final destiny

▨   Areas with Kurdish majority today

Scale   Km. 0 100 200
         Miles 0 50 100 150

numbers of Parthian settlers, the military might of whose empire had overwhelmed the
Seleucid Hellenistic empire in the Middle East. The Parthians were cultural cousins of
the Kurds, and along with the Greeks, likely constituted a majority of the urban
population of southern Kurdistan and Luristan. This area in fact came to be known as
Pahla (after the ethnic name of the Parthians: *Partha>Paltha>Palh>Pahla*). The legacy
of the Greek settlers is found today in the folk tradition of theatrical plays, gymnasia, and
wrestling matches, as well as in the tradition of naturalistic sculpture. The Parthian
legacy can be found in the name of one of the two surviving Kurdish language groups,
Pahlawâni (see **Language**), which the Parthians adopted as their own. It is also evident
in the name of the *Fayli* Kurds, and in the term for honor and manliness, *Pahlawân* (see
National Character).

Easily discernible from the surviving classical sources for the next period of migrations
is a continuous northwest flow of Kurdish tribes from the southeast (Map 29). This lasted
approximately from the 4th century BC to the 5th century AD.

There are six bodies of evidence that demonstrate this.

1) Almost every Kurdish tribe mentioned in the far southeastern Zagros in Fârs is later
encountered solely or simultaneously in central, and later northern, Kurdistan.

2) Armenian early histories are full of indirect reports of influential foreign aristo-
cratic/feudal families who established themselves in Armenia as early as the 3rd century
BC. Most, if not all, of these families had Iranic names, which coincide with Kurdish
tribal names from the regions to the south and southeast of Armenia.

3) In the early geographies, such as those of Strabo and Ptolemy, the names of
numerous localities in northern and western Kurdistan are corrupted forms of Kurdish
tribal names ending with *vand* or *wand,* a south Kurdish tribal designation, as opposed to
kân/gân/ân, a north Kurdish designation. Almost all of those tribes that appeared over
2000 years ago with southern tribal suffixes to their names have since the end of the

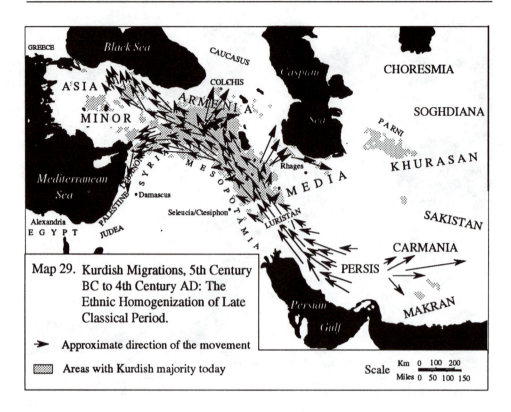

Map 29. Kurdish Migrations, 5th Century
BC to 4th Century AD: The
Ethnic Homogenization of Late
Classical Period.

➤   Approximate direction of the movement

▨▨   Areas with Kurdish majority today

medieval period switched to the northern suffixes. Only in southern Kurdistan and in
Luristân (which is no longer Kurdish) and the southern Zagros do the southern suffixes
still prevail.

4) The tribal denominator *zom* (often misread as *rom* or *ram*), reported by the early
Islamic sources for the Kurdish tribes of the southern Zagros, is now found exclusively in
the north-central and northern Zagros in Kurdistan. The term, pronounced *zoma* in
modern Kurdish, signifies a summer grazing camp (of nomads).

5) Religions, ideas, and Kurdish dialects indigenous to southern Kurdistan begin to
appear in northern and western Kurdistan with increasing frequency beginning in the 4th
century BC.

6) History's first encounter with tribes such as the Bagrâvand (Bakrân), Tigrânavand
(Tirikân), Hadhabâni, Shaddâdân, and Mamakân (Mamikon), in the Armenian sources,
locates them to the south and southeast of the Armenian frontiers. These same sources
later report them solely or simultaneously in northern Armenia. The Bagrâvands, for
example, appear first in the 4th century BC near the Jabal Sanjâr-Mosul region (*Naphates
Mons*), then on the upper Tigris in the 3rd century BC (when Ptolemy records them),
followed by the northwest environs of Lake Vân, in the 1st century AD, and northern
Armenia and southern Georgia in the 3rd century AD. In south-central Kurdistan near
the modern town of Sulaymânia, the most southerly evidence of the Bakrâns is found in
the names of the plains and towns of Bakrâwâ and Bakrajo. Etymologically, it is possible
to connect the ancient Bagrâvandenes with the Bajrâwân or Bajalân tribes of southern
and central Kurdistan. The Bajrâwâns and Bajalâns are still Gurâni-speaking, and follow
the ancient Kurdish Cult of Angels (as the ancient Bagrâwands are likely to have done).
They are now found near Mosul on the Tigris, i.e., on the southern limits of Ptolemy's
Bagrauandene Regio, as well as near Khânaqin in southern Kurdistan.

The connections of the Bakrân tribe with the Bagrâtid royal houses of Armenia and later Georgia, and the Tirikân tribe with the Armenian king Tigrân the Great (r. 140-55 BC), are discussed in detail under **Tribes** and **Classical History**. The evidence of these links also sheds further light on the general direction of Kurdish migrations.

It has traditionally been held that the Armenian king Tigrân was of non-Armenian origin. The early medieval Armenian historian Moses of Chorene (or Movses Khorenat'se), who lived sometime between 490 and 760 AD, relates that the ancestors of Tigrân came to Armenia, having had difficulties with the Median king Âzhi Dahâk (r. 584–549 BC) to whom they were related, and in whose realm they had lived. Moses thus places the original home of Tigrân's family and clan somewhere in southern Kurdistan. By the time of Moses, *Media* (Armenian *Mâr*, Kurdish *Mâi*, Persian *Mâh*) had come to signify only the heartland of ancient Media, i.e., southern Kurdistan and northern Luristân. The departure route of the Tigrân clan, therefore, was in a southeast-northwest direction.

This reconstruction can be further supported by the fact that Ptolemy has *Tigranuan* for the country south of Lake Vân and immediately east of the country of the Bagrauande (Bakrân) tribe. This is the area Tigrân's family/clan was supposed to have dominated prior to its rise to the Armenian throne. This place name can be reconstructed as *Tigrânavand.* The suffix of the tribal name, *vand,* is readily recognized for its southern Kurdish origin.

Several important Kurdish tribes that made this long-distance journey north and northwest merit special attention, as they played notable historical roles in the region, and little has been written about them. These are the Mamakâns, Gelus, Dilams, and Hadhabânis. The list of historically important tribes could be extended to include the Shabânkâra (Shwânkâra/Shwân), the Khalkân (Qalkhân), the Zangi (Zangana), and more.

The historical link of between the Armenian-speaking medieval Mamikonian clan and the Kurdish-speaking Mamakân and the Mamesh tribes (respectively of northern and central Kurdistan), and the Luri-speaking Mamasani of the southern Zagros further substantiates the direction of early Kurdish tribal movements. Only a long-distance migration could account for the more than 1000 miles separating various branches of this old tribe.

The tribe neighboring the modern Mamakân, the populous Jalâli, has in fact made this very same long-distance trek. The Jalâlis are first mentioned in early medieval times only in Fârs and the far southern Zagros. They have since spread nothwestward, and are now found, in addition to the southern Zagros (as the Gelu or Kuh Giluyah tribes, or medieval Jiluyah), in the central Zagros (as the Galâwand, Kalâlawand, and Jalâlawand) and the northern Zagros (the Jalâlis).

In addition to the Jalâlis, another branch had earlier split from the Gelu/Gelo tribes of the southern Zagros, migrating north in the course of the 3rd century BC, and settling the western Alburz mountains and the Caspian sea lowlands. The Gelus imparted their name to modern Gilân, which until the 3rd century BC was called Cadusia. Beginning with the works of Strabo, Plutarch, and Pliny, the land is more commonly referred to as the land of the *Geloi.*

The migrating Gelus left their imprint on many other places as they slowly passed through the Zagros chain, before finally settling on the Caspian rim. There are too many place and tribal names with the element *gelu* and its variations in Kurdistan to require any further substantiation.

Another important Kurdish tribe to follow the Gelus to the western Alburz were the Dilams (medieval Daylamites), whose vanguard arrived in the Alburz with the Gelus in the 3rd century BC. Unlike the Gelus, however, the Dilams continued to receive more immigrant kinsmen in the following centuries. These came from the regions of the upper Tigris river basin in Anatolia, where the bulk of the Dilams had previously settled. The process continued until the 4th century AD and the next great episode of Kurdish migration.

While Armenia, and to a lesser extent Georgia and Aran to northeast of Kurdistan, were gradually being settled by these Kurdish immigrants, Commagene, Cappadocia, and

Pontus to the far northwest were also receiving massive numbers of immigrants. The Kurdish Pontian king Mithridates, in a single alliance against the Romans, received the allegiance of 14 of these tribes and fielded their irregular tribal fighters in his expeditions into Greece and Ukraine (see **Classical History**).

A comparatively large volume of literature pertinent to this episode of historical migrations and settlements is preserved in the later Syriac sources, which are compilations and summaries of earlier Aramaic archives of the royal houses of central Kurdistan, like Adiabene and Karkhu (Kirkuk). These documents were later transferred to the Nestorian Christian church archives around the 6th century AD (see **Christianity**).

In all, twelve clans are known to have settled in the Garmiyân-Kirkuk region during the Parthian period. Of particular interest, however, are the tribal/family names of the leaders of three of these: Virâz, Burzân, and Paren, who "immigrated into [Kirkuk] region with their clan and the great families" (Pigulevskaya 1963). These are also the names of three of the seven major aristocratic houses of Parthia, each of which was deeply involved in the internal and external policies of that state. These three names are now preserved in the modern Kurdish tribes or confederacies of Barâz, Bârzân, and Pirân.

The prevalent southeast-northwest movement appears to have in time thinned out the Kurdish population of the far southern, and eventually no longer Kurdish, regions of Luristân, Bakhtiyâri, and Gelu (Kuh Giluyah), and the highlands of Persis/Fârs.The massive departure could have been a reflection of economic-ecological distress, which made staying in the southeast Zagros a disadvantage. It could also have been the aftermath of an economic boom, which had earlier stimulated demographic growth in the area, which in decline forced the surplus population to migrate in search of better conditions. Likewise, an economic-ecological advantage to the northern Zagros, Pontus, and Taurus systems could have acted as a magnet, attracting the bulk of the Kurdish emigrants from the southeast. Whatever the causes, by the end of the 5th century AD, they no longer existed.

The continuous arrival of the southern Kurds, and the resultant positive demographic growth primarily in northern and western, but also central, Kurdistan, had resulted by the beginning of the 4th century AD in a large population surplus in those regions. This culminated in an out-migration that took Kurds to every neighboring region and beyond in the Middle East. For this episode of Kurdish migrations, northern and western Kurdistan was the springboard. It lasted from approximately the 4th century to the 11th century AD. In both this and the previous episode of Kurdish migration the movements were so gradual that they were seldom noticed by the inhabitants of the lands that received this steady stream of Kurdish immigrants. For example, the "Kurdish settlment of Armenia," writes Ter-Ghewondian, "was so unobtrusive, that its beginning is difficultly traceable."

The Daylamites and the Rivands, for example, were the results of two massive emigration pulses. The Daylamites, whose vanguard had already colonized the western Alburz four centuries earlier, moved out in such large numbers this time that they not only overran the rest of the neighboring Alburz mountains south of the Caspian sea, but burst out to spread over large tracts of the eastern Islamic lands. At this time the Daylamites even managed, according to the accounts of medieval Muslim traveler Nâsir Khusraw, to populate an entire city quarter in far-off Cairo by the 11th century, while the Rivands populated all of northern Khurasan, thenceforth the eponymous "Rivand Heights" (Map 30).

The same outflow of Kurdish people can account for the considerable pre-Islamic Kurdish population in Lebanon and in coastal Syria, where we know large numbers lived as Christians in the cities of Baalbek and Latakia. After Baalbek fell to Muslim conquerors in the 8th century, some of these refugees retreated to Antioch and Tarsus inside the

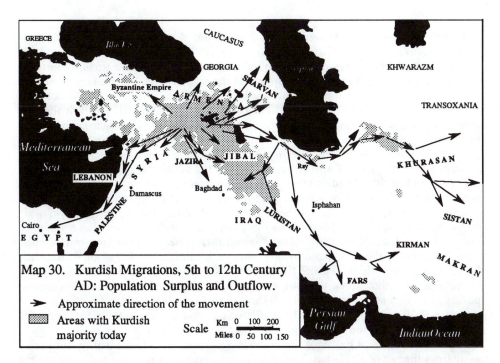

Map 30.   Kurdish Migrations, 5th to 12th Century AD: Population Surplus and Outflow.

➤   Approximate direction of the movement

▨▨   Areas with Kurdish majority today

Scale   Km 0   100   200
        Miles 0   50   100   150

shrinking Byzantine Empire. The non-Christian, Alevi Kurds remained, and even increased their demographic weight with fresh Kurdish immigrants (Cahen 1940). Most of these Kurds were later assimilated and became the ancestors of the modern Alevi Arabs of coastal Syria, where they constitute a vast majority today.

In southern Kurdistan, classical Middle Persian sources, as well as Greco-Roman works on geography and later medieval Muslim accounts, all point to a large and vibrant Kurdish society stretching deep into the southern Zagros almost to the Straits of Hormuz. For example, Ibn Hawqal, in his geographical work *Surat al-'Ard* (written ca. AD 980), provides a list of 33 "better-known" Kurdish tribes in Fârs (southern Zagros), adding that their total was over 100, numbering 500,000 families. Ibn Hawqal was himself a native of Nisibis (modern town of Nesibin in western Kurdistan) and must have known what he meant when referring to Kurds in his work. Ibn Balkhi, a native of Fârs, a century and a half later in his geographical work *Fârsnâma* (ca. AD 1116), gives a list of five tribes (or tribal confederacies) for the Kurds there, each, he writes, 100,000 families strong.

Most of these tribes are still extant today and their names, even to the extent of their subdivisions and clans, can be matched with these early lists given for Kurdish tribal names of the southern Zagros. These fall into three groups: 1) those tribes that are still Kurdish today, like the Shabânkâra and the Gurân, but live in the central and/or northern Zagros, 2) those that are present but no longer Kurdish-speaking, like the Lurs and Giluya who live in the southern Zagros, 3) those that are present in both forms, like the Kurdish-speaking Mâmash and the Luri-speaking Mamasani (both offshoots of the medieval Mamasan tribe of the southern Zagros).

By the end of the 9th century AD, large population surpluses and their consequent emigrations had stretched the Kurdish-inhabited areas to their historical peak. The medieval historian Mas'udi (AD 893-965) gives a short list of 16 major Kurdish tribes in his work *Al-Tanbih,* and reports the extent of the land inhabited by the Kurds to have been in his time Fârs, Kirmân, Sistân, Isfahân, Khurâsân, Jibâl (central and northern Zagros), Mâhât (Media, i.e., Luristan and Kirmânshâh), Hamadân, Shahrazur

(Sulaymânia), Azerbaijan, Armenia, Ârân, Bâb'l Abwâb (Sharvan), Jazira, Bilighân (east-central Anatolia), Syria, and the (Syrian) Gates (Antioch-Adana). Kurds are today a majority in six of these regions, a large minority in four others, and a small minority in the rest. Areas in which many Kurds appear in the early reports, but are now present in only small numbers, are those of the southern Zagros, in Fârs, Kirmân, Sistân (i.e., modern Seistân and Baluchistân), and Isfahân. The only district from which they are entirely absent is Bâb'l Abwâb (northern Sharvân, i.e., Russian Daghistan). The strong presence of ethnic Kurds in these regions was the crucial element in the rise of the medieval Kurdish dynasties that ruled large segments of the eastern Islamic world.

Large portions of the Kurdish population in the southern Zagros gradually but permanently lost their Kurdish ethnic identity. It now appears that, by about the 10th century, a populous Persian-speaking tribe from northern Afghanistan or southern Tajikistân wandered into the southern Zagros and settled the region (many Turkic nomads, like the Qashqa'i, also came via this route much later). This tribe has come to be known as the Bakhtiyâris. With relative speed, they appear to have transmitted their Islamic religion to the local, basically non-Muslim, Kurdish tribes and along with it their Persian language, which became the basis for the modern Luri-Bakhtiyâri dialects. Starting in the 11th century, the southern Zagros is mentioned less and less by contemporary observers as being Kurdish. Fakhr al-Din Gurgâni, who versified the ancient romance of *Vis o Râmin* (ca. AD 1040-1050), is among the first authors to distinguish between the Lurs and the Kurds.

The southern Zagros has since then increasingly taken on a Luri identity and pulled away from the rest of Kurdistan. This same process is also taking place today among the Laks, who are progressively distancing themselves from the rest of the Kurds. The religious and linguistic metamorphoses of these Kurds seem to have been simultaneous.

Interestingly, the Lurs and Bakhtiyâris on occasion still identify themselves as Kurds, or as closely related to them. Many local toponyms include the word *kurd*, as in the Bakhtiyâri provincial capital of *Shahri Kurd* ("City of the Kurds"), or in the district and river of "Kurdistan" in the Mamasani Luri region near the Persian Gulf. Further, the vocabulary of Luri is still primarily Kurdish, while the verb system and syntax are Persian.

It is also appropriate to consider the question of Baluchi ethnicity at this point. The Baluchi national folk stories and the histories written by pre-modern Baluchis contend that they are descended from the Kurds. The most important of the tales is the *Kurdgalnâmak* ("The Book of Kurdish Folk"), written in AD 1640 by Akhund Muhammed Saleh Zangana Baluch (Ahmadzai 1986). There is also the Daptar Sha'ar or Shajar "chronicle of genealogies," an ancient ballad popular among all 17 major Baluchi tribes. The ballad tells of a common origin for the Kurds and the Baluch, who later separated, each assuming a new identity (Dames 1907, Harrison 1981). To this one may add the question of the origin of the Baluchi language. It is, like Kurdish, a northwest Iranic language (see **Language**, Fig. 2), even though its domain is in linguistic isolation in the extreme southeast of the Iranic world, near the banks of the Indus river in Pakistan. The Baluchis are now separated by over 1000 miles from their nearest linguistic kinsmen, the Kurds.

There is absolutely no historical record of the existence of the Baluchis prior to the 5th century AD, while other ethnic groups (such as the Gedrosians and the Makas, referred to by the ancient Greek sources as the *Ichthyophagi*, "the fish eaters"), are well known to have lived in what is now Baluchistan. The Baluchis' appearance coincides with the period of Kurdish population surplus and the northwest outflow from the southern Zagros. Chosroes I is said in the *Shâhnâma* to have encountered the Baluchis and the Daylamites on his return from his Indian campaigns—rendering the southern Zagros a logical and geographically plausible point of origin for them, as it is the midpoint on the direct route between India and the Sasanian capital at Ctesiphon.

The Shabânkâra Kurdish presence in Kirmân, the region neighboring Baluchistan, is attested historically from the 8th to the 14th century. Medieval Muslim authors like Ibn Hawqal and Ibn Khalkân (himself a Kurd from Arbil) assert that the Baluch are descended from Kurdish immigrants. The great northwestward Kurdish migrations from the 5th century BC to the 5th century AD may very well have had a smaller spur pushing in the opposite direction, i.e., east toward modern Kirmân, Sistan, and Baluchistan (Map 29). The impetus for this uncharacteristic eastern migration may have been the aforementioned campaigns of the Sasanian Chosroes I. In any case, these Kurds later evolved their own separate ethnic identities, as did the other Kurds of the southern Zagros. An alternative hypothesis, advanced by Bosworth (1976), is that the Baluchis neighbored the Daylamites and migrated to their present location from the the Caspian Sea region. While this theory implies the same close connection between the Baluchis and the Kurds, it is much less plausible than the theory here entertained. After all, Baluchi movements are documented to have progressed from west to east, as required by placing their ancestry in the southern Zagros, not north to south, as Bosworth's theory would require. The Baluchis are nonetheless now an independent ethnic group with only historical and linguistic ties to the Kurds.

An unexpected and unfortunate result of this general trend of ethnic metamorphosis in the southern Zagros has been the misconception it has produced among modern historians and scholars, who read extensive medieval reports on vast numbers of Kurds in that area. These reports lead them to suspect that the term *Kurd* in earlier times must have meant any individual or group of people leading an economic life based on herding and pastoralism. This hypothesis is based primarily on the fact that almost no ethnic Kurds live today in the southern Zagros. This is a facile conclusion, since no one has ever carried out a study on the Kurdish demographic and migratory patterns to substantiate so sweeping an assertion (see **National Identity**).

Starting in the 11th century and continuing for about four hundred years, Kurdistan was settled by some Arabs and later larger numbers of Aramaeans and Turco-Mongolians. Kurds themselves, on the other hand, were emigrating in other directions at about the same time. There are a few Arabic, and many Aramaic and Turco-Mongolian, place-names found in Kurdistan today. Except for a few small Turkmen and Aramaean (now known as Assyrian Christian) (see **Christianity**) enclaves in Iraqi Kurdistan and a shrinking Jewish population, these settlers have been thoroughly assimilated into the Kurdish people.

Western Kurds prospered greatly under the early Ayyubids (12th century), and expanded into many of the historically Kurdish realms that had been lost through deportations in earlier periods, particularly on the eastern Mediterranean rim and in Mesopotamia. Lands that were lost by the Kurds to Muslim Arabs and Christian Aramaeans under the Umayyads and the Byzantines were reclaimed at this time. The Amanus range and the Amiq valley, for example, were conquered for the Kurds by the Ayyubid Sherkoh in AD 1149. Antioch and Alexandretta were conquered in AD 1188 by king Saladin himself, allowing Kurds to return to cities they had helped build 14 centuries earlier.

The Kurds pushed farther south toward the historic Crusaders' fortress Croc de Chevallier (or *Hisn al-Akrâd*, Arabic for the "Fortress of the Kurds") in the western coastal mountains of Syria. Even Lebanon received Kurdish settlers after a hiatus of over three centuries. Although these were all later arabized, they left behind marks of their presence: the overwhelming majority of the inhabitants of the mountains and Syrian coastal regions, including Syrian President Assad, are of the Alevi religion (see **Alevism**).

This new wave of Kurdish settlers brought to Lebanon and coastal Syria Kurds whose names today, although thoroughly arabized, can easily be traced to their Kurdish tribal origins. The prestigious Lebanese families of Barâzi/Berâzi, Jibrân/Gibrân, and Jumbalât have preserved these Kurdish tribal names, which are still extant today in Kurdistan proper as well. The many basic similarities between the Druze religion and the Cult of

Angels, particularly Alevism, indicate, at the very least, a period of profound contact between the followers of the two religions in the past.

The Egyptian encyclopedist Shahâb al-Din Fadlullâh al-'Umari provides, ca. AD 1338, a very detailed and valuable study of the Kurdish tribes of this period in his work Masâlik al-Absâr. His recording of the Kurdish tribal locations and movements fills the historical gap between the earlier works, like those of Mas'udi and Ibn Hawqal, and the first pan-Kurdish history and tribal lists of Sharaf al-Din Bitlisi in 1596-97.

The episode of massive emigration of Kurds to regions outside Kurdistan reached its conclusion by the end of the 13th century. The next period, extending from the beginning of the 14th century to the present, is one of internal migration and homogenization under a new identity.

The most striking feature of this internal migration is the gradual expansion into the rest of Kurdistan of the Kurmânji-speaking Kurdish nomads (Map 31). These were earlier restricted to the area between Lake Urmiâ and Lake Vân, with the district of Hakkâri as their heartland. They gradually filled the countryside of Kurdistan from their original area of concentration. They drove out, or forced into serfdom, the sedentary, agriculturalist Kurds who were almost exclusively Dimili- or Gurâni-speaking and overwhelmingly followers of the Cult of Angels. These sedentary Kurds were gradually pushed back into the towns and cities of Kurdistan by the nomads, but were eventually assimilated into the culture of the nomads. Except for the present Dimili and Gurân regions in the far northern and far southern Kurdistan, the Kurds and Kurdistan have generally taken on a Kurmânji-speaking, Sunni Muslim identity (see **Religion** and **Language**).

Special attention must be given to Armenia in any discussion of Kurdish demography and population movements, as nearly half of the historical Armenian territory has gradually and effectively been incorporated into Kurdish ethnic territories (in northern Kurdistan) through millennia of Kurdish migrations and settlements (see Map 4).

As already observed, the Kurdish settlement of Armenia proper can be traced to at least 2300 years ago. Prior to Islamic times, Kurdish immigrants seem to have in large part assimilated into the Armenian community, leaving behind their tribal names. The continuing immigration of Kurds into Armenia from the 5th to the 11th century AD, however, eventually brought about a change in the ethnic composition of the land. As early as the 6th century, Jewish Talmudic scripture, particularly the *Targum,* consistently interprets *Ararat,* the traditional heartland of Armenia, to mean Kurdistan, and no longer Armenia (Targums of Genesis 8:4, Isaiah 37:38, and Jeremiah).

By about the beginning of the present millennium, unassimilated Kurdish tribes were living in every corner of the Armenian plateau. They were found in large numbers living around the historic Armenian city of Dvin north of Yerivan by the middle of the 10th century, and farther north at Ani, the capital of Bagratid Armenia, by the late 11th century. These Kurds became the power base for several Kurdish dynasties that ruled this entire region for centuries. By the time their rate of immigration had slackened (the middle of the 14th century), the Kurdish population in Armenia had stabilized. While the city and town dwellers in Armenia remained primarily Armenians, the countryside was progressively being kurdified.

Under pressure from the Turkic nomads who were passing into the Byzantine lands from the east, large numbers of Armenians moved to Cilicia on the Mediterranean, where they established a state of their own. This encouraged emigration, further reducing the Armenian component of the ancient Armenian homeland. The Kurdish proportion of the overall population rose as a direct result.

The destructive effects of the 16th-17th century wars and mass deportations affected the Armenians as profoundly as the Kurds. More Armenians, however, moved away on their own accord, as conditions deteriorated on the Armenian plateau. This process continued until the late 19th century, with the result that the agriculturalist, urban-

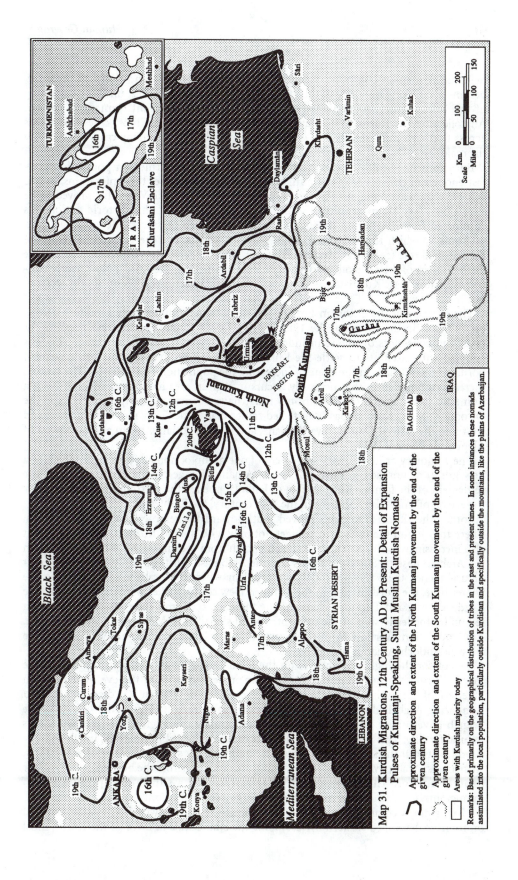

Map 31. Kurdish Migrations, 12th Century AD to Present: Detail of Expansion
Pulses of Kurmanji-Speaking, Sunni Muslim Kurdish Nomads.

⌐ Approximate direction and extent of the North Kurmanj movement by the end of the
   given century

⋯ Approximate direction and extent of the South Kurmanj movement by the end of the
   given century

☐ Areas with Kurdish majority today

Remarks: Based primarily on the geographical distribution of tribes in the past and present times. In some instances these nomads
assimilated into the local population, particularly outside Kurdistan and specifically outside the mountains, like the plains of Azerbaijan.

oriented Armenian community, under centuries of nomadic and political pressure, became a shrinking minority in their ancient homeland. Despite this, until the beginning of the 20th century, Armenians constituted the most important element in eastern Anatolia after the Kurds. While few were left in the countryside, most cities and towns across northern Kurdistan had large Armenian populations, in many cases constituting the majority.

Born to better health care, education, and nutrition, the Armenian population grew fast enough in the course of the 19th century to not only offset the emigrations, but to achieve a numerical majority in the immediate vicinity of Lake Vân. This proved to be short-lived (see **Demography**). By the end of World War I, this historic nation was eliminated from the region through Ottoman-sponsored massacres, deportations, and pogroms, in which Kurdish tribal chiefs, religious leaders, and mercenaries played more than a small role (see **Early Modern History**). This rendered the Armenian plateau a de facto domain of the only other surviving native population: the Kurds. Now nearly two-thirds of northern Kurdistan is in essence kurdified sections of central and western historic Armenia.

The faltering of the Ottoman Empire, which sustained uninterrupted military defeats on all fronts in the course of the 19th century, forced Istanbul to increase pressure for taxes and conscripts on the semi-independent pastoralist tribes of Kurdistan. This was coupled with attempts to settle the Kurdish nomads who lived on the fertile western borders of Kurdistan, in the hope of increasing the population and revenue. The tenfold increase in population that normally occurs in a given area after the transition from a nomadic to an agricultural economy must have been an alluring prospect for the Ottomans. Many Kurdish pastoralists fled rather than settle. They moved southwest and west into the eastern Taurus toward Adana, and into the Amanus north and northwest of Aleppo (de Planhol 1959).

The voluntary or involuntary settlement of one group of nomads opens the niche for a new group of nomads to move in. In the Amanus Range on the Mediterranean, the settlement of the famous Kurdish clan of Janbulât opened the surrounding highlands for the arrival of a new Kurdish tribe in the 19th century, the Rashwand.

Some other Kurdish nomads moved south toward the remote Jabal Sanjâr in Jazira. There they found themselves in contact not only with the old Kurdish Yezidi clans, but also increasingly with Arab nomads fleeing north from the onslaught of the Wahhâbis in the Arabian deserts. Since the Kurds and the Arab pastoralists basically occupy different natural niches, there was not much of a problem: where the Arabs used a pasture in the winter time, the Kurds used it in the summer. New confederacies were formed to include Kurdish, Arab, and Turkmen clans sharing the same economic interests. Many of them fell under the leadership of the influential Kurdish Milân or Melli tribal administration. Any population overflow from these eastern Syrian confederacies moved west to settle the rich Antioch-Amanus region.

Except for the higher elevations on the Jabal Sanjâr heights (the stronghold of the Yezidi Kurds), Jazira was unsafe for permanent settlement. On the eve of the French takeover of the Syrian Mandate in 1922, there were only a few Kurdish villages and wandering Arab Bedouins in all of the lower Jazira region (Hourani 1947, 80). The French government took it upon itself to repopulate this region, well-known for its natural fertility. This coincided with a demographic upheaval in Anatolia, in which hundreds of thousands of people were on the move. A steady stream of Assyrians, Armenians, Arabs, Syriacs, Turkmens, and Kurds moved across the borders into Syria for protection from the Turkish army. Jazira received a substantial population of immigrants, of which Kurds constituted the largest single portion.

Most of the incoming ethnic Arab immigrants—Muslim as well as Christian—moved on to more developed western Syria, tipping the ethnic scale in favor of the Kurds, most of whom remained behind.

With the steady westward departure of the Arabs, Armenians, and Assyrians, Jazira has now gained a distinctly Kurdish character, which will continue, barring a massive deportation of Kurds from the region. This is not as unlikely as it may seem, since many of these Kurds have been denied Syrian citizenship, even after more than three generations of residency, on the grounds that many of them are "recent" arrivals from beyond the modern borders of Syria.

Further Readings and Bibliography: T. Cuyler Young, Jr., "The Iranian Migration into the Zagros," *Iran* V (1967); R.H. Dyson, "Architecture of the Iron I Period at Hasanlu in Western Iran and its Implications for Theories of Migration on the Iranian Plateau," in *Le plateau iranien et l'asi centrale des origines à la conquête islamique* (Paris: Colloques internationaux du centre national de la recherche scientifique, No. 567, 1976); N. Pigulevskaya, *Goroda Irana v Pannem Crednevekovie* (Leningrad, 1955), in French translation, *Les Villes de l'Etat Iranien* (Paris, 1963); Aram Ter-Ghewondian, *The Arab Emirates in Bagratid Armenia*, trans. N. Garsoian (Lisbon: Livraria Bertrand, 1976); Moses Khorenats'i, *History of the Armenians*, trans. Robert Thomson (Cambridge: Harvard University Press, 1978); Albert Hourani, *Minorities in the Arab World* (London: Oxford University Press, 1947); Ismet Vanly, "Le déplacement du pays Kurde vers l'ouest, X-XV siècles, étude de géographie et de sociologie historieques," *Actes du XXIX Congrès International des Orientalistes* (Paris, 1973); Agha Naseer Khan Ahmadzai, "Akhund Muhammed Saleh, the author of Koordgal-Nâmak," *Newsletter of Baluchistan Studies* 3 (Napels, 1986); C.E. Bosworth, "The Kufichis or Qufs in Persian History," *Iran* XIV (1976); Claude Cahen, *La Syrie du Nord* (Paris: Institut farançais de Damas, 1940); Rene Dussaud, *Topographie historique de la Syrie antique et Medievale* (Paris, 1927).

EMIGRATIONS & DIASPORA

In the past quarter century, the Kurds have been progressively moving out of the economically depressed rural regions to settle first in the major towns within Kurdistan, and then in the primary urban magnets within the boundaries of the countries in which they presently live. In Turkey, the greater Istanbul region is receiving the largest number of Kurds, followed by Ankara and Adana, with Izmir being a distant fourth. In Iran, too, the largest Kurdish movements are within the boundaries of Kurdistan, followed by migration into metropolitan Teheran. There are much smaller movements into the petroleum-producing cities of Âbâdân and Ahvâz in the province of Khuzistân in the south, and Tabriz in Azerbaijan in the north. Tabriz basically attracts Kurds from Iranian Kurdistan north of Sanandaj.

In Iraq, the Kurds have been urbanizing rapidly, with local Kurdish cities keeping pace with Baghdad in attracting immigrants. With the Iraqi petroleum industry concentrated in the Kurdish city of Kirkuk, Kurds have been competing with non-Kurds in the job market and to regain an ethnic majority in the city and its environs. Voluntary Kurdish population movements in Iraq, however, are dwarfed by the deportations of Kurds by various Iraqi governments, and must be viewed in that context (see **Deportations & Forced Resettlements**).

Immigration outside the five sovereign states that share Kurdish land has also increased in recent years. Israel, Lebanon, and the Persian Gulf states, and beyond the Middle East, Germany, Austria, France, Sweden, Australia, and the United States, attract the majority of Kurdish immigrants.

Estimates of the number of Kurds outside Kurdistan are understandably imprecise. Turkish government spokesman Kaya Toperi asserted in an American National Public Radio interview on March 1, 1991 that of "about 7-12 million people of Kurdish origin living in Turkey, two thirds live outside the southeastern regions." Kurds believe that between a third and a half of their population in Turkey has already moved outside the traditional boundaries of Kurdistan (Vanly 1986). Other evidence, not the least of which is the dynamics associated with the explosive demographic growth of the Kurds in Turkey, also points toward this rather startling probability . If the Euphrates river is accepted as the western and northern boundary of Kurdistan proper in Turkey, then it is quite likely that more than half of the Anatolian Kurds live outside this region and, presumably, in diaspora in other parts of Turkey. Of these, nearly half now likely live in the territories immediately to the north and west of the Euphrates, in the Taurus and Pontus ranges, including the cities of Adana and Sivas. The other half are likely to be found in the central Anatolian enclave and the major cities of western and central Turkey, most importantly Istanbul, Ankara, and Izmir. Barring any drastic change in Turkey, this trend will continue to bring more Kurds to other parts of Turkey in the foreseeable future — a development which will bring to ordinary Turks more first-hand awareness of their Kurdish compatriots.

Since no one carries a Kurdish passport, it is equally difficult to track down Kurds in countries to which they are not indigenous. Many estimates put the number of Kurds presently in Lebanon at around 50,000. If this is the case, proportionately Lebanon now has far more Kurds (6% of the total population of Lebanon) than there are in the former territories of the Soviet Union (0.14%), where segments of the Kurdish mainland are actually located. This is not surprising in light of the historical Kurdish settlements in Lebanon (see **Historical Migrations**).

Various Kurdish organizations place the number of Kurds living in European countries between one-half and three-quarters of a million. In the United States, the first Kurdish immigrants arrived in the upper Ohio Valley and the industrial centers of eastern Michigan in the early 1930's. They were refugees from the wars and uprisings in eastern Anatolia and the aftermath of the Khoyboun insurrection. They numbered around 1,000 individuals (Bedir Khan and Bletch 1930) and appear to have assimilated. The next wave of Kurdish refugees and immigrants to the United States had to wait until the 1970's and the collapse of the Kurdish uprising in Iraq under General Bârzâni.

There are presently at least 35,000 Kurds in the United States, the large majority of whom are of Iranian origin. In the course of the Iranian revolution and its aftermath, about 750,000 Iranians immigrated to the United States. Kurds constitute about 12% of the total population of Iran. It is not, therefore, unreasonable to expect that approximately 3% of the Iranians living in the United States are Kurdish. This results in a rough estimate of 23,000 Iranian Kurds living in the United States. Adding half as much to this figure to account for Kurds from other sections of Kurdistan, which contain 76% of all Kurds, a total of 35,000 Kurds for the United States is a conservative figure.

Various Kurdish organizations in the diaspora have embarked on the systematic education of children and the production of print material in Kurdish, with various degrees of assistance from local governments. In Sweden, the government has devised its own comprehensive educational program for its Kurdish immigrants, and now publishes textbooks, newsprint, and other materials in both North and South Kurmânji and in two alphabets, catering to the Kurdish immigrant communities from Iraq and Turkey (see **Language** and **Education**).

In France and Austria, and to a lesser extent Germany, government funds have been made available to help with the publication of Kurdish language materials, as well as with other cultural and educational activities. These efforts are, however, far behind the unique Swedish program in both scope and degree of support.

While some financial and technical help has also been forthcoming in Canada (particularly for Kurdish textbooks and education), in Australia and the United States, where much larger Kurdish communities reside, none has been, or is likely to be, provided. The result has been the conspicuous near-absence of Kurdish cultural and educational activities in both countries. The only center for Kurdish studies in the Western Hemisphere, the Kurdish Library and Museum in Brooklyn, New York, for example, is funded entirely by private donations.

Further Readings and Bibliography: A valuable reference book on the achievements and engagements of Kurds in diaspora is Robin Schneider, ed., *Kurden im Exil: Ein Handbuch kurdischer Kultur, Politik und Wissenschaft* (Berlin: Berliner Institut für Vergleichende Sozialforschung, dem Haus der Kulturen der Welt und medico internationa, 1991); Marcel Bazin et al, *Gilân et Âzarbâyjân Oriental: Cartes et Documents Ethnographiques* (Paris: A.D.P.F., 1982); Ismet Ch. Vanly, *Kurdistan und die Kurden,* vol. 2, *Türkei und Irak* (Göttingen: Gesellshaft für bedrohte Völker, 1986); Sureya Badir Khan and Chirug Bletch. *La Question Kurde* (Cairo, 1930); Sharaf al-Din Bitlisi, *Chèref-nameh [Sharafnâma] ou Fastes de la nation kourde,* French trans. Charmoy, 2 vols. (St. Petersbourg, 1868-75).

DEPORTATIONS & FORCED RESETTLEMENTS

Forced deportations have played a major role in Kurdish history. Since at least the second millennium BC and the emergence of the first empires of the Akkadians and Assyrians, mass deportations of the populations of conquered Kurdish territories have been the norm (Wright and Johnson 1975). The necessary historical background for this section is provided under **History,** as well as under **Historical Migrations.**

Regardless of the nature of the policies that have promoted deportations, they have wrought important demographic changes, as they have normally been conducted in tandem with the immigration of other groups to fill the vacated space. The earliest known deportations of Kurds, conducted by the Assyrians, are surprisingly well-documented. Oded counts 18 instances of mass deportations from southern and central Kurdistan (Madaya) and 12 instances from eastern Kurdistan (Manna) in the Neo-Assyrian phase of that empire (745-612 BC) alone. Many of these deportees were settled on lands near the three successive capitals of Assyria (Ashur, Kalhu, and Nineveh, all on the upper Tigris, facing the foothills of central Kurdistan), while those already living there were sent as far as the Mediterranean and the region of Unqi (future Antioch). Many other peoples were forcibly brought in to settle their vacated homes.

On balance, more people were moved into the metropolitan regions of Assyria from the outlying provinces than were deported (Oded 1979). Large numbers of these people, however, did not survive the ordeal, because they lacked resources to support themselves while they acclimated themselves to the new land. Only those who were settled in the cities thrived (e.g., the Jews).

Because of its proximity to Assyrian nerve centers, central Kurdistan suffered the most. In one instance, 65,000 people were deported from the region of modern Sulaymânia (ancient city-state of Namri) in central Kurdistan. This is a tremendous number, perhaps nearly the entire population of the region, considering that the estimated total population for the whole of Kurdistan at this time was only about 1.5 million (see **Demography**).

The formerly populous central Kurdistan was apparently so depopulated by this and 14 additional mass deportations that, as his first act after his conquest of the Assyrian Empire, the Median king Cyaxares brought in a large number of Sagarthians from the region of southern Kurdistan and northern Luristân to populate the land.

Evidence of the deportations and resettlements of this period can also be found in unconventional sources. According to the Talmud, the Assyrians introduced into Kurdistan some Jewish deportees of the first exile. These were not, however, numerous.

Some Middle Persian sources suggest Kurdish deportations, particularly in the later Sasanian era. In addition to the deportation of a number of the Bârzânis to the province of Carmania (modern Kirmân), the Baluchis were forced en masse into the far-off volcanic wastes of Makrân (now Baluchistân) by Chosroes I Anoshervân (r. AD 531-579) and Chosroes II Aparviz (r. AD 591-628). Since the Baluchis were already in the process of migrating, the Sasanian actions may have resulted only their changing direction eastward, rather than following the other Kurds who were migrating toward the northwest at this time. The Sasanians further resettled the Kirkuk region with Neo-Elamite Khuzis from Mishân/Maysân region several times during the course of the third century AD.

During the Islamic period, the Byzantine Empire, benefitting from the decline of Muslim military might in the course of the 10th to 12th centuries, extended its borders once again to cover all of Anatolia to the borders of the Caucasus, as far as the eastern and southern borders of modern Turkey. They soon engaged in a ruthless deportation and slaughter of non-Christian populations of the area, which was almost entirely Kurdish. In the area west of the Euphrates, the upper Halys (Kizilirmâq) basins, and the eastern Taurus, they succeeded in uprooting the ancient Kurdish inhabitants of Commagene, Cappadocia, eastern Pontus, and to some extent, the Jazira region. In their place, the Byzantines, beginning with Emperor Nicephorus Phocas (r. AD 963-969) engaged in a less-than-successful program of repopulating these former Kurdish lands with Christian Aramaeans, whom the Byzantine authors called "White Syrians."

The list of cities earmarked by Nicephorus for such repopulations offers a glimpse of the size of the evacuated area and the havoc it must have inflicted on the native Kurdish population. Malâtya, Maras, Urfâ, Kayseri, Sivas, and Erzincan, as well as Diyârbakir, Mardin, and Nesibin in the Jazira region, are just a few examples. Their strategy of deportation and repopulation soon proved to have fatal consequences for the Byzantines themselves, however. Despite their attempts to repopulate the area, it was nearly vacant when, less than a century later, a flood of Turkic nomads broke into Anatolia following the Battle of Manzikert (1071), and quickly gained control of the region the Byzantines had emptied, literally unopposed. The earlier Kurdish inhabitants, left unmolested, would naturally have resisted the invasion, and the area would not have provided a fertile breeding ground for these nomads, who multiplied there in overwhelming numbers and eventually overtook the Byzantine state. The Kurds are beginning peacefully and organically to reclaim these areas after ten centuries of absence.

Following the battle of Chaldirân (1514) and up until the signing of the Treaty of Zohâb (1639) between the warring Persian and Ottoman Empires, Persia and, to a lesser degree, the Ottoman Empire pursued a disastrous policy of forced depopulation of northern and western Kurdistan. This policy was targeted to achieve five primary goals. Kurds were exiled 1) to break and fragment troublesome, or potentially troublesome, tribes; 2) to press the Kurds into service as border guards for vulnerable frontiers of the Empire outside Kurdistan; 3) to help populate a state-favored region outside Kurdistan suffering from a manpower deficiency; 4) to remove a population with uncertain loyalty to the state, and finally, 5) to make a territory utterly inhospitable for an enemy troop crossing, by removing its entire population and destroying its means of agricultural production—the so-called scorched earth policy (Perry 1975).

Removal of the population from along their borders with the Ottomans in Kurdistan and the Caucasus was of strategic importance to the Safavids. They likely deemed it a matter on which the very survival of the Empire depended. Hundreds of thousands of Kurds, along with large groups of Armenians, Azeris, and Turkmens, were forcibly removed from the border regions and resettled in the interior of Persia. As the borders moved progressively eastward, as the Ottomans pushed deeper into the Persian domains, entire Kurdish regions of Anatolia were at one point or another exposed to horrific acts of despoilation and deportation. These began under the reign of the Safavid Shâh Tahmâsp I (r. 1524-1576). Between 1534 and 1535, Tahmâsp began the systematic destruction of the old Kurdish cities and the countryside. Crops were set alight and irrigation works wrecked. Wells and qanats were filled in or poisoned. When retreating before the Ottoman army, Tahmâsp ordered the destruction of crops and settlements of all sizes, driving the inhabitants before him into Azerbaijan, where they were later transferred permanently, nearly 1000 miles east, into Khurâsân. Some Kurdish tribes were deported even farther east, into Gharjistân in the Hindu Kush mountains of present day Afghanistan, about 1500 miles away from their homes in western Kurdistan.

The magnitude of Safavid destruction can be glimpsed through the works of the Safavid court historians. One of these, Iskandar Bayg Munshi, describing just one episode, writes in the *'Âlam-ârâ yi 'Abbâsi* that Shâh Abbâs I, in furthering the scorched earth policy of his predecessors, "set upon the country north of the Araxes and west of Urmia, and between Kârs and Lake Vân [i.e., northern Kurdistan], which he commanded to be laid waste and the population of the countryside and the entire towns rounded up and led out of harm's way." Resistance was met "with massacres and mutilation; all immovable property—houses, churches, mosques, crops... was destroyed, and the whole horde of prisoners was hurried southeast before the Ottomans should counterattack" (Perry 1975). Many of these Kurds ended up in Khurâsân, but many others were scattered into the Alburz mountains, central Persia, and even Baluchistân. They became the nucleus of several modern Kurdish enclaves outside Kurdistan proper, in Iran and Turkmenistan.

Despite having the upper hand in their confrontation with Safavid Persia, the Ottomans were not by any means above such destructive actions. Their deportations, though not nearly as massive as those sponsored by the Safavids, began earlier. No sooner had western Kurdistan been incorporated into the Ottoman domain, following the Battle of Châldirân, than Sultân Selim I (the Grim), deported several populous Kurdish tribes into central Anatolia, south of modern Ankara. In their place, he settled a few, more loyal, Turkmen tribes. While the deported Kurds became the nucleus of the modern central Anatolian Kurdish enclave, the Turkmen tribes in Kurdistan eventually assimilated.

The events at the 16th and 17th centuries were also decisive in that they effected a fundamental cultural realignment, from the dominance of the sedentary, mainly Pahlawâni-speaking Kurds, to the prevalence of the nomadic, primarily Kurmânji-speaking Kurds in northern and western Kurdistan. This process had already begun as a direct result of the less visible 16-17th century shifts in the international trade routes (see **Trade**). It was exacerbated by the much more visible military ravaging of the land and people. These events wiped out the agriculturalist economy of the area, and the nomadic Kurmânj were left as the only viable Kurdish group to spread and scratch a living off the destitute land.

From 1639 and the signing of the Treaty of Zohâb between the Ottomans and Persia, a relative calm descended upon Kurdistan and its autonomous principalities, only to be broken in 1722.

The fall of the Safavids provided the Ottomans with the opportunity to annex the rest of Kurdistan from Persia. The energetic founder of the Afshârid dynasty of Persia, Nâdir Shâh, challenged the Ottoman takeover in Kurdistan and Iraq. The dark, post-Châldirân years were all but back, this time ravaging southern, eastern, and central Kurdistan—the areas that had escaped the previous two centuries of destruction of the northern and western parts of the country. These now became the primary battlefields between the two warring empires. Cities and town were destroyed, agricultural communities were looted, and the sedentary farmers forced to flee before the armies. The last bastions of the old Kurdish culture and civil life, largely unaffected by the fate of northern and western Kurdistan in the previous two centuries, were thus extinguished.

The physical destruction of these new regions was inevitably followed by the forced relocation and deportation of the inhabitants. Large numbers of Kurds from these areas found themselves deported to the Alburz mountains and Khurâsân, as well as the heights in the central Iranian Plateau. The Laks suffered most. At this time the last remnant of the ancient royal Hadhabâni (Adiabene) tribe of central Kurdistan was removed from the heartland of Kurdistan and deported to Khurâsân, where they are still found today (Map 32). Among the Laks deported to Khurâsân was the Zand tribe of the Deh Pari district of southern Kurdistan. From among them rose Karim Khân Zand, who replaced the Afshârids in 1750 and founded the last Kurdish royal house comparable to the medieval Kurdish dynasties of the Ayyubids or the Daylamites.

Most of the new enclaves resulting from these deportations were jumbles of Kurdish and non-Kurdish groups, dialects, religions, and customs, carelessly thrown together, and remain so to the present time. An ethnographic map of the Kalât region in the Khurâsâni enclave reveals just one of these terminal points in the 16-18th century episode of deportations. In an area the size of Manhattan Island are found (in addition to Turkmens, Azeris, Lurs, and Persians) Kurds who speak North and South Kurmânji, Laki, Gurâni, and Dimili, and practice Sunni and Shi'ite Islam, Yârsânism, and Alevism. Yezidism also is practiced near the Khurâsâni town of Dughâ'i, by Kurds deported from Siirt.

The valor and energy of these Kurdish mountaineers has often marked them for military service in the Babylonian, Persian, Greek, Arabian, Turkish, and even Russian armies. A Kurdish regiment is partly credited for the liberation of the Belarus capital of Minsk from Nazi forces. This regiment was composed of the descendants of those Kurds captured during the Crimean War and settled by the Russians in Smolensk in western Russia. In some cases, large segments of the Kurdish population were transferred to far-off borders of an empire to garrison it against intrusions. The result is the presence of many small Kurdish communities spread across vast stretches of the mountain systems of central and southwestern Asia, on the ethnic boundaries of old warring nations. The Kurds of the Bampur region of Baluchistân and the Hamkaw Kurds of the Bukhârâ and Ferghâna regions, for example, are two surviving communities of garrison Kurds.

Religious persecution of the Yezidis, Bâbis, and other non-Muslim Kurds has very often taken the form of massacres and deportations. Many massacres were carried out against the Yezidis under the Ottomans in the course of the 17th and 18th centuries. These massacres were revisited on the Yezidis in the middle of the 19th century, resulting in their flight into Russian territories in the Caucasus. Lescot counts 20 major massacres of the Yezidis between 1640 and 1910 alone! (see **Yezidism**). The massacres of the Bâbis, and the resulting exodus, likely wiped out this flourishing community in Kurdistan in the late 19th century (see **Bâbism & Bahâ'ism**).

Since the beginning of the 20th century, the magnitude of the deportations has grown once again. Large communities of Kurds were dispersed throughout Turkey by the Turkish Republican army in response to their uprising during and after World War I. Large numbers of Kurds from Darsim and the Murâd River basin were dispersed in small units throughout ethnically Turkish regions of Turkey, particularly the Aegean Sea rimland, from where up to one million ethnic Greeks had earlier been deported, in the aftermath of World War I. The wide dispersion was of course intended to facilitate speedy assimilation of these Kurds into their predominantly Turkish surroundings. Over one hundred thousand were also pushed over the borders of the new Turkish Republic into neighboring states (see **Integration & Assimilation**).

In the Soviet Union, Josef Stalin, in accordance with his notorious ethnic deportation policies during and after World War II, displaced a majority of the Kurds of the Soviet Caucasus, relocating them in Central Asia, Kazakhstan, and Siberia.

Syria, claiming that the Kurds, despite several thousand years of local existence, are newcomers and squatters, deported nearly a third of its Kurds in the 1960s, pushing some toward its borders and others into the interior, as far as the cities of Hama and Damascus. Syria had in fact received a large Kurdish refugee community from Anatolia after the Turkish Republican forces began operations against rebellious Kurdish populations in the course of the 1920s and 1930s. Many of these Kurds, however, moved on to Lebanon, Palestine, Jordan, and Egypt, where they can still be found today leading wealthy and successful lives. Jordan alone now has about 15,000 Kurds, a few of whom have even married into the Jordanian royal family.

Syria (since the 1960s), Iraq (since the late 1970s), and Turkey (since the early 1980s) have all created empty security zones along their borders in Kurdistan by resettling the population elsewhere. These zones are as much as 20 miles wide in Iraq. By physically

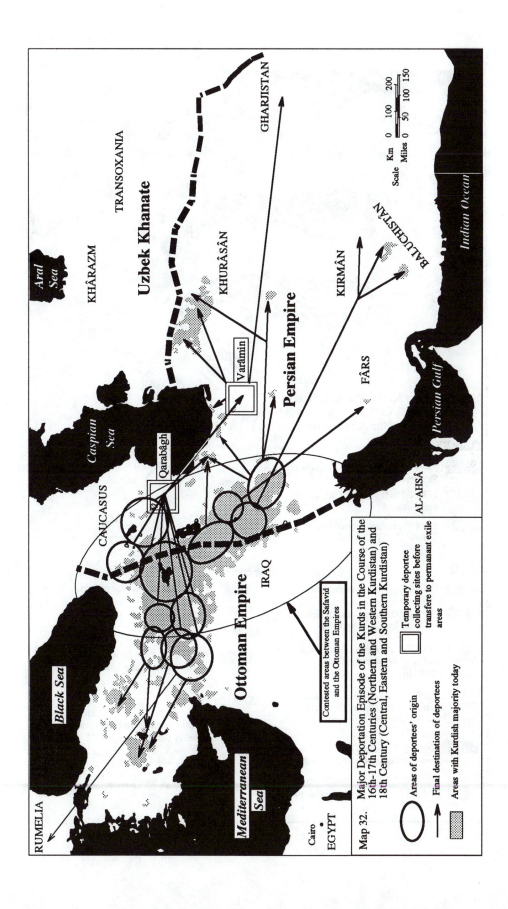

Map 32. Major Deportation Episode of the Kurds in the Course of the 16th-17th Centuries (Northern and Western Kurdistan) and 18th Century (Central, Eastern and Southern Kurdistan)

Contested areas between the Safavid and the Ottoman Empires

Temporary deportee collecting sites before transfere to permanant exile areas

◯ Areas of deportees' origin

→ Final destination of deportees

▓ Areas with Kurdish majority today

RUMELIA

Black Sea

Mediterranean Sea

Cairo
EGYPT

Ottoman Empire

IRAQ

Caspian Sea

Aral Sea

KHÂRAZM

CAUCASUS

Qarabâgh

Varâmin

TRANSOXANIA

Uzbek Khanate

KHURÂSÂN

GHARJISTÂN

Persian Empire

KIRMÂN

FÂRS

BALUCHISTÂN

Persian Gulf

AL-AHSÂ

Indian Ocean

Scale   Km   0   100   200
         Miles 0   50   100 150

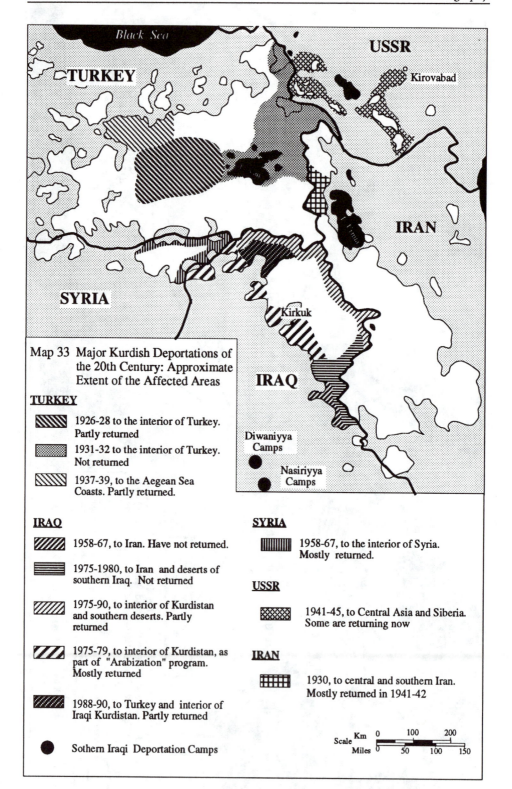

Map 33 Major Kurdish Deportations of
        the 20th Century: Approximate
        Extent of the Affected Areas

TURKEY

1926-28 to the interior of Turkey.
Partly returned

1931-32 to the interior of Turkey.
Not returned

1937-39, to the Aegean Sea
Coasts. Partly returned.

IRAQ

1958-67, to Iran. Have not returned.

1975-1980, to Iran and deserts of
southern Iraq. Not returned

1975-90, to interior of Kurdistan
and southern deserts. Partly
returned

1975-79, to interior of Kurdistan, as
part of "Arabization" program.
Mostly returned

1988-90, to Turkey and interior of
Iraqi Kurdistan. Partly returned

● Sothern Iraqi Deportation Camps

SYRIA

1958-67, to the interior of Syria.
Mostly returned.

USSR

1941-45, to Central Asia and Siberia.
Some are returning now

IRAN

1930, to central and southern Iran.
Mostly returned in 1941-42

Scale Km 0   100   200

Miles 0   50   100   150

separating the Kurds from their kinsmen across the borders, it is apparently hoped they will be rendered incapable of helping one another in their frequent national uprisings. In the cases of Iraq and Syria, unsuccessful attempts were made to populate these areas with Arabs (Map 33).

Since the 1980s Turkey has marked certain troublesome areas of Kurdistan, like Darsim, for depopulation using the pretext of a "forest protection" law. It is doubtful that Turkey will go ahead with full enforcement of these depopulation plans, as the military government has been replaced by a civilian one.

In Iran, under Reza Shah (r. 1925-41), some Kurdish tribes were deported as far away as Fârs and Kirmân. Parts of the Jalâli tribes deported to Fârs in the late 1920s have chosen to remain there, in a small enclave west of Shirâz, while the rest returned to Kurdistan after the Allied invasion of Iran during World War II. After clashes between the government and Iranian Kurdish insurgent forces in the 1980s, reports of some deportations surfaced. If true, they must have been very small, since not much has been made of them by any Kurdish political organization.

The state of Iraq, in little over fifty years of existence, has committed violent acts of deportation that dwarf all others since the Treaty of Zohâb. In recognition of their paramount strategic importance to Baghdad's economic and military security, the Iraqi leadership earmarked two Kurdish communities for the first episode of deportation. The first was the Laki-speaking Faylis community (ancient Pahlas). The domain of these Kurds stretched along the Diyâla river, from the Iranian borders almost to the northeast suburbs of Baghdad. The Iraqi government, disputing their citizenship (most Fayli have historically lived in Iranian territories), deported over 50,000 Faylis across the border into Iran.

The second, and more problematic, case was that of Kirkuk district. With its rich oil fields and many refineries, Kirkuk has been the center of the Iraqi petroleum industry. Baghdad and the Iraqi Kurds have long disputed the sharing of its revenues. Because of the vital importance of Kirkuk to the Iraqi economy, various Iraqi regimes have attempted to increase the Arab ethnic component in the city and region. Kirkuk has traditionally had a minority of Arab, Nestorian (Assyrian), Jewish, and Turkmen residents, with concentrated pockets of these ethnic groups in the plains to the north and southwest of the city. Iraq has engaged in the deportation of the Kurds from the city and its environs, in tandem with incentives designed to augment the Arab minority populations of Kirkuk. (Of course, the economic attraction of Kirkuk did more to bring Arab settlers than any government-sponsored program. Approximately 100,000 Kurds have been removed from the area in this way, although it is unclear how successful Baghdad's repopulation policies have been. Today, it is unlikely that the city itself has a Kurdish majority, and the immediate countryside is witnessing the progressive expulsion of indigenous Kurdish villagers.

The cases of Kirkuk and the Fayli Kurds proved to be just a prelude to much more serious acts of deportation. Since the mid-1960s, Iraqi Kurds have been forced to migrate in great numbers, most to neighboring countries. Internal exile has created in the southern Iraqi deserts near Diwâniyya, Nâsiriyya, and Ramâdi a Kurdish community of several hundred thousand.

The developments following the Persian Gulf War of 1991 forced more Kurds out of their home region in Iraq. At present, nearly a third of the Iraqi Kurds live in exile, either in neighboring countries or in deportation camps within Iraq. This may not change much in the near future.

Further Readings and Bibliography: John Perry, "Forced Migration in Iran During the Seventeenth and Eighteenth Centuries," *Iranian Studies*, VIII-4 (1975); Bustenai Oded, *Forced Migrations and Deportations of People in the Assyrian Empire* (Wiesbaden: Reichert, 1979); Editors, "De la question Kurde, la loi de deportation et de dispersion des Kurdes," *Hawar* 8 (Damascus,

1934); H. Wright and G. Johnson, "Population Exchange and Early State Formation in Southwestern Iran," *American Anthropologist* 77 (1975); Sharaf al-Din Bitlisi, *Chèref-nameh [Sharafnâma] ou Fastes de la nation kourde*, French trans. Charmoy, 2 vols. (St. Petersburg, 1868-75); Robert Conquest, *The Nation-Killers: The Soviet Deportation of Nationalities* (New York: Macmillan, 1970).

INTEGRATION & ASSIMILATION

Peoples have been and shall continue in the future naturally and organically to assimilate or be assimilated into other peoples at various stages of their collective lives. Kurds are no exception, and do not require a separate treatment. It is the forced assimilation of peoples by states that merits special attention here.

A major example of voluntary assimilation of the Kurds is the ongoing case of the Laks. In the past few centuries a segment of the Kurdish nation, the Laks of southern Kurdistan, have been progressively assimilating into their neighboring ethnic group, the Lurs. The Laks still speak a Kurdish dialect, distinct from Luri, which is itself a dialect of Persian. The Laks practice the native Kurdish religion of Yârsânism, while the Lurs are Shi'ite Muslims (see **Language** and **Religion**). Despite these differences, large numbers of Laks now prefer to be counted as Lurs, and are switching their religion and language as well. No state forced this conversion.

Desiring ethnic homogeneity—a prerequisite for the European model of the nation-state—every state in which fragments of the Kurdish nation live today has moved to assimilate the Kurds, as well as other minority populations, into the ruling ethnic group. The exceptions, of course, are where the Kurdish population is insignificant, as in Armenia and Georgia, or where the population is used for other political purposes, as in post-1975 Syria.

The mechanisms employed to achieve this goal have been primarily brute force, and sometimes highly visible, facile schemes, periodically introduced by central state bureaucrats. Means of suppressing the Kurdish culture, history, and language, to the extent of criminalizing the very use of the ethnic name *Kurd*, have been devised and incorporated at various times in the past 70 years into the laws of local states. Except in Iraq, education in the Kurdish language has been strictly denied. Meanwhile, sociologically and economically, Kurdistan has been neglected, regressing and becoming detached from the mainstream. The hope of these states is that Kurds will see the disadvantage of remaining Kurds and assimilate. This has not happened.

One of the earliest and most important ethnic propagandists in the Turkish Republic, under Atatürk, was Sukru Mehmet Sekban, himself a Kurd. He fabricated a history of the Kurds, complete with linguistics, designed to embed the Kurds in the utterly alien Turkic family of peoples, seemingly to spare them the unpleasantness of remaining an ethno-linguistic minority in a hostile social environment.

In 1933, Sekban wrote:

> To get to the point, why should we be afraid of being assimilated linguistically into the other groups? Weak minorities who have assimilated into a strong majority have always fared better. This alone is enough to save them from discrimination.... From the end of the Great War until now [1933], Kurdish language has been the medium of instruction in all elementary schools of Iraqi Sulaymânia district. The benefits attained from this have been nil. What would those who finish these elementary schools do? In what language can they continue their education? Up to date, only few books or articles have been published in this [Kurdish] language, and we must at once admit that no practical benefit is emanating from this attempt.... If the Kurdish language in the best of conditions is propagated for a hundred years, it will not be upgraded to the level of [the language of] civilized nations.... Does the Kurdish nation prefer to be run by dead generations who have left it no worthy heritage? We

must honestly admit that the idea of educating the Kurdish nation in its mother tongue is no longer feasible or desirable... and the self-defeating fanaticism in this regard is to be thus discarded....

However, the British historian Lord Kinross observed, 40 years after the enactment of laws prohibiting education in minority languages in Turkey, that they had achieved the opposite results. In the extreme eastern provinces of Turkey bordering on Iraq and Iran, most Kurdish parents were observed to insist on teaching their children only Kurdish, and had less desire to acquire formal education for them. Lack of a standard and up-to-date education has in turn inhibited progress in minority home regions and prolonged the group's socioeconomically underprivileged and non-integrated position. The Kurds as a whole have turned inward, becoming largely defiant of any change dictated by the Turkish government (see **Education**).

A report by the Turkish National Commission on Education, dated 1959, makes it plain the authorities have been well aware of this fact, and some of them critical of it. It reads,

If [part] of the people living in Turkey today [i.e., the Kurds] are poorer and more backward than others it is not because of the climate of the country nor the character of the individuals. It is because of the lack of education.... The improvement and development of the Turkish soil depends on the development of the people living on it. No development project which does not start with educational development can succeed.

Quite a few Kurds have been deported from their homes to faraway corners of various states in the past and present (see **Deportations & Forced Resettlements**). These have nearly always been relocated en masse in a new locality. On rare occasions, as in Turkey during the deportations of 1923-1938, Kurds were dispersed in groups of just a few families to each alien community, with the hope that isolation and loneliness would break the will of these people to retain their identity. They would then assimilate once and for all for their own and their children's sake. But for all the miseries inflicted on the people, very little if any assimilation can be shown to justify the continuation of this practice.

A law passed in 1932 ordered the deportation, but particularly the dispersion, of the Kurds in Turkey, apparently to force their assimilation. The law provided that

Four separate categories of inhabited zones will be recognized in Turkey, as will be indicated on a map established by the Minister of the Interior and approved by the other Ministers.

Zone one will include all those areas in which it is deemed desirable to increase the density of the culturally Turkish population; zone two will include those areas in which it is deemed desirable to establish populations which must be assimilated into Turkish culture; zone three will be territories in which culturally Turkish immigrants will be allowed to establish themselves, freely but without the assistance of the authorities; zone four will include all those territories which it has been decided should be evacuated and those which may be closed off for public health, material, cultural, political, strategic or security reasons." (cited in Challiand 1980)

Deported Kurds were to be dispersed so thinly as to prevent the establishment of villages where Kurds constituted a majority, and such that they could not constitute more than one-tenth of the overall population of any district to which they were moved. The law, as a means for assimilation, failed.

A third generation descendant of a resettled family, himself raised in the United States, recounted to this author the saga of his family. They were "uprooted from Tunceli

[Darsim] region in Turkey and relocated to a hillside overlooking the Aegean Sea, where they could not understand a word of the spoken [Turkish] language of the local villagers. Despite the kindness of new neighbors, and relative generosity of the local magistrate, they remained feeling as prisoners for twenty-five years, until they felt they could return to Kurdistan once again." Faced with the depressed economy of their former home, lack of adequate education or opportunity for advancement, and the overbearing surveillance of the local people by the authorities, the second generation of the family moved to Western Europe as guest workers. The third generation, most born and raised in Europe, sought and received advanced education in Europe and the United States. They still express determination to "do something" for their ancestral homeland and people, and refuse to allow their children to forget "who they really are."

History reveals a poor success rate for programs of forced assimilation, while it is rife with cases of voluntary assimilation (Izady 1990). Kurds are not an exception to this phenomenon. One can point to many examples of natural assimilation in the Kurdish past, and there will be similar ones in the future. Many Kurdish tribes, such as the Shaqâqis and Kurdânli of Azerbaijan, the Laks of Russian Daghistan, and the al-Shuyukh of the Antioch basins, as well as most of the now-Arab Alevis of Syria, have lost their Kurdish identities and have assumed new ones. Presently, some Kurdish groups, like the Shatrânlu of north-central Iran and the aforementioned Lak population of southern Kurdistan, are in the advanced stages of peaceful and organic assimilation.

The list of modern Middle Eastern personages descended from naturally assimilated Kurdish groups is a long one, and in some cases reveals historical irony. Abdullah Jevdet and Is'hak Sukuti, two founding figures in the Young Turks movement; Zia Gükalp, the "father of pan-Turkish nationalism" (Ramsauer 1957, Heyd 1950, Berkes 1959); Ismet Inönü, a colleague and prime minister of Atatürk and the man who oversaw the holocaust of Kurdish Darsim; and General Kenan Evren, the military President of Turkey in the early 1980s and the architect of the renewed wave of oppression against the Kurds of Turkey, all were assimilated Kurds. The current President of the Turkish Republic, Turgut Özal, now admits to having a Kurdish grandmother.

In Iraq, the list of assimilated Kurds includes President Abdul Karim Qasim, who overthrew the Iraqi monarchy and placed the Kurdish sun disk in the center of the Iraqi state flag (see **Modern History**). Saddam Hussein himself is partly Kurdish through his father's family (revealingly, his brother's name is Bârzân). In Syria President Assad, and the leaders of the other Alevi Arabs like him, as well as the Atrash family are at least partially of Kurdish origin. In Lebanon the Druze political and spiritual leaders of the Jumbalât family, poet Khalil Gibrân, and Shi'ite religious commentator Jurgi Zeidân (1861-1914) are also assimilated Kurds (see **Tribes** and **Historical Migrations**).

In Iran, where suppression of Kurdish culture and identity is least obtrusive, and socioeconomically the Kurds are most integrated into mainstream society, assimilation has been the most common. Of course, the closeness of the dominant Persian culture of Iran to Kurdish culture facilitates such assimilations. However, the assimilation of most Iranian Kurds has not progressed to the point where they lack memory of their Kurdish past, even among those who have lived outside Kurdistan and not spoken Kurdish for generations. Many major Iranian national figures in literature, art, politics and administration, and the armed forces have Kurdish tribal surnames, reminders of their Kurdish origins. The most important secular political party in Iran, the prestigious National Front, is led by Karim Sanjâbi; the prominent opera singer Perry Zangana, and the popular playwright Ali Muhammad Afghani, all introduce themselves as ethnic Kurds, even though none speaks Kurdish.

Further Readings and Bibliography: L. Molyneux-Seel, "Journey into Dersim," *Geographical Journal* 44-1 (1914); G. Perrot, "Les Kurdes de Haimaneh," *Revue des deux Mondes* 55 (1865);

Mehrdad Izady, "Persian Carrot and Turkish Stick," *Kurdish Times* III-2 (1990); United States Helsinki Watch Committee, *Destroying Ethnic Identity: The Kurds of Turkey* (New York: USHWC, 1988); Lord Kinross, *Within the Taurus* (London, 1954); Lord Kinross, *Atatürk: The Rebirth of a Nation* (London: Weidenfeld, 1964); Martin van Bruinessen, "The Ethnic Identity of the Kurds," in Peter Andrews, ed., *Ethnic Groups in the Republic of Turkey* (Wiesbaden: Reichert, 1989); Sukru Mehmed Sekban, *La question kurde. Des Problèmes des minorités* (Paris: Les Presses Universitaires de France, 1933); G. Challiand, ed., *People without a Country* (New York: Zed, 1980); Ernest Ramsauer, *The Young Turks* (Princeton, 1957); Uriel Heyd, *Foundation of Turkish Nationalism* (London, 1950); Niyazi Berkes, *Turkish Nationalism and Western Civilization* (New York: Columbia University Press, 1959); F. McDermott and J. Short, *The Kurds* (London: Minority Rights Group, 1975).

DEMOGRAPHY

No demographic study, detailed or otherwise, specifically focusing on the Kurds has ever been conducted. There are, on the other hand, many valuable studies of the population dynamics and demographic trends of other ancient and contemporary Middle Eastern populations. The Kurdish numbers at any given time in history can be inferred from these. Being physically in the center of the region, Kurdistan is included in almost every demographic study of the Middle East. The difficulty is in determining how many of the people of any given era and area were ethnic Kurds. The method employed here is first to count all those who lived or are living in the Kurdish mountains, and then to present the case that they are Kurds, or otherwise.

In the modern era, the problem is less complicated, but far from simple. Local censuses rarely provide the ethnic breakdown of populations, and when they do, they very often cannot be taken at face value for reasons set forth above; see **Integration & Assimilation** and **National Identity.**

In the absence of regular, reliable, and frequent censuses, scholars and demographers have been forced to deal with very rough estimates based on past counts of varying reliability, using various models to interpret a myriad of raw provincial and national statistics. The only figures beside the provincial totals available from local governments have been the counts for nomadic and semi-nomadic Kurdish tribes. The settled, but particularly the urban, Kurdish citizenry have often been counted as members of the dominant nationality in each state.

As an additional obstacle to any attempt to use untreated state censuses for the calculation, T.F. Aristova observed over a generation ago that because "the census is made for the purpose of tax-collecting or in connection with army recruitment, the [mobile] tribes try to dodge it and frequently migrate over the frontier at the time of a census" (Aristova 1958). Some pastoralist tribes, like the Harki, who move across several international frontiers, have been counted in more than one state census. Furthermore, Turkish statistics count as Kurdish only those tribes who admit Kurmânji Kurdish as their mother tongue, and that only until 1965. In all five states where they live, according to Aristova, "the figures given for the Kurdish population end up to be considerably lower than the actual figure."

The result is radical variation among the figures given for the total number of Kurds in the present century. In fact, the population figures for Kurds have become a heated political issue, as some believe that population figures indicate the political or economic power of a group. Furthermore, it is often asserted that the national origin, and thus the allegiances, of any given researcher play a major role in the population figures he or she provides for the Kurds. But little correlation can be shown between national origin and the figures given by any author. The erratic figures provided by most bespeak a lack of information and/or research rather than personal feelings for the Kurds. As an example, in the period between 1980 and 1986 Pelletiere (an American) provides the lowest figure of 7-7.5 million for all Kurds, followed by Sabar (an Israeli) who gives 7.6 million. Deschner (a German) gives "more than 15 million," More (a Frenchman) 20.1 million, while Vanly (a Kurd) gives 20 million (excluding the Kurds of diaspora), and Eickelman (another American, citing British sources) reports the highest figure, 23.5 million. Meanwhile Kurdoyev, himself a Soviet Kurd, reported no Kurds whatsoever for the Soviet Union of 1957!

For the number of Kurds in Turkey alone, Kaya Toperi, spokesman for President Özal of Turkey, a country that had historically denied the very existence of ethnic Kurds on its territories, in an interview with American National Public Radio on March 1, 1991, provided a figure of 7-12 million for all those people of Turkey "with Kurdish affiliation." Toperi upped his figure to "12-14 million" in three weeks time in another NPR broadcast interview. He further indicated that only about "a third of these people [i.e., the Kurds in Turkey] live in the eastern provinces." The highest numbers for the Kurds, at least those in Turkey, are thus provided by the least expected person, a Turk, speaking for the highest authority in that country. The lowest figure for the Kurds of Turkey, 3 million, is given by an American (Pelletiere 1984). In fact, Pelletiere gives a figure of 8 million for the Kurds of Turkey in 1991—an inexplicable jump of over 250% in 7 years, and demonstration of the confusion and uncertainty over the Kurdish population in that and many other studies.

A lack of awareness of up-to-date state statistics, and of the basics of demographic dynamics, are the major causes for the confusion observed in the works of most authors who report population figures for the Kurds. For example, MacDonald in 1990, after providing figures of 5 million for the Kurds of Iran and 9 million for Turkey, states that the Kurds represent around 3% of the total Iranian state population, and 12% of Turkey. For such an equation to work, the total Iranian population must have been assumed by MacDonald to be 167 million, and that of Turkey to be 75 million in 1990. The official state figures for Iran and Turkey in 1990 were 55.6 million and 56.7 million, respectively.

The confusion need not be there, at least not in such magnitude, as there were and are state censuses from which a good approximation of the Kurdish population totals can be ascertained. The task requires only standard demographic modeling techniques and the availability of national and international data for neighboring ethnic groups as a control mechanism. In this way, a fairly detailed study of Kurdish demographic trends since at least the late 1920s can be carried out and valid future projections made.

The summary presented below is the result of the first demographic study of the Kurds, carried out by this author. When determining their numbers, the definition set forth in the **Preface** has been the guideline in considering a group Kurdish or otherwise: the study respects the word of anyone who claims to be a Kurd. Questions pertaining to the geographical distribution of the Kurds have been treated in the section on **Plotting the Geographical Distribution of Kurds**. Once these questions have been answered, the task is rather straightforward. Local and non-local censuses, studies, informed estimates, and so on have been used for the figures given here, as are the paradigms of other similar local and non-local populations for whom established and reliable numbers are readily available. The necessary historical background for this section is found under **History**, while the sections on **Historical Migrations** and **Deportations & Forced Resettlements** are important in understanding the demographic evolution of the Kurds, and ought to be consulted first.

It is not by accident that Kurdistan has always been a populous land, with occasional population surpluses and emigrations (Smith and Young 1982). Being the locus (or near it) of many profound technological innovations conducive to population growth, such as the domestication of many animals and the development of agriculture, it has seldom lagged behind neighboring regions in demographic growth. Additionally, the land's vast soil, water, timber, and mineral resources have always been able to sustain and promote a large population. The mountain ranges of Kurdistan have served as natural fortifications against frequent outside invasion, hence against the sharp population fluctuations that result from war, until of course the present century. As late as AD 1800, there were as many Kurds (3.51 million) as Egyptians (3.5 million, according to the bureaucrats accompanying Napoleon in Egypt in 1799). Today, the Kurds are fewer than half as many (ca. 28 million) as the Egyptians (ca. 57 million).

In early antiquity, the faster growth rates of the Mesopotamian and Levantine populations were steadily reducing the Kurdish proportion of the overall Middle Eastern population. The slip bottomed out at about 12% of the total around 2000 BC, and then began to reverse itself (see Table 2 and Figure 1).

In the course of the 2nd and 1st millennia BC, progressive waves of Indo-European-speaking nomads inundated the land. This immigration lasted approximately 1500 years, ending by the 4th century BC (although eastern Kurdistan continued to receive Aryan immigrants until the 2nd century AD, in the form of the Alans from the European steppes of the northern Caucasus). This reduced growth rate of the total population by converting portions of Kurdistan from a high-population-density, settled agricultural economy to a low-population-density nomadic economy. The demographic weight of the Kurds in the Middle East increased (from 12% to 12.5%), however, since the populations of the vast territories of the Iranian Plateau, central Asia, and central and western Anatolia suffered even greater losses than the Kurds. Only the neighboring peoples of Mesopotamia and the Levant continued to grow at impressive rates throughout the period of Aryan immigration into the Middle East, albeit at slower rates than before.

At the conclusion of this episode, the population began to grow again, in the 4th century BC. The southern Zagros—very much a part of the Kurdish ethnic home from the 7th century BC to 12th century AD (when it entered a decisive period of ethnic metamorphosis; see **Historical Migrations**)—experienced at this time a great population surplus of migratory nomads. The southern Zagros is physically capable of sustaining a very large number of pastoralists. It is well sheltered from external hostilities, and rich in natural resources, including high-grade pastures. Even today the largest concentration of pastoralist nomads in this part of the world is found in the southern Zagros.

Beginning with the 4th century BC and lasting until the 5th century AD, wave after wave of Kurds migrated northwestward, from the southern Zagros to the central and northern Zagros, western Alburz, eastern Taurus, and Pontus mountains. A spur also went eastward into the Makrân region (modern Baluchistan). Between 0.5 and 0.75 million people (20-30% of all Kurds at the time) could have migrated northwestward in this internal Kurdish migration episode.

By about the beginning of the 5th century AD northern and western Kurdistan, at the receiving end of this migration, in turn entered a period of great population surplus, resulting in a massive outburst of Kurdish emigrants and the establishment of many

Table 2: DEMOGRAPHIC EVOLUTION OF THE KURDS IN THE MIDDLE EAST, 4000–500 BC.

Date	Total Mid East*	Total Kurds	Kurdish % of Mid East Totals
4000 BC	1 million	0.15 million	15
3000	2.5	0.32	13
2000	5.5	0.66	12
1000	9	1.12	12.5
500	12	1.77	12.5

Remarks: The figures for the total Middle Eastern population in 3000, 2000, and 1000 BC are adopted from C. McEvedy and R. Jones (1978), pp. 123-5; figure for 4000 BC is this author's estimate. For figures supplied for 500 BC, see the sources for Table 4.

*For this demographic study, North Africa is excluded from the Middle East.

Fig. 1. Kurdish Demographic Trends, 600 BC to AD 1900.

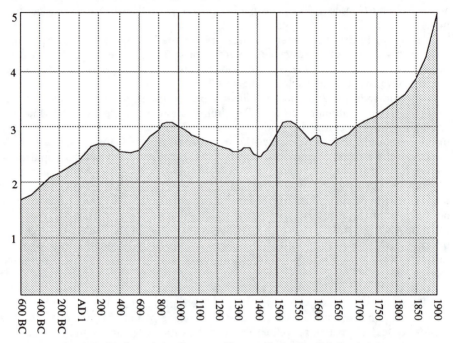

Source: Regional population figures used here to calculate Kurdish population
of any given era are in part based on C. McEvedy and R. Jones (1978).

Kurdish enclaves outside Kurdistan. The process ended only in the 11th century, when large numbers of Turkic nomads arrived from the east. These migrants used Kurdistan primarily as a stopping point on their way farther west into Byzantine and Mesopotamian lands. The dislocation and damage to the lives and property of the sedentary Kurdish population, brought about by the massive Turkic nomadic influx, translated into negative demographic results.

The Turkic nomadic movements abated by the end of the 14th century, just in time for the Black Death to take its toll on the Kurdish population at the end of the 14th and beginning of the 15th centuries. Along with western Anatolia and the Caucasus, Kurdistan suffered the most from the bubonic plague, the spread of which was retarded by the harsher desert climate of the rest of the Middle East. It was by no means, however, as devastating on the Kurdish population as it was in Europe.

If the theories that attribute the prevalence type A blood in a given region to the recurrence of bubonic plague, and type B to cholera, are true, then Kurdistan must historically have suffered much more from cholera than the bubonic plague. Type B blood is the most common type in Kurdistan, followed by A (see **Physical Anthropology**). Population adjustments for the two major outbreaks of bubonic plague, in the 6th and 14th centuries AD, although nowhere near as great as in Europe, must be made nevertheless. The relative dearth of type O blood, seemingly resistant to smallpox, may hint at the infrequency of that disease in Kurdistan. Downward adjustments of the Kurdish population figures need not be made when massive outbreaks of smallpox are recorded for the neighboring populations and lands.

At the end of the cycle of nomadic dislocation and epidemics, around 1425, the Kurdish population bottomed out at about 2.48 million—its lowest since AD 50. The population made a surprising rebound in the following century, gaining 20% by 1520 to reach a high of 3.1 million. Most neighboring populations also experienced similar fast growth at about this time.

Two factors quickly reversed this positive demographic trend among the Kurds: 1) the collapse of the traditional trade-based economy due to the shift in international trade routes from land to sea, bypassing Kurdistan, and 2) the many long wars (including the scorched earth policy of Persia in its defense against the expanding Ottoman Empire) and episodes of massive population deportations. The economic decline and physical devastation of most parts of Kurdistan in the course of the next two centuries caused a reduction in the Kurdish population to 2.7 million by 1638 and the signing of the peace Treaty of Zohâb between the two warring empires.

Following the treaty, the population began to rebound, but very slowly. This slowness was due first to the increase of nomadism among the Kurds, who in the course of the preceding centuries had found settled agriculture to be a high-risk profession, as the farmers were susceptible to frequent looting, capture, deportation, or enslavement by the imperial forces or brigands who roamed the Kurdish marches. It bears repeating that, demographically, an agricultural economy can easily sustain 10 times as many people per unit of land than nomadism.

The shrinkage of the economy due to the stoppage of international trade dramatically slowed the recuperation of the settled agricultural economy in Kurdistan, and hence the return of higher population density. Only by 1725 did Kurdistan regain the population it had over two centuries earlier in 1520.

A new episode of wars and deportations rather briefly befell southern and central Kurdistan, earlier unscathed, from 1725 to 1750, which further retarded its already sluggish growth rates. This last episode, however, had a far greater impact on the culture of Kurdistan than on its demographic growth. It destroyed all that was left of the earlier urban-based culture and its associated educated middle class, which had earlier been wiped out in northern and western Kurdistan during the Perso-Ottoman wars of the preceding centuries. Nonetheless, the high of 3.1 million Kurds in AD 1525 was again reached, and perhaps surpassed, by 1750. Growth now picked up momentum and was sustained until 1914 without any important interruptions.

By the beginning of the 19th century, the modern world finally made itself felt in Kurdistan with the expansion of the Russian Empire into the Caucasus. New technologies, modes of production, and better health care, among other advances brought by the Europeans into the East, caused an explosion in the natural growth rates of the Kurds and neighboring populations. International trade, this time northward with Russia, returned to Kurdistan, albeit on a moderate scale. The agriculturalist economy thus began a comeback, at the expense of the nomadic economy, heralding the final decline of the nomadic economy. As a result, the population jumped to 3.9 million by 1850 from 3.51 in 1800, and boomed to 5.04 million by the beginning of the 20th century.

These seemingly fast growth rates were dwarfed by the rates registered in the first decade of the present century, after which another period of demographic decline began in Kurdistan, at the start of World War I. By 1914, the Kurds had already begun to lose demographic ground to their major neighboring ethnic groups, the Turks and Armenians in particular. The war only intensified it. By 1920 the decline was most obvious, with its causes being as much the widespread massacres, deportations, famines, and epidemics as the devastation of the Kurdish economy and basic sanitation. A glance at the magnitude of these demographic losses can be obtained from the following.

In the course of World War I, the four Ottoman provinces of Vân, Bitlis, Diyârbakir, and Elâzig alone lost, respectively, 62%, 42%, 26%, and 16% of their non-Christian (that is, excluding the predominantly Christian Armenian and Assyrian inhabitants), and primarily Kurdish, population. Large numbers of these losses were due to death, but surely not all, as often depicted. For these four provinces, the total non-Christian loss

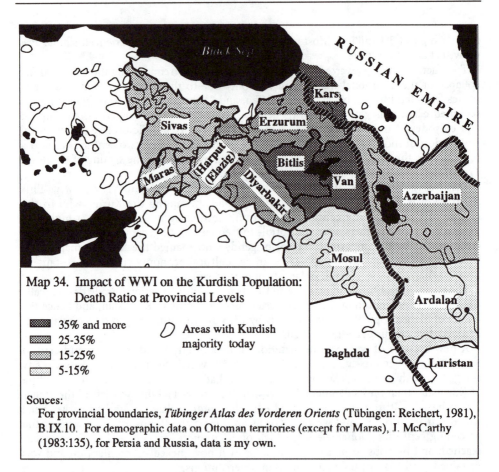

Map 34. Impact of WWI on the Kurdish Population:
Death Ratio at Provincial Levels

35% and more
25-35%
15-25%
5-15%

Areas with Kurdish
majority today

Souces:
For provincial boundaries, *Tübinger Atlas des Vorderen Orients* (Tübingen: Reichert, 1981),
B.IX.10. For demographic data on Ottoman territories (except for Maras), J. McCarthy
(1983:135), for Persia and Russia, data is my own.

amounted to 611,000 (McCarthy 1983). Of this figure, perhaps 450,000-500,000 were due
to death, of which it is reasonable to assume that between 350,000 and 400,000 were
Kurds, as they constituted the predominant non-Christian element of the population of
these provinces.

On the loss of Kurdish lives in other provinces, we can only speculate, as no reliable
figures can be found from local censuses. The problem is compounded by the heavy
population transfers that took place during, and shortly after, the war. Quite likely, the
province of Kârs lost the highest percentage of all. Changing hands several times between
1914 and 1923, the human and ethnic face of the Kârs province was totally remade in this
short span of time, preventing any meaningful estimations of its true losses to death or
migration. The total loss of Kurds in all the Ottoman and Russian provinces as well as
Persia can be safely estimated at about 500,000, including casualties attributable to both
the World War I and its aftermath, from 1914 to 1925. This represented nearly 10% of
the 1914 Kurdish population (Map 34).

From 1914 to 1930, the Kurdish population actually decreased in absolute numbers,
but far more so in relative numbers. This was at a time when, excepting the Armenians,
every other major ethnic group in the area was increasing its numbers in both absolute
and relative terms. The relative demographic loss of ground by the Kurds continued until
1950, when it stopped and then, by 1955, reversed itself (Table 3).

Since the middle of the 1960's the Kurdish demographic growth has picked up
increasing momentum. The Kurds are steadily regaining their former demographic
position, representing 15% of the overall population of the Middle East in Asia. This has

Table 3: Kurdish Demographic Trends in the 20th Century.

Year	TURKEY			IRAN			IRAQ			SYRIA			CAUCASUS & CENT. ASIA	Total Percent Change Over	
	All	Kurds	%	All	Kurds	%	All	Kurds	%	All	Kurds	%	Kurds	Kurds	Previous Decade
1900	13.3	2.99	22.5	10	1.2	12	2.25	.61	27	1.75	.17	10	.07	5.04	
1910	14.2	3.15	22.2	11.8	1.35	11.5	2.29	.64	28	2.0	.18	9	.06	5.38	6.75
1920	13.1	2.85	21.7	10	1.3	13	2.5	.67	27	2.1	.18	8.6	.05	5.05	6.13–
1930	14.4	2.95	20.5	12.1	1.51	12.5	3.0	.75	25	2.25	.29	12.9**	.07	5.57	10.3
1940	17.8	3.39	19.1	13.8	1.66	12	3.8	.87	23	2.5	.26	10.4	.13	6.31	13.29
1950	20.9	3.97	19	17.5	2.1	12	4.77	1.1	23	3.25	.32	9.8	.12	7.61	20.6
1960	27.8	5.25	18.9	22.6	2.71	12	6.5	1.46	22.5	4.43	.41	9.2	.16	9.99	31.27
1970	36.0	7.04	19.5	28.7	3.5	12.2	9.8	2.25	23	6.6	.59	9	.23	13.61	36.24
1980	46.0	9.78	21.3	39	4.8	12.4	12.1	3.15	25*	9.1	.83	9.1	.28	18.84	38.43
1990	56.7	13.65	24.1	55.6	6.6	12.4#	18.8	4.4	23.5*	12.6	1.16	9.2	.34	26.15	37.21

All populations in millions. Figures have been rounded

Remarks: For the states like Iran which conduct their general census in mid-decade, the figures for the end of the decades are my calculations based on their average annual growth rates.

* Large numbers of Iraqi Kurds have been forced into the neighboring countries, particularly Iran since 1975. While most will eventually return, some are bound to stay or move outside the Middle East. The number of Kurds remaining in Iraq can now (1991) be as low as 3.5 million, constituting only about 21.1% of the total Iraqi population of 16.6 million (the total Iraqi figure of 18.8 of 1990 should be reduced by 2.6 million to account for the flight of the Kurds and nearly 1.5 million Arab guest-workerers and the Shi'ites, plus heavy war-related casualties of nearly 0.2 million, then adjusted for the natural growth for the one year, 1990-91 period).

** Mainly due to influx of Kurdish refugees from Anatolia. Abut 50,000 of these moved on to Lebanon, Jordan and Palestine in the course of the next 15 years.

\# The percentage of Kurds in the total Iranian population would have fallen between 1970 and 1990 (due to slower natural growth rates than the state average), if it was not for the influx of the Iraqi Kurdish refugees in that period who have settled, seemingly permanently, in Iran.

Sources (in addition to those provided for the text): For the state demographic data of the period 1900-present: *World Development Report* (1986), Turkey, James Spitler and Michael Roof, *Detailed Statistics on the Urban and Rural Population of Turkey: 1950-2000* (1982).

been primarily the result of what has effectively been a policy of socioeconomic apartheid in Turkey. The policy has inadvertently spawned a demographic phenomenon that has already wreaked havoc with the ethnic composition of other states that have pursued similar policies. While the advanced health care systems in Turkey have drastically reduced infant mortality rates and extended the longevity of all of its citizens, the socioeconomic system has fostered much lower rates of education and socioeconomic underdevelopment of the backward Kurdish regions of the east, as compared to western Turkey. There are much lower literacy rates and job opportunities for the Kurds in general and the fertile Kurdish women in particular. At a time when the Turkish state system for the past 40 years has steadily cut down the infant mortality rates for the Kurds, little incentive has been given to the would-be mothers to practice birth control for the potential of a better life or a career. While ethnic Turks are reducing their fertility rates to the levels of the European countries, the Kurdish citizens of Turkey are experiencing the runaway fertility rates common to the rest of the Middle East.

The same phenomenon that is increasingly turning Turkey more Kurdish, was largely responsible for turning South Africa from a nation nearly 38% white at the turn of the century to 16% white in 1970 and just about 10% today. At the grand level, Europeans who accounted for over a third of the world population in 1900, constitute only 9% of the world total today.

For the purposes of this study, the Kurdish demographic growth in Turkey has been estimated based on Middle Eastern demographic trends (as compared to what would be expected for the ethnic Turks, who have been maintaining very low, steadily declining, European rates; see Table 4b). I have utilized average Syrian, Iraqi, and Iranian state annual growth rates, and applied them to the entire Kurdish population for the past 20 years. An exception was made for the decade of the 1960's, when the Turkish state average was applied to the total Kurdish population. This was done because, as the Kurds in Turkey grew faster than the Turks in the 1950's, they were growing slower outside Turkey. These factors made the Turkish state average rate a reasonable figure.

This Kurdish demographic growth is now manifesting itself in geographical terms as well, particularly in Turkey. The general westward economic attraction in Turkey has been gradually shifting the Anatolian Kurdish demographic center of gravity westward—away from the Zagros and towards the Taurus and Pontus mountains. The cities there are becoming large Kurdish urban centers (see **Urbanization & Urban Centers**), reversing a Byzantine act that expelled the Kurds from the area about 1100 years earlier.

Despite the confusion over the total number of Kurds, by consensus, Kurds are believed to constitute the fourth largest ethnic group in the greater Middle East, after the Arabs, Persians, and Turks, in that order.

The largest concentrations of Kurds are now in Turkey (52% of all Kurds), Iran (25.2%), Iraq (16.8%), Syria (4.9%), and the Commonwealth of Independent States (1.1%). The Iraqi Kurds constituted about 17.5% of all Kurds until 1975. The large number of Iraqi Kurds who subsequently settled in Iran as war refugees have been properly subtracted from the Iraqi Kurdish totals, and added to that of the Iranian Kurds, as they have for all practical purposes acclimated and permanently settled in that state. The figure of 16.8% thus reflects this earlier loss of Iraqi Kurds, but not the far more serious losses of the late 1980's and 1991, the ultimate course of which has yet to be completed. It is doubtful that presently any more than 12% of the total Kurds still live on the territory of the state of Iraq.

FUTURE TRENDS

Future Kurdish demographic trends can be projected along the lines of projected growth rates for Syria, Iraq, and Iran. Instead of averaging the three state growth rates, as was done for the period 1970-1990, *the median point of the three is employed here for this purpose.* The demographic relevance of these states to the Kurds is obvious. Overall Kurdish demographic growth in the near future is therefore assumed here to match that of the Syrian state average for the period 1990-2000, that of Iraq for 2000-2020, and halfway between that of Iran and Iraq 2020-2050. Since Iran is projected to register annual growth rates from 2020 onward far larger than the other two, a conservative midpoint between the Iranian and Iraqi rates is a better choice than the true median in this case. Because the calculated growth figures for the Kurds are just median points, naturally in any given period there will be neighboring populations who are actually growing faster, as there will be those who are growing slower, than the Kurds. Table 4b summarizes these comparative calculations.

John Maynard Keynes once observed that "the great events of history are often due to slow changes in demography, hardly noticed at the time." Kurds may prove this thesis one more time. Barring a catastrophe, Kurds will become the third most populous ethnic group in the Middle East by the year 2000, displacing the Turks. Furthermore, if present demographic trends hold, as they are likely to, in about two generations' time the Kurds will also replace the Turks as the largest ethnic group in Turkey herself, re-establishing an Indo-European language (Kurdish) as the principal language in that land—as it had been from the time of the Hittites to the demise of the Byzantines.

The total number of Kurds is now growing by roughly 1 million people per annum, which should increase to 1.5 million per annum after the year 2000 and remain at that level until around 2020. Afterwards, the annual growth rates should begin a gradual but steady decline, falling to just below 1 million per year after 2035, and half as much by 2045. Zero growth should be reached between 2055 and 2065, when the Kurdish population will commence a long-term decrease in absolute numbers on the way to the postmodern demographic maturity (Table 4a).

Further Readings and Bibliography: P. Smith and T. Cuyler Young, "The Force of Numbers: Population Pressure in the Central Zagros 12000-4500 BC," *The Hilly Flanks, Essays on the Prehistory of Southwestern Asia* (Chicago: The Oriental Institute of the University of Chicago Press, 1982); B.B. Spooner, ed., *Population Growth: Anthropological Implications* (Cambridge: Harvard University Press, 1972), particularly, P. Smith and T. Young's article, "The Evolution of Early Agriculture and Culture in Greater Mesopotamia: A Trial Model"; P. Smith, "Iran 9000-4000 BC," *Expedition* 13 (1971); J.B. Bridsell, "Some Population Problems Involving Pleistocene Man," *Population Studies: Animal Ecology and Demography, Cold Spring Harbor Symposia in Quantitative Biology* 22 (Cold Spring, Colorado, 1957); T. Cuyler Young, "Population Dynamics and Philosophical Dichotomies," in L.D. Levine and T.C. Young, Jr., eds., *Mountains and Lowlands: Essays in the Archaeology of Greater Mesopotamia* (Malibu, California: Bibliotheca Mesopotamica, vol. 7, 1977); Ahmad Sousa, *Atlas of Iraq* (Baghdad, 1953); Peter Andrews, ed., *Ethnic Groups in the Republic of Turkey* (Wiesbaden: Ludwig Reichert Publisher, 1989); T.F. Aristova, "Poyezdka k Kurdam Zakavka'ya" ("A Visit to the Kurds of Transcaucasia") *Sovetskaya Etnografiya* VI (Moscow,

TABLE 4A. KURDISH PRESENT AND NEAR FUTURE DEMOGRAPHIC TRENDS.

Year		1990			2000			2020			2050	
State	Total Pop.	Total Kurds	% Kurdish	Total Pop.	Total Kurds	% Kurdish	Total Pop.	Total Kurds	% Kurdish	Total Pop.	Total Kurds	% Kurdish
Turkey	56.7	13.7	24.1	65.9	18.7	28.4	87.5	32.3	36.9	105.8	47.0	44.4
Iran	55.6	6.6	12.4	73.9	9.0	12.6	130.6	16.2	12	192.5	23.1	12.1
Iraq	18.8	4.4	23.5	26.5	6.4	24	44.8	10.9	24.5	62.2	15.0	25
Syria	12.6	1.3	9.2	17.2	1.6	9.2	28	2.7	9.8	33.7	3.9	11
CIS*		0.3			0.5			0.9			1.1	
Totals		26.3			36.2			63.0			90.2	

TABLE 4b. COMPARATIVE POPULATION GROWTH RATES, PAST AND NEAR FUTURE.

	Past State Population Growth: Annual Rates (%)			Projected State Population Growth: Overall Rates (%)		
				1990-	2000-	2020-
State	1965-73	73-84	84-90	2000	2020	2050
Turkey	2.5	2.2	2.1	16.2	32.7	20.9
Iran	3.0	3.1	3.6	32.9	76.7	47.4
Iraq	3.3	3.6	3.9	41.0	71.8	38.8
Syria	3.4	3.4	3.8	36.5	62.8	20.4
KURDS	3.5	3.8	3.7	36.5	71.8	43.1

All populations are in millions.
All figures rounded to the nearest decimal point.
* CIS, The Commonwealth of Independent States, refers to the territories of the former Soviet Union, dissolved in 1991.
Source: Present state population figures and their projected growth trends are based on *World Population Data Sheets* (Washington, DC: Population Reference Bureau, annual report sheet for 1990).

1958); *Annual Abstract of Statistics, 1970* (Baghdad: Government of Iraq, 1971); *Statistical Abstract 1973* (Damascus: Government of Syria, 1973); *Population Census 1970* (Damascus: Government of Syria, 1972); *World Population Data Sheets* (Washington, DC: Population Reference Bureau, annual report sheet for 1990); James Spitler and Michael Roof, *Detailed Statistics on the Urban and Rural Population of Turkey, 1950-2000* (Washington: US Bureau of the Census, International Demographic Data Center, 1982); Justin McCarthy, *Muslims and Minorities: The Population of Ottoman Anatolia and the End of the Empire* (New York: New York University Press, 1983); Kemal Karpat, *Ottoman Population, 1830-1914: Demographic and Social Characteristics* (Madison: University of Wisconsin Press, 1985); Günther Deschner, *Saladins Söhne, Die Kurden–das betrogene Volk* (Munich: Droemer Knaur, 1983); S. Pelletiere, *The Kurds, An Unstable Element in the Gulf* (Boulder, Colorado: Westview, 1984); Dale Eickelman, *The Middle East: An Anthropological Approach* (Englewood Cliffs: Prentice-Hall, 1981); Ismet Vanly, *Kurdistan und die Kurden*, vol. 2, *Türkei und Irak* (Göttingen: Gesellschaft für bedrohte Völker, 1986); Scott MacDonald, "The Kurds in the 1990s," *Middle East Insight* vii-1 (1990); K.K. Kurdoyev, "Kurdy," *Narodr Mira, Narody Predney Azii*, Izd-vo AN/SSSR (Moscow, 1957); Christiane More, *Les Kurdes Aujourd' hui: Movement National et Partis Politiques* (Paris: Éditions L'Harmattan, 1984); M.A. Cook, *Population Pressure in Rural Anatolia* (Oxford: Oxford University Press, 1977); Vital Cuinet, *La Turquie d'Asie*, 4 vols. (Paris, 1890-94); Colin McEvedy and Richard Jones, *Atlas of World Population History* (Harmondsworth: Penguin, 1978); *Köy Envanter Etüdleri*, (Village inventory studies [of Turkey]," in Peter Andrews, ed., *Ethnic Groups in the Republic of Turkey* (Wiesbaden: Reichert, 1989); an excellent resource on the Iranian Kurds remains A. Razmara, ed., *Geographical Dictionary of Iran*, 10 vols. (Teheran: The Iranian Armed Forces Geographical Bureau, 1949-51). The text is in Persian, and still in print.

URBANIZATION & URBAN CENTERS

Kurdistan contains the archaeological remains of some of man's earliest experiments with urbanization. A number of the most ancient sites that can be referred to as cities, and not villages, are found in Kurdistan. An early city is distinguished from a village when it can be demonstrated that it contained a sophisticated society composed of various classes and gilds, controlled a set territory for basic supplies of consumer goods, generated its own economic growth on the basis of its controlled resources, and had some standing defense force or militia. To these qualifications was later to be added writing, first for recording commercial transactions and later for other needs (see

Prehistory & Early Technological Development).

Most, if not all, of these early cities gradually expanded their area of control into the surrounding smaller communities of villages and other settlements, forming in effect a city-state. The city-states in their turn expanded, even absorbing other city-states, until they was subsequently formed what can be termed kingdoms, for which the original cities served as the capital.

A large number of ancient sites in Kurdistan qualify by this definition as having been cities. Some better-known sites are Çayönü (western Kurdistan), Jarmo and Tapa Gawâra (central Kurdistan), Ganj Dara, and Godin (southern Kurdistan), all founded prior to 5000 BC. Many more urban sites of lesser age dotted the Kurdish landscape before the closing of the prehistoric era (ca. 3000 BC), with the most important being the sites of Seh Gâbi and Hâji Firuz.

By the beginning of the historic era, urbanization had become the norm in Kurdistan. Kurdish cities, with few exceptions, remained small in number of inhabitants. They usually had about one-tenth the number of residents of the average contemporary Mesopotamian city. But there were far more of them in Kurdistan.

Another characteristic of these early cities in Kurdistan is rather graphically, recorded in the Assyrian bas reliefs of the 9th-7th centuries BC. In the myriad of cities the Assyrians sieged and pillaged in the Kurdish highlands, there appears to have emerged a uniquely Kurdish style of urban planning as well (see **Architecture & Urban Planning**).

Some contemporary Kurdish cities trace their extraordinarily long histories to these early urban settlements. Modern Hamadân, Arbil, and Malâtya are the ancient Ecbatana, Arba Ilu (Greek and Latin Arbela), and Melidi (Greek and Latin Melitene). Many of these cities boast continuous habitation in the range of 4000 years. In fact, imposing mounds marking the ancient settlements are still in the heart of Hamadân, Arbil, Malâtya, Shâhâbâd, and Kirmânshâh.

The majority of modern Kurdish cities, however, can trace their history with clarity and certainty only to the beginning of the classical period (5th century BC). Kangawar (ancient Cancubar), Dinawar (Dun), Kirind (Carina), Saqqez (Sacaes), Sulaymânia (Shahrazur), Kirkuk (Karkhu de Bêt Salukh), Shahrabân (Satrap), Diyârbakir (Amid), Urfâ (Ruhha), and Mardin (Mardis) are among these.

The late classical and early medieval periods are well-documented periods of Kurdish history due primarily to the various types of record-keeping in the Kurdish cities (see **Classical History**). It is tempting to interpret this wealth of urban records as an expansion in urbanism per se. However, it can be explained as the result of better preservation of historical records for the cities of the era. But there is additional evidence to support the notion that the rate of urbanization did in fact increase.

Both native and foreign sources carry many direct accounts of town building by monarchs such as the Sasanians and others in the area of Kurdistan. There is also evidence of population movements into these new cities from the surrounding countryside as well as far off lands. The case of Kirkuk is already mentioned in the section **Deportations & Forced Resettlement**.

The comparatively strong urban nature of Kurdish society extended well into the early medieval and Islamic periods. A decline however set in by about the 12th century. This coincides with a massive influx of Turkic nomads into the country and moving through it toward the west. A speedy conversion of the Kurdish economy to a low density, marginal nomadic economy from the beginning of the 16th century, and the frequent wars, deportations, and depopulations of the countryside, turned the surviving Kurdish cities into strongly fortified and shrunken urban islands in a vast sea of overtly anti-urban, pastoralists. The disruption of the overland east-west trade by wars and then its transfer to marine transportation over the southern seas provided the coup de grâce for the ancient and traditional urban centers in Kurdistan.

Imposing and picturesque castles and fortresses dot the mountain tops of northern and western Kurdistan. Far from being just military outposts or tribal chieftains' castles, these are the surviving relics of the early modern Kurdish cities' adjustment to a militantly anti-urban countryside. Despite their small size, capable of housing only a few thousand inhabitants at the most, these are actual towns or cities, many of which boasted a local aristocracy who fostered art and culture. Almost every luminary in Kurdish cultural life of the early modern times was nurtured and supported in these castle-like towns and cities. Mullay Jaziri and Ahmad Khâni are two of the most prominent examples (see **Literature**).

The urban centers in Kurdistan are just beginning to recover from nearly 800 years of decline. Since the 1950s the rate of urbanization has began to increase.

There is now one Kurdish city with a population of nearly one million (Kirmânshâh/Kermânshâh/*Kirmâshân*), two with around half a million (Diyârbakir/*Diyârbakr* and Kirkuk/*Karkuk*), five with between a quarter and half a million (Malâtya, Urfâ/Sanliurfa, Arbil/Erbil/Irbil/*Hawlar*, Sulaymânia Suleimania/*Slemâni*, and Hamadân), and 18 with between 100,000 and 250,000 people (Tunçeli/Dersim/*Darsim*, Bingöl/*Chapakhchur*, Mus/*Moush*, Agri/Karakuse/*Kusa*, Sanandaj/*Senna*, Mahâbâd/Sauj Boulagh/*Sablâkh*, Shâhâbâd/Hârunâbâd/Islâmâbâd/*Shââbâd*, Khânaqin, Mardin, Adiyâman, Ardahân, Elâzig/*Kharput*, Erzincan/*Arzingân*, Gaziantep/Antep, Dohuk/Dahuk, Kifri, Quchân/Qochân, and Polatli). (The standard spelling of each city name is followed by other common variant names and spellings. The Kurdish name, if different from standard form, is given in italics.) (See Maps 35 and 36.)

Like education, urbanization is a good indicator of the involvement or retreat of the Kurds from the national lives and mainstream of the local states. Using available state statistics on urbanization and education, an interesting trend emerges. It indicates a direct correlation between the rate of education and urbanization, while the rate of education is itself directly correlated to level of the use of the Kurdish language as the medium of instruction (see **Education** and **Integration & Assimilation**). Only in Iraq and the territories of the former Soviet Union have the Kurds enjoyed that educational privilege, and there they show the highest rates of urbanization among all Kurds. In Turkey, on the other hand, where the Kurds enjoy the least recognition for their ethnic identity, culture, and language, and are exposed to the most vigorous attempts at assimilation, Kurdish regions and the Kurds in general are the least urbanized, and sinking to levels less than half that of the national average.

In Iran, the state census of 1986 found the national average rate of urbanization to be 54.2%. In the Kurdish provinces of West Azerbaijan, Kordestan, Kirmânshâhân, and Ilâm, on the other hand, 45.8%, 39.6%, 56.28%, and 40.8%, of the populations, respectively, were classified as urban. These are, however, misleading figures. If we were to exclude the mixed populations of the two largest cities of Kirmânshâh and Urmiâ from these figures, as they are not reflective of typical urbanization trends of the Kurds by themselves, the percentages for West Azerbaijan and Kirmânshâhân would sink to 32.% and 36%, respectively, making the Kurdish provinces the least urbanized of the 24 Iranian provinces, with the sole exception of the small Kuh-Giluya province with its large pastoralist population. Even the desolate wastelands of Baluchistan turn out to be more urbanized than Kurdistan.

The neighboring provinces to Kurdistan that have large Kurdish populations, like Hamadân and Luristân, also show low urbanization levels, of 37.1% and 46.6%, respectively.

Unlike education, no strong correlation is observed between the economic integration of Kurdistan into local states and the Kurdish level of urbanization. In Iran, for example, despite greater economic integration in the Kurdish regions, the Iranian Kurds and their home provinces are still the least urbanized of all Iranian minorities and regions.

Overall, Kurds remain far less urbanized than the other major ethnic groups in Iran, Turkey, and Syria, and slightly less urbanized than average in Iraq.

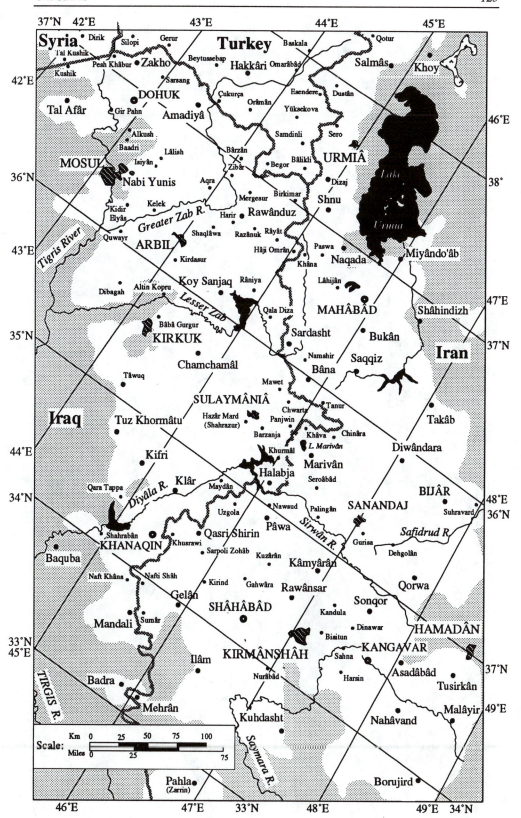

Map 35: Cities and Towns in Southern, Central, and Eastern Kurdistan.

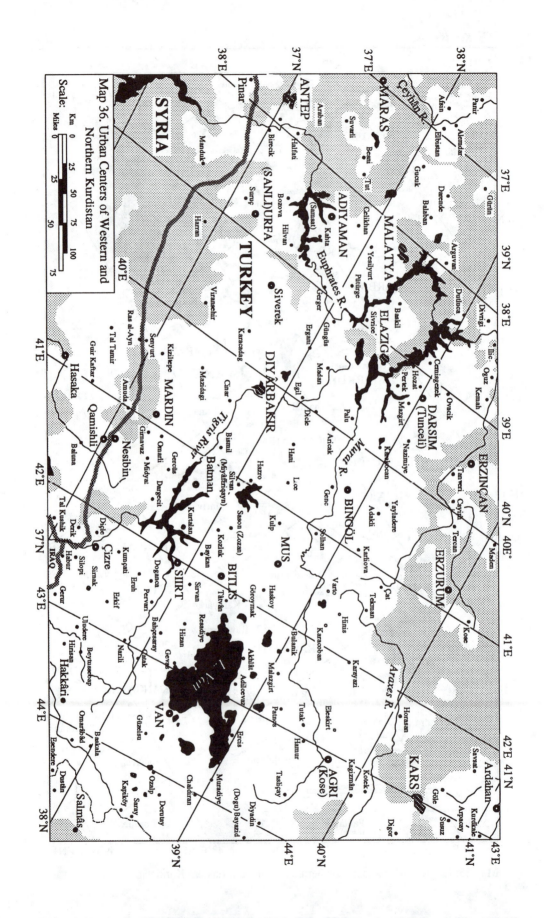

Map 36. Urban Centers of Western and Northern Kurdistan

Scale:

Km 0   25   50   75   100

Miles 0   25   50   75

While the Kurdish cities are expanding, albeit at moderate rates, hundreds of Kurdish villages and smaller towns have been destroyed in the course of the wars and struggles that have taken place on Kurdish lands in Iraq and to a lesser extent Iran over the past 17 years. Most of the inhabitants of the destroyed villages and smaller towns have been forced into the cities, or in the case of Iraq deported outside Kurdistan. Iraqi Kurdistan has suffered rather catastrophically, with many parts of Iranian Kurdistan close behind. The intermittent waves of Iraqi Kurdish refugees into Iran have greatly swollen the population of the Kurdish cities in that country. This is in addition to those Iranian Kurdish villagers from the border regions who sought refuge in the cities after the start of the Iran-Iraq war in 1980. The Iranian government gives, for example, a figure of 267,000 for the Iraqi Kurdish refugees alone who have been settled in Kirmânshâh since 1988, pushing the totals for that city to nearly one million inhabitants. Iranian state censuses do not normally count the refugees with the native inhabitants of the Iranian cities. Many Kurdish cities in Iran, therefore, are officially inhabited by fewer people than in actuality, with Sardasht, Bâna, Marivân, Pâwa, and Bukân officially registering only between a half to one-third of those who actually live there. The totals for these cities can be adjusted to near actuality, since fairly detailed official figures for the location and number of refugees are available.

The Syrian-, Turkish-, and Soviet-administered regions of Kurdistan have suffered little or not at all from these recent upheavals, which has allowed for normal rates of urbanization.

Kurdish demographic growth in many Turkish cities on the peripheries of Kurdistan and beyond, meanwhile, is changing their ethnic composition. All cities along the eastern flanks of the Taurus range from Erzincan and Elâzig to Malâtya, Antep, and Maras should have a Kurdish majority by now, or will by the end of this decade. These cities are the first stops in the westward movement of large masses of Kurdish economic migrants (see **Modern Emigrations & Diaspora**). Those who choose to stay become the source of an additional Kurdish element in the cities' ethnic composition. Being on the fringes of the "Wild East," the cities in the eastern Taurus regularly lose many Turks, but attract very few to replace them. They are fast becoming the largest Kurdish cities, outranking any in the deep mountains. It is now possible that even populous Diyârbakir may soon lose its position as the largest Kurdish city in Anatolia, either to fast-growing Malâtya or Antep.

To the far north, while the smaller towns of Ardahân, Ârpâchây, and Göle are Kurdish in ethnic composition, the large and strategic city of Kârs, with a population nearing 300,000, has retained the features of a centralist, non-Kurdish outpost of western Turkey in the deep east. The city is only beginning to experience the weight of job-seeking Kurdish immigrants. The countryside around Kârs has already been Kurdified to an advanced degree.

Farther afield, Kurds have been settling in large numbers in the Turkish cities of Adana, Ankara, and Istanbul. There they have established populous ethnic quarters for themselves. In fact, metropolitan Istanbul probably houses more Kurds than any other city in Turkey or elsewhere, including in Kurdistan itself!

The same migration patterns observed in Turkey are fast changing the ethnic composition of Hamadân and Kirmânshâh, as well as other Iranian cities formerly with largely non-Kurdish populations, such as Urmiâ, Shâhâbâd, and Kangawar (see **Ethnic Minorities in Kurdistan**).

The city of Kirkuk presents an interesting contrast. The center of the Iraqi oil industry, Kirkuk almost certainly now has an Arab plurality. Kirkuk has always had a mixed population. The city's spectacular economic expansion in the past half century could have turned Kirkuk into the largest Kurdish urban center in general. While government intervention to prevent that from happening has certainly been a factor in retarding Kurdish demographic expansion in the city, the present ethnic plurality in Kirkuk is much more the result of the city becoming a natural magnet for job-seekers from across Iraq. Similar ethnic shifts can be observed in the petroleum cities of Iran, like Ahvâz,

Mâhshahr, and Âbâdân, where the indigenous Arab population has been overwhelmed by the job-seeking immigrants from across the country, including Kurds.

Mosul, after Baghdad the second largest city in Iraq, is becoming predominantly Kurdish, with the influx of Kurdish war refugees being the primary cause. The city is surrounded on three side by the Kurds, with the quarter of Nabi Yunis (ancient Nineveh) on the east bank of the Tigris having been almost exclusively Kurdish since before the turn of the century. With a meager ethnic Arab population nearby, and little to attract Arab immigrants from afar, Mosul's rapid population growth is attributable only to its increasing numbers of Kurds. These are mainly refugees from over two decades of war in the highlands, and the destruction of hundreds of Kurdish villages on the heights over-looking Mosul. It is almost certain that like Antep, Malâtya, and Kirmânshâh, Mosul now has a Kurdish majority, or will by the end of this decade, and is replacing Arbil as the largest predominantly Kurdish urban center in Iraq.

Also like Antep, Malâtya, and Kirmânshâh, Mosul remains a multi-ethnic city with a strong cosmopolitan outlook different from that of the Kurdish cities deep in the mountains. Perhaps these are the cities of the future for the Kurds, as more and more of them receive higher education and expect more from their city life than an escape from war and subsistence.

Further Readings and Bibliography: Special note must be made of Gwyn Williams, *Eastern Turkey: A Guide and History* (London: Faber & Faber, 1972), for the historical background and current conditions of cities in western and northern Kurdistan in Anatolia. Also A.H.M. Jones, *The Cities of the Eastern Roman Provinces* (Oxford, 1937); Evliyâ Chelebi, *Siyâhatnâma: Narrative of Travels in Europe, Asia, and Africa*, 3 vols., trans. Joseph von Hammer (London, 1834-50); *The Population and Household Census, 1986* (Teheran: Iranian Census Bureau, 1987), "the secret edition"; William M. Masters, "Rowanduz: A Kurdish Administrative and Mercantile Center," unpublished doctoral dissertation (Ann Arbor: University of Michigan, 1953); R.H. Dyson, "The Death of a City (Hasanlu)," *Expedition* 2.3 (1960); R.H. Dyson, "Hasanlu and Early Iran," *Archaeology* 13 (1960); R.H. Dyson, "Excavating the Mannaean Citadel of Hasanlu...," *Illustrated London News* (September 9, 1961). An excellent resource on the Iranian Kurds, remains A. Razmara, ed., *Geographical Dictionary of Iran*, 10 vols. (Teheran: The Iranian Armed Forces Geographical Bureau, 1949-51). The text is in Persian, and still in print.

ETHNIC MINORITIES IN KURDISTAN

Within the boundaries of Kurdistan are, and have since time immemorial been, various non-Kurdish ethnic minorities (Map 37). Some, like the Assyrians and the Qarapâpâq, call their enclaves in Kurdistan their primary homes. Turkish, Persian, Arab, Turkmen (Turcoman), and Armenian minorities on the other hand have their primary homelands outside Kurdistan.

Kurdoyev in 1957 estimated the number of minorities living in Kurdistan to constitute about a quarter of the total inhabitants. In 1980, Vanly put the Iraqi Kurdistan minority population at 8.6% of the total, with half of them, i.e., 130,000, being Turkmens (Challiand 1980, 206, n. 3). It would at any rate be difficult, if not impossible, to arrive at exact numbers for the non-Kurdish minorities living deep in Kurdistan.

It is clear, however, that far fewer non-Kurds live in Kurdistan today than did only a century ago. Then, vast numbers of Armenians, Assyrians, Turks, Turkmens, Arabs, and Azeris lived within the territories of Kurdistan proper. World War I changed all this. By 1925, the Armenians had all either been killed or had fled, leaving behind a tiny community of about 10,000 people where there had been nearly half a million at the turn of the century. The Assyrians (a new, and inaccurate name coined by the Western missionaries for the ancient, mainly Aramaic-speaking, Nestorian Christians of the area), who once resided in much larger numbers in Kurdistan from the environs of Mosul to the shores of Lake Vân and Lake Urmiâ, fled the region after the massacres of the late 19th

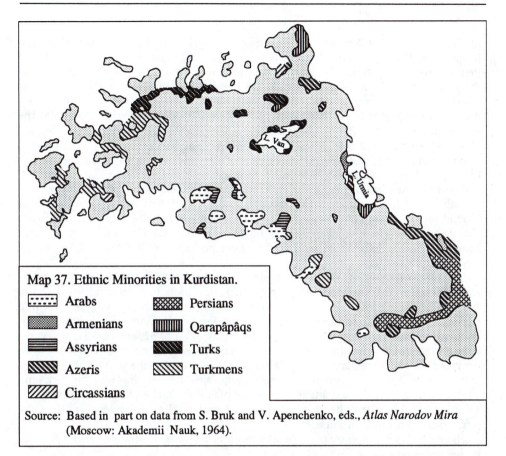

Map 37. Ethnic Minorities in Kurdistan.

Arabs		Persians	
Armenians		Qarapâpâqs	
Assyrians		Turks	
Azeris		Turkmens	
Circassians			

Source: Based in part on data from S. Bruk and V. Apenchenko, eds., *Atlas Narodov Mira* (Moscow: Akademii Nauk, 1964).

and early 20th centuries. They now reside only on the peripheries of Kurdistan, near Salmâs and Urmiâ in Iran, near Dohuk, Arbil, and Mosul in Iraq, and Qamishli, Mardin, and Siirt in Syria and Turkey. There are perhaps 250,000 Assyrians living on the territories of Kurdistan proper.

It is not easy to determine whether Kurdish Jews have been an ethnic minority or just a religious minority (like the Alevi or Yezidi Kurds), as they culturally have been more conservatively Kurdish than many non-Jewish Kurds. Their areas of concentration today, at any rate, are mainly in Iranian Kurdistan, in the towns of Sanandaj, Kirmânshâh, Sahna, and Hamadân. The populous Kurdish Jewish community of Iraq, once living from Kirkuk to Arbil and Zakho, migrated to Israel in the course of 1950s and 1960s under pressure from Baghdad.

The majority of Turks living in northern and western Kurdistan have been streaming out of the land since the 1960s. Being of the ruling ethnic group, they have found few reasons to stay in the most backward regions of the Turkish Republic among increasingly hostile natives, with their increasing guerrilla activities and the overbearing presence of the military. Many northern and western Kurdish cities that once bustled with Turkish-speaking immigrants from the Balkans are steadily seeing these emigrate west and out of Kurdistan. They had originally settled in Kurdistan at the end of World War I and had filled a niche left vacant by the removal of the urban and agriculturalist Armenian community. The shrinking number of these Turks living in Kurdistan as a minority is perhaps between 1 and 1.25 million people.

The Azeris and particularly the Qarapâpâq have recently had an uncordial relationship with the Kurds. The latter, a Turkic-speaking, Shi'ite people, are found in three pockets in Kurdistan, east of Ardahân and southwest of Agri in Turkey, and in and around Naqadeh in Iran. The largest pocket is that in Iran. The Qarapâpâq immigrated into Persia/Iran after it lost the Caucasus to the Russians in the 19th century. They settled in the Sulduz region south of Lake Urmiâ. Their center is the town of Naqadeh, between Mahâbâd and Shnu (near the historic Mannaean ruins at Hasanlu). As newcomers, they displaced the Kurds from those regions they came to occupy. With the fall of the monarchy in Iran in 1979 and the end of army surveillance of the region, bitter fighting between the Kurds and the Qarapâpâq for control of the Sulduz region and the town of Naqadeh ensued and has continued intermittently to this day. An educated guess of the total number of Qarapâpâqs in Kurdistan is 100,000.

While the Azeri minority in the Bukân region of eastern Kurdistan (southeast of Mahâbâd) has been at odds with the Kurds, the Azeri pockets in northern Kurdistan around Mt. Ararat and the towns of Agri and Kârs have been living rather harmoniously with the Kurds. There are also pockets of Azeris found near Hamadân, Sunqur, and Sahna in southern Kurdistan in Iran. There are perhaps 150,000 Azeris living in the territories of Kurdistan.

The Turkmen minority is concentrated in two major areas: in Iraq, where they live in small pockets in the Kurdish foothills from Kifri and Kirkuk to Arbil and Mosul, and in Turkey from Elâzig to Malâtya and Antep. The number of Turkmens living in all of Iraq is around 360,000, half of them perhaps living in Kurdish territories. This shows a quadrupling of their numbers since 1947, when a state total of 92,000 Turkmens was reported in the Iraqi census (Batatu 1978, 40). On the other hand no reliable figures can be provided for the Turkmens living in Kurdistan of Turkey, as the population censuses there did not distinguish between different Turkic-speaking peoples (e.g., the Turks and Turkmens), except for the nomads. The ethnic breakdowns, at any rate, ceased after the 1965 census. There may be as many as 1 million Anatolian Turkmens living in the territories of Kurdistan in Turkey.

There are also two pockets of Circassians, west of Kâgizmân and south of Antep, numbering perhaps no more than 50,000 souls.

In south and southeastern Kurdistan, a Persian-speaking minority of between 400,000 and 500,000 is present today. Most of these are assimilated Shi'ite Kurds who have given up Kurdish as their primary language when they adopted their religion—a phenomenon encountered many times before as a result of religious conversions in the history of the Kurdish people (see **Historical Migrations** and **Christianity**). In fact, until about a generation ago, Kirmânshâh, the largest city in all Kurdistan, had a solid Persian-speaking majority. Hamadân may still have one!

A large number of wealthy Persian or Persianized Kurdish families have already left the territories of Iranian Kurdistan for the country's major cities and/or overseas, taking with them material and intellectual wealth. The state land reform programs of the 1960s worked as shock therapy to the Persian-speaking upper- and upper-middle-class residents of Iranian Kurdistan, who hastily departed en masse from these economic outbacks once they had few land interests to keep them there. The vacuum was willingly and quickly filled by well-to-do Kurdish tribal chiefs and local entrepreneurs, which changed the ethnic character of many Iranian Kurdish cities and their urban lifestyle (Map 37).

The number of Arab minorities living in Kurdistan is hard to estimate, as it has fluctuated wildly with politically motivated attempts by the Syrian and Iraqi governments to introduce Arab settlers into Kurdistan, and with their subsequent withdrawals upon cessation of the state-sponsored efforts. The indigenous Arab minority in Kurdistan is found primarily near Urfâ, Mardin, and Siirt in Turkey and near Arbil, Kirkuk, and Khânaqin in Iraq. Kirkuk almost certainly now has an Arab plurality (see **Urbanization & Urban Centers**). There is a minority of perhaps one-half million Arabs living in all of Kurdistan. The new settlers have proven to be too transitory to count.

Loyal to its pan-Turkic ideology, Ankara has been quick to admit Turkic refugees into its territories. They have been mostly settled in non-Turkic Kurdistan. The most recent arrivals were about 5000 Kirghiz from the Afghan high Pamirs, fleeing Soviet invading forces. The Kirghiz were settled near Lake Vân in northern Kurdistan. Earlier, larger numbers of Kazakhs, Tatars, and Uzbeks from central Asia had been settled by Ankara, respectively, in the environs of Vân, Antep, and Urfâ. These need not be counted as indigenous ethnic minorities in Kurdistan, and should be treated as the recently settled Arabs in Syria and Iraq, as a transitory occurrence.

Further Readings and Bibliography: Peter Andrews, ed., *Ethnic Groups in the Republic of Turkey* (Wiesbaden: Reichert, 1989); Paul Magnarella, "A Note on Aspects of Social Life among the Jewish Kurds of Sanandaj, Iran," *Jewish Journal of Sociology* XI.1 (1969); G. Challiand, ed., *People Without a Country* (London: Zed, 1980); Walter Fischel, "The Jews of Kurdistan, a Hundred Years Ago," *Jewish Social Studies* (1944); Hanna Batatu, *The Old Social Classes and the Revolutionary Movements of Iraq* (Princeton: Princeton University Press, 1978).

General Bibliography

Huntington Ellsworth, "The Valley of the Upper Euphrates River and Its People," *Bulletin of the American Geographical Society of New York* 34 (1902); Ahmad Sousa, *Atlas of Iraq* (Baghdad, 1953); C.J. Edmonds, *Kurds, Turks and Arabs* (London: Oxford University Press, 1957); Henry Field, *The Anthropology of Iran* (Chicago: Field Museum Press, 1939); Henry Field, *The Anthropology of Iraq* (Cambridge: Harvard Peabody Museum of Anthropology, 1952); W.E. Ainsworth, *Travels and Research in Asia Minor* (London: 1842); J.C.A. Johnson. "The Kurds of Iraq," *Geographical Magazine* 11:50–59 (1940); Mark Sykes, *The Caliph's Last Heritage* (New York: Arno Press, 1973, reprint of the 1915 London edition); R.H. Dyson, "Ninth Century [BC] Man in Western Iran," *Archaeology* 17 (1964); D. Kinnane, *The Kurds and Kurdistan* (London: Oxford University Press, 1964); *Kurdish Times*, semi-annual journal of the Kurdish Library, Brooklyn, New York. 1985-present.

Chapter 5

RELIGION

OVERVIEW

The infusion of an Indo-European (Iranic) language, culture, and genetic element into the Kurdish population over the two millennia preceding the Christian era also entailed the incorporation of Aryan religious practices and deities into indigenous Kurdish faith(s). Zoroastrianism, Judaism, Manichaeism, and Christianity successively made inroads into Kurdistan. The most holy of Zoroastrianism's three grand fire temples, that of Âzargushasp, was built at the holy site of Ganzak (modern Takâb) in eastern Kurdistan in the northern environs of the Kurdish city of Bijâr. The imposing ruins of the temple are still extant. Despite this, Zoroastrianism did not succeed in converting any appreciable proportion of the Kurds. In fact, it was the indigenous Kurdish religions that, in addition to deeply influencing Zoroastrianism, on two instances attempted to absorb that religion.

There also existed a large community of exiled Jews in Kurdistan from the time of the Neo-Assyrian Empire. These exiled Jews, according to the Talmud, were granted permission by the Jewish authorities to proselytize and succeeded spectacularly in converting nearly all of central Kurdistan to Judaism. Christianity was even more successful. Large numbers of Kurds in far western and central Kurdistan converted to Christianity. The introduction of Christianity was soon followed by Islam, which added further to the religious diversity of Kurdistan.

From various state statistics, ethnographic field work, and independent observations set forth in the bibliography, Table 5 quantifying the religious composition of Kurdistan has been constructed (Map 38). (Further information on the provincial boundaries is provided under the entry **Internal Subdivisions**).

Very valuable background information on Islam, its denominations, cults, and movements, as well as on non-Islamic religions that have influenced or come into sustained contact with Islam during and shortly before the Islamic era can be found in the *Encyclopaedia of Islam*, 2nd edition (1960-present). The 1st edition (1913-36) should also be considered, as the second edition is not yet complete. *Encyclopaedia Britannica* is also a valuable resource, particularly for the pre-Islamic religions and movements, such as Zoroastrianism, Mithraism, Manichaeism, and the Mazdakite movement.

Further Readings and Bibliography: A. Gabriel, *Religionsgeographie von Persien* (Vienna, 1971); K.E. Müller, *Kulturhistorische Studien zur Genese pseudo-islamisheer Sekterngebilde in Vorderasien* (Wiesbaden, 1969); Thomas Bois, *Connaissance des Kurdes* (Beirut: Khayats, 1965); *Köy Envanter Etüdleri* ("Village Inventory Studies [of Turkey]") in Peter Andrews, ed., *Ethnic Groups in the Republic of Turkey* (Wiesbaden: Reichert, 1989); *Annual Abstract ofStatistics, 1970* (Baghdad: Government of Iraq, 1971); *Statistical Abstract 1973* (Damascus: Government of Syria, 1973); *Population Census 1970* (Damascus: Government of Syria, 1972); *The Population and Household Census, 1986* (Teheran: Iranian Census Bureau, 1987), "the secret edition," text available in English. An excellent resource on the Iranian Kurds, remains A. Razmara, ed., *Geographical Dictionary of Iran*, 10 vols. (Teheran: The Iranian Armed Forces Geographical Bureau, 1949-51); the text is in Persian, and still in print.

TABLE 5. RELIGIOUS COMPOSITION OF THE ADMINISTRATIVE UNITS WITH A KURDISH POPULATION, BY PERCENTAGE OF POPULATION

Province	Islam		Cult of Angels			Christian	Other
	Sunni	Shi'ite	Alevi	Yârsân	Yezidi		
TURKEY							
Adana*#	72.7%		27.3%				
Adiyaman	77.8		22.2				
Âgri	95	5					
Amasya*	69		31				
Antep	96.1		3.9				
Antioch*	62		38				
Bingöl	86.7		13.3				
Bitlis	98		2				
Cankri**	99		1				
Çurum*	83.4		16.6				
Diyârbakir	96.6		3.4				
Elâzig	87.5		12.5				
Erzincan	93.7		6.3				
Erzurum*	93.7		6.3				
Hakkâri	99			1			
Gümüshane**	95.5		4.5				
Kayseri**	97.5		2.5				
Kârs	84.8	8.2	5			2	
Kirshehir*	92.3		7.8				
Konya*	98.2		1.8				
Malâtya	72.2		28.8				
Maras*	79.5		20.5				
Mardin	95.2		2.5		5	3	
Nevshehir*	95		5				
Nigde**	97		3				
Siirt	86		4		6	4	
Mus	90		10				
Sivas*	67.5		32.5				
Tokat*	75.5		24.5				
Tunçeli/Darsim	13.4		86.6				
Urfâ#	95.1		3.9				
Vân	95	4				1	
Yozgat*	97.7		2.3				
IRAN							
E. Azerbaijan**	8.8	76.9		14.2			
W. Azerbaijan	35	55		9		1	
Gilan**	15.3	75.6		9.2			
Hamadân*	17	77.8		4			1.2 (Jewish)
Ilâm	34	46		20			
Khurâsân*	17	68	4	2	1		8 (Ismâ'ili)
Kirmânshâh	47.1	13.8		37.3			10.8 (Jewish)
Kordestan	70	13		16			1 (Jewish)
Luristan*	8.6	71.4		20			
Mazandaran**	21.1	71.1		7.8			

TABLE 5. RELIGIOUS COMPOSITION OF THE ADMINISTRATIVE UNITS WITH A KURDISH POPULATION, BY PERCENTAGE OF POPULATION (*continued*)

Province	Islam		Cult of Angels			Christian	Other
	Sunni	Shi'ite	Alevi	Yârsân	Yezidi		
IRAQ							
Arbil	94					6	
Diyâla	52.5	47.5					
Dohuk	80.5	6.5			6.5	6.5	
Kirkuk#	87.5	8.3				4.2	
Mosul (Nineveh)	78.5	6			10	5.5	
Sulaymânia#	97.5					2.5	
SYRIA							
Hasaka (Jazira)	73				3.5	23.5	
Deyr az-Zor*	97					3	
Aleppo*	85						132 (Ismâ'ili)
Hama**	58.6		22			9.4	10 (Druze)
Latakia**	24		64			12	
Hims**	60		16			24	
Idlib**	38		47			15	

For provincial boundaries, see Map 4.

Legend: Provinces without asterisks have a Kurdish majority. One asterisk denotes provinces with a large Kurdish minority. Two asterisks denote provinces where Kurds constitute 10-20% of the total population. See Remarks for provinces with # sign.

Remarks: In Turkey, religious designators such as Çeferi/Ja'fari, Qizilbâsh, Alevi, and Nuseyri/Nusayri are applied loosely to various branches of Alevism. There are very few, primarily Azeri, followers of the standard Imâmi Shi'ism in Turkey, with concentrations are in Âgri, Kârs, and Vân provinces in northern Kurdistan. In all other regions, those reported by such religious designators have been counted here as Alevis. A good deal of confusion and false reporting mar these censuses, as even the followers of the minority religions report varying local appellations for the same religion; some are simply apprehensive about reporting their actual religion out fear of harassment, and falsely report themselves as followers of the mainstream, state religion. The provinces of Urfâ and Antep in Turkey and Sulaymânia, Diyâla, and Kirkuk in Iraq are good examples of areas where the followers of minority religions (Alevism and Yârsânism, respectively), practice this religious dissimulation. Figures of 25-30% Alevi for Urfâ and Antep are conservative estimates, as are the 15-20% Yârsân for Sulaymânia, Diyâla, and Kirkuk. In the late 1970s the Iraqi province of Kirkuk was disbanded. Kirkuk city and its immediate environs formed the new province of Tamim. The rest of the territories were incorporated into a newly created province, Salâh al-Din (Saladin), with its capital at Tikrit, and other neighboring provinces. Spellings here follow the official state spellings of the names of the localities.

ISLAM

About three-fifths of the Kurds, nearly all of them Kurmânji speakers, are today at least nominally Sunni Muslims of the Shafi'ite rite. There are also followers of mainstream Imâmi (Twelver) Shi'ite Islam among the Kurds, particularly in and around the cities of Kirmânshâh, Kangawar, Hamadân, Qurva, and Bijâr in southern and eastern Kurdistan in Iran, and in much smaller numbers in and around Malâtya, Adiyâman, and Maras in far western Kurdistan in Turkey. There are a large number of Shi'ite Kurds in the Khurâsâni enclave as well, but they are not a majority there, as some sources have erroneously reported. The Shi'ite Kurds number no more than 1 to 1.5 million, i.e., between 5 and 7% of the total Kurdish population.

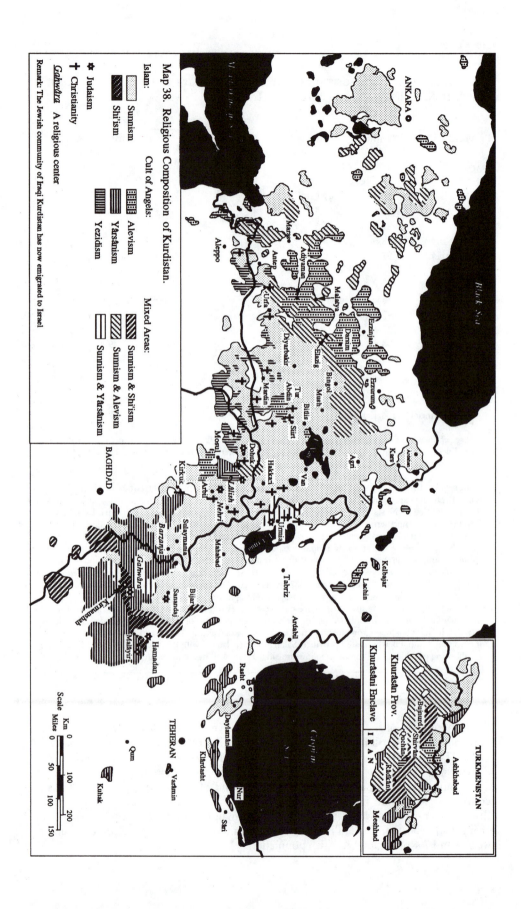

Map 38. Religious Composition of Kurdistan.

Islam:

☐ Sunnism

▨ Shi'ism

Cult of Angels:

▦ Alevism

▧ Yarsanism

▥ Yezidism

Mixed Areas:

▨ Sunnism & Shi'ism

▨ Sunnism & Alevism

▥ Sunnism & Yarsanism

✿ Judaism

✝ Christianity

Gahwara   A religious center

Remark: The Jewish community of Iraqi Kurdistan has now emigrated to Israel

The Shafi'ite Sunni rites emerged among the Kurmânj in medieval times when Iran was also primarily Shafi'ite Sunni Muslim. Arriving from the east toward the end of the medieval period, the Turkic tribes that proceeded to populate the better part of Anatolia brought with them the Hanafite rite prevalent in central Asia. The Hanafite rite became quite influential in the formerly Christian Byzantine lands to the west of Kurdistan, but did not change the Shafi'ism of the Kurds. It did, however, succeed in introducing the Naqshbandi Sufi order, an order indigenous to central Asia, into Kurdistan (see **Sufi Mystic Orders**). Kurdish Shafi'ite Muslims now constitute the single largest community of adherents to this once pervasive Sunni rite in the northern Middle East. They are now sandwiched between the Shi'ite Persians and Azeris on the east, Hanafite Sunni Turks on the west and north, and Hanafite Arabs of Syria and northern Iraq (the birth place of Hanafism per se) on the south.

Kurdistan straddles the very heartland of Islam, coming within 50 miles of Baghdad and 200 miles of Damascus, the two medieval cultural and spiritual capitals of the Islamic caliphates. The land was among the first to be breached by the Muslim forces, as early as the 7th century AD. Despite this centrality, there are very few mosques to be seen in Kurdistan, including in the cities. Why so?

Until at least the 12th century the Kurds were mostly, and rightly, reckoned as non-Muslims by influential medieval Muslim writers like Nizâm al-Mulk, Abu Mansur al-Baghdâdi, and Ibn Athir, who referred to the Kurds as *mushrikin*, i.e., polytheists. It appears that Islam touched Kurdistan rather superficially, and primarily on its peripheries. While there existed a notable minority of Kurdish Muslims, the majority adhered to the old religions (Cult of Angels, Judaism, and Christianity) resisting conversion until a gradual change in the socioeconomic life of the predominantly agriculturalist Kurdistan began to take shape from the 12th to the 15th centuries, and the destructive migration of the Turkic nomads through Kurdistan (see **Historical Migrations).**

The fact that most early Kurdish Muslim thinkers and men of fame come from cities like Dinawar, Suhraward, and Hamadân, or tribes like the Khalkâns and Fadhlâns, all bordering on the neighboring Muslim ethnic groups, further strengthens the contention that the majority of the Kurdish Muslims were relatively late converts to Islam, perhaps as late as the 16th century. This time coincides with the onset of an extended socioeconomic decline in Kurdistan, which may indicate a lack of the necessary stability and finances to construct durable and/or monumental mosques, accounting for their dearth today.

By the end of the 15th century, the old religions had been undercut steadily by the socioeconomic stress caused by the influx of nomads. From the beginning of the 16th century, the expansion of these nomads came at the expense of settled agriculturalists. The deterioration of their strength enabled the native Kurmânji-speaking Kurdish nomads to expand their dominance of the Hakkâri region (southwest of Lake Urmiâ) to cover most of Kurdistan. The Kurmânj were Shâfi'ite Sunnis, and as they expanded their power and numbers they expanded their religion, Islam. They gained the decisive momentum in the beginning of the 16th century, with the collapse of the trade routes through Kurdistan and its disruption of the Kurdish economy (see **Early Modern History, Nomadic Economy**, and **Trade**). The Kurmânj nomads soon overwhelmed and converted the sedentary, Pahlawâni-speaking, non-Muslim Kurds in most of Kurdistan. This pattern of intertwined linguistic and religious change had also occurred earlier, when Kurds of the southern Zagros mountains assumed new identities when they converted to Shi'ite Islam. These southern Kurds gave up their Kurdish language for Persian, and became the ancestors of the modern Lurs and other ethnic groups in the southern Zagros (see **Integration & Assimilation**). Kurdish society is now approaching a period of homogenization under the Kurmânji language, through conversion to Sunni Islam of the Shâfi'ite rite.

The lateness of their conversion should not however be interpreted to discount the importance of Islam to the Kurds, particularly now and specifically in major cities and towns where the majority of inhabitants truly adhere to conventionally recognized Islamic denominations. In fact, even in medieval times Kurds produced many Muslim thinkers and authors whose works are of great value to the entire Islamic world. Kurds like al-Dinawari, Ibn Athir, Ibn Fadlân, Ibn Khalkân, Suhrawardi, and Ba'di ul-Zamân al-Hamadâni are well known for their contributions to Islamic civilization (see **Medieval History**).

Since their conversion to Islam, conflict has existed between Muslim Kurdish groups following various Islamic denominations, and particularly between the Sunnis and the Shi'ites. This is not, however, any different in nature, intensity, or frequency from similar factional conflicts in other parts of the Muslim world. In the region around the city of Kirmânshâh in southern Kurdistan, for example, where Imâmi Shi'ism is the religion of the plurality, annual feasts are held in which effigies of 'Umar, the Muslim caliph revered by the Sunnis, is burned with fanfare (see **Popular Culture**). This is done despite the presence of many Sunni Kurds in the city and region, and sometimes just to provoke them. Kurdish Shi'ism, with its extremist traits, has created a large body of provocative rituals, figures of speech, and literature just for the purpose, going back to the vigorous re-introduction of extremist Shi'ism in Persia under the later Safavids, whose Kurdish connections and background are discussed below under **Cult of Angels** (see also **Early Modern History**).

The suppression of the Shi'ites by the Sunnis has been much more pervasive in Anatolia than in Iran, where for centuries the Shi'ite Persian government would have harshly punished such acts. In Anatolia, when the Ottoman sultan Selim the Grim embarked in the early 16th century on a series of widespread massacres of Shi'ite and Alevi inhabitants (Turkmen as well as Kurd), the Sunni Kurdish clergy provided a willing helping hand in the pogroms.

In the last decades of the 19th century, and particularly the early decades of the present, the fervor of the Germanic thinkers to rediscover their "Aryan" roots led them to study, elaborate, and glorify Aryan religions over the Semitic Judeo-Christian religions. The religions of India and the Zoroastrianism of Persia were prime points of departure for these "Aryan nationalists." The Kurdish intelligentsia, which frequented European capitals and were strongly influenced by their trends, came to view Islam—the other Semitic religion— as their fellow Germanic "Aryans" viewed Judaism and Christianity. Abjuring Islam, the "Arab" religion, the Kurdish literary-cultural journal *Hewâr* (published 1932-43, see **Press & Electronic Mass Media**) championed Yezidism as the native Kurdish religion that had kept its native purity despite centuries of aliens' suppressions. Their erroneous supposition was that Yezidism was a direct offshoot of Zoroastrianism, the "Aryan" religion glorified by the Germanic authors.

The degradation of Islam and the downplaying of its relevance to Kurds (or rather Kurdish nationalism) was a well-developed vogue until the end of World War II and the violent death of Aryanism in the ashes of the Third Reich.

Despite this, many educated Kurds continued their fascination with the pre-Islamic religions of their people, paying misplaced attention to the primarily Persian religion of Zoroastrianism as a source of inspiration. The poet Jagarkhwin (1903-84) exalted Zoroastrianism at the expense of Islam for a good deal of his life and work. It was only towards the end of his life, and a change of tides in the Middle East toward an Islamic identity, that he tilted toward Islam, albeit a vague, idealized, non-Arabian, clergy-free Islam.

Even today, there are many older Kurdish intellectuals whose fascination with Zoroastrianism, Yezidism, and other native religions is equaled only by their distaste for Islam. Now, however, they have to be more careful in openly attacking Islam at a time when the religion's radical revival happens to be a chief preoccupation of many governments and political groups in the area.

Further Readings and Bibliography: Martin van Bruinessen, "Kurdischer Nationalismus und Sunni–Schi'i Konflikt," in *Geschichte und Politik religiöser Bewegungen im Iran, Jahrbuch zur Geschichte und Gesellshchaft des Mittleren Orients* (Berlin/Frankfurt, 1981).

CULT OF ANGELS

Most non-Muslim Kurds follow one of several indigenous Kurdish faiths of great antiquity and originality, each of which is a variation on and permutation of an ancient religion that can loosely be labeled the "Cult of Angels," *Yazdâni* in Kurdish. The actual name of the religion is all but lost to its modern followers, who retain only the names of its surviving denominations. The name *Yazdânism* or *Cult of Angels* is a variation of the Kurdish name of one of its isolated branches, *Yezidism*, which literally means "the angelicans." There are some indications that Yazdânism was in fact the name of the religion before its fragmentation. An even older name for this creed may have been *Hâk* (or *Haq*), which is the name given by this religion to its pre-eternal, all-encompassing deity, the Universal Spirit. A brief argument in favor of the former view is presented in this section under **Yezidism**.

Only three branches of the Cult of Angels have survived from ancient times. They are Yezidism, Alevism, and Yârsânism (also known as *Aliullâhi* or *Ahl-i Haq*). Alevism now also encompasses Nusayrism, which is followed primarily by a minority of Arabs in Syria and most of the Arab minority in Turkey.

All denominations of the Cult, past and present, hold a fundamental belief in luminous, angelic beings of ether, numbering seven, that protect the universe from an equal number of balancing dark forces of matter. Another shared belief, and a cornerstone of the Cult, is the belief in the transmigration of souls through numerous reincarnations, with reincarnations of the deity constituting major and minor avatars.

The Cult believes in a boundless, all-encompassing, yet fully detached "Universal Spirit" (*Haq*), whose only involvement in the material world has been his primeval manifestation as a supreme avatar who, after coming into being himself, created the material universe. (*Haq*, incidentally, is not derived from the Arabic homophone *haqq*, meaning "truth," as commonly and erroneously believed.) The Spirit has stayed out of the affairs of the material world except to contain and bind it together within his essence. The prime avatar who became the Creator is identified as the Lord God in all branches of the Cult except Yezidism, as discussed below. Following or in conjunction with the acts of creation, the Creator also manifested himself in five additional avatars (*Bâbâ* or *Bâb*, perhaps from the Aramaic *bâbâ*, "portal" or "gate"), who then assumed the position of his deputies in maintaining and administering the creation. These are the archangels, who with the Creator and the ever-present Spirit, number the sacred Seven of the First Epoch of the universal life. This epoch was to be followed by six more, a new epoch occurring each time the soul or essence of the avatars of the previous epoch transmigrates into new avatars, to again achieve with the Spirit the holy number 7. Following these original seven epochs and major avatars, new, but minor, avatars may emerge from time to time. However, their importance is limited, as are their contributions, to the time period in which they live.

In this century three individuals have risen to the station of *Bâb*, or "avatar": Shaykh Ahmad Bârzâni (supposedly a Muslim), Sulaymân Murshid (a Syrian Arab Alevi) (see **Modern History**), and Nurali Ilâhi (a Yârsân leader). Their impact, however, has been ephemeral. This was not the case with another avatar who appeared a century earlier.

In the 19th century, Mirzâ Ali Muhammad, now commonly known as *The Bâb*, rose to establish the religion of Bâbism, which soon evolved into the world religion of Bâhâ'ism. The religion spread at the same wild-fire pace as Mithraism in classical times, from the Persian Gulf to Britain in less than a century's time (see **Bâbism & Bâhâ'ism**).

The rites and tenets of the Cult have traditionally been kept secret from non-believing outsiders, even when followers were not subject to persecution. In the present century an appreciable number of the scriptures of various branches of the Cult of Angels have been studied and published, allowing for better understanding of the nature of this native Kurdish religion, as well as the extent of its contribution to other religions.

The Cult is a genuinely universalist religion. It views all other religions as legitimate manifestations of the same original idea of human faith in the Spirit. The founders of these religions are examples of the Creator's continuous involvement in world affairs in the form of periodic incarnations as a new prophet who brings salvation to the living. Thus, a believer in the Cult has little difficulty being associated with Islam, Christianity, Zoroastrianism, or any other religion, as to him these are all just other versions of the old idea. He also has little difficulty in passing as a follower of any one of these religions if need be. Other religions that view themselves as unique systems of approach to the divinity, with an exclusive monopoly on truth, are viewed as unique as the images in a kaleidoscope: they are unique only in the configuration of their elements, but are all identical in that the elements that are involved in forming each image were supplied by the Creator at the moment of the universal Genesis of the material world. Hinduism and its similar cosmopolitan approach to other religions come readily to mind.

Meanwhile, the Cult has always been apt to absorb other religions, whole or in part, that have come into contact with it. To do so, new branches of the Cult have formed by incorporating into their dynamic cosmogonic system of continuing avatars the highest personages of these external religions. Alevism, for instance, was formed in the process of the Cult's movement to swallow Shi'ite Islam beginning in the 15th century. Such movements, which recur throughout the history of the Cult, should not be interpreted as organized and sinister efforts directed by a central, priestly body in the Cult. Far from it, the Cult as a whole could not have been any more indifferent to such events. These movements were all spontaneous creations of various segments of the followers of the Cult who through intensive exposure to an outside religion would in time adopt and adapt enough of it to be able to pass as insiders, raise a messianic scepter, and try to overtake that neighboring religion.

Several old, and now extinct, movements and religions also appear to have begun their existence as branches of the Cult of Angels, under circumstances similar to those that gave rise to Alevism. Among these, with due caution and reservation, one may place the Gnostic religions of Mithraism and Zorvânism, and the socioeconomically motivated messianic movements of the Mazdakites, Khurramiyya, and the Qarmatites. The Cult also has fundamentally influenced another Gnostic religion, Manichaeism, as well as Ismâ'ili (Sevener) Shi'ism, Druzism, and Bâbism, and to a lesser extent, Zoroastrianism, Imâmi Shi'ism, and Bahâ'ism. The Mithraist religious movement seems now to have been a guise under which Cult followers attempted to take over the old Greco-Roman pantheistic religion, with which the Cult had been in contact since the start of the Hellenistic period in the 4th century BC. Mithraism succeeded impressively. By the time of Constantine and the prevalence of Christianity, Mithraism had become so influential in the Roman Empire that it may be that the Roman state observance of the birth of the god Mithras on December 25 inspired the traditional dating of the birth of Christ. This date was the one on which the Universal Spirit first manifested itself in its prime avatar, Lord Creator, whom Mithraism presumed to be Mithras.

The Yezidi branch of the Cult of Angels, and the Nusayri movement within Alevism, still retain vestiges of this primary position of Mithras, particularly in their festivals and annual communal religious observations.

Despite the shrinking of its earlier domain and loss of ground to Islam, the Cult still influences all the Kurds at the levels of popular culture and quasi-religious rituals. The reverence for Khidir or Nabi Khizir "the living green man of the ponds," is a well-accepted practice among the Muslim Kurds. Khidir's shrines are found all over Kurdistan beside natural springs (see **Folklore & Folk Tales**). The Muslims have connected the lore of Khidir to that of the Prophet Elijah, who like Khidir, having drank from the Fountain of Life, is also ever-living. An earth and water spirit, the immortal Khidir (whose name might mean "green" or a "crawler") lives within the deep waters of the lakes and ponds. Assuming various guises, Khidir appears among the people who call upon him to grant them their wishes.

Many communal and religious ceremonies belonging to various faiths of the Kurds take place at Khidir's shrines, which are a transreligious institution (see **Popular Culture** and **Festivals, Ceremonies, & Calendar**). Khidir's longevity is symbolized in the longevous pond turtles found at the ponds and springs where his shrines are located. As such, realistic, but more often stylized, turtles are common motifs in Kurdish decorative and religious arts (see **Decorative Designs & Motifs**). The feast of Khidir falls in the spring, when nature renews itself. The exact observation date, however, varies from religion to religion, and even community to community. All branches of the Cult observe the feast, as do many Muslim commoners.

In ancient times the Cult came to be regarded as a contender to the ascendancy of early Zoroastrianism. This must have been before the end of the Median period, and the movement to overtake Zoroastrianism was perhaps sponsored by the last Median ruler, Rshti-vegâ Âzhi Dahâk (r. 584–549 BC). There is now compelling evidence that the slaying of Zoroaster himself and the overthrowing of his patron king Vishtaspa were at the hands of the troops of King Rshti-vegâ Âzhi Dahâk, as he advanced eastward into Harirud-Murghâb river basins in northwest Afghanistan in 552 BC. This did not help Âzhi Dahâk's reputation among the early Zoroastrians. The Median king Âzhi Dahâk has since been assigned a demonic character and is seen as the arch villain in both Zoroastrianism and the Iranian national mythology and epic literature, like the *Shâhnâma*. In fact, *Azhdahâ* has become the only word in the Persian language for "dragon." The controversial title *Âzhi Dahâk* for the last Median king was already known to Herodotus, albeit in a corrupted form, as *Astyages*.

A lasting legacy of this encounter between the two religions was the Cult's introduction of a hereditary priestly class, the Magi, into the simpler, priestless religion that Zoroaster had founded.

Zoroastrianism and the Cult of Angels share many features, among which are the belief in seven good angels and seven "bad" ones in charge of the world, and a hereditary priestly class. These common features are natural results of the long and eventful contact between the two religions. Other common features may be the result of the religious imprint of the Aryan settlers of Kurdistan, whose original religion must have been the same as that which the Prophet Zoroaster later reformed and reconstituted into the religion of Zoroastrianism. In its present form, however, the Cult shows the greatest mutuality with Islam, which has been its neighbor for the past 14 centuries. Nearly a thousand years after the first attempt on Zoroastrianism, followers of the Cult made another, less successful, bid to take over, or eliminate, Zoroastrianism. This was in the form of the Mazdakite movement.

The cult or movement of Mazdak rose in the 5th century AD in response to the rigid social and economic class system instituted by the Zoroastrian state religion of Sasanian Persia. The movement spread out from the Zagros region led by a native son, Mazdak, who eventually even succeeded in converting the Sasanian king Kavât or Qubâd (r. AD 488-531).

The Mazdakites' fundamental belief in the social equality of people, still largely present in the Cult of Angels, gave this religion special attraction to the poor and the objects of discrimination. Mazdak (whose name may mean "lesser Mazdâ," with Mazdâ being the shortened form for the name of the Zoroastrian supreme god *Ahurâ Mazdâ*), preached communal ownership of many worldly possessions, and was accused of having included women in this same category—an accusation of sexual promiscuity still levied on the Cult of Angels. The practice of communal ownership has prompted many modern writers to flamboyantly brand the cult of Mazdak as the first world communist system (see **Classical History**). In this religion was also embedded a militancy that continued to manifest itself in several socioreligious movements in the Islamic era, and indirectly through the militant Shi'ism of modern times.

Despite, or perhaps because of, their earlier successes, the Mazdakites were soon subjected to widespread massacres towards the end of Kavât's rule ca. AD 528 (as he had by then reverted to Zoroastrianism). Under the rule of Kavât's son and successor, Chosroes I Anoshervân, pogroms were extended to all corners of the country, prompting the king soon to declare them all destroyed. Far from being destroyed, the movement resurfaced, albeit fragmented, after the destruction of the staunchly Zoroastrian Sasanian Persian Empire. Mazdak remains one of the two patron saints of the populous Khushnow Kurdish tribe in central Kurdistan (Sykes 1908, 457).

Muslim rulers in their turn had to face and put down successive waves of economically driven messianic religious movements originating in this same area of Jibâl (Arabic for "[Zagros] mountains," i.e., old Media). The most important movement, that of the *Khurramiyya*, was led by religious and military leader Bâbak. The Khurramiyya believed in transmigration of souls, especially those of their leaders and religious figures. Bâbak and his followers, like Mazdak and the Mazdakites earlier, were known for their practice of communal ownership of all properties and means of economic production, and lack of social distinctions.

Simultaneously with Bâbak, whose headquarters were among the migrant Kurdish tribes in Azerbaijan, a Kurd named Nârseh (known to the medieval Muslim historian Mas'udi as "Nasir the Kurd"), led a Khurrami uprising in southern Kurdistan (the heartland of the Cult of Angels), which was finally put down under the 'Abbâsid caliph Mu'tasim. Muslim historian Tabari reports that about 60,000 of Nârseh's followers were killed by the Muslims, forcing the rest, along with Nârseh, to flee into the Byzantine Empire in AD 833 (see **Medieval History**).

The hallmark of the Mazdakites and the Khurramis was their use of the color red for their banners and clothing. They were thus called the *Surkhalamân*, "the people of red banners," or *Surkhjâmagân*, "the people of red cloths." This signature reappeared in the 14th and 15th centuries in another movement from among the followers of the Cult, when the Alevis came to be called the *Qizilbâsh*, or "the red heads," from their red headgear (see **Alevism** and **Medieval History**).

After its suppression under the early 'Abbâsid caliphs, an offshoot of Khurramiyya appeared in southern Iraq and later in Lahsâ or Ahsâ (modern Al-Ahsâ in eastern Saudi Arabia). These were called the Qarmatites, and shared with the parent movement the ideals of socioeconomic equality, as well as its cosmogony and theology. The medieval Ismâ'ili traveller Nâsir Khusraw records such practices of the inhabitants of Lahsâ as communal ownership of property and pointing to the connection between the old Mazdakite movement and Qarmatism. A hotbed of "schism," Lahsâ remains a predominantly non-Sunni region in the otherwise fanatically Sunni Saudi Arabia. The population is now reported to be mainstream Imâmi Shi'ite, which may well turn out to be the same kind of inaccurate generalization as that which classified the Cult of Angels itself as a Shi'ite Muslim sect.

In the 15th century, Muhammad Nurbakhsh, whose Sufi movement turned out to closely parallel the tenets of the Cult of Angels (see **Sufi Mystic Orders**), came from Lahsâ. In the early 19th century, another mystic from Lahsâ, Shaykh Ahmad Lahsâ'i, moved to Persia to lay the foundations for the Bâbi movement of the middle of the 19th century. A socioeconomic, messianic movement with striking similarities to the old Mazdakite movement, the ideas of Shaykh Ahmad (which were popularized by Ali-Muhammad Bâb), on which it was based, share at least as much with the Cult of Angels as did the Nurbakhshi movement (see **Bâbism & Bahâ'ism**).

All branches of the Cult, from the Mazdakites to the modern-day Alevis, have been commonly accused of sexual promiscuity. The Muslims believe they share their women at their communal religious gatherings. Even today the fiction of this notorious ceremony (called *mum söndü*, "candle blown out" in Anatolia, or *chirâgh kushân*, "killing of the lights" in Iran) is used by the Cult's Muslim neighbors to demean its followers. The accusation is levied against many other religious minorities connected in various ways to the Cult of Angels, such as the Ismâ'ilis in Afghanistan (Canfield 1978), the Alevis of Turkey (Yalman 1969) and Syria, and the Druze of the Levant (Eickelman 1981). Oddly, even scholars of the stature of Henry Rawlinson, Macdonald Kinnier, and G.R. Driver chose to believe rumors of this ceremony. Driver compares it with the oriental *Bona Dea* at Rome, and declares it even more shameless (Driver 1921-23). Rawlinson states that, although he did not believe it was still practiced in his time (1836), he thought it had been until half a century earlier. He further adds that it must have been the remnant of the ancient worship of fertility deities found in the cults of Mithra and Anahita, and also in the cult of Sesostris, which practiced the worship of genitalia. Kinnier claimed to have witnessed, if not actually participated in, one in 1818.

The followers of all branches of the Cult of Angels have ritual gatherings called *Jam*, *Âyini Jam*, or *Jamkhâna* (spelled *Çemhane* in Turkey), in a designated enclosure where holy scripture is recited, religious masters speak, and community bonds are renewed by the shaking of hands of all those present. Social equality is demonstrated by the forbidding of any hierarchical seating arrangements. The gatherings are closed to non-believers for fear of persecution, and the secrecy enshrouding the ceremony may have been the cause of the myth of communal sexual improprieties. The fact that women now are forbidden even to enter the Jamkhâna by some branches of the Yârsân is a reaction to these accusations, even though it runs against the grain of Kurdish society and its traditionally high status of women (see **Status of Women & Family Life**).

The minor Jam ceremonies occur once every seven days. The all-important major Jam occurs once a year, at different times for different branches of the cult, as discussed under their entries below.

In the Islamic era the religion has influenced and been influenced by many branches of Islam, particularly by the Shi'ism of the Imâmi (Twelver) and the Isma'ili (Sevener) sects. The most important and lasting contribution of the Cult of Angels to Islam, however, came at the time of the Qara Qoyunlu dynasty of eastern Anatolia and western Iran (1380-1468), as well as during the formative early decades of the Safavid dynasty, beginning in AD 1501. The dynasty's founder, Ismâ'il I, had strong Alevi sentiments, and in fact claimed to be an avatar of the Divinity. He is still revered by the Alevis as such, and as a *Sâhabi Zamân*, a living "Time Lord." It took many generations of Safavid endeavor to adjust to, and largely expunge, the elements of the Cult of Angels from their original religion. They did succeed, however, and the traditional, standard Imâmi Shi'ite Islam has since dominated Persia/Iran. Nonetheless, every impartial report concerning the faith and practices of the early Safavids points toward the Cult of Angels (Alevism in particular), and not Shi'ite Islam, as their religion.

To distinguish themselves from these non-Muslim "infidels," the mainstream Imâmi Shi'ites began from the start of the 16th century to refer to themselves as *Ja'fari* (after the 6th Shi'ite imam, Ja'far al-Sâdiq), instead of by their earlier, and cherished, title: the Shi'a. *Shi'a*, short for *shi'at al-'Ali*, is Arabic for "the party of Ali," Muhammad's son-in-law. Convinced that the names *Alevi* and *Aliullâhi*, by which these non-Muslim Kurds, and later Turkmens and Arabs, called themselves, are derived from the name of imam Ali (a notion fortified by the semi-deification of Ali, as one of the most important earthly avatars of the Universal Spirit, by two out of three branches of the Cult of Angels), the Imâmi Shi'ites opted for the less-than-desirable, but safer title of *Ja'fari*. By the time of the fall of the Safavids in 1720, this had become the almost exclusive title observed by mainstream Shi'ites, so real was their fear of association and confusion with the manifestly non-Muslim Alevis and Aliullâhis. To their chagrin, some Alevis in Anatolia began to embrace the name *Ja'fari* in the 20th century, and have reported themselves as such to the Turkish census takers (see Table 5, Remarks).

The ability of the Cult to adapt and absorb alien religions through its belief in the transmigration and reincarnation of souls again reminds one of Hinduism. Indian Buddhism was absorbed by Hinduism when the latter declared Buddha to be yet another, albeit important, avatar of the Spirit, just as Vishnu, Shiva, and Rama are. Some Hindus did unsuccessfully claim such status for the Prophet Muhammad as well.

The "high-jacking" of Ali and Muhammad for a while seemed to have given the Cult the means it needed to absorb Shi'ite Islam from the beginning of the 15th century to the time of the Ascension of Abbâs the Great on the Safavid throne in AD 1588. His enthusiastic sponsorship of the mainstream Imâmi Shi'ite theologians, attracted from as far away as Medina, Lebanon, Mesopotamia, and Khurâsân, finally blew away the smoke screen of Ali-worship by the Cult of Angels. Abbâs' Islamic scholars codified and strictly delineated Imâmi Shi'ism within its traditional boundaries prior to the Cult's offensive. The most important of these Shi'ite theologians, Allâma Majlisi, goes to great lengths to damn the followers of the Cult of Angels in his seminal treatise upholding traditional Shi'ism, *Bihâr al-Anwâr*. Despite all this, Shi'ism in its modern form bears the influence of the Cult in its rituals, specifically those that are considered the most offensive and unorthodox by the Sunnis. After all, it was under the sharp and punishing pressure of the Qara Qoyunlu and the early Safavids (i.e., in their "Alevi period") that most Muslims of Iran and the Caucasus were converted from Sunnism. The later reforms and introduction of traditional Shi'ism after the 17th century never succeeded in doing away with the imprint of the Cult of Angels on the common practice of the religion. The Cult survives today in the radicalism, economic and social egalitarianism, and martyr syndrome of Iranian and Caucasian Shi'ism, but not so much of Iraqi Shi'ism. The inhabitants of what is now Iraq were mostly Shi'ite before the arrival of the revolutionary Alevis out of Anatolia and never converted to Alevism. Iraq was not, however, left unaffected by the Cult. It was another branch of the Cult, Yârsânism, that had more peacefully been influencing Mesopotamia since the early days of Islam.

In words once interpreted as slander, but that now appear to have been true, the famous 15th century Sunni theologian, Sufi master, and poet, Abdul-Rahmân Muhammad Jâmi (in the *Rashahât-i Jâmi*) refers clearly to the "Shi'ites" he encounters in Baghdad as the "people of *Dun ba Dun*" (a fundamental religious tenet of the Cult, denoting continuous reincarnation of the soul; see **Yârsânism**). Jâmi habitually respects the traditional Shi'ite Muslims of central Asia and his home province of Khurâsân. His great antagonism toward the "Shi'ites" of the western Middle East, including Baghdad, is demonstrated by his adamant refusal to call them Shi'ites, but instead *Râfidi*, i.e., "the apostates." This and the similarly hostile reception of western Shi'ism by the Sunni theologians of eastern Islamdom (who well tolerated traditional Imâmi Shi'ism), occurred at a time when the Cult of Angels was busily absorbing traditional Islamic Shi'ism.

The Shi'ite beliefs in many saints, the messiah, a living *Sâhib al-Zamâm*, "Time Lord," and the like, all naturally appeal to the followers of the Cult of Angels. The Cult embraces all such notions, except that of a messiah to come at the end of the world. It has not, therefore, been difficult for them to pass themselves off as Shi'ites if need be. Even today, some branches of the Cult of Angels comfortably declare themselves bona fide Shi'ite Muslims, despite the fact that their fundamental beliefs clash with the principles of Islam as set forth in the Koran.

The Cult contains an impressive body of cosmogonical and eschatological literature, which is best preserved in the Yârsân branch, and is discussed under **Yârsânism**. The number 7 is sacred in this religion, and is the number of heavens, the number of luminous angels (as well as of their opposing dark forces of matter), the number of major avatars of the Universal Spirit, the number of epochs in the life of the material world, and the number of venerable families that maintain a hereditary priestly office in the religion. At the heart of number 7 also lies another, more sacred but less often employed, number: 3, which denotes things pertaining to the almighty himself. These numbers of course are sacred, more or less, in many other religions and disciplines of Middle Eastern origin as well. We need only remember the Trinity in Christianity, and the veneration of the number 7 in traditional astrology. What is missing from the Cult of Angels is the veneration of the number 12, which is sacred to Judaism, Christianity, and Islam (e.g., 12 tribes of Israel, apostles of Christ, Shi'ite imams).

Fasting requirements in this religion are limited to three days, while prayers are required only on the occasion of the communal gathering of Jamkhâna. Dietary laws vary from denomination to denomination, but are lax, or rather vague, at best. Alcohol and ham, for example, are often permitted because they are not directly prohibited in the scripture.

The Cult is fundamentally a non-Semitic religion, with an Aryan superstructure over-laying a religious foundation indigenous to the Zagros. To identify the Cult or any of its denominations as Islamic is a simple mistake, born of a lack of knowledge of the religion, which pre-dates Islam by millennia. Even though there has been strong mutual impact of the Alevi and Yârsân branches of the Cult and Shi'ite Islam, it is equally a mistake to consider these branches as Shi'ite Muslim sects, or vice versa.

The causes of this common mistake are several, but most important is the high station of Ali, the first Muslim Shi'ite imam, in both Yârsânism and Alevism. Through the ele-vation of Ali to status of primary avatar of the Spirit, Alevism and Yârsânsim have earned the title *Aliullâhi* (those who deify Ali) from their Muslim neighbors. The ongoing practice of religious dissimulation—like the Muslim *taquiyah*—has been also an impor-tant factor in confusing outsiders. The Cult's past attempts to absorb Shi'ism through pretensions of a shared identity have also confused many a hapless historian. As extremist Shi'ites, or *ghulât*, was how the embarrassed Muslim neighbors of the followers of the Cult used to identify them. Today, if asked, most Muslims would readily call Cult followers (with the exception of the Yezidis) Shi'ite Muslims of a "peculiar" kind.

The dwindling number of followers of the Cult over the past 4 centuries, coupled with the religious dissimulation of their leaders, who have openly and persistently called the Cult a Shi'ite Muslim sect, have relegated the question to the realm of unimportance for Muslims. The exception is, perhaps, the Kurdish Muslims themselves, whose persecution of Cult followers in the 19th and early 20th centuries was instigated by the fame- and follower-seeking, demagogue Muslim mullahs. These Muslims alone have kept up the pressure on Cult members (see **Early Modern History**).

Unlike many major religions, the Cult lacks a divinely inspired, single holy book. In fact such a book would have been out of place, given the multiplicity of the avatars of the Spirit, and the fact that revelation and reincarnation are an on-going affair in this regen-erative religion. Instead there are many venerated scriptures, produced at various dates, in various languages, and covering various themes by holy figures in the Cult. In fact Nurali Ilâhi, himself a minor avatar and the author of the most recent "holy scripture," the Burhân (see **Yârsânism**), passed on in 1975. Lack of a single holy book has not by any means hindered the Cult from developing a most impressive cosmogony, catechesis, eschatology, and liturgy, which are shared with minor variations in all denominations of the Cult to this day.

Good and evil are believed by the Cult to be equally important and fundamental to the creation and continuation of the material world. The good Angels, are therefore, as venerable as the bad ones, if one may call them so. In fact, without this binary opposition the world would not exist. Cold exists only because there is also its opposite, warm; up is what it is only because there is also down. Good would cease to exist if evil ceased to balance its existence. "Knowledge" and "awareness" in man exist only because good and evil exist in equal force, to be used as points of reference by man to comprehend and balance his being. Good, traditionally represented by the symbol of a dog and evil by the symbol of a serpent, join each other in a dog-headed serpent to represent the embodiment of the act of world creation: the mixture of ether and matter, good and evil, and all other opposites that make up this world. Some reports by European travellers of the late 19th and early 20th centuries regarding the veneration of dogs by the Alevis, if true, may point to worship of the symbol of good, since there is plenty of evidence of veneration of the symbol of the serpent (and hence evil) in the Yezidi arts, particularly at their shrines in Lâlish (see **Yezidism**).

The symbol of a dog-headed serpent finds its precedent in the Kurdish art of the Mannaean period of the 9th century BC. Side-by-side representation of the dog and serpent symbols is already well-known through the ancient Mithraic temple art from England to Iran.

The Cult does not believe in a physical hell or heaven, filled with devils or angels to come at the end of time. The horrors of hell and pleasures of paradise take place in this world as people reincarnate after death into a life of bounty and health or conversely into one of misery and destitution, depending on the nature of the life they lived within their previous body. At the end of time, however, only the righteous and complete "humans" who succeed in crossing the tricky bridge of final judgment (*Perdivari*) will join the eternity of the Universal Spirit. The failed souls will be annihilated along with the material world forever.

The Cult's belief in the figurative nature of hell and heaven is shared prominently by many Sufi orders, but particularly those that have come under the influence of the Cult (see **Sufi Mystic Orders**).

In addition to their attempt to absorb Shi'ite Islam, in the past thousand years, the followers of the Cult of Angels went through a period of successful proselytization of the Turkmens of Anatolia and the Arabs of the Levantine coasts of the eastern Mediterranean. There are also notable groups of Azeris, Gilânis, and Mâzandarânis who follow the Cult (Table 5).

It must be noted, however, that not all non-Kurdish followers of the various branches of this religion are just foreign converts. While most non-Kurdish followers of the Alevi branch of the Cult in Anatolia are actually Turkmen converts, the Arabs of the southern Amanus mountains and the Syrian coastal regions are in large part assimilated Kurds who inhabited the region in the medieval period. The same is true of the followers of the Cult in Azerbaijan, and in Gilân and Mâzandarân on the Caspian Sea, most of whom are the descendants of assimilated Kurds who have lost all traces of their former ethnic identity short of this religion (see **Historical Migrations** and **Integration & Assimilation**). The multilingualism of the sacred works of this religion may be the result of a desire to communicate with these ethnically metamorphosed followers of the Cult, and to convey the Word to all interested people in the tongue most native to them. This practice is also found in the Manichaean (now extinct), Druze, and Ismâ'ili religions, all of which have had strong past contact with the Cult of Angels.

In the past the religion has also lost major communities of adherents: almost all the Lurs have gone over to mainstream Shi'ite Islam, while the population in Kurdistan itself has become primarily Sunni Muslim. The Laks are fast following the suit of the Lurs. This religious change seems almost always to parallel a change in language and lifestyle among the affected Kurds. The Lurs went from various dialects of Gurâni Kurdish to Persian, an evolved form of which they still speak today. Most of the agriculturalist Kurdish followers of the Cult of Angels switched from Pahlawâni to Kurmânji and its dialects when converting to Islam. Except for the Mukri regions around the town of Mahâbâd, the area now dominated by the South Kurmânji dialect of Sorâni (see **Language**) was a domain of

Yârsânism and the Gurâni dialect until about three centuries ago (see **Historical Migrations**), while the domain of North Kurmânji was primarily that of the Dimili language and Alevi faith until the 16th century.

At the turn of the century, 33-40% of all Kurds followed this old religion. The proportion of the followers of the Cult converting to Islam has slowed down in this century, and now about 30-35% of all Kurds follow various branches of the Cult. More statistics are provided below under relevant denominations of the Cult.

The followers of the Cult have been the primary targets of missionary work, particularly Christian. Christian missionaries began work in Kurdistan on various denominations of the Cult as early as the 18th century. These produced the earliest Kurdish dictionaries, along with some of the earliest surviving pieces of written Kurdish, in the form of translated Bibles (see **Literature**). The missionaries have traditionally found these Kurds (who were mostly agriculturalists) more receptive to their works than the Muslim Kurds (who were mostly pastoralist nomads). Even today, the primary focus of the Christian and Bâhâ'i missionaries remains the Kurds following the Cult.

Further Readings and Bibliography: A. Christensen, *Le règne du roi Kawadh I et le communisme mazdakite* (Copenhagen, 1925); O. Klima, *Mazdak* (Prague, 1957); F. Altheim, *Ein asiatischer Staat* (Wiesbaden, 1954); M. Rekaya, "Mise au point sur Thèophobe et l'alliance de Bâbek avec Thèophile (839/840)," *Byzantia* 44 (1974); J.B. Bury, *A History of the Eastern Roman Empire from the Fall of Irene to the Accession of Basil I: AD 802-867* (Brussels, 1935); H. Grègoire, "Manuel et Thèophobe et l'ambassade de Jean le Grammairien chez les Arabes," in A. Vasiliev, *Byzance et les Arabes*, vol. 1 (Brussels, 1935); J. Rosser, "Theophilus' Khurramite Policy and Its Finale: The Revolt of Theophobus' Persian Troops in 838," *Byzantia* 6 (1974); W.A. Wright, "Bàbak of Badhdh and al-Afshin during the Years 816-41 AD: Symbols of Iranian Persistence against Islamic Penetration in North Iran," *Muslim World* 38 (1948).

Yârsânism. The followers of Yârsânism, also known as the Yârisân, Aliullâhi, Ali-Ilâhi (i.e., "those who deify Ali"), Alihaq, Ahl-i Haqq ("the People of Truth") or Ahl-i Haq ("the People of the Spirit" [*Hâk* or *Haq*]), Shaytânparass (devil-worshippers), Nusayri ("the Nazarenes," i.e., Christians), etc., are concentrated in southern Kurdistan in both Iran and Iraq. Their domain roughly coincides with that of the Gurâni (including the Laki) Kurdish dialect, with some major exceptions. The faith is loosely divided at present into two or three, very unequal sects.

1) The Ahl-i Haq have been increasingly identified with mainstream Shi'ite Islam, yet follow for their religious instruction the mystic order led by Nurali Ilâhi (himself a minor avatar, d. 1974) and his father Ni'matullah Jayhunâbâdi. Nurali Ilâhi is the author of the venerated book *Burhân*, which serves as the religious manual for the Ahl-i Haq. Despite Ahl-i Haq's apparent enthusiasm to at least appear to have merged with mainstream Imâmi Shi'ism (or claim that the religion is an independent Shi'ite sect), a short review of the Burhân and study of the discourses of Nurali Ilâhi and his father leave not a shred of doubt that this is only a pretense intended to protect the Ahl-i Haq from the wrath of their Muslim neighbors. As late as the 1920s, as Nurali relates, the Muslims were lynching and crucifying Yârsân followers.

2) The Tâyifasân have only recently begun to associate with the pragmatic approach and teachings of Nurali vis-a-vis Islam. However, they are not as enthusiastic about an open association with Shi'ism as Ahl-i Haq. Nurali claims the Tâyifasân to be his followers, not very different from the Ahl-i Haq. These two groups are the most urban and urbane of the Yârsân sects, and show the most influence from modern Iranian society. Their small branch in Iraq follows their lead.

3) The traditionalists consist of the commoners and village folk, who constitute the overwhelming majority, and call themselves the Yârsân, but also on occasion the Nusayri

or Aliullâhi. They are the most readily targeted for abuse by their Muslim neighbors, but they are also the ones who are the most faithful to the tenets of the ancient religion. They make no pretense to be Muslims. Since they constitute by far the largest group, the appellation *Yârsân* here is considered to represent this entire branch of the Cult of Angels. The name is believed by the Yârsâns to have evolved from *yâr-i sân,* "the companion, or people of the Sultan," i.e., Sultan Sahâk. This seems to be a folk etymology, and the true meaning waits to be discovered.

Yârsânism possesses an impressive body of religious cosmogony. It holds that the world was created when the Universal Spirit (*Haq*) who resided in *Azal,* "Pre-Eternity," in (or as) a pearl, manifested itself in a primary avatar (*Zâti Bashar*) the Lord God (*Khâwandagâr*), and signaled the First of the Seven Epochs (*Biyâbas*) of universal life. The Lord God then proceeded to create the world. The Spirit further manifested itself in five secondary avatars (*Zâti Mihmân*), to form the Holy Seven with the Spirit itself. And this was the original Epoch of Creation, the *Sâjnâri,* or "Genesis." (See Table 6.)

The First Epoch was followed by another six (one Zâti Bashar and five Zâti Mihmân). In each one the Spirit manifested itself in six new avatars, to form the seven for that epoch of the universal life.While the avatars of the First Epoch can be closely matched by name to the archangels of the Semitic religions, the avatars of the Second Epoch, which begins with Ali as the primary avatar, are all Muslim figures, except for Nusayr. Nusayr may be interpreted as referring to the "Nazarene," i.e., Jesus Christ, or as Nârseh, the minor avatar who later came to be known as Theophobus (see **Classical History**). The Third Epoch belongs to Shâh Khushin or Khurshid, "the Sun," that is, the God Mithras or Mihr and his cycle (see also **Folklore & Folk Tales**).

The Fourth Epoch begins with Sultan Sahâk, whose accompanying avatars are primarily Jewish figures, like Moses, David, and Benjamin. The avatars of the Seventh Epoch bear names followed by the Turkic honorific title *beg,* "master." These changes in the character and origin of the names of the avatars of each epoch may reflect the social and historical events that were occurring in the national life of the Kurds at the time. Possible influential events include the outbreak of the Mithraist movement (2nd century BC to 3rd century AD) in northern and western Kurdistan; the introduction of the Judeo-Christian tradition into central Kurdistan in the 1st century BC and in the rest of Kurdistan up to the 7th century AD; the coming of Islam in the 7th century; the Turkic invasions of the 12th-15th centuries; and the nomadization of Kurdish society in the 17th-19th centuries (see **History**).

The names of the avatars of the Fifth Epoch may also signify early medieval revolutionary movements within the Cult. The name of the primary avatar of the epoch, *Qirmizi,* meaning "the Red One," may be either Bâbak or Nârseh. The red clothing and banner of these revolutionaries have already been mentioned above. The element *yâr,* "companion, disciple," found in the names of the two secondary avatars of this epoch was commonly found in the given names of individuals in the early medieval period. A relevant example is *Mâzyâr* (*Mâh Yazd Yâr,* meaning "the companion of the Angel of Media"), the name of a Cult revolutionary who rose up simultaneously with Bâbak and Nârseh in the Caspian Sea regions (Rekaya 1973). There was, meanwhile, a secret society or brotherhood of plebeians and their revolutionary reformers operating in nearby Baghdad under the title the *Ayyârs,* "the companions."

The avatars of the Fourth Epoch and Sahâk himself are now held by the Yârsâns to have been the most important of the Spirit's manifestations after the First, and ethereal one, headed by the Lord God. The Alevis consider the Second Epoch and Ali to occupy this primary station, while the much-corrupted Yezidi cosmogonical tradition entitles Shaykh Adi and his avatars to that place of importance, even though it is not clear to which Epoch they are assigned.

Khâwandagâr, Ali, and Sahâk form a Supreme Three within the Seven for the Yârsâns;

the Alevis have Khâwandagâr, Ali, and Bektâsh (see **Sufi Mystic Orders**); while Lucifer, Adi, and Yezid serve the purpose for the Yezidis. The Yezidis place Lucifer or Malak Tâwus among the avatars of the primary or First Epoch. On Table 6 this translates into Lucifer replacing Khâwandagâr himself, as otherwise Lucifer would not both fit in the First Epoch and have Adi as one of his primary avatars in the following Epochs. Each manifestation reincarnates into his or her successor in station in the next Epoch. Thus Khâwandagâr reincarnates into Ali in the Second Epoch, into Shâh Khushin in the Third, into Sultân Sahâk in the Fourth, and so on.

In each epoch there is a female avatar of the Universal Spirit, a reflection of the higher status of women in the Kurdish culture and tradition (see **Status of Women & Family Life**).

The greatest personage in Yârsânism, Sultan Sahâk, is with increasing frequency referred to as *Sultan Is'hâq*, i.e., an Islamicized form of Isaac, by some apologetic Ahl-i Haq and Tâyifasây. This title would obviously fit rather nicely with the other Judaic names of the avatars of the Fourth Epoch. In his new garb, Sahâk, or "Is'hâq," is contended to have been born sometime between the 11th and 13th centuries in the venerated city of Barzanja, southeast of Sulaymânia (now the center of the Qâdiri Sufi order; see **Sufi Mystic Orders**. In fact Shaykh Mahmud, the Qâdiri Sufi master who following World War I led a 12-year-long revolt against the British administration in Iraq and subsequently proclaimed himself the "King of Kurdistan" (see **Modern History**) claimed to be descended from a brother of Sultan Sahâk in the twelfth generation. The traditionalist Yârsâns, on the other hand, believe Sahâk to have been superhuman, a supreme avatar of the Universal Spirit, who lived many centuries, possessed mysterious powers, and lives on as a protective mountain spirit in caves on the high peaks.

Sahâk is the much corrupted form of *Dhahâk* or *Dahâk*, which also served as the royal title of the last Median ruler, Rshti-vegâ Âzhi Dahâk (see **Ancient History**). The name is encountered in various versions throughout the classical and medieval periods in the Zagros region, and everywhere else that the Kurds happened to settle, including Armenia. There is a St. Sâhâk Bartev, an Armenian Catholicos who lived in the late 4th and early 5th centuries AD; there are many other luminaries in early medieval Armenia with this name. At the time Armenia was receiving a large number of Kurdish immigrants from the southeast (see **Classical History** and **Historical Migrations**).

According to Yârsânism, humans are the end product of the worldly evolutionary journey of the soul. The soul begins its journey by entering inanimate objects. Upon completion of that experience, the soul lives within plants, then animals. Eventually, the soul enters the body of a man or a woman. Thus he or she contains four natures: those of objects, plants, animals, and mankind. At the moment of entry into the human body, the soul begins a new transmigratory journey, which can last for 1001 reincarnations, equivalent in time to the 50,000 years allotted to the universe. This is called the *Dun ba Dun* stage (variously interpreted to mean "oblivion to oblivion," i.e., indicating movement from one mortal body to another, or "garb to garb," implying the same thing). At the end of this evolutionary journey, a man/woman reaches salvation and becomes a human, a holy, perfect being worthy of his/her new station in the high heavens and his/her total union with the Universal Spirit.

Salvation in Yârsânism is the responsibility of the individual. The community has no responsibility to help one reach humanity. Even the assistance provided by religious teachers and masters is voluntary guidance and not a duty. The presence or absence of this guidance at any rate has no bearing on the status of the soul of the pupil. Theoretically it is possible for man to reach the high station of humanity through a single life period of high endeavor. Conversely, it may require the entire cycle of 1000 reincarnated lives (the last life after the one-thousandth is the life of salvation and does not count in the Dun ba Dun). Sinning individuals may be reincarnated in the regressed form of an animal, the life of which is not then counted among the 1000 lives. Nor is

Universal Spirit (Hâq)	Epoch	Avatars (Bâbâ)					
		Primary (Zâti Bashar)	Secondary (Zâti Mihmân)				Female
	1	Khâwandagâr	Jibrâ'il	Mikâ'il	Isrâfil	Izrâ'il	?
	2	Ali	Salmân	Qanbar	Muhammed	Nusayr	Fâtima
	3	*Shâh Khushin (Mithras)	Bâbâ Buzurg	Kâka Redâ	Pir Shâliyâr	Bâbâ Tâhir	Mâmâ Jalâla
	4	*Sultan Sahâk	Khidir (Benyâmin)	Dâwud	Pir Musi *Bâbâ Yâdgâr	**Ibrâhim Tayyâr	Dâyirâk Razbâr
	5	Qirmizi (Shâh Ways)	Qambar Dastawar	Yâri Jân	Yâr Ali	Shâh Swâr	Zar Bânu
	6	MuhammadBeg (Nurbakhsh)	Kâ Mahrijân	Kâ Malak	?	Qara Pust	Dusti
	7	Âtish Beg	Jamshid Beg	Almâs Beg	Alâdin Khân	Abdâl Beg	Pari Khânim

Legend: * Conceived without a father
** Conceived without a mother
? Too many or no candidates

Sources: *Khazâna, Shâhnâma-i Haqiqat,* and *Burhân.*

TABLE 6: COSMOGONICAL EPOCHS AND THE AVATARS OF THE UNIVERSAL SPIRIT IN YARSANISM.

reincarnation into the body of a newborn who dies before reaching 40 days of age counted. If after the 1000 lives of Dun ba Dun or at the end of universe's 50,000 years (which ever comes first) a soul has not yet succeeded in elevating itself to the station of a human, then it will be judged, along with other failed souls, at the Final Judgment or *Pardivari,* "the bridge crossing."

Because of this strong belief in reincarnation, the dead are scarcely mourned by the Yârsâns, as they are expected to return soon, if not immediately, in the body of a newborn. Indeed, it was not uncommon until relatively recently for priests to try to identify the exact newborn to whom the soul of a deceased person had transmigrated.

Like other branches of the Cult of Angels, Yarsânism does not have a divine holy book as such. They possess instead a body of sayings, or *kalâm,* and traditions, or *deftar,* which they treat as their holy scriptures. These have been composed at various times and languages, each at an epoch-making turn in the long history of the religion. The most important kalâm is that of *Saranjâm* ("Conclusion") also known as the kalâm of *Khazâna* (perhaps meaning "Repository"), and contains the sayings of Sultan Sahâk, his contemporary saints, and other Yârsân religious figures who preceded him. This is considered to be the paramount work and supersedes all others in authority. The work is in verse and written in the Awrâmani dialect of Gurâni (see **Language**). Other kalâms and deftars are in Gurâni, but also in Luri, Persian, and various Turkic dialects. Other major works are the *Dawrai Bahlul,* ascribed to the mysterious Bahlul Mâhi (Bahlul the Median) of the 8th century AD, written in verse in an archaic form of Gurâni. *Shâhnâma-i Haqiqat,* by Ni'matullah Jayhunâbâdi Mukri and the *Burhân* by Nurali Ilâhi, both are, on the other hand, written recently in Persian with a smattering of Gurâni and Koranic quotations in Arabic.

The center of Yârsânism is deep inside the Gurân region at the town of Gahwâra (or Gawâra), 40 miles west of Kirmânshâh. The shrine of Bâbâ Yâdigâr, in an eponymous village 50 miles northwest of Gahwâra, now serves as one of Yârsânism's holiest sites. Two days before the festival of the new year, or New Ruz (see **Festivals, Ceremonies, & Calendar**), believers visit the shrine and participate in chants that assume the form of a dialectic on the principles of Yârsânism. The religious teacher and master, or *pir*, recites a formula posing a question, which is answered by the believers by another formula. The tradition of dialectics in religious discourse and ceremonial chants has deep roots in the Zagros region. It is also found in the Zoroastrian religious commentaries of the *Zand-i Avestâ* and the poetic style of all peoples inhabiting the Zagros chain. A ritual also practiced by the Yârsâns on this occasion is the sacrifice of a rooster. (To the Yezidis, the rooster serves as the venerated announcer of the Sun, so to them this Yârsân practice would be a sacrilege beyond all bounds.)

Despite the impressiveness of what remains of the religious beliefs and tradition, much more has been forgotten, garbled, and fabricated in all branches of the Cult of Angels. The most important religious terminologies, cycles of events, and pivotal points of the religion are derived from popular etymologies, common superstitions, pseudo-histories, and plain fabrications by the imaginative minds of the Yârsân religious masters, the *pirs*. The important cosmogonical events of *Sâjnâri* and *Perdivari* are celebrated and venerated with very little knowledge of even their literal meaning beyond a flimsy popular etymology.

The striking physical attribute of the followers of Yârsânism is the tradition among men of not cutting or trimming their mustaches. In fact, they are allowed to grow to extreme sizes. The beard, on the other hand, is always shaved. The habit is prohibited by Islam (according to which the mustache must always be kept very short) but became the outward hallmark of the extremist Shi'ites, who adopted it from the Alevis. The faces of the Safavid kings, clean-shaven other than their great bushy mustaches as they are recorded in the paintings of the period, could be those of any of the followers of the Cult of Angels as seen today. The habit is no longer practiced by the mainstream Shi'ites because it is disallowed under Islam. The practice has thus once again become the exclusive habit of the followers of the Cult of Angels, particularly the Yârsâns and the Yezidis.

The followers of Yârsânism are now found in one large concentration in southern Kurdistan and many secondary concentrations outside Kurdistan proper, in the Alburz Mountains, Azerbaijan, and Iraq (see Table 5). The famous medieval poet Bâbâ Tâhir and the 19th-century poet Adib al-Mamâlik were adherents of this faith. (In fact, Bâbâ Tâhir is among the secondary avatars of the Third Epoch.) The Sârili, the Kâka'i, and the Bazhalân (also known as the Bajalân and the Bajarwân) Kurds, occupying in separate pockets the area between Qasri Shirin, Kirkuk, and Mosul, practice some variations of Yârsânism as well. Presently the followers of Yârsânism constitute roughly 10-15% of the Kurds.

Further Readings and Bibliography: V. Minorsky, "Ahl-i Haqq," in *The Encyclopaedia of Islam*; Mohammed Mokri, *Le Chasseur de Dieu et le mythe du Roi-Aigle* (Wiesbaden: Otto Harrassowitz, 1967); Shâh-Nâma-ye Haqîqat, French commentary and partial translation by Mohammad Mokri (Paris: Institute Français d'Iranologie, Bibliothèque Iranienne, 1971); Robert Canfield, "What They Do When the Lights Are Out: Myth and Social Order in Afghanistan," paper presented at the ACLS/SSRC Joint Committee on the Near and Middle East Conference on Symbols of Social Differentiation (Baltimore, 1978); Reza M. Hamzeh'i, *The Yaresan: A Sociological, Historical and Religio-Historical Study of a Kurdish Community* (Berlin: Klaus Schwarz Verlag, 1990); W. Ivanow, *The Truth-Worshippers of Kurdistan: Ahl-i Haqq Texts* (Leiden: Brill, 1953); V. Minorsky, "Notes sur la secte des Ahlè Haqq," *Revue du Monde Musulman* 40–41 (1920 and 1921); Mohammed Mokri, *Recherches de kurdologie: Contribution scientifique aux études iraniennes* (Paris: Klincksieck, 1970); Dale Eickelman, *The Middle East: An Anthropological Approach* (Englewood Cliffs: Prentice-Hall, 1981); Henry Rawlinson, *Journey from Zohab to Khuzistan* (London, 1836); Henry Rawlinson, "Notes on a march from Zohab," *Journal of Royal Geographic Society* (London, 1839); John Macdonald Kinnier, *A Geographical Memoir of the Persian Empire* (London, 1813); John Macdonald Kinnier, *Journey through Asia Minor, Armenia and Koordistan, in the years 1813 and 1814* (London, 1818); Edith Porada, "Of Deer, Bells and Pomegranates," *Iranica Antiqua* vii (1967); Mohammed

Mokri, *L'Esotérisme kurde* (Paris, 1966); Matti Moosa, *Extremist Shiites: The Ghulat Sects* (Syracuse: Syracuse University Press, 1988); M. Rekaya, "Mâzyâr: Résistance ou intégration d'un province iranienne au monde musulman au milieu du IXe siècle ap. J.C.," *Studia Iranica* 2 (1973).

Alevism. A majority of the Dimila Kurds of Anatolia and some of their Kurmânji-speaking neighbors are followers of another denomination of the Cult of Angels. These have been called collectively the Alawis ("the Followers of Ali"), the Alevis ("the People of Fire," implying fire-worship or Zoroastrianism, from *alev,* "fire"), the Qizilbâsh ("the red heads," from their red head gear; see **Costumes & Jewelry**), and the Nusayri (which can be interpreted as the "Nazarenes," implying Christianity, or as the "followers of Nârseh," the early medieval Kurdish revolutionary of the Khurrami movement who settled with his followers in Anatolia). See Medieval History). The Alevis believe in Ali as the most important primary avatar of the Universal Spirit in the Second Epoch of the universal life (see **Yârsânism**), hence their exaggerated feelings for this first Shi'ite Muslim imam. This may be the root of their communal appellation, just as the title *Aliullâhi* ("the deifiers of Ali") serves as one of the titles the outsiders call the Yârsâns. A point to note is that unlike in Yârsânism, Ali is a double figure in Alevism. Alevis join the Imâm Ali and the Prophet Muhammad together to form *Alimuhammad,* who is then considered a single avatar, albeit with double manifestations. The founder of the Safavid dynasty, Shâh Ismâ'il I, often referred to himself in his writings with the formula "Alimuhammad," when he was not calling himself *Haq,* the Spirit.

Despite the importance of Ali in the religion and its modern communal appellation, Alevism remains a thoroughly non-Islamic religion, and a part of the Cult of Angels. Like other branches of the Cult, the fundamental theology of Alevism sharply contradicts the letter and spirit of the Koran in every important manner, as any independent, non-Semitic religion might.

Alevism is now also practiced by many Syrian Arabs, where Alevis constitute over 13% of the total population of the state. In Syria they are more often known as the Nusayris and are the predominant religious group in coastal Syria, centered on the ports of Latakia and Tartus. Ethnic Kurds were once numerous here and are still found not just to the north, but also to the east, toward the city of Hama. The Alevi Arabs are thus a mixture of Arab converts and assimilated Kurds (see **Historical Migrations**). The current president of Syria, Hafez al-Assad is an Alevi (more precisely, a Nusayri; see below). Under the French Mandate, this section of Syria was made autonomous for this religious reason.

Many Turkmens of Turkey, who neighbor the Kurds in the Taurus and Pontus mountains near the cities of Adana, Sivas, Tokat, and Amasya are also adherents of Alevism. Contrary to the Syrian case, the non-Kurdish Alevis of Anatolia are primarily Turkic converts and not assimilated Kurds. Along with the Kurdish Alevis, these Turkmens were the backbone of the armed forces that powered the rise of the Safavids of Persia (see **Early Modern History**). There may now be as many Turkmen Alevis as Kurds, if not actually more. The Shabaks, who live to the immediate south-southeast of Mosul in central Kurdistan, neighboring the Yârsân Bajalâns, also practice a form of this Dimili Alevism.

Dimili Alevism bears closer links to ancient Aryan cults than does Yârsânism. Its rites include daily bowing to the rising sun and moon and the incantation of hymns for the occasion. The communal ritual gathering of Jamkhâna is observed by these Dimili Alevis as the *Âyini Jam,* "the Tradition of Jam." The major Jam, or the grand annual communal gathering, coincides with the great Muslim Feast of Abraham that concludes the Hajj pilgrimage to Mecca and includes the sacrifice of a lamb. Jam (known as *Jamshid* in Zoroastrianism and *Yamâ* in the Veda) was the great Aryan hero in the tradition of the Zoroastrians to whom is ascribed the creation of the feast of New Ruz—the Kurdish and Iranic new year. The myth holds that Jam was sacrificed at the end of his own days to the rising sun by none else than Âzhi Dahâk. In fact, in the renowned Iranic national epic, the *Shâhnâma* of Firdawsi, Jamshid is depicted as "the worshipper of the Sun and Moon" (chapter on the Advent of Zoroaster, line 71), as are the Alevis.

The *Âyini Jam* constitutes basically the same religious occasion as that of Jamkhâna of the Yârsâns and Jam of the Yezidis. The Alevis, despite the verbal torments of outsiders, still allow full participation of women in their rituals and religious gatherings, particularly the occasion of the major Âyini Jam. This is therefore the specific occasion to which outsiders point for their accusation of the communal sex ritual of the "candle blown out" mentioned earlier.

Some Dimili Alevis, as well as the Yezidi clans, still maintain the ancient Iranic rite of worshipping the deity represented as a sword stuck into the ground. Mark Sykes in 1908 mentions this practice among a few Dimili tribes: the Bosikân, Kuriân, and apparently also the Zekiri, Musi, and Sarmi, but he adds that at the time the last three no longer practiced it. This rite is mentioned by Herodotus for the Iranic Scythians and Sarmatians (kinsmen of the Kurds and other Iranic peoples) in Ukraine of 2300 years ago. (The resemblance between the Dimili tribal name Sarmi and the that of Sarmatians is also worthy of note.) The image of the sword stuck in the ground or a rock is of course similar to that of the British Excalibur and King Arthur. There is a strong possibility that the two are related. In AD 175, Roman emperor Marcus Aurelius assigned a legion of Sarmatians from Pannonia (modern Hungary) to serve in England and Scotland (the Sarmatians' commander's name was Lucius Artorius Castus!). According to Nickel, the basic elements of the legend may have been introduced into Britain by these Sarmatian settlers, and the familiar story of Excalibur may thus be akin to this Dimili Alevi religious practice. The Dimila are the last Iranic people still practicing the ancient rite.

Some modern European travellers have reported, as hearsay, that some Qizilbâsh worship a large (black) dog as the embodiment of the deity (Driver 1921-23). Even though Driver's account is rather derogatory toward the Alevis and to the practice, of which he clearly does not approve, veneration of the dog as a symbol of good (the serpent standing for evil) is a very ancient rite. The binary opposition in which the dog and serpent symbols represent the basic poles is found in almost all Gnostic religions of the old, particularly Mithraism (Jonas 1963).

The divine reverence for Ali practiced by the Alevis became the most conspicuous religious sign of the Qara Qoyunlu and the early Safavid dynasties. Added to their other non-Islamic rites and beliefs, this alienated them from the Muslim surroundings, to which they sought to extend their political domination and their Alevi religion under the pretense of Shi'ism. They were commonly referred to as the Qizilbâsh, a name still carried by the modern Alevi Dimila Kurds of east-central Anatolia—the area where the movement began in the 15th century.

To form the critical human force necessary for the outburst of the Alevis in the 15th and 16th centuries, two factors proved crucial: 1) the unprecedented demographic gains by the Kurds in the period between 1400 and the 1520's (see **Demography**), and 2) the earlier successful conversion to the Cult of Angels of vast numbers of the neighboring Turkmen tribes of Anatolia and the Caucasus. The early patrons of this Alevism, better known to historians as extremist Shi'ites, were the Turkmen royal house of Qara Qoyunlu, which ruled basically the entire area of contemporary Iran, as well as the Caucasus and eastern Anatolia (see **Medieval History**). The inclinations of the Qara Qoyunlu toward the Cult of Angels and away from Islam were too clear at their own time. Even today, the last remnant of the royal Turkmen Qara Qoyunlu tribe living in ex-Soviet and Iranian Azerbaijan are followers of the Cult of Angels according to Minorsky. The list of the primary Kurdish tribes that participated in the Safavid Alevi revolution included the Shâmlu, Shaykhâwand, Shâdlu, Khâjawand, Zafrânlu (Za'farânlu), Stâjlu (Istâjlu), and Quvânlu (Qovâ). All these tribes are still extant and Kurdish (see Table 1).

The red headgear that gave the name *Qizilbâsh,* Turkic for "red heads," to these socioreligious revolutionaries, are still worn among the Alevi Dimila Kurds. Among the non-Alevi Kurds, it finds its last remnants in the tradition of the Bârzânis. The chiefs of the Bârzâni Confederacy, who have traditionally commanded high religious leadership as well, carry the exclusive privilege of wearing red turbans to their family as a sacred tradition (see **Costumes & Jewelry**). This red color was also the hallmark of the Mazdakite and the Khurramite movements, which are the direct predecessors of Alevism.

As in Yârsânism, some branches of Alevism have for various reasons grown ever closer to the mainstream Shi'ite Islam they helped form in its current state in the course of the 15th-17th centuries. The most transformed branches of Alevism are similar in their association with Shi'ism to the Ahl-i Haq followers of Nurali Ilâhi (see **Yârsânism**). Even at their most advanced stage of convergence, neither the Ahl-i Haq nor the Alevis qualify as Shi'ites or Muslims by any Koranic standards.

Alevism was a disfavored religion in the Ottoman Empire, whose ruling sultans wore the mantle of the Prophet Muhammad and championed the cause of orthodox Sunni Islam. The Alevis were exposed to many massacres and state-sponsored pogroms immediately after the annexation of eastern Anatolia from Persia under the Ottoman sultan Selim in 1514.

Despite this, the Alevis have seen far less oppression than the Yezidis. This has been due to their larger numbers. Even today followers of this religion constitute roughly 20% of all Kurds.

The centuries-long underprivileged status of the Alevi community under the Ottomans and the suspicion of their Persian sympathies was inadvertently carried over into the Turkish Republican period after 1922, even though the Republic confessed total secularism, and Persia/Iran had ceased to be a threat. Only recently has it occurred to Ankara that there is no logic in disfavoring the Alevis, and the Bektâshi Sufi order which is strongly associated with it. On the contrary, there is much to be lost by continuing the old anti-Alevi policies. These policies have turned the Alevi Kurds (who saw themselves discriminated against on two counts, being Kurds and being Alevis) into some of the most radical insurgents and most extremist of all political groups. The rebellious attitude of these contemporary Alevis towards an oppressive state reminds one of the earlier movements by the followers of the Cult of Angels (e.g., the Mazdakites and the Khurramis), and the radicalism it has imparted to Shi'ism.

Alevism is now recognized in Turkey as an "indigenous" Anatolian religion worthy of respect. Cloaked in nationalist garb, and a useful counterweight to the rising militancy among the Sunni Muslims, Ankara even officially sponsors some Alevi festivals (see **Festivals, Ceremonies, & Calendar**).

Attention must be also given to Nusayrism, the branch of Alevism that was formed by the introduction of Arabian values into the practice of the Cult of Angels when it was introduced into the Syrian coastal regions by immigrating Kurds. Since Nusayrism is now followed by peoples who do not consider themselves to be ethnic Kurds, a brief observation of its tenets is all that is given here. Instead of Ali, Nusayrism takes Salmân to be the most important avatar of the Spirit after the Lord God. Salmân was a Persian companion of the Prophet Muhammad. Other Islamic figures fill in the Second Epoch (the most important earthly one) of the universal life, as they do in Alevism. The dates of the major annual celebrations of the Nusayris closely parallel those of the Yezidis, with New Ruz (March 21), Mithrâkân (called *Mihrajân* by the Nusayris, October 6-13), the Feast of Yezid (December 25) all being celebrated. The fourth celebration, observed on the occasion of the Tiragân by the Yezidis in late July, is replaced by *Sada* among the Nusayris, and is held in January about the time of the Christian feast of Epiphany.

The marked difference between Nusayrism and Alevism, and in fact the rest of the Cult of Angels, is not in their theology but in their sociology, particularly their treatment of women. In a very un-Kurdish fashion, but on par with other Semitic religions, women are held in a very low station by the Nusayris. They actually believe women, like objects and animals, lack souls, and that the soul of a sinful man may reincarnate into a woman after his death, so that he may spend one life span in the purgatory of a woman's soulless body. In fact, while retaining Fatima, daughter of the Prophet Muhammad, on the list of the major avatars of the Spirit, Nusayris turn the name into *Fâtim*, a masculine form of Fatima's name. They believe her to have been a man, manifesting himself as a woman only to give birth to Ali's sons and imams, Hasan and Husayn. This is a clear challenge to the high status that women enjoy in virtually all other branches of the Cult of Angels, belief in which requires the presence of one female Major Avatar in every stage of reincarnations of the Spirit, as set forth in Table 6 (see also **Status of Women & Family Life**).

Further Readings and Bibliography: P.J. Bumke, "Kizilbas Kurden in Dersim (Tunçeli, Türkei):Marginalität und Häresie," *Anthropos* 74 (1979); "The Kurdish Alevis: Boundaries and Perceptions," in Peter Andrews, ed., *Ethnic Groups in the Republic of Turkey* (Wiesbaden: Reichert, 1989); N. Yalman, "Islamic Reform and the Mystic Tradition in Eastern Turkey," *European Journal of Sociology* 10 (1969); F.W. Hasluck, "Heterodox Tribes of Asia Minor," *Journal of the Royal Anthropological Institute of Great Britain and Ireland* 51 (1921); Matti Moosa, *Extremist Shiites: The Ghulat Sects* (Syracuse: Syracuse University Press, 1988); James Reid, *Tribalism and Society in Islamic Iran, 1500-1629* (Malibu: Undena, 1983); Klaus Müller, *Kulturhistorische Studien zur Genese pseudo-islamischer Sektengebilde in Vorderasien* (Wiesbaden: Franz Steiner Verlag, 1967); P. Butyka, "Das ehemalige Vilayet Dersim," *Mitteilungen der kaiserlich-königlichen Geographischen Gesellschaft* 35 (Berlin, 1892); Peter J. Bumke, "Kizilbasç-Kurden in Dersim (Tunceli, Türkei): Marginalität und Häresie," *Anthropos* 74 (1979); Krisztina Kehl-Bodrogi, *Die Kizilbasç/Aleviten: Untersuchungen über eine esoterische Glaubensgemeinschaft in Anatolien* (Berlin: Klaus Schwarz Verlag, 1988); Rev. Henry H. Riggs, "The Religion of the Dersim Kurds," *Missionary Review of the World* 24 (1911); Hanna Sohrweide, "Der Sieg der Safaviden in Persien und seine Rückwirkungen auf die Shiiten Anatoliens im 16. Jahrhundert," *Der Islam* 41 (1965); Melville Charter, "The Kizilbash Clans of Kurdistan," *National Geographic Magazine* 54 (1928); Trowbridge, "The Alevis," *Harvard Theological Review* (1909); Helmut Nickel, "The Dawn of Chivalry," in Ann Farkas et al., eds., *From the Land of the Scythians* (New York: Metropolitan Museum of Arts, n.d.); Richard Antoun and Donald Quataert, eds., *Syria, Society, Culture, and Polity* (Albany: SUNY Press, 1991); Albert Hourani, *Minorities in the Arab World* (London: Oxford University Press, 1947); L. Molyneux-Steel, "Journey into Dersim," *Geographical Journal* 44-1 (London: 1914); M. Rekaya, "Mise au point sur Thèophobe et l'alliance de Bâbek avec Thèophile (839/840)," *Byzantion* 44 (1974); J. Rosser, "Theophilus' Khurramite Policy and Its Finale: The Revolt of Theophobus' Persian Troops in 838," *Byzantia* 6 (1974); Hans Jonas, *The Gnostic Religion* (Boston: Beacon, 1963).

Yezidism. The followers of the Yezidi religion, who have variously referred to themselves also as the Yazidi, Yazdâni, Izadi, and Dasna'i, have often been pejoratively referred to by outsiders as "devil worshippers." They constitute less than 5% of the Kurdish population. At present they live in fragmented pockets, primarily in northwest and northeast Syria, the Caucasus, southeast Turkey, in the Jabal Sanjâr highlands on the Iraqi-Syrian border, and regions north of the Iraqi city of Mosul.

As a branch of the Cult of Angels, Yezidism places a special emphasis on the angels. The name *Yezidi* is derived from the Old and Middle Iranic term *yazata* or *yezad*, for "angel," rendering it to mean "angelicans." Among these angels, the Yezidis include also Lucifer, who is referred to as *Malak Tâwus* ("Peacock Angel"). Far from being the prince of darkness and evil, Lucifer is of the same nature as other archangels, albeit with far more authority and power over worldly affairs. In fact, it is Malak Tâwus who creates the material world using the dismembered pieces of the original cosmic egg, or pearl, in which the Spirit once resided.

Despite the publication of (reportedly) all major Yezidi religious scriptures, and the availability of their translations, the most basic questions regarding the Yezidi cosmogony are left to speculation. For example, it is left to deductive reasoning to figure out in which epoch of the universal life Lucifer belongs, or what his exact station is. He naturally cannot be the same as the Universal Spirit, as the Spirit does not enter into the act of creation. In Yârsânism and Alevism it is Khâwandagâr, the "Lord God," who as the first avatar of the Spirit undertakes the task of *Sâjnâri*—world genesis. It is tempting to concluded that Lucifer replaces Khâwandagâr himself in the Yezidi cosmogony. Two Yezidi holy scriptures, *Jilwa* and *Mes'haf*, both discussed later, substantiate this conclusion. The following translations of these texts are adopted almost entirely from Guest (1987). *Jilwa* reads, "Malak Tâwus existed before all creatures," and "I (Malak Tâwus) was, and am now, and will continue unto eternity, ruling over all creatures....Neither is there any place void of me where I am not present....Every Epoch has an Avatar, and this by my counsel. Every generation changes with the Chief of this world, so that each one of the chiefs in his turn and cycle fulfills his charge. The other angels may not interfere in my deeds and work: Whatsoever I determine, that is." The implied attributes are all those of Khâwandagâr in Yârsânism and Alevism. Mes'haf asserts, "In the beginning God [which must mean the Universal Spirit] created the White Pearl out of his most precious Essence; and He created a bird named *Anfar*. And he placed the pearl upon its back, and dwelt thereon forty thousand years. On the first day [of Creation], Sunday, He created an angel named 'Azâzil, which is Malak Tâwus, the chief of all...." Mes'haf goes on to name six other angels, each created in the following days of this first week of creation in the First Epoch. The names of these angels closely match those of Yârsânism and Alevism, as given in Table 6. The problem is that there are *seven* rather than six avatars, leaving out, therefore, the Spirit himself from the world affairs. This is, however, the result of the later corruption of the original cosmogony, perhaps under Judeo-Christian influence. The rest of the opening chapter of the Mes'haf provides a version of human origin close to the Judeo-Christian story of Adam and Eve, and their interaction with Satan, even though Satan, here Lucifer, serves them only as an honest councillor and educator. Thereafter, he is left in charge of all creatures of the world.

The real story of the First Epoch however surfaces rather inconspicuously, in a single sentence at the end of the Mes'haf's first chapter. As it turns out, the sentence is very much in agreement with the basic tenets of the Cult of Angels. It reads, "From his essence and light He created six Avatars, whose creation was as one lighteth a lamp from another lamp." It is then safe to assume that the original Yezidi belief was that Lucifer was the primary avatar of the Universal Spirit in the First Epoch, and the rest of the cosmogony of the Cult of Angels remains more or less intact. Lucifer himself, in the form of Malak Tawus, "Peacock Angel," is represented by a sculptured bronze bird. This icon, called *Anzal*, "the Ancient One," is presented to worshippers annually at the major *Jam* at Lâlish.

Lâlish and its environs are also the burial site of Shaykh Adi, the most important personage of the Yezidi religion. Adi's role in Yezidism is similar to those played by Sahâk in Yârsânism and Ali in Alevism. To the Yezidis, Shaykh Adi is the most important avatar of the Universal Spirit of the epochs following the First Epoch. Adi being a primary avatar, he is therefore a reincarnation of Malak Tawus himself. In its modern, garbled form, Adi is assigned a founding role in Yezidism, and interestingly is believed to have lived at about the same time in history as Sultan Sahâk is believed by the modern Yârsâns, i.e., sometime in the 12-13th centuries. (This is about the same time that Bektâsh of Alevism is believed to have lived and founded that branch of the Cult.) Both Adi and Sahâk are believed to have lived well in excess of a century.

In addition to the main sculptured bird icon Anzal, there are six other similar relics of the Peacock Angel. These are called the *sanjaqs*, meaning "dioceses" (of the Yezidi community), and each is assigned to a different diocese of Yezidi concentration. Each year these are brought forth for worship to the dioceses of Syria, Zozan (i.e., Sasoon/Sasun or western and northern Kurdistan in Anatolia), Sanjâr, Shaykhân (of the Greater Zâb basin), Tabriz (Azerbaijan), and Musquf (Moscow, i.e., ex-Soviet Caucasus). The sanjaqs of Tabriz and Musquf no longer circulate, since there are not many Yezidis left in Azerbaijan, and the anti-religious Soviet government did not permit the icon to enter the bustling Yezidi community of the Caucasus.

Like other branches of the Cult of Angels, Yezidism lacks a holy book of divine origin. There are however many sacred works that contain the body of their beliefs. There is a very short volume (about 500 words) of Arabic-language hymns, ascribed to Shaykh Adi himself and named *Jilwa*, or "Revelation." Another, more detailed book is the *Mes'haf i Resh*, "the Black Book" in Kurdish, which has been credited to Adi's son, Shaykh Hasan ibn Adi (b. ca. AD 1195), a great-grandnephew of Adi.

Mes'haf is the most informative of the Yezidi scriptures, as it contains the body of the religion's cosmogony, catechesis, eschatology, and liturgy, despite many contradictions and vagaries (far more than in the works of the Yârsâns). The Mes'haf may in fact date back to the 13th century. Mes'haf was written in an old form of Kurmânji Kurdish. Kurmânji in the 13th century was primarily restricted to its stronghold in the ultra-rugged Hakkâri highlands (see **Kurmânji**). But Hakkâri is in fact exactly were the most ardent followers of Adi and Hasan arose. Adi himself, despite the Yezidi's belief that he was born in Bekaa Valley of Lebanon, came to be called *Adi al-Hakkâri* ("Adi of Hakkâri").

Of the Yezidis' four major annual celebrations (see **Festivals, Ceremonies, & Calendar**), two are of special interest here, the Jam and the feast of Yezid.

The most important Yezidi feast is the seven-day-long feast of *Jam*, when the bird icon of Anzal is presented to the worshippers. It occurs between the 6th and 13th of October, which is obligatory to all believers to attend, and is held at Lâlish, north of Mosul, the burial site of Adi and other important Yezidi holy figures, including Hasan. It coincides with the great ancient Aryan feast of *Mithrâkân* (Zoroastrian Mihragân, Nusayri Mihrajân; see **Alevism**), held customarily around the middle of October. Ancient Mithrâkân celebrated the act of world creation by the sun god Mithras, who killing the bull of heaven, used its dismembered body to create the material world. On the occasion of the feast at Lâlish, riding men pretend to capture a bull, with which they then circumambulate the Lâlish shrine of *Shams al-Din* (the "Sun of the Faith"), before sacrificing the bull and distributing its flesh to the pilgrims.

Yezid, a puzzling personage, is venerated by the Yezidis in a somewhat confused fashion. Yezid is credited with founding Yezidism (the religion, obviously, shares his name), or to have been the most important avatar of the Spirit after Malak Tâwus (some even claiming he is the same as Malak Tâwus). He is occasionally identified by the Yezidis as the Umayyad caliph, Yazid ibn Mu'awiyya (r. AD 680-683), the archvillain to Shi'ite Muslims. This faulty identification is encouraged by the Syrian and Iraqi governments (who hope thus to detach the Yezidis from other Kurds, and to connect them instead with the Umayyads, hence the Arabs). It has also prompted the leading Yezidi family, the chols, to adopt Arabic costumes and Umayyad caliphal names. Yet, far from being the 'Umayyad caliph, the name is certainly derived from *yezad*, "angel," and judging by its importance, he must be *the* angel of the Yezidis. This comical confusion, which permeates the Yezidi leadership to the extent that they doubt their own ethnic identity, is not unexpected, given the intensity of their persecution in the past, and the destruction of whatever religious and historical literature Yezidism may have had in the past, in addition to the little that remains today.

Is it possible that Malak Tâwus, who created the material world in Yezidi cosmogony by utilizing a piece of the original cosmic egg or pearl that he had dismembered earlier, originally represented Mithras in early Yezidism, and only later Lucifer? The second most important Yezidi celebration points toward this possibility. It is held between middle and late December and commemorates the birth of Yezid. His birthday at or near the winter solstice, links him to Mithras. (Mithraism did after all expand into the Roman

Empire from this general geographical area in the course of the first century BC, and Mithras' mythical birth was celebrated on December 25 as already has been discussed.) The celebration parallels in importance the major Jam ceremony in October. It is commemorated with three days of fasting before the jubilees.

In the Yezidi version of world creation, birds play a central role in all major events—too numerous in fact to permit summary here. The reverence of the Yezidis for divine manifestations in the form of a bird, the Peacock Angel, and the sacredness of roosters are just two better-known examples. What is fascinating, but less known, is that within 30 miles of the shrines of Lâlish are the Shanidar-Zawi Chami archaeological sites of central Kurdistan, where the archaeologist Solecki has unearthed the remains of shrines and large bird wings, particularly those of the great bustards, dated to 10,800±300 years ago. The remains are indicative of a religious ritual that involved birds and employed their wings, possibly as part of the priestly costume (Solecki 1977).

The representation of bird wings on gods was later to become common in Mesopotamian art, and particularly in the royal rock carvings of the Assyrians, whose capital Nineveh can literally be seen on the horizon from Lâlish. The artistic combination of wings and non-flying beings like humans (to form gods), lions (to form sphinxes), bulls (to form royal symbols), and horses (to form the Pegasus), as well as wing-like adornments to priestly costumes, are common in many cultures, but the representation of the supreme deity as a full-fledged bird is peculiarly Yezidi. The evidence of sacrificial rites practiced at ancient Zawi Chami may substantiate an indigenous precursor to modern Yezidi practice.

The bird icon of Lâlish has always been readily identified, as the name implies, as a peacock. However, there are no peacocks native to Kurdistan or this part of Asia. In light of the discoveries at Zawi Chami, the great bustard is a much more likely the bird of the Yezidi icon. The great bustard (Kurdish *shawât*) is native to Kurdistan (see **Flora & Fauna**). It too possesses a colorful tail, similar to that of a turkey (similar to, though much smaller than, that of a peacock, which is seen on the icon). The great bustard far more logically suits the archaic tradition of the Yezidis than does the peacock, a native bird of India.

The practice of bowing three times before the rising sun and chanting hymns for the occasion is practiced by the Yezidis, as among the traditional Alevis (Nikitine 1956). The Yezidis also practice the rite of embracing the "very body of the sun," by kissing its beams as they first fall on the trunks of the trees at the dawn (Kamurân Ali Badir-Khân 1934).

Another Alevi hallmark, the representation of the deity in the shape of a sword or dagger stuck into the ground, is also found among the Yezidis, albeit not for worship but to take oaths upon it (Alexander 1928, Bellino 1816).

In addition to an entrenched aristocracy, the social class system of the Yezidis shows interesting similarities to the rigid social stratification of the Zoroastrian Sasanian Empire. Zoroastrian priests forbade anyone who did not belong to the priestly or princely class to gain literacy, and traditionally Yezidism barred such luxury altogether. (Some Yarsans also believe that this should be so, and also practice it.) In fact, it has been asserted that until the beginning of this century only one man among the Yezidis, the custodian of the *Jilwa,* knew how to read (Guest 1987, 33). This ban is largely gone now, although through force of habit the Yezidi commoners are still not keen on literacy.

Interestingly, the wealthier Yezidi shaykhs and mullahs wear Arab bedouin clothes and headdress, speak both Arabic and Kurdish, and usually have Arabic names. The poorer Yezidi social and religious leaders, on the other hand, have Kurdish names, speak only Kurdish, and wear Kurdish traditional clothes and headgear (Lescot 1938).

Leadership of the Yezidi community has traditionally rested with one of the old Kurdish princely houses, the Chols, who took over in the 17th century. They replaced the line of rulers who claimed descent from Shaykh Hasan, the author of Mes'haf. They are supported financially and otherwise by every Yezidi. The priestly duties reside, as in Yârsânism, with the members of the seven hereditary priestly houses, which include the Chols.

The relative smallness of the current Yezidi community can be misleading. At the time of Saladin's conquest of Antioch, the Yezidis were dominant in the neighboring valleys in the Amanus coastal mountains, and by the 13th and 14th centuries Yezidis had expanded their domains by converting many Muslims and Christians to their faith, from Antioch to Urmiâ, and from Sivâs to Kirkuk. They also mustered a good deal of political and military power. In this period, the emirs of the Jazira region (upper Mesopotamia) were Yezidis, as was one of the emirs of Damascus. A Yezidi preacher, Zayn al-Din Yusuf, established Yezidi communities of converts in Damascus and Cairo, where he died in 1297. His imposing tomb in Cairo remains to this day. Of 30 major tribal confederacies enumerated by the Kurdish historian Sharaf al-Din Bitlisi in *Sharafnâma* (1596), he contends seven were fully Yezidi in times past. Among these tribes was the historic and populous Buhtâns (the *Bokhtanoi* of Herodotus).

An early Muslim encyclopedist, Shahâb al-Din Fadlullâh al-'Umari, declares as Yezidi in AD 1338 also the Dunbuli/Dumbuli. This reference carries a very important piece of information, which can be the only known reference to the Cult of Angels before its fragmentation into its present state and the loss of its common name. Since the Dunbuli were a well-known branch of the Alevi Daylamites, and since the reporting by al-'Umari is normally astute, the declaration of this tribe as Yezidi may indicate that at the time the appellation *Yazidi* ("angelicans') was that of the Cult of Angels in general. (The historical designation *Yazdâni* here for the Cult of Angels has been used to avoid confusion with the modern Yezidism.)

There have been persistent attempts by their Muslim and Christian neighbors to convert the Yezidis, peacefully or otherwise. The Ottoman government and military schools recruited many Yezidis, who were then converted to Sunni Islam, while in the mountains the Yezidis maintained their faith. A petition submitted in 1872 to the Ottoman authorities to exempt the Yezidis from military service has become the *locus classicus* on the subject of Yezidi religious codes and beliefs (for the English translation of the text, see Driver 1921-23).

Failing peaceful conversion, the Ottomans carried out massacres against the Yezidis in the course of the 17th and 18th centuries. The massacres recurred in Ottoman domains in the middle of the 19th century, resulting in a great migration of Ottoman Yezidis into the Russian territories in the Caucasus. Twenty major massacres between 1640 and 1910 were counted by Lescot (see **Deportations & Forced Resettlements**).

Many Yezidis escaped into the forbidding mountain areas, but others converted, at least nominally, to Sunni Islam. The Ottoman Land Registration Law of 1859 particularly pressed for conversion by refusing to honor ownership claims of Yezidis. Many Yezidi shaykhs, who were the primary property owners, maintained their lands and property by converting. The Yezidi leaders whose holdings were in the inaccessible higher mountains were spared the need for conversion, and so were the landless sharecroppers or herders. Before 1858, the Yezidis in the Antioch-Amanus region on the Mediterranean littoral numbered 200,000, constituting the majority of the inhabitants. In 1938, Lescot counted only 60,000—a small minority.

Even today the Yezidis are still subject to great pressure for conversion. There is now also a movement to strip the Yezidis of their Kurdish identity by either declaring them an independent ethnic group apart from the Kurds or by attaching them to the Arabs. Hence, the Yezidis are now called "Umayyad Arabs" by the governments of Iraq and Syria, capitalizing on the aforementioned confusion that exists among the Yezidis with respect to the irrelevant Umayyad caliph Yazid ibn Mu'awiyya.

Most Yezidis are now in Syria, in the Jazira region and the Jabal Sanjâr heights, and in the Afrin region northwest of Aleppo. The next largest population of Yezidis is found in the Caucasus, where up to half the Kurds are followers of Yezidism. In Iraq, where the holiest Yezidi shrines of Lâlish are located, they are found in a band from eastern Jabal Sanjâr toward Dohuk and to Lâlish, northeast of Mosul. There used to be a large number of Yezidis in Anatolia, prior to the massacres of the last century. Those who now live within the borders of Turkey are thinly spread from Mardin to Siirt, and from Antioch and Antep to Urfâ. There are also a relatively small number of Yezidis in Iran, particularly between the towns of Quchân and Dughâ'i in the Khurâsâni enclave, and in Azerbaijan province.

Further Readings and Bibliography: R.H.W. Empson, *The Cult of the Peacock Angel* (London, 1928); E.S. Drower, *Peacock Angel* (London, 1941); G.R. Driver, "The Religion of the Kurds," *Bulletin of the School of Oriental and Studies* II (1921-23); John S. Guest, *The Yezidis* (New York: KPI, 1987); Isya Joseph, *Devil Worship* (Boston, 1919); Alphonse Mingana, "Devil-worshippers: Their Beliefs and their Sacred Books," *Journal of the Royal Asiatic Society* (1916); R.C. Zaehner, *Zurvân: A Zoroastrian Dilemma* (New York: Oxford University Press, 1955); R. Lescot, *Enquête sur les Yezidis de Syrie et du Djebel Sindjar, Mémoires de l'Institut Français de Damas*, vol. 5 (Beirut, 1938); Hugo Makas, *Kurdische Studien*, vol. 3, *Jezidengebete* (Heidelberg, 1900); Ralph Solecki, "Predatory Bird Rituals at Zawi Chemi Shanidar," *Sumer* XXXIII.1 (1977); Rose Solecki, "Zawi Chemi Shanidar, a Post-Pleistocene Village Site in Northern Iraq," *Report of the VI International Congress on Quaternary* (1964); Sami Said Ahmed, *The Yazidis: Their Life and Beliefs*, ed. Henry Field (Miami: Field Research Projects, 1975); E.S. Drower, *Peacock Angel: Being Some Account of Votaries of a Secret Cult and Their Sanctuaries*. (London, 1941); Cecil J. Edmonds, *A Pilgrimage to Lalish* (London: The Royal Asiatic Society, 1967); Theodor Menzel, "Ein Beitrag zur Kenntnis der Jeziden," in Hugo Grother, ed., *Meine Vorderasienexpedition 1906 und 1907*. Vol. 1. (Leipzig, 1911); Basile Nikitine, *Les Kurdes, etude sociologique et historique* (Paris, 1956); Kamurân Ali Badir Khân, "Les soleil chez les Kurdes," *Atlantis* 54, vii-viii (Paris, 1934); Constance Alexander, *Baghdad in Bygone Days, from the Journals of the Correspondence of Claudius Rich... 1808-1821* (London, 1928); Charles Bellino letter, 16 May 1816, to Hammer, included in *Fundgruben des Orients* 5 (1816).

SUFI MYSTIC ORDERS

An overwhelming majority of Muslim and non-Muslim Kurds are followers of one of many mystic Sufi orders (or *tariqa*). The bonds of the Muslim Kurds, for example, to different Sufi orders have traditionally been stronger than to orthodox Muslim practices. Sufi rituals in Kurdistan, led by Sufi masters, or *shaykhs*, contain so many clearly non-Islamic rites and practices that an objective observer would not consider them Islamic in the orthodox sense.

The Sufi shaykhs train deputies (*khalifa*), who represent and supervise the followers of various districts in the name of the shaykh, collecting allegiance, and dues, for the shaykh. Anyone may follow a shaykh, but to actually join the order of a specific shaykh, he/she must go through a process of initiation. These members (*murids*) then participate in many rituals, including the Sufi dances, chants, and prayers. When necessary they will go into combat for their shaykhs. Shaykh Ubaydullâh, Shaykh Sa'id, Shaykh Ahmad Bârzâni, and Shaykh Mahmud Barzanji, among others, were Sufi masters who asked for and received armed support from their murids in their political adventures (see **Early Modern** and **Modern History**).

The close shaykh-murid relationship is also an excellent vote-gathering mechanism for modern democratic elections. As such, in Turkey at least, the shaykhs curry favor with various political parties by delivering their followers' votes (van Bruinessen 1991).

Three of the stormiest and most controversial early movements within Sufism were led by Husayn ibn Mansur Hallâj (crucified AD 922), 'Ain al-Qudât Hamadâni (crucified AD 1131), and Shahâb al-Din Suhrawardi (crucified AD 1191). They all preached ideas anti-thetical to the basic tenets of established Islam, and in astonishing conformity with the Cult of Angels. Hallâj, for example, claimed himself to be an avatar of the divinity, by which he proclaimed in his famous formula, *anâ'l haqq*, Arabic for "I am the Haq [the

Spirit]," out of the belief in the unity of creation, and that all creatures are ultimately the manifestations of the same original Universal Spirit. He thus also declared Lucifer to have been redeemed and elevated to the highest universal station, as in Yezidism. He was subjected to exquisite tortures before being crucified in Baghdad. At present there is a shrine dedicated to Hallâj in the sacred Yezidi religious center and shrine complex at Lâlish, next to the tomb of Shaykh Adi.

Hamadâni's ideas revolved around the "unity of existence"; that is, like Hallâj, he believed that all creations are manifestations of the original, Universal Spirit. The Spirit is also aloof from events in this world, as the Cult of Angels believes the Spirit to have remained aloof after his original—and final—reincarnation into Lord God, the creator of the material world. His idea of successive reincarnation, and the redemption of Lucifer, added to his other non-Islamic preachings, qualified him for burning on a cross by the Muslim authorities when he was 33.

The same general ideas of Hallâj and Hamadâni are echoed in the work of Suhrawardi. Suhrawardi's Gnostic teachings under the rubric of the School of *Ishrâq*, "illumination," bear so much influence from the Cult of Angels that it is rather an extension of that religion (albeit with strong Hellenistic and Mesopotamian influences) than an Islamic Sufi movement. There exists a hymn by Suhrawardi, entitled *Al-Hurakhsh al-Kabir*, "The Great Sun [Deity]," which is to be made daily to the rising sun, asking for a personal book at the end. Echoes of the daily Cult prayer to the rising sun can unmistakably be heard in this hymn. "Thou art the strong and victorious Hurakhsh," writes Suhrawardi, "the vanquisher of the dark...the king of Angels...the proprietor of the incarnate lights of existence by the power of the obeyed God, the luminous matter...the learned scholarly philosopher, the greatest sacred son of the corporeal lights, the successor of the light of lights in the material world...I beg [him]...so that he might beg his God and God of gods...[to give me a boon]" (Mo'in 1962). His idea of the evolution of the worshipper's soul into that of the Divinity, although not as pronounced as that in the Cult of Angels, finally cost him his life at the age of 38, at the instigation of the Muslim ulema and at the hands of another Kurd, the Ayyubid prince of Aleppo, in AD 1191. Like Hallâj, Hamadâni and Suhrawardi have been elevated to the station of minor avatars of the Universal Spirit in the Cult.

Hallâj was born in Baghdad from parents who had migrated from the Fârs region in the southern Zagros, where tens of Kurdish tribes were present at the time (see **Historical Migrations**). The influence of the Cult of Angels on Hallâj's beliefs is, however, much easier to establish than his ethnic affiliation. This is not so, however, with Hâmadâni or Suhrawardi. Hamadâni was born and lived in Hamadân in southern Kurdistan. Suhrawardi was from the town of Shahraward (often misread as Suhraward), between Shahrazur (modern Sulaymânia) and Zanjân, 15 miles east of Bijâr. Suhraward's population, according to the medieval Islamic geographer Ibn Hawqal, was, like today, predominantly Kurdish.

About 300 years later another follower of the Cult of Angels popularized another controversial and stormy Sufi movement. Muhammad Nurbakhsh (the "bestower of light") began his preaching in the middle of the 15th century. He was from Lahsâ (modern Ahsâ in oil-bearing eastern Saudi Arabia). Lahsâ had been a hotbed of extremist movements, like those of the Qarmatites in early Islamic times, whose socioeconomic ideologies, as well as their belief in the transmigration of the soul, connected them with the earlier Khurramiyya and Mazdakite movements of the Zagros region (see **Cult of Angels**). His connection with the Cult of Angels was revealed when he was given the mantle of *Hamadâni*. Like Hallâj and Suhrawardi, Nurbakhsh also claimed to be a minor avatar of the Universal Spirit, of the line that included the Prophet Muhammad in the Second Epoch of the universal life (see Table 6). He proclaimed himself a *Mahdi*, "deliverer, messiah," and further claimed his father's name to have been *Abdullâh* (like that of the Prophet Muhammad). He named his son *Qasim*, so his own title would be *Abul-Qasim* (again, like that of the Prophet). He also claimed supernatural powers consistent with those expected of an avatar in the Cult of Angels, and blasphemy in Islam. For this and other unorthodox utterances, he was attacked by the mainstream Sunni and Shi'ite ulema, among them, his contemporary Abdul Rahmân Jâmi. He did not, however, meet the dire end of his three predecessors, Hallâj, Hamadân, and Suhrawardi.

Arriving in Kurdistan, Nurbakhsh announced himself also to be the new caliph of all Muslims. The Kurds minted coins in his name (AD 1443). He was arrested by the Timurid king Shâhrukh and imprisoned in Herât, but was released in AD 1444. Nurbakhsh died of natural causes, perhaps only because his movement occurred at the height of the Cult of Angels' offensive on Shi'ite Islam in the 15th century, and existence of powerful Alevi dynasties in the area.

Nurbakhsh's son and successor, Qâsim, was favored by the founder of the Safavid dynasty, Ismâ'il I, and he and the Nurbakhshi movement increasingly came to reflect the religious evolution through which the Safavids were going in the course of the 16th and 17th centuries (see **Early Modern History**). The Nurbakhshi Sufi order has evolved from there into a bona fide Shi'ite order, with its membership from among the Kurds being primarily Shi'ite, but with most members being non-Kurds. There are also many Yârsân followers in this order.

The oldest Sunni Sufi order still followed by the Kurds is the Qâdiri, named after its founder, Abdul-Qâdir Gilâni (also Gaylâni, Kaylâni, or Khaylâni) (AD 1077-1166). Many important Kurdish religious families are presently, or are known in the past to have been, members of this order. The Qâdiri order has been in steady retreat since the start of the 19th century, under pressure from another Sufi order, the Naqshbandis.

The Tâlabâni tribe, the Patriotic Union of Kurdistan party, its leadership, and most people in the southern sectors of Iraqi Kurdistan and in eastern Kurdistan (in Iran) are Qâdiris. The order's headquarters are in the sacred ancient town of Barzanja near Sulaymânia. Shaykh Mahmud, leader of many Kurdish uprisings against the British Mandate of Iraq, was also the leader of the Qâdiri Sufi house of Barzanji (see **Modern History**).

A more recent arrival into Kurdistan is the Sunni Naqshbandi order, founded by Bahâ al-Din Naqshband of Bukhârâ (AD 1317-1389) and introduced from central Asia, perhaps by the Turkic tribes and/or Turkic *Bakshis*, whence they were arriving in these parts of the Middle East since the 12th century (see **Historical Migrations**).

Today, the people in northern, and to some extent western, Kurdistan follow the Naqshbandi order, while central and eastern Kurdistan are still Qâdiri. The Bârzâni tribe is led by Naqshbandi Sufi masters, who exercise temporal, as much as spiritual, influence in their area. Until late in the last century, however, the Bârzânis and all other tribes and clans in these areas of Kurdistan were followers of the Qâdiri order. This and many other conversions to the Naqshbandi order were the direct result of the energy and fervor of one Mawlânâ Khâlid.

In 1811 Mawlânâ Khâlid (b. 1779), a Kurdish Naqshbandi shaykh (of the Jaf tribe) from Shahrazur (modern Sulaymânia) set out on a furious bout of proselytization by appointing a myriad of deputies across Kurdistan and beyond. These deputies then proceeded, after Khalid's death in 1827, to appoint their own deputies. In a short span of time, north central Kurdistan, along with its influential religious center of Nahri/Nehri, near Rawânduz, was lost by the Qâdiri order for good. The change has been so recent and abrupt that the most important Sufi religious family there still bears the name of Gaylâni or Khaylâni (after Abudl-Qâdir Gilâni). The Iraqi Kurdish Democratic Party and its Bârzâni leadership are thus of Naqshbandi Sufi affiliation.

Under President Özal's government (himself of a Naqshbandi family), the Naqshbandis have staged a comeback in Turkey after many decades of official banning and persecution, following Shaykh Sa'id's uprising of 1925 (see **Modern History**).

Sufi lodges (*khânaqâs*) pepper Kurdistan, and are much more common in fact than mosques or any other places of religious ritual (except, perhaps, for the sacred trees and ponds dedicated to Khidir) (see **Popular Culture**).

Non-Muslim Kurds also follow Sufi orders of their own, or any one of the Cult orders, which are at least nominally known to be Shi'ite Sufi orders (as, for example, are the Nurbakhshi and Ni'matullâhi orders). The Alevis in western and northern Kurdistan are predominantly of the Bektâshi/Baktâshi order. The order traditionally claimed to be a Sunni Muslim order, since none else was permitted under the Ottomans. But the followers of this order remained almost exclusively Alevi, with adherents among Kurds and non-Kurds all the way to Bulgaria, Albania, and Bosnia. The influence of this order on the life of the Alevi Kurds is profound. One of the most important festivals observed by the Alevi Kurds is that of Hâji Bektâsh, the founder of the Bektâshi Sufi order and one of the most important of the primary avatars of the Spirit in Alevism. While long suppressed, the Turkish government, within whose domain the bulk of the Bektâshis live, now allows, and sometimes officially sponsors, these Alevi feasts. A reason may be the influence of Turkish President Özal. Even though Özal's own family is of Naqshbandi background, they are natives of the largely Kurdish city of Malâtya, where both Naqshbandi and Bektâshi orders are present.

The Bektâshis are more commonly, and indirectly, known in the West through their "Whirling Dervishes," whose white costumes and conical white hats are familiar to most Westerners interested in the Asian religions and practices. The most important center of the Bektâshis is the site of the shrine of the great Sufi master and poet, Mevlânâ (more accurately, Mawlânâ Jalâl al-Din Balkhi, also known as Al-Rumi), in the city of Konya, near the southern fringes of the central Anatolian Kurdish enclave.

The Qâdiri order also practices elaborate dances and plays musical instruments alongside chants, not dissimilarly from the Bektâshi Whirling Dervishes. The Naqshbandis, on the other hand, have traditionally been far more given to meditations and chants to reach the state of ecstasy that is the hallmark of all Sufi orders. The Bektâshis are famous for their dance and music, and use the chants as the supplements to these.

A rather peculiar order, the Rafâ'is, should also be mentioned, as they are in a sense a mystic order. Their strong belief in the ability of the soul to transcend the physical body at the will of any well-trained mind provides for ceremonies that include walking barefoot on hot coal, swallowing swords, and driving sharp objects through one's own flesh, and in all cases, seemingly coming out unharmed.

Further Readings and Bibliography: N. Yalman, "Islamic Reform and the Mystic Tradition in Eastern Turkey," *European Journal of Sociology* 10 (1969); S.H. Nasr, *Shihâbaddin Yahyâ Sohrawardî* (Paris: Institut Français d'Iranologie, Bibliothèque Iranienne, 1970); John Kingsley Birge, *The Bektashi Order of Dervishes* (London: Luzac, 1937); Martin van Bruinessen, "Religious Life in Diyarbekir: Religious Learning and the Role of the Tariqats," in Martin van Bruinessen and H. E. Boeschoten, eds., *Evliya Çelebi in Diyarbekir* (Leiden: Brill, 1988); Hamid Algar, "The Naqshbandi Order: A Preliminary Survey of Its History and Significance," *Studia Islamica* 44 (1976); Hamid Algar, "Said Nursi and the Risala-i Nur," *Islamic Perspectives: Studies in Honour of Sayyid Abul Ala Mawdudi.* (London, 1978); Halkawt Hakim, "Mawlana Khalid et les pouvoirs," in Marc Gaborieau, A. Popovic, and T. Zarcone, eds., *Naqshbandis: Historical Development and Present Situation of a Muslim Mystical Order* (Istanbul-Paris: Isis, 1990); Albert Hourani, "Shaikh Khalid and the Naqshbandi Order," in S. M. Stern, A. Hourani, and V. Brown, eds., *Islamic Philosophy and the Classical Tradition* (Oxford: Oxford University Press, 1972); Sherif Mardin, *Religion and Social Change in Modern Turkey: The Case of Bediuzzaman Said Nursi* (Albany: State University of New York Press, 1989); Wheeler Thackston, *The Mystical & Visionary Treatises of Suhrawardi* (London: Octagon, 1982); J.S. Trimingham, *The Sufi Orders in Islam* (New York and London: Oxford University Press, 1971); Martin van Bruinessen, "Religion in Kurdistan," *Kurdish Times* IV:1-2 (1991); 'Ain al-Qudât al-Hamadâni, *The Apologia*, A. J. Arberry, ed. and trans., as *A*

Sufi Marty (London: George Allen and Unwin, 1969); Muhammad Mo'in, "Huraxs," in W.B. Henning and E. Yarshater, eds., *A Locust's Leg: Studies in the Honour of S.H. Taqizadeh* (London: Percy Lund, 1962).

JUDAISM

The history of Judaism in Kurdistan is ancient. The Talmud holds that Jewish deportees were settled in Kurdistan 2800 years ago by the Assyrian king Shalmaneser III (r. 858-824 BC). As indicated in the Talmud, the Jews eventually were given permission by the rabbinic authorities to convert local Kurds. They were exceptionally successful in their endeavor. The illustrious Kurdish royal house of Adiabene, with Arbil as its capital, was converted to Judaism in the course of the 1st century BC, along with, it appears, a large number of Kurdish citizens in the kingdom (see Irbil/Arbil in *Encyclopaedia Judaica*). The name of the Kurdish king *Monobazes* (related etymologically to the name of the ancient Mannaeans), his queen *Helena,* and his son and successor *Izates* (derived from *yazata,* "angel"), are preserved as the first proselytes of this royal house (Ginzberg 1968, VI.412). But this is chronologically untenable as Monobazes' effective rule began only in AD 18. In fact during the Roman conquest of Judea and Samaria (68-67 BC), it was only Kurdish Adiabene that sent provisions and troops to the rescue of the beseiged Galilee (Grayzel 1968, 163)—an inexplicable act if Adiabene was not already Jewish (see **Classical History**). Many modern Jewish historians like Kahle (1959), who believes Adiabene was Jewish by the middle of the 1st century BC, and Neusner (1986), who goes for the middle of the 1st century AD, have tried unsuccessfully to reconcile this chronolgical discrepancy. All agree that by the beginning of the 2nd century AD, at any rate, Judaism was firmly established in central Kurdistan.

Like many other Jewish communities, Christianity found Adiabene a fertile ground for conversion in the course of 4th and 5th centuries. Despite this, Jews remained a populous group in Kurdistan until the middle of the present century and the creation of the state of Israel. At home and in the synagogues, Kurdish Jews speak a form of ancient Aramaic called *Suriyâni* (i.e., "Assyrian"), and in commerce and the larger society they speak Kurdish. Many aspects of Kurdish and Jewish life and culture have become so intertwined that some of the most popular folk stories accounting for Kurdish ethnic origins connect them with the Jews. Some maintain that the Kurds sprang from one of the lost tribes of Israel, while others assert that the Kurds emerged through an episode involving King Solomon and the genies under his command (see **Folklore & Folk Tales**).

The relative freedom of Kurdish women among the Kurdish Jews led in the 17th century to the ordination of the first woman rabbi, Rabbi Asenath Bârzâni, the daughter of the illustrious Rabbi Samuel Bârzâni (d. ca. 1630), who founded many Judaic schools and seminaries in Kurdistan. For her was coined the term *tanna'ith,* the feminine form for a Talmudic scholar. Eventually, Mâmâ ("Lady") Asenath became the head of the prestigious Judaic academy at Mosul (Mann 1932).

The tombs of Biblical prophets like Nahum in Alikush, Jonah in Nabi Yunis (ancient Nineveh), Daniel in Kirkuk, Habakkuk in Tuisirkân, and Queen Esther and Mordecai in Hamadân, and several caves reportedly visited by Elijah are among the most important Jewish shrines in Kurdistan and are venerated by all Jews today.

The Alliance Israélite Universelle opened schools and many other facilities in Kurdistan for education and fostered progress among the Jewish Kurds as early as 1906 (Cuenca 1960). Non-Jewish Kurds also benefitted vastly, since children were accepted into these schools regardless of their religious affiliation. A new class of educated and well-trained citizens was being founded in Kurdistan. Operations of the Alliance continued until soon after the creation of Israel.

Many Kurdish Jews have recently emigrated to Israel. However, they live in their own neighborhoods in Israel and still celebrate Kurdish life and culture, including Kurdish festivals, costumes, and music in some of its most original forms.

Further Readings and Bibliography: *Encyclopaedia Judaica*, entries on Kurds and Irbil/Arbil; Louis Ginzberg, *The Legends of the Jews, 5th ed.* (Philadelphia: The Jewish Publication Society of America, 1968); Jacob Mann, *Texts and Studies in Jewish History and Literature*, vol. I (London, 1932); Yona Sabar, *The Folk Literature of the Kurdistani Jews* (New Haven: Yale University Press, 1982); Paul Magnarella, "A Note on Aspects of Social Life among the Jewish Kurds of Sanandaj, Iran," *Jewish Journal of Sociology* XI.1 (1969); Walter Fischel, "The Jews of Kurdistan," *Commentary* VIII.6 (1949); André Cuenca, "L'oeuvre de l'Allance Israélite Universelle en Iran," in *Les droits de l'éducation* (Paris: UNESCO, 1960); Dina Feitelson, "Aspects of the Social Life of Kurdish Jews," *Jewish Journal of Sociology* I.2 (1910); Walter Fischel, "The Jews of Kurdistan, a Hundred Years Ago," *Jewish Social Studies* (1944); Solomon Grayzel, *A History of the Jews* (New York: Mentor, 1968); Paul Kahle, *The Cairo Geniza* (Oxford, 1959); Jacob Neusner, *Judaism, Christianity, and Zoroastrianism in Talmudic Babylonia* (New York; University Press of America, 1986).

CHRISTIANITY

The early history of Christianity in Kurdistan closely parallels that of the rest of Anatolia and Mesopotamia. By the early 5th century the Kurdish royal house of Adiabene had converted from Judaism to Christianity. The extensive ecclesiastical archives kept at their capital of Arbela (modern Arbil), are valuable primary sources for the history of central Kurdistan, from the middle of the Parthian era (ca. 1st century AD). Kurdish Christians, like their Jewish predecessors, used Aramaic for their records and archives and as the ecclesiastical language.

The persecution of the Christians in the Persian Sasanian Empire extended to Kurdistan as well. It was only after the conversion of the Empire's Christians to the eastern Nestorian church (from St. Nestorius, d. AD 440) and their break with Rome and Constantinople in the 6th century that they were given a measure of safety. At the time of the advent of Islam in the 7th century, central Kurdistan was predominantly Christian.

Anatolian Kurds, on the other hand, responded in two distinct manners to this new religion. The westernmost Kurds, i.e., those of Pontus and the western regions of Cappadocia and Cilicia in central and northern Anatolia, converted to Christianity before the 7th century. Their conversion, it turned out, was to cost them in the long run their ethnic identity. They were wholly Hellenized before the arrival of the Turkic nomads in Anatolia in the 12th century. The Kurds of eastern Anatolia, including eastern Cilicia and Cappadocia, and all those east of the Euphrates resisted conversion, and were punished for it by the Byzantines.

When in the 8th and 9th centuries the Byzantines deported and exiled the non-Christian populations from their Anatolian domain, Kurds suffered the most. The Cappadocian and Cilician Kurds were deported in toto (see **Deportations & Forced Resettlements**).

Christianity's effect on southern Kurdistan appears to have been marginal, but clear. The influence of Christian tenets on Yârsânism, which goes beyond the influences that would have been exerted via Islam, point to a direct exchange between the two religions.

With the waning and isolation of Christianity in Kurdistan and the Middle East following the expansion of Islam, the dwindling Christian Kurdish community began to renounce its Kurdish ethnic identity and forged a new one with its neighboring Semitic Christians. The Suriyâni (Nestorian) Christians of Mesopotamia and Kurdistan, who have recently adopted the ethnic name *Assyrian*, are a Neo-Aramaic-speaking amalgam of Kurds and Semitic peoples who have retained the old religion and language of the Nestorian Church, and the court language of the old Kingdom of Adiabene. A large number of these Suriyâni Christians lived, until the onslaught of World War 1, deep in mountainous northern Kurdistan, away from any ethnic or genetic influence of the Semitic Christians of lowland Mesopotamia. Their fair complexion, in marked contrast to that of their Semitic "brethren" in the Mosul region, also bears witness to their Kurdish origin.

Yet they speak Neo-Aramaic and insist on a separate ethnic identity. In the matter of language, the Christians in Kurdistan share the use of Neo-Aramaic with the Kurdish Jews.

Not all Christian Kurds found it necessary to exchange their Kurdish identity for their faith. The medieval Muslim historian and commentator Mas'udi reports Kurds who were Christians in the 10th century. In 1272 Marco Polo wrote, "In the mountainous parts [of Mosul] there is a race of people named Kurds, some of whom are Christians of the Nestorian and Jacobite sects, and others Muhammadan" (*Travels*, I.vi). These are in fact Christian Kurds, as Polo earlier in his work distinguishes the non-Kurdish Christian population of the region.

There are records of missionary conversion of the Kurds to Christianity as early as the 15th century, a notable example being Father Subhalemaran (Nikitine 1956, 231). Many other missionaries have been sent from Europe and later America into Kurdistan since that time, with some of them producing the earliest studies of Kurdish language and culture, including dictionaries (see **Early Modern History**). Religious changes have almost always has entailed language change (see **Classical History** and **Historical Migrations**). Most Kurds who converted to Christianity eventually switched to Armenian and Neo-Aramaic, and were thus counted among these ethnic groups. A good example of this process was observed at the end of the World War I.

At the time of the fall of the Ottoman Empire a considerable number of Christians who spoke only Kurdish left the area of western and northern Kurdistan for the French Mandate of Syria. There, having been told they "must be Armenian" if they were Christian, they were counted and eventually assimilated into the immigrant Armenian community of Syria and Lebanon.

Some non-Christian Kurds of Anatolia and even central Kurdistan still bless their bread dough by pressing the sign of the cross on it while letting it rise. They also make pilgrimage to the old abandoned or functioning churches of the Armenian and Assyrian Christians. This may well be a cultural tradition left with the Kurds through long association with Christian neighbors, or very possibly it stems from the time that many Kurds themselves were Christians.

Today there remain an uncertain number of Kurdish Christians, particularly in the districts of Hakkâri in north-central Kurdistan, Tur Abdin in western Kurdistan, and among the Milân and Barâz tribal confederacies in western Kurdistan in Turkey and Syria. In 1908 Sykes reports at least 500 Kurdish Christian families of the Piniânishli tribe in the Hakkâri district, whose leaders insisted they were an ancient community converted before the advent of Islam. Of the Hawerka tribe of Tur Abdin 900 families are listed as Christian, along with 700 more families from various other tribes in this region. Sykes is, however, silent on the number of Milân Christians. Despite this, the question remains whether these and others are the modern descendants of the larger and more ancient Kurdish Christian community, or whether they are relatively recent converts by Christian Armenians, Assyrians, and Western Christian missionaries. Many centers for these recent proselytes were set up during the 19th and early 20th centuries in and around Bitlis, Urfâ, Mosul, Urmiâ and Salmâs, to name a few. Likely, the Kurdish Christian population is an even mix of the ancient population and modern converts.

An educated guess for the total number of Christian Kurds (excluding the Assyrians, whose claim to a separate ethnic identity must be honored) would place them in the range of tens of thousands, most of them living in Turkey.

There is a renewed interest among the active Christian organizations in Europe, but particularly in the United States, to carry missionary work to Kurdistan. In fact, one of the first languages of the East into which the post-Renaissance Europeans translated the Gospel was Kurdish. New editions and new translations of the New Testament into North Kurmânji (Bâhdinâni) are being attempted now. These translations and endeavors are targeted towards the Kurds in Turkey, as has been the case since the time of Father Subhalemaran.

The reason has been the faulty assumption of these missionary organizations that the Kurds of northern and western Kurdistan in Anatolia, having been under Byzantine rule prior to Muslim occupation, were mostly or all Christians, but that the other Kurds were not. The missionaries probably would find more fertile ground in central and part of southern Kurdistan, on the territories of the former Christian Kurdish kingdoms of Adiabene and Karkhu b't Salukh (Kirkuk), but not in northern and western Kurdistan, whose non-Christian inclinations made the Byzantines deport the populace in earlier times.

Further Readings and Bibliography: Asahel Grant, *The Nestorians, or the Lost Tribes* (London, 1841); Thomas Laurie, *Dr. Grant and the Mountain Nestorians* (Cambridge, 1853); Helga Anschütz, *Die syrischen Christen vom Tor 'Abdin* (Würzburg: Reinhardt, 1984); Michel Chevalier, *Les montagnards chrétiens du Hakkari et du Kurdistan septentrional* (Paris: Département de Géographie de l'Université de Paris-Sorbonne, 1985); John Joseph, *The Nestorians and Their Muslim Neighbors* (Princeton: Princeton University Press, 1961); John Joseph, *Muslim-Christian Relations and Inter-Christian Rivalries in the Middle East: The Case of the Jacobites in an Age of Transition* (Albany: State University of New York Press, 1983); G.P. Badger, *The Nestorians and their Rituals* (London, 1892); Marco Polo, *Travels*, ed. John Masefield (London: Dent, 1975); Basile Nikitine. "Les Kurdes et le Christianisme," *Revue de l'Histoire des Religion* (Paris, 1929); William Ainsworth "An Account of a Visit to the Chaldeans Inhabiting Central Kurdistan, and of an Ascent of the Peak of Rowandiz (Tur Sheikhiwa) in the Summer of 1840," *Journal of the Royal Geographical Society* XI (1941).

BABISM & BAHA'ISM

Bâbism was formed in Persia in 1844 by Mirzâ Ali Muhammad (1819-1850), the *Bâb*, or "the portal" (to the Deity). *Bâb*, or *Bâbâ*, standing for "avatar," is of course the title by which the Cult of Angels refers to the major reincarnations of the *Haq*, or the Universal Spirit. A native of Shirâz in Persia, Bâb became a follower of Shaykh Ahmad Ahsâ'i, who had settled in Kirmân in southeast Persia from Ahsâ. Ahsâ (the medieval Lahsâ, the eastern coastal regions of modern Saudi Arabia) was a bastion of the socioreligious movement of Qarmatites, which was strongly influenced by the Cult of Angels, particularly the Mazdakite movement. (From Ahsâ also came in the 15th century the mystic Muhammad Nurbakhsh, whose connection with the Cult of Angels has already been set forth in the section on **Sufi Mystic Orders**.)

Shaykh Ahmad, and hence the Cult of Angels, had a profound influence on Mirzâ Ali Muhammad Bâb. In fact, Shaykh Ahmad Ahsâ'i was in Kirmânshâh in southern Kurdistan, the ancient heartland of the Cult, when he announced the reincarnation of the Spirit in Bâb as his new avatar. This was on the occasion of the death of his own son Ali, when Shâykh Ahmad told his disciples: "Grieve not, O my friends, for I have offered up my son, my own Ali, as a sacrifice for the Ali whose advent we all await. To this end have I reared and prepared him" (Nabil-i A'zam 1932). Bâb was born in the same year, supposedly carrying the soul of the Shaykh's son as well as his name. Bâb was the bearer of the name and soul of the Shi'ite imam and the primary avatar of the Second Epoch, Ali. The later inclusion of *Muhammad* in his first name also brought Bâb to the exact station of the primary avatar in Alevism, *Alimuhammad* (see **Alevism**).

The Bâbis, particularly the Kurdish Bâbis, believed in the transmigration of the soul, as do followers of the Cult of Angels. They did not mourn the dead, as they believed the soul of a dead Bâbi, after spending a few days in a transitional stage, enters the body of another Bâbi, usually a newborn. The transmigrations were believed to have started long ago, particularly the souls of the religious leaders, which were supposed to have resided in the bodies of the Shi'ite saints and martyrs of earlier times. The Bâbis too were accused of engaging in communal sex, in the "candle blown out" ceremony (see **Cult of Angels**) and were persecuted in Persia with such severity that by comparison the savage repressions of the Yezidis by the Ottoman Empire seem relatively benign.

The involvement of the ethnic Kurds in Bâbism was relatively strong. One of the earliest major Bâbi communities was Kurdish, numbering about 5000 and inhabiting the area between Bâsh Qala and Qotur in Hakkâri in north-central Kurdistan on the Perso-Ottoman border. However, in July 1850, when the Persian Qajar king Nâsir al-Din ordered the execution of the Bâb in Tabriz, it was the Shiqâqi Kurdish and Armenian troops who carried out the order.

Bâbism soon evolved into the universalist Bahâ'ism under the direction of Mirzâ Husayn Ali, *Bahâ'u'llâh* ("the Glory of God"). For two years before his proclamation of the new religion and his mission in April 1863, Bahâ'u'llâh lived in the Kurdish city of Sulaymânia (less than 30 miles from Barzanja, the legendary birthplace of the Cult of Angels), earning his livelihood by providing Muslim religious services to the local people under the pseudonym *Dervish Muhammad*. Many of the coins he gave to people as festival presents are still cherished for their healing power. In one of his books, *Iqân*, Bahâ'u'llâh paints a vivid and interesting picture of his retreat in the "wilderness" of Kurdistan.

A Kurdish Bahâ'i, Muhammad Zaki al-Kurdi, established the first Kurdish publishing house in 1920 in Cairo. He took over the publication of the first Kurdish newspaper/journal, *Kurdistan* (published first in Istanbul in 1898 without his involvement) after it moved to Cairo after the start of World War I. Some of the most important works of Bahâ'i literature, such as J.E. Esslemont's *Bahâ'ullâh and the New Era*, have been translated into the dialects of Sorâni (by Husein Jawdat) and Gurâni (anonymous).

Bahâ'ism has done much to distance itself from the militancy of Bâbism. In the form of a new world religion, it has also tried to shed itself of the Shi'ite Islamic and Cult of Angels (particularly, Yârsânist) influence so apparent in Bâbism. Minorsky preserved and translated in 1920 just one Bahâ'i polemical tract directed against the Yârsâns. Several paramount aspects of the Cult, however, remain apparent in modern Bahâ'ism: 1) universalism, that is the belief that other religions are an extension of a same original idea of faith, and that all are equally respectable; 2) the belief that all prophets and holy figures of other religions are manifestations of the same supreme Deity or Spirit, from Buddha and Zoroaster, to Moses, Jesus, and Muhammad; 3) the belief that the Word and, supposedly the soul, is conveyed to these prophets through an intermediary archangel(s); 4) the practice of a mandatory ritual communal gathering at *Mahfels,* similar to the ceremony of Jam in the Cult, but every 19th day; 5) social and class liberalism, and a high status of women, including their right to serve on high religious councils. The de facto female avatar of the Bâbi cycle of primary incarnations, Tâhira Qurratu'l Ayn, removed her veil in public in 1849 to "signal the equality of women with men as a basic principle of the new Bâbi religion" (see **Status of Women & Family Life**).

With its attention directed to the world level, little Bahâ'i proselytization has been conducted in Kurdistan—a naturally fertile ground for this new religion that carries such fundamental affinities with Kurdish religious and social values and tradition. There are only a few thousand Kurdish Bahâ'is, spread over southern and central Kurdistan today. Of the number of Bâbis, if there are any left, even an educated guess is hazardous.

Further Readings and Bibliography: Muhammad Zarandi Nabil-i A'zam, *The Dawn-Breakers, Nabil's Narrative of the Early Days of the Bahâ'i Revelation,* trans. and ed. Shoghi Effendi, (New York, 1932); J.E. Esslemont, *Bahâ'u'llâh and the New Era* (Wilmette, Illinois: Bahâ'i Publishing Trust, 1980, reprint of the 1923 original); E.G. Browne, *A Traveller's Narrative written to illustrate the Episode of the Bab,* 2 vols. (London, 1891); E.G. Browne, *Materials for the study of the Babi Religion* (London, 1918); E.G. Browne, "Bâbis of Persia," *Journal of Royal Asiatic Society* xxi (1898); Abbas Amanat, *Resurrection and Renewal: The Making of the Babi Movement in Iran, 1844-1850* (Ithaca: Cornell University Press, 1989); V. Minorsky, "Notes sur la secte des Ahlè Haqq," *Revue du Monde Musulman* 40–41 (1920 and 1921).

Chapter 6

LANGUAGE, LITERATURE, & PRESS

LANGUAGE

Kurdish vernaculars are members of the northwestern subdivision of the Iranic branch of the Indo-European family of languages. Many Kurdish words are cognate with English, such as *gama=game, mâra=marry, stâra=star, rubâr=river, dol=dale* or *valley, brâ=brother, mong=moon, snoy=snow, firo=free* (of charge), *standin=to stand, sur=sure,* and the like. The major language nearest to Kurdish, however, is Persian, the state language of Iran, Afghanistan, and Tajikistan. The close relationship between Kurdish and Persian is similar to that between German and Danish.

Kurdish vernaculars divide into two primary groups: 1) the Kurmânji group, composed of two major branches, Bâhdinâni (or North Kurmânji) and Sorâni (or South Kurmânji) and 2) the Pahlawâni (or Pahlawânik) group, also composed of two major branches, Dimili (or Zâzâ) and Gurâni (Figure 2 and Map 39). These are further divided into scores of dialects and subdialects as well. Some of them, like Awrâmani and Laki (both major dialects of Gurâni), have large bodies of written literature that span more than a thousand years.

The name *Kurmânj* has been proposed by Minorsky to have evolved from the combination of *Kurt* and *Mând*, together meaning "Median Kurd." This may be less plausible than contending theories asserting that it may have evolved from *Kurt* and *Manna*, i.e., "Mannaean Kurd." The original home of Kurmânj was the Hakkâri region, which falls nicely within the territories of the ancient Mannas (see **Ancient History** for the Mannas).

The common appellation *Pahlawâni* for Gurâni, Dimili, and other related dialects of the old language of the Kurds has now fallen out of use by the Kurds and the non-Kurds. *Pahlawâni* used by the medieval authors, and is here revived out of the need for a common name to cover all these dialects.

The term *Pahlawâni* itself has clearly evolved from *Pahlawand*, i.e., "that of Pahla." Pahla comprised southern Kurdistan and northern Luristan, perhaps the original home area of the language. The suffix *wand* has already been discussed in the section on **Tribes**. The word *Pahla* is still preserved in corrupted form in the Kurdish tribal name *Fayli*, who incidentally still reside in southern Kurdistan, in the old Pahla region.

Lacking a state apparatus to undertake the task of creating a standard Kurdish language, the Kurds continue to speak a myriad of dialects, despite many unsuccessful attempts by Kurds to create such a standard national language (see **Education** and **National Identity**).

If we were to compare the Kurdish language group to the Romance languages, the relationship between Kurmânji and Pahlawâni would be like that between French and Italian. Just as these Romance languages are the modern offshoots of Latin with various degrees of evolution from the original parent tongue, the modern Kurdish vernaculars are the offshoots of a single, now lost, archaic language that may loosely be called

INDO-EUROPEAN FAMILY OF LANGUAGES

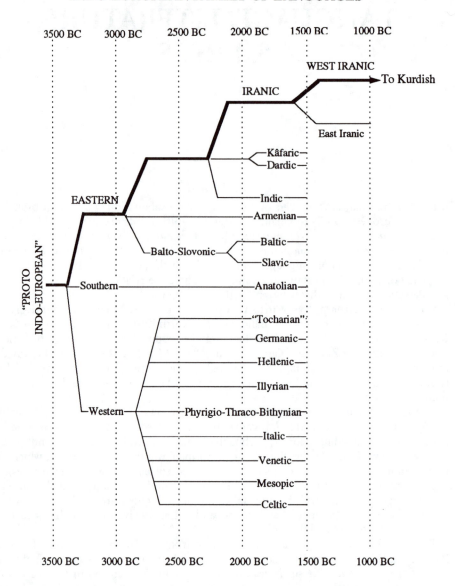

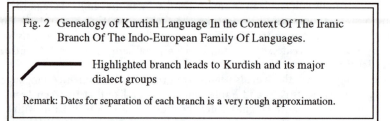

Fig. 2 Genealogy of Kurdish Language In the Context Of The Iranic Branch Of The Indo-European Family Of Languages.

Highlighted branch leads to Kurdish and its major dialect groups

Remark: Dates for separation of each branch is a very rough approximation.

IRANIC BRANCH OF THE INDO-EUROPEAN FAMILY OF LANGUAGES

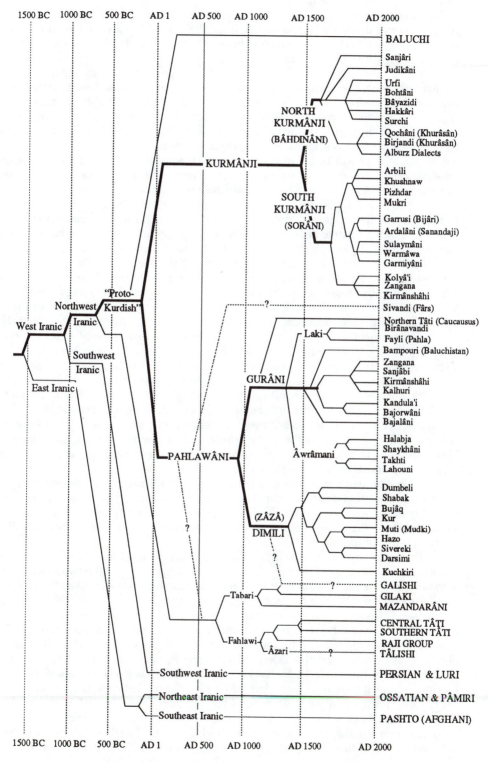

* Only The Kurdish Group Is Shown In Detail.

"Median" or "Proto-Kurdish" (Figure 2).

Kurmânji and Pahlawâni, like French and Italian, now qualify as two bona fide languages, and not dialects of the same language. Their variations are far too great by any standard linguistic criteria to warrant classification as dialects of the same language. Moreover, the level of mutual understanding between the speakers of the two is at best about half. These two Kurdish languages presently are spoken by very uneven segments of the Kurdish nation, with Kurmânji being the vernacular of about three-quarters of all Kurds, and Pahlawâni of the rest. This is the direct result of the major historical movements of people in Kurdistan since the middle of the classical era, as well as the introduction of new religions, which often resulted in alteration of the local speech as well as culture and economy (see **Historical Migrations** and **Religion**). These changes are manifest not just in the language of the Kurds, but in their entire social and cultural spectrum (see **Internal Subdivisions**). The extent of literature and the writing system employed in each of the Kurdish vernaculars are discussed under **Literature** and **Education**.

To add to this complexity, there is no standard nomenclature for the divisions of Kurdish vernaculars, not just in the works of Western scholars but among the Kurds themselves. All the native designators for local languages and dialects are based on the way the spoken language of one group sounds to the unfamiliar ears of the other. The Dimila and their vernacular, Dimili, are therefore called *Zâzâ* by the Bâhdinâni-speakers, with reference to the preponderance of *z* sounds in their language (Nikitine 1926). The Dimila call the Bâhdinâni dialect and its speakers *Kharawara*. The Gurâns refer to the Sorâni as *Korkora* and *Wâwâ*. The Sorani speakers in turn call the Gurâns and their vernacular, Gurâni, *Mâcho Mâcho*, and refer to the tongue and the speakers of Bâhdinâni as *Zhe Bâbu*. How the speakers of these vernaculars refer to their own language is even more interesting. The Gurâns call their language *Kurdi*, i.e., "Kurdish." But so do the common speakers of Sorâni. This is the name they use for their languages, and not their local dialects, for which they would produce a traditional name on demand. The speakers of North Kurmânji (or Bâhdinâni) call their *language* in general Kurmânji, and never *Kurdi* (Kurdish). This is quite interesting, as North Kurmânj speakers by themselves constitute, as was mentioned earlier, the numerical majority of the Kurds. It is instead the Gurâns (in toto) followed by the South Kurmânj (the majority) who call their language "Kurdish." The Dimila call their language Dimili among themselves, and Zâzâ when speaking to a non-Dimila Kurd or anyone else.

The more educated Kurds have now come to call these dialects and languages more or less by the titles that appear in this work. The only exception is the survival of the pejorative designator *Zâzâ* for the Dimili language and the Dimila people. This name has so far withstood the many attempts of educated Kurds to replace the old names with a proper nomenclature.

The linguistic situation in Kurdistan is in reality less complex than the above classification and terminology may imply. The basic similarity between the two branches of Kurmânji, i.e., Bâhdinâni and Sorâni, is very strong, and the speakers of each can communicate with the other to a reasonable degree, which increases markedly with a few days of practice. This stems from the fact that North and South Kurmânji separated from one another in comparatively recent times—perhaps as recently as 400-600 years ago.

Within each of the two Kurdish languages, various degrees of linguistic evolution are observed among their respective dialects. In Kurmânji, for instance, while Bâhdinâni retains the older gender distinction, Sorâni has lost all vestiges of gender. The Awrâmani dialect of Gurâni, likewise, has noun genders, while Laki has lost them completely. On the other hand, the ergative construction (verbs agreeing with object rather than subject) is present in all dialects of Kurmânji, but Pahlawâni does not use this grammatical construction.

Some linguists in the past have tended to label Kurmânji (North and South branches) the "real Kurdish," thus declaring the Pahlawâni branch non-Kurdish. If by *non-Kurdish*

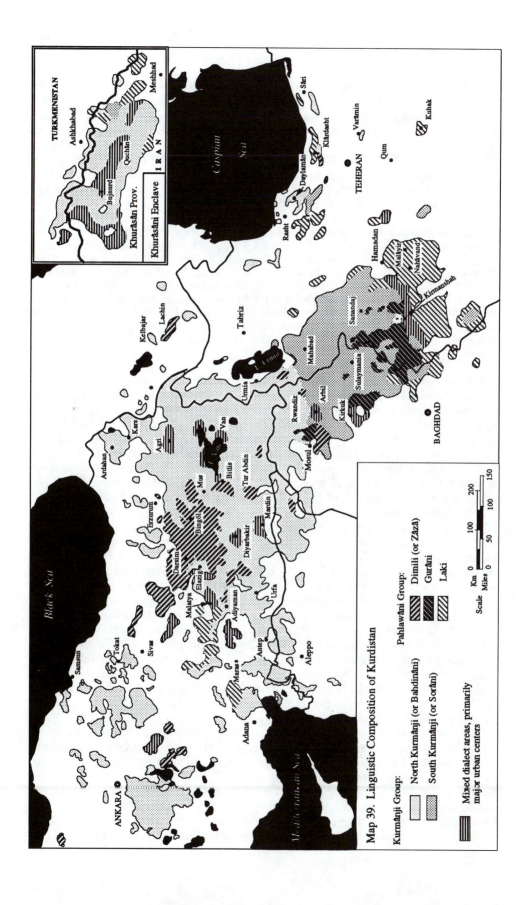

Map 39. Linguistic Composition of Kurdistan

Kurmânji Group:

- North Kurmânji (or Bahdinâni)
- South Kurmânji (or Sorâni)

Pahlawâni Group:

- Dimili (or Zâzâ)
- Gurâni
- Laki

- Mixed dialect areas, primarily major urban centers

Scale
Km 0   100   200
Miles 0   50   100   150

is meant non-Kurmânji, then such assertions are true. However, this is quite ironic in that, as noted above, it is the Gurân who always call their language *Kurdi,* or "Kurdish," while the vast majority of the Kurmânj (the supposedly "real" Kurds), never do. But the assertion that the *speakers* of Pahlawâni are not ethnic Kurds is born only of a lack of proper knowledge of the history and society of the Kurds. The Gurâns and the Dimila are the oldest identifiable branches of the Kurdish nation—much older in fact than the Kurmânj. They have been called, and having been calling themselves, Kurds since before the advent of Islam in the 7th century (see **Classical History**). However their language may be classified for linguistic purposes, the people remain Kurdish.

Further Readings and Bibliography: D.N. MacKenzie, "The Origins of Kurdish," *Transactions of the Philological Society* (London, 1961); Mohammed Mokri, "Kurdologie et Enseignement de la Langue Kurde en URSS," *Revue de la Société Ethnographie de Paris* (1963); C.J. Edmonds, "Some Developments in the Use of Latin Characters for the Writing of Kurdish," *Journal of the Royal Asiatic Society,* 2 parts (London, 1931 and 1933); Amir Hassanpour, "The Language Factor in National Development: The Standardization of the Kurdish Language, 1918-1985," unpublished doctoral dissertation (Urbana, Illinois: University of Illinois, 1989); Basile Nikitine, "Kurdish Stories from My Collection," *Bulletin of the School of Oriental and African Studies* IV (1926-28); V. Minorsky, "The Gûrân," *Bulletin of the School of Oriental and African Studies* XI (1943-46).

Kurmânji. The vernacular with the largest number of speakers is Kurmânji (or Kirmâncha), spoken by about three-quarters of the Kurds today. Kurmânji is divided into North Kurmânji (also called Bâhdinâni) and South Kurmânji (also called Sorâni).

North Kurmânji, or Bâhdinâni, is the language of most of the Kurds of Turkey and almost all of the Kurds of Syria and the former Soviet Union, as well as being the predominant language of the Kurdish enclave in northern Khurâsân in Iran (Map 39). In fact, North Kurmânji alone is spoken by a little over half of all Kurds, making it the most common Kurdish vernacular. There are at present about 15 million speakers of North Kurmânji. Major subdialects of North Kurmânji are Buhtâni, Bâyazidi, Hakkâri, Urfi, and Bâhdinâni proper.

South Kurmânji, or Sorâni, is the language of a plurality of Kurds in Iran and Iraq, with about 6 million speakers. Major subdialects of South Kurmânji are Mukri, Ardalâni, Garmiyâni, Khushnow, Pizhdar, Warmâwa, Kirmânshâhi, and Arbili (or Sorâni proper). A line can be drawn to divide Sorâni-speaking areas into a Persianized southeastern section and a more orthodox northwestern section, running from Bijâr to Kifri. The ergative construction in the Persianized Sorâni has begun to disappear, while it is being retained in the non-Persianized northwestern section. Also, under the influence of Arabic and Neo-Aramaic languages, the northwest section of Sorâni has acquired two fricative sounds (faucalized pharyngeal fricative 'ayn, and hâ), absent from other Kurdish, and in fact Indo-European languages. Realizing this, the Iraqi Kurds tend to expunge these sounds from their Kurdish to move away from their Semitic Arab neighbors and overlords. In Iran, where few Kurds can pronounce the sounds and even fewer have them in their dialect, the tendency is the reverse. This is to distinguish their increasingly Persianized language from Persian.

Since the last century many formerly Gurâni-speaking tribes in the Kirmânshâh region have partially switched to South Kurmânji, although they retain much of the vocabulary, syntax, and mood of the Gurâni in their new language. This has prompted many linguists to consider this a new branch of Kurmânji, independent of Sorâni altogether. Since the transition is exceedingly gradual and no boundaries can be drawn to separate the two (as can be drawn between North and South Kurmânji), the Kurmânji of Kirmânshâh should be considered a division of Sorâni and not a new branch.

Many tribes in the Kirmânshâh region have both Sorâni and Gurâni speakers among them.

The Kalhur, Zangana, Sanjâbi, and Nankeli tribes are among these. Figure 2 thus contains the dialect designators Kalhuri and Kirmânshâhi in both the Sorâni and Gurâni branches.

As a major Kurdish tongue, Kurmânji is relatively recent. It has achieved its present position by replacing Pahlawâni as the language of the majority. Like Pahlawâni, Kurmânji is descended from the old Median or "Proto-Kurdish." Kurmânji remained for a very long time the language spoken only by the Kurdish nomads in the mountains of the Hakkâri region west of Lake Urmiâ. It was not until the beginning of the 14th century and the progressive nomadization of Kurdistan that it expanded. It had begun to expand rapidly by the middle of the 16th century, when the destruction of the agriculturalist economy and massive deportations of the sedentary Kurds, coupled with the loss of overland trade routes through Kurdistan, paved the way for a fundamental change in Kurdish society (see **Early Modern History**). As the nomads gradually expanded from the Hakkâri region into various corners of Kurdistan, they carried with them, and in time imposed upon the remaining agriculturalists, their Kurmânji language. With it they also introduced Sunni Islam of the Shafi'ite rite as the predominant religion of the land.

Kurmânji first advanced out from Hakkâri through Bâhdinân to Mosul. This divided Kurdistan into a Dimili northern half and a Gurâni southern half, with Kurmânji in the middle. The expansion then continued into the Dimili linguistic domain, as it was the first to experience the full force of the socioeconomic calamities of the early modern times. The Bâhdinân dialect of Kurmânji in time became the predominant language of northern and western Kurdistan. The assault on the Gurâni domain began in the early 18th century with the onset of the socioeconomic disruption of this part of Kurdistan through wars and deportations. The Sorâni dialect and the nomads carrying it expanded from the Sorân region (modern Arbil-Rawanduz area) into central and eastern Kurdistan, replacing Gurâni. The hegemony of the Pahlawâni language over Kurdistan was thus gradually broken by Kurmânji, which was expanding from the geographical center. Pahlawâni was in time pushed into its present limited domains on both extreme ends of Kurdistan.

Pahlawâni. To the far north of Kurdistan along the upper courses of the Euphrates, Kizilirmaq, and Murat rivers in Turkey, the Dimili branch of Pahlawâni (less accurately but more commonly known as Zâzâ) is spoken by about 4.5 million Dimila Kurds. The larger cities of Darsim (now Tunçeli), Chapakhchur (now Bingöl), and Siverek, and a large proportion of the Kurds of Bitlis, are Dimili-speaking. There are also smaller pockets of this language spoken in various corners of Anatolia from Adiyâman to Malâtya and Maras, in northern Iraq (where the speakers are known as the Shabaks) and northwest Iran (the tribes of Dumbuli and some of the Zarzâs) as well. The language seems in late classical and early medieval times to have been more or less spoken in all the area now covered by North Kurmânji in contiguous Kurdistan. Its domain also stretched west into Pontus, Cappadocia, and Cilicia, before a sustained period of assimilation and deportations obliterated the Kurdish presence in the area in the Byzantine period (see **Integration & Assimilation**). The Dimili further retreated from its former eastern domains to its present limited one under pressure from the advancing North Kurmânji-speaking pastoralist Kurds. This loss of ground, which started at the beginning of the 16th century, continues to this day.

Dimili is closely related to Gurâni, a relationship indicative of a time when a single form of Pahlawâni was spoken throughout much of Kurdistan, when after the late classical period, Kurdistan was homogenized through massive internal migrations (see **Classical History** and **Historical Migrations**). At that time the domain of the Pahlawâni language was uninterrupted across Kurdistan. Today, in only one place, around Mosul, do Gurâni (in the form of the Bajalân dialect) and Dimili (in the form of the Shabak dialect) still neighbor each other. The main bodies of Dimili- and Gurâni-speaking Kurds are now at the extreme opposite ends of Kurdistan.

Major dialects of Dimili are Sivereki, Kori, Hazzu (or Hazo), Motki (or Moti), Shabak, and Dumbuli. The dialect of Gâlishi now spoken in the highlands of Gilân on the Caspian Sea may be a distant offshoot of Dimili as well, brought here by the migrating medieval Daylamites from western and northern Kurdistan.

Dimili has served as the prime language of the sacred scriptures of the Alevis, but not the exclusive one. Despite this, not much written material survives to give an indication of the older forms of Dimili and its evolution. The documents come from rather unexpected sources: the early medieval Islamic histories. Ibn Isfandiyâr in his history of Tabaristân, for example, preserves passages in the language of the Daylamite settlers of this Caspian Sea district, which resembles modern Dimili.

In far southern Kurdistan, both in Iraq and Iran, in an area from Halabja and Marivân to Dinawar, Hamadân, Kirmânshâh, and Khânaqin, all the way to Mandali, Gurâni predominates. It is also the language of the populous Kâkâ'i tribe near Kirkuk and the Zanganas near Kifri. The Kurdish colony of western Baluchistân is also primarily Gurâni-speaking. There are also populous pockets of Gurâni found in the Alburz mountains. A major dialect of Gurâni, i.e., the prestigious Awrâmani, now spoken in a small pocket between the towns of Halabja, Marivân, and Pâwa, was once the predominant language of central Kurdistan, where now South Kurmânji (Sorâni) is spoken. The language of sedentary farmers and old urban centers, it was the language of the important Kurdish princely house, that of Ardalân, until its fall in 1867. Most of the popular and polished poetry written under the auspices of the Bâbân princely house of central Kurdistan, even though itself a house of South Kurmânji speakers, was written in this dialect, until the beginning of the 19th century. The switch to South Kurmânji is traditionally ascribed to the reign of the early 19th-century Bâbân prince Abdul-Rahmân Pâshâ.

Gurâni and its dialects began their retreat in the 17th and 18th centuries and are now still under great pressure from South Kurmânji speakers. With the avalanche of the Iraqi Kurdish refugees, nearly all speakers of South Kurmânji, into eastern and southern Kurdistan in Iran, the process of Gurâni dilution and assimilation has been hastened tremendously. Kirmânshâh, once the center of the Gurân, is now a multi-lingual city, and very likely has a South Kurmânji plurality. The population of Halabja, the northernmost outpost of the language, and the former seat of the Houses of Ardalân and Bâbân, was annihilated by chemical warfare in 1988. It now houses more than 100,000 refugee Kurds, who speak almost exclusively South Kurmânji. In fact, the Gurani-speaking Pâwa, Nowsud and, ancient Awrâman, opposite Halabja on the Iranian side of the border, have also been overrun by these refugees.

The past expanse of Gurâni can still be detected in pockets of Gurâni-speaking farmers from the environs of Hakkâri in Turkey to Mosul (the Bajalâns/Bajarwâns), and to Shahrabân—less than forty miles northeast of Baghdad. Other major dialects of Gurâni, besides Awrâmani and Bajalâni, are Kalhuri, Nânkeli, Kandula'i, Sanjâbi, Zangana, Kâkâ'i (or Dargazini), and Kirmânshâhi. Today, there are roughly 1.5 million Gurâni speakers in Iran and Iraq.

Laki. This vernacular is just a major dialect of Gurâni and is treated here separately not on linguistic grounds, but ethnological. The speakers of Laki have been steadily pulling away from the main body of Kurds, increasingly associating with their neighboring ethnic group, the Lurs. The phenomenon is most visible among the educated Laks and the urbanites—in the countryside, the commoners still consider themselves Kurds in regions bordering other parts of Kurdistan, and Laks or Lurs where they border the Lurs. The process is a valuable living example of the dynamics through which the entire southern Zagros has been permanently lost by the Kurds since the late medieval period: an ethnic metamorphosis that converted the Lurs, Gelus, Mamasanis, and Shabânkâras into a new ethnic group (the greater Lurish ethnic group), independent of the Kurds (see **Integration & Assimilation**).

Laki is presently spoken in the areas south of Hamadân and including the towns of Nahâwand, Tuisirkân, Nurâbâd, Ilâm, Gelân, and Pahla, as well as the countryside in the districts of Horru, Selasela, Silâkhur, and the northern Alishtar in western Iran. There are also major Laki colonies spread from Khurâsân to the Mediterranean Sea. Pockets of Laki speakers are found in Azerbaijan, the Alburz mountains, the Caspian coastal region, the Khurâsâni enclave (as far south as Birjand), the mountainous land between Qum and Kâshân, and the region between Adiyâman and the Ceyhân river in far western Kurdistan in Anatolia. There are also many Kurdish tribes named Lak who now speak other Kurdish dialects (or other languages altogether) and are found from Adana to central Anatolia in Turkey, in Daghistân in the Russian Caucasus, and from Ahar to the suburbs of Teheran in Iran (see **Tribes**).

The syntax and vocabulary of Laki have been profoundly altered by Luri, itself an off-shoot of New Persian, a Southwest Iranic language. The basic grammar and verb systems of Laki are, like in all other Kurdish dialects, clearly Northwest Iranic. This relationship is further affirmed by remnants in Laki of the Kurdish grammatical hallmark, the ergative construction. The Laki language is therefore fundamentally different from Luri, and similar to Kurdish.

There are at least 1.5 million Laki speakers at present, and possibly many more, as they are often counted as Lurs.

Further Readings and Bibliography: W. Ivanow, "Notes on Khorasani Kurdish," *Journal and Proceedings of the Asiatic Society of Bengal,* new series, XXIII:1 (1927); Ch. Bakaev, *Yazik Azerbaidzhanskii Kurdov* (Moscow: Akademi Nauk, 1965); Ch. Bakaev, *Govor Kurdov Turkmenii* (Moscow: Akademi Nauk, 1962); Karl Hadank, *Mundarten der Gûrân, besonders das Kândûlâî, Auramânî und Bâdschâlânî* (Berlin, 1930); Karl Hadank, *Mundarten der Zâzâ, Hauptsächlich aus Siwerek und Kor* (Berlin, 1932); Karl Hadank, *Untersuchungen zum Westkurdischen: Bôtî und Êzâdî* (Leipzig, 1936); Peter Andrews, ed., *Ethnic Groups in the Republic of Turkey* (Wiesbaden: Ludwig Reichert, 1989); Mehrdad Izady, "A Kurdish Lingua Franca?," *Kurdish Times* II-2 (1988); Hugo Makas, *Kurdische Studien: 1) Eine Probe des Dialektes von Diarbekir, 2)Ein Gedicht aus Gâwar, 3)Jezidengebete* (Heidelberg, 1900); Age Meyer Benedictsen, *Les Dialectes d'Awromân et de Pâwä* (Copenhagen, 1921); D.N. MacKenzie, *The Dialect of Awroman (Hawrâmân-î Luhôn): Grammatical Sketch, Texts, and Vocabulary* (Copenhagen: Kongelige Danske Videnskabernes Selskab, 1966); P. Pikkert, *A Basic Course in Modern Kurmanji* (Genk, Belgium: Alev Books, 1991).

LITERATURE

Kurdish is heir to a rich and extensive, but now mainly oral, literature extending back into pre-Islamic times. A large portion of the written literature has been lost to over eight centuries of nomadic dislocation into and through Kurdistan, leaving behind only fragments. Although now spoken by a minority of Kurds, Gurâni is claimant to the oldest extant literary pieces in Kurdish. Pahlawâni in general, and particularly Gurâni and its dialects, once enjoyed an unusual status as the language of high culture and literature. In all dialects of Kurmânji, *Gurâni* now simply means "lyric poetry" or "balladry." This vernacular, along with its dialect Awrâmani, was in fact until early modern times the language of polite society and belles lettres in most of Kurdistan, irrespective of the dominant local dialect. The Kurdish princely house of Ardalân (1168-1867) spoke Gurâni until its final removal. Not surprisingly, all of the oldest surviving literary pieces in Kurdish are in Pahlawâni.

Bâbâ Tâhir (1000-1054) of Hamadân is one of the very first poets in the East to write *rubaiyat,* the medium of Omar Khayyam's fame. Bâbâ Tâhir's rusticity and mastery of both Laki/Gurâni and Persian have rendered his works unusually dear to the common people of both nations. His particular poetic meter is perhaps a legacy of the pre-Islamic poetic tradition of southern and central Kurdistan. Many Yârsân religious works and Jilwa, the holy hymns of the Yezidi prophet Shaykh Adi, are also in this style of verse. Bâbâ Tâhir himself has now ascended to a high station in the indigenous Kurdish Cult of Angels as one of the avatars of the Universal Spirit.

The lyricist Parishân (d. ca. 1398), Muhammad Faqih-Tayrân (1590-1660) of the town of Makas (from whom survive many folk tales), Mustafâ Basârâni (1641-1702), Muhammad Kandulayi (late 17th century), Khâna Qubâdi (1700-1759), Mirzâ Almâs Khân and Mirzâ Sharif Kulyâyi (mid-17th century), Shaydâ Awrâmi (1784-1852), Ahmad Beg Kumâsi (1796-1889), and Muhammad Wali Kirmânshâhi (d. ca. 1901) are just a few of the better-known poets in Gurâni and its dialects of Awrâmâni and Laki.

Nevertheless, some of the greatest works of Kurdish secular literature presently extant in toto are in the North Kurmânji dialect. Except for Ali Hariri, all other Kurmânji poets of whom we know and whose works are extant today began their careers after the beginning of the wars and deportations of the 16th century (see **Early Modern History** and **Deportations & Forced Resettlements**).

Although works in Kurmânji are generally of recent writing, a Yezidi religious work, the *Mes'haf i Resh*, is in a classic form of Kurmânji (closer to Bâhdinâni than Sorâni), and could well have been written sometime in the 13th century. It is held to have been written by Shaykh Hasan (born ca. AD 1195), a nephew of Shaykh Adi ibn Musâfir, the sacred prophet of the Yezidis (see **Yezidism**). If this date can be further authenticated, Mes'haf will be the oldest piece of literature in Kurmânji, predating anything else in that vernacular by hundreds of years.

Some of the earliest Kurmânji poets and lyricists whose works are extant are Ali Hariri, from the town of Harir near Rawânduz in the Hakkâri (1425-1490?); Mullâh Ahmad (1417-1494) of Hakkâri, the author of *Mawlud*, a collection of verse and an anthology; Salim Salmân, who composed his romance of *Yusif u Zulaykha* in 1586; Shaykh Ahmad (1570-1640), better known as Mullâ-i Jaziri (or Malây Jaziri) of Buhtân, who is considered one of the greatest of all Kurdish poets; and Ismâ'il of Bâyazid (1654-1710), who compiled a small Kurmânji-Arabic-Persian glossary for the use of the young, entitled *Gulzhen*, and several poems.

The epic drama of *Mem o Zin* (more properly, *Mami Âlân o Zini Buhtân*), versified in 1696 by Ahmad Khâni (1650-1706) of the Khâniyân tribe of Hakkâri, who settled early at Bâyazid in northern Kurdistan, embodies a wealth of mythological and historical events in the national life of the Kurds and idealizes their national aspirations.

Mem of the Âlân clan and Zin of the rival Buhtân clan are two lovers whose union is prevented by a certain Bakr of the Bakrân clan. Mem eventually dies; then, while mourning the death of her lover on his grave, Zin falls dead of grief and is duly buried next to him. Fearing for his life when his role in the tragedy is revealed, Bakr takes sanctuary between the two graves. Unimpressed, the people slay Bakr. A thorn bush soon grows out of Bakr's blood, sending its roots of malice deep into the earth between the lovers' graves, separating the two even after their death.

The heroic epic *Ballad of Dem Dem* is a mythologized story of the actual siege of the fortress of Dem Dem in eastern Kurdistan, defended by the Kurdish prince of Barâdost, *Khâni Zarrin Panja*, "the Khân with the Golden Arm," against the Safavid King Abbâs I in the 17th century. The epic is alive with vivid and graphic, but mostly symbolic, descriptions of the actual battles and the heroic resistance of the defenders. The association of the Khân with the siege is chronologically problematic, but the literary value of the epic stands out on its own. The spirit of the *Dem Dem* readily reminds one of the personal faceoffs of the honor-bound heroes of the Trojan war, and of the stubborn and desperate resistance of the defenders of Massada to the last man and woman (see **Early Modern History**).

Chargars or bards, travel widely to bring to their audience the wealth of hundreds of *chariga*, versified epics like the *Dem Dem* and *Mem o Zin*, and other popular pieces of literature (see **Music**).

In comparison to North Kurmânji, South Kurmânji has only lately produced its own works of literature. In fact, none is known before the early 19th century and the works of Mustafâ Kurdi (1809-1866), coming at least 1000 years after the earliest extant Gurâni works. The first substantial works in South Kurmânji, beginning with those of Hâji Qadir Koy'i of Koy Sanjaq in central Kurdistan (1817-1897), capitalize more on their patriotic themes than their literary value, which is at any rate hardly comparable with the works of the giants of North Kurmânji, such as Hariri, Khâni, or Jaziri. A major exception is of course Shaykh Rizâ Tâlabâni (1835-1909) whose wit, playfulness, and lampooning of those who crossed him (of which, judging by his works, there happened to be many) renders him a delight to read (Edmonds 1935).

Mention must be made of the discovery a few decades ago of a parchment containing many lines of Kurdish poetry in the South Kurmânji (Sorâni) dialect. The poem speaks of Zoroastrian Kurds being oppressed by invading Arab Muslims, who put out the fire temples and destroyed the old virtues. Much importance has been attached to this parchment, as it is held to date back to the original 7th-century Muslim invasion. This parchment is doubtless a forgery, as 1) it is in a Sorâni dialect that would not be developed for another 1000 years (Gurâni would have been the logical language, if the parchment were authentic), 2) the Kurds of central Kurdistan, where the parchment is alleged to have been found, were largely Christians at the time of the Muslim invasion (see **Christianity**), with the remainder being mostly Yârsâns (Zoroastrians and Jews constituted marginal populations); 3) no scientific examination of the parchment for dating and authentication has ever been presented, and no photographs of the piece are available to examine the alphabet used in its writing. Likely the work of a hapless nationalist hoaxter, the parchment was presumably meant to provide "history" for Kurdish written literature, particularly in the Sorâni dialect.

One reason that South Kurmânji did not produce written literature earlier is of course its closeness to North Kurmânji. Any work produced in latter dialect would have been readily accessible to the speakers of South Kurmânji. But also, it is only in the past two centuries that South Kurmânji has spread to occupy the crucial areas of central and eastern Kurdistan at the expense of Gurâni, thus gaining a large number of speakers and hence the potential and the status required for a literary language. In fact the greatest of the South Kurmânji-speaking princely houses, the Bâbâns, used Gurâni exclusively for their court language and literature until the beginning of the 19th century.

The present unusual importance of South Kurmânji is the outcome of several, equally unusual, historical events. The fragmentation of Kurdistan was a primary cause, as it rendered South Kurmânji the language of the majority of Kurds in Iraq and a plurality in Iran. With the added relative freedom it received in Iraq for its development, South Kurmânji has flourished with a disproportionately large volume of printed material produced in those two countries in the last 75 years, while North Kurmânji has been stifled in its main domain in Turkey for this same period.

A brief survey of the works of the Kurdish poets whose works have been preserved shows that in the 1000 years up to the beginning of the present century, 19 have been written in Gurâni, 10 in North Kurmânji, and 8 in South Kurmânji—not a surprising statistic when one notes the former extent and importance of Pahlawâni. Despite its very late start, South Kurmânji has produced over four-fifths of the literary works in Kurdish in the 20th century—as befits the most dynamic dialect of Kurdish today.

Over the course of the present century, the Kurdish language has come under a great deal of pressure. The publication of Kurdish has been forbidden in Syria and, until relatively recently, in Iran. Since the founding of the Turkish Republic, even speaking

Kurdish was illegal in Turkey, and punishable by imprisonment—a state policy in force intermittently until, in December 1990, president Ozal of Turkey announced the legalization of spoken Kurdish for domestic, and only domestic, use. When this was made law in the Turkish parliament in February of 1991, there were hysterical mass demonstrations in Ankara by academics who opposed the measure. Unimpressed, the Turkish government further liberalized the use of Kurdish language, allowing Kurdish-language publications. This instantly meant the appearance of Kurdish-language newspapers and magazines (see **Press & Electronic Mass Media**), even though under official supervision. Education, however, is still not included in these positive developments in Turkey, but there are signs indicating that a renaissance of Kurdish literature is on its way in Turkey, a country where over half of all Kurds live today.

In Iraq, on the other hand, a great body of published work in South Kurmânji has been produced with central government assistance and approval. A Kurdish university founded in Sulaymânia has been functioning for a few decades, providing a bilingual curriculum in Arabic and Kurdish, and fostering literature written in South Kurmânji (i.e., Sorâni).

The Soviet Kurds, despite (or perhaps because of) their small numbers, were given an elementary and advanced education in Kurdish and other relevant languages of the Soviet Union for many decades. A number of better-known pieces of Kurdish literature also appeared in that country, but these were often targeted as propaganda pieces to attract Kurds from beyond the Soviet borders, rather than having been written just to benefit the small, widely dispersed population of Soviet Kurds. Upon the dissolution of the Soviet Union in 1991, and the emergence of new independent states in the Caucasus and central Asia, it is doubtful that the Kurds will enjoy the same generous treatment from their local, now sovereign, ethnic neighbors. These are already at war with each other (Georgians vs. Ossets and Abkhâz, Armenians vs. Azeris, etc.), and promotion of Kurdish literature is not high on their agendas.

In Iraq and Iran a modified version of the Perso-Arabic alphabet has been adapted to the phonetic peculiarities of Sorâni and is used for publications. The Kurds of Turkey have recently embarked on an extensive campaign of publication in the North Kurmânji dialect of Kurdish from their publishing houses in Europe, in the hope that it may trickle back to their deprived kinfolk in Turkey. They have adapted a modified form of the Latin alphabet for this purpose, first championed by Prince Kamurân Badir Khân in the course of 1930 when he embarked on its creation. The Kurds of the Soviet Union first began writing Kurdish in the Armenian alphabet in the 1920s, followed by Latin in 1927, then Cyrillic in 1945, and now in both Cyrillic and Latin. Gurâni and Laki continue to use the Persian alphabet without any change. There is likely only one modern publication in Dimili—a newspaper, *Tayrâ*, published in Austria—and that employs the Latin-based alphabet of North Kurmânji developed by the European Kurdish diaspora. However, recent liberalizations in Turkey may change this. Since late 1991, a Kurdish news journal, *Rozhnâme*, published in Turkey, has carried two pages of news in Dimili—the other 38 pages are in North Kurmânji. Both use the same Latin-based alphabet as used for their European publications.

It seems that in the absence of a standardized pan-Kurdish language, an alphabet that least reflects the vocalic system of various Kurdish dialects would serve to reach a wider audience since it would mask dialectal differences (see **Education**). Any piece of Kurdish literature recorded in a Latin- or Cyrillic-based alphabet would achieve the reverse. These writing systems possess a relatively exact recording of short and long vowels and diphthongs. The vowel-starved Perso-Arabic alphabet, on the other hand, does the job rather nicely by its vague or non-recording of many vowels, and inexact consonant representation. When and if a standard pan-Kurdish language is adopted, then a Latin-based alphabet may be appropriate.

Further Readings and Bibliography: B. Nikitine and E .Soane, "Tale of Suto and Tato: Kurdish Text with Translation and Notes," *Bulletin of the School of Oriental Studies* III (London, 1923-25); B. Nikitine and E .Soane, "Kurdish Stories from My Collection,"*Bulletin of the School of Oriental Studies* IV (London, 1948); R. Lescot, *Textes Kurdes. Deuxe`me Partie: Mamé Alan* (1942); Alexandre Jaba, *Recueil de Notices et Récits kourdes* (St.Petersburg, 1860); Abdul-Kader Amin (collected by), *Kurdish Proverbs* (New York: Kurdish Library, 1989); C.J. Edmonds, "A Kurdish Lampoonist: Shaikh Riza Talabani," *Journal of the Royal Central Asian Society* XXII (1935)

EDUCATION

Of all the major nationalities in the Middle East, only the Kurds have yet to adopt a standard language commonly accepted and learned by all branches of that nation. Despite many attempts by Kurds and even non-Kurds (e.g., Edmonds 1931 and 1933), the fact that the nation remains physically fragmented, embattled, and mutually isolated has brought these efforts to nought (Izady 1988; Hassanpour 1989). At present then, the problem remains not just whether Kurdish is used for formal education, but also which Kurdish?

The development of a standard, pan-Kurdish language would serve as an indispensable vehicle for both the transmission of ideas and convergence of the disparate Kurdish cultural and literary heritage. The experiments of the neighboring Arabs, Turks, and Persians can serve as guides as to how this can be achieved. Before the creation of the modern standard Arabic (based on the classical language of the Koran, or the *Fus'hâ*) Arabs from different corners of the Arabia and North Africa had at least as much difficulty communicating with each other as Kurds do today. Their local dialects had indeed evolved to the same levels of mutual incomprehensibility.

Kurdish does not possess works of the stature of the Koran or of the Persian classical literature to guide its standardization. But this can be interpreted as a blessing in disguise. The production of a great amount of valuable literature has almost always rendered the language static and sensitive to change, hostile even to the introduction of new technological terminologies (as in the case of modern French). Kurdish should not have this problem.

Standardization of Kurdish will at most cause the loss of a minute amount of literature that is important to the Kurdish heritage while benefiting and uplifting the Kurdish national identity immeasurably.

Regardless of which dialect of Kurdish is used for educating the Kurds, the first noticeable aspect of education, or lack of it, in Kurdistan is the direct correlation between the use of Kurdish in the school curriculum and the level of literacy. There is also a direct correlation between the levels of education and social integration, as can be demonstrated by the level of urbanization in various parts of Kurdistan (see **Urbanization & Urban Centers**).

Since their incorporation into Iraq after the end of World War II, Iraqi Kurds have received eduction at the elementary and high-school levels in Kurdish as well as the state language, Arabic. A university was established for the Iraqi Kurds at Sulaymânia. The university was recently relocated to Arbil.

The employment of Kurdish in the universal educational system in Iraqi Kurdistan has produced very notable results: Kurds there have by far the highest literacy rate and are the most educated of all Kurds, with the sole possible exception of the small Soviet Kurdish community.

Despite a state average for literacy among its citizens over the age of 6 being 61.96% in 1986, the Iranian Kurdish provinces on the other hand registered 47.18%, 39.6%, 56%, 52%, and 57.28% for West Azerbaijan, Kordestân, Kirmânshâhân, Ilâm, and the neighboring, partly-Kurdish, Hamadân, respectively. Kurds are the least literate of the major nationalities in the country, and only the desolate Baluchistân ranks lower in literacy than the Kurdish regions among the 24 provinces of Iran in the 1986 census. The ancient Kurdish city of Qasri Shirin registered the lowest rate of literacy for any urban site in Iran, with only 9.87% of its citizens over the age of 6 qualifying as literate. Even the remote port of Châh Bahâr in Baluchistan had a 21.2% literacy rate for the same age bracket.

The Persian language has traditionally been the medium of instruction in Iran at all levels. Prior to the Islamic Revolution of 1979, any publication in the minority languages was also discouraged but, except for newsprint, not banned. The Revolution changed this situation by giving the constitutional right to all minority languages to be utilized in the press and mass media. Teaching ethnic literature in schools at all levels was also allowed. This is yet to be put into widespread practice, however. Schools and institutions of higher learning continue their Persian-only curricula. The primary gain from this new constitutional change was that non-Persian languages can now be freely published, and are.

Kurds have benefited from this change of state language policy, and the positive results of this should be visible in the 1996 Iranian state census on education.

In Turkey, the use of the Kurdish language, particularly teaching or publishing in Kurdish, has been forbidden since March 3, 1924—about a year after the signing of the Treaty of Lausanne, which awarded Anatolian Kurdistan to Turkey (see **Modern History**). This restriction has been in clear violation of the word and spirit of the Treaty, which provides in Article 38, "No restrictions shall be imposed on the free use by any Turkish national of any language in private intercourse, in commerce, religion, in the press, or in publications of any kind or at public meetings."

In the course of the 1950s the restrictions were partially and unofficially relaxed, allowing even for the appearance of some publications in Kurdish. This positive policy was reversed and further toughened in the 1980s. In view of the restrictions noted above, there is no role for Kurdish in education in Turkey.

The difference between the level of education of Kurds and that of other citizens of Turkey is even more marked than in Iran, with the Kurds of Turkey attaining less than half the national average for education, and less than a third of that in those provinces dominated by ethnic Turks. A few officially sanctioned Kurdish newspapers and journals were allowed to appear by the end of 1991, and if the positive steps taken in the course of 1990-91 are followed by more liberalization to include education and free publications, the level of Kurdish literacy and subsequent socioeconomic integration will rise dramatically—a phenomenon advantageous for both the Turkish state and her Kurdish citizens (see **Integration & Assimilation**).

Large communities of Kurds from Turkey who now live in Western Europe as guest workers, immigrants, or refugees have embarked on an impressive program of educating Kurdish children in their own language (see **Modern Emigrations & Diaspora**) To this end, they use the Latin-based alphabet. This alphabet was first developed and introduced by two members of the Kurdish Rozhaki-Badirkhânid princely house, Jalâdat Ali and Kâmurân. They originally used the alphabet to publish the journals *Hawâr/Hewâr* (1932-43) and *Ronahi* (1935), which they smuggled out of French Syria and into Turkey. This alphabet has since been the medium of publication of the Kurds of Turkey when they get the chance to publish, in or outside Turkey.

The enthusiasm of the Anatolian Kurdish diaspora for seeing material in their own language has translated itself into a prodigious quantity of textbooks, newsprint, and scholarly works, coming mainly out of print shops in Germany, France, Austria, and Sweden.

It is difficult to provide trustworthy figures for the literacy levels of the Syrian Kurds, as their regions are included in much larger, Arab-dominated provinces. But, judging by the trends in the other four fragments of Kurdistan and in light of the absence of Kurdish as a medium of education, it is highly improbable that they average anything near the literacy levels of the Arabic-speaking Syrians.

The smaller community of the Soviet Kurds in Armenia and Georgia, on the other hand, has enjoyed a long tradition of receiving education in their own language at various levels. They are very likely the most literate of all Kurds. On the other hand, in Soviet Azerbaijan, Turkmenistan, Kazakhstan, Uzbekistan, and Kirghizistan no such education is available. In fact, the Kurds in Azerbaijan and Turkmenistan have been subject to local republic-sponsored assimilation programs and have vanished from their state statistics since the end of World War II. It can be speculated that in light of the familiar restrictions on the language of education, fewer Kurds here tend to seek formal education than their compatriots in Armenia and Georgia.

Further Readings and Bibliography: *A Statistical Reflection of the Islamic Republic of Iran* (text in English), Publication No. 4 (Teheran: Ministry of Planning and Budget, Center for Statistics, 1987); *The Population and Household Census, 1986* (Teheran: Iranian Census Bureau, 1987), the "secret edition"; Lord Kinross, *Within the Taurus* (London, 1954)

PRESS & ELECTRONIC MASS MEDIA

The first Kurdish paper, *Kurdistan,* was published in Istanbul in Ottoman Turkey in 1898 by Prince Medhat Beg and other representatives of the prestigious Rozhaki-Badirkhânid Kurdish princely house of Buhtân. The paper was soon forced to close, but it later reopened in Cairo, and finally moved its headquarters to Europe. It is still published. A short-lived newspaper, *Ta'âvun,* appeared in Ottoman Turkey in 1908, but was also forced to close. These were followed by a monthly newspaper (also named *Kurdistan*) printed first in Urmiâ, Persia/Iran, in 1912 under the editorship of another Badirkhânid prince, Abdul Razzâq. He was soon banished by the Russians, in whose sphere of influence northern Persia laid at the time. When this paper ceased publication in 1914, *Yekbun* and *Rozhi Kurd* had already begun publication, in 1913.

Following these beginnings, the frequency of publication and the number of titles of Kurdish papers and journals continued to grow. Some titles of note were *Bangi Kurd* (1914), *Zhin* (1918), *Tigeyishtini* (1918-1919), *Kurd dar sâli 1340* (1921), a new *Rozhi Kurd* (1921), *Peshkawtin* (1920-22), *Rozhi Kurdistan* (1922-23), *Bangi Kurdistan* (1922-23), *Bangi Haq* (1923), *Umidi Istiqlâl* (1923-24), *Diyâri Kurdistan* (1925-26), and a literary journal *Zari Kirmanji* (1926).

The number of Kurdish-language newspapers, journals, and magazines becomes too large after this date to make it possible to note every single one. A valuable annotated survey of the early Kurdish press was carried out by C.J. Edmonds in the course of the 1920s and 1930s, and it indicates the energy with which the Kurdish press (and publishing in general) began its life (Edmonds 1924, 1937, and 1945). Currently, over a hundred titles are printed in Kurdistan and the diaspora in the Kurdish language, or foreign languages, but totally dedicated to Kurdish issues. Despite the ban on Kurdish print material in various local countries and at various times, the Kurdish press has always managed to filter through to people, signaling the impracticability of such bans.

The predominant dialect used by these Kurdish presses of earlier years was naturally North Kurmânji, as these Kurds constituted the majority then, and still do. Their Anatolian home was also physically the closest part of Kurdistan to industrialized Europe, allowing them to benefit more from the new trends and ideas there. The advent of the Turkish Republic and its repressive linguistic policies soon shifted this dramatically in favor of South Kurmânji and Iraq. This predominance continues to this day, except that it has become less conspicuous since the beginning of the 1980s and the reappearance of a myriad of material in North Kurmânji in Europe. Dimili (Zâzâ) has now a newspaper *Teyrâ*, which is published out of Austria, while newsprint has yet to appear in Gurâni.

Many Kurdish cities now have radio and television stations of their own, but the frequency of their broadcasts in Kurdish varies from none in Turkey to most times in Iraq. Iran falls in between these two extremes.

Here are not included clandestine, all-Kurdish radio stations that are transitory, highly politicized, and at any rate irrelevant to the development of the Kurdish culture and society. It is highly doubtful, for example, if all the clandestine Kurdish radio stations put together have affected the development of the Kurdish worldview more than the American-produced soap operas that pipe in Western values via Persian, Turkish, or Arabic languages (dubbed) into the Kurdish home. No clandestine Kurdish television station exists.

Kurdish music can be heard on radio stations in northern Syria, while the Iraqi radio and television stations in Kurdistan had (before the Gulf War) comprehensive daily Kurdish language programs. Their Iranian counterparts give only portions of their daily time to purely Kurdish material, while both national stations in Baghdad and Teheran quite regularly broadcast Kurdish music and songs, if not daily. Even radio Meshhad in the Iranian Khurâsân has a regular, one-hour daily program in Kurdish to serve the Khurâsâni Kurdish enclave.

Kurdish newsprint is allowed in both Iraq and Iran, as long as it carries the same items in the state's official language as well. While some important Iranian newspapers have begun carrying their major stories in both Persian and Azeri (the language of the second most populous ethnic group), Kurdish has yet to attain this very important recognition.

Following the positive steps taken by the Turkish government to allow the use of spoken Kurdish (the Language Law of 1991), there have appeared since December 1991 a few Kurdish-language publications in Turkey after decades of having been banned. A Kurdish newspaper, *Rojname* (Kurdish *Rozhnâma*, or "newspaper"), with 38 pages in North Kurmânji and two pages in Dimili, and a magazine of culture, *Deng* ("voice" in Kurdish), entirely in North Kurmânji, are among the publications that have just been introduced in Turkey. To Kurds used to the glacial pace of change in the negative state policies of Ankara, these improvements are happening at a dizzying pace, too fast indeed for many of their intellectuals and commoners to even begin forming an opinion about all the good news.

Further Readings and Bibliography: Amir Hassanpour, "The Language Factor in National Development," unpublished doctoral thesis (Urbana: University of Illinois, 1989), particularly chapter 7; C.J. Edmonds, "A Kurdish Newspaper: Rozh-i-Kurdistan," *Journal of the Central Asian Society* XI-i ((1924); C.J. Edmonds, "A Bibliography of Southern Kurdish, 1920-36," *Journal of The Royal Central Asian Society* XXIV (1937); C.J. Edmonds, "Bibliography of Southern Kurdish, 1937-1944," *Journal of the Royal Central Asian Society* XXXII (1945). Some very valuable surveys of the Kurdish press and journalism have appeared in Kurdish and other Middle Eastern languages (except for Edmonds, I am unaware of anything comprehensive or otherwise in English). Some of these are Abduljabbâr Jabbâri, *History of Kurdish Journalism* (Sulaymânia, Iraq, 1970); Najmadin Malâ, "History of printing press in Sulaymânia," *Zhin* 30-1232 (Baghdad, 1955); Muhammad Malâ-Karim, "Brief Review of the Open Kurdish Press," *Al-Ta'âkhi* (Baghdad, June 15, 1970); Alâuddin Sajjâdi, *History of Kurdish Literature* (Baghdad, 1971); Jamâl Khazânadâr, *Kurdish Journalism Guide* (Baghdad, 1973).

General Bibliography

A valuable survey of works done on the topic of Kurdish languages to 1960 is Ernest McCarus, "Kurdish Language Studies," *The Middle East Journal* (Washington, Summer 1960). Joyce Blau's work *Les Kurdes et le Kurdistan: Bibliographie Critique, 1977-1986* (Paris: Institute Français de Recherche en Iran, 1989), is an extensive annotated bibliography of titles that have appeared on Kurds, but most specifically on their literature, language, and political affairs. A good portion of the cited works are in English and other European languages. Another good source is the *Kurdish Times*, semi-annual journal of the Kurdish Library, Brooklyn, New York, 1985-present.

Chapter 7

SOCIETY

NATIONAL IDENTITY

Among their most important qualifications for nationhood are the Kurds' long common historical experience, their common worldview, common national character, integrated economy, common national territory, and collective future aspirations. Even among many modern nations are not found so many common elements to qualify them as a distinct nation. The only difference is that these sovereign nations possess, often as a result of the mere whim of their former European colonizers, a sovereign government. And because of their lack of an independent national government, every other genuine claim to nationhood by the Kurds has been cast in doubt.

External challenge to the Kurdish national identity takes the form of doubts cast on its antiquity and the discounting of its modern authenticity and value. Most such challenges are state-sponsored, but by no means all. Many scholars, equipped only with a superficial and rudimentary knowledge of the Kurdish past, have been quick to allow such challenges as well. The external challenges, in general, take on three forms, and are analyzed as follows.

1) *Modern Kurds are different from those ancient people who lived in the territory of Kurdistan, as they are not now identical with those earlier people in matters of language or religion.* It is quite legitimate to ask why all the people who lived in the area of Kurdistan in ancient times are collectively to be considered Kurds, since we now know that the culture and national character of the Kurds was altered and their language totally changed with the coming of the Aryans and subsequent immigrants. In this respect one can very properly compare the Kurds to the Egyptians. Ancient Egyptians too spoke a language different from the Arabic they have come to adopt and cherish since the advent of Islam. Many new genetic elements have been introduced into their nation, and their national character has undoubtedly been altered by the Islamic ethos and codes of conduct, of which the Egyptians have been the very champions since the 10th century of the common era. In matters of religion, Egyptians practiced pharaonic cults before becoming Christians and later Muslims. Even today Egypt has the largest Christian population in the Middle East, comprising about 10% of its total. Despite these past ethnic metamorphoses and their present heterogeneity, few people deny that the modern Egyptians are the inheritors and descendants of the ancient Egyptian people and civilization. The relationship of the modern English-speaking Irish to their Gaelic heritage is not any different. Examples are many, and in this respect the Kurds are similar to any ancient people who have over time adopted new languages or been influenced, even fundamentally, by new cultures and traditions.

Like practically every other large nation, past or modern-day, Kurds are the end product of the convergence and assimilation of many ethnic groups into one. They similarly demonstrate vestiges of an earlier culture underlying their contemporary culture, or practiced by small communities that have not yet forfeited the old, and once pervasive, cultural ways. In Egypt, the Coptic Christians are, for example, the last vestiges of a Coptic-speaking, Christian Egypt that has now been to a large extent reduced to a substratum of the modern, largely homogenized, Arabic-speaking, Muslim Egyptian culture.

There have since the 6th millennium BC been at least four eras of national homogenization in Kurdistan, each under a new and reconstituted identity. The last episode began with the breakup of the medieval, Pahlawâni-speaking, agriculturalist society of Kurdistan that practiced the Cult of Angels. The steady expansion of the Kurmânji-speaking, Sunni Muslim, pastoralist nomads from the Hakkâri region in northern Kurdistan is close to completion today, with roughly three-quarters of all Kurds now tracing the roots of their contemporary culture and identity to this process. The Pahlawâni speakers, reduced to about one-quarter of the total Kurds, therefore, have no stronger claim to be the sole heirs of the old culture and heritage of Kurdistan than the Copts do to the Egyptian culture and heritage, nor conversely are they any less Kurdish than the modern Copts are Egyptian.

More examples of such national cultural evolution and identity can be cited. The major ethnic neighbors of the Kurds, the Persians, the Turks, and the Arabs, have acquired their present cultural identities through a very similar accumulative process. The ethnic cousins of Kurds, the Persians, who are now spread from the borders of China and India to Mesopotamia, and boast an identifiable culture, language, history, and territory, are the end product of the convergence of many obscure, but also illustrious and historic, ethnic groups, such as the Bactrians, Soghdians, Kushans, Carmanians, eastern Medes, and so on. These latter groups were never just footnotes to history, and yet for all practical purposes, are correctly identified as ethnic Persians starting with the Islamic era.

The "Arabs" of Egypt, Iraq, and Greater Syria carry their pre-Islamic Coptic and Aramaean heritage into their new Arab identity without any contradiction or trouble. The Turkmens in Turkey are in the advanced stages of convergence with the Turks, which now forms the basis of a common Turkish identity in that state.

2) *The term* Kurd *used by the ancient, classical, and medieval sources was not an ethnic designator, as were ethnic names like Armenian or Persian, but rather a general term meaning "shepherd."* Faced with historical reports on far-flung Kurdish populations, in areas that are not predominantly Kurdish today, many modern scholars of Middle Eastern history readily assert that the term *Kurd* as used in the ancient and medieval sources was a designator of a life-style, and not an ethnic name. Most modern works trying to place the Kurds in history convey to their readers that any pastoralist mountain nomad was called a Kurd by the classical and medieval authors regardless of ethnic affiliation. Consequently, even when some entity is identified as *Kurd* or *Kurdish* by these valuable primary sources, the report does not necessarily make the entity a part of the *ethnic* Kurdish past.

This rather facile misconception was shared, though with reservations, by this author as well (Izady 1986). It has stemmed from insufficient knowledge of Kurdish historical migrations. Large numbers of Kurds have throughout the past few thousand years been settling new lands, some surviving as Kurds and others as-similating (see **Historical Migrations**). But the doubt thus cast on the reality of the Kurdish position in history has never withstood the following re-examination:

a) There has been no mention of Kurds in an area where presently there is not at least a small Kurdish population, or where a definitive case cannot be made for their origin in one of numerous (and ongoing) Kurdish migrations or deportations.

b) The Zagros mountains are the loci of the overwhelming majority of reports of the ancient Kurds. Kurds still constitute a majority of the inhabitants of the Zagros.

c) Many Turkic pastoralist groups, like the Qashqâ'is, Afshârs, Inânlu, and Qaragözlu, to name just a few, have dwelt in the Zagros mountains for at least the past 500 years, displaying an economic life identical to that of the Kurds, but have never been referred to as Kurds at any stage of history.

d) The Iranic groups frequently referred to as Kurds in the early sources are the tribes of the southern Zagros—the Shabânkâras, the Mamasanis, the Gelus, the Boyr Ahmads, and the Lurs. These all were actually Kurdish before their assimilation in the past 1000 years. They still maintain the array of Kurdish tribal subdivisions and names, proving they were once part of the same nation (see **Integration & Assimilation** and **Tribes**).

The Kurds mentioned in the classical and medieval sources were bona fide ethnic Kurds, and the forbearers of the modern Kurds and/or those who have acquired separate ethnic identities in the southern Zagros since the end of the medieval period.

3) *Kurds lack a common language and a common religion to bind them together as a single national group.* In fact this can be elaborated further. Today, Kurdish society remains heterogeneous in almost all those aspects that normally form the basis of an ethnic identity, such as religion, language, modes of economic production, and coherent homeland. At present, for example, the level of verbal understanding between many Kurdish dialects is no better than between French, Italian, Spanish, and Portuguese. Physically, Kurds are also a multi-racial group. The very land and people have been denied physical unity for the past three generations: a time sufficient to create most of the sovereign nations we have come to recognize at the world level today.

Many religions and their denominations are followed by the Kurds, and the Kurdish economy has always been diverse, with nomadism and intensive agriculture, as well as urban-based services, manufacturing, and commerce, existing side-by-side for at least the last millennium. Detailed accounts of these topics are provided throughout this handbook.

This degree of diversity would contradict any claim to ethnic distinctiveness. In their pluralism Kurds are not alone, but only if they are viewed as a nation with internal diversity and not as a subsidiary ethnic minority. Ethnic minorities are distinguished from a majority by the particular and unitary nature of their language, religion, or race, and not by their multiplicity. Kurds are a multi-lingual, multi-religious, multi-racial nation, but with a unified, independent, and identifiable national history and culture. Unlike that of an ethnic minority, Kurdish culture is not a local subsidiary of the larger national culture of a majority, nor is Kurdish history an extension of a more universal national history claimed by some majority group.

In their internal diversity, Kurds resemble closely the Arabs, as they too comprise a multi-racial, multi-cultural, multi-religious, and multi-lingual nation. Standard Arabic, or *fus'hâ*, based on classical Arabic literature like the Koran, is not the native language of any living Arab. The levels of mutual understanding among the native speakers of various modern descendants of the old Arabic language from Mauritania and Morocco to Lebanon, Iraq, and Oman are similar to the levels of understanding among various Kurdish vernaculars. No doubt is cast on the Arab identity of those groups of people who choose to claim it, despite these levels of diversity, primarily because the governments that rule the Arab lands strongly promote such a unified identity.

Nations, in order to develop and enhance their heritage and national life, need freedom of action over their wherewithals, the lack of which, although not fatal, is adverse to the nation's growth. Such freedom can be found within the framework of local autonomy, as it was traditionally available to the Kurds under the suzerainty of the old multi-ethnic empires, or outright sovereignty of the modern kind. The standardization and the governmental fostering of a common literary language, fus'hâ, has achieved for the Arab people unity in a pan-Arab identity. The Arabs now share the cumulative achievements of all the segments of the larger nation, submerging the disparate elements within their newly formed common identity only in this century.

The present century has, in contrast, brought Kurdistan a degree of effective fragmentation never before experienced by the Kurds. With the advent of modern states in the Middle East and well-guarded national boundaries, the movement of Kurds and exchange of ideas and culture among the five fragments of Kurdistan have become exceedingly difficult. This situation has been aggravated by the reserved or hostile relations between the countries under whose jurisdiction the Kurds live.

In many respects contemporary Kurdistan demonstrates signs of a retarded national evolution. Its people are bewildered in regards to their collective national identity. In short, they stopped evolving in the early 1920s, while the neighboring nations grew and evolved to create a uniform national ideology, culture, language, national history (true or invented), ethos, and political culture. As an example, even major national festivals in Kurdistan are celebrated in so many different ways and at so many different times that the definition of *national* becomes a puzzle when applied to these events, and a source of embarrassment to the Kurds themselves (see **Festivals, Ceremonies, & Calendar**). For a Kurd from Kirmânshâh in Iran to communicate with a Kurd from Arbil in Iraq, Afrin in Syria, or Diyârbakir in Turkey, it is necessary to use a third languages beyond simple greetings, which raises many eyebrows if non-Kurds happen also to be present. Similar embarrassing situations would exist among Arabs of various countries, if the fus'hâ were to be eliminated as a vehicle of communication.

There are also in existence two "national" flags for Kurdistan, neither one of which carries anything particularly Kurdish. In fact, two ancient Kurdish motifs have appeared on the standards of the Arab League (the eagle of king Saladin) and the state of Iraq. Between 1959 and 1963, the Iraqi flag carried a golden sun disk, surrounded by crimson rays, numbering the sacred seven. This Iraqi state flag was far more culturally Kurdish than either current Kurdish flag (see **Modern History**).

Further Readings and Bibliography: Martin van Bruinessen, "The Ethnic Identity of the Kurds," Peter Bumke "The Kurdish Alevis: Boundaries and Perceptions," and L. Nestmann, "Die ethnische Differenzierung der Bevölkerung der Ostttürkei in ihren sozialen Bezügen," in Peter Andrews, ed., *Ethnic Groups in the Republic of Turkey* (Wiesbaden: Reichert, 1989); Mehrdad Izady, "The Question of an Ethnic Identity," *Kurdish Times* I.1 (Spring 1986).

NATIONAL CHARACTER

U.S. Ambassador William Eagleton, Jr., could have written the following as a concise observation of any average Kurd, although he wrote specifically about General Mustafâ Bârzâni (see **Political Culture & Leadership**): "[he] quickly grasped the essence of a situation and exercised diplomatic and military cunning in achieving his objective. Less commendable characteristics were [his] egotism, opportunism, shortsightedness, and intractability" (Eagleton, 1963). American journalist Dana Adams Schmidt adds the following to this picture: "His remarks often had a cryptic, delphic quality. He liked to convey his ideas by telling stories" (Adams Schmidt 1964, 197).

Often suspicious of strangers and strange things, Kurds are nonetheless quick to reverse themselves and trust them. The Kurds as individuals and as a nation can tell long stories of "dishonorable" betrayals by peoples and groups they openly trusted. They never, however, can stand criticism for their apparent naivete.

The Pahlawân. The ideal Kurdish character is perhaps best crystallized in the image of the *pahlawân*, the cavalier and gentleman who must constantly substantiate his claim to nobility by demonstrating extreme bravery, wit, and magnanimity. The romantic tradition of the pahlawân is similar to that of Sir Walter Scott's heroes. Perhaps for this reason, Westerners from Lord Curzon and C.J. Edmonds, to Justice William O. Douglas and journalist Dana Adams Schmidt, to the American and British soldiers guarding the Kurdish refugee camps in Turkey and Iraq, have found the Kurds personally appealing.

However, the average Kurd is averse to, and in some quarters thought to be incapable of, group work and group planning. He is basically an atomist, believing in individualism as the only way to live like the proverbial "soaring lone eagle above the crest of the mountains." In fact the rugged and isolating terrain of Kurdistan is the prime culprit behind the Kurdish inclination toward individual enterprise and strict self-reliance.

The Kurd prides himself on precision and attention to detail, a characteristic which often distinguishes him from his ethnic neighbors. Many early Kurds are famous because of this characteristic. The detailed, specific, and refreshingly unbiased reports of the medieval Kurdish traveller to Scandinavia, Ibn Fadlân, and the treatment of the metallurgical processes of nations by Dinawari find their worth in this particular characteristic.

A joyous, free-spirited, basically unbiased individual, a Kurd once warmed up to somebody, will literally give his all to that person. With generosity bordering on recklessness, fortunes can be lost in entertaining absolute strangers, and murderous fights can break out between old friends as to who should have the honor of paying for a service enjoyed by them both.

Kurds are romantic and often reckless in love. To kill one's self or a contender for love is believed to be just another dangerous part of the sweet game, an attitude well reflected in Kurdish literature and folk stories. Kurds are said to show a strong, almost melancholic attachment to their mates for life, although this should not by any means be interpreted to mean that they do not have other consorts and liaisons to the very end of their days.

Kurds are warm and generous towards guests in their house. But their hospitality quickly runs thin if they are unable to "play" together with them. A stuffy, dry, and over-serious person will find himself quickly turned off by the playfulness or simple light-heartedness of even the oldest Kurdish patriarch—and vice versa. The fastest way to lose a Kurd's heart and mind is to sermonize on the virtues of decorum and berate his notion of a flamboyant or dreamy existence.

Honor, on the other hand, is always dearer than life itself, and commitment to anything by an oath of honor requires one to attain both or neither. Valor is considered the most valuable character of an individual, for man as well as woman, and is a prerequisite of honor. The result of a struggle is far less important than the way it is conducted, and therefore to show valor in the conduct of the exploit is praised whether one wins or loses. In the aftermath of the 1991 Persian Gulf War, it was not a surprise to those familiar with the Kurdish character to see Kurdish refugees first and foremost blaming their own leaders and not their non-Kurdish enemies for their predicament. The leaders had dishonored them all by pushing them into a situation where in less than three years, they twice had to commit an unthinkable act (for a pahlawân): they were forced to flee. Earlier, in 1975, when Kurdish general Bârzâni ordered them to retreat after the collapse of their uprising, most peshmergas could not fathom the meaning of, far less follow, this utterly uncharacteristic command, which ran against the very grain of their individualistic ethos. They stayed behind and were slaughtered defending their image as "cavaliers and gentlemen."

Being self-sufficient is also considered to be an integral part of the sacrosanct code of honor. Wealth as the insurer of financial autonomy (ergo, generosity) is strived for by all. It is not considered crude to add "wealthiness" to a list of one's personal qualities, even in written communications. Despite the value attached to manliness and masculine strength, the common Kurds of the countryside bulge up their stomachs (demonstrating that they are well-fed, and therefore wealthy) rather than the muscles of their chest as a preferred sign of being "mighty."

In defense of his religious convictions, the Kurd can be fanatical, even though he may not know exactly what it is he is defending. Left alone, he hardly ever performs religious duties when they do not serve other, parallel social functions. He respects religious figures such as pirs, shaykhs, mullahs, and the like, as part of the hierarchical pyramid of social respect, as he also respects tribal chiefs or members of local princely houses. While Kurds have often been noted by outsiders for their religious fanaticism, very seldom have they been noted for their religiosity.

The Mountains. As a community, Kurds are a niche-oriented people. Their history and culture are so intertwined with the mountains that the ethnic identity of a Kurd on the plain becomes a contradiction in terms. Kurds themselves have a saying: "Level the mounts, and in a day the Kurds would be no more." The two have become so inextricable that it is said that "The relation between a Kurd and his mountain habitat is like a farmer to his farm: one has no meaning without the other" (Siaband 1988). To a Kurd the mountain is no less than the embodiment of the deity: mountain is his mother, his refuge, his protector, his home, his farm, his market, his mate, and his only friend. This intimate man-mountain relationship shapes the physical, cultural, and psychological landscape of Kurdistan more than any other factor. Such a thorough attachment to and indivisibility from their natural environment is the source of many folk beliefs that all mountains are inhabited by the Kurds.

Every populous Kurdish tribe that has in historical times settled the flat neighboring regions, plains or plateaus, has quickly assimilated into the surrounding ethnic group (see **Tribes**, **Historical Migrations**, and **Deportations & Forced Resettlements**). In the mountains, on the other hand, their relative isolation has rendered the Kurds a lively, diverse nation largely resistant to assimilation. Over the course of several thousand years of Kurdish history—a time long enough for many other ethnic groups to have assimilated entirely into a dominant culture—the Kurds have remained a distinct people. Conversely, almost all who settled among them in the mountains—Scythians, Alans, Aramaeans, Armenians, Persians, Arabs, Mongols, Turkmens, and Turks—have been kurdified beyond recognition.

Just as the mountains create autonomy for the Kurds, they often prohibit easy communication between them. Meaningful intercommunal exchanges, let alone frequent communication over long distances between remote tribes, is still a rarity in the daily lives of the Kurds. Interpersonal and intercommunal quarrels mark the history of the Kurds over the past several centuries. Many of these quarrels are the result of physical and psychological distance. The mountains have broken down the language of the Kurds to a babble of dialects, their religions to a case study in diversity, and their art and costumes to a zoo of colorful variety.

Because of this diversity, in the past, and some may argue even today, the Kurds have never achieved sufficient unity to produce even the prototype of an organized pan-Kurdish political movement for independence. Let us note the fact that the individual Kurd has always felt very independent in his highlands, across which he travelled freely from one "country" to another. Indeed, the movement of the Kurds across the highlands had, until recently, been that of pastoral tribes who could traverse several international boundaries in the quest for fresh grazing lands.

The Jāsh. Kurdish life in its traditional setting is perhaps too organic, too close to nature, to permit the evolution of the vices, machinations, and maneuvering basic to the creation of successful political figures. On those rare occasions when individual Kurds—such as King Saladin and Karim Khan Zand—have become politically prominent, their benevolence and innocence have been their undoing, and they have at any rate moved to set the center of their empires outside of Kurdistan, among non-Kurds and with their help.

To become a good politician it has been necessary to leave mother-mountain and descend to the cities of the plains, where politicking is a well-developed craft. When, and if, an expatriate returns to the mountains, he will no longer be trusted wholeheartedly by the common people; it is as if he has lost his virtue by leaving the apron of mother-mountain and living among the crafty plains people. These men always seem eager to tell the Kurds how quickly they can succeed once they become non-Kurdish in every way (see **Integration & Assimilation**). Indeed, Kurds living in the plains cities are seldom considered to *be* Kurds by those living in the highlands, and are not trusted to be leaders. To know the secrets of the mountains, the passes, rivers, and caves; to know the tribal customs; and to be brave, are essential characteristics of Kurdish chiefs and leaders.

Often the Kurds living on the plains are perceived as foreign agents, insiders trained to obliterate all that is held dear by the Kurds. Any common Kurd can name a few of these "mercenary, plains-stricken" Kurds, known as the *jâsh*, "the donkeys," embracing the sinister aims of outsiders wishing to annihilate the Kurdish homeland and people. This notion is exemplified in two pieces of ancient literature: the tale of Enkidu in the Sumerian epic of Gilgamesh, and in the early medieval romance-tragedy of Shirin and Farhâd.

Mythological Farhâd is a Kurdish sculptor who carves the living rock of the mountains. He falls in love with a woman called Shirin, the queen of Persia and wife of the mighty 7th-century king Chosroes II (see **Popular Culture** and **Folklore & Folk Tales**). Shirin comes from the capital of Ctesiphon on the plains of Mesopotamia, and has just recently had a pleasure garden-palace constructed for herself on the Kurdish foothills at Qasiri Shirin ("the Palace of Shirin").

Farhâd leaves the mountain for the maddening love of Shirin (even today love is said to be the most common reason young Kurds who visit the towns and cities of the plains fail to return to the highlands). Farhâd is asked by Shirin to destroy the mountains, his home and his heart, by symbolically leveling the venerable Mount Bisitun ("the Abode of the God") to prove his commitment. Knowing the mountains and their strong and weak points, Farhâd works furiously at the task. He soon learns, however, that Shirin has betrayed his love, "as is the habit of the plains people." Shamed by his betrayal of his homeland and the defiling of the mother mountain, Farhâd throws himself off the same Mount Bisitun he had set out to obliterate.

Over two thousand years earlier than Farhâd, another man from the Kurdish mountains goes through the same disillusionment when he opts for the ways of the plains people. The story of Enkidu comes from the Mesopotamian epic of Gilgamesh, first put into writing over 4000 years ago. The story provides us also with a glimpse of how the ancestors of the modern Kurds were perceived by outsiders then as compared to now. The similarities are quite surprising. As the oldest literary piece describing the character of an inhabitant of the Kurdish mountains, the epic is fascinating. Almost all the following synopses of the story are from N.K. Sandars' translation (1972).

Gilgamesh is the semidivine king of the Sumerian city-state of Uruk (only several tens of miles away from Ctesiphon, where King Chosroes and Queen Shirin of the Farhâd story resided). Gilgamesh longs for a companion who can match him in power and character. The gods arrange for a "nature man," Enkidu, to emerge from the "Cedar Forests" in the Zagros mountains (see **Environment & Ecology**). As he is described in Sandars' translation, "'There was virtue in him of the god of war, of Ninurta himself. His body was rough, he had long hair like a woman's; his [golden] hair waved like the hair of Nisaba, the goddess of corn.... He was innocent of mankind; he knew nothing of the [plains] land." The animal trappers complain, "He ranges over the hills with wild beasts and eats grass; he fills in the pits which [we] dig and tears up [our] traps set for the game; he helps the beasts to escape and now they slip through [our] fingers."

To tame Enkidu, they all agree they should get a woman, "a wanton from the temple of love... and let her woman's power overpower this man." It is hoped that love of a woman of the plains will cause him to lose his natural innocence, "for when he murmurs love to [the woman from the plains] the wild beasts that shared his life in the hills will reject him, he who was born in the hills."

After a sensual introduction to the ways of the plains, Enkidu is rejected by all his familiar friends: the wild creatures of the mountains. Sad and weak, he listens as his new-found mate sermonizes him: "You are wise, Enkidu, and now you have become like a god. Why do you want to run wild with the beasts in the hill? Come with me. I will take you to strong-walled Uruk... there Gilgamesh lives, who is very strong, and like a wild bull he lords it over men." When he has spoken he asks the woman to take him to Gilgamesh, the lord of Uruk. There Enkidu could proclaim in his presence, like a true pahlawân, "I am the strongest here, I have come to change the old order, I am he who was born in the hills, I am he who is strongest of all."

Enkidu soon softens to the ways of the plains, grooming himself and admitting fear into his heart. For the first time he eats bread and drinks wine, as the woman slowly entices him to "become a [civilized] man."

Making a complete turnaround from his days as the protector of nature, when he destroyed the animal trappers' snares and filled their pits, he takes arms to "hunt the lion so that the shepherds could rest at night. He caught wolves and lions and the herdsman lay down in peace; for Enkidu had become their watchman" (see the account of Ziâ Gökalp, Mehmet Sekbân, Ismet Inönü, and Abdul-Karim Qâsim, in **Integration & Assimilation**).

He also becomes a devoted friend of Gilgamesh, who longs to destroy the "Cedar Forest" of the mountains, and its protective spirit Humbâbâ, for his personal glorification. Gilgamesh asks Enkidu to lead him back to his former home and refuge. Enkidu naively agrees.

With the help of the gods of the plains and Enkidu's knowledge of secrets of the mountains and woods, Gilgamesh corners Humbâbâ, the "blaze," the protector spirit of the woods and the mountains. Reacting to Enkidu's treacherous complicity with Gilgamesh, Humbâbâ chides him as having turned from a free-spirited mountain man to "a hireling, dependent for your bread." Ashamed, Enkidu further incites Gilgamesh to kill Humbâbâ and destroy the Forest. Together they bring down Humbâbâ: "Now the mountains were moved and all the hills, for the guardian of the forest was killed." Enkidu leading, they advance on the most sacred parts of the forest, where "They attacked the cedars... while Gilgamesh felled the first of the trees of the Forest, Enkidu cleared their roots as far as the banks of Euphrates."

Gilgamesh is glorified as the "conqueror of the Blaze [Humbâbâ]," and as the "wild bull who plundered the mountain." Enkidu falls sick, and on his death bed bitterly curses the woman whose love had entrapped him in the first place. In moment of profound recognition, he realizes that she has led him to betray everything of importance to him, including his wife back in the mountains and their seven children (for the significance of this number, see **Cult of Angels**), whose existence he reveals for the first time, in tears.

Before he dies, however, in the spirit of a pahlawân, Enkidu even forgives the woman of the plains, admitting that he had enjoyed his transformed life with her after all.

The parallels with the story of Shirin and Farhâd are illuminating to say the least, as they demonstrate the ethos of both Kurdish and non-Kurdish peoples. It appears that little has changed in the way they have perceived each other throughout ages.

Further Readings and Bibliography: Abdul-Kader Amin (collected by), *Kurdish Proverbs* (New York: Kurdish Library, 1989); Major E. Noel, "The Character of the Kurds as Illustrated by Their Proverbs and Popular Sayings," *Bulletin of the School of Oriental Studies* I-iv (London, 1917-20);

Basile Nikitine, "Kurdish Stories from My Collection," *Bulletin of the School of Oriental and African Studies* IV (1926-28); William Eagleton, Jr., *The Kurdish Republic of 1946* (London: Oxford University Press, 1963); , Dana Adams Schmidt, *Journey Among Brave Men* (Boston: Little, Brown, 1964); Captain Bertram Dickinson. "Journeys in Kurdistan," *Geographical Journal* 35 (1910); C.J. Edmonds, *The Kurds, Turks and Arabs* (London: Oxford University Press, 1957); C.J. Edmonds, "Shah Bazher and the Basin of the Qalachuwalan," *Geographical Journal* 123 (1957); W.R. Hay, *Two Years in Kurdistan: Experiences of a Political Officer, 1918-1920* (London, 1921); Margaret Khan, *Children of the Jinn: In Search of the Kurds and their Country*. (New York: Seaview Books, 1980); Captain F.R. Maunsell, "Kurdistan," *Geographical Journal* 3-2 (1894); Major E. B. Soane, "The Southern Kurd," *Journal of the Central Asian Society* 9.1 (1922); Mrs. Lindfield Soane, "A Recent Journey in Kurdistan," *Journal of the Royal Central Asian Society* 22.3 (1935); B. Nikitine and E.B. Soane, "The Tale of Suto and Tato," *Bulletin of the School of Oriental and African Studies, London Institute* III (1923-25); Nizâmi, *Chosroès et Chirin*, French trans. of the Persian original by Henri Massé (Paris: Bibiothèque des Oeuvres Classiques Persanes, No. 2, 1970); Ph. K. Hitti, "The Origin of the Druze People and Religion with Extracts of their Sacred Writings," *Columbia University Oriental Studies* 28 (New York, 1928); *The Epic of Gilgamesh*, N.K. Sandars trans. and ed.(Baltimore: Penguin, 1972); Martin van Bruinessen, "The Kurds Between Iran and Iraq," *Middle East Report* (July-August 1986); C.L. Brown and D. Itzkowitz, eds., *Psychological Dimensions of Near Eastern Studies* (Princeton: Darwin, 1977); A.M. Hamilton, *Road Through Kurdistan* (London: Faber and Faber, 1958); J.C.A. Johnson, "The Kurds of Iraq," *Geographical Magazine* (1940); Mark Sykes, *The Caliph's Last Heritage* (London: Macmillan, 1915); Samande Siaband (pen name used by M. Izady), "Mountains My Home," *Kurdish Times* II.2 (1988); C.J. Rich, *Narrative of a Residence in Koordistan, and on the Site of Ancient Nineveh; with Journal of Voyage Down the Tigris to Baghdad*. London, 1836; Lieut. Col. J. Shiel, "Notes on a Journey from Tabriz, through Kurdistan via Vân, Bitlis, Se'ert and Erbil, to Suleïmaniyeh, in July and August 1836," *Journal of the Royal Geographical Society* 8 (1838); Michael Crichton, *Eaters of the Dead: The Manuscript of Ibn Fadlan Relating His Experiences with the Northmen in AD 922* (New York: Knopf, 1976).

SOCIAL ORGANIZATION

The forbidding mountains and rugged terrain of Kurdistan have engendered semi-isolated communities in the fertile valleys and plateaus, each with its own unique linguistic and social traits. Just as the mountains have largely protected the Kurds from outside influences—and threats—they have also hindered communication, fostering cultural heterogeneity.

The earliest records of civilized habitation in Kurdistan coincide with the invention of agriculture in the region. Kurdistan boasts some of the earliest settled agriculturalist communities in the world. To administer the fast expanding population soon after the transition to an agricultural economy (standard estimates are that it would have increased around tenfold), generating a far larger economy, and more trade, necessitated military protection for the bounty. Organized states were thus formed, with urban life soon becoming a by-product. A substrata of settled agriculturalists has always been present ever since the agricultural revolution in Kurdistan (see **Prehistory**).

At times lack of security and nomadic dislocations have forced the agriculturalists to give ground to the nomads, but never so thoroughly to account for anywhere less than half the overall domestic production of goods in the Kurdish economy. Engaging in a labor-intensive mode of production, agriculturalists by their sheer numbers remained the majority in the Kurdish society even at the very height of nomadic shift in the 18th and early 19th centuries.

It has been suggested by various authors of the earlier decades of this century that the agriculturalist, settled Kurds may actually constitute a different race from the nomads and represent an aboriginal population of the land who have survived the onslaught of many centuries of nomadism. Missing from this observation has been the fact that Kurdistan, like many neighboring lands, has never seen a society made of agriculturalists or nomads alone. The existence of strong physical variations among social classes can be seen in other societies as well, such as the inhabitants of many Pacific Islands. The seemingly racial distinction among classes is largely the outcome of the superior nutrition, hygiene, and lifestyle of the nomads. But not all of it is attributable to environmental factors (see **Physical Anthropology**).

"Tribes" more often were pastoralist, and performed more as a social block of associations and allegiances than as economic organizations. Only within the walls of the cities would tribal affiliations weaken, but even the sedentary farmers in the countryside maintained close association with tribes from whom they received protection and direction. An increase in the number of raiding nomads in the countryside, the existence of war or the threat of war with an outside force, or the emergence of an extortionist individual or clan was enough to push the non-tribal people, even those in the cities, to seek a tribal affiliation and buy their security by paying tribute to an agreeable and capable tribal chief. The allegiance of the majority of the inhabitants has until recently been, therefore, to their extended families and then to their own tribe or clan. Beyond the bounds of tribe, a Kurd only infrequently showed any allegiance to nation, state, or any other entity.

Even religion has played a secondary role to this all-important social feature. As much as one finds the tribal surnames carried by modern Kurds and their leaders, the ancient Kurds, as far as recorded history can relate, did the same. The Kurd has found his identity, his security, and his livelihood in the tribe, and has paid his tributes, moral and material, to the tribal chief. The local chief then struck alliances or entered into tribal confederations with other groups, which in turn gave support to the local Kurdish principalities. These principalities in turn paid varying degrees of homage to the dominant kingdoms and empires as they came and went. More often, however, the principalities exercised outright independence, even in the midst of mighty empires, occasionally paying tributes to far-away capitals that could command suzerainty over the land.

This arrangement was the best that outside powers could hope for. In view of the limited technology of the pre-modern times, it was physically impossible to rule directly, from a far-off imperial capital, the homes of the citizens or even the local chieftains, particularly in areas as inaccessible as the Kurdish highlands. This traditional restriction of central governmental rule, to a very loose and exclusively political dominance, allowed the Kurds every vestige of independence short of annual tributes in kind and soldiers, and worked to everybody's satisfaction.

The dawn of the industrial age and the spread of advanced technology in armaments, transportation, and communication into the region eventually rendered local autonomous principalities and even chieftains an unnecessary and costly detour on the route to collect revenue and manpower for the imperial and colonial governments of the Middle East. By the middle of the 19th century went the last of the autonomous Kurdish principalities, followed in less than three-quarters of a century by the demise of the autonomous tribal chiefs. The *coup de grâce* came rather abruptly and harshly at the end of World War I, when the traditional power structure was replaced by the five governments that inherited the fragments of Kurdistan.

The new states set out on a systematic program of social and political subjugation of the autonomous Kurdish lands into their central system of modern government and economy. Bloody frictions resulted from the attempts of the state government to wrest from the Kurds their historical autonomy and freedom of domestic action, which is as natural to them as *snoyi zissân*, "the fall of snow in winter." The states' efforts, however, can be shown to be impracticable. Kurdistan shows every sign of a land and a people who are under foreign occupation and not just an ethnic group living in an integrated state or states dominated by a majority group. In fact, the degree of freedom enjoyed by the Kurds for thousands of years was nothing less than de facto independence, even at those times when they were vassal principalities within larger empires.

Most Kurds, even the highly educated ones, still reserve their strongest loyalties for their family-clan leaders. The leaders and patricians of even the smallest of clans enjoy an impressive degree of respect among the members. Even today, every Kurdish political party leader sees various degrees of need to consult these tribal patricians for every major decision. After all, their guerrilla fighters do come from these very clan and tribal subdivisions, and respect and consultation with their local representatives encourage them to stay the ranks. Even the most politically modernized party, the PKK in Turkish Kurdistan, is not exempt from this rule. To circumvent the ideological contradictions, the PKK has now managed to legitimize its relationship with those clan leaders whom it finds necessary to consult by calling them "progressive," as distinguished from those who do not cooperate and are therefore "reactionary" clan leaders (see **Political Parties**).

With rampant nomadism long gone from the land, these clan chiefs and tribal chieftains should properly be referred to as a local political elite, similar to those with more politically current titles in all independent states, with whom politicians at the national level must deal with for local votes of confidence and support. They are the power brokers, and being the "local boys," are much more trusted to protect the local people's interests. This has not escaped the attention of modern Kurdish political leaders, and all of them without exception, and including the modernist PKK and KDP-I, consult these local traditional elites at different levels.

Further Readings and Bibliography: Frederick Barth, *Principles of Social Organization in Southern Kurdistan* (Oslo: Vorgensen, 1953); William M. Masters, "Rowanduz: A Kurdish Administrative and Mercantile Center," unpublished doctoral dissertation (Ann Arbor: University of Michigan, 1953); John M. Smith, "Turanian Nomadism and Iranian Politics," *Iranian Studies* XI (1978); Messoud Fany, "La Nation Kurde et son évolution sociale," unpublished doctoral dissertation (Paris: University of Paris, Faculty of Law, 1933); J. F. Bestor, "The Kurds of Iranian Baluchistan: A Regional Elite," unpublished masters thesis (Montreal: McGill University, 1979); Edmund Leach, *Social and Economic Organization of the Rowanduz Kurds* (London: London School of Economics, Monographs in Social Anthropology III, 1940).

STATUS OF WOMEN & FAMILY LIFE

Commenting in 1923 on the social characteristics of the Kurds, G.R. Driver, a British Kurdologist, scorns the settlement of the previously pastoralist Kurds of Cilicia (in central Taurus on the Mediterranean) for having brought out their "worst characteristics," that "the women go unveiled and are allowed great freedom, but most of the hard manual labour falls on them." Of the other Kurds he writes: "Kurdish women are comparatively free to come and go as they like; they are wooed and won by open courtship, for almost all tribes they are unveiled. They are not in the least degree cautious to hide themselves and even admit male servants into their houses. In the resulting union the wife plays no secondary part and is regarded as 'the pillar of the house.' They are treated as equals by their husbands and regard with contempt the slavish estate of [traditional] Turkish women."

If not approving of the freedom of Kurdish women, the Victorian Driver concedes that "the morality of the women is famous, and almost all tribes punish adultery with death; prostitution is almost unknown, and it is even asserted that there is no (indigenous) word in Kurdish for a prostitute." (Of course Driver was wrong in presuming that the oldest profession was not practiced among the Kurds, or that their language lacks words for it: it is practiced and there are several Kurdish words for its various types, even though some of them are derived from neighboring languages.)

To better evaluate the traditional status of women in Kurdish society, it is useful to examine their role in certain fields that are usually dominated by men, such as the military, politics, finance, and religion.

Among the Qutils, who are among the ancient ancestors of the Kurds (see **Ancient History**), it was the women who often commanded the army (R. Ghirshman 1954, 44).

Nearly 2000 years after the Qutils, the Greco-Roman historian Plutarch reports local people in northern and western Kurdistan fiercely defending their home from the invading Roman troops, in the 1st century BC. Among these native forces he emphasizes the existence of fighting "Amazon" women. Women under arm, anathema to the Greeks and Romans, always evoked for them the legend of the Amazons, which incidentally, and by all accounts, had their homeland in this same general geographical area (Plutarch, *Fall of the Roman Republic: Pompey*).

In the same campaigns, Plutarch reports a female consort of the Kurdish Pontian king Mithridates who, dressed in traditional colorful Kurdish dress (which he erroneously calls Persian), made an impressive display of military prowess in defense of the Pontian state besieged by the Roman general Pompey. "Mithridates himself, however, with 800 cavalry had, at the very beginning of the attack, cut his way right through the Romans and made his escape. His escort soon scattered in different directions and he was left with three companions. Among these was his concubine Hypsicrateia, a girl who had always shown the spirit of a man and always been ready to take any risk. For this reason the King used to give her the masculine name of Hypsicrates"

The evidence of the military prowess of the women in Kurdistan is, however, much older than the written records. At the 12,000-year-old cemeteries at Shânidar in central Kurdistan (famous for its Neanderthal remains) the only adornments found buried with most female skeletons were well-ornamented knives. In one such grave the knife was made of a bone haft and a flint blade set in bitumen (Roaf 1990, 30).

The Zand dynasty (AD 1750-1794), the last major Kurdish dynasty of the Middle East, employed women extensively in its military campaigns for the throne of Persia. Even the founder of the dynasty, Muhammad Karim Khân, fully adhered to this ancient Kurdish custom. He and his soldiers enjoyed the military support of their brides, who fought alongside them as they routed invading Afghan forces. The Afghan officers ridiculed the Zands for this, accusing them of "hiding behind their women's skirts."

The participation of women in the military continues today in Kurdistan, as nearly all Kurdish political parties (except for the fundamentalist Islamic parties) who command a fighting peshmerga guerrilla group include women in their ranks. Women guerrillas are found in the the the largest numbers in the formidable peshmerga force of the PKK party in Anatolia (see **Political Parties**), whose actual combat participation record is similar to that which prompted Plutarch to report 2100 years ago of the "Amazon" women soldiers in the exact same area of Anatolia: western and northern Kurdistan.

In politics Kurdish women have been similarly active from the earliest times. The last ruler of an important medieval Kurdish Daylamite dynasty, the Buwayhids of Ray (modern Teheran), was a woman, Sayyida "Mâmâ" Khâtun. For nearly 30 years she safeguarded the kingdom from the onslaught of the Turkic nomads and their mighty Ghaznavid king, Mahmud, through a combination of courage, wit, and diplomacy. She ruled until the passing of the reign to her son Majd al-Dawlah in 1029 AD, which rang the death knell for the dynasty.

In early modern times Kurdish women figured prominently in politics and leadership. Examples of female Kurdish political figures are far too many to permit a listing. Among the better-known ones are Lady Kara Fâtima of the city of Marash in far western Kurdistan in Commagene, who represented the Kurds in the mid-nineteenth century at the Ottoman court in Constantinople. A full-page sketch commemorating the arrival, holding a lance and accompanied by her 300 cavalier retinue appeared on the front page of the *Illustrated London News* of April 22, 1856. In the same decade the Ottoman government had to face a Kurdish woman, the last autonomous ruler of Hakkâri region in northern Kurdistan, while the Ottoman armed forces had to deal with Mâmâ Pura Halima of Pizhdar, Mâmâ Kara Nargiz of the Shwân tribes of central Kurdistan, as well as Mâmâ Persheng of the populous Milân tribe of western Kurdistan (Nikitine 1956). The

Russian forces advancing into north-central Kurdistan in 1916 also found a woman, Mâmâ Mariam, widow of the Naqshbandi shaykh Muhammad Sadiq leading the defense of the historic-religious town of Nahri/Nehri. The last Kurdish military leader to succumb to the Persian army of Rezâ Shâh of Iran in 1928 was also a woman, heading the Harki tribe.

The well-cultured Âdila Khânem was the chief of the most important and populous Kurdish tribe of central Kurdistan, the Jâf, until her death in 1924. She hired the legendary E.B. Soane as her Persian scribe, whose descriptions provide a great deal of insight into the traditional place of women in Kurdish society. He once described Âdila herself as a "lioness." Âdila Khânem's palace at Halabja remained the last relic of the traditional princely architecture in central Kurdistan until the city's destruction in 1988 (see **Recent History**).

In religion women again play a primary role. The native Kurdish Cult of Angels includes a female among the six Major Avatars of the Universal Spirit in every one of the seven epochs of the life of the material world (see **Yârsânism**). Some of the sacred scriptures of the Cult were written by women, such as Mâmâ Nargiz Shahrazuri (b. AD 1313), herself a Minor Avatar of the Universal Spirit.

Of the 1145 Sufi followers of the early 20th century Yârsân holy man and religious leader Ni'matullâh Jayhunâbâdi, about 500 were women, according his son and successor Nurali Ilahi. In fact the above-mentioned Mâmâ Fara Fâtima herself claimed to be a famale avatar of the Spirit in the 19th century.

The participation of women in the communal religious practices of the Cult was perceived by non-Kurds to be an anomaly. The freedom with which women participate in functions reserved routinely for men in the surrounding communities and their religions, was not, and still is not, easily tolerated. This has been the cause of many accusations of sexual impropriety levied against the Kurdish followers of the religion (see **Cult of Angels**). Despite millennia of accusations of scandal, women are still required to participate in all religious rituals in the Alevi and Yezidi communities. The followers of Yârsânism have partially relented to pressure from the surrounding populations and less liberal religions. Some denominations of Yârsânism, particularly those that have drawn close to Shi'ite Islam, have now banned women's participation in communal gatherings taking place indoors.

The Bâbi movement, which carries a great deal of influence from the Cult of Angels, also holds a liberal view of women (see **Bâbism & Bahâ'ism**). In 1849, Tâhira Qurratu'l Ayn, the de facto female avatar in the Bâbi cycle of primary reincarnations, removed her veil in public to "signal the equality of women with men as a basic principle of the new Bâbi religion" (Fischer 1978). Tâhira's action was in fact a replay of a similar episode in AD 922, when upon the crucifixion of Cult mystic Hallâj, his sister removed her veil in public in Baghdad (see **Sufi Mystic Orders**).

The high social status and relative freedom of Kurdish women adopted by the Kurdish Jews gave rise in the 17th century to the first woman rabbi, the famous Rabbi Asenath Bârzâni (see **Judaism**). In fact, it was Queen Helena of the Kurdish kingdom of Adiabene who, after converting to Judaism, is traditionally held to have been instrumental in the conversion of her royal husband and later the kingdom.

Financially, women have enjoyed a much more secure position than they do in neighboring ethnic groups. Even though Kurdish families remain patriarchal, patrilineal, and patrilocal, upon the death or disgrace of the male head, the matriarch customarily assumes his property and social station. The existence of male offspring has seldom prevented a Kurdish matriarch from succeeding her husband as the head of a family.

Marriages have not traditionally been arranged, but as observed by Driver (see above), the woman and men choose each other. Only out of political or financial necessity have there been arranged marriages.

Ironically, in recent decades, many Kurdish men have tried to assimilate the values of the more powerful ethnic neighbors, for the sake of "modernization," and have attempted to limit the freedom of the women in their households and in society. Veils are more frequently being forced upon Kurdish women in the cities and larger towns. These are the Kurds who have most fully assimilated into the prevailing state cultures. This "modernization" is unlikely to succeed in restricting the traditional liberal attitudes of the Kurdish society toward women, since the next wave of modernization should also bring with it the even newer trend of women's liberation and social equality. Nonetheless, the millennia-old Kurdish traditions persist in the remoter parts of Kurdistan. In fact among some isolated contemporary tribes, such as the Kurasonni (on both sides of the Turkish-Iranian border between the towns of Khoy and Vân), the birth of a female child is more celebrated than that of a male.

Further Readings and Bibliography: Henny H. Hansen, *The Kurdish Woman's Life: Field Research in a Muslim Society, Iraq* (Copenhagen: Ethnografiske Kaekke, no. 7, 1961); Henny H. Hansen, *Daughters of Allah: Among MuslimWomen in Kurdistan* (London, 1960); Mohammed Mokri, "Le Mariage chez les Kurdes," *Revue de la Société d'Ethnographie* (Paris, 1962); T.F. Aristova, "Ocherki kul'tury i byta kurdskikh krest'yan Irana" ("A Sketch of the Culture and Way of Life of the Kurdish Peasants in Iran"), *Trudy Etnografii Miklukho-Maklaya* 39 (Moscow, 1958); Paul Magnarella, "A Note on Aspects of Social Life among the Jewish Kurds of Sanandaj, Iran," *Jewish Journal of Sociology* XI.1 (1969); R. Ghirshman, *Iran: From the Earliest Times to the Islamic Conquest* (Baltimore: Pelican, 1954); Ziba Mir-Hosseini, "Impact of Wage Labour on Household Fission in Rural Iran," *Comparative Journal of Family Studies* 18.3 (1987); Walter Fischel, "The Jews of Kurdistan," *Commentary* VIII.6 (1949); Dina Feitelson, "Aspects of the Social Life of Kurdish Jews," *Jewish Journal of Sociology* I.2 (1910); Ziba Mir-Hosseini, "Changing Aspects of Economic and Family Structures in Kalardasht, A District in Northern Iran," unpublished doctoral dissertation (Cambridge: Department of Social Anthropology, Cambridge University, 1980); A. Salar, "A Kurdish Boyhood," *Kurdish Times* IV.1-2 (1991); Basile Nikitine, *Les Kurdes, etude sociologique et historique* (Paris, 1956); Michael Roaf, *Cultural Atlas of Mesopotamia and the Ancient Near East* (New York: Equinox-Oxford, 1990); M. Fischer, "On Changing Concept and Position of Persian Women," in L. Beck and N. Keddie, eds., *Women in the Muslim World* (Cambridge, Massachusetts: Harvard University Press, 1978).

General Bibliography

Two excellent works on the social psychology of the Kurds and the cultural-environmental roots of their social behavior and organization are Abdul-Kader Amin (collected by), *Kurdish Proverbs* (New York: Kurdish Library, 1989) and Samande Siaband (pen name used by M. Izady), "Mountains My Home," *Kurdish Times* II.2 (1988); Witold Rajkowski, "A Visit to Southern Kurdistan," *Geographical Journal* 107.3-4 (1946); A valuable earlier work is that of C.J. Edmonds, *Kurds, Turks, and Arabs* (London: Oxford University Press, 1957). B. Nikitine, *Les Kurdes. Etude Sociologique et Historique* (Paris, 1956); Henny Hansen's work, *The Kurdish Woman's Life: Field Research in a Muslim Society, Iraq* (Copenhagen: Ethnografiske Kaekke, no. 7, 1961) sheds light on more than the status of Kurdish women, and should prove valuable reading. A more specific bibliography on the social and political organization of the Iranian Kurds is provided in the work of Wolfgang Behn, *The Kurds in Iran: A Selected and Annotated Bibliography* (London: Mansell, 1977); Hanzelka Jiri and Miroslav Zikmund, *Kurdistan: Land der Aufstände, der Legenden und der Hoffnung* (Prague: Artic Praha, 1962); and the *Kurdish Times*, semi-annual journal, Brooklyn, New York, Kurdish Library, 1985-present.

Chapter 8

POLITICAL &
CONTEMPORARY ISSUES

NATION-STATES & KURDISH NATIONALISM

Kurds now live as minorities in five independent states—many more, if the former Soviet republics in the Caucasus and central Asia gain their full independence. Kurds are indeed a numerical minority in all the sovereign states where they live today. The resemblance of the Kurds to other national ethnic minorities ends with this. By any other standard, Kurds constitute a vibrant and diverse nation, and individually and collectively demonstrate symptoms of a major nation under foreign occupation. The endemic conflicts of the Kurds with their administering governments, the formation and liquidation of numerous Kurdish political parties, and their susceptibility to popular uprisings, wars, declarations of independence, as well as deportations set the Kurds apart from other ethnic minorities living in these same states, and most others across the globe (see **Early Modern, Modern,** and **Recent History; Deportations & Forced Resettlements**; and **Political Parties**).

By comparison, the same qualities that made the Germans a nation, even though they were never united before 1871 in a single German state, are present among the Kurds. What the Kurds lack as a "nation" in the contemporary sense is a sovereign government. By every other accepted standard the Kurds are a major nation.

All that has been done by the organized state apparatuses to create a nation out of the disparate peoples they inherited within their newly formed boundaries in Turkey, Syria, Iraq, and Iran is fundamentally missing to the Kurds. In fact these very same states have done all that they could to stop the growth of Kurdish society as a distinct and separate national entity, and often to destroy its distinctions altogether. They have attempted to bury the Kurdish past, figuratively as well as literally, deny any originality to the ancient Kurdish culture, and prevent original research on any topic of national importance to the Kurds. Moreover, they have created and forced on the Kurds false identities such as "Mountain Turk" in Turkey and "Umayyad Arab" in Syria and Iraq (for the Yezidi Kurds). Their separate existence in Iran, Soviet Azerbaijan, and Turkmenistan has simply been denied. These efforts have done plenty to confuse even the Kurds themselves.

Most efforts of the governments now administering fragments of Kurdistan have been directed toward the creation of an effective and universal national identity to bolster political unity and to create nation-states on the European model. In Turkey, Syria, and Iraq, the terms *Turk* and *Arab*, formerly used pejoratively for country bumpkins and desert nomads, are now promoted through a process of historicism, pseudo-linguistics, and myth to create a new and collective national identity. They have blurred or distorted other historical realities in order to arrive at the simple view that the "nation" in its contemporary form has existed as an identifiable and unified body since time immemorial, and has been one of the primary contributors to world culture.

Where do Kurds fit in this mixed picture? Since it is clear that the Kurds are not Arabs or Turks, all attempts to fabricate a pseudo-identity to make them so have been half-hearted, clumsy, and at the end a failure. In Iran, Kurds fit rather nicely in the pan-Iranian views of the government, as the Kurdish culture and language are indeed Iranic. Not only does the Iranian government find it easy to explain the Kurdish identity within the larger family of Iranic peoples, but its support for the Kurds beyond its boundaries has been susceptible to a pan-Iranist rationales (as well as any other rationale suitable at the time). Shah Muhammed Reza Pahlavi referred to the Kurds as "the purest of all Aryans, and one of the most noble races of the Iranians." To him and most other elites, *Iranian* was synonymous with *Persian*.

As Teheran maintains, Kurds are in fact, like the Persians, an Iranic people in speech and culture. With the confusion that now exists even in the scientific circles regarding the terms *Iranian* and *Iranic* (notions as distinct as *German* and *Germanic*), Kurds are understandably uncertain what, beyond the bounds of their language, is exclusively theirs and not Iranian, which is progressive coming to mean *Persian*. It is therefore an easy task for the Kurdish to sort out their lot from the others in Turkey, Syria, Iraq, and the Commonwealth of Independent States, but not so in Iran.

Another important difference between Iran and other states is that the Iranian Kurds have a long history as part of an Iranian state. European colonial authorities invented Syria, Iraq, and even Turkey out of the wreckage of the Ottoman Empire in the aftermath of World War I, where no such states had existed before. Kurds ended up within these new states only because an independent Kurdistan turned out not to be useful to British or French colonial administrators. The Iranian Kurds have been living within the boundaries of Persia since at least the 16th century. The only difference is that the same state has come to be called Iran since 1935.

Many important national figures in past and present Iran have been unassimilated Kurds. The most prominent Iranian political party prior to the Islamic Revolution, the National Front (founded by the Premier, Dr. Muhammed Mussadegh), has been chaired for the past two decades by Karim Sanjâbi, a Kurd from Kirmânshâh. Many important writers, artists, and social figures at the national level have also been ethnic Kurds. These have climbed up the social ladder, however, because they have pursued a pan-Iranian agenda and not a Kurdish one. To do otherwise, would mean quick reprisal and ostracism.

Constituting only about 12% of the total population of Iran, and with little hope of increasing this proportion (see **Demography**), Iranian Kurds also find themselves divided between contiguous Kurdistan and the Khurâsâni enclave over 600 miles away, as well as in many other populous pockets in the Alburz mountains. Regional differences further distinguish those Kurds in the Iranian portions of contiguous Kurdistan, hampering the development of a unified voice to argue the case of the Kurds in Teheran (see **Internal Subdivisions**).

In Iraq too, many Kurds have held high political positions, and there have been Kurdish vice presidents to various Iraqi presidents. Because of the recent origin of the Iraqi state, dating only to 1932 (the year when the British mandate ended), and the lack of an entrenched political elite, the regimes in Baghdad have never felt it possible to exclude representatives from other ethnic groups. The Sunni Arabs, who have held power in Baghdad since independence, represent only about 18% of the total Iraqi population, a percentage less than that of the Kurds (23.5%). One can openly remain a Kurd and acquire high political and social standing in Baghdad if he supports the government absolutely. Only the very inner circles of power (including the highest-ranking military posts) are reserved for the Sunni Arabs. And this has had security and nepotism as its source rather than ethnic chauvinism. There is no state ideology that excludes from upward social mobility the Kurds or any other person based solely on ethnic affiliation. The pan-Arabism intermittently championed by Baghdad has been more rhetorical than real, as witnessed by the recent destruction of Arab Kuwait at the hands of the Iraqi

"Arabs" (a number of which, perhaps as many as 15% of the regulars, were naturally Kurdish conscripts).

Even the much-maligned President Saddam Hussein has not brought punishment on the Kurds, or anyone else for that matter, because of who they are, but rather what they have done in challenging his authority. Members of his family and clan (the Tikritis) suspected of disloyalty have invariably met the same fate as would a common Kurdish farmer deep inside the mountains guilty of the same offense.

The future is uncertain for the Iraqi Kurds. It will take more than a continuation of the status quo to bring back into the international community a fully sovereign and territorially intact country. Yet the majority of the Kurds in Iraq have been living either outside the direct rule of Baghdad or completely independent of it since March 1991. The shocked and (debatably) awakened Kurds of Iraq can hardly be imagined to allow themselves to again be administered from Baghdad. They made this clear by their massive exodus when it seemed Baghdad was about to reassert its control over their territories in the spring of 1991.

After a year of near independence in the "liberated" parts of Iraq, the Kurdish political parties have again squandered the opportunity to show the outside world that an autonomous or an independent Kurdistan is a workable idea, that left to themselves the Kurds are capable of providing law and order and looking after the needs of the citizens in the territories under their control. Their one-year record is an embarrassing series of failures in the administration and economic management of the region. While they have been squabbling with their local political rivals, civil security has been all but forgotten, and smuggling has become the prime industry. If the dream of the Iraqi Kurds for self-government is to be realized, it will surely take more than what is already there in political and diplomatic talent.

The idea of a separate Kurdish identity, in the future, as in the past, will clash the most with the state ideology in Turkey. While the names *Iran, Iraq,* and *Syria* are not ethnic-based country names, *Turkey* is. By definition, *Turkey* means "the land of the Turks." Yet for the Kurds from Turkey to refer to themselves as "Turkish Kurds" is a contradiction in terms. How can a Turk be a Kurd? This contradiction may have been foreseen by the advocates of Anatolianism in 1924-25 (Andrews 1989). Their point of view was propelled not so much by concern for the Kurds and other non-Turkish minorities in the new republic, but by their grander pan-Turkic ideals. It was argued that the terms *Turk* and *Turkey* defined all people of Turkish race and all lands inhabited by them, i.e., the mythical Turân. "We are Anatolians," they argued, "Anatolia is our homeland, our nation is the Anatolian nation" (Tachau 1962, 167-8). Whatever their true motives, Anatolia, a neutral term, could have avoided the subsequent radicalism and ethnic chauvinism born of the state name *Turkey.*

Conceding to the inadequacy of the ultimately ethnocentric terms *Turkey* and *Turkish,* the 1982 Turkish constitution, article 66, thus declares: "A Turk is someone associated with the Turkish State by the ties of Nationality." There is no ethnic affiliation specified here, and legally a Turk could be an ethnic Kurd. It is only in practice that this is still interpreted as meaning that only ethnic Turks live, or ought to be living, in Turkey. To this end, an act of Turkish parliament passed in 1930 prohibited official usage (such as before the courts of law), publication, education, and electromagnetic propagation or broadcasting in the Kurdish language. Such acts were punishable by imprisonment. The ban was enforced with varying vigor in the past, sometimes applied even to domestic usage of Kurdish. This rather unenforceable gag rule was relaxed in the 1950s, when the slow Kurdish demographic decline (relative to non-Kurds) gave the deceiving impression that the Kurds were assimilating (see **Demography**). Noting a reversal of the trend, the Turkish governments brought back the restrictions in the mid-1960s and further reinforced them in the 1970's and particularly the 1980s.

From December 1990 to March 1991, presidential consent to a new act of the Parliament again allowed Kurdish to be used publicly. A few Kurdish publications, including newsprint have appeared in Turkey (see **Language, Literature, & Press**). These are the most drastic and positive steps taken since the early 1950s to reconcile the two major ethnic groups of the Republic of Turkey—a sign that things can improve at a relatively rapid pace for the Kurds living in that state, and in a peaceful manners.

It is a fact widely known in Turkey that nearly a fifth of the Turkish Members of Parliament are unassimilated Kurds. Important figures in politics, the military, and every other walk of civic life in Turkey have been Kurds, some assimilated to be sure (see **Integration & Assimilation**), but by all evidence, the majority are unassimilated. They have been made well-aware that they are safe as long as they do not mention anything else concerning their ethnic affiliation. With the recent official recognition of spoken Kurdish, Ankara itself has reinstated the word *Kurd*. This could very well indicate a broadening of its interpretation of the clause in the Turkish constitution that states that a *Turk* means anyone who is a citizen of Turkey.

This step toward a more equitable social and political order is perhaps inescapable when a nation develops toward social and political maturity. One should also think of the possibility that when (but less *if* than ever before) Turkey is admitted to the European Community, the majority of the Kurds living today will also be transferred along with that state into the EC, placing their fate more in the hands of Brussels than Ankara. If Turkey is barred from the EC, it may be a longer and more arduous road, but the democratization trends set in motion since the beginning of 1991 signal a more promising future for the Kurds in Turkey.

The Syrian treatment of the Kurdish ethnic identity has ranged from strong support and encouragement under the French Mandate to equally strong suppression and deportation of the people under the independent Syrian government before the takeover by President Assad in 1968. Assad has reinstated a measure of ethnic tolerance. There have been two main reasons for this latest shift. First, Damascus appears to have realized that the three fragments of Kurdistan along Syria's northern and northeastern borders with Turkey and Iraq are incapable of presenting a credible challenge to state authority there, while the Kurds could be used to score points against Turkey and Iraq. More and more expressions of Kurdish ethnic identity have been allowed, albeit under tight official control. Second, with the Assad government also representing a Syrian minority, the Alevis, it needs to court many different ethnic groups to retain power. Nevertheless, Kurds in Syria will continue to benefit or hurt from the actions of the Kurds outside the Syrian borders, depending on how they affect the fortunes of Damascus.

In the former Soviet Union, Kurds were found only in fragmented pockets, mostly along its borders in the Caucasus and central Asia. The Kurds living in the Armenian and Georgian Republics, a population only in the range of tens of thousands, have traditionally received admirable levels of cultural autonomy. In the Republics of Azerbaijan and Turkmenistan they have seen deportations and denial of their separate identity. This may not change in the near future despite the independence of these new states.

Faced with this fragmentation, widening social and cultural diversity among the fragments of their nation, and the outright denial of their national rights, the Kurds have become a very politicized and embattled people, usually at odds with their local governments and squabbling among themselves. Their precarious existence on the border regions of these states has more than once caught the Kurds in a political or physical crossfire. A major force in the Middle East for millennia, the Kurds nonetheless, despite their fragmentation, remain a vital nation steadfastly resisting assimilation and elimination.

With the breakup of the Soviet Union and the emergence of a dozen new independent states in the area, the Kurds are just realizing that international boundaries are not as sacrosanct as they used to be, especially in their neighborhood. The fluid political situation in the better part of the Eurasian land mass from Slovenia to Korea and Yemen is demonstrating that many new possibilities, formerly rejected as radical and subversive, can now routinely be considered by the international community where ethnic groups and their basic human and national rights, including independence, are concerned.

Further Readings and Bibliography: Ismail Besikci, "State Ideology and the Kurds," *Middle East Report* (July-August 1988); Peter A. Andrews, *Ethnic Groups in the Republic of Turkey* (Wiesbaden: Ludwig Reichert, 1989); Sureya Bedir Khan, *The Case of Kurdistan Against Turkey* (Philadelphia: Kurdish Independence League, 1928); F. Tachau, "The Search for National Identity among the Turks," *Die Welt des Islams* 8 (Leiden, 1962); Martin van Bruinessen, "Kurdischer Nationalismus und Sunni–Schi'i Konflikt," in *Geschichte und Politik religiöser Bewegungen im Iran, Jahrbuch zur Geschichte und Gesellshchaft des Mittleren Orients* (Berlin/Frankfurt, 1981); Ferhad Ibrahim, *Die Kurdische Nationalbewegung im Irak: eine Fallstudie zur Problematik ethnisher in der Dritten Welt* (Berlin: Klaus Schwarz Verlag, 1983); Christiane More, *Les Kurdes Aujourd'hui: Mouvement National et Partis Politiques* (Paris: Éditions l'Harmattan, 1984); Theodore Nash, "The Effect of International Oil Interests upon the Fate of Autonomous Kurdish Territory: A Perspective on the Conference at Sèvres, August 10, 1920," *International Problems* 15, 1-2 (1976); McDermott and Short, *The Kurds* (London: Minority Rights Group, 1975); U.S. Helsinki Watch Committee, *Destroying Ethnic Identity: The Kurds of Turkey* (New York: USHWC, 1988).

GEOPOLITICS

The geopolitics of Kurdistan has effectively precluded the formation of an independent Kurdish nation in this century. Currently stretching over five international boundaries, Kurdistan resembles an arching shield of highlands, which separated the Middle East from the advance defense lines of the Soviet Union in the Caucasus for 74 eventful years. With the dissolution of the Soviet Union, an unclear future looms on the northern horizons of the Middle East, with Kurdistan continuing to serve as a buffer zone.

The Kurds have had the dubious distinction of being the only ethnic group in the world with indigenous representatives in four contending world geopolitical power formations: the Arab world (in Iraq and Syria), NATO (in Turkey), the Warsaw Pact and the Soviet bloc (in Soviet Caucasia), and the South Asian-Central Asian bloc (in Iran and Soviet Turkmenistan). The Kurds and their fate in the 20th century must be understood within the context of power politics among these world blocs and their shifting points of interest.

For world powers to help the Kurds in order to pressure Iran meant to indirectly but seriously press Turkey's eastern flank with the USSR, with clear ramifications for NATO security. To help the Iraqi Kurds is to assist Iran and Syria indirectly in their long-standing antagonism toward Baghdad, and again worry Turkey. The Arab bloc, at any rate, has found it unpalatable to have non-Arab minorities in Iraq or Syria wooed by out-side forces. For the West, not to help the Kurds at all meant to leave them to seek aid from the Soviet Union, or to push the Kurds towards terrorism as the only other alternative for furthering their cause. The demise of the Soviet Union has removed this northern card from the Kurdish leaders' deck, but the present fluid situation can revert to its old form, or find a new and unfamiliar shape.

Kurdistan as the primary watershed in an otherwise dry Middle East is of critical importance to the states that now administer it. Further, nearly all the Syrian and Turkish petroleum deposits are in Kurdistan, while the old Kirkuk fields in Iraq constitute about one-third of that state's total petroleum reserves (see **Natural Resources: Oil**). In fact these very same economic concerns likely were the prinicipal reason Britain chose to short-circuit the process set in motion by the Treaty of Sèvres for an independent Kurdistan after World War I. Because of the strategic and economic importance of the oil-bearing territories of central Kurdistan, Britain incorporated them in its Mandate of

Iraq, allowing the rest to be annexed by Turkey in return (see **Modern History**).

A further impediment to their national well-being is that the Kurds lack natural friends in their immediate vicinity. In this respect they contrast markedly with the Palestinians, who are surrounded and generally supported by other Arabs and serve as a unifying cause for pan-Arabists. The Kurds share an ethnic identity with none of their sovereign neighbors. The Kurds are victims of their own strategic location and world geopolitical concerns. They remain friendless locally and internationally.

At the same time the Kurds are divided by their dispersal into so many geopolitical blocs, each with a distinct state culture and weltanschauung whose influence they cannot entirely escape. Today the eastern and southern Kurds are expected to follow the Islamic, traditionalist ideology of Iran, while the Iraqi and Syrian Kurds, on the other hand, are obliged to adapt their heritage and justify their existence under the radical Arabism of these two anti-Western states. In Anatolia, Kurdish culture faces a Turkey with a southeast European outlook and a staunchly pro-Western, modernist government.

These cultural, economic, and political forces are pulling the segments of the Kurdish nation in various directions. If not stopped, in the long run they will undoubtedly undermine the cultural coherence and national identity of the Kurds, creating new nations out of the single old one.

Considering all the benefits and liabilities that holding on to the Kurdish territories and expanding population have and will have for the administering states of the Middle East, what would actually happen if Kurdistan were to become wholly or in part independent? What would be the geopolitical, economic, and social ramifications of an independent Kurdistan for the states from whose present territories such a sovereign Kurdistan might hypothetically emerge? Who would be the winners and who the losers?

Let's start with Turkey, where the majority of Kurds live today. Were a greater pan-Kurdish sovereign state to emerge that included all contiguous territories in which Kurds predominate today, the Turkish Republic would actually fare better economically, socially, and internationally than now. Kurdistan is economically the most depressed part of Turkey, and its society is the most conservative, most procreative, least educated, and least integrated portion of the otherwise European Turkey. It does not require much sophistication to see that for Turkey to shed such an area and population, it would be shedding only liability. In fact, in losing Kurdistan, peninsular Turkey would become as European sociologically, demographically, economically, and historically as any country in southeastern Europe, if not actually more. Trimmed of its deeply Asiatic, and poorest, parts in Kurdistan, peninsular Turkey would almost certainly be admitted into the European Community, paving a very clear road for Turkey in Europe. Kurdish strategic water resources would also become irrelevant to Turkey, as no major river in the reconfigured Turkey would depend for any appreciable part of its waters on the Kurdish highlands. The Tigris-Euphrates system, for example, flows south from Kurdistan into Iraq and Syria, and the Araxes and Kura east into Armenia and Georgia. The high Taurus mountain system effectively separates geologically and hydrologically Kurdistan from peninsular Anatolia. Turkey would lose the potential sale of the Kurdish waters to the thirsty Arab countries farther south, but such earnings would never compensate for the expense of upkeeping Kurdistan.

The dissolution of an unworkable and economically unviable polity has in fact just occurred in the state neighboring Turkey: the Soviet Union. Overlooking the current difficulties born of many decades of economic mismanagement, Russia is already faring better in the realm of social and human rights, and should fare better economically than when it held onto its empire, which drained Russian wealth in order to pay for the upkeep of the poor dominions in central Asia and the Caucasus. Trimmed of Kurdistan, Turkey would have a much higher per-capita income, higher literacy rates, much lower population growth rates, a much more modern transportation system, and less reason to pile up cases of human rights abuses. In fact, it would also have fewer neighbors in Asia to worry about. The land borders in Asia of such a reconfigured Turkish state would be solely with a sovereign Kurdistan and Georgia. Turkey, in short, would be the biggest winner in the geopolitical scenario of an independent Kurdistan.

For Iran, on the other hand, the loss of most of its Kurdish territories (the Khurâsâni enclave could not conceivably be included in the Kurdish state, because of its distance from contiguous Kurdistan) would likely mean further dissolution of that state along its ample inter-ethnic seams. Iran would cease to exist as it has since ancient times. The state is basically made up of ethnic minorities. The consent to let go of the Kurds, their third largest ethnic group, would leave little justification for Teheran to keep the other dozen or so ethnic groups within its borders. The northern Azeris have already established their own independent state on the former territories of the Soviet Union. The more numerous Iranian Azeris might find it meaningless to stay on if pieces start falling away from the Iranian state body. They might well opt for unification with the independent northern Azerbaijan. We need not to look into economic ramifications for Iran, as the political ones are dire enough. Iran would turn out to be the biggest loser if a pan-Kurdish sovereign state were to form.

Syria would lose its pockets of Kurdish lands, with little overall affect on the state, except perhaps a bruised sense of "nationalism." The loss of Kurdish territories to Syria could be well compensated by a transfer to that state of those Arab-inhabited territories of the Harrân Plain (southeast of Urfâ) and south of Mardin. These areas are now part of Turkey, but out of geographical necessity would be included within Kurdistan in any Turkish-Kurdish disassociation arrangement. Syria would then become almost totally Arabic speaking, with little or no overall territorial loss. Economically, all the disjointed Kurdish territories in Syria are of less economic value than the fertile cotton fields of the Harrân Plain alone.

Iraqi consent to let go of its Kurdish territories, with their rich natural and agricultural resources, would mean a good deal of economic loss to that state. The loss of the petroleum fields of Kirkuk, its refineries, and other facilities would be dearly missed. But there is much more oil in southern, Arab Iraq, and the loss of Kirkuk oil would be forgotten sooner than later. It would be the loss of its strategic hold on the headwaters of the Tigris' major tributaries, which would put it at the mercy of an independent Kurdistan for three-quarters of its river water supply, that could not be forgotten sooner or later. Both the Tigris and the Euphrates form in Kurdistan, and receive no other tributaries of note once outside the Kurdish mountains. The question of control over its water resources should be of great worry to any government in Baghdad, and loss of its Kurdish territories would be most dearly felt because of water, not oil.

The entire Iraqi state has had a tormented modern history due mainly to the Kurdish question, and all parties would breathe in relief once a disassociation had taken place. Like Syria, Iraq too would become almost totally Arabic speaking, but less wealthy, and much less secure.

Kurdish-inhabited regions of the Caucasus have not been connected with contiguous Kurdistan since the middle of the 19th century and the massive influx of Armenians into the khanate of Erivân (later Russian Armenia). These regions could not be expected to join an independent Kurdistan, unless the inhabitants chose to emigrate and settle in such a hypothetical state.

Kurdistan per se should fare very well as an independent state. It would have vast water and agricultural resources. Its petroleum reserves are well-developed, with refineries, pipelines, and exporting facilities on the Gulf of Alexandretta already in place. It would be one of the biggest countries in the entire Middle East, and potentially one of the wealthiest as well, if the above assumptions are correct. It would border at least on seven sovereign countries, and would by necessity be a major player in Middle Eastern affairs.

Further Reading and Bibliography: Chris Kutschera, "Le Mouvement National Kurde," *Military Review* 6-6 (1981); Theodore Nash, "The Effect of International Oil Interests upon the Fate of Autonomous Kurdish Territory: A Perspective on the Conference at Sèvres, August 10, 1920," *International Problems* 15, 1-2 (1976).

POLITICAL CULTURE & LEADERSHIP

Increasingly in the past 150 years, the loyalties of the majority of the world's peoples, traditionally reserved for local political elites, have been redirected to ever higher and narrower groups at the top of the political pyramid, namely, to the leaders of the nation-state. Allegiances previously reserved for religious, regional, or tribal leaders tend to have been steadily undercut or eliminated by national political figures to promote a political culture and leadership with the widest base of support.

Through a combination of several historical events, the Kurds as a nation have experienced the reverse. Among the Kurds, the leadership has progressively represented a more narrow popular base and a more localized agenda. As among the major neighboring ethnic groups, the creation of a Kurdish political culture with an agenda aiming at a pan-Kurdish polity had already begun in the early 19th century. This is evident in the nationalistic works of Kurdish political elites such as Koy'i (see **Early Modern History**). Simultaneously, there still existed a number of old native principalities with many characteristics of statehood in the modern sense. These principalities naturally received allegiance from all the subjects within their domains, irrespective of their religious or tribal affiliation and economic status. Kurdish principalities were in essence mini-states in the modern sense. In all likelihood they could have evolved into modern nation-states had they survived the past 150 years. However, this was not to be.

Advances in technology made it possible by the middle of the 19th century for the Ottoman and Persian empires to seek, and progressively enforce, direct central rule. This resulted in the gradual elimination of the autonomous Kurdish principalities within their control. The last major house to fall was that of the Ardalâns, in 1867 (see **Early Modern History**).

This power vacuum at the local level was filled by the next layer of elites and people of influence, i.e., religious figures like the mullahs, qadis, and shaykhs. The loyalty of common Kurds regressed to these secondary elites, who could command the loyalty of only a limited number of citizens of the multi-religious, multi-cultural Kurdish nation. These religious leaders resisted Ottoman and Persian encroachment on Kurdish autonomy. After the mid-19th century, only religious and tribal leaders led the Kurdish against increasingly obtrusive state presences.

Sociologically and economically, the middle of 19th century brought yet another, even more decisive event: the previous three centuries' of expansion of nomadism was reversed in favor of settled agriculture. This undercut the authority of nomadic chieftains and their military power, which often translated into political power at the local levels. By this time, while the religious leaders were unchallenged in expanding agricultural communities in the valleys, they exercised only limited authority in the higher mountains among the nomads and semi-nomads. Progressive settlement of the nomads resulted in expansion of the influence of these religious leaders at the expense of their tribal competitors. By the beginning of the 20th century, their authority was largely unopposed within the Kurdish political hierarchy, despite their highly controversial ideology and social conduct. Alarmed by their increasing influence, the central governments administering Kurdistan effectively eliminated this stratum of the Kurdish power pyramid, much as they had done with the principalities.

The regression continued until local tribal leaders were left as the highest remaining native source of authority. A tertiary layer of elites, tribal leaders could muster an even smaller popular base than the religious leaders. Their political dominance continues largely to this day.

Faced with the erosion of their power base through the settlement of the nomads and the much faster numerical growth of the settled peasants, many important tribal leaders came to realize the importance of religious status. Through actual training in the religious laws or otherwise via Sufi mystic leadership, many tribal leaders were able to tap into the source of the wider popularity of the religious leaders The chiefs of the Bârzâni, particularly Shaykh Ahmad, are good examples of this phenomenon.

To these political developments one must add that the rugged terrain of Kurdistan also fosters strong individualism among the citizens. This has resulted in limited authority being ceded to any collective administrative body by individuals, that is, only the minimum necessary to maintain the basic social and defensive functions. The tribal organization is often the highest level of allegiance to which an individual Kurd is willing to consent.

Consequently, what Kurds now possess is, to a large extent, a tribal, fragmented, and highly localized political culture and leadership. A pan-Kurdish, urban-based political platform that can command loyalty from the majority of Kurds is only recently emerging.

Current Political Elite. By the time the last purely religious Kurdish leader, Shaykh Mahmud, was put down in 1932, the tribal leaders had reasserted their political primacy, in part due to the absence of any native competitors. Some of them formed political parties, and the others provided guerrilla forces for political leaders in return for a voice in their decisions. In this way, the tribal leaders became the highest form of native political authority, and the Westernized, modern Kurdish political elite and parties have inevitably had to reckon with them, if not directly represent their interests.

Tribal leaders are by no means reactionary or uneducated country folks. College education, often at Western universities, is almost universal among the family members of the chiefs. As the older generation passes, the new Kurdish tribal chiefs boast as much education and worldliness as any national-level politician in a recognized state.

While no modern Kurdish party leader has seen the test of a ballot, Kurdish political parties are legitimized through their dealings with traditional tribal representatives, who allow them to learn of the views of the common people. The tribe and clan leaders, being in close contact with their citizen clients, are the sources of indigenous legitimacy. Until a democratic and representative political body replaces them, it appears that a large part of Kurdistan will retain these tribal elders as local representatives in all political negotiations on Kurdistan. The process of legitimizing political decisions is inherently democratic as it requires consultation of the primary Kurdish political leaders and political parties with local elites, who in turn reflect the grass-roots needs and views. In this manner, public opinion is made available to the modern Kurdish political leaders who obviously cannot call national elections or take public opinion polls in Kurdistan. The modern leaders therefore must gain information and support from the traditional tribal leaders in order to survive and be able to speak for some portion of the common Kurdish citizenry.

Even the parties on the political Left have worked overtly or covertly with the tribal and religious leadership, while criticizing them simultaneously as feudal and reactionary.

Despite the long list of modern Kurdish political parties (see **Political Parties**), the highest point of loyalty for the majority of Kurds remains with these traditional political structures, resulting in the strong—though rapidly changing—tribal character of Kurdish politics and leadership. Almost anyone of political importance in Kurdistan carries a tribal title for his surname (in addition to any religious titles, as noted above). Jalâl Tâlabâni, Mustafâ Bârzâni, Masoud Bârzâni, Rasul Mâmand, and Abdul-Rahmân Qassemlou, all of whom carry the names of their respective tribes as their last names, are only the best known.

Allied commanders in the "security zone" established in Iraqi Kurdistan following the Persian Gulf War were surprised and then frustrated when they realized they had to deal with each and every clan and tribe leader to gain the cooperation of the Kurds in their activities. They were surprised to find these grass-roots leaders as well informed, and crafty, as other representative politicians elsewhere in the world.

The negative aspects of the traditional tribal-style politics are its tendencies toward conservatism, nepotism, sectarianism, and provincialism. Modern Kurdish political leaders such as Jalâl Tâlabâni (PUK) and Abdul-Rahmân Qassemlou (KDP-I), despite their Western education and long European residence, have achieved unimpressive records in doing away with the old tribal affinities and loyalties within their parties. The long-standing rivalry between the southern parts of Iraqi Kurdistan, the domain of the PUK, and the northern parts, the domain of the KDP, illustrate the failure of either of these "modern" parties to appeal to Kurds regardless of tribal affiliation. Some authors have blamed differences between the spoken dialects of the two regions; others have blamed the interregional differences between the popular Sufi orders for the discord. However, the dialectal differences between the two branches of Kurmânji are too minor, particularly in Iraq, to explain such a rift. Moreover, there is a similar rift between the Iranian KDP and Komala, as well as between the PUK and the Iraqi Komala, all of which are run by South Kurmânji-speaking, Qâdiri Sunni Muslim leaders. The problem more likely is the limited scope and appeal of these parties outside their own tribes and regions, where they neither know the local issues nor are known by the citizenry.

Since these modern political leaders behave (and are perceived by their followers) as neo-tribal leaders, their image, particularly in Iraqi Kurdistan, has been that of the concerned father rather than of the political leader that can be voted in or out of office by virtue of their portfolio of performance. As long as they are doing what they can, they have the loyalty of their people; that is, of course, as long as they maintain the fundamental virtues associated with such leaders: courage, loyalty, dignity, and magnanimity. Neither wisdom nor diplomacy are fundamental requirements (see **National Character**). As such, their mistakes seldom weaken their position as leaders. They may be perceived as bad leaders, but they are leaders nevertheless, and continue to receive support, even reverence.

In the last five years of his life, for example, General Mustafâ Bârzâni ran into the following problems. He suggested in 1975 that Kurdistan should become the 51st state of the United States (van Bruinessen 1986), a suggestion that would have cast doubt on the sanity, let alone political competence, of any other political leader anywhere else in the Third World. His acceptance of financial help from the CIA in an era when the United States did not enjoy a good image in the area (following the Vietnam and 1973 Arab-Israeli wars) was widely publicized. His catastrophic misjudgment in trusting the Shah of Iran, combined with his decision to switch from guerrilla to conventional tactics against the far superior Iraqi state war machine, precipitated a military fiasco that doomed the costly Kurdish uprising in Iraq of 1975.

Any one of these mistakes might have been sufficient to speed any other Middle Eastern leader into political disgrace. Yet General Bârzâni continued to be followed and is still revered and mythologized by most Kurds. This seeming oddity is the direct result of his image as the leader, a father of the extended tribal family—an insider who could commit gross mistakes and show repeated misjudgment and still be forgiven, like any other traditional tribal leader and a typical pahlawân (see **National Character**).

The lingering of tribalism in modern Kurdish politics has also inevitably led to careerist leaders who have never seen the test of a ballot—even internally within their parties. It is not by coincidence, for example, that when General Bârzâni died his sons acceded to the leadership of the KDP without election.

In Turkey, major tribal confederacies have weathered away under pressure from the Turkish government over the last three generations. The smaller tribes and clans remain much less affected, but have dwindled in influence because many of their members either emigrated or were deported to western Turkey and its major cities. This includes between one-third and one-half of the Kurds in Turkey (see **Emigrations & Diaspora**). A by-product of this has been the formation in Turkey of the only Kurdish political parties in the modern sense (i.e., not dependent on tribal fealty).

Relatively speaking, the Kurdish political leadership in Turkey is the most modern and up-to-date in every sense. In the PKK and its leadership, for example, one encounters the prolific production of ideological and educational publications, exemplary discipline and training of staff and guerrillas, and the use of terror, when need be, against enemies, Kurds and non-Kurds. This last activity, an accepted tactic in the modern world of radical political ideology, is of course absent from the traditional, almost extended-familial, tribal political culture.

Regionalism. There is a major chasm, or series of chasms, in the Kurdish political culture that must be spanned in order for pan-Kurdish aims to be achieved: the wide variations in "weltanschauung" and social ideals of the five regions of contiguous Kurdistan (see **Internal Subdivisions**). Different styles of political leadership evident in Kurdistan tend to predominate in different regions. In fact reviewing the character of the Kurdish political parties, their leadership, and their style of conduct is the quickest way of discerning the strength of regional differences within the Kurdish nation.

In northern Iraqi Kurdistan, the Bârzâni-led KDP represents an ethos embodying the northern Kurdish tradition. It is familial, with firm grass-roots connections through tribal and local elders and community leaders. The Barzanis are religious, with their followers being traditionalist and inward-oriented people. In consulting tribal elders on all important decisions, they continue the tradition of tribe-based democracy. They treat their followers as members of the same extended family.

In central Kurdistan in Iraq, the Tâlabâni-led PUK represents a more urban, modern, and outward-looking populace, with a strong connection to southern Kurdistan in Iran. The party is less religious, as is characteristic of these parts of Kurdistan, and its leaders seldom consult local tribal or religious leaders. They view the KDP and its followers from a position of sophistication and modernism, scorning the tribal, religious, and peasant affinities of their informal northern counterparts, the "hillbillies," who never cease to be an embarrassment and who never lose an opportunity to lose an opportunity.

This view of PUK is well shared by many common Kurdish citizens of this area, who populate some of the most ancient urban centers of Kurdistan and can pride themselves of a clear and venerable history stretching for thousands of years. Meanwhile they never fail to confess their admiration for honesty, valor, generosity and "natural looks" of their rougher northern compatriots.

The northerners' view of the Tâlabâni-led PUK is equally contradictory. They consider the PUK to be an effete organization, more concerned with looks than substance, and led by people whose preferred means are treachery rather than valor and who seldom are willing to give their lives for their honor. Nonetheless, they admire the sophistication and cosmopolitanism of these southerners, and envy the very same "sophisticated looks" they spend so much time smearing. This view of the PUK is more or less identical to that which most northern Kurds of Iraq think of their southern Kurdish compatriots in that country.

The Iranian KDP, with its base in eastern Kurdistan, is less tribal, and while counting on support from local patricians and chieftains, is elitist. Reflecting its constituents' feelings, the party leaders bear an unflattering view of the neighboring Kurds of central, but particularly northern, Kurdistan, as basically hard-minded, bearish characters, as barely educated, uncivilized tribal people whose long association with the alien Arab and Turkic cultures has rendered their social behavior an embarrassment and their culture adulterated. They "authenticate" this by noting that most Kurds of Turkey and Iraq have no grasp of the meaning or the background of the Kurdish culture and history. The Iranian Kurds find themselves superior in all elements of culture and believe their sub-tlety sets them apart from the "unpolished hillmen." At the same time, these eastern

Kurds look for political leadership from the "crude and rough, but also trustworthy, solid, witty, and can-do" Kurds of Iraq.

The southern Kurds distance themselves from other Kurds even farther. Most, if not all, find Kurdistan too small and unpromising a place to "waste their political or cultural talent," and find Baghdad or Teheran, if not Vienna, Paris, or New York, to be preferable locales. Even today, there is no exclusively Kurdish political party to speak of in the south, as the elite find outlet for their political ambitions outside Kurdistan, in the national capitals. For example, Karim Sanjâbi, an unassimilated Kurd from Kirmânshâh, has long been the head of the all-important Iranian National Front Party (founded by Muhammad Mossadegh). The political culture of the southern and eastern Kurds is Iranian in outlook, and far more easily understood in the context of the state's political culture than any pan-Kurdish one.

The reason for the divisions between the political culture of the Iranian Kurds and those of Iraq are obvious, though not widely known. So much attention has been focused on the modern, post-World War I division of Kurdistan that most scholars have come to thoroughly neglect another, far older dividing line in Kurdistan, separating the Iranian Kurds from the rest. The Iranian Kurds have been living in that polity not since the end of World War I, but since at least 1514 and the Battle of Châldirân. In fact these Kurds have lived under many Iranian dynasties (some of them of Kurdish origin) since ancient times. In the process, the Iranian Kurds have absorbed from—and contributed much to—the Iranian national political culture and social ethos, more than to the larger Kurdish political culture.

The contact between the Iranian Kurds and their ethnic kin was and remains through central Kurdistan in Iraq, an area that traditionally has served as a crucial bazaar of ideas from various segments of Kurdistan.

The Kurds of western Kurdistan are even more isolated from the other Kurds, and have developed a distinct political culture of their own. The heavy-handed Turkish suppression of communication between Kurds in Turkey and the rest of Kurdistan is only a part of the reason for their separateness. Much more important reasons are their history and geography. As such, the western Kurds are novelties to the other Kurds and vice versa. It is only now, with the advent of global communication, that these Kurds are truly discovering and being discovered by their fellow Kurds.

The difference is neither language nor religion, as they share these with other regions of Kurdistan. Rather it is their outlook—a Mediterranean orientation and tilt toward the West—that has rendered this most populous Kurdish subdivision so different. Most mutual feelings have been those of discovery and curiosity than criticism or praise, including on political and social grounds.

The western Kurdish political leader, Abdullâh Öcalan has recently come to be revered among many Kurds outside Turkey (his home ground), not so much because of any deep knowledge that these other Kurds have of him or of the political culture he represents, but rather because his outlook and methods are exotic in comparison to their own familiar, and supposedly failed, ones. Öcalan has done little in inter-regional politics to attract Kurds outside his own cultural region in Anatolia. But since Anatolia is the origin of over half of all Kurds living today, he could have an easier time achieving a pan-Kurdish political platform than did Bârzâni. Additionally, Öcalan's Mediterranean political culture and quasi-Western political conduct are fast mythologizing him and his political party in the eyes of the other half of the Kurdish nation that lives outside Anatolia and Turkey, in the same fashion in which Mustafâ Bârzâni was earlier elevated, despite his political shortcomings, to the highest station in the all-Kurdish political pantheon.

Further Readings and Bibliography: Very valuable primary resources are the detailed tape interviews with many Kurdish leaders and political figures on deposit in the Oral History Archives at the

Kurdish Library in Brooklyn, New York. Wadie Jwaideh, "The Kurdish Nationalist Movement: Its Origins and Development," unpublished doctoral dissertation (Syracuse, 1960); Chris Kutschera, *Le mouvement national kurde* (Paris: Falmmarion, 1979); R. Olson, *Emergence of Kurdish Nationalism* (Austin: University of Texas Press, 1989); Martin van Bruinessen, *Agha Shaikh and State: On the Social and Political Organization of Kurdistan* (Rijswijk: Europrint, 1978); Martin van Bruinessen, "The Kurds between Iran and Iraq," *Middle East Report* (July-August 1986); Fredrik Barth. *Principles of Social Organization in Southern Kurdistan* (Oslo: Brodrene Vorgensen, 1953); Martin van Bruinessen, "The Kurds in Turkey," *MERIP Reports* 16.141 (1986).

POLITICAL PARTIES

The political parties and movements of modern Kurdistan are too numerous to cover in their entirety here. Only the most important and lasting parties that have operated primarily on the territories of Kurdistan will, therefore, be treated.

Like other places in the world where many parties are struggling for the limited available support of their constituents, and carry ideologies and promote goals not too dissimilar from one another, inter-party feuding and rivalry have been a common feature of the history of the Kurdish political parties. What is different is that in Kurdistan these feuds on occasion become armed skirmishes between the parties' guerrillas. These extreme instances, however, have been few and short-lasting.

No definitive data are available on the membership numbers of the Kurdish political parties. Occasionally they have issued membership cards, but all been forced to organize fighting guerrilla groups, and it is the number of fighting men and women each commands that should be taken as the clearest indicator of how popular a party and its policies are with the Kurdish citizens.

The popular Kurdish term *peshmerga* is commonly used for the guerrillas and militias in Iraqi Kurdistan, but is also spreading to other Kurdish groups outside Iraq. The term means "self-sacrificer." It is one of strong affection, even romance. It is used often by Kurdish mothers, vowing to become their children's *peshmerg,* i.e., to give their life for the health and security of their children. The term and concept have deep roots in Kurdish history. References to these guerrilla/militia forces in Kurdistan are encountered twice in the present work: in ancient times, during the Median campaigns in Assyria, and in classical times, when Kurds were defending themselves against the Persian Sasanian king Ardashir I (see **Ancient** and **Classical History**).

For the sake of simplicity, all political parties here are viewed within the context of the states of Iran, Iraq, Turkey, and Syria, with relevant observations on their interactions where appropriate. The necessary historical background on these political events is provided in the sections on **Modern** and **Recent History**.

IRAN

Kurdish Democratic Party (KDP). The party was established in December 1945 in Mahâbâd by President Qâzi Muhammed in conjunction with the establishment of the Kurdish Republic in eastern Kurdistan (December 1945 to December 1946). As the oldest extant Kurdish political party, the KDP merits special attention. In little less than half a century, the party has experienced a combination of events that are representative of those affecting all other subsequent Kurdish political parties, save the experience of being extinguished.

In the year of its formation, 1945, the KDP was joined by the Iraqi Kurdish leader, Mullâh Mustafâ Bârzâni, who brought some of his tribal forces into Mahâbâd territory to support it. After the fall of the Republic in December 1946 and the execution of Qâzi Muhammed at the hands of Iranian troops, the KDP was forced underground and into relative inactivity.

The KDP-I and other Iranian political parties experienced a renaissance during the upheavals of 1951-53, which culminated in the removal of the Shah by the premier Mossadegh, and his subsequent reinstatement by a military coup d'etat. The KDP, along with all the other agitating parties, had to go underground once again.

The party was also forced to change its name to KDP-I (*I* for Iran) after Mustafâ Bârzâni, upon his return to Iraq from the Soviet Union in 1957, claimed "KDP" as the title of the branch of the party he had encouraged to form in Iraq in 1946 and was consolidating under his own leadership, as will be discussed later.

The KDP-I, because of its inability to operate within Iranian territory, focused its attention on events in Iraqi Kurdistan, and, despite grievances against Bârzâni, followed his lead until the late 1960s. The ever-growing connection between the Shah and Bârzâni, out of the latter's need for backing in his deteriorating relations with Baghdad, eventually pushed the KDP-I away from its Iraqi counterpart. It reoriented itself to the problems of the Kurds in Iran after 1973.

Despite the similarity of their names, the Iranian KDP, a basically urban, elitist party with moderate tribal connection, has fundamentally very little in common with the Iraqi KDP, which is a traditionalist party with very strong tribal allegiances. The KDP-I is moderately left-wing, and except for the first year of its existence (1945-46), has only advocated autonomy for the Kurdish region "within a democratic Iran."

The relationship between the Iranian KDP and its Iraqi counterpart remains quite uncordial. The Iraqi KDP forces have often been accused by their Iranian counterparts of routinely cooperating with the Iranian government to undermine their party and movement, and to expand their influence into the Iranian Kurdish territories.

In 1980, a split occurred within the KDP-I's own central cadres, over the decision to cooperate with or oppose the policies of the Revolutionary government in Teheran. A small group sided with the mainstream communist party of Iran, the *Tudeh*, in their support of Teheran. The main body of the KDP-I, under the chairmanship of Abdul-Rahmân Qassemlou, a Czech-educated economist, soon opened hostilities with the government forces. The military campaign did not fare well, and in late 1983, the KDP-I was forced to reach an entente with the Iraqi government and Jalâl Tâlabâni's Patriotic Union of (Iraqi) Kurdistan (PUK). Qassemlou and Tâlabâni were old acquaintances who had studied together in Prague. Despite this, the KDP-I leadership distrusted the PUK. It feared being branded a traitor if it tacitly allied itself with Baghdad, which was at war with Iran and most Iraqi Kurdish parties. Thus, it was never able to gain full support from either the PUK or Baghdad, and was eventually defeated by Iranian government forces in 1984.

The KDP-I remained under the leadership of Dr. Qassemlou, until his mysterious July 1988 assassination in Vienna, where he was about to enter into peace talks with Teheran's representatives. The leadership has now passed to Dr. Saeed Sharafkandi.

The number of armed forces commanded by the KDP-I has varied from time to time. At the height of its war on the Revolutionary government of Teheran from 1979-81, it claimed about 12,000 men under arm. The present numbers may be reckoned only in hundreds.

Far from being an all-encompassing Kurdish political party, the KDP-I, or any other single Kurdish political party for that matter, has never mustered the allegiance of more than a small minority of Iranian Kurds, primarily because of strong regional and socio-cultural differences between the extreme northern sectors of Iranian Kurdistan and the deep south, not to mention between those regions and the populous enclave in far-away Khurâsân. The KDP-I, KDP, PUK, Komala, and other parties are anathema to an Iranian Kurd from southern Kurdistan, who traditionally dismissed them on every ground of importance to him, from their economic plans, to their religious affiliation, their spoken dialects, their provincial ethos, their extremism, and their tribal orientation. The Khurâsâni Kurd might, at best, just have heard of these parties. In any case, the only area in which the KDP-I can claim any real numerical strength is in the area between Urmiâ, Mahâbâd, and Marivân (see Map 40).

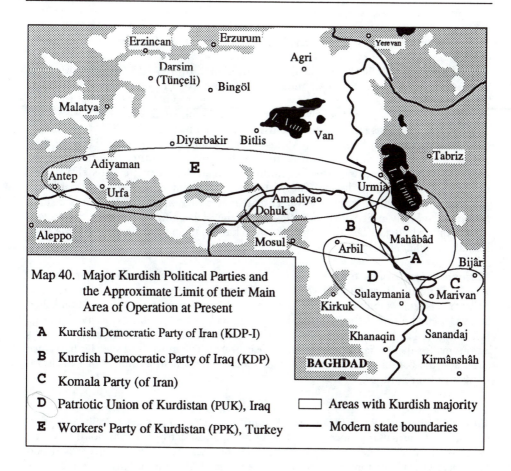

Map 40. Major Kurdish Political Parties and
the Approximate Limit of their Main
Area of Operation at Present

A Kurdish Democratic Party of Iran (KDP-I)

B Kurdish Democratic Party of Iraq (KDP)

C Komala Party (of Iran)

D Patriotic Union of Kurdistan (PUK), Iraq

E Workers' Party of Kurdistan (PPK), Turkey

☐ Areas with Kurdish majority

—— Modern state boundaries

There is, and has been, plenty of room for the KDP-I to expand within Iranian Kurdistan, if it is able to shed its strong regional character and cultural parochialism. The party has a long and noteworthy history of adapting to internal and external challenges, and may prove to be more than just a localized phenomenon if it chooses to change.

In December 1991 some Iranian newspapers carried articles reporting preliminary talks between Teheran and Dr. Sharafkandi on the subject of establishing a dialogue between the KDP-I and the government. Considering that the last chairman of the KDP-I lost his life in a similar situation, Sharafkandi may need to think twice before appearing for any such "dialogue."

Komala. In September 1942, three years before the birth of the Kurdish Republic of Mahâbâd, a nationalist political party named *Komala* ("society" in Kurdish) was formed by urban middle-class Kurdish intellectuals. Komala was eventually transformed into the Iranian KDP at the time of its formation in 1945. From its ashes, however, quickly rose a new party, strongly Marxist-Leninist, also named Komala.

Along with almost everything else about the Komala, the very name of the party is enigmatic. The late chairman of the KDP-I, Qassemlou, wrote in 1980 that *Komala* stood for "*Komala Jiânı Kurdistan,*" i.e., "the Council on Rebirth [sic] of Kurdistan" (Challiand 1980, 118). Van Bruinessen, on the other hand, believes that the name stands for "*Komalay Shoreshgeri Zahmatkeshani Kurdistani Iran,*" or "Organization of Revolutionary Toilers of Iranian Kurdistan" (1986, 18). *Komala* in Kurdish has the same double meaning as the term "society" in English; it means "society" at large, and a political or social club or association.

Both Komala and the KDP-I challenged Iranian authority in Kurdistan after the Revolution, but Komala has never mustered the same level of support and followers as the KDP-I. At times, as in 1985, the two parties have engaged in bloody combat with one another, even when under attack by Iranian central government forces.

In 1991 Komala was reported to have fissioned into a majority faction led by Mansur Hekmat and a minority by Abdullâh Mohtadâ (or Mohtadi). It is not clear if this will be a permanent division, or if the two factions will rejoin. Like other Marxist-Leninist movements, the collapse of the Communism has undercut or perhaps eliminated Komala's ideological legitimacy. The party is likely to replace soon the old bankrupt ideology with something more native. The main area of Komala's operation is a small region in the Marivân-Sanandaj district, south of the KDP-I home territory.

As with the Iranian KDP, the Iranian Komala has found an Iraqi counterpart, the Iraqi Komala, a child of the 1970s.

National Organization. In late 1979, a Sunni Muslim religious leader from Mahâbâd, Shaykh Izziddin Husayni (Husseini), led a popular struggle against the policies of Teheran's Islamic Republic. Despite being hunted by government forces, he established in 1983 a group called the "National Organization," which at times received a large following. It has evolved into a leftist organization linked with the Komala. It seeks autonomy for the Iranian Kurds, to an unclear degree. The movement's leader has, since 1984 and the consolidation of the central Iranian government authority in Kurdistan, lived in exile in Europe.

IRAQ

Kurdish Democratic Party (KDP). The Kurdish Democratic Party has since its inception in 1946, but particularly since the 1960s, been the most active Kurdish political party. While still in Mahâbâd under the Kurdish Republic, Mullâh Mustafâ Bârzâni had encouraged the formation of a "branch" of the Iranian KDP in Iraq. This was done in the southern sector of Iraqi Kurdistan, by Ibrâhim Ahmad, a lawyer and intellectual from Sulaymânia, and the future father-in-law of Jalâl Tâlabâni (see below). Ibrâhim Ahmad led the Iraqi KDP firmly until 1958, and more or less nominally until Bârzâni's internal coup in 1964 led to his ouster.

In 1958, the KDP was actually legalized in Iraq, and Bârzâni was invited to return following the fall of the monarchy and the establishment of the Iraqi Republic under Qâsim. Three years earlier, while still expatriate, Bârzâni had been made the honorary president of the KDP, while Ahmad continued to run the actual affairs.

After his return to Iraq, Bârzâni increasingly interfered in KDP internal affairs, although as its honorary president he was not entitled to do so. His reasons, besides desiring the actual leadership for himself, were two-fold: 1) KDP was dominated by the urban elitist Kurds of the southern sector of Iraqi Kurdistan (see **National Character** and **Political Culture & Leadership**), and 2) it leaned too far to the left. His challenge to the central committee of the KDP came to a head in 1964, when each faction declared the other expelled from the party. Having the military power to support his side, Bârzâni came out the winner, and the chairman of the reconstituted, moderately rightist, Kurdish Democratic Party of Iraq. His forces drove the armed guerrillas loyal to Ahmad's old party apparatus across the border into Iran, thus becoming unopposed in Iraqi Kurdistan. Ahmad's exiled force became the nucleus of the future Patriotic Union of Kurdistan under Jalâl al-Din Tâlabâni.

The expanding influence and power of the KDP encouraged Bârzâni to increasingly challenge Baghdad's authority, sometimes needlessly. He had already signed a pact with

Baghdad on Kurdish autonomy in 1970 (see **Recent History**). By 1974 and the start of open war with the Iraqi armed forces, the party could at times field up to 30,000 well-armed guerrilla fighters. Neither the sheer number of its guerrilla forces nor assistance from foreign governments could compensate for bad generalship and the inflexibility of the party cadres and Bârzâni himself. In 1975 the KDP-led Kurdish uprising in Iraq collapsed, precipitating an exodus of the top party leaders and a large number of civilians and guerrillas into Iran. The Iranian government set up a suburb of Teheran for KDP refugees, where many of them are still found today. Government stipends were set up for party leaders, and Iranian passports were provided to refugees. For this the KDP was greatly indebted to Teheran, and it has paid them back by performing many overt and covert proxy actions for them, from acts of sabotage behind Iraqi lines during the Iran-Iraq war, to helping Iranian troops put down Iranian Kurdish uprisings.

After the death of Mullâh Mustafâ of cancer while under treatment in the United States in 1978, the leadership of the party passed to his eldest son, Idris, and upon Idris' death in 1987, to his second eldest son, Masoud.

At present the KDP can muster around 15,000 guerrilla fighters. Its power base is in the northern sector of Iraqi Kurdistan, home to the Bârzâni tribe (one of the oldest in Kurdistan; see **Tribes**), but by no means limited to it. It operates and has supporters in other sectors of Iraqi Kurdistan, and still enjoys respect and some following even outside Iraqi Kurdistan, thanks to the legendary image of Mustafâ Bârzâni.

The KDP operates a radio station, the *Voice of Iraqi Kurdistan*, which now appears to be broadcast from within the Kurdish territories in Iraq. In 1980 the KDP struck an anti-Baghdad alliance of convenience with the Iraqi Communist Party (ICP) and the United Socialist Party, and at the end of the Gulf War, with its rival Kurdish political party, the Patriotic Union of Kurdistan. This alliance is still holding as these pages are being written.

Patriotic Union of Kurdistan (PUK). The Iraqi KDP is now rivaled in Iraq by the Patriotic Union of Kurdistan (PUK), a party based in the southern sector of Iraqi Kurdistan.

The military forces and the faction of the KDP led by Ibrâhim Ahmad, which were driven out by Bârzâni in 1964, returned to Iraq in 1965 under the leadership of Jalâl al-Din Tâlabâni, the son-in-law of Ibrâhim Ahmad. Jalâl came from the ruling family of the Tâlabâni tribe, which has produced a number of well-known literati, religious figures, and political leaders in the past. He initially reconciled with Bârzâni and joined forces with him. However, he soon realized his own and his faction's eclipse under the expanding shadow of Bârzâni, who had also begun to receive increasing amounts of military and financial support from Teheran. Tâlabâni eventually broke with Bârzâni, branding him as "tribal, feudal, and reactionary" (van Bruinessen 1986, 22). Bârzâni attacked his forces.

In order to survive the all-out assault by Bârzâni, Tâlabâni did the unthinkable: he joined forces with Baghdad in 1966, then fighting the native Kurdish guerrillas of a Bârzâni-led uprising. Tâlabâni was heavily and bitterly criticized. The untimely arrival of Ibrâhim Ahmad in Baghdad from his exile in Teheran did not help Tâlabâni's image either. In the two-year period ending in 1970, Tâlabâni remained a secondary figure in Kurdish politics with little to show vis-a-vis the towering image of Bârzâni, despite his daring activities and unorthodox initiatives.

The peace and autonomy agreement between Baghdad and Bârzâni signed in 1970 (see **Recent History**) threw the Tâlabâni faction into political limbo once again. Not welcome in Baghdad any more since an accord had been reached with Bârzâni, Tâlabâni returned to Bârzâni's folds, this time staying there until the 1975 final defeat of Bârzâni and the KDP-led general uprising. This time not only Tâlabâni, but almost every other member of Bârzâni's coalition deserted him, most establishing political movements of their own.

Tâlabâni did the same of course, most willingly. In the summer of 1976, Tâlabâni, then Bârzâni's representative in Damascus, established there the Patriotic Union of Kurdistan (PUK), a coalition between the Iraqi Komala, the Socialist Party (or Movement) of Iraq (SPI) (later the Socialist Party of Kurdistan, SPK), and Tâlabâni's faction of the KDP.

To gain strength against the superior forces of the KDP, the PUK needed to expand its membership. The party's internal political platform was expanded to accommodate almost every group of Kurds, with as many political ideologies and agendas. This ideological pluralism continues today. The party has conservative, center, and Marxist factions, all working within the framework of the PUK.

A bloody clash between KDP and PUK armed forces in Bârzâni home territory in spring 1978 caused havoc within the PUK. Nearly 800 of its top military leaders and guerrillas were killed, executed, captured, or turned over to the Turkish or Iraqi government for later execution.

Upon the departure of the SPK from the PUK, Tâlabâni scrambled for new alliances, forging one with the Iranian Komala in 1979. He also hoped to ally himself with the prestigious KDP-I, which was under attack by both Iranian forces and the Bârzânis. He partially achieved such an alliance in 1981, but as soon became apparent, he had sided with the losing side.

In 1983, objecting to the crossing of KDP-aided Iranian forces into Iraqi Kurdistan, Tâlabâni opened talks with Baghdad again, while his forces engaged in battle with both the SPK and the Iraqi Communist Party. The old accusations of treason were leveled at Tâlabâni again.

Tâlabâni did negotiate a generous accord with Baghdad in 1985, but, under intense pressure from Turkey, Baghdad never signed it. PUK forces opened hostilities with government troops. Komala instantly split from the PUK, and the party was splintered once again. The party's membership and support were suffering steadily.

Tâlabâni has on a number of occasions negotiated, unsuccessfully, with the central Iraqi government for a settlement on Kurdistan, all with disappointing results. The latest of these began in cooperation with the KDP, soon after the end of the Gulf War (see **Recent History**). The latest round of negotiations also broke down before the end of 1991.

The PUK now claims about 4000 guerrillas and a good support base among the local Kurdish civilians in the southern sector of the Iraqi Kurdistan. This is a reversal of its fortunes for the better.

Socialist Party of Kurdistan (SPK). Disgruntled with Tâlabâni's military misjudgment, the Socialist Movement of Kurdistan, which had lost most heavily in the 1978 bloody clash between the Tâlabâni and the Bârzâni forces, split from the PUK. Led by Rasul Mâmand, the party joined with Mahmud Osmân (Uthmân), an old but disillusioned ally of Mustafâ Bârzâni, to form the United Socialist Party of Kurdistan (USPK, or simply SPK) in winter 1979. This coalition lasted only until 1981, when both Mahmud Osmân and Rasul Mâmand went their separate ways, with Mâmand carrying the main body and name of the party with him. At its height, the SPK could field about 1700 combatants.

The SPK was routinely accused of kidnapping Westerners working in Iraq, and releasing them for ransom. The party has struck alliances in the past with many other Iraqi and Kurdish political parties, particularly the KDP, and has engaged in feuding with the others, particularly the PUK and Iraqi Komala. Fights broke out between PUK forces and the SPK in 1983, resulting in heavy losses of personnel and leadership of the SPK. The SPK's platform has shifted from "self-determination for Kurds" outside the framework of the state to "autonomy for Kurds" in a democratic Iraq.

Komala. Having come into a tumultuous existence at a moment of great difficulty in Iraqi Kurdistan in the early 1970s, the Iraqi Komala party proved to be as bedeviled by internal quarrels and hostilities with other local Kurdish political parties as the Iranian Komala. It gained prestige when it organized grass-roots resistance to the Iraqi government deportation of the villagers living near the Iranian borders following Bârzâni's defeat. It brought fame to the PUK coalition which it joined in the same year.

Democratic People's Party of Kurdistan (DPPK). This party was formed in 1981, and has been in alliance with the PUK for most of its existence. The party's founder and chairman is Muhammed Mahmud Abdul-Rahmân, better known by his nick-name, *Sami.* Like many other Kurdish leaders in Iraq, Sami was an old, loyal ally of Mustafâ Bârzâni, and stayed with the reorganized KDP and Bârzâni's sons Idris and Masoud until 1979, when, citing Idris' penchant for authoritarianism, he broke off from the KDP to form the DPPK.

Iraqi Communist Party (ICP). To these purely Kurdish political parties in Iraq must also be added the Iraqi Communist Party (ICP), which although not primarily Kurdish, relies heavily on Kurdish support and has many high-ranking Kurdish members. About one thousand Kurdish guerrilla fighters serve under the ICP, constituting almost all the fighting force it has.

Postscript. The horrific treatment of the Kurdish civilians by the Iraqi war machine in 1988 and the following two years gradually brought the Iraqi Kurdish political parties to realize the need for a comprehensive alliance among them, even one of convenience, if there was to be any chance of meaningful survival. All the more often-feuding Kurdish parties in Iraq, in fact almost all Iraqi political parties, struck a loose alliance of convenience with one another at the end of the Persian Gulf War in the hope of bringing down their common enemy, Saddam Hussein. There was also an unexpected new threat, the rise in popularity of the Turkey-based PKK Kurdish party in Iraq, and of its leader, Öcalan, who it appears is fast gaining the pan-Kurdish prestige once enjoyed by Mustafâ Bârzâni. As this work was being completed, this alliance was, more or less, still holding.

TURKEY

Khoyboun. The earliest Kurdish political party in the modern sense is the Khoyboun, established by Kurdish aristocrats and intellectuals in Paris in 1918. It later moved its headquarters to French Syria. It declared a Kurdish government in exile in 1927, and proceeded to direct an uprising inside Turkey in 1928, where it had moved its headquarters. It was thoroughly defeated in its stronghold at Mount Ararat in 1930, and its leader Ihsân Nuri Pâshâ went into exile in Teheran. Kurds in Turkey had to wait for another 37 years before forming another political party.

Kurdish Democratic Party (KDP-T). In 1967, under the leadership of Fâ'ik Bucak (pronounced Bu.châk), a lawyer from Urfâ, was established the Kurdish Democratic Party of Turkey. The party was formed on the model of the Iraqi KDP and maintained cordial relations with it. The KDP-T was repressed by Ankara, which increased its military presence in the Kurdish regions in Anatolia for this purpose. Bucak was assassinated in July 1968. His colleague and successor, Sa'id Elci (pronounced El.chi) met the same fate in 1970 in his exile in Iraqi Kurdistan. The party split in 1969, and a splinter led by a "Dr. Divân" formed a more radical, leftist group, asking for total independence of Kurdistan from Turkey as well as other neighboring states.

Workers' Party of Kurdistan (PKK). In 1974 a Kurdish splinter group emerged from the Turkish Revolutionary Youth party. It formally announced its existence as a separate party in 1978, after which it moved its headquarters and base of operations from Ankara into Kurdistan, in 1979. It called itself the Workers' Party of Kurdistan (in Kurdish, *Pârtiya Kârkerâna Kurdistân*, or PKK).

Founded as a Marxist-Leninist party, it declared its aims to be not merely freedom for Kurdistan, but also freedom from "feudalism, colonialism, and class distinction." It has thus disputed the legitimacy of Kurdish chieftains and their forces as much if not more than the Turkish state apparatus. Both have been targets of PKK attacks. The PKK's attitude towards traditional Kurdish authorities, however, has progressively softened since the late 1980s. With the collapse of world Communism, the PKK now may have to revise its obsolete Marxist ideology to one focusing more on indigenous Kurdish values and "bourgeois" national aspirations.

The PKK is still the only Kurdish political party with no tribal chief in its central committee. It has strived for and received the loyalty of the large Kurdish lower class, to which it is much more familiar than the elitist political parties. But having come to realize the grave jeopardy in which they place civilians when asking or forcing them to provide assistance, PKK guerrillas live primitive lives in the mountains and woods, under more brutal conditions than any other Kurdish guerrilla group.

Like any political party, in order to survive in the long term, the PKK has had to swim at least marginally with the prevalent social currents. The party has now distinguished "progressive" tribal leaders from the "reactionary," the apparent basis for distinction being the presence or absence of support for the PKK (van Bruinessen 1988, 44). In this way, the PKK has bettered its chances for survival.

In recent years, the PKK, has also come to change its radically dismissive attitude toward religion, recognizing it as an important social force, and has tried to coopt religion to its own ends. Religious personages are, like the tribal ones, now divided into "progressive" and "reactionary" camps in the PKK worldview.

Since its creation, the PKK has always been led by Abdullah Öcalan (pronounced Oh.ch.âlân). Öcalan is known affectionately as "Apo," in accordance with the Kurdish tradition of giving nicknames made of the shortened form of individuals' first names (*Apo* for *Aptollâ*, his first name as pronounced in Kurdish). Apo, incidentally, also means "uncle" in Kurdish, thus giving his name a doubly affectionate meaning. In fact, PKK party members are best known in Turkey as the "Apocu" (pronounced Apoh.chu), Turkish for "Apo's folks."

The PKK's activities were brought to a halt after the military coup of 1980 in Turkey and the declaration of general martial law in the Kurdish provinces, which in some districts lasts until today. The party moved many of its activities into the Kurdish communities in Western and Northern Europe, where it found fertile ground among Kurdish young people thirsting for action. In addition, the PKK set up bases in Syria and the Syrian-controlled Bekaa Valley in Lebanon. There it received training from Palestinian guerrilla groups, which it put into use upon its return to Turkey in the summer of 1983. Many Turkish military installations and Kurdish citizens thought to have cooperated with the government were attacked by the PKK. Since 1980, the PKK has also been receiving support from the Iraqi KDP, and it began using bases in northern Iraqi Kurdistan for its attacks inside Turkey. This precipitated the 1983 Turkish invasion of northern Iraq to isolate the PKK and punish the KDP. Neither goal was achieved.

From 1984 to 1991, the PKK's activities inside Turkey were progressively curbed by the powerful presence of the Turkish army and the enforcement of martial law in the most restless of the Kurdish provinces. Infrequent skirmishes, kidnapping, and inflammatory rhetoric mark the PKK's ground activities in this period. This was to change dramatically.

Following the Gulf War and the disappearance of central authority from the border regions of Iraqi Kurdistan, the PKK intensified its use of those territories for its activities. This was done without the tacit approval of the Iraqi KDP, which controls the border areas.

The Iraqi KDP and PUK have been seeking Ankara's favor in dealing with Baghdad, and have not wanted to jeopardize at this juncture their newly won entente with Turkey for the sake of the PKK (or any other Anatolian Kurd for that matter). The PKK publications have bitterly attacked the KDP, but particularly the PUK, for their "reactionary, collaborating and treasonous" conduct regarding their dealings with Ankara. The PUK was also accused of committing "political harlotry" in selling themselves to the next highest bidder, now that Teheran's gravy train had stopped going to them. What was not mentioned in the PKK's criticisms was that the same gravy train was now arriving at its headquarters.

As they had done in 1983, Turkish forces crossed Iraqi borders in 1991 to hunt for PKK guerrillas. They also casually intruded into Iranian territories for the same purpose, being rather sure that the Iranians, like in 1983, would not make an issue out of a minor border crossing for their mutual interest of snuffing out rebellion. They were very wrong, and their action put Iran, like Syria, squarely behind the Kurdish forces operating in Turkey, which meant basically the PKK. As the relationship between Ankara and Teheran progressively deteriorates over a growing number of clashing points of interest, including the fluid political situation in the Caucasus and central Asia, the formerly friendly neighbors are arming each other's dissidents. While Ankara is now helping the Iranian Mujâhidin guerrillas and instigating unrest in Iranian Azerbaijan, the PKK is bound to receive even more help from Teheran than it does now. The firm support by Iran for the PKK may translate into an open alliance between the Iraqi KDP and the PKK, which would be a doomsday scenario as perceived in Ankara. This would benefit both. Such an alliance would strengthen the KDP's position vis-a-vis the PUK in Iraq, while adding the well-equipped, war-hardened KDP peshmergas to those of the PKK operating in Turkey from Iraqi bases.

The PKK commands roughly between 10,000 and 15,000 peshmergas, with the highest number of female recruits of any Kurdish guerrilla group (see **Status of Women & Family Life**).

In the diaspora, the PKK's achievements hardly hint at its military nature back home. The printing houses of the PKK have poured out Kurdish language literature and newsprint in prodigious quantity, with impressive regularity and comprehensive scope, so as to bedazzle anyone familiar with the dearth of Kurdish-language printed material and the customary cultural aloofness of the Kurdish political parties. The nearly 70 years of suppression of Kurdish print and education in Turkey has found a relief valve in the PKK.

Kurdish Socialist Party of Turkey (KSPT). In 1974, the same year in which the PKK was formed, the Kurdish members of the Turkish Workers' Party, formed a new and purely Kurdish Marxist party, named the Kurdish Socialist Party of Turkey (KSPT). Many of its members have been imprisoned since its founding, and the party secretary, Kemâl Burkay, lives in exile outside Turkey. For most of its existence, KSPT activities have been primarily among the Kurdish diaspora in Europe, which falls outside the parameters of this work.

Komkâr. The only other party coming close to the stature of the PKK is Komkâr. The party was founded by the Anatolian Kurdish diaspora in Germany and Sweden. It has produced a large body of quality printed literature for and by the Kurds, and merits a good deal of attention if only on this ground. Komkâr remains fundamentally a party of European Kurdish immigrants, with little or no grounds of operation in Kurdistan per se. As such, Komkâr and its history fall outside the scope of this work.

Islamic Party of Kurdistan (PIK). This is a Sunni-led organization, with a politico-religious agenda. In more recent times, however, the party leaders have busied themselves with Kurdish nationalism rather than Islamic issues. Its official organ, *Judi* (an allusion to the Talmud's reference to Mount Judi in Kurdistan as the original resting place of Noah's Ark), reflects this inclination well. The party's main loci of operation are in those boundary regions in Turkey's Kurdistan where different religions overlap, such as the Sunni-Alevi Malâtya and Elâzig and the Yezidi-Christian-Sunni Siirt and Bâtmân.

Pârtizân. This party closely resembles the ICP in Iraq, with the same type of relationship to the Kurds. It is a Turkey-wide radical Left organization whose members are almost exclusively of Alevi background, and it has attracted the allegiance of many Kurdish Alevis. Alevi Kurds have maintained a very strong and disproportionate presence in its leadership and membership. The Alevis have been made to feel as outcasts in Turkey on two grounds, religion (among the their Sunni Kurdish brethren) and ethnic affiliation (as Kurds among the mainly ethnic Turkish society of Turkey). Understandably, the Alevis desire to be considered true equals by their fellow Kurds and the Turkish citizenry at large. The secular Left has been an answer to the insecurity that these non-Muslim Kurds have been made to feel among the political Right and even the center, which is often led by leaders of Sunni religious background, be they Kurdish or Turkish.

SYRIA

Kurdish Democratic Party of Syria (KDP-S). The non-contiguous nature of the Kurdish regions in Syria has hampered any attempt to give a unified facade to Kurdish needs and aspirations as a distinct nationality, even within the framework of the Syrian state. Syria has served far more often as a springboard for Kurdish political parties coming from Turkey and Iraq than for indigenous movements. The extent of the use of Syria by those non-local Kurdish political parties can be ascertained from the survey above. Khoyboun, PUK, and PKK are just the better-known cases.

In 1957, however, a "branch" of the Kurdish Democratic Party was formed in Syria, 10 years before a similar formation in Turkey. The party's platform promoted cultural and domestic autonomy for the Kurds within the framework of the Syrian state. The KDP-S was outlawed and its leaders and some members imprisoned in 1959, the period of Colonel Sarâj's administration of Syria during its brief union with Egypt. No other Kurdish political party of note has emerged in Syria.

Further Readings and Bibliography: Very valuable primary sources are the detailed tape interviews with many Kurdish leaders and political figures on deposit in the Oral History Archives at the Kurdish Library in Brooklyn, New York. An excellent reference book on the Kurdish political and semi-political organizations in Kurdistan and diaspora is Robin Schneider, ed., *Kurden im Exil: Ein Handbuch kurdischer Kultur, Politik und Wissenschaft* (Berlin: Berliner Institut für Vergleichende Sozialforschung, dem Haus der Kulturen der Welt und medico international, 1991), section 3; Gerard Challiand, ed., *People Without a Country* (London: Zed, 1980); *Echo of Iran* (Teheran: Echo of Iran Press, various issues, especially the annual almanacs); Great Britain, Office of the Civil Commissioner, *Personalities in Kurdistan* (Baghdad, 1919), and also *Personalities* for *Mosul, Arbil, Kirkuk*, and *Sulaimaniyyah* (Baghdad, 1922-23); Ferdinand Hennerbichler, "Iran's Kurdish Rebellion and its Leaders," *Swiss Review of World Affairs* 29 (March 1980); UK, Foreign and Commonwealth Office, "The Kurdish Problem," Background Brief, (London, July 1986); Chris Kutschera, *Le mouvement national kurde* (Paris: Flammarion, 1979); Chris Kutschera, "Le Mouvement National Kurde," *Military Review* 6-6 (1981); Christiane More, *Le Kurdes d'aujourdhui: Mouvement national et partis politiques* (Paris: Editions l'Harmattan, 1984); Martin van Bruinessen, "The Kurds between Iran and Iraq," *Middle East Report* (July-August 1986); Martin van Bruinessen, "Between Guerrilla War and Political Murder: The Workers' Party of Kurdistan [PKK]," *Middle East Report* (July-August 1988); Martin van Bruinessen, "The Kurds in Turkey," *MERIP Reports* 16.141 (1986); Marvin Zonis, *The Political Elite of Iran* (Princeton: Princeton University Press, 1971); Ismet Vanly, *The Kurdish Problem in Syria* (Chicago: Committee for the Defence of the Kurdish People's Rights, 1968).

General Bibliography

Of the two works of special value one is regrettably as yet unpublished, the doctoral dissertation of Wadie Jwaideh, "The Kurdish Nationalist Movement: Its Origins and Development" (Syracuse, 1960). The other is Martin van Bruinessen, *Agha Shaikh and State: On the Social and Political Organization of Kurdistan* (Rijswijk: Europrint, 1978). Of a more specific nature are William Eagleton, *The Kurdish Republic of 1946* (New York, 1963), which is a valuable case-study of the Kurdish political process as it took place during the course of World War II at Mahâbâd; Edith Lytle, *A Bibliography of the Kurds, Kurdistan and the Kurdish Question.* (Monticello, Illinois, Council of Planning Librarians, No. 1301, 1977); *Kurdish Times*, semi-annual journal of the Kurdish Library, Brooklyn, New York, 1985-present; *Studia Kurdica*, semi-annual publication of the Centre de Recherches de l'Institut Kurde, Paris, 1984-present (text appears in English, French, and the primary Middle Eastern languages).

Chapter 9

ECONOMY

NATURAL RESOURCES

Oil. Kurdistan has among the largest oil reserves in the Middle East and the world. With about 45 billion barrels, Kurdistan contains more and larger proven deposits than the entire United States, and ranks 6th in the world. These reserves are spread over a thin band on the margins between the high mountains and the foothills, from far southern Kurdistan to extreme western Kurdistan near the Mediterranean Sea (see Map 41).

In the south, the fields of Nafti Shâh-Naft Khâna in far southern Kurdistan straddle the Iran-Iraq border. The Nafti Shâh field (renamed Naft Shahr after the Iranian Revolution of 1979) near Qasri Shirin feeds a refinery in Kirmânshâh. The Nafti Shâh-Naft Khâna field has been under production for over half a century and is now nearing exhaustion. This and the expansion of the refining capacities at both Kirmânshâh and Khânaqin have necessitated the import of crude from other fields for refining at these facilities. A pipeline now connects the Kirmânshâh refinery to Hamadân and the Iranian state network of oil pipelines. Likewise, the Khânaqin facility receives additional crude from Kirkuk via a pipeline. While the Nafti Shâh-Naft Khâna field is nearing exhaustion, the adjoining rich natural gas field of Tanga Bijâr, which stretches south from Nafti Shâh toward the town of Sumâr in Iran, has yet to be tapped.

Still farther south, the oil of the richer Pahla-Dehlurân field (only partly under Kurdish-inhabited areas) is piped to Ahvâz and the Iranian ports on the Persian Gulf.

By far the most productive Kurdish petroleum fields are at Kirkuk in central Kurdistan in Iraq. Oil here seeps naturally up to the ground and served as a source of bitumen and naphtha for ancient civilizations. Ignited by lightning, the natural fires there were venerated by various local religions, particularly Zoroastrianism. The Kirkuk fields were the principal reason for the inclusion of central Kurdistan into the British Mandate of Iraq (Nash 1976). Without this natural resource, it is almost certain that the Mosul Vilayet, as central Kurdistan was then called, would have been allowed to go to Kemalist Turkey—if they still wanted it without the oil (see **Deportations & Forced Resettlements**).

New fields are routinely discovered and tapped in central Kurdistan, with fields at Chiâ Surkh and Jambur being major examples.

A separate northern field stretching from Mosul into Syria has also been brought under production. This is the area the ancient geographer Claudius Ptolemy named *Niphates Mons*, i.e., the Naphtha (petroleum) Mountains. The productive fields on the Iraqi side of the area at Mushorab, Ain Zalah, Butmah, and Sâsân are now mostly tapped and joined to the main Iraqi pipelines. The Iraqi government has over the years constructed a vast network of oil pipelines, internally and in neighboring states. These include with Red Sea outlets at Yanbu in Saudi Arabia, Persian Gulf outlets at Mina al-Bakr and Khor al-Amaya in Iraq, and Mediterranean outlets at Tartus in Syria and Dörtyol-Yümurtalik in Turkey. The pipeline through Turkey has proven to be the most reliable and profitable in

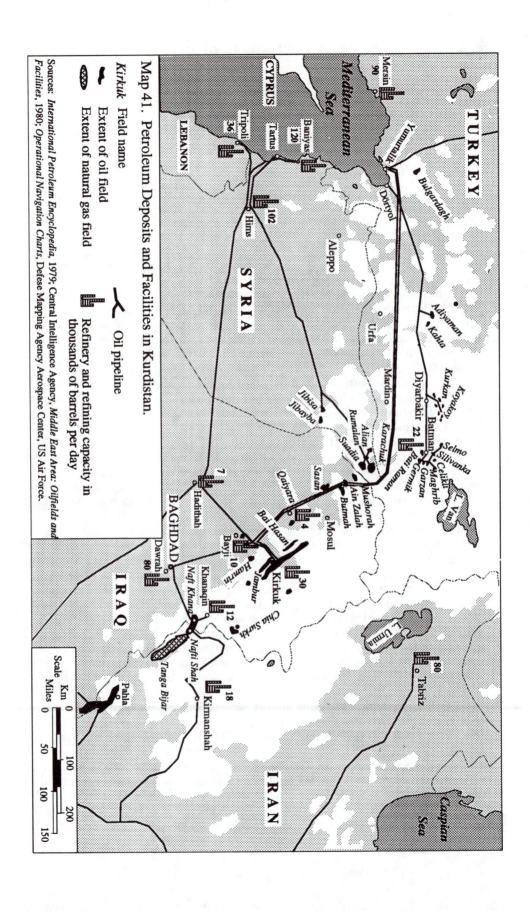

Map 41. Petroleum Deposits and Facilities in Kurdistan.

Kirkuk Field name

⌒ Oil pipeline

▱ Extent of oil field

▱ Extent of natural gas field

🏭 Oil field

🏭 Refinery and refining capacity in thousands of barrels per day

Sources: *International Petroleum Encyclopedia*, 1979; Central Intelligence Agency, *Middle East Area: Oilfields and Facilities*, 1980; *Operational Navigation Charts*, Defense Mapping Agency Aerospace Center, US Air Force.

Scale

Km 0   50   100   100   150

Miles 0   100   200

the past decade. With the Persian Gulf facilities destroyed in 1980, intermittently between 60% and 90% of all Iraqi oil exports passed through this single pipeline. After the opening of the Yanbu pipeline in 1986, this proportion stabilized at about 60% until 1991 and the total blockade of Iraqi oil exports. In the late 1980s, the pipeline became a double artery. It crosses almost exclusively Turkish Kurdistan all the way to the Mediterranean.

With the discovery of the giant oil fields of southern Iraq, the Kirkuk fields have also lost the vital importance they once had to the Iraqi state economy. While almost all Iraqi oil once came from Kurdistan, now only a third of the state's reserves are Kurdish. Kurdish fields in Iraq contain 36 billion barrels of reserves, out of a total of 90 billion barrels of proven reserves in all of Iraq. This development may in fact remove the strong objection of the central Iraqi government to sharing title to and revenues from the fields with the Kurds and various Kurdish autonomous local administrations which have been intermittently set up in central Kurdistan. It also may herald a time when Kurds will have even fewer valuable cards in their deck to bargain for economic and political concessions from Baghdad.

The same geologic formations that yield the Kurdish oil fields of Iraq north of Mosul continue on across the border into Syria in the Jazira region. The fields of Alian, Rumalan, Suadia, and Kara Chuk are now tapped, along with the Jubayba and Jibisa fields in the Sajar district farther south. Their yields are the only ones of note in Syria, and they are connected via a collecting pipeline to the Syrian heartland.

What little petroleum is produced in Turkey is from the Kurdish fields. The richest are in an area centered on the town of Bâtmân east of Diyârbakir. Many small fields have been brought into production in the mountains around the town, and a collecting pipeline system brings the yield to the Bâtmân refinery. Another pipeline connects Bâtmân with the oil fields of Diyârbakir, located in an arc north of the city. Farther west at Adiyaman two primary fields have been brought under production and connected to the previous fields and facilities via another pipeline, and southwest to the port of Dörtyol on the Mediterranean.

So far Kurdish oil has not been produced in quantities large enough to satisfy the needs of the.internal market in Turkey, but promising formations continue to be prospected in this section of Kurdistan.

Further Readings and Bibliography: *The International Petroleum Encyclopedia, 1979*; Christopher Ryan, *A Guide to the Known Minerals of Turkey* (Ankara: Mineral Research and Exploration Institute of Turkey, 1960); I. Altin et al., *Ölçekli Türkiye Jeoloji Haritasi* ("Explanatory Text of the Geological Maps of Turkey"), sheets published loose at 1:500,000 scale for each Turkish province, accompanied by explanatory texts (Ankara: Mineral Research and Exploration Institute of Turkey, 1960-70); *Middle East Area: Oil Fields and Facilities* (Washington: U.S. Central Intelligence Agency, 1980), a sheet map at 1:4,500,000; Theodore Nash, "The Effect of International Oil Interests upon the Fate of Autonomous Kurdish Territory: A Perspective on the Conference at Sèvres, August 10, 1920," *International Problems* 15, 1-2 (1976).

Other Minerals. The Zagros and Taurus mountains were known to the ancients as a source of many metal ores, particularly copper, chromium, and iron. The development of some of humanity's earliest metallurgical technologies, which transferred the human race from the stone age into the revolutionary metal ages (copper, bronze and iron, successively), took place at the 8000 year-old site of Çayönü near Diyârbakir in western Kurdistan (see **Prehistory & Early Technological Development**). Modern mining operations continue on the old track, producing some 2% of the world's copper and 8% of the chromium in 1970. The ancients also recovered a great deal of silver and some gold from the Zagros mines, but both silver and gold are now produced solely as by-products of copper ore refining in western Kurdistan in Turkey. The Adiyaman-Malatya region of far western Kurdistan is rich in iron ore, and has been producing at very high rates by Middle Eastern standards for almost two decades.

The world's largest deposit of rock sulfur, located southwest of Arbil at Sharqat, has recently been brought under production by the Iraqi government. A relatively large amount of sulfur was already produced in central Kurdistan as a by-product of petroleum and natural gas refining at Kirkuk and Khânaqin in Iraq, as well as Kirmânshâh in Iran. Sulfur is one of the main ingredients in soil fertilizers and pesticides, but is also used as the main ingredient for gun power and in several military poison gases. Ironically, the raw materials for the chemical weapons used on the Kurdish population by the Iraqi military may well have been harvested from the land's own mineral wealth (see **Recent History**).

Because of the varied geological formations of the land, many igneous, metamorphic, and sedimentary rocks for construction are available in abundance. Decorative stones, such as travertine, marble, diorite, and granite, as well as limestone for cement, are some examples.

Further Readings and Bibliography: C. Ryan, *A Guide to the Known Minerals of Turkey* (Ankara: Mineral Research and Exploration Institute of Turkey, 1960); I. Altin et al., *Ölçekli Türkiye Ceoloji Haritasi* ("Explanatory Text of the Geological Maps of Turkey"), sheets published loose at 1:500,000 scale for each Turkish province, accompanied by explanatory texts (Ankara: Mineral Research and Exploration Institute of Turkey, 1960-70); O. Kühn, et al, "Oberkreide aus Kurdistan," *Neues Jahrbuch für Mineralogie, Geologie und Paläontologie Beilagebände* 83 (1940).

Water. In an otherwise water-starved region, Kurdistan is blessed with abundant precipitation. The generous regime has made Kurdistan one of the few watersheds of the Middle East. Rivers like the Tigris, Euphrates, Khâbur, Tharthâr, Ceyhân, Araxes, Kurâ, Safidrud, Karkha, and their major tributaries spring from the mountains of Kurdistan. Those rivers that are entirely or nearly entirely in Kurdistan are usually of historical importance to the Kurds. Among these are the Murat (Arasân) and Buhtân rivers in northern and western Kurdistan (in Turkey); the Peshkhâbur, the Lesser and the Greater Zâb, and the Sirwân/Diyâla in central Kurdistan (in Iraq); and the Jaghatu (Zarrinarud), the Tâtâ'u (Siminarud), the Zohâb (Zahâb), and the Gâmâsiyâb in southern Kurdistan (in Iran) (Map 42).

The wealth of glacial and snow fields as well as the favorable geological properties of the land produce what is a common feature in most areas of Kurdistan (except in the volcanic north): exceptionally powerful springs. Sarâb Ghambar in southern Kurdistan, for example, emerges from the ground already a bona fide river, with a capacity of 650 gallons per second. The river flows over 400 miles to the Persian Gulf and is the source water of the Saymara-Karkha river system. The preponderance of Kurdish towns and villages with the prefix Sarâb or Kâni (spring in Kurdish) in their names commemorates this bounty of springs. While the Kurdish rivers are the lifeblood of the lowland Middle Eastern economies, it is the springs that serve as the main source of artificial irrigation and domestic water for the Kurds. The largest Kurdish city, Kirmânshâh, collects its tap water exclusively from the spring fields around the city.

The regulation of the flow of river waters is more for the benefit of the non-Kurdish users on the lowlands than the Kurds of the mountains. As such, many hydraulic projects now dot Kurdish watercourses, and many more projected.

The most important of these are in the Tigris-Euphrates catchment area. In central Kurdistan, two large dams at Darbandi Khân (on the Sirwân-Diyâla) and Dokhân (or Dokkân on the Lesser Zâb) double as major hydroelectric sources for the Baghdad metropolitan region. In northern and western Kurdistan in Turkey, the multi-billion-dollar Southeast Anatolian Project (GAP, from its Turkish acronym) envisions damming the Tigris, the Euphrates, and their tributaries to provide regulated water for irrigation of

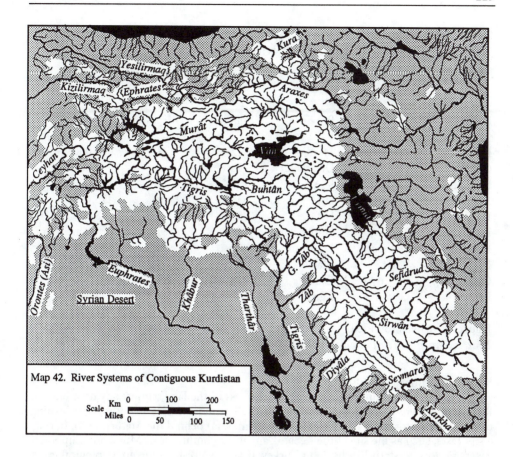

Map 42. River Systems of Contiguous Kurdistan

Scale Km 0 100 200
Miles 0 50 100 150

the parched lowland plains and to provide inexpensive electricity for domestic and industrial use. The water is also seen as a cash commodity, for it is to be sold through the
so-called peace pipeline, which is projected to run 1,700 miles from Turkey to the thirsty
countries of the Middle East, as far south as Kuwait and Saudi Arabia (Gregory 1991).
The source water for the pipeline is to be the Ceyhan-Seyhan river system in the east-
central Taurus mountains. It is doubtful that these rivers could provide the necessary
resources for the the project, and the Euphrates basin may eventually become the main
supplier for this export scheme.

Many of the dams have already been completed, including the mammoth Atatürk Dam
on the Euphrates near Urfâ, which is by far the largest in the GAP and the fifth largest in
the world. When complete, the GAP will consist of 13 major hydroelectric and irrigation
projects (seven in the Euphrates basin, six in the Tigris). GAP envisions irrigating over 4
million acres of land and producing 24 megawatt-hours of electricity per year. The fact
that in the 40 years prior to the GAP the state brought only 1.4 million acres of land
under artificial irrigation in all of Turkey, and produced only 34 megawatt-hours of electricity nationwide in 1985, might highlight the importance of GAP.

The filling of the Atatürk Dam reservoir in 1990, with its final capacity exceeding the
total annual discharge of the Euphrates, or even the Nile, showed the importance of
Kurdish waters for other economies down on the plains as well (Table 7). Turkey all but
halted the flow of the Euphrates into Syria and Iraq, to whom the river is of vital national
economic importance, for two months. The swift mobilization of the Syrian armed forces
(Angus 1989) and the threats and counter-threats flying between Ankara, Damascus, and
Baghdad vividly demonstrate the strategic importance of water in the Middle East, and

TABLE 7. DAMS PRESENTLY UNDER CONSTRUCTION OR RECENTLY COMPLETED IN WESTERN AND NORTHERN KURDISTAN IN ANATOLIA.

Dam	River	Province	Capacity (Billion ft^3)	Electricity (Megawatts)	Irrigation Acreage
Dumluca	Bugur	Mardin	12	0	6,000
Göksu	Göksu	Diyârbakir	56	0	9,000
Memzelet	Ceyhân	K. Maras	256	120	116,000
Atatürk	Euphrates	Urfâ	2,535	2,400	2,175,000
Hacihidir	Hacihidir	Urfâ	42	0	8,500
Kiralkizi	Tigris	Diyârbakir	449	90	n.a.
Kuzgun	Serceme	Erzurum	83	20	130,000
Polât	Polât	Malâtya	63	0	7,000
Özlüce	Perisuyu	Elazig	228	160	0
Patnos	Gevi	Âgri	82	0	12,500

Figures have been rounded.
Source: *Statistical Yearbook of Turkey*, 1989.

Kurdistan as one of its most important sources.

Due to the extraordinary archaeological richness of the land, almost any dam built in Kurdistan drowns a portion of Kurdish history. The most glaring loss was the drowning of the entire historic city of Samsat (ancient Samosata) behind the Atatürk Dam. In only a few cases, such as the site of the Keban Dam at the confluence of Murat and Euphrates Rivers in northwestern Kurdistan in Turkey, have any pre-flooding archaeological excavations been made. One can only guess the magnitude of the loss of the historical remains in sites like the Darbandi Khân Dam near Halabja in Iraq—the very historic heartland of Kurdistan, where more ancient mounds per square mile are known to exist than in the rich Mesopotamian plain. Vast archaeological wealth has thus been lost forever by flooding the very same mountain valleys where civilization in Kurdistan first took root nearly 11,000 years ago.

Many natural lakes of various sizes, most with great potential for tourism, can be found in Kurdistan. Lake Zarivâr near Marivân in eastern Kurdistan, surrounded by forested mountains and attractive shores, is just one of these sites. Lake Vân in northern Kurdistan is the world's fourth largest non-saline body of water by volume. The lake's surrounding country, rich with archaeological and architectural monuments, is an ideal tourist spot, well suited for commercial development. Fifteen miles west of the shores of Lake Vân is the crescent-shaped Lake Nimrod, formed at the bottom of Mt. Nimrod (called *Nimrut Dagh* on Turkish maps, but not to be confused with the archaelogical site of Nimrut Dag in far western Kurdistan, north of Adiyaman), a volcanic caldera 8 miles in diameter and surrounded by vertical cliffs half a mile high. The lake ranks among the most attractive natural sites in all of Kurdistan.

Further Readings and Bibliography: *Doomed by the Dam: A Survey of the Monuments Threatened by the Creation of the Keban Dam Flood Area*, Faculty of Architecture, Publ. No. 9 (Ankara: Middle East Technical University, 1967); Robert Whallon, *An Archaeological Survey of the Keban Reservoir Area of East-Central Turkey*, Memoirs of the Museum of Anthropology, No. 11 (Ann Arbor: University of Michigan Press, 1979); Daniel Stoll and Joyce Starr, eds., *The Politics of Scarcity:*

Water in the Middle East (Boulder: Westview, 1988); Joyce Starr and Daniel Stoll, *U.S. Foreign Policy on Water Resources in the Middle East* (Washington: The Center for Strategic and International Studies, 1987); John Kolars and H. Mitchell, *The Euphrates River* (Carbondale: University of Illinois Press, 1990); Thomas Naff and Ruth Matson, eds., *Water in the Middle East: Conflict or Cooperation?* (Boulder: Westview, 1984); Thomas Naff, "Water: An Emerging Issue in the Middle East?" The Annals of the American Academy of Political Scientists (November 1985); "Middle East: Water Issues in the 1990's," testimonies submitted to the U.S. House [of Congress] Subcommittee on Europe and the Middle East, Washington, June 26, 1990; Joseph R. Gregory. "Liquid Asset," *World Monitor* 28 (November 1991); Joyce Starr, "Water Wars," *Foreign Policy* 82 (Spring 1991). Angus Hindley, "Battle Lines Drawn for Euphrates," *Middle East Economic Development* (October 13, 1989).

AGRICULTURE

Kurdistan's wealth of high-grade pasture lands has long made it suitable for a pastoralist economy, but it is equally suitable in many areas for intensive agriculture. Unlike the woodlands and the heavy damage they have sustained, the pasture lands have remained in reasonably good condition and continue to be a productive source of animal feed (see **Flora & Fauna**). The rich pastures have always ensured that in all historical periods, regardless of how dominant the agricultural sector, there have been nomadic herdsmen exploiting this economic niche to its fullest.

Although many pasture lands are suitable for agriculture, in many others, especially on the steep slopes and hard-to-reach plateaus, pastoralist herding is the only viable use of the resources. In many areas, various other elements, such as high elevation (hence, short growing seasons), inavailability of suitable sources of water, unsuitable soil properties, etc., can make impossible the conversion of a given pasture land into agricultural land. Even terracing of the slopes, which has been practiced there since the 8th millenium BC, is limited by the availability of deep top soil. These pastures would produce nothing if not used by the pastoralist nomads and/or for seasonal shepherding by otherwise settled farmers. Even today there are some Kurds who practice pastoral life, tapping a valuable resource (see **Nomadic Economy**). The range of such seasonal shepherding operations remain by necessity quite limited. The herd remains within a few days walking distance of their home base, and the more remote and inaccessible pastures are slowly forced out of production. The pre-modern nomads before them had no such limitations.

Large and fertile mountain valleys, on the other hand, provide ample space for agriculture. Despite its mountainous nature, Kurdistan has more arable land proportionately (28% of its total surface area) than the majority of Middle Eastern countries. Expansive river valleys create a lattice work of fertile fields in Kurdistan, except in the region of the central massif. This may very well explain the fact that agriculture was almost surely invented in Kurdistan, as was the domestication of almost all basic cereals and livestock, with the notable exceptions of cows and rice (see **Prehistory & Early Technological Development**). Since then, the economy has always had an agricultural base, albeit with varying degrees of importance.

A great variety of cereals and vegetables have traditionally been grown in Kurdistan, but wheat and barley are the most common. Rice has more recently been given growing preference, and it is displacing bread as the basic food of choice of the Kurdish middle class.

Cash crops like tobacco, sugar beets, and cotton are playing a growing role in the local economy. The tobacco is of good quality, with pipe tobacco (also the tobacco of choice for water pipes) of the region being in great demand throughout the Middle East.

On the rich soil of the foothills, where plenty of sunshine and long growing seasons are coupled with runoff from the mountains, cotton has become the cash crop of choice. In western Kurdistan in Turkey, large swaths of land earmarked for development under the GAP project (see **Natural Resources: Water**), particularly in the Middle Euphrates basin (Atatürk Dam region), are to be given to cotton production. As the level of cotton production in Kurdistan of Syria and Iraq also rises, it is expected that the plant will play a growing role in the Kurdish economy in the decades to come.

Sugar beets were introduced for large-scale plantation farming in the middle of the last century. Many sugar refining mills of various sizes are found now in Kurdistan, processing sugar for local and state markets (see **Industries**).

Olives are a localized cash crop, and grow primarily in western Kurdistan toward the Mediterranean Sea. Fats and oils for cooking and other uses have traditionally come from dairy sources, rendering olive oil more of a delicacy than a dietary necessity.

A few basic crops introduced into Kurdistan relatively recently are opening a fast-growing niche for themselves. Maize, soy beans, and sunflowers are primarily cash crops. They supply state markets for vegetable oil, but also a growing portion is now used as poultry feed in that fast-expanding industry. Potatoes, grown on the poorer and glacial soils, are consumed locally and beyond.

Many fruit and nut trees grow naturally in the Zagros-Taurus forests (see **Flora & Fauna**). Pistachios, almonds, hazel nuts (filberts), chestnuts, and acorns have traditionally been collected from these natural growths. Much larger crops are progressively being collected from the cultivated groves. Located in the natural habitat of these trees, these groves yield prolifically.

Wild berries, particularly black and white mulberries, are found in almost every village, but are not yet produced in large quantities for market. Mulberries, and to a lesser extent barberries, are currently the berries of choice. Dried, they are used throughout the year.

The fruits, including grapes, are grown in large tracts of land. Some quantity is also collected from wild stands. They play an important role in the Kurdish diet, particularly in their dried forms.

Evidence of the importance of fruits and nuts in the diet of the ancient Kurds comes from the 2800-year-old archaeological site of Hasanlu in eastern Kurdistan. There was found ample evidence of quince (of species Cydonia oblonga), several kinds of pear (Pyrus communis), apples (Pyrus malus), and a variety of apricot or almond (of genes Prunus), indicative of the importance of fruits in the local diet (Harris 1989).

The dried fruits are the fastest-growing cash commodities, outranking even cotton and tobacco in their total cash value. In 1981, for example, Iranian Kurdistan produced an agricultural (non-animal) surplus worth approximately $221 million. Of this, $89 million was in fresh and dried fruit products. Cereals were second in value (Iran State Statistics, 1986). The expanding international market for fresh and dried fruits has outpaced the local market for these commodities, turning it into a bona fide industry. The products, now processed and packaged with international standards in mind, promise yet a larger role for dried fruits in the local economic output.

Growing wild in abundance in the oak forests, truffles (*chema*), the prize of any gourmand chef in the West, are a food for the poor in Kurdistan. Kurdish truffles can at least rival the lucrative Japanese *shiitake* mushrooms in the U.S. and European food markets, becoming a valuable source of specialty food export.

A healthy agricultural export industry will more than any other single economic sector help the Kurdish economy in balancing its cash flow and maintaining a healthy economy. The agricultural cash commodities represent a far more rational and attainable means of converting the presently static, subsistence-level Kurdish economy into the vibrant trading economy it was before the beginning of the 16th century. Additionally, the income generated from agriculture percolates down to the household levels, benefiting the largest number of people, and helping not just the larger producers, but also the average village growers.

Livestock. Included in agricultural production are animal products. The most important animals have been traditionally sheep and to a lesser extent goats. Goats are not a readily marketable commodity anymore, and they cater to special needs for their hair and wool, particularly the angora goat, the source of mohair. Their numbers, once in millions, are steadily dropping due to a shrinkage of the market and the extensive damage they cause to the pastures and wood lands.

Sheep on the other hand are not only expanding in numbers, but they are also gaining in importance as an export commodity. The meat can now travel to distant internal and external markets, refrigerated or frozen, generating vast income for the Kurdish producers. The Middle Eastern market preference for fresh meat guarantees a ready market for Kurdish fresh lamb—a market presently denied to geographically more remote international producers like Argentina, New Zealand and Australia, whose live sheep exports to the area becomes economical only after the local annual live supplies have run out.

The wool used for local weaving now supports a growing mechanized textile industry. Sheep have always been the most import source of wool and continue to be even more so at present.

Cows and bulls are found in moderate numbers in the villages, supplying milk and meat, but also pulling power. As mechanical motors replace them, the trend for drinking cow's milk instead of sheep's should prevent any drastic drop in the bovine population, if not actually increase it.

The traditional excellence ascribed to Kurdish dairy products in medieval reports, however, pertain only to the sheep products. Local cheeses, yogurt, curds, buttermilk, butter, and clarified butter (*rowan*, used exclusively for cooking) have a distinctly pleasant flower-like scent that has been the traditional hallmark of the Kurdish dairies, but more in the past than now.

Increasing numbers of livestock are fed by farm byproducts—hay, stalks, and the like—and no longer graze the wild flower beds that naturally imparted the distinctive scent of dairy products.

Wild pigs and boars are very common, but are shunned in the meat market, as ham is forbidden by the Islamic dietary laws, and the non-Muslim Kurds have been reluctant to add one more point of friction to their delicate relationship with the Muslims. In the more remote areas, boars and pigs are consumed by hunters of all religious affiliations. They are not however sold in the market. Even though there is a good potential for the export of pork products to nearby Europe, it is doubtful that there is much future for this industry in Kurdistan.

While the prospects for expanding the economic output of the pastures are at the end limited, the farm lands and orchards have vast potential to meet local dietary needs and as exportable commodities. Great tracts of fallow pasture lands can be brought under intensive agriculture using the rich surface, subsurface, and precipitant water resources.

Further Readings and Bibliography: Mary Virginia Harris, "Glimpses of an Iron Age Landscape: Plants at Hasanlu," *Expedition* 31.2-3 (1989); E. R. Guest, C. C. Townsend, and A. al-Rawi, eds., *Flora of Iraq*, 6 vols. (Baghdad: Ministry of Agriculture, 1966-85); B. Gilliat-Smith and W.B. Terril, "On the Flora of the Near East," *Bulletin of Miscellaneous Information of the Royal Botanic (Kew) Gardens* 7-10 (1930).

NOMADIC ECONOMY: A POSTSCRIPT

It is rather late to speak of a Kurdish nomadic economy, at a time when less than 3% of the total population still practice this economic life style. This was not so, however, until the recent past.

Pastoral life style and economy must have come into existence in the Zagros mountains after the formation of settled agricultural communities which domesticated the prerequisite animals and plants (Garthwaite 1978). For the remainder of history, nomads always lived along side the settled agriculturalists and the urbanites. Like all other nomads, they practiced banditry and highway robbery, particularly in the rougher economic times. Their exploits made the name *Kurd* almost synonymous with *bandit*.

The settled Kurds suffered far more from the lack of security perpetrated by the elusive, highly mobile, and unpredictable nomads than ever did non-Kurds or travellers in transit. At the height of international trade through Kurdistan in the medieval period, the local Kurdish principalities maintained an acceptable degree of control over the exploits of the nomads. They depended on the trade for revenue, and their coffers were quick to reflect any relaxation of their vigilance. After the calamitous shift of the international trade routes to the southern seas (see **Trade**), the general decline of the Kurdish national economy gave the nomads more incentive to rob, while drastically undercutting the resources of the local organized states to combat it. By the late 18th century there was little left to rob, even from the settled Kurds, except from couriers and the few impoverished Armenian merchants who still had to use some of the abandoned old trade routes of Kurdistan.

The lack of an organized state security force allowed the settled farmers to fall easy prey to the highly mobile, vastly more fit, and better-fed nomadic warriors (Smith 1978), who wreaked havoc with every operation conducive to a settled agricultural economy. Large numbers of farmers found themselves enslaved by the nomadic lords and taken away. Many town dwellers faced the same unpleasant prospects. Many, if not most, non-pastoral people found it necessary to become clients of some mighty nomadic tribe for protection and also to gain a guaranteed commercial relationship with the increasingly wealthy pastoralist economic entities.

To the nomads themselves, banditry was just a diversion, even though a highly visible one. In fact, by the opening of the 18th century, with the steady reduction in the quantity and value of the output of the sedentary Kurds, the general welfare of the economy had progressively came to depend on the animal products and hand-made fabrics produced by the nomads.

It is conceivable that at the height of nomadism in the 18th century, up to 1 million Kurds, i.e., about 30% of the population, were nomads (see **Demography**). This is indeed a very high figure, accounting for the political and military power the nomads exercised over the settled farmers and the urban Kurds. Such proportions would have meant an almost empty Kurdish countryside, with agricultural communities few and far apart. The formerly tilled land would have been taken over by the nomads who came grazing through once or twice a year. This is consistent with what one reads in the accounts of eyewitnesses like Evliyâ Chelebi, who report the land almost empty, the farms abandoned, and the local settled communities living in castles and high-ground fortresses for protection. Northern Kurdistan, in particular, bore the brunt of this, and the results can still be observed today (see **Internal Subdivisions**).

Kurdistan was not alone in this devastation. Many neighboring communities were also suffering dearly from the stoppage of land trade and frequent wars, which had become cataclysmic with the introduction of cannons into the area. The frequency and boldness with which these ruthless nomads raided settlements and caravans so alienated the sedentary people that it came to be utterly inconceivable to them that they and the nomads could be related. They would readily find more in common with a similarly settled Armenian, Turk, Arab, or Turkmen than with a "fellow" nomad Kurd who had made a peaceful life a distant dream.

By the beginning of the 19th century, almost every settled agriculturalist and urbanite in the Middle East had forgone the old ethnic designators because of the nomads, using instead the name of a native city or province. The old ethnic designators *Kurd, Arab, Turk,* and *Turkmen* had come to mean almost exclusively a nomad to them—an unpolished, semi-wild wanderer who was the scourge of the land and an instrument of lawlessness and destruction. Not until the early 20th century were these old ethnic names exonerated and promoted.

The nomadic population of the Kurds were the last from a major ethnic group in the Middle East to be settled, and thus the Kurds were the last to begin commmonly using the old ethnic term for their entire nation again. Even now, the very old urban Kurds who remember bygone wanderers shun the term *Kurd*, just as the modern Turks, despite all that has been done in exoneration of the term *Turk*, still use it in intimate conversation to mean a country bumpkin or a lout.

The turn came toward the middle of the 19th century, when the rural sedentary population registered a 25% natural increase while the nomads did not. The nomads could not retain their domination in the face of such increases. The ratio was now 4 sedentary farmers to 1 nomadic Kurd, and the gap was fast increasing.

The forced sedentarization programs introduced in Turkey and Iran beginning in the 1920's were the beginning of the end for the nomads and their traditional modes of economic production. The overwhelming majority of the pastoralist Kurds were forced to settle down, and only a few marginal tribes managed to continue their migratory life. After the 1941 abdication of Rezâ Shâh in Iran and the Allied occupation of the land, some sedentarized tribes, Kurds and non-Kurds alike, returned to their former economic life. But this did not last. The time had passed for the great pastoralist, transhumant life, and no amount of resistance could turn back time. Pastoralism was doomed, and has now left behind just relics of its former primacy.

Some shepherds still take great flocks of sheep and goats to summer and winter pastures, but they are no longer accompanied by the other members of the community, who now are farmers, villagers, or even city dwellers. The untilled, or untillable, land is now being brought under agricultural production, which adds markedly to the economic and nutritional well-being of the Kurdish society.

With the economic shift all but complete, the great Kurdish tribal names, formerly exclusive to great pastoral tribes and their sedentary clients, are now only social designators similar to the use of clan names in modern Ireland, denoting one's point of origin in the land and often one's political allegiances (see **Tribes** and **Political Parties**).

Further Readings and Bibliography: John Masson Smith, "Turanian Nomadism and Iranian Politics," *Iranian Studies* XI (1978); G.R. Garthwaite, "Pastoral Nomadism and Tribal Power," *Iranian Studies* XI (1978); Fredrik Barth, *Principles of Social Organization in Southern Kurdistan* (Oslo: Brodrene Vorgensen, 1953); William Masters, "Rowanduz: A Kurdish Administrative and Mercantile Center," unpublished doctoral dissertation (Ann Arbor: University of Michigan Microfilms International, 1953); E.R. Leach. *Social and Economic Organization of the Rawanduz Kurds* (London: London School of Economics and Political Science, 1940); Douglas Johnson, *The Nature of Nomadism* (Chicago: University of Chicago Press, 1969).

INDUSTRIES

Marco Polo writes of the Kurds of the area between Mus, Mardin, and Mosul, and reports they produced cotton "in great abundance, of which they prepare the cloths called *boccasini,* and many other fabrics.The inhabitants are manufacturers and traders" (*Travels,* I.vi). The exportable manufactured goods of Kurdistan are limited to handicrafts, which can only serve as souvenirs and specialty items. There is no mass production of textiles for export anywhere in Kurdistan. In fact, textiles are net imports. This is despite the local wealth of natural wool and cotton. Very little traditional cloth weaving has remained in Kurdistan, despite the past luster of this industry. Only the fabrics used for floor coverings, pile rugs, kelims, and felt rugs, are still produced in relatively large quantities. Their export potential is very good, particularly for the rustic, village types. Their "wild" designs and "natural" looks are considered virtues in the Western rug market, catering to those who find the sophistication of Persian and other similar rugs with a machine-made quality too perfect for their tastes. The future for the Kurdish hand-made rug exports is promising, but they cannot possibly be expected to perform better than, say, Persian rugs, which were worth $7.2 billion in 1990 in export markets. The maximum annual export income that could be expected from this industry would fall in the range of hundreds of millions of dollars, a disappointing figure for the most important manufactured item in Kurdistan.

Other traditional fabrics, used for making the nomadic tents, and the saddle blankets and trinkets long associated with horse riding, are all but gone. There is very little use left for these fabrics, and the export market for them is even more limited (see **Rugs & Fabrics**).

Petroleum refinement is easily the most valuable and developed modern industry in Kurdistan, with mining being the second. Nearly half of the 2.1 million barrels per day exported by Iraq in 1990 came from the major Kurdish fields. This and production from other smaller fields in Kurdistan could translate into $7-10 billion per annum in foreign currency income. The refined oil productions and petrochemicals can potentially raise this figure considerably. The income from other mineral exports, particularly from western Kurdistan in Turkey, was less than $1 billion in the same period.

Both these industries, however, have been developed to benefit the larger economy of Iraq and Turkey. Only in Iran has the Kurdish oil industry been directly geared to benefit the local people, and this is because of the limited oil resources of the region. The extensive, modern refineries at Kirkuk and Khânaqin in Iraq, and Batman in Turkey are maintained and operated with little relevance to Kurdistan per se, except to provide employment for unskilled laborers. Even at this level the work force is ethnically thoroughly mixed, as the higher, secure wages of the oil industries attract workers from many far away places.

The mining of other important minerals such as copper, iron, and chromium in Turkey also follows the pattern of the oil industry there, i.e., the mines are operated and maintained only insofar as their yields can be shipped out of Kurdistan, with litte effect on the local economy beyond providing employment for unskilled local laborers.

The lighter industries, such as construction materials, sugar, and textiles, on the other hand have much more relevance to the local Kurdish economy. The textile mills in Bisitun, in southern Kurdistan in Iran, satisfy a substantial portion of the local Kurdish market for cloth. Similarly, the sugar mills, tapping the fast-expanding sugar beet production, and the cement factories of central Kurdistan have far more relevance to the current Kurdish economy than the oil industry has, and will continue to do so in the foreseeable future.

Beyond these light industries, Kurdistan has a long way to go to satisfy its needs for modern industrial commodities and manufactured goods locally. However, except for Turkey, the industrial sectors of the states of the Middle East, in particular Iraq and Iran, also fall well short of satisfying their local needs, and much industrial development will have to take place to wean these economies from their current massive imports of modern manufactured goods from the industrial countries. Kurdistan, being among the least developed and least industrialized sections of these states, has to import only marginally more manufactured goods than the state economies of which it is a part.

Further Readings and Bibliography: Glenn M. Fleming, "The Ecology and Economy of Kurdish Villages," *Kurdish Times* IV 1-2 (1991); F. Barth, *Principles of Social Organization in Southern Kurdistan* (Oslo: Vorgensen, 1953); Ziba Mir-Hosseini, "Some Aspects of Changing Economy in Rural Iran: The Case of Kalardasht, A District in the Caspian Provinces," *International Journal of Middle Eastern Studies* 19 (1987); H.L. Rabino, "A Journey in Mazandaran (from Resht to Sari)," *Geographical Journal* 42 (1913); J.B. Noel, "A Reconnaissance in the Caspian Provinces of Persia," *Geographical Journal* 57 (1921); Marcel Bazin and Christian Bromberger et al., *Gilân et Âzerbâyjân Oriental: Cartes et Documents Ethnographic* (Paris: Éditions Recherche sur les civilisations, 1982); Ziba Mir-Hosseini, "Impact of Wage Labour on Household Fission in Rural Iran," *Comparative*

Journal of Family Studies 18.3 (1987); X. de Planhol, "Le boeuf porteur dans le Proche-Orient et l'Afrique du Nord," *Journal of the Economic and Social History of the Orient* XII.3 (1969); Z. Mir-Hosseini, "Changing Aspects of Economic and Family Structures in Kalardasht, A District in Northern Iran," unpublished doctoral dissertation (Cambridge: Dept. of Social Anthropology, University of Cambridge, 1980); E. R. Leach. *Social and Economic Organization of the Rowanduz Kurds.* (London: London School of Economics and Political Science, 1940); Marco Polo, *Travels,* John Masefield, ed. (London: Dent, 1975); E.J. Keall, "Political, Economic, and Social Factors on the Parthian Landscape of Mesopotamia and Western Iran: Evidence from Two Case Studies," in L.D. Levine and T.C. Young, eds., *Mountains and Lowlands: Essays in the Archaeology of Greater Mesopotamia* (Malibu, California: Bibliotheca Mesopotamica, vol. 7, 1977).

TRADE

Archaeological evidence amply demonstrates that Kurdistan was, as far back as 10,000 years ago, a trading society. The artifacts and remains of materials of very distant manufacturing origins point to the role that trade had played in the economy of Kurdistan, but more importantly and less perceptibly, in its technological development (Beale 1973).

The crossing of the Cape of Good Hope by Vasco da Gama in 1497 heralded a shift toward sea transportation for commercial traffic, which had before that time used long-established land trade routes, such as the Silk Road between East and West, which crossed Kurdistan.

Cessation of commercial traffic, and its by-product, cross-cultural exchanges of technological and economic achievements, resulted in a stagnant economy, static technology, and a country ever more remote from the international consciousness. The quality and volume of local manufacturing declined catastrophically, left with only limited local markets. The physical and administrative infrastructure that supported and in turn profited from the commercial traffic through Kurdistan also withered. The historical backdrop for these events is provided in the sections on **Early Modern**, **Modern**, and **Recent History**.

It is only now that Kurdistan is recovering from the many centuries of progressive isolation that followed. The return of international commercial traffic since the 1960s, albeit in a more limited scope, and the revitalization of the old Kurdish trade routes is undoing what their diversion had done since the 16th century, and at an astonishing pace. The brisk overland trade from the oil-rich states of Iran and Iraq (and to a lesser extent the countries further east and south) with the European markets has revived Kurdistan as a bridge for that lucrative trade. The rebuilding of the Kurdish transportation infrastructure has outpaced any other material or industrial improvement of the country.

The heaviest traffic now passes through northern and western Kurdistan in Turkey, joining the markets of Iran (the Bâzargân-Agri, Qotur-Vân, and Sero-Yüksekova crossings) and Iraq (Mosul-Peshkhâbur-Cizre crossings) to those of Europe. In 1990 the total value of commodities (including oil) that passed through Kurdistan stood at approximately $23 billion. The main arteries of Hamadân-Kirmânshâh-Baghdad and Gali Ali Beg-Qala Diza-Mosul are bracing for a similar acceleration of heavy commercial traffic when the Iran-Iraq borders are opened. The Kurdish commercial arteries have played a vital role in the economies of both of these countries, whose ports were closed or heavily damaged in the course of their 8-year war (1980-88).

The traffic, sometimes backed up for tens of miles at the borders, prompted Turkey to give some attention to improving the roads in Kurdistan, as it was bringing such a large income in transit fares. But its meager improvements were not enough to satisfy Iran and Iraq, whose trucks and trains have to struggle with the third- and fourth-class roads, with delays, and with physical damage to their equipment and commodities. Both nations offered assistance to Turkey to improve its Kurdish roads. The largest bridge in the Middle East, the rail crossing between Iran and Turkey, was built in northern Kurdistan at the Qotur Canyon, with full Iranian funding. But much greater investment by the

Turkish government is needed to improve the situation. As a result of the 1991 Gulf War, these improvements will be delayed, but they can no longer be avoided.

In addition to roads, many pipelines have been built over the Kurdish territories to carry petroleum and petroleum products from Middle Eastern sources to Western markets. Others are projected for the near future.

In comparison to the importance of the return of international commercial traffic to Kurdistan, the resumption of large-scale trade in Kurdish mineral deposits and other natural resources plays only a secondary role. In fact, despite the mineral wealth of the land, the agricultural sector has the greatest potential for enriching the domestic Kurdish economy through participation in this renewed international trade (see **Agriculture**).

The most valuable by-product of investment in the transit trade is the impetus it gives to rebuilding the local subsidiary infrastructure. In comparison, mineral wealth can be exported with little requirement of improving local infrastructure. Many urban-based improvement programs, such as the laying of foundations for modern utilities, have been sponsored by Baghdad, which is far more negligent of its Arab, Shi'ite south. Of all the regions of Kurdistan, the Iraqi ones are the best developed in terms of modern infrastructure and transportation, although telecommunication is better developed in the Iranian Kurdistan.

There have been two conflicting trends in Iraqi Kurdistan: one of great expansion, and the other of vast destruction. Oddly enough, quite often while Baghdad has been rebuilding one section of Kurdistan it is destroying others, even ones it had already rebuilt. A large number of villages and smaller towns have been bulldozed out of existence, and the population moved into more manageable larger towns and cities in Iraqi Kurdistan. The August 1988 large-scale use of chemical agents on the Kurdish population in the Dahuk-Zakho-Amâdiya triangle north of Mosul can be explained only in the context of Baghdad's desire to secure the overland commercial links with Europe that it had only recently built. All the major roads, rails, and petroleum pipelines of Iraq into Turkey and beyond pass through this triangle, and the restive Kurdish population may have paid with their lives in this instance for the reopening of commercial traffic through their land.

Infrastructurally, Kurdistan of Turkey is the least developed, and since it constitutes the largest section of Kurdistan, with over half of its population, the overall level of these modern improvements in Kurdistan remains below the national averages of Iran, Iraq, Syria, and Turkey, despite the vast improvements in the Iraqi and Iranian sections.

Further Readings and Bibliography: H. Weiss and T. Cuyler Young, Jr., "The Merchants of Susa: Godin V and Plateau-Lowland Relations in the late Fourth Millennium B.C.," *Iran* XIII (1975); L.D. Levine, "East-West Trade in the Late Iron Age: A View from the Zagros," in *Le plateau iranien et l'asie centrale des origines à la conquête islamique,* No. 567 (Paris: Colloques internationaux du centre national de la recherche scientifique, 1976); T.W. Beale, "Early Trade in Highland Iran: A View from a Source Area," *World Archaeology* 5:2 (1973); G.A. Wright, *Obsidian Analysis and Prehistoric Near Eastern Trade: 7500 to 3500 BC* (Ann Arbor: University of Michigan Press, 1969).

EMPLOYMENT

Despite much lower rates of urbanization and education, Kurds demonstrate a high level of employment within their local states (see **Urbanization & Urban Centers** and **Education**).

With a state employment average of 22.3% of the population over the age of 6 in Iran, the Kurdish provinces of West Azerbaijan, Kordestân, Kirmânshâhân and Ilâm registered employment rates of 22.99%, 21.13%, 19.17%, and 17.59%, respectively, with partly Kurdish Hamadân registering 23.34%. If we consider the large refugee population of Ilâm and Kirmânshâhân brought about by the Iran-Iraq war, overall rates for Kurdistan in Iran rise to the 30% level, highest among the 24 Iranian provinces, even ahead of the Persian-dominated provinces of Kirmân and Fârs.

Employment statistics in Iran, as in other countries of residence of the Kurds, can be misleading if not qualified by other factors. For the past 30 years, the explosive population growth in the countryside, coupled with the limited investment and improvements in the agricultural sector (the largest employer), has been pushing more and more people into local urban centers and beyond. A growing proportion of able-bodied young people are emigrating out of Kurdistan altogether, maintaining only for a while their economic connection with their native land through cash remittance. The result is twofold:

1) There is decreased pressure on the limited local job markets, which are adequate to employ most of those who choose to stay behind despite the lower wages and the generally depressed economy. 2) Many of those who have sought employment outside of Kurdistan are counted as unemployed in non-Kurdish locales. This naturally gives higher employment figures in the Kurdish territories in Iran as well as Iraq, Turkey, and Syria. The local rates of employment, therefore, should not by themselves be taken as automatically implying wealth and a lively economy. They can, however, be taken to mean greater socioeconomic mobility than is common among traditional ethnic groups in the Kurdish-inhabited countries.

Cash remittance by the Kurds employed outside Kurdistan may explain the rather odd statistics that place the Kurdish provinces of Iran and Iraq near the top of the national scales for per-household expenditure. Kurdish households in Turkey might well show the same trend, even though I could find no relevant statistics.

The fact that most estimates place nearly a third of the Kurds outside Kurdistan (see **Emigrations & Diaspora**), indicates in part the continuing imbalance between the number of job-seekers and the potential of employment in local job markets. Many labor-intensive modern industries have yet to make their way into Kurdistan, and the petroleum and mining industries (see **Industries**) hire fewer people than even the traditional rug industry. Agriculture remains the most important economic sector for employment, and the fastest growth in the job market can be attained by stimulating it.

The agricultural scheme planned under the aegis of the GAP project (see **Natural Resources: Water**), could quell the emigration of young Kurdish job-seekers in Turkey, and develop the local economy by injecting it with extra cash. There are more and more agricultural laborers, as agro-industrial projects like GAP foster the cultivation of cotton, tobacco, and sugar beets spread in Kurdistan in general and Kurdistan of Turkey in particular.

With the increase in cash injected into the Kurdish economy, an increasing number of Kurds are finding local employment in services, particularly transportation. The service-oriented middle class is the most dynamic sector of Kurdish society today. As the wages and income earned through agriculture and a revitalized transportation system reinvigorate the petrified local markets of Kurdistan of Turkey with renewed local demand, more and more Kurds may choose to stay in eastern Anatolia rather than flood the western Turkish cities.

Further Readings and Bibliography: *The Population and Household Census, 1986* (Teheran: Iranian Census Bureau, 1987), the secret edition; Yacqub Sarkis, *Tobacco in Iraq: Its Existence and Cultivation a Little Before Three Hundred Years Ago* (Baghdad: 1941); Marcel Bazin and Christian Bromberger et al., *Gilân et Âzerbâyjân Oriental: Cartes et Documents Ethnographic* (Paris: Éditions Recherche sur les Civilisations, 1982).

General Bibliography

Jürgen Roth, *Geographie der Unterdrückten: die Kurden* (Hamburg: Rowohlz, 1978); M.A. Cook, ed., *Studies in the Economic History of the Middle East* (1970); *Kurdish Times*, semi-annual journal of the Kurdish Library, Brooklyn, New York, 1985-present; *Studia Kurdica*, semi-annual publication of the Centre de Recherches de l'Institut Kurde, Paris, (1984-present) with text in English, French, and the primary Middle Eastern languages.

Chapter 10

CULTURE & ARTS

POPULAR CULTURE

Kurds are fortunate to have some of the most visible aspects of their popular culture authenticated to remote antiquity. Some sections of well-known pieces of ancient literature read like compendiums to a lost encyclopedia of the Kurdish ethnic character and culture, as soon as one has identified the site of the events and the characters involved.

The most interesting evidence of the unusual antiquity of the Kurdish popular culture is in fact the oldest. Digging for the paleolithic remains at the Shanidar Caves of central Kurdistan, the archaeologist R. Solecki complains throughout the first few chapters of his excavation report book, *Shanidar: The First Flower People* (1971), of the preoccupation of his local Kurdish manual workers with wild flowers. He watches in exasperation while the Kurds continue attaching flower bouquets to their axes and picks, the water trucks, caves' walls, and of course to their already riotously colored costumes (see **Costumes & Jewelry**). He fascinates his readers when he reports laboratory results showing that a 56,000-year-old Neanderthal man, uncovered from the cave by his flower-bedecked Kurdish workers, was buried in a bed of flowers of many kinds. Old habits die hard.

This national preoccupation with flowers, or rather their colors, is one of the strongest traits of the Kurdish national culture, consistent in every niche and corner of the land and in every segment of the society—more uniform and pervasive than any other single national characteristic or trait.

This may well go back to the roots of Kurds' way of treating nature as she inhabits the mountains, like a loving treatment of one's living mate, or more: one's own doppelgänger. The rocks, the waterfalls, the animals, plants, the spirits, and the personages who inhabit them are each a constituent part of nature's whole that in its totality a Kurd seeks to simulate as a mirror image—an authentic doppelgänger. Many of these elements are revered and held in religious respect. Almost any large solitary tree growing by a spring or a natural pond is heavy with pieces of colorful cloth and ribbons fastened to its branches as a sign of vigil for a wish. The tree, the pond, and the animals living in and around them are all important elements in the picture of nature as a whole, one that is just a material reflection of the ethereal Universal Spirit. These entities often house lesser spirits, including the souls of human beings on their evolutionary passage up to the station of "human," or conversely, the spirit of those humans who are demoted to receive punishment for their previous evil lives (see **Religion: Yârsânism**). As such, they must be respected and kept from being needlessly defiled. The most important of the nature spirits is by far Khidir, "the living green man of the ponds" (see **Folklore & Folk Tales**).

The rich colors of the landscape: rocks, lichens, flowers, the varied nature of the plant and animal life all have been combined and used by this people to create a taste known pejoratively or complimentarily as "Kurdish." But any traditional Kurd will find this a compliment, a recognition of an important national trait most readily discerned by outsiders. Riotous and gaudy colors, many, many of them, thrown together seemingly haphazardly, with absolutely no control or care to match them, is the trademark of the Kurdish taste. It makes a Kurd stand out in any crowed of conventionally dressed people, in the ancient times as now. Plutarch made note of this colorfulness when singling out the costumes of the consort of the Pontian Mithridates V (*Lives: Pompey*).

Many modern appliances making it to Kurdistan are "house-broken" by being instantly painted in various colors. Graves are covered by brightly colored, gaily patterned fabrics until the time that flowers can grow on it to give rest to the soul of the dead. It is sadly amusing to non-Kurds present at the burial of a Kurdish infant that the body is treated in a fashion that a Western observer can explain only by the term *gift-wrapped*. The bright flower-patterned burial shroud is supplemented by colored bows.

Their colors are also what distinguish unmistakably the modern Kurdish paintings from others in the area and the world: the painter has seemingly no notion of "matching and coordinating" his colors, or even controlling his greed for more and more of them. The modern Kurdish painter Mansoor Ahmed announced to the audience at a recent exhibition of his works in Göttingen, Germany, "For me painting is a way of altercation and coping with a given situation. In association with colors I find my distant home, I find my own self" (see **Sculpture & Painting**).

As far as this author is aware, old Kurdish culture, as preserved in the tenets of the native Cult of Angels, is the only culture which ascribes specific colors to the seven days of the week: Sunday is red, Monday black, Tuesday white, Wednesday blue, Thursday purple or violet, Friday green, and Saturday yellow. In fact the seven divine avatars of the Universal Spirit in this religion have their own specific colors as well, with the supreme deity represented by color combination of white and blue (compare these with the seven concentric wall colorings of the the ancient Kurdish cities in **Architecture & Urban Planning**).

The themes of Kurdish folklore are those events that have taken place as a part of nature, in relation to nature, or about nature. Even the epics and war stories exalt the ultimate superiority of nature and the interconnection between man and nature. Two important cases of this man-nature relationship in the folklore are the stories of the self-alienated sculptor Farhâd and the ancient protagonist Enkidu (see **National Character**). But even in the more recent epic of *Mem o Zin*, this relationship plays its part. From the blood of Bakr, the slain antagonist, grows, as if expectedly and naturally, a thorn bush, which sends down its roots of malice between the adjoining graves of the two lovers, separating them after their death (see **Literature**).

The subject of religion is rarely used in Kurdistan to create derogatory literature and ceremonies. The exception is the Shi'ite regions and the ceremony of *omar sowzân*, i.e., the burning of Umar. Umar was the third Muslim Caliph in the 7th century. He is highly respected by the Sunnis, but the subject of abuse by all Shi'ites, who consider him a usurper. Effigies of Umar are burned at stakes on the anniversary of his assassination in the Shi'ite-dominated regions of Kurdistan, but particularly where Sunnis are also present in some numbers. A large number of abusive rhymes and signing accompany the ceremony, giving it on the whole rather a carnival air, as children's participation is also encouraged. Many folk theaters also participate to make the occasion as splendid—and abusive to the Sunnis—as possible (see **Theater & Motion Pictures**). Bloody riots can break out, ending in tragedies for all sides, but every year the ceremony is repeated. Paradoxically, under the revolutionary Islamic Shi'ite rule in Iran, the ceremony has been banned, in an attempt to reduce the degree of alienation of non-Shi'ites from the regime.

Certain Sufi orders, like the Rafâ'is (see **Sufi Mystic Orders**), or quasi-Sufi orders practice some ancient rites of magical quality. They entail drum beatings, chanting of names and formulas, and bodily motions meant to bring about a state of trance in which the physical body may be tormented and tortured without any pain brought on to the subject or any lasting effects after the process is completed and the state of trance is broken. Driving swords and other sharp objects into the limbs, tongues, and the sides of the trunk take place at such moments of ecstasy. Fire walking or flame inhaling are also reported to be common practices.

Faith-healing also takes place at just such ceremonies, but the belief in its curing power is not as strong or as widespread as, say, in the church-based faith-healing ceremonies in the United States.

Further Readings and Bibliography: R. Solecki, *Shanidar: The First Flower People* (New York: Alfred Knopf, 1971); Patty Jo Watson, *Archaeological Ethnography in Western Iran* (Tucson: University of Arizona Press, 1979); Margaret Kahn, *The Children of the Jinn* (New York: Seaview, 1980); Dana Adams Schmidt, *Journey Among the Brave Men* (Boston: Little, Brown, 1964); A.M. Hamilton, *Road Through Kurdistan* (London: Faber and Faber, 1937); W.R. Hay, *Two Years in Kurdistan* (London: Sidgwick and Jackson, 1921), William O. Douglas, *Strange Lands and Friendly People* (New York, 1951); Roderic Hill, *The Baghdad Air Mail* (London: Edward Arnold, 1929); E.B. Soane, *To Mesopotamia and Kurdistan in Disguise* (London: Johny Murray, 1912); Sally Binford, "A Structural Comparison of Disposal of the Dead in the Mousterian and Upper Paleolithic," *Southwestern Journal of Anthropology* XXIV-2 (1968); Marcel Bazin and Christian Bromberger, et al., *Gilân et Âzerbâyjân Oriental: Cartes et Documents Ethnographic* (Paris: Éditions Recherche sur les civilisations, 1982); J.C.A. Johnson, "The Kurds of Iraq," *Geographical Magazine* 11 (1940); Mark Sykes, *The Caliph's Last Heritage* (New York: Arno Press, 1973, reprint of the 1915 London edition); Henry Rawlinson, *Journey from Zohab to Khuzistan* (London, 1836); Major Frederick Millingen, *Wild Life Among the Koords* (London, 1870).

FOLKLORE & FOLK TALES

The largest body of Kurdish folk tales can be grouped together as "Kurdish winter stories." These all happen in long, cold, and if one is not very cautious, dangerous Kurdish winters. They are full of maxims and punch lines regarding the proper coping with the hazards of the season and ways to avoid them by learning from the failures and victories of various characters in the stories. They are quite simple and attractive stories, masterfully hiding their witty finale from the guesses of the listeners.

Children's stories keep close to natural events, with bears, still abundant in the forests, playing the combined role of many other animals that appear in other children's literature the world over. In the stories for adults, bears, beavers, foxes, and in fact the trees, all are intelligent beings like people, with sophisticated lives and codes of honor. In these stories, for example, any fine-looking man or woman is thought susceptible to being kidnapped by some beauty-loving bear for a mate. The bear takes care of the person and feeds and intelligently tends to his or her needs, except for one: freedom. These stories always end with a tender observation on the bear's intelligence, kindness, amorousness, and "humanity" upon its eventual killing to free the captive. These animals are presented in the stories as being able to master the human language, by which they can outwit the cleverest of humans, or when by donning human costumes a bear can pass as one.

In fact in one story, the bear is depicted as a human being who, in order not to host a stranger who has just dropped in, hides himself under a heap of wool he has just sheared from his sheep. He instructs his wife to let the stranger know that he cannot be entertained, as her husband is away. The stranger just happens to be none other than the nature spirit Khidir himself, who always travels in disguised form (see below). All-knowing Khidir replies that in fact the man of the house is not present, since the one who is hiding under the wool is no longer a man. To the inhospitable man's body instantly adheres the wool he is hiding under. He loses the power of speech, and becomes the first bear. Learning his lesson, the bear is a very honorable creature, who having been human once, still understands human language but can no longer talk back.

To the folk stories may be added those of religious character, of which the Kurds have a rich repertoire. The most common ones are those connected with Khidir. Khidir, his name meaning "green" or "crawler," is an omnipresent personality which permeates the land and water environments. He dwells primarily in deep, still ponds. As one of the major avatars of the Universal Spirit, Khidir is omniscient, and possesses considerable supernatural powers, but particularly over the natural forces, plant and animal kingdoms. He can also be called to come to a person's help, if he/she performs a special cleansing ceremony (see also **Festivals, Ceremonies, & Calendar**). One who desires a visit by Khidir must prepare for 40 days, as if for a visit by a great guest. The house, even the garden and the sidewalks outside the house door, must be cleaned, and foods and condiments prepared every day. If the ritual is done properly and to the liking of Khidir, he appears on the 40th day in a disguised form. It is up to the person to recognize Khidir and ask for a boon. Admittedly, Khidir is very tricky (his arrival is marked by an overwhelming sleepiness descending on the hapless boon-seeker) and ingenious in his disguises, and seldom does anyone get to recognize him until it is too late and Khidir is gone.

Another important figure with a fair number of folk stories surrounding him is Shâh Khushin, a major avatar of the Spirit. The folk story of the birth of Shâh Khushin is particularly important since it sheds a good deal of light on the less clear stories and legends in the Mithraic (Sun God) cycle of creation, as they are preserved in surviving texts regarding this ancient, Gnostic religion. The strong religious symbolism of this story is worthy of special note.

In the story Shâh Khushin is conceived when his mother, the virgin Mâmâ Jalâla, at the daily ritual of bowing before the rising sun, is impregnated by a sun ray, which enters her throat when she sinfully yawns during the ritual. When signs of pregnancy become apparent, Jalâla's father orders her six brothers (adding up to the holy seven including herself) to murder her for the shame she has brought to the family. Their sword-bearing arms are petrified in the air before they can strike her. A voice is heard from within her, with which the fetus declares himself a new (bâbâ) avatar of the Spirit. The pregnancy lasts only 21 days (i.e., the multiplication of the two sacred numbers 3 and 7; see **Cult of Angels**).

At the time of her labor, Khushin emerges from his mother's mouth as a radiant speck of light, which then lands in a golden basin provided for the birth, changing into a fully conversant man-child. News of a hostile army arriving to destroy the land is immediately heard. Trying to escape, the radiant child cannot be picked up, even though a hundred men are put to the task. They try instead to hide the infant under a golden basin for protection, but he cannot be lifted, as he seems to be the earth itself. Mâmâ Jalâla speaks, asserting that the only way to move the child is to let him ride on a bull, sitting still in his gold basin. They did so and thus moved on. Khushin grew up to assume his role as avatar of the Spirit at age 32, and disappears under the waves of the Gâmâsiyâb River at the age of 61, where he lives forever.

All the elements of symbolism in this story are familiar to anyone familiar with the cosmogonical tradition of ancient Mithraism: the conception by a sun ray, the bull , and the golden basin.

Stories like these are among the most valuable pieces of literature that can cast light into the darker periods of Kurdish history and culture. The folk story about the the virgin birth of Khushin may also help clarify the reason behind the immaculate conception of other important divine avatars in the Cult of Angels, some of whom were conceived without a father or mother. In fact other interesting correspondences between the legend of Shâh Khushin and some other religions can be observed. His annunciation at age 32 is one year short of the age at which Christ is believed to have been taken to the Cross, and his disappearance below the waters at age 61 is one year short of the age at which the Prophet Muhammad is considered to have died.

There are also various folk stories connected with the very question of the origin of the Kurdish nation. Some of these stories have been known for so long as to have been recorded by the medieval authors. The most famous one, not surprisingly, connects the Kurds with the king Âzhi Dahâk (see **Cult of Angels**). The story, as it is recorded in the epic *Shâhnâma*, maintains that the Kurds sprang from the imprisoned young men who were secretly set free by two stewards of Âzhi Dahâk. They were given goats and sheep by the former for their livelihood, hence also the origin of herding among the Kurds. The Kurdish Jews maintained that the Kurds were instead the outcome of another event, involving king Solomon. The folk story holds that Solomon, who ruled over all mankind, beasts, and genies, sent the latter to collect for his harem 100 of the most beautiful maidens on earth. Their accomplishment of the task coincided with the death of Solomon, upon which the genies took the maidens for themselves and settled in the inaccessible mountains. The offspring of these strange marriages were the Kurds, who in their elusiveness resemble their genie forefathers and in their handsomeness their foremothers. The pejorative title "children of the jinn [genies]" is still occasionally given to the Kurds by many of their ethnic neighbors.

Many early Islamic historians give account of folk beliefs that connected the Kurdish origins with some Arab forefathers. The interesting point in these is the fact that they almost always have two persons, one named "Kurd" and the other "Mard," among the folk genealogies for the Kurds. Mards were of course a very old and large community that populated western Kurdistan (the city of Mardin still preserves their name). The combination of the two names in these genealogies might possibly hint at an early ethnic merger and homogenization. Some other folk tales maintain that the Kurds are the descendants of the lost tribes of Israel.

Further Readings and Bibliography: Abdul-Kader Amin (collected by), *Kurdish Proverbs* (New York: Kurdish Library, 1989); M. Mokri, *L'Arménie dans le Folklore kurde* (Paris: Librairie Kliencksieck, 1964); D.N. MacKenzie, *Kurdish Dialect Studies*, vol. II, *Texts and Folk Stories* (London: Oxford University Press, 1962); Major E. Noel, "The Character of the Kurds as Illustrated by Their Proverbs and Popular Sayings," *Bulletin of the School of Oriental Studies* I-iv (London, 1917-20); Basile Nikitine, "Kurdish Stories from My Collection," *Bulletin of the School of Oriental and African Studies* IV (1926-28).

FESTIVALS, CEREMONIES & CALENDAR

The Kurdish calendar is a solar one, consisting of 365 days, with the remaining natural few hours being marked by a leap year every fourth year. It starts with the exact first day of spring (March 20 or 21, depending on the Gregorian calendar), and has been set on an astonishingly accurate footing by none else than Omar Khayyam, the Persian mathematician and astronomer, better known in the West for his quatrain poetry, the *Rubbayat*. Except for the names of the months and the original starting year, the Kurdish calendar is identical to those of the ethnic Persians and other Iranic peoples.

In this calendar the first six months of spring and summer are each 31 days long, and those of fall and winter are 30 days each. The exception is the last winter month (the 12th in the annual calendar), which is 29 days normally, but 30 in the leap years. The months coincide with the 12 zodiacal signs, i.e., the first month is identical with the duration of Aries, the second with Taurus, the third with Gemini, and so on. The names of the Kurdish months are *Khâkalewa, Bânamar, Jozardân, Pushpar, Galâwezh, Kharmânân, Razbar, Khazalawar, Sarmâwaz, Bafranbâr, Rebandân*, and *Rashama*. The calendar begins with the year that marks the fall of the last Kurdish kingdom of the classical era, the House of Kayus (or the Kâvusakân dynasty), in AD 380 (see **Classical History**) plus an enigmatic seven extra years. The extra seven years may be connected with the veneration with which the number is held in the native Kurdish religions and would be the time needed for the reincarnation of the souls of departed leaders (see **Cult of Angels**). It is now (AD 1992) the year 1605. This calendar has been variously called *Kurdi* (Kurdish) or *Mây'i* (Median). An alternative beginning for the calendar is the common Muslim era, marked by the Prophet Muhammad's departure from Mecca to take up residence at Medina (July 16, 622 AD), and is now (AD 1992) the year 1371 of *Hajira*.

As expected, this native calendar is strongly promoted by the Kurdish nationalists, while the pan-Islamic lunar calendar is allowed to serve Muslim religious purposes. In reality, however, depending under which administrative jurisdiction they live now, the Kurds seldom get to use their native calendar, which clashes, with notable exception of Iran, with the official state calendars.

In Iraq and Syria, the Western Gregorian calendar is observed unchanged for all governmental purposes, except for the nomenclature of the months, which is replaced by the ancient Aramaic. In Turkey and the territories of the former Soviet Union, the Gregorian calendar is used without any change.

In Iran the old Zoroastrian calendar, identical in every way to the native Kurdish calendar (except for the nomenclature), is used by the state. As with the Kurdish calendar, it is also the year 1371 of Hajira in the Iranian state calendar (AD 1992).

With such a diversity of calendars in official use, the average Kurd is expectedly confused about the timing if not the importance of traditional festivals and ceremonies— even the primary ones.

The all-important Kurdish national festival remains that of the new year, or *New Ruz* (pronounced "naw rooz" in northern Kurdistan, "ni roz" in western Kurdistan, and "no rooz" in the south), on March 21. This is a long ceremony that may stretch over a period of one week or more.

Many specific foods and condiments are prepared in advance, special flowers are grown for the occasion (narcissuses, tulips, and hyacinths), and pussy willow and quince branches covered with fresh buds are cut and made to adorn the feast. New cloths are worn, and some old pottery is broken for good luck. People visit each other's houses, and old feuds and misunderstandings are to be set to rest because of the occasion. Gifts are given by seniors to their juniors in age, and the high-ranking social figures are paid visits, and brought gifts.

In southern, eastern, and central Kurdistan New Ruz festivals are preceded by a few days by another observation of a very interesting night ceremony. Bonfires are lit on the rooftops or in the streets to mark the passing of the dark (winter) season, and the arrival of the light (spring) season. Fire crackers and missiles are lit to scare off the evil spirits, and a thought is given to the deceased, who are believed to visit their living relatives and to rejoice in their happiness.

In western and northern Kurdistan, this ceremony is known as *Tuldân* (possibly from the verb *tul haldân,* Kurdish for "atonement"). It is observed by lighting two lamps and keeping them lit until the following morning. It is believed in these parts of Kurdistan that the holy and mysterious figure Khizir Ilyâs or Khidir Nabi, loosely identified with the Prophet Elijah, visits all homes during the night in which the two lamps are kept lit. He brings gifts of blessings, happiness, and longevity to those he visits (see **Folklore & Folk Tales**). The religious background of these festivals is provided in the section on **Religion**.

Since the establishment of the Turkish Republic and the change of its common Julian calendar to Gregorian, the ceremony of Tuldân among the Kurdish community there has been pushed back from March 9 to February 14. Among some remoter communities, Tuldân is observed much earlier than the vernal equinox—as early, in fact, as the winter solstice. The exiled Kurdish communities in the central Alburz mountains (having arrived there largely from Anatolia around 400 years ago) celebrate Tuldân on August 31.

In other ceremonies attached to Tuldân, torches are lit and carried in the streets, celebrating the triumph of an ancient, unknown monarch over his enemies and that of the people. It has unconvincingly been suggested by modern Kurdish intellectuals that Tuldân may mark the occasion of the triumph of the mythical Aryan hero Feridon over the demon Dahâk, as set forth in the Zoroastrian holy book the *Avesta*. In such assertions these sources neglect the fact that, in their indigenous myths, Dahâk is the Kurdish hero, and Feridon the villain! A more unlikely explanation provided by the Kurdish general and historian Ihsân Nuri Pâshâ is that the occasion marks the triumph of the Median king Cyaraxes the Great over Madyes, the Scythian usurper of his throne and kingdom (c. 625 BC). Nuri Pâshâ provides no argument to support this implausible suggestion.

The populous Shakâk, Begzâda, and Jalâli tribes do not observe the New Ruz or Tuldân festivals, and instead attach great importance to the Islamic festivals of the *Id Fitr* (end of the fasting month of Ramadan) and the Feast of Abraham (*Id Adhâ* or *Qurbân Bâyrâm*), marking the annual conclusion of the *Hajj*, the Muslim pilgrimage to Mecca. There are many other festivals observed locally by various Kurdish groups, such as those religious festivals and holidays of the Sunni and Shi'ite Muslims, as well as Yezidi, Yârsân, and Alevi occasions. Festivals such as that of Khizir Ilyâs or Khidir Nabi (a detached part of the larger Tuldân festival), even though non-Islamic like New Ruz, are observed widely by Muslim Kurds, even by the Shakâk, Begzâda, and Jalâli, who do not observe Now Ruz.

Except for the pan-Kurdish New Ruz, and to a lesser degree, the Tuldân, the pre-Islamic festivals are far more popular among the followers of the Cult of Angels than Islam. Of the four religious feasts of the Yezidis, for example, two correspond by a few days more or less to the great Aryan festivals of Now Ruz (Yezidis observe it in mid-April instead of the customary March 21), *Tiragân* (Yezidis observe it on July 30 instead of the customary July 5). Messina has documented the observance of Tiragân among the Kurds of Adiabene of the 3rd century AD (Messina 1938).

Of the two other feasts, and the most important one for the Yezidis is the seven-day-long feast of *Jami Mazin*, or "Great Jam," which occurs between the 6th and 13th of October. The fourth festival, called for the birth of Yezid, coincides, with a few days' discrepancy, with the birth or emergence of the god Mithras on December 25. The connection between these two feasts and the ancient cult of Mithraism is discussed under **Yezidism**.

To avoid persecution, and when not holding secret observance of them, the non-Muslim Kurds have at various times tried, for their community's safety, to give an Islamic appearance to their indigenous religious festivals by matching them with Islamic feasts. The matching of *Âyini Jam*, celebrated by the Dimila Alevis, to the Islamic Feast of Abraham, and the Yârsâns' and Alevis' adoption of Ali (the first Shi'ite Muslim imam) as the patron of their religion, and the attribution to him of the origin of almost all their festivals, are just such precautionary measures.

In Iran, home to many other Iranic peoples like the Kurds themselves, most Kurdish festivals are identical to the state and national festivals. Thus Kurds have not found the observances of their festivals a grounds for political friction. In Iraq, New Ruz is an official state holiday. In Syria, where an Arab Alevi, Hafez al-Assad, is the president, the Kurdish New Ruz is again not an alien celebration, even though it is not a recognized state holiday. The Arab Alevis celebrate New Ruz just as the Kurds do. There has been, however, some reports of harassment of the celebrating Kurds in the past.

In the Soviet Union, all non-Communist, local celebrations were suppressed in favor of the state-sanctioned celebrations of Communist historical events. In addition to the Kurds, the celebration of New Ruz is also common among all the indigenous Muslim populations of the former Soviet Union, from the Volga Tatars and Bâshkirs to the Azeris and Turkmens, Uzbeks, Tâjiks, and Kâzâkhs of central Asia. These are the nationalities who have been deeply influenced by Iranic culture. With the recent demise of the Soviet Union, there is unlikely to remain any state-imposed restrictions on celebrating Kurdish or any other local feasts.

Again, only in Turkey do Kurds find themselves most disadvantaged. Many Kurdish festivals, such as the New Ruz and Tuldân, have taken the form of strong anti-government political expressions. This and every other Kurdish festival was strictly forbidden by state laws, and the defiant participants in the celebrations had even been shot at. Recently, however, the Turkish government has extended recognition to the Alevi religion and the festivals associated with it, such as the festival of Hâji Bektâsh, the founder of the Bektâshi Sufi order (see **Recent History**). On occasion now, Ankara even officially sponsors these Alevi feasts. Other Kurdish celebrations are no longer forbidden, but discouraged.

Interestingly, on American Public Radio on the occasion of the New Ruz of 1991, every jubilant citizen of Diyârbakir, even the elders, when asked the meaning behind the New Ruz missed the correct answer. Besides being the beginning of a new year on the Kurdish calendar, all the tradition and folklore behind the New Ruz appeared to have been lost to them, even those in Diyârbakir, the so-called capital of Turkey's Kurdistan. As a matter of course this was quickly blamed on the Turkish state policy of discouraging anything Kurdish for so many years. It should however be noted that a more oppressive regime in the neighboring Soviet Union never succeeded in confusing the many nationalities of the former USSR who also celebrated the New Ruz. After 70 years of Communist suppression, these too resumed its observation in 1991. This represented an even longer denial than to the western and northern Kurds in Turkey. No evident confusion regarding the meaning or the history of the feast of New Ruz, however, is encountered among these ex-Soviet nationalities. The truth may then lie more with the fact that New Ruz was never as involving an occasion in western and northern Kurdistan (areas north of the ancient north-south cultural divide; see **Internal Subdivisions**) as in other parts of Kurdistan.

Many other Kurdish traditions taken for granted by the Iranian and Iraqi Kurds have also been little more than curiosities in far western and northern Kurdistan in Turkey. Since these latter sections of the Kurdish nation together constitute the majority of the Kurds, it persuades one to ask the question as to which Kurdish traditions are to be taken as national and which as local in Kurdistan, regardless of their external prestige. Is Tuldân, which is practiced widely by the northern and western Kurds, i.e., the majority of the Kurds, not to replace New Ruz as the most important Kurdish national celebration? Perhaps New Ruz has just been getting better press because of the prominence that its staunchest adherents—the Iraqi and Iranian Kurds—have been enjoying through their more frequent popular uprisings.

Whatever the earlier influence of the New Ruz celebration, the western and northern Kurds seem to have resolved to celebrate this national festival, at least as a unifying political expression. As such, every passing year witnesses a larger (and sometimes violent) participation of the Kurds in this and other long-forbidden ethnic celebrations in Turkey.

Family-level celebrations vary even more widely in their conduct and importance than the national ones. Marriages and funerals are important events. Marriage may take up to seven days of celebrations for the well-to-do families, or may be a single-day event for the common villagers. Gifts are exchanged between the wedding families. The bride brings with her a dowry equal to the ceremonial bride price and the agreed-upon alimony to be collected if the marriage ends in divorce. On the seventh day of the marriage, the couple visits close relatives, receiving more presents for their new lives.

The death of a person is remembered on the third, seventh, and 40th days and the first anniversary. This ceremony as it is observed by the more conservative families can be quite an unsettling practice to behold, as the women deeply scratch their faces with their fingernails periodically, bloodying their cheeks and foreheads. Mud or clay is poured on the head, creating a most pitiful scene. The French archaeologist and traveller Jacques de Morgan reports a funeral scene in which the head of the dead is struck by a club "to let out the evil spirit trapped inside" (1895, 39-40). This ancient practice, also common to many neighboring ethnic groups, is now gone.

The ceremony of circumcision of male children calls for a celebration. Traditionally, it takes place late in the summer "when cantaloupes are in season," about 5 years after the birth of the child. In much more localized, and limited numbers, female children are subjected to clitoridectomy by some followers of the Cult of Angels. The actual act of excision is done without celebration, and if possible, under certain venerated trees by the shrines of Khizir, "the living green man of the ponds" (see **Cult of Angels**). The practice continues in extreme secrecy and very limited numbers to this day, as it is abhorred by the overwhelming majority of Kurds, who are afraid of its potential to give them a "bad name." According to United Nations data, clitoridectomy is practiced in 26 African and in more isolated cases in most Middle Eastern countries, affecting about 100 million women overall. There are no clear ideas as to the place or time of the origin of this practice.

Further Readings and Bibliography: Mohammed Mokri, *Les rites magiques dans les fêtes du "Dernier Mercredi de l'Année" en Iran* (Teheran: Teheran University Press, 1963); Mohammed Mokri, "Le Mariage chez les Kurdes," *Revue de la Société d'Ethnographie* (Paris, 1962); Jacques de Morgan, *Relation sommaire d'un voyage en perse et dans le kurdistan* (Paris, 1895); P. G. Messina, "La celebrazione de Tiragan in Adiabene," *Proceedings of the International Congress of the Orientalists* (Rome, 1938).

DANCE

Traditional Kurdish dance falls within the tradition of hand-holding group dances observed from the Balkans to Lebanon, the Caucasus, and Iran. This dance formation is called *govand* or *gowand* in Kurdish (more familiar to the Western audience through the Lebanese *Dabka* dance). It is almost always a form of round dancing, with a single or a couple of figure dancers often added to the geometrical center of the dancing circle. The Kurdish dancers on the circular path consist, usually, of alternating men and women holding hands and colorful handkerchiefs, in a semi-circle, and moving around the circle with the leading and trailing persons waving their kerchiefs in elaborate motions. The leading individual often accentuates the customary steps and motions for the dance by displaying more energy or even by adding to the standard moves some of his own personal liking.

The group dances divide into two distinct groups. The slow and graceful types are performed by the hand-holding dancers pulling close together and pressing their shoulders tightly against each other, performing the most elaborate and complicated steps of any group dancing. They occasionally change direction, by facing their leading partner to his/her back, while never breaking their original hand hold. They reverse this back and forth several times. In some slow dances, performers hold the hands of every second person on their side by passing their arms behind their immediate dancing partner to each of their sides. Whenever the man-woman-man-woman formation is possible, this last style result in all men holding each others' hands, while the women achieve the same thing from behind each other. This principle is the same as fabric weaving, and in fact the dancers resemble weaving when performing.

In the fast dances, the performers loosen up their holds on each other, and gradually spread out as the dance tempo increases. In this style of dancing too the performers alternately face the center of the circle or the back of their leading partner when moving around the circle.

When the two individual figure dancers are present at the center of the dancing circle, they face each other, and weaving to and fro the kerchiefs, perform certain customary steps, including dropping down to the ankles and popping up straight in quick succession, as is better known in the Caucasian dances. More often, however, the center figure dancers relay through their steps and mime a story of love. In one, the dancing girl refuses the love of the dancing man who offers her successively money, jewelry, and a sword. But she accepts him when he offers her the stem of a flower (see **Popular Culture**).

A great many variations of the styles are present in different parts of Kurdistan, with the style of northwest Kurdistan, i.e., of the Dimilas of Darsim, being the most elaborate.

Among the better-known fast dances are the *Hây Nara, Yâla, Niri, Darsim, Shaykhâne, Chupi,* and *Halparika.* In *Chupi,* the figure dancers in the center sometimes use sticks to perform a dance that depicts a mock face off between two lovers fighting for the favor of their mutual beloved, or simply a mock battle scene.

The dancers are usually accompanied by the sound of a drum (*Duhul*), and a powerful oboe (*Surnâ/Zurnâ*). Less often a tambura is added to the musical ensemble, or instead of the *Surnâ* (see **Music**). In southern Kurdistan, especially, the musicians often double as singers, adding popular lyrics to their dancing music.

Dancing has become more and more a social and political statement among the Kurds. With their culture having been strongly discouraged or banned for generations in Turkey, and for a long time in Syria, to dance Kurdish is to break the local oppressive rules and assert the group's identity. As such, one sees Kurdish fighters, the *peshmerga,* dancing in their guerrilla uniforms, and Kurdish politicians, academics, and professionals dancing in their Western attire all the same at any gathering—in or outside Kurdistan— all making the same statement. General Mustafâ Bârzâni, the legendary Kurdish leader, used to say, "One who cannot dance is not a Kurd."

Despite this, individual dancing is becoming more popular, as the global village gradually consumes Kurdistan as well. The younger generation in the major cities has already made up its mind, and except for the traditional ceremonies, festivals, or making a nationalistic statement, has gone over to the Western modern style of dancing.

Further Readings and Bibliography: T.F. Aristova, "Poyezdka k Kurdam Zakavka'ya," *Sovetskaya Etnografiya* VI (Moscow, 1958).

THEATER & MOTION PICTURES

There exists a very old tradition of village theater in Kurdistan, with its center of gravity in southern and parts of eastern Kurdistan. The surprising wealth of indigenous theatrical styles, stories, and forms surviving until now has translated into the emergence of a large number of contemporary playwrights, novelists, cinematographers, and actors, who have found exceptional success and fame in Iran (where eastern and southern Kurdistan are basically located).

If we had to place the roots of this art in Kurdish history, we may look at least as far back as the Hellenistic period (4th to 2nd century BC). At that time a large number of Greek city-states were established in the Zagros mountains, with their numerical center of gravity in modern Luristân. These Greeks and their Hellenized fellow citizens soon developed their favorite pasttimes: theater and gymnasia. Whatever the source, these two remain the favorite pasttimes of the common Kurds, in the form of village theater (primarily in southern and eastern Kurdistan) and wrestling matches in the village squares and gymnasia in the cities (all over Kurdistan).

Despite their popularity, these theatrical presentations are simple in theme and therefore easy to stage. In one such play in southern Kurdistan, the local miller powders his beard with flour and becomes the old man of the plot, and a boy wraps a scarf borrowed from a female relative around his face to represent a female character. A piece of rock plays the role of valuable merchandise, a pillow to which a rope is fastened serves as a pet goat, and a heavy-set woman walks on her hands and feet and moos to represent a cow. A light-weight old woman rides on her hip as the owner of the cow. Each villager brings in a few items to serve as relevant props, and when a player is worn down in the middle of the show, he or she is replaced by another villager, and all provide a joyous and comical time for the crowd.

The *Kulaka Kâli* (the pumpkin planting) or *Bussân Bussân* (vegetable garden) is a two-man show. In one version of this, one of the actors hides behind the other and stretches his arms from under the arms of the other, pretending that his arms are the that of the player. The person in front hides his arms behind himself. While the man in front tells a story, the one behind makes clever hand gestures befitting the story, amusing the spectators.

In another form of two-actor play, a pantomime in fact, the actors engage each other in comical, slapstick corporal abuse, which always end with a moral message, not too dissimilar from moralistic endings along Chaplinesque lines.

Finally, there are plays in which the conversations are all in verse, and the players need to memorize the lines in advance.

Some plays include puppet shows intermingled with real people. Rods are driven into the sleeves and legs of costumes, and handled from behind as life-size marionettes. The mixed play and puppet shows and the versified plays are, however, fewer in frequency than the others, as they require a good deal of advance preparation on the part of the players and a dexterity that only a few in the community may be able to muster.

The plays also serve as a source of income for those members of the village community who do not farm, such as the village guards, barbers, and the bath keeper, if there is one. At the end of harvest season in autumn, they enact a play in which they appear at the doorsteps of the village houses (entering the yard, if there is one) and feign an argument and fight between a man and his wife over household expenses, while others play the role of the children, mediators, etc. What is collected helps the actors with their winter provisions.

The shadow theater, *Kosa Kâli*, is far less popular in the south than in western and northern Kurdistan, where it predominates over other forms of folk theater. In fact in Anatolia since the 16th century the ethnic Turks have with much enthusiasm adopted this form of theatrical art, which they call *Karagoz*, "dark eyes." There is no consensus as to the origins of the shadow play in Kurdistan or the Middle East in general. It likely is not, however, Egyptian, as is sometimes held, since even the name of the shadow play in Egypt is a corrupted form of the Turkish. There are some indirect remarks by Plato that suggest that he was familiar with the art. But even this would only confirm the antiquity of shadow theater in the region, and not its origin.

These indigenous Kurdish plays are totally different from the Shi'ite tradition of passion plays in Iran and Iraq, and among the small Kurdish Shi'ite community, they are just a welcome addition to these theatrical presentations. The passion plays are, at any rate, absent from among the non-Shi'ite Kurds.

The tradition of village theater seems to be a natural counterpart to the long tradition of balladry and travelling storytellers so embedded in the popular culture of the Kurds (see **Music**). One would naturally expect the wealth of traditional Kurdish theater to have prompted the production of a large body of modern literature to explore it. To the best of my knowledge, this has yet to happen, at least in Western languages. Many works dealing with traditional Kurdish theater are available in Kurdish and other Middle Eastern languages, however. The most recent works are those of Ali-Ashraf Dervishiân, himself a novelist, playwright, amd writer of children's stories, who has collected a wealth of native Kurdish village theatrical plays. In volume two of his work, *Kurdish Fables, Theatrical Plays and Games* (1988), Dervishiân gives the plots of many plays and reports on the preparation, production, and staging of them.

One may cite this kind of native background for those Kurdish themes as having served to produce two highly acclaimed motion pictures in Turkey and Iran. *The Husband of Miss Gazelle*, a novel by Ali Muhammed Afghani (a native of Kirmânshâh), was based on the life of a Kurdish woman whose husband marries a second wife. It caused a sensation in Iranian literary circles in 1961 and became an enduring best-seller in the country. Its clear theatrical qualities enabled it subsequently to be adapted for theater, television, and a popular motion picture. *Yol,* Turkish for "path," was produced by the Anatolian Kurdish filmmaker Yilmaz Günay, highlighting the effects of a depressed economy and an undereducated society on personal relationships among common people, including women's family and social conditions as Kurdistan moves into the modern world. Günay's work received major international awards, being acclaimed as a masterpiece, while the producer himself was serving a term in prison in Turkey.

Despite their highly acclaimed talent, Afghani and Günay both use almost exclusively Kurdish themes and in this respect can be artistically labeled as "provincial." They seldom, if ever, detach the plot or the players in the productions from their Kurdish sentiments and thus never treat any character as just a person, but rather as a Kurdish person. This is not however a universal phenomenon among Kurdish playwrights and film producers.

Further Readings and Bibliography: Valuable biographies of some Kurdish playwrights and film directors living overseas are found in Robin Schneider, ed., *Kurden im Exil: Ein Handbuch kurdischer Kultur, Politik und Wissenschaft* (Berlin: Berliner Institut für Vergleichende Sozialforschung, dem Haus der Kulturen der Welt and medico international, 1991), section 2; see also Ali-Ashraf Dervishiân, *Kurdish Fables, Theatrical Plays, and Games* (Teheran: Nashr-i Ruz Publisher, 1988), text in Kurdish and Persian.

DECORATIVE DESIGNS & MOTIFS

The earliest time for which enough archaeological evidence is available to propose the existence of a reasonably unified artistic school in Kurdistan is the Halaf Period (ca. 6000-5000 BC). A clear artistic unity is immediately observed in the decorative motifs of the painted potteries of almost all the peoples inhabiting the modern Kurdish lands from the Amanus Range on the Mediterranean to the ancient mound of Ali Kush on the south of Kurdistan. The southern limits of Halaf culture coincided with the limits of dry farming and the beginning of the flat plains, as do the limits of Kurdistan. The northern borders of this culture are less well known, due to less archaeological investigation in the off-limits, strategic northern and northwestern Kurdistan in Turkey (Map 12). The degree of basic artistic unity among the people of Halaf culture has made some actually propose the existence of a distinct ethnic group who practiced it (Roaf 1990, 51).

Halaf culture is most commonly known for its wealth of attractively and colorfully painted pottery, fired in two-chamber kilns. It is not difficult to see the wealth of local wild flowers as the models for most of these design, and a further surprise is the survival of many of those Halaf period basic designs until the present day in the motifs of Kurdish textiles and decorations (Mellaart 1975).

Because of its distinctive designs and notable craftsmanship, Halaf pottery is relatively easy to identify. As such, it has been found in many localities outside the boundaries of this culture, pointing to an active trade between Kurdistan and the outside economies at this early period—a practice which strongly supported the overall Kurdish economy until the beginning of the 16th century AD (see **Trade**).

The Halaf culture is followed by the Hurrian period in Kurdish cultural history, which started about 3000 BC and lasted until the coming of the Indo-European immigrants into Kurdistan and the aryanization of Kurdish society and culture in about the middle of the 2nd millennium BC (see **Historical Migrations**). The Hurrian cultural period carries strong marks of exchange with the neighboring peoples, and evidence of brisk trade of merchandise and ideas between Kurdistan and Mesopotamia, the Iranian Plateau, and beyond (Mellink 1966). The artifacts of the end of the Hurrian period found at the archaeological sites of Ziwiya and Hasanlu mark the transitional time from this period into the Aryan cultural period, which still continues in Kurdistan to this day.

Artifacts found at the village of Ziwiya in eastern Kurdistan (ancient Mannaean city of Izzibia) incorporate some of the most interesting designs of these ancient Kurds. The "Ziwiyeh Treasure," as the find is known to art galleries around the world where its priceless objects are still being sold off, contains not just the temporal links between modern Kurdish decorative designs and motifs with those of the Halaf culture, but also crucial clues the religious art and mythology of the ancient Kurds (Godard 1950). The Ziwiya treasure is supplemented by the rich finds at yet another Mannaean city at Hassanlu (east of Shnu and north of Ziwiya), dating to about the same time as the former (9th century BC). Hasanlu finds provide crucial comparison and supporting evidence for any artistic and cultural hypotheses that can be drawn based on either one of these finds alone (Dyson and Voigt 1989).

But it is not necessary to rely solely on ancient pottery for evidence of this continuity. Contemporary body markings may serve as totally different, and yet living, examples of the resiliency of many other motifs. It is reasonable to believe that the first decorative expressions by mankind involved self-grooming and body painting, with relevant supernatural and magical powers subsequently attached to them. Yet body painting, from the common use of colored cosmetics to more permanent tattoos, are still with us everywhere in the world today.

Kurdish men and women frequently wore tattoos (*kutra'i* in Kurdish), and continue to do so with less frequency to this day. Some figurines from the Halaf culture, for example, carry markings on the breast and face which can be interpreted as body markings (von Oppenheim 1931; Field 1958).

Most if not all tattooing is done nowadays for its magical and perceived healing properties, and much less for beauty (Field 1958, 24). As such, each motif has the value of a verse or a holy formula which cannot be altered without losing its power. These markings are of considerable antiquity, and are "living" examples of many ancient design motifs preserved in this way.

Many surviving tattoo styles and motifs support this hypothesis, telling of a relationship between them and the motifs used for other religious or secular purposes. The male tattoo motifs of combs and the sun and seven stars, for example, are also found adorning the outer walls of the Yezidi shrine of Shaykh Adi at Lâlish (see **Yezidism**). The turtle tattoo motif, a symbol of longevity, recalling holy Khidir (see **Yârsânism**) is also found commonly, and in various degrees of stylization, in the characteristically Kurdish field design, the *minâ khâni.* The symbol combining a dog, a serpent hole, and the sun disc used by the Yezidi women is a fascinating reminder of this combination in the ancient Mithraic religious sculptures (the sun god Mithras killing the bull of heaven, from whose blood springs a serpent and a dog, the symbols of balancing forces of good and evil).

Kurdish decorative motifs fall within two distinct groups: 1) those with no connection to naturally occurring (geometric) forms, 2) those which use natural forms as models, with various degrees of subsequent stylization. A village artist may use these both side-by-side or separately for difference objects. A city craftsman is inclined to separate these from one another. A city rug, for example, may use stylized animal and floral motifs, but it is the tribal and village rugs and kilim which also include non-organic, often magical, motifs along with any other motif in the same product.

Presently, both of these motif groups can be distinguished as Kurdish, particularly in the art of rug weaving. While the antiquity of these motifs can be established for their native roots, their occurrence outside Kurdistan establishes past episodes of migration and even, as in the case of Halaf culture, the direction of the trade routes.

Further Readings and Bibliography: Robert Dyson and Mary Voigt, eds., "East of Assyria: The Highland Settlement of Hasanlu," *Expedition* 31:2-3 (1989); I.J. Winter, "Perspective on the 'Local

Style' of Hasanlu: A Study in Perspective," in L.D. Levine and T.C. Young, eds., *Mountains and Lowlands: Essays in the Archaeology of Greater Mesopotamia*, vol. 7 (Malibu, California: Bibliotheca Mesopotamica, 1977); James Mellaart, *The Neolithic of the Near East* (New York: Scribner, 1975); André Godard, *Le Trésor de Ziwiyè, (Kurdistan)* (Haarlem: Publications du service archéologique de l'Iran, 1950); Edith Porada, "Of Deer, Bells and Pomegranates," *Iranica Antiqua* vii (1967); Edith Porada, "The Hasanlu Bowl," *Expedition* 1.3 (1959); M.J. Mellink, "The Hasanlu Bowl in Anatolian Perspective," *Irancia Antiqua* VI (1966); M.J. Mellink, "Hurriter Kunst," *Realexikon der Assyriologie* 514 (1972-75); Pierre Amiet, "Un vase rituel iranien," *Syria* XLII (1965); R.H. Dyson, "Problems of Protohistoric Iran as seen from Hasanlu," *Journal of Near Eastern Studies* 24 (1965); P. Amandry, "A propos du trésor de Ziwiyé," *Iranica Antiqua* VI (1966); Edith Porada, "A Fragment of a Gold Applique from Ziwiye and some Remarks on the Artistic Traditions of Armenia and Iran during the Early First Millennium BC," *Journal of Near Eastern Studies* 19 (1960); C.K. Wilkinson, "Treasures from the Mannean Land," *Bulletin of the Metropolitan Museum of Art* (New York, April 1963); R.D. Barnett, "Median Art," *Iranica Antiqua* II.1 (1962); A.D.H. Bivar, "A Hoard of Ingot-Currency of the Median Period from Nush-i Jan, near Malayir," *Iran* IX (1971); P.R.S. Moorey, "A Note on Pre-Achaemenid Standard-Tops from Western Iran," *Iran* XV (1977); Henry Field, *Body-Marking in Southwestern Asia* (Cambridge, Massachusetts: Peabody Museum, 1958); Max von Oppenheim, *Der Tell Halaf* (Leipzig, 1931); Michael Roaf, *Cultural Atlas of Mesopotamia and the Ancient Near East* (New York: Equinox-Oxford, 1990); O.W. Muscarella, "Comments on the Urkish Lion Pegs," in G. Buccellati and M. Kelly-Buccellati, eds., *Mozan I: The Soundings of the First Two Seasons*, vol. 20 (Malibu, California: Bibliotheca Mesopotamica, Undena, 1988).

RUGS & FABRICS

The appearance of rugs in the ancient Middle Eastern records coincides with the arrival of the Aryans and other Indo-European speaking tribes, such as the Mitannis, Medes, and Hittites. These nomads from the cold northern Eurasian steppes likely introduced the art of rug weaving (at least that of the pile rugs) into Kurdistan and other vast localities they settled (see **Historical Migrations**). The earliest evidence of pile rugs is from a circa 14th century BC orthostat, excavated at the Hittite site of Alaça Hüyük in central Anatolia, and an Egyptian wall painting from the reign of Amen-hotep IV (Akhenaton) and his Mitanni Aryan queen, Nefertiti (r. 1369-53 BC). The preponderance of evidence of pile rugs begins, however, with the "Black Obelisk" of the Assyrian king Shalmaneser III (r. 858-824 BC). It depicts a tribute of pile rugs of considerable weight (two of them are shown being carried on thick poles, resting on the shoulders of two men), with the fringes (omnipresent in the pile rugs) hanging from the ends. The rug bearers have been identified by their clothing as the inhabitants of the lands to the northwest of Assyria, i.e., western Kurdistan, where earlier the Mitannis had their kingdom (see **Ancient History**).

The design motifs and the artistic provenance of the rugs brought to the Assyrian - markets can also be ascertained, thanks primarily to the local rock carvers, who chose to adopt them for decorating stone palace floors. Most of these surviving "stone rugs" carry motifs similar to modern Kurdish motifs, such as the garden squares, latch-hooked diamonds, and crab/turtle motifs. As to the general design styles, the *minâ khâni*, *chwârsuch*, *pirgul*, and *raqa âwita* are all present (Akasheh 1992). Of all prominent modern Kurdish rug designs, only *mâsi âwita* is missing from these ancient Assyrian records. The details of these styles and motifs are given below.

Cloth weaving in Kurdistan, by contrast, has a far longer documented history than that of pile rugs. The earliest evidence of weaving in the modern sense, i.e., the tabby weave, comes from impressions on clay from the Aceramic Neolithic Period (8500-7000 BC) left at the urban site of Jarmo near modern Sulaymânia in central Kurdistan (Roaf 1990, 28). These are in fact the oldest records of cloth weaving in the modern sense anywhere in the world. Their practically modern looks tell, however, of a much earlier beginning in yet undiscovered loci for this technology. By contrast, the contemporary evidence of weaving found at the cave of Nahal Hemar in Israel, a contemporary of Jarmo, consists of the primitive twisting of the weft threads around the warps—a technique known as twining.

The weaving industry in Kurdistan continued into the historic period, with the products appearing more frequently, as royal presents to the Assyrian royal court since the 10th century BC. The tradition of fine weaving continued in Kurdistan until at least the end of the medieval period (15th century).

Marco Polo writes of the area between Mus, Mardin, and Mosul (western Kurdistan), as the locality where "cotton is produced in great abundance, of which they prepare the cloths called *boccasini*, and many other fabrics" (*Travels*, I.vi). On the other end of Kurdistan in the west, Marco Polo again relates, of the markets of Kaysari (Caesaria) and Sivas (Sebastia), "The best and handsomest carpets in the world are brought here, and also silks of crimson and other rich colors." Seven centuries later, in the 19th century, the famous archaeologist Niebuhr, describing this same section of western Kurdistan, speaks of its manufacture of flax and cotton, and "a species of silk called *kas* or *kes*, which grow on trees" (*Voyage*, II.268). As to the weaving goods presented at the markets of Mosul, Marco Polo reports, "Mosul and muslin, [is] a sort of cotton cloth, and the name of *the country* where much of it is manufactured." He includes under the term *muslin* "All those cloths of gold and silver and of silk which we call muslin...."

In a tradition which stretches to this day among the Western merchants, particularly those of rugs and fabrics, Marco ascribes the handicraft to the city or locality where it was marketed, not where it was manufactured. Thus, when he writes of all the hoards of goods he encounters at the markets of the late medieval Mosul, "[they] are all manufactures of Mosul." His passage should be interpreted, "they are all marketed at Mosul." His own and that of Neibuhr's alone are enough to place the site of the manufacture of many of these woven goods not just in the Kurdish regions surrounding the cosmopolitan Mosul, but northern, western, and even central Kurdistan as well.

In the late medieval times, Mosul was one of the greatest entrepôts of eastern commerce, and probably the most important market for Kurdish goods, even surpassing Tabriz. As in the time of Marco Polo, Kurdish rugs and other weaves still are marketed in the bazaars of Mosul, Sivas, and Kaysari, among other neighboring large cities.

Even though silk now has much diminished in production and importance, cotton is still the most important cash crop of this region of Kurdistan (see **Agriculture**), rivaling wool as the raw material for local weaving needs.

The Kurdish economy began to shrink soon after Marco Polo's visit, a process that did not cease until late in the last century. This was primarily due to the almost complete stoppage of international commercial traffic through Kurdistan (see **Trade**). The income and the dynamic momentum trade imparted to the local economy and technology gave way to a subsistence economy and a negative trend in the cumulative and available native technology. Gone from the Kurdistan of Marco Polo were the world-class fabrics and techniques for producing them. Five centuries after the Venetian's visit, Kurdish textiles had sunk to the level of the least refined (more politely called "rustic and bold") of all local products, which some new travellers and visitors defined as "barbaric" or "wild" (Eagleton 1988, 38).

The production of hand-made cloths has all but ceased in Kurdistan. Except for scarfs and a few other minor goods, which utilize the limited Kurdish silk production, every inch of cloth used by the Kurds is either imported or machine-made locally. The manufacture of hand-made rugs, flat as well as pile, and exquisite embroidery, is, however, a teeming and lucrative industry in modern Kurdistan.

The kind of embroideries produced in Kurdistan are of the kind in which the foundation material is completely covered by the embroidery work and stitches, creating a thoroughly new background and design from the foundation. Chain stitching is almost the sole method of executing the overall embroidery, done on a soft herringbone weave wool background. Wool is almost the sole material used for larger pieces, resulting in a coarser product with larger designs than can usually be achieved with finer yarns of silk or cotton. Silk and cotton are used for smaller works, such as hats and handbags. The predominant background color is brilliant red or scarlet, with madder roots or cochineal bugs serving as the dye source. Other colors are generally bright and showy. The motifs are varied. They can be arabesque (northern Kurdistan), floral-animal (central and western Kurdistan), or floral-animal-human (eastern and southern Kurdistan). While the designs employed in Kurdish kilims can find their way into the embroideries, the standard rug motifs are thoroughly, and surprisingly, missing. In fact the closest thing to designs of people and animals on the embroideries of eastern and southern Kurdistan remind one of the Paleolithic petroglyphs. They are so close that the sense of *déjà vu* is unavoidable in one who as seen the former and beholds the latter.

Embroideries can range in size from small appliques to enormous, 14 x 6 foot wedding mats, made of one single embroidery work. Embroideries are found most commonly in eastern and central Kurdistan, where they are employed for producing any item of fabric decorations, from belts and skull caps to saddle blankets and decorative mats. The recent rush to benefit from outside markets, especially exports to the West, has made many Kurdish craftsmen adapt the old embroidery styles to new articles that were never part of the old native repertoire. Among these, the most notorious are the ever-present flat handbags that are now made of embroidery, but also many woven like miniature pile rugs. These bags sell well to unsuspecting foreign visitors who are looking for not-too-exotic native handicraft. There now also appear full jackets and skirts—in fact anything which might sell. For these, the craftsmen often use a black cotton back, and a cotton front piece with factory-printed designs already on them. The embroidering then follows the nameless, obscure designs that happen to appear on the printed cotton that might have struck the fancy of the modern craftsman. In this way, they are further accommodating the non-native tastes of the buyers with their accustomed designs.

Flat weave rugs, or kilims, are much more easily produced, far more affordable, and less durable than the pile rugs. They are not fundamentally different from any cloth, as they are woven just the same, but with much thicker warps and wefts. They are not knotted, as this is the hallmark of the pile rugs. They are generally more colorful and bolder in design than Kurdish pile rugs, which themselves are famous for just such properties.

A type of Kurdish kilim is made out of two matching pieces, sewn to each other on their sides. These kilim are produced on very small, portable, hand looms, between 1 and 1.5 feet in width, which were used by the wandering nomadic women, riding on draft animals, effectively putting into economic production a time which would otherwise have been lost in idleness. The long, narrow pieces were then joined to each other to get a standard size kilim. The problem was that the uneven tension of the warps, caused by the small size and constant bumps, wreaked havoc with the finished products. In the best of times, the pieces barely matched each other at the joint, and the whole product was warped before and after the joining of the pieces. These fetched the lowest prices, and were used solely by the nomadic producers or the most indiscriminate of buyers. This is not true any longer, as the "naturalness" and the authentic "wild, ethnic" appearance of these most crude pieces are their charm in the postindustrial markets of the West.

Even to an untrained eye, two types of Kurdish pile rugs can be distinguished immediately, one a finely woven, intricately designed, often curvelinear, city type, and the second a coarse-woven, coarsely designed, angular, village or tribal type.

Despite this dichotomy, the overall design style and motifs of these two types are basically the same; an indicator that we are not dealing with two different schools of design, and cultural backgrounds, but the same school of design with two different socioeconomic backgrounds.

As such, the rugs and fabrics can serve as a barometer of Kurdish economic health and social class structure. A fascinating observation is recorded in this regard by Anahid Akasheh (1986), who points to the absence of "ordinary" weaves in Kurdistan: They are either very strong, durable, and coarse in texture, with simple and naturalistic motifs, or extremely fine, delicate in texture, and highly stylized in motifs. She sees this phenomenon as a reflection of the market, which in turn reflects the social class structure of Kurdistan. A two-tier society consisting of 1) a subsistence economy, and the associated nomads and farmers to whose needs were suited the first kind of fabrics, and 2) a ruling aristocratic class of khâns, emirs, and princes who supported and received the very best. The absence of an urban-based middle class, or even wealthy farmers, in the past **four or five** centuries of Kurdish history precluded anything in between. Akasheh's hypothesis is well founded, and is witnessed in this work as well (see **Social Organization** and **Early Modern History**).

The fine specimens of the 18th and 19th century rugs of Bijâr and Sanandaj (Senneh) that have survived tell of a city-based industry which could have catered only to the most discriminating of tastes. This tradition is largely gone, as is the native Kurdish aristocratic class which supported it. The more recent efforts, for commercial purposes, to retrieve the lost and to preserve the little which remains of this ultra-refined past in the modern workshops of Sanandaj are mere whistlings in the dark.

Kurdish rugs are (or rather were) easy to identify, as their general design style and the primary motifs have largely been particular to the Kurdish artists. The primary motifs were *harshang* (crab), *raqa* (pond turtle), *kisal* (land turtle), *mâsi âwita* (fish and lotus, also known as *Herâti*), *gul* (latch-hooked diamonds), *chwârsuch* (squares or cross roads) *shâkhi* (deer antlers), *gulâla* (roses), and *lawlâw o kâjina* (lotus and pine cones, also known in the West as the bread loaves and wine glass motif). The gul, mâsi âwita, and lawlâw o kâjina motifs are used frequently by the neighboring ethnic weavers, albeit in altered form. The lotus in the lawlâw o kâjina motif is V-shaped in Kurdish rugs, while it looks like a U or is completely flat-bottomed in the Caucasus, where also it is often used. The fish and lotus design is now also common in Azerbaijan in a highly stylized form. The latch-hooked diamonds are used by tribal groups neighboring the Kurds, and it is not easy to tell their diamonds apart (Figure 3).

The general design styles must be divided into those of the border(s) and that of the field or the arena. In the field's design, the most important are the diamond medallions (a diamond at the center of the rug, with four quarter diamonds, each at one corner of the rug). The *pirgul* (full rosettes), *minâ khâni* (royal aster), and *chwârsuch* (square, crossroads) styles are the most important, and authentic, Kurdish rug designs. The early existence of these three Kurdish styles is known by their appearance in the same ancient Assyrian floor engravings noted above.

The medallion and *hawri* (clouds) are foreign styles adopted by the Kurdish weavers. Individual Kurdish motifs are commonly adapted to these non-native styles, such as the mâsi âwita for the medallion style, and shâkhi for the hawri style. The highly prized pieces from the weaving centers of Bijâr and Senneh (Sanandaj) very often use the medallion style, in which the very highly stylized turtle, and fish and lotus, are used for motifs.

Pirgul is a tightly packed aggregation of smaller rosettes or other rounded motifs, filling symmetrically and uninterrupted the entire field of the rug. The chwârsuch fills the entire field with squares, evenly spaced, and placed within a network of grid lines (hence the parallel name, *crossroads*). Various motifs can then appear inside the squares. The minâ khâni is a style in between the densely packed pirgul and the well-spaced, angular chwârsuch. The motifs are large and well spaced (like chwârsuch), but curvilinear and free floating (like pirgul). The motifs used in minâ khâni range almost the entire spectrum. The most common ones are the pond and land turtles, crabs, and latch-hooked diamonds.

Minâ khâni has been called the most typical of all Kurdish styles of rug design. It is certainly more versatile in accepting diverse individual motifs, but it is no more typical or

A. Border Motifs

Lotus & Pine Cones (Tribal)

Lotus & Pine Cones (City)

Crab (Tribal)

Turtle & Scorpions (City)

B. Field Motifs

Fish & Lotus

Land Turles (incorporating lotus and pine cone motifs)

Pond Turtle

Rose

Turtle

Crab

Land Turtle ("Anchor")

Latch-hooked Diamond

Zozan Diamond

(By permission of A. Akasheh)

Fig. 3. Kurdish Rug Motifs.

authentic than the other two styles.

For the borders, the motifs can be any of the ones used for the field, with the turtle, pine cones, and lotus being the most favored.

Many Kurdish rug weaving designs have been transplanted to far-away lands by the migrating or deported Kurds. Like visiting cards, these design motifs have been left behind long after the assimilation of these Kurds into the local group or their subsequent return to Kurdistan. The Varâmin weaving center southeast of Teheran, for example, produces in its rugs some of the most authentic harshangi, minâ khâni, and turtle motifs, and yet the craftsmen are ethnic Persians. Only some minor Kurdish communities of 16th-century deportees still live in the mountains overlooking Varâmin from the north, and none produce rugs, much less the fine specimens of that town (see **Tribes**). The Kurdish motifs have obviously been adopted by the town's craftsmen, many of whom could well be long-assimilated Kurds. Varâmin rugs and others like them can be a puzzle to anyone trying to identify them without a basic knowledge of the ethnic and artistic history of the town and its Kurdish connections of the past.

The attractive, highly stylized turtle motifs used extensively in the borders of the finest rugs of Senneh and Bijâr have now been adopted by the neighboring ethnic weavers and are commonly used in Persian and other fine rugs. The same is also true of the fish and lotus motif which is increasingly showing up in the borders and fields of the non-Kurdish Tabriz, Arak, and Sarouk rugs of Iran.

The lustrous wool from the upper chest areas of the sheep is the preferred raw material for rug weaving. The yarn for the warp in Kurdish rugs is almost exclusively made from two strands of Z spun and S plied wool. In fact, other variations, like three-strand yarn in the warp of rugs, can normally be taken to disqualify a rug as having a Kurdish origin, if the design and motifs alone do not do that in a given case (Eagleton 1988, 59). Cotton replaces wool for more intricate pieces, following the same style of spinning and number of strands.

The knots in the pile rugs of Kurdistan employ both of the standard systems, symmetric (Turkish) and asymmetric (Persian) knots. The knotting methods are better known in the West by their traditional, and perplexingly erroneous, names of *Ghiordes* (symmetric) and *Senneh* (asymmetric). Ghiordes was a minor rug-weaving town in western Anatolia, and Senneh is of course modern Sanandaj, capital of eastern Kurdistan. Only the very finest Kurdish rugs employ the asymmetric Persian knot, suitable for very delicate weaves and intricate designs. The pile rugs of the ethnic Persians use almost nothing but this knot, and if it is to be called after a city, any one of the more important rug-producing Persian cities of Isfahan, Kashan, or Kirman would surely be more fitting than Sanandaj. This knotting technique is naturally not suitable for the coarse tribal rugs which are intended to be durable products under harsh conditions. The Senneh and Bijâr rugs produced under the tutelage of the Kurdish Ardalân princely house naturally used this technique for valuable pieces to adorn mansions and palaces of the rich (Cecil-Edwards 1953). The average Kurdish rug uses the Turkish knot (named so since almost every Turkic tribal weaver uses this technique). It is stronger than the asymmetric Persian knot, and by its very nature capable of only half the fineness of the former. Kurdish tribal rugs that are in demand in the market employ this type of symmetric knotting.

The high pile of many of these rugs, and their shagginess, may explain the pejorative term the city dwellers have traditionally given tribal Kurdish rugs: "bear rugs."

In Middle Eastern markets, typical Kurdish rugs were the stuff of the poor. As such, and ironically, they occupied a lucrative niche in the local market that the other weavers did not care to, or could not, fill economically. Inexpensively and prolifically produced "bear rugs" brought large volumes of cash into the pre-modern Kurdish economy, enticing the producers to keep high levels of production, which continue to this day. The Kurdish stuff of the poor now has found rich and enthusiastic buyers in the Western, postindustrial, societies. The simplicity, honesty, playfulness of colors, and motifs (and a good deal of mistakes in the execution of the designs) have suddenly become virtues in the eyes of those who have seen too much order of the machine kind. The bear rug is now all in vogue, and market forces are taking it past the buying range of its traditional buyers, the local poor.

Further Readings and Bibliography: The most valuable general work on rugs, including Kurdish rugs, remains that of A. Cecil-Edwards, *The Persian Carpet* (London: Duckworth, 1953). Works of William Eagleton, *An Introduction to Kurdish Rugs and Other Weavings* (New York: Interlink, 1988), Anahid Akasheh, "Woven Skies, Woven Lands: Kurdish Textiles as an Expression of Social Structure," *Kurdish Times*, I.1 (1986) fill the remaining gap. Also, Ora Schwartz, "Jewish Weaving in Kurdistan," *Journal of Jewish Art* 3-4 (1977); Marco Polo, *Travels*, ed. John Masefield (London: Dent, 1975); R. Pfister, "Le rôle de l'Iran dans les textiles d'Antioné," *Ars islamica* XIII-XIV (1948); Anahid Akasheh, *The Archaeology of the Kurdish Rugs* (New York: Kurdish Library, 1992); R.S. Ellis, "Mesopotamian Carpets in Modern and Ancient Times: Ancient Near Eastern Weaving," *American Journal of Archaeology* 80 (1976); Yanni Petsopoulos, *Kilims: The Art of Tapestry Weaving in Anatolia, the Caucasus and Persia* (London: Thames and Hudson, 1979); Anthony Landreau, "Kurdish Kilim Weaving in the Van-Hakkari District of Eastern Turkey," *Textile Museum Journal* 3:4 (1973); Michael Roaf, *Cultural Atlas of Mesopotamia and the Ancient Near East* (New York: Equinox-Oxford, 1990).

COSTUMES & JEWELRY

The riotously colored costumes, a time-honored cultural trait which has made the Kurds the butt of jokes for non-Kurds, tell of a direct environmental influence on the Kurdish psyche and taste. The same influence can be credited for the development of exquisitely painted, colorful potteries of the Halaf culture in Kurdistan, 8000 years earlier (see **Designs & Motifs**).

The colors and busy motifs of the costumes are so natural in the context of the colorful and varied Kurdish countryside that one may very well consider them a form of camouflage on the part of the native population in non-snowy seasons. "This colour of the hills" wrote the writer and traveller Vita Sackville-West, passing through Kurdistan in 1926, "cannot be exaggerated in variety, richness, and unexpectedness. I have never seen anything to equal it. The rockier portions looked painted, artificial; patches of blue-green rock appeared, looking as though they been sprayed with copper sulfate – copper over-grown with verdigris; rocks of pale malachite; then a ridge of blood-red rock; rocks of porphyry." (Sackville-West 1926, 72). In fact the all-white, heavy winter costumes used in many areas by men may fortify the notion that this colorfulness has a protective adaptation as one of its roots.

Besides the exaggerated colorfulness, there exists nothing which can be called a typical Kurdish costume. The costumes vary from region to region in composition, cut, and material. Two general domains can readily be recognized, however: 1) western Kurdistan, and 2) southern, eastern, and central Kurdistan. Northern Kurdistan has representatives from both of these regions, intermixed (see **Internal Subdivisions**).

In western Kurdistan costumes are tight. Men wear stove-pipe pants and smallish vests over tight shirts. The color black with gold embroidery is favored. The costumes have an unmistakable southeast European, Balkan look to them. Red fez or red skull caps are worn by men, to which sometimes are added small turbans, wrapped so that the red cap or fez can be seen from the top. From this practice may have come the appellation Qizilbâsh, red heads for the the modern Kurdish Alevis and the military forces which gave rise to the Safavid royal house of Persia in the 16th century (see **Early Modern History**). The red headgear in the form of red turbans also distinguishes the Bârzâni clan chiefs to this day (Figure 4).

Women in western Kurdistan do not use turbans, but tight, long scarfs, often in solid

Figure 4. Costumes of Western Kurdistan and Parts of the Khurâsâni Enclave and Northern Kurdistan.

Figure 5. Costumes of Southern, Eastern and Central Kurdistan.

colors. The woman's costume is made of many pieces worn over one another, with a little bit of each showing from underneath the subsequent pieces. The cloths are often of solid colors, but by no means any less riotous than the ones with designs in the rest of Kurdistan.

After three generations' of limits on Kurdish ethnic costumes in Turkey, northern Khurâsân, oddly enough, is where one must look for the genuine costume design of the Anatolian Kurds, not Anatolia itself. The transplanted Kurdish community of Khurâsân, which came from western and northern Kurdistan in the course of the 16th and 17th century deportations, preserves in its isolation the costume tradition of a Kurdistan long gone: the tight fit of the west, decorated with the busy motifs of the rest of Kurdistan (see **Deportations & Forced Resettlements**).

In southern, central, and eastern Kurdistan fits are predominantly loose. The baggy pants of the men are brought together at the ankles by a strap or an elastic band. This same type of pants when used in northern Kurdistan loses the ankle tightness, taking a bell-bottomed shape. One can know he is crossing into the northern Kurdish cultural domain on the middle course of the Greater Zâb river by noting only the sharp change in the shape of men's trousers around their ankles.

Men's collarless shirts open in the front, and their sleeves end in long conical attachments, which are rolled back on the wrist and then wrapped around it and knotted. A vest and/or an unconstructed jacket of soft material (and a long overcoat in colder times) is worn over the shirt. The sleeves' extension is then wrapped over them all at the wrist. A very long waist band is then wrapped around the top of the pants, which in its turn are pulled over the lower ends of the shirt, vest, jacket, etc. (except for the long overcoat). The headgear is a small conical skull cap around which is wrapped a turban, utilizing a large square piece of cloth, first folded into a triangle and then, at the line of folding, again folded several times to produce a long strip about 5 inches wide. This is then wrapped around the head to make the turban. The starting end of the turban cloth is allowed to hang loosely from just behind the right ear (Figure 5).

To this basic costume is added many trimmings and extra pieces, depending on the locality. The turban in northern Kurdistan, for example, took on truly enormous proportions by the early 20th century, using tens of yards of material, with the end product not easy to balance on the head because of its sheer size. The waist band also gradually grew to enormous size. Early photographs of Kurdish khâns in this century are rather comical in this respect. Men in southern Kurdistan use very colorful, but particularly shiny, material for their costumes, with the Sanjâbi tribal costume being literally dazzling in the sun.

The woman's costume was basically the same as that of the man, except that it had a finer, and constructed, jacket, and a dress which was worn between the shirt and the vest. Everything else stayed the same, including the headgear of turbans. In central, and partially eastern, Kurdistan, the cloth which is wrapped as a turban is worn like a long, loose scarf by women over their skull caps, with the difference that the material used is usually a very fine, diaphanous cloth.

A large amount of jewelry was worn by men and women in the past in Kurdistan, and is still worn by women today. The sheer variety can be overwhelming. The Harki tribal women's jewelry is considered the most elaborate, involving several pounds of precious metals and stones for the rich, and a similar weight of less precious material for the less rich, made into hundreds of strands, beads, and plaques, to adorn the owner, literally, from head to toe. This has been an ancient habit in Kurdistan. In the 12,000-year-old cemeteries at Shânidar (famous for the much-earlier Neanderthal remains) where the Harki nomads summered until very recently, a skeleton of a child was discovered with 1500 small beads around its head alone (Roaf 1990, 30).

The jewelry today serves as the family savings for traditional Kurdish families. Even today these items are sold as easily, and commonly, as funds are withdrawn from a bank savings accounts, and used to finance activities such as the purchase of a piece of land or a child's education. Women's (or men's) jewelry is thus treated not as a personal possession, but a family asset and savings.

There are many other local variations in costume, but none are represented beyond the boundaries of certain tribes or localities to merit a review at this general level. Under the influence of the two mainstream Kurdish costume styles, these and other local variations, like the local dialects and customs, are fast disappearing. Many have already done so in the course of this century.

Travellers like Sykes have kept for posterity in their description many interesting local Kurdish costumes which now have disappeared. The traditional Kurdish costume of Jabal Sanjâr heights, for example, consisted of a pointed brown felt cap, sometimes with ear straps hanging on the sides, a white shirt of cotton cut square at the neck and with no opening in front, a cloak of gazelle skin or light brown leather, rawhide sandals, and a leather belt. Male and female members of the very large Jibrân tribe of western Kurdistan shaved the top of their heads where the skull cap rested. "The men wear the most extraordinary clothes," observed Sykes of the Jibrâns in 1908, "something after the fashion of East-end costermongers, pearl buttons, black velvet collar and cuffs, baggy trousers, sash, and among the well-to-do, a collar and tie; on the head is worn an enormous white felt tarbush about 1 foot high bulging out like a busby; around this is turned a very small turban of silk."

The old Yezidi pointed cap from Jabal Sanjar is clearly Scytho-Alanic headgear. An ancient example of it can be found on the colossal representation of the god Mithras at the ruins of Nimrut Dagh in western Kurdistan. The monument was built by the Kurdish king Mithradates Kallinikos of Commagene (69-34 BC). Only the god Mithras, of all the deities represented at Nimrut Dagh, wears this particular headgear. In view of the special connection observed between the god Mithras and Yezidism (see **Religion**), this additional evidence of the costume may be worth further investigation. The survival of this Scytho-Alanic headgear among the Yezidis may even be of help in reconstructing the pattern of early settlements of these Aryan tribes in Kurdistan (see **Historical Migrations**).

The Kurdish jewelry and costume have been shown to carry a lot of history behind their designs and style of use. The archaeological finds of actual jewelry specimens, such as those from Ziwiya, and the depiction of jewelry and costumes in the ancient rock carvings still extant in Kurdistan (e.g., those at Tâqi Bustân, Sarpuli Zohâb, and Nimrut Dagh), document the survival of many ancient forms in jewelry to this day (Peck 1969). Ackerman (1938) believes that, in general, there is present a strong influence from the Sasanian period on Kurdish jewelry as well. Ala-Firouz et al. (1977) document a direct influence of Sasanian royal attire on the modern Kurdish costume, particularly in belts and skullcaps, utilizing the available ancient rock carvings in Kurdistan. What is not elaborated in any of these case studies is the direction of the influence, or whether one should be talking of the influence of one on the other. They fail to see that the local artists (like the legendary rock sculptor Ferhâd; see **Literature**) who executed these ancient carvings could have been naturally inclined to use their own familiar clothing articles as models, particularly for secondary items and trimmings. Alternatively, one can see instead the items which Ackerman, Peck, and Ala-Firouz prove to have an affinity with modern Kurdish costumes and jewelry as simply the common Kurdish costume of that time, and the native ancestors of the modern ones. There is no need to discover any foreign influence because of their appearance in the Sasanian-commissioned memorial rock carving in Kurdistan.

Further Readings and Bibliography: E.H. Peck, "The Representation of Costumes in the Reliefs of Taq-i Bustan," *Artibus Asiae* 31 (1969); Iran Ala-Firouz, *A Survey of Persian Handcraft*, ed. Jay Glick and Sumi Hiramoto-Gluck (Teheran and Tokyo, 1977); Vita Sackville-West, *Passenger to*

Teheran (London: Hogarth, 1926); R. Berliner and P. Borchart, *Silberschmiedearbeiten aus Kurdistan* (Berlin, 1922); A.S.M. Chirvani, *Islamic Metalwork from the Iranian world, 8th–18th century* (London: Victoria and Albert Museum, 1982); H.E. Wulff, *Traditional Crafts of Persia* (Cambridge: M.I.T. Press, 1966); Ora Schwartz Be'eri, "Kurdish Jewish Silvercraft," *Kurdish Times* IV.1-2 (1991); Edith Porada, *Ancient Iran* (New York, 1965); Géza Fehérvari, *Islamic Metalwork of the Eighth to the Fifteenth Century* (London/Boston 1976); Phyllis Ackerman, "Jewelry in the Islamic Period," in Arthur U. Pope, *A Survey of Persian Art* (London/New York, 1938); Mark Sykes, "The Kurdish Tribes of the Ottoman Empire," *The Journal of the Royal Anthropological Institute of Great Britain and Ireland* XXXVIII (London, 1908); Michael Roaf, *Cultural Atlas of Mesopotamia and the Ancient Near East* (New York: Equinox-Oxford, 1990).

SCULPTURE & PAINTING

While some modern Kurdish artists have used sculpture as an avenue for expressing their inspirations, it has been in painting that they have excelled, and it is painting which merits a good amount of attention—belatedly, that is.

It is fascinatingly easy for anyone familiar with the "Kurdish taste" for colors to identify modern Kurdish paintings (see **Costumes & Jewelry**). Several young Kurdish painters are now producing a wealth of works mainly in European diaspora, and only recently have they received the recognition from their people and art-lovers the world over that they so richly deserve.

The painting styles fall within two general categories: a modern abstract to cubist style, and a revivalist, old miniature painting style of the traditional East. Judging by the quality of work, it seems the former style has been more successful in gathering attention and praise than the latter, which at any rate is not specifically Kurdish.

The theme of these paintings has conveniently also fallen into two categories: a nationalistic, "socially committed" theme, and one which varies from artist to artist, from still-life to garden scenes, which I call "free-style." The "socially committed" style uses Kurdistan as its theme, endeavoring to serve the land and the people by depicting their problems and celebrating their achievements, homeland, and daily life. Even mountains by themselves are not presented without attaching a patriotic meaning to them. The scenes abstractly represent guerrilla fighters, village life, the hardships that common people still have to face daily, and the like.

The limitations on subjects and the distractions brought about by the attempt to send an artistically irrelevant, but politically loaded message via artwork has made the quality suffer. Even though perfect for presentation at human rights conferences and nationalistic meetings, artistically they cannot compete with the work of the "free painters," who have let only the limits of their imaginations bound their artistic expression, and not political considerations. Every pixil of the canvas is attended to, carefully not deprived of a showy presentation of its own. The artists do not seem worried a bit about the taste of their potential viewers and critics in the West. They are sure the Kurds love them. And they do.

Of the socially committed painters, the works of Gara Rasul (b. 1955 in Kirkuk, now living in Germany) are of special note.

The verve, colorfulness, and sometimes the craze of the free-style paintings of Remzi (b. in 1932, now living in France) make them seem to have a hard time staying bound within the picture frames limiting them. The background wall paper of a still-life presentation of a fruit bowel by Remzi is so busily and vibrantly covered with flower designs that one finds the term *still life* a bit ironic. Even simple shadows fall victim to Remzi's "Kurdish taste." A representation of an ornate red chair has shadows in purple, green, and yellow, on a black floor, against an orange wall.

Among the other free painters, the works of Mansoor Ahmed (b. 1955, in Kirkuk, now living in Germany) are of special note.

Even the more sober, socially committed painters are not immune to this color madness, and far from it. The face of one elderly village man in a portrait done by Zudi Sardar (b. 1953 in Iraq, now living in the United States), is sectioned off to flash with solid and composite colors, with no apparent role but to inadvertently tell the viewers of the ethnic background of the painter.

Even though the works of modern Kurdish painters are beginning to receive cautious first note in the art circles of Europe, none has so far been shown in the United States, despite many visits by Kurdish artists. They are facing stiff competition from other ethnic painters from Latin America that have rather saturated the market for this line of artistic work. This is despite the fact the works by the Kurdish painters are as far from the Latin American ones as the physical distance separating their homelands from one another.

In fact many Kurdish artists have tried to fight the label *ethnic* on their works, asking to be judged by their artistic merits, of which there are plenty. So far, ethnic painters and paintings they have remained. Remzi's works have very little ethnicity in them, that is, none which has been introduced intentionally by the artist. But the artist's nationality so far has automatically been an ethnic label on him and every other Kurdish painter.

Hasan Tunç (pronounced Tun.ch, b. 1950 in Darsim, now living primarily in Sweden) falls within the old tradition of the multifaceted artist of the East. He is a first-class painter of the free style, an accomplished sculptor, and a gifted jewelry maker. His last talent is in keeping with the jewel-making tradition of his home region of Darsim.

Despite the current fascination of many Kurdish artists with painting, and large-scale production, not much archaeological material, such as frescoes or other kinds of wall painting, has so far turned up to help trace the roots and evolution of the art of painting in Kurdish history. The reverse is true of sculpture.

Kurdistan is very rich in archaeological rock carvings, bas reliefs, and free-standing ancient sculptures and figurines, stretching back to prehistoric times. In fact, the oldest folk hero of Kurdistan is Farhâd/Ferhâd, a sculptor who fashions the living rocks of the mountains (see **National Character** and **Folklore & Folk Tales**).

The history of sculpture, particularly of rock reliefs, is indeed long in Kurdistan. The colossal statues of the mountain temples of Nimrut Dagh in western Kurdistan (north of Adiyaman) are impressive evidence of the antiquity and importance of sculpture in the art of old Kurdistan. Some of the oldest architectural monuments in Kurdistan are also fashioned into the cliffs as grottos. The grottos of Dav Dukhtar, Dukkâni Davud, Tâqi Gira, and the Tâqi Bustân complex are only the better-known examples. Sculpting the mountains seems to have been the popular way of sculpting. Even the colossi at Nimrut Dagh are attached at the base of the mountains. This physical attachment of the artistic work to the mountain confirms the relationship of the Kurdish psyche to the mountains, as already presented under **National Character**.

Despite the impressive archaeological record, contemporary Kurdish artists have done little in the field of sculpture worth mentioning. Zudi Sardar's sculptures take a definite second row in comparison to his paintings. In the case of Hasan Tunç's sculptures, despite their surprising delicacy and attractiveness, in absolute artistic value, they rank behind his sculpted jewelry pieces and his painting.

Further Readings and Bibliography: W. Kleiss, "Zur Topographie des 'Partherhanges' in Bisutun," *Archäologische Mitteilungen aus Iran, Neue Folge* 3 (1970); H. Luschey, "Zur Datierung der sasanidischen Kapitelle aus Bisutun und des Monuments von Taq-i Bostan," *Archäologische Mitteilungen aus Iran, Neue Folge* 1 (1968); S. Fukai and K. Horiuchi, "Taq-i Bustan I-II," *The Tokyo University Iran-Iraq Archaeological Expedition Reports* 10-11 (Tokyo, 1969, 1972); W. Hinz, "Das sasanidische Felsrelief von Salmas," *Iranica Antiqua* V (1965); W. Hinz, "Das sasanidische Felsrelief von Tag-e Qandil," *Archäologische Mitteilungen aus Iran, Neue Folge* 6 (1973); E.H. Peck, "The Representation of Costumes in the Reliefs of Taq-i Bustan," *Artibus Asiae* 31 (1969); L. Vanden Berghe, "De ikonografische Betekenis van het sassanidisch Roksrelief van Sarab-i Qandil

(Iran)," *Mededelingen van het Kon. Akad. van Wetenshappen van Belgie* XXXV.1 (1973); B. Hrouda et al., "Die Felsreliefs (Sarpoli Zohab) I-IV," *Iran. Denkmäler* (Iran, Felsreliefs C, 1976), Lief. 7; H. von Gall, "Neue Beobachtungen zu den sog. medischen Felsgräbern," *Proceedings of Second Annual Symposium of Archaeological Research in Iran* (1974); W. Hinz, "Das sassanidische Felsrelief von Salmas," *Iranica Antiqua* V (1965); Robin Schneider, ed., *Kurden im Exil: Ein Handbuch kurdischer Kultur, Politik und Wissenschaft* (Berlin: Berliner Institut für Vergleichende Sozialforschung, dem Haus der Kulturen der Welt und medico international, 1991), section 2.

ARCHITECTURE & URBAN PLANNING

The construction of permanent houses had to wait until the invention of agriculture, as hunter-gatherer societies had no need for such abodes as they followed their prey or the ripening wild crops. Caves served as shelters. The invention of agriculture and the domestication of animals, in contrast, necessitated the construction of permanent houses near the cultivated fields. It is only logical to look for the earliest evidence of man-made housing accommodations in the same areas where the invention of agriculture took place. The earliest records of architectural construction are in fact those of the Proto-Neolithic period (9300-8500 BC) at Qermez Dera and Karim Shâr in central Kurdistan, contemporaneous with the oldest strata at Jericho. These were rounded mud huts, half sunk into the ground. Molds to make mud bricks were already in use in Kurdistan, but still absent in Jericho.

During the Halaf Period (6000-5400 BC), construction of houses once more returned to the older, circular plan (called *tholoi*), abandoning the rectangular, multi-room housing plan of the preceding 2000 years. These enclosed, rather small, spaces of about 15-25 feet in diameter are believed to have served as single-family units, with rectangular additions to one side to possibly house domestic animals. The materials used for the houses were different, depending on the average annual rainfall of the locality. Mud bricks, rubble stones, and timber were variously used. While the mud houses possibly had domed mud roofs, evidence also abounds that others, such as those at Yârim Tepe, used wooden rafters for flat roofs. The modern Kurdish domestic village architecture is not any different, as mud bricks and domed roofings are employed in the drier zones, while rubble stone walls and wood beam roofs serve the wetter, higher zones. Styles hybridizing both of these methods are found today in the zones in between these two extremes, as were also found in the Halaf period.

The incoming Medes and other Indo-European-speaking peoples surely adapted from the ancient Kurds many vestiges of their art and culture. The elements of urban planning and architecture can readily be identified and documented. The Assyrian bas reliefs depicting Kurdish cities besieged by Assyrian forces, all show a basic design of the cities, built on hills with many (usually seven) concentric walls sectioning the city all the way to the top of the hill, where the palace/temple is located. The same design is reported by Herodotus for the famous garden palaces of the Medes at Hamadân (ancient Ecbatana), where each one of these concentric city walls was painted differently (gold, silver, blue, white, purple, red, and black, from top to bottom). Between the walls were placed houses of the citizens, gardens, flower beds, and presumably, livestock shelters. This design, or *pairi daeza,* from ancient Iranic, very likely Median, words meaning "walled all around," has given rise to the modern words *paradise* in European languages (through Greek), *firdaws* (heaven) in the Koran, modern Persian *jâliz* (vegetable garden), Kurmânji Kurdish *parez* (vegetable garden), and Gurâni Kurdish *pardez* (flower garden). The last exposed remnants of the outer two walls (i.e., the black and the red walls) of the Median capital, the original "Paradise," were extant in Hamadân until 1967.

The lavish use of colors in Kurdish art is already elucidated in various other sections in this chapter, and the liberal use of colors in the city structures is only a continuation of the same phenomenon.

The later Mesopotamian ziggurats, particularly the Elamite, Assyrian, and Neo-Babylonian, are miniature designs of an entire city from the Kurdish mountains. These lowlanders built artificial miniature "mountains" of god with concentric levels of buildings to crown them, on top of which stood the temple. The walls were painted in many colors, with the Assyrian ziggurat of Dur Shârukin (modern Kurdish village of Khorsâbâd, northeast of Mosul) preserving the Kurdish color combination in the seven-story edifice.

The mountain-top location of the capital of the classical Kurdish kingdom of Commagene at Nimrut Dagh (Mt. Nimrud, north of Adiyaman in western Kurdistan) already meets the first criterion of Kurdishness, of construction on a round hill. Further excavation of the site is likely to add the concentric walls to complete the design.

It is not so much the layout of modern cities and towns that is characteristically Kurdish, as their location on the landscape. Like the old settlements depicted in the ancient bas reliefs, their modern counterparts also cling to the hilltops, mountainsides, and even cliffs, in sheer defiance of the rationality which would have prescribed the plains nearby (see **National Character**).

In northern Kurdistan, near the medieval town of Bâyazid (meaning "Lord Angel," modern Dogubayezit), on a rocky outcrop opposite Mt. Ararat, an immense palace complex with a small private mosque, built by the Kurdish prince Is'hâq Pâshâ in 1784, has survived. The complex is a multi-level, solid masonry structure with domes, minarets, several monumental gates, and multi-level courtyards and stables. The palace's artistic style includes Caucasian, Persian, Syrian, and Anatolian architectural elements in one harmonious mold, which is built, like the palaces of the pre-Aryan Kurdish rulers, or those of the Medians, on the top of a high rocky hill. Despite the clear foreign influence on the surface decoration, the plan and the general design of the complex favorably compare to a classical hill-top palace complex in far southern Kurdistan: the Qala Yazdigird (the "City of Angels"). Not much of the superstructure remains at the Qala Yazdigird, but the ground plan, the masonry, and the layout of this supposedly Sasanian structure clearly anticipate the supposedly Ottoman complex of Is'hâq Pâshâ in northern Kurdistan 2000 years later.

Is'hâq Pâshâ's complex was well preserved until the early decades of this century. At the fall of the Khoyboun uprising, the palace was looted and partially sacked by Turkish Republican forces. It has been left to the elements ever since.

After the destruction in Sulaymânia of the all-important palace of Hamid Beg, the last Bâbân prince during the Iraqi revolution of 1958, Lady Âdila's palace at Halabja remained the last relic of the traditional princely architecture in central Kurdistan (see **Early Modern History**). This was also destroyed, along with the historic city of Halabja during the spring 1988 warfare.

The princely mansions of the Ardalâns and their main palace in Sanandaj, on the other hand, have partially survived, albeit in much altered form. They served as government buildings after the removal of the Ardalâns in 1867. Their interiors were mostly rebuilt to suit their new bureaucratic function. One of the more elaborate mansions has been rather carefully renovated, and now serves as the Sanandaj Museum.

Structurally, these relics of the old princely times are all multi-storied, with stone being the main construction material. Even in southern and eastern Kurdistan, where under Persian influence bricks are employed frequently, stones are often cut to the size and shape of bricks, and then used in their stead. No such mocking adaptation is needed in northern or western Kurdistan, where large masonry blocks are commonly used in large structures. Stone rubble serves the small private houses and village huts. The imposing jet black basalt megaliths forming the city wall of Diyârbakir (ancient Amid) were noted by the Greco-Roman writers. They are still standing to a large extent in situ, as a clue to another aspect of yet unstudied Kurdish architecture and town planning.

Further Readings and Bibliography: E.J. Keall, "Qal'eh-i Yazdigird. A Sasanian Palace Stronghold in Persian Kurdistan," *Iran* V (1967); E.J. Keall, "Qal'eh-i Yazdigird: The Question of its Date," *Iran* XV (1977); R.H. Dyson, "Architecture of the Iron I Period at Hasanlu in Western Iran and its Implications for Theories of Migration on the Iranian Plateau," in *Le plateau iranien et l'asi centrale des origines à la conquête islamique* (Paris: Colloques internationaux du centre national de la recherche scientifique, No. 567, 1976); T. Cuyler Young, "Thoughts on the Architecture of Hasanlu IV," *Iranica Antiqua* VI (1966); C.L. Goff, "Excavations at Baba Jan, the Architecture of the East Mound," *Iran* XV (1977); Glenn M. Fleming, "The Ecology and Economy of Kurdish Villages," *Kurdish Times* IV.1-2 (1991).

MUSIC

It is only natural to expect to find old roots in Kurdish music, reaching down into ancient times. With clarity, the Kurdish musical heritage can be traced to medieval times, when many first-class native musicologists wrote on the modal music system of the Middle East. Two of these musicologists readily stand out: Safi al-Din Urmawi, author of *Kitâb al-Adwâr* and *Risâla al-Sharafiya,* and Muhammad al-Khatib Arbili, author of *Jawâhir al-Nizâm fi Ma'rifat al-Aghâni.* Urmawi (d. 1294) is considered the founder of the "Systematist" school of music (Wright 1978). This school concentrates on analysis of, among other features, the intervals and scalar sequences of intervals in the modal music prevalent in the Middle East. His work is by consensus considered to be one of the most seminal, systematic works on Middle Eastern musicology. While Arbili pays some attention to Kurdish musical characteristics, Urmawi wrote nothing specifically on the Kurdish musical heritage. He concentrated on the musical school of the high society in Baghdad of the last days of the 'Abbâsid caliphate. It was only after the sack of Baghdad, and his capture by the Mongol forces, that he wrote the *Risâla al-Sharafiya* at the appointment of the cultured Mongol grand vezir Nasir al-Din Tusi. In this work he does survey the ethnic musical heritage of the Iranic peoples (including the Kurds) and the Arabians.

Much more is found on Kurdish music in the medieval Ismâ'ili treatise, the *Rasâ'il Ikhwân al-Safâ.* The *Rasâ'il* clearly distinguishes between the Kurdish musical heritage, in terms of scales, melodies, instruments, and those of the Persians, Arabians, and a few others who are mentioned.

Several Kurdish musicians also climbed in the medieval period, among which Zeriyâb is noted for his bringing of the eastern musical tradition to Muslim Spain and training local musicians in his familiar styles. The Mawsilis, Ibrâhim and Is'hâq, two Kurdish Jewish converts to Islam, were musicians and musicologists who played prodigiously and wrote several first-rate works on the local music styles of Mesopotamia and the Iranic world.

Modern Kurdish music is the inheritor of the medieval Kurdish musical heritage which nurtured and gave rise to these artists and researchers in the field. Even though little has been written on or by Kurds on their music since these early days, Kurdish music has maintained a variety and richness that sometimes confuses even Kurdish listeners when for the first time they hear a piece coming from an opposite end of Kurdistan, or very high up in the mountains.

While no record tells how important singing was to the overall music of medieval Kurdistan, the fact that the Mawsilis and Zeriyâb were singers as well as instrumentalists may indicate the interconnection between the two. In modern Kurdish music, at any rate, adding words to the instrumental sounds is considered as essential and necessary to make music as plucking the strings of the tambura, striking the drum, or blowing into the flute. Songs are the only complete form of music.

The lyric must also have a point, must tell a story, and traverse an accepted course, just as the the melodies should have their own preludes, crescendos, and finales. As various melodies within a set mode are traversed by the music, the words must have a plot and a narrative structure. Kurdish folk songs, in short, are stories told in the company of music. In fact, even when the words are not uttered, the music associated with these songs take on a form of "silent" song to any Kurdish listener, with the music alone telling the story.

Conversely, songs can be just the singing of words without the accompanying musical instruments. In this case, the singer "plays" the music in the lulls within the lyrics by singing monosyllabic words of no meaning, like *lo lo lo* or *le le le*, to fulfill all the requirements of a "song." In southern and eastern Kurdistan these monosyllables of northern and western Kurdistan lose their consonants. In one southern style, *tura khweni*, "singing of sadness," which as the name implies is reserved for melancholic and sad occasions, they cease to be syllables altogether, becoming soft vowel sounds pronounced after one another in succession and in a melodic fashion, staying in full concordance with a standard mode. Occasionally, the instrument-less "musician" includes a sorrowful word or two in the tura khweni.

Kurdish story songs employ four distinct themes: heroic, amorous, religious, and now also political. The heroic songs, the Kurdish chansons de geste, traditionally glorified the valor of heroes from the past and the legends of their chivalry as true Pahlawâns (see **National Character**). Following the division of Kurdistan in this century, this style has been given increasingly to include political and nationalistic lyrics, aimed at arousing the nationalist feelings among the listeners. Poems of classical Kurdish lyricists with patriotic themes, seldom if ever put into songs, are now being actively dug up and fitted to songs to supplement the myriad of modern patriotic jingles, as the welcome "originals." In the former Soviet Union, the Kurds fitted such themes to the Soviet propaganda "Song of the Komsomol" and the "May Song" (Aristova 1958). These modern vulgarities have left the traditional balladeers quite unaffected. They have become the last repository of the oral heritage of their nation, in ever retreating corners of Kurdistan.

During the Parthian period (247 BC to AD 227), there was present an elaborate network of bards and popular storytellers, the *gosân*, in the area, among which the tradition of *Mithrakân*, or the Mithraic legend of world genesis, played an important role. But, the tradition of bards and balladry is present among almost all Indo-European cultures and those deeply influenced by them, such as the Turkic cultures. If there is a need to identify a beginning of this art and tradition in Kurdistan, then with due caution the arrival of the Aryans into Kurdistan may be a possible time.

A traveling Kurdish balladeer, or *chargar,* sings of epic heroes and their exploits on the battlefield of love as commonly as war. The epics, or *chariga*, they sing playing a tambura, or a *kemâncha.* The number of charigas a chargar can present is a point of pride for him. In fact the chargars can present many versions of the same epic story, such as the better-known epic of *Mem o Zin* (see **Literature**). Other popular stories are the tragic romance of *Shirin o Ferhâd,* and the heroic *Ballad of Dem Dem.*

If occasion requires, the balladeer engages in non-musical storytelling as well, albeit punctuated with occasional singing of the rhymed lines. Any one of the more popular "winter stories" can serve the purpose (see **Popular Culture** and **Folklore & Folk Tales**).

Most, but not all, modern Kurdish singers continue to sing while playing instruments themselves. This was the traditional way, but is steadily becoming less frequent, as Kurdish music is played with orchestras arranged in a quasi or genuine Western format. In their choice of language, modern singers fall into two clear categories: those who for nationalistic or other motivations sing Kurdish only, and those who have gained fame outside Kurdistan and sing primarily non-Kurdish, but continue to sing Kurdish alongside. These two categories can loosely be used to categorize modern Kurdish painters as well. Of the first group, Temo Izzidin, Arif and Hesen Cizrewi, Arame Tigran, Shirin, and finally Shevân Perver, are the best known. Most, but not all of these singers and song writers are also socially active, and sing to further the national aspirations of the Kurds.

Of the second group, Perry Zangana, Faqih Tayrân, Shahrâm Nâziri, Husayn Alburzi, and the Kâmkâr brothers are better-known names. Among these artists, Perry Zangana, for example, is an accomplished opera singer who also has adapted Kurdish folk songs to modern instruments. She quite regularly surprises her unsuspecting audience by finishing her performances with a Kurdish song, be it a performance of a Western aria or a Persian *ghazal.* Feqi Teyrâ's exceptional talent and use of most common and over-looked Kurdish melodies, including the lullabies, presented with a good deal of theatrics, captivate his Turkish, Western, and Kurdish audiences all the same.

The lyric content and the nature of a song can be known by the name with which the musician/singer refers to the piece about to be presented. The song style *gorâni* (named after the ethnic Gurân Kurds) is often in the form of quatrains and is reserved for relatively long love songs, not too dissimilar to Western arias. *Kalhuri* (named after the historic Kurdish nomadic tribe of Kalhurs) is the style of singing ascribed to, and revolving around the themes pertinent to, travellers, hunters, and common workers. *Bayts* are single lines, made of two rhyming hemstitches, and are also dedicated to love themes. Bayts sometimes come from the works of the better-known poets of the past. *Dilok* is a collection of very short lines of poetry sung to dance music, while *hayrân* is a singing style used to relate the pains of parting and the sorrow of unfulfilled love. *Qatâr* is a formal singing of a standard melody with all its trimmings and properties (Schneider 1991). The *bariti* is sung in a chorus. It can be fit to a dance tune or a modern political propaganda anthem. The style used by the Sufi dervishes for singing their religious, mystic songs is *laya,* while *lawk* is the singing style for the heroic tales of the chargars.

The traditional instruments used varied greatly from the cities to the countryside. They still do to a certain degree. The instruments used in non-urban folk music were the *zornâ* (a powerful oboe), *juzala* (a double clarinet), *tambur* (tambura), *pik* (reed flute), *dahol* (a large, double-sided drum), and a *tumbalak* (small kettle drum). Of more localized nature is the *shimshâl* or *shamshâl* (a large reed flute).

Sâz is the name given to many different, but ordinary string instruments from one corner of the land to the other. There is no way to identify a sâz without knowing the provenance of it. To complicate this, in the Kurdish urban centers, *sâz* stands for the Persian sitar-like instrument *Târ,* or is simply a generic term for any musical instrument. Overlooking this seemingly complicated semantics and technical jargon, the joyous sound of a zornâ accompanied by a dahol or a tumbalak is the most common musical sound one should expect to hear coming from the direction of Kurdistan.

The travelling bards use only a tambur or *kamâncha* (a violin-type instrument, played upright like a cello). Many more instruments were used in the urban-based music, local or foreign.

Like Indian music, Kurdish music explores the octave. It has a modal structure similar to the music of the Persians and most central Asians and Afghans. The term for mode is both *dessga* (Persian *dastgâh*) or *maghâma* (Arabic *maghâm*). The most common traditional mode used is the *bayât-i Kurd,* the Kurdish scale. This scale is utilized widely under the same name by many of Kurdish ethnic neighbors. Some have argued that this mode is the only mode that Kurdish music uses (or should be using). If one were to accept that traditional Kurdish music employed but only a single mode, it can only reflect the antiquity of the music which has survived in its pristine simplicity until today. But of the single mode this music is not. Every single lullaby sung by Kurdish mothers, for example, is in the mode of *Homâyun,* which immediately belies the single-mode hypothesis. The mode of bayât-i Kurd, at any rate, is the same as the *Flamenco* mode of the Spaniards or the *Dorian* mode of the ancient Greeks, with no telling the direction of the influence, if there was one. Within the mode or modes, of course, vast numbers of melodies are played out by the Kurdish musicians, who improvise freely to the delight and admiration of their listeners. Even though improvisation is the hallmark of the Kurdish musicians, they must, and do, strictly observe the standard modes and melodies. Common people may not know how to play music, but can easily tell when the accepted boundaries of the melodies are trespassed by an inexperienced musician.

The history of Kurdish music is better documented for the medieval period, than anytime before or, surprisingly, after. The Ismâ'ili treatise *Risâlât Akhwân Safâ* includes the tradition of Kurdish music along with Persian and Arabian among the four traditions that it explores (Wright 1978). The information the *Risâlât* imparts is invaluable for the study of the evolution of Kurdish music and the reach and distinct heritage it draws upon.

Kurdish music today shows great regional diversity in style and mood. This must have always been so, recognizing the far-flung expanse of the land and difficulty in communication over the rugged landscape. Northern and western Kurdistan have a definite Anatolian flavor in their music, easily reminding one of Turkish, Greek, and Balkan music. The northeastern style is rather difficult to tell apart from traditional Armenian and Caucasian music except for the words of course. The music of the areas of Kurdistan neighboring Arab lowlands, particularly in Syria and Iraq, picks up the fast and joyous tempo of the traditional Arab music of the Fertile Crescent. In southern and eastern Kurdistan, the influence of the musical style of the Iranian plateau, including the multi-modal structure, is so strong that it completely sets the Kurdish music from this area apart from the rest. This is not surprising, as the area had been part of the state of Persia/Iran since at least the 16th century. This style is the most melancholic and subtle of all Kurdish musical styles.

For a Kurd to listen to his national music is an experience not easily open to description. He has to reconcile himself that "all these are Kurdish music," even though the variations are so strong, tell of so many different sources of influence and experiences, and so many variant tracks of evolution to render him worried about the single identity of Kurdish music. But as is the story with the musical style of nations spread over long stretches of territory, neighboring different peoples, cultures, and musical styles, Kurdish music carries all these influences in their pristine form. Had Kurdistan not been effectively fragmented, and a native centralized governmental mass electronic media and school of music been available, the past 75 years would have definitely homogenized (and made dull) the exciting diversity still present in Kurdish music.

Now that Kurds from various segments of the fragmented land communicate with each other in diaspora, and as the radio and television airwaves breach the formidable state boundaries, Kurdish music should be expected to belatedly, and regrettably, start on a path to homogenization and standardization.

Bibliography and Audio Records: The music collection at the Kurdish Library in Brooklyn, New York, is of special value. Also, Ralph Solecki, *Kurdish Folk Songs and Dances* (New York: Ethnic Folkways Library, Album No. FE 4469, 1955); Christian Poche and Jochen Wenzel, *Musical Sources: Kurdish Music* (Berlin: UNESCO Collection, Modal Music and Improvisation VI-4, n.d., a Phillips music record); T.F. Aristova, "Poyezdka k Kurdam Zakavka'ya" ("A Visit to the Kurds of Transcaucasia") *Sovetskaya Etnografiya* VI (Moscow, 1958); Robin Schneider, ed., *Kurden im Exil: Ein Handbuch kurdischer Kultur, Politik und Wissenschaft* (Berlin: Berliner Institut für Vergleichende Sozialforschung, dem Haus der Kulturen der Welt und medico international, 1991), section 2; O. Wright, *The Modal System of Arab and Persian Music: AD 1250-1300* (Oxford: Oxford University Press, 1978).

General Bibliography

A very valuable reference book on the Kurdish artists in diaspora is Robin Schneider, ed., *Kurden im Exil: Ein Handbuch kurdischer Kultur, Politik und Wissenschaft* (Berlin: Berliner Institut für Vergleichende Sozialforschung, dem Haus der Kulturen der Welt und medico international, 1991), section 2; L.D. Levine and T.C. Young, Jr., eds., *Mountains and Lowlands: Essays in the Archaeology of Greater Mesopotamia* (Malibu, California: Bibliotheca Mesopotamica, vol. 7, 1977); P.R.S. Moorey, ed., *Excavation in Iran, the British Contribution* (Oxford: Oxford University Press, 1972); R.D. Barnett, "Median Art," *Iranica Antiqua* II.1 (1962); *The Cambridge Ancient History*, 3rd ed. (New York: Cambridge University Press, 1964); R. Ghirshman, *Iran. Protoiranier, Meder, Achämeniden* (Munich: Universum der Kunst, 1964); T.F. Aristova, "Ocherki kul'tury i byta kurdskikh krest'yan Irana" ("A Sketch of the Culture and Way of Life of the Kurdish Peasants in Iran"), *Trudy Etnografii Miklukho-Maklaya* 39 (Moscow, 1958); *Kurdish Times*, semi-annual journal of the Kurdish Library, Brooklyn, New York, 1985-present.

About the Author

Mehrdad Izady is currently a lecturer in the Department of Near Eastern Languages and Civilizations at Harvard University. He has undergraduate degrees in History, Political Science, and Geography and masters degrees in International Affairs, Geography, and Middle Eastern Studies. His doctorate is in Middle Eastern Studies from Columbia University. He has lectured widely and testified before two U.S. Congressional subcommittees on the Kurds. He has published extensively in the *Kurdish Times* as well as *The Middle East Journal*. He has also contributed to the *Encyclopedia of Asian History* and has published maps on the distribution of Kurds.